ASPEN P

2007 Medicare Handbook

Judith A. Stein and Alfred J. Chiplin, Jr., Editors

Successful challenges to improper denials of Medicare coverage and necessary health services are possible. The *2007 Medicare Handbook* provides information and practical tips designed to extend coverage under the Medicare law to all who are entitled, regardless of their medical condition or economic status. The *Handbook* addresses coverage criteria and advocacy strategies across the spectrum of services available under the Medicare program—including hospital services, outpatient services, skilled nursing services, home health care, hospice care, physician services, durable medical equipment, and other services. The *2007 Medicare Handbook* also provides access to relevant Medicare law and regulations, case law developments, agency manuals, and other program-implementing materials, along with practical information about how to use these materials. Armed with this information, beneficiaries and their advocates can formulate an effective response to protect their rights to Medicare and access to necessary health care.

2007 EDITION HIGHLIGHTS

This edition of the *Handbook* comes at the beginning of the second year of the Medicare Prescription Drug Benefit, Medicare Part D. This edition addresses the myriad problems associated with this new benefit, including Part D design and implementation issues, the special problems Part D has posed for persons eligible for both Medicare and Medicaid and for other low-income Medicare beneficiaries, and changes in Medigap policies occasioned by the new drug benefit.

Further revisions in the 2007 Edition address other Medicare changes, including:

- Restoration of a cap on Medicare payments for physical, speech, and occupational therapy caps;

- Increased payments to managed care plans;

- New rules for Power Operated Vehicles used as wheelchairs;

- The new 2007 income-based Part B deductible increase and other premium and co-payment updates;

- Additional information about transferring the Medicare administrative law judge (ALJ) function from the Social Security Administration (SSA) to the Department of Health and Human Services and beneficiary experiences and

advocacy developments concerning this important change in Medicare law and practice;

- Updated discussion of extending time periods for issuing redetermination and reconsideration decisions in the Medicare administrative review process; and

- Expanded and updated discussion of Medicare's coordinated care options, including managed care, collectively known as the *Medicare Advantage* (MA) program.

12/07

For questions concerning this shipment, billing, or other customer service matters, call our Customer Service Department at 1-800-234-1660.

For toll-free ordering, please call 1-800-638-8437.

2007
MEDICARE
HANDBOOK

ASPEN PUBLISHERS

2007 MEDICARE HANDBOOK

CENTER FOR MEDICARE ADVOCACY, INC.

Judith A. Stein, Esq.
and
Alfred J. Chiplin, Jr., Esq.
Editors

Contributing Authors
Mary T. Berthelot
Alfred J. Chiplin, Jr.
Toby S. Edelman
Vicki Gottlich
Sally Hart
Ellen L. Lang
Pamela A. Meliso
Patricia B. Nemore
Brad S. Plebani
Lara Stauning
Judith A. Stein

 Wolters Kluwer
Law & Business

AUSTIN   BOSTON   CHICAGO   NEW YORK   THE NETHERLANDS

This publication is designed to provide accurate and authoritative information in regard to the subject matter covered. It is sold with the understanding that the publisher is not engaged in rendering legal, accounting, or other professional services. If legal advice or other professional assistance is required, the services of a competent professional person should be sought.

—From a *Declaration of Principles* jointly adopted by
a Committee of the American Bar Association and
a Committee of Publishers and Associations

Printed in the United States of America

1 2 3 4 5 6 7 8 9 0

ISBN 0-7355-6012-9
ISSN 1530-8979

About Wolters Kluwer Law & Business

Wolters Kluwer Law & Business is a leading provider of research information and workflow solutions in key speciality areas. The strength of the individual brands of Aspen Publishers, CCH, Kluwer Law International and Loislaw are aligned within Wolters Kluwer Law & Business to provide comprehensive, in-depth solutions and expert-authored content for the legal, professional and education markets.

CCH was founded in 1913 and has served more than four generations of business professionals and their clients. The CCH products in the Wolters Kluwer Law & Business group are highly regarded electronic and print resources for legal, securities, antitrust and trade regulation, government contracting, banking, pension, payroll, employment and labor, and healthcare reimbursement and compliance professionals.

Aspen Publishers is a leading information provider for attorneys, business professionals and law students. Written by preeminent authorities, Aspen products offer analytical and practical information in a range of specialty practice areas, from securities law and intellectual property to mergers and acquisitions and pension/benefits. Aspen's trusted legal education resources provide professors and students with high-quality, up-to-date and effective resources for successful instruction and study in all areas of the law.

Kluwer Law International supplies the global business community with comprehensive English-language international legal information. Legal practitioners, corporate counsel, and business executives around the world rely on the Kluwer Law International journals, loose-leafs, books and electronic products for authoritative information in many areas of international legal practice.

Loislaw is a premier provider of digitized legal content to small law firm practitioners of various specializations. Loislaw provides attorneys with the ability to find the legal information they need, when and where they need it, by facilitating access to primary law as well as state-specific law, records, forms and treatises.

Wolters Kluwer Law & Business, a unit of Wolters Kluwer, is headquartered in New York and Riverwoods, Illinois. Wolters Kluwer is a leading multinational publisher and information services company.

ASPEN PUBLISHERS SUBSCRIPTION NOTICE

This Aspen Publishers product is updated on a periodic basis with supplements to reflect important changes in the subject matter. If you purchased this product directly from Aspen Publishers, we have already recorded your subscription for the update service.

If, however, you purchased this product from a bookstore and wish to receive future updates and revised or related volumes billed separately with a 30-day examination review, please contact our Customer Service Department at 1-800-234-1660, or send your name, company name (if applicable), address, and the title of the product to:

ASPEN PUBLISHERS
7201 McKinney Circle
Frederick, MD 21704

Important Aspen Publishers Contact Information

- To order any Aspen Publisher title, go to *www.aspenpublishers.com* or call 1-800-638-8437.
- To reinstate your manual update service, call 1-800-638-8437.
- To contact Customer Care, e-mail *customer.care@aspenpublishers.com*, call 1-800-234-1660, fax 1-800-901-9075, or mail correspondence to Order Department, Aspen Publishers, PO Box 990, Frederick, MD 21705.
- To review your account history or pay an invoice online, visit *www.aspenpublishers.com/payinvoices*.

CONTENTS

*A complete table of contents for each chapter
is included at the beginning of the chapter.*

Chapter 11 Prescription Drug Coverage

PREFACE

The Medicare Program remains a national success story. Despite significant recent changes to its structure, the program continues to provide a core set of health coverage benefits for older people and people with disabilities throughout the country. Successful challenges to improper denials of Medicare coverage and necessary health services continue to be essential to assuring access to services and program flexibility, based upon a common set of benefits and legal standards. Further, advocacy is more important than ever to ensure that the program is responsive to the needs of beneficiaries. It is in this context that *2007 Medicare Handbook* addresses Medicare coverage and appeal issues. The information and advocacy recommendations are designed to extend coverage under the Medicare law to all who are entitled, regardless of their medical diagnosis or economic status.

The *2007 Medicare Handbook* is intended as a guide for attorneys and other advocates. Its premise is that knowledgeable legal advocates, working in concert with physicians and other health care providers, can ensure that all Medicare beneficiaries receive the coverage to which they are entitled. It addresses coverage criteria and advocacy strategies across the spectrum of services available under the Medicare program—including hospital services, outpatient services, skilled nursing services, home health care, hospice care, physician services, durable medical equipment, and other services. Importantly, the coverage criteria should be the same, whether the beneficiary is in the traditional Medicare program or receives coverage through a Medicare managed care organization. Careful, assertive advocacy is particularly important for persons with chronic conditions who are too often erroneously denied Medicare coverage and are therefore left without adequate health care.

The *2007 Medicare Handbook,* which includes a full discussion of Medicare prescription drug coverage (Chapter 11, "Prescription Drug Coverage"), provides new information learned by the authors during the first year of the program's implementation, providing insight into Part D's complexities and identifying areas where advocacy efforts are particularly needed.

As in the past, timely, informative written notice of beneficiary coverage and appeal rights are a major emphasis of the *2007 Medicare Handbook*. A proper notice should explain the reason for a denial, reduction, or termination of services and the process for appealing.

The *2007 Medicare Handbook* provides access to relevant Medicare law and regulations, case law developments, agency manuals, and other program implementing materials, along with practical information about how to use these materials. Armed with this information, beneficiaries and their advocates should be able to formulate an effective response to protect their rights.

The authors hope that the *2007 Medicare Handbook* will illuminate the importance of maintaining Medicare as a universal program that provides a defined set of benefits and services for all beneficiaries. By maintaining a program with uniform benefits and coverage standards, we are also better able to obtain proper coverage and necessary health care for each individual beneficiary.

Judith A. Stein, Esq.
Executive Director
Center for Medicare Advocacy, Inc.
November 2006

ABOUT THE CENTER FOR MEDICARE ADVOCACY, INC.

The Center for Medicare Advocacy, Inc., founded in 1986, is a nonpartisan, nonprofit organization. The Center provides education, analytical research, advocacy, and legal assistance to help elders and people with disabilities obtain fair access to Medicare and necessary health care. It focuses on the needs of Medicare beneficiaries, people with chronic conditions, and those in need of long-term care. The Center provides training regarding Medicare and health care rights throughout the country and serves as legal counsel in litigation of importance to Medicare beneficiaries nationwide.

The Center's national headquarters is in Mansfield, Connecticut, and its Data Unit is in Norway, Maine. The organization also has a law and policy office in Washington, D.C., which enhances the Center's ability to address national health care policy, research, and advocacy. In addition, the Center employs a consulting attorney who is located at the Arizona Center for Disability Law in Tucson, Arizona, affording the Center additional Medicare litigation and disability law expertise.

The Center is staffed by attorneys, nurses, legal assistants, information management experts, and technical assistants. Staff members provide analysis, written and electronic materials, and legal services, and they host an informative, and regularly updated, Web site at *www.medicareadvocacy.org*. A complete list of the organization's publications and products is available upon request.

Each year, the Center represents thousands of individuals in appeals of Medicare denials. The work of the Center includes responding to more than 7,000 calls annually, producing educational and self-help materials, and pursuing Medicare coverage for dually eligible beneficiaries (individuals who are eligible for both Medicare and Medicaid). The organization also provides the legal training and support for Connecticut's state health insurance and assistance program, known as CHOICES.

The Center's staff members act as consultants and trainers for individuals and groups interested in learning about health care rights, Medicare coverage and appeals, and Medicare advocacy projects. The Center collaborates widely with a variety of state and national organizations on health care policy matters, litigation, and litigation support.

To learn more about the Center and its work and to obtain important information about Medicare, health care rights, and related issues, visit the Center's Web site at *http://www.medicareadvocacy.org*.

ACKNOWLEDGMENTS

The authors gratefully acknowledge the staff of the Center for Medicare Advocacy, Inc., who helped in the production of this book and who provide constant professional support and assistance to us and to our clients. In particular, we thank Jacqueline Bender, Susan Morrison, Elizabeth Maldanado, and Susan Collins for their patient and varied assistance in the production and distribution of our material.

The Center for Medicare Advocacy, Inc., also recognizes and thanks Legal Counsel for the Elderly, Inc., of the AARP, which published the original version of much of the writing in this book. The material was written by Center for Medicare Advocacy attorneys and published in 1990 as the *Medicare Practice Manual*. It serves as the basis for this publication. Legal Counsel for the Elderly graciously released its copyright control over the writing and encouraged us to update the work and to prepare it for a new publication.

Finally, we acknowledge the Center for Medicare Advocacy's coordinator of this project, Alfred J. Chiplin, Jr., who keeps us on track and on time and who maintains his special blend of intelligence, decency, and good humor throughout the process.

The Authors
November 2006

CHAPTER 1

AN INTRODUCTION TO MEDICARE COVERAGE AND APPEALS

§1.01 HISTORY AND OVERVIEW

Medicare is the country's only national health insurance program. Individuals entitled to Social Security retirement insurance who are 65 years of age or older and individuals entitled to Social Security disability benefits for not less than 24 months are eligible to participate in Medicare. Individuals entitled to Railroad Retirement benefits or Railroad Retirement disability benefits and individuals with end-stage renal disease (ESRD) and amyotrophic lateral sclerosis (ALS) are also entitled to participate.[1] In addition, individuals who are not otherwise eligible for Medicare, but who are over age 65, may purchase coverage by paying a monthly premium.[2] Since January 1, 1983, most federal employees may count their government work toward eligibility for the Medicare hospital insurance program, Medicare Part A.[3]

Passed in 1965 as Title 18 of the Social Security Act,[4] Medicare was intended to pay some of the cost of some health care services in order to ensure access to a basic level of health care for the aged.[5] Medicare was always intended as a health insurance program. It was, and continues to be, based upon a private health insurance model. Medicare requires deductibles and copayments by the insured, and it pays only a portion of the cost of certain services for certain patients. Claims must be submitted to an insurance company or other entity, acting as an agent for the government, for approval prior to payment, and payments are usually made directly to the health care provider.

Unlike Medicaid, or Title 19 of the Social Security Act,[6] neither Medicare eligibility nor program payment is currently predicated upon the income or assets of the beneficiary.[7] Medicaid is a shared state-federal program, paid in part by both entities, and administered by state agencies with federal oversight. Medicare, on the other hand, is entirely a federal program, and benefits are paid from entirely federal sources. Both programs are overseen by the Centers for Medicare and Medicaid Services (CMS), formerly known as the Health Care Financing Administration (HCFA), a component of the United States Department of Health and Human Services (HHS).

---

[1] 42 U.S.C. §1395c. *See* 42 C.F.R. §§406.12 and 406.13, regarding qualifying due to disability or end-stage renal disease. Persons with amyotrophic lateral sclerosis (ALS) can qualify for Medicare without the 24-month waiting period effective July 1, 2001. *See* Pub. L. No. 106-554, 115 (signed into law Dec. 21, 2000).

[2] 42 U.S.C. §1395i-2.

[3] 42 U.S.C. §426(a)(2)(c), (b)(2)(c); 42 C.F.R. §406.15.

[4] 42 U.S.C. §§1395 *et seq.*

[5] Whitman v. Weinberger, 382 F. Supp. 256 (E.D. Va. 1974). Coverage for certain individuals deemed permanently disabled for 24 months was added in 1972. Social Security Amendments of 1972, 201(a) (1972).

[6] 42 U.S.C. §§1396 *et seq.*

[7] Starting in January 2007, however, individuals with incomes $80,000 or more per year and couples with incomes of $160,000 or more per year will have to pay a greater share of the Part B premium.

Since Medicare is a national program, Medicare procedures and qualifying criteria should not vary significantly from state to state. When they do, advocates should be alert to be certain that there are valid reasons for the discrepancies.

[A] The Medicare Program in Transition

Over the past several years, Congress has added new features and limitations to the Medicare program. The Balanced Budget Act of 1997 (BBA'97)[8] created a new Medicare Part C, also known as the Medicare + Choice program, now known as Medicare Advantage (MA).[9] Medicare Part C added a variety of managed care and other financing options for Medicare-covered services, while retaining the original Medicare program.

Medicare Part C allows for coordinated care plans, including Health Maintenance organizations (HMOs), Provider Service Organizations (PSOs), and both local and regional Preferred Provider Organizations (PPOs), as options for receiving coverage. Other options include Medical Savings Accounts (MSAs),[10] Private Fee-for-Service plans (PFFSs), and Private Religious-Fraternal Order plans. While these options were allowed commencing January 1999, in most areas of the country only managed care plans, including HMOs and PPOs, and PFFS plans developed.

BBA '97 also created, outside the MA program, an option for "private contracts" between physicians and their Medicare patients for the receipt of Medicare-covered services for which no Medicare payment will be made. Physicians entering into such contracts must agree not to accept Medicare reimbursement for any Medicare-covered service for two years.[11]

In December 2000, Congress passed another bill that made significant adjustments to the Medicare Program. The Medicare, Medicaid, SCHIP Benefit Improvement & Protection Act of 2000 (BIPA)[12] returned some of the funds to providers and HMOs that were reduced by BBA '97, and made some minor enhancements for beneficiaries.

The most recent changes occurred at the end of 2003 with the enactment of the Medicare Prescription Drug, Improvement, and Modernization Act of 2003 (MMA).[13] This Act included sweeping changes to the Medicare program.

---

[8] Pub. L. No. 105-33 (Aug. 5, 1997).

[9] Medicare Part C, Pub. L. No. 105-33, §4001, enacting Social Security Act 1851–1859. As discussed later, Medicare+Choice was renamed "Medicare Advantage" (MA) in December 2003. *See* Section 201, of the Medicare Prescription Drug, Improvement, and Modernization Act of 2003 (MMA), Pub. L. No. 108-173 (Dec. 8, 2003).

[10] MSA plans will be available for the first time in January 2006.

[11] Pub. L. No. 105-33, 4507, amending 1802 of the Social Security Act, 42 U.S.C. §1395a.

[12] Pub. L. No. 106-554 (Dec. 21, 2000).

[13] Pub. L. No. 108-173 (Dec. 8, 2003).

It provided Medicare beneficiaries with some limited assistance to pay for prescription drugs through a new Medicare Part D. The law also changed the name of private plans offered under Medicare Part C, from Medicare+Choice to "Medicare Advantage," and created a few additional benefits for certain beneficiaries. However, MMA also began a major restructuring of the traditional Medicare program, relying heavily on private insurance to deliver benefits. In addition, it increases beneficiary cost-sharing responsibilities.

[B] An Historical Perspective

BBA '97, BIPA, and MMA were not the first alteration of the Medicare program. Since its enactment in 1965, Medicare has been revised several times by Congress, often to increase coverage. In 1972, for example, coverage was extended to the disabled.[14] Also in 1972, coverage was extended to skilled nursing facility patients needing skilled rehabilitation rather than only to those in need of skilled nursing.[15] In 1980, Congress removed the requirement that home health patients have a prior hospitalization in order to receive Medicare home health coverage; Congress also removed the 100-visit limitation on home health coverage.[16] Despite this apparent congressional intent to increase coverage, Medicare criteria are often strictly interpreted by those who administer the program, and denials for many types of care are the norm rather than the exception.

An exception to the movement by Congress to enlarge Medicare coverage occurred in 1989, with the repeal of the Medicare Catastrophic Coverage Act of 1988 (MCCA).[17] Signed into law in July 1988, MCCA was the most significant revision and enhancement of the Medicare program since its inception. The law increased the amount of coverage available in all care settings, established some limits on beneficiary cost-sharing responsibilities, and added new benefits. The law also altered the manner in which Medicare was financed by looking only to those eligible for the program to pay for the new benefits. MCCA added to the monthly Part B premium. In addition, MCCA required a payment of a set amount for every $150 of tax liability, not to exceed a certain limit each year. This payment, which quickly became known as the Medicare surtax, was mandatory for all those eligible for Medicare, even if they did not participate in the program or did not need the new

---

[14] Social Security Amendments of 1972, 201(a) (1972).

[15] *Id.* 238(a).

[16] Omnibus Budget Reconciliation Act of 1980, 930(b), (g); 94 Stat. 2599, 2631 (1980). Note: The Balanced Budget Act of 1997 (BBA '97), Pub. L. No. 105-33, 4611, established a prior institutionalization requirement for payment of home health services and a 100-visit limit on post-institutional home health services for payment under Part A for persons entitled to benefits under Parts A and B. Other home health care for these individuals is paid under Part B. *See* discussion of the Medicare Home Health benefit, *infra*.

[17] Pub. L. No. 100-360 (1988).

benefits. This payment mechanism proved to be the death knell of MCCA; almost all of the Medicare components of MCCA were repealed in December 1989.[18]

As discussed above, Congress altered the Medicare program again in the BBA '97. As discussed throughout this text, this Act created a variety of options for receiving Medicare coverage. It also made other significant changes, which have had the effect of limiting some payments and services.[19] The revisions in the home health program, for example, created a prior hospitalization requirement for Part A coverage, established a home health spell of illness benefit period, added a 100-visit coverage limit per spell of illness under Part A for persons with both Part A and Part B coverage, and shifted the cost of care over 100 visits to Medicare Part B. The restructuring of the home health payment system, together with uncertainty about how to interpret the law, reduced the availability of home health services.

The 2003 MMA greatly expands the role of private insurance companies in Medicare. Prescription drug benefits under the new Part D are available only through private insurance companies and not through Medicare itself. In an effort to increase enrollment in managed care and other private insurance options, Congress created new private plan options under Part C. Congress also further increased funding to all private plans, paying them more money per enrollee than Medicare would pay if the enrollee had remained in the traditional program. In addition, Congress in MMA changed the way actuaries calculate the solvency of the Medicare program. This change has the potential to create unnecessary concerns about the security of Medicare and could, in future years, result in Congress's reducing benefits directly or by requiring individuals to pay more for their Medicare-covered services.

§1.02   FINANCING

Part A of the Medicare program is financed largely through federal payroll taxes paid into Social Security by employers and employees. Part B is financed by monthly premiums paid by Medicare beneficiaries and by general revenues from the federal government. In addition, Medicare beneficiaries share the cost of the program through copayments and deductibles that are required for many of the services covered under both Parts A and B.

Medicare beneficiaries must also share in the costs of the Medicare Advantage program, although in some of these plans the beneficiary's cost sharing may be modest. The beneficiary share is permitted to increase under the law as long as the increases do not exceed the actuarial value of the cost sharing that would be

---

[18] Medicare Catastrophic Repeal Act of 1989, H.R. 3607 (1989), Pub. L. No. 101-234 (Dec. 13, 1989). Note: The Qualified Medicare Beneficiary Program and the Medicaid spousal impoverishment provisions were not repealed.

[19] *See* Pub. L. No. 105-33, 4611 *et seq.*, amending 1812 of the Social Security Act, 42 U.S.C. §§1395d *et seq. See also* BBA '97 home health care discussion *infra.*

applicable, on average, to individuals who are not members of a Medicare Advantage plan.[20]

§1.03   ADMINISTRATION

The Medicare program is administered by CMS, under the direction of the Secretary of HHS. It has 10 regional offices throughout the country that oversee the program for their areas; CMS contracts with private organizations, usually insurance companies, to review claims and make payment. These entities are known as fiscal intermediaries (now called "Administrative Contractors") for Part A skilled nursing facility, home health, and hospice cases; Quality Improvement Organizations (QIOs), formerly peer review organizations (PROs), for hospital cases; and carriers (now called "Administrative Contractors") for all Part B cases. Qualified Independent Contractors (QICs) began reviewing Part A reconsiderations in 2005; they began reviewing Part B reconsiderations in 2006. Medicare Advantage determinations are made by the private insurance companies that offer the plans and then may be reviewed by a private entity under contract with CMS.[21]

In the traditional Medicare system, these entities review coverage decisions issued by providers under their authority and issue notices known as initial determinations from which a beneficiary can appeal. Except for inpatient hospital cases, intermediaries and carriers make initial determinations and issue payments when Medicare coverage is available. In hospital cases, QIOs make the initial determinations but do not issue payment; instead, they authorize the appropriate intermediary to issue payment when coverage criteria are met. QIOs, intermediaries, and carriers are all responsible for making decisions in the first stage of the appeal process, known as redeterminations.

Initial coverage decisions for beneficiaries enrolled in Medicare Advantage plans are made by the plan itself.[22] The HMO is required to apply CMS policy and coverage rules when making its coverage decisions. Reviews of unfavorable plan decisions are handled by the private contractor.

CMS guides the claim review, decision, and payment process by issuing health insurance coverage manuals as well as various mailings, bulletins, guidance, and memoranda. These writings purport to interpret the statute and regulations, but sometimes go beyond interpretation and create criteria that are more restrictive than the Medicare Act. Practically, the manuals and other unpublished directives from CMS form the basis for the coverage decisions that affect most beneficiaries.

---

[20] 42 U.S.C. §1395w-24(e).

[21] The MMA also included changes to the administration of Medicare. By 2011, all claims will be reviewed by Medicare Administrative Contractors (MACs) chosen by CMS through a competitive bidding process.

[22] We use the terms "Medicare managed care plans" and "HMOs" generically to refer to all plans under Medicare Part C, including PPOs and PFFS plans.

Advocates should be alert to discrepancies between standards established by CMS and those established by the Medicare Act and regulations.[23] Where detrimental discrepancies exist, they may be the grounds for appeals or federal court challenges. Importantly, administrative law judges and federal judges rely on the Medicare statute and regulations, not on CMS's guidelines, though recent regulatory changes require ALJs to give greater deference to CMS guidelines than was given in the past. Thus, many cases have been won on appeal to an administrative law judge (ALJ) that were denied initially and at reconsideration based on CMS rules. Furthermore, successful challenges to CMS's restrictive criteria have been brought in United States District Court as violating the due process clause of the Fifth Amendment to the United States Constitution, the Medicare Act and regulations, and the Administrative Procedure Act.[24]

Advocates should also watch for discrepancies that may exist between standards enforced by CMS's regional offices, intermediaries, and carriers. Since Medicare is a federal program, beneficiaries should not be subject to more restrictive criteria in one region of the country than in another.

§1.04   ENROLLMENT AND ELIGIBILITY

Generally, individuals who are 65 and are entitled to Social Security or Railroad Retirement benefits are automatically entitled to and enrolled in Medicare Part A and will be deemed to have also enrolled in Part B.[25] Persons who are not yet receiving Social Security or Railroad Retirement benefits must enroll in Part A during an initial enrollment period, which begins in the third month before the person reaches age 65 (or reaches age 65 and becomes a U.S. citizen, or a permanent resident who has lived continually in the United States for the five years immediately preceding application for Medicare). The initial enrollment period extends for the next seven months.[26]

An application for Social Security or Railroad Retirement will also suffice for Medicare. A separate application is not necessary. Individuals who take early retirement under Social Security will be automatically enrolled in Medicare when they attain age 65.

---

[23] New Medicare appeals regulations require administrative law judges to give deference to CMS program guidance. 42 C.F.R. §§405.1062.

[24] *See* Grijalva v. Shalala, 153 F.3d 1115 (9th Cir. 1998), *vacated and remanded,* 526 U.S. 1096, 119 S. Ct. 1573, 143 L. Ed. 2d 669 (1999); Healey v. Shalala, Civ. Action No. 3:98 CV 418 (DJS) (Mar. 2000); Linoz v. Heckler, Medicare & Medicaid Guide (CCH) 35,876 (9th Cir. 1986); Duggan v. Bowen, 691 F. Supp. (D.D.C. 1988); Fox v. Bowen, 656 F. Supp. 1236 (D. Conn. 1987); Hooper v. Sullivan, Medicare & Medicaid Guide (CCH) 37,985 (D. Conn. 1989); Sarrassat v. Bowen, No. C88-20161 (N.D. Cal. 1989).

[25] Social Security Act 406, 42 U.S.C. §1395p(f).

[26] 42 U.S.C. §1395i-2(a); 42 C.F.R. §406.21(b).

Those who are 65 but who delay receipt of Social Security benefits may still enroll in Medicare but must file an application. Individuals who have been entitled to Social Security or Railroad Retirement disability benefits for 24 months are entitled to Medicare but also must apply to enroll in the program. Applications may be made with Social Security after receiving disability benefits for 21 months.[27] Effective July 1, 2001, the 24-month waiting period is eliminated for disabled persons diagnosed with amyotrophic lateral sclerosis (ALS, also known as Lou Gehrig's disease).[28]

Medicare coverage can be extended up to 78 months after disability benefits are terminated if the beneficiary is engaged in an approved nine-month trial work period after a period of disability.[29] The previous period of disability benefits will count toward the 24-month eligibility requirement, should the beneficiary seek to reestablish Medicare eligibility.

Individuals who miss the initial enrollment period must wait for a general enrollment period to enter Medicare Part B. The general enrollment period is the first three months of each calendar year (January 1 through March 31). Medicare Part B benefits do not begin until July of that year.[30]

The new Part D prescription drug benefit, which became effective January 1, 2006, requires individuals who want drug coverage to affirmatively enroll in a prescription drug plan. The initial enrollment period for individuals who had Medicare Part A and/or Part B, or who first became eligible for Part A and/or Part B through February 2006, ran from November 15, 2005, through May 15, 2006. Subsequently, the initial enrollment period for Part D corresponds to the individual's initial enrollment period for Part A.[31] Individuals who do not enroll during their initial enrollment period or who want to change the plan in which they have enrolled may do so during the annual coordinated enrollment period for Part C plans, November 15 through December 31 of each year.[32]

Penalties apply for late enrollment under Part A, Part B, and Part D. Under Part A, a ten percent penalty, based on the monthly Part A premium price, is imposed for every month of late enrollment up to twice the number of months for which the beneficiary has failed to enroll.[33] Under Part B, a 10 percent penalty is also imposed. The penalty is for each full year (12-month gap) of late enrollment.[34] Unlike Part A, there is no end point to the penalty under Part B. Under Part D, the penalty is the greater of an amount that is actuarially sound for each uncovered month or 1 percent of the national average monthly beneficiary base

---

[27] 42 U.S.C. §1395p(g).

[28] BIPA, Pub. L. No. 106-554, 115 (Dec. 21, 2000).

[29] 42 C.F.R. §406.12(e)(2).

[30] 42 C.F.R. §§406.21(c), 407.12(a)(2).

[31] 42 C.F.R. §423.38(a).

[32] 42 U.S.C. §1395w-101(b).

[33] 42 U.S.C. §1395i-2(c)(6).

[34] 42 U.S.C. §1395r(b); 42 C.F.R. §408.22.

premium for each uncovered month, whichever is greater. As with Part B, there is no end point to the penalty.[35]

Medicare has established a special enrollment period (SEP) for persons who do not purchase Medicare Part B at age 65 because they (or their spouse) are covered under an employer's large group health plan.[36] The special enrollment is generally defined to include each month in which a person is enrolled in a group health plan as described in Sections 1862(b)(1)(A)(v) and 1862(b)(1)(B)(iv) of the Social Security Act and to end with the last day of the eighth consecutive month after the person is no longer enrolled.[37]

A SEP is also available to eligible Medicare beneficiaries who are members of a qualified HMO.[38] In addition, BBA '97 created a six-month SEP for disabled workers who lose benefits under a group health plan. The SEP for these individuals starts the first day of the month in which the termination of benefits occurs.[39]

Individuals who delay enrolling in a Part D plan because they have creditable drug coverage, i.e., drug coverage that is as good as Medicare, through another source also have a special enrollment period if that drug coverage ends. There are additional SEPS that allow individuals to change drug plans at times other than the annual enrollment period, under limited circumstances.[40]

[A] Medicare Advantage (HMO, PPO, and PFFS) Eligibility and Enrollment

Beneficiaries have the option to receive their Medicare coverage through a participating private Medicare Advantage plan in areas where those plans are available. In order to do so, beneficiaries must be enrolled in both Part A and Part B.[41] Beneficiaries enrolled only in Medicare Part B are not eligible to enroll in a Medicare Advantage plan. The beneficiary must live within the service area served by the HMO[42] and must not be enrolled in any other Medicare-participating HMO.[43]

---

[35] 42 U.S.C. §1395ww-113(b). In 2007 the late penalty will be $1.91.

[36] 42 U.S.C. §1395p(i); 42 C.F.R. §406.24.

[37] 42 U.S.C. §1395p(i)(3)(A), (B).

[38] 42 U.S.C. §1395i-2(c)(7); *see* definition of eligible individual, 42 U.S.C. §1395i-2(a).

[39] 42 U.S.C. §1395i-2(c)(7); *see* definition of eligible individual, 42 U.S.C. §1395i-2(a).

[40] [Reserved]

[41] 42 C.F.R. §422.50(a).

[42] For this discussion, the term "HMO" is used interchangeably with "Medicare Advantage." Generally, a Medicare Advantage plan acts as an insurer of health care and/or as a provider of comprehensive health care services to its enrollees. Medicare Advantage plans receive a capitated payment from Medicare for each enrollee in return for providing all Medicare covered services.

[43] 42 C.F.R. §§422.2, 422.50(b). The service area, as defined by CMS, is the geographic area for which CMS grants its approval for the plan to enroll eligible individuals. A service area generally consists of a full county or counties. In 2006, regional PPOs serving multiple states became available in some areas of the country.

Medicare Advantage plans must provide the services currently available under Medicare Parts A and B. Plans must pass on to beneficiaries any cost savings achieved through efficient plan administration in the form of additional benefits, including a reduction in the Part B premium. Medicare Advantage plans may offer supplemental benefits for which a separate premium is charged, but the separate premium may not vary among individuals within the plan and must not exceed certain actuarial and community rating requirements.

To enroll, the beneficiary must file an application with a participating HMO. Filing an application does not guarantee enrollment. To ensure fairness in the enrollment process, each application must be dated when it is received and processed in chronological order by date of receipt. Under Medicare regulations, the HMO is required to provide prompt notification to the applicant in writing of acceptance or denial.[44]

The HMO may deny enrollment only if acceptance of the individual (1) would require the HMO to exceed its overall enrollment capacity; (2) would cause the enrollment to become substantially nonrepresentative of the general population in the HMO's geographic area; or (3) would prevent the HMO from complying with the terms of its contract with CMS.[45] HMOs may choose to close enrollment. However, unless HMOs receive a "capacity waiver" from CMS, they must accept applications from certain beneficiaries, such as those who move into the geographic area.

Generally, application decisions may not be based on the age or health of the applicant.[46] However, ESRD patients may only enroll as new enrollees in a special needs Medicare Advantage plan that serves people with chronic conditions or those dually eligible for Medicare and Medicaid. Individuals who develop ESRD while already enrolled in an HMO may remain in the plan. If the HMO requires periodic re-enrollment, they must also be permitted to re-enroll.[47] Enrollment in the HMO continues until such time as the enrollee is disenrolled voluntarily or involuntarily.[48]

Issues of disenrollment are a critical concern, particularly when costly care and services are involved. Medicare has established specific regulatory requirements defining the circumstances for involuntary disenrollment. They include the failure to pay premiums or deductibles as required, a permanent move outside the HMO's service area, fraudulent statements on behalf of the enrollee leading to enrollment, and disruptive behavior that impairs the HMO's ability to provide services. Beneficiaries must be provided notice and appeal rights information before disenrollment.[49]

---

[44] 42 C.F.R. §422.60.

[45] *Id.*

[46] 42 C.F.R. §422.10.

[47] 42 C.F.R. §422.50(a)(2).

[48] 42 C.F.R. §422.74.

[49] 42 C.F.R. §422.74.

[B] Process for Exercising Choice of Medicare Advantage Plan

Beneficiaries can elect to enroll or disenroll from a Medicare Advantage plan only in accord with certain limitations.[50]

1. If there are one or more Medicare Advantage plans offered in an individual's service area at the time the individual first becomes entitled to benefits under Part A and enrolled under Part B, the individual may make an election during an initial election period. Coverage under the Plan becomes effective as of the first date on which the individual may receive coverage, i.e., the month in which the individual becomes entitled to Medicare A and B.

2. "Lock-in" rules, so called because beneficiaries become "locked in" to the choices they made during the previous November's annual enrollment period, became effective on January 1, 2006. A beneficiary could change plans at any time during the first six months of 2006, January through June, in addition to the annual election period. Starting in 2007 and continuing thereafter, a beneficiary may only change plans during the first three months of the year, January through March, in addition to the annual election period.[51]

3. All beneficiaries may make an election during an "annual, coordinated open enrollment period." This annual election will permit beneficiaries to enroll or disenroll from the various offerings during the period from November 15 through December 31 each year.

4. Certain "special election periods" apply only if (a) the Medicare Advantage plan was terminated; (b) the beneficiary ceased to be eligible for enrollment in such plan; (c) the beneficiary demonstrated that the plan violated its contract with Medicare; or (d) some other exceptional circumstance exists.

5. Beneficiaries in the traditional Medicare program who do not make a plan election during the annual election period remain in the original program. If an individual does not make an election and is in an HMO, that individual will remain in the HMO. Elections become effective January 1 of the following year. However, a beneficiary who was previously covered by original Medicare and who elected a Medicare Advantage plan will, if hospitalized as of the effective date of the election, have that hospitalization covered by original Medicare until discharge. Note that this special rule applies only to hospital stays; all other ongoing Medicare-covered services should be covered by the Medicare HMO.

6. CMS must conduct a special educational and publicity campaign every November to inform beneficiaries about Medicare Advantage election procedures.[52] At the time of enrollment and every year thereafter, Medicare

---

[50] 42 U.S.C. §1395w-21(e).

[51] 42 U.S.C. §1395w-21(e)(2).

[52] 42 C.F.R. §§422.50–422.80.

Advantage plans must disclose to enrollees in their service area the number and mix of participating doctors, emergency service options, out-of-service coverage, procedures for obtaining emergency services, optional supplemental coverage and costs, prior authorization rules, grievance and appeals procedures, quality assurance mechanisms, number of grievances and appeals and their disposition, and a summary of the method of compensating doctors.

§1.05 COVERAGE

The Medicare Act allows for coverage when the services received are medically "reasonable and necessary for the diagnosis or treatment of illness or injury or to improve the functioning of a malformed body member."[53] Medicare coverage is *excluded* by statute for custodial care, except in the case of hospice services.[54] These requirements, that the care be medically reasonable and necessary for treatment or diagnosis, and that the care be "skilled," are often strictly interpreted by those who administer the Medicare program; they create the most frequent obstacles to coverage.

With the enactment of MMA, Medicare has four parts: Part A, Part B, Part C, and Part D. Part A covers inpatient hospital care, inpatient care in a skilled nursing facility, home health care services, and hospice care.[55] Part B covers medical care and services provided by physicians and other medical practitioners, durable medical equipment, a variety of outpatient care services, and home health services not otherwise covered under Part A.[56] Medicare Part C, originally known as Medicare+Choice and now called Medicare Advantage (MA), added a variety of systems for the *financing* of Medicare covered health services. These Medicare Advantage options must offer the core package of benefits available under Parts A and B, plus additional benefits.[57] Starting in 2006, Medicare Part D adds a limited prescription drug benefit offered through private insurance plans. Part D only specifies the deductible, copayment, and out-of-pocket limits for the drug benefits. Private insurers may set their own drug formularies and premiums, and they may

---

[53] 42 U.S.C. §1395y(a)(1)(A). Note: The "improvement" criteria only apply to coverage for a "malformed body member."

[54] 42 U.S.C. §1395y(a)(9).

[55] 42 U.S.C. §§1395c, 1395d.

[56] 42 U.S.C. §§1395j, 1395k.

[57] 42 U.S.C. §1395w-21 *et seq.* (Plans must pass on to beneficiaries 75 percent of cost savings achieved through efficient plan administration, in the form of additional benefits, including payment of the premium for drug coverage or a reduction in the Part B premium. 42 C.F.R. §422.266. In addition, under some circumstances, plans may offer supplemental benefits for which a separate premium is charged, but the separate premium may not vary among individuals within the plan and must meet certain actuarial and community rating requirements.)

even vary the cost sharing as long as the drug package they offer is the actuarial equivalent of the statutory standard benefit.[58]

[A] Part A

[1] Hospital Coverage

A beneficiary is entitled to 90 days of Medicare coverage for hospital care during each benefit period, or "spell of illness," after the beneficiary meets the deductible ($992 in 2007). A spell of illness begins when a beneficiary receives Medicare-covered inpatient hospital care and ends when the patient has spent 60 consecutive days outside the hospital (or skilled nursing facility) or remains in the health care institution but does not receive Medicare-covered services for 60 consecutive days.[59]

In addition, the beneficiary is entitled to 60 days of hospital care as a "lifetime reserve." Once exhausted, lifetime reserve days may not be replenished. If the patient remains in the hospital beyond the 60th day, he or she is responsible for a daily coinsurance amount for days 61 to 90 ($248 per day in 2007). The coinsurance for lifetime reserve days is even heftier ($496 per day in 2007).

In 1983, Congress established a prospective payment system (PPS) for Medicare reimbursement of inpatient acute care hospital services.[60] Care in Medicare-certified rehabilitation and psychiatric hospitals and hospital units is exempt from the DRG (diagnosis-related group) system. Under PPS, Medicare payment is made at a predetermined, specific rate for each discharge. All discharges are classified according to a list of DRGs. The list contains approximately 500 specific DRGs. Each DRG is assigned a dollar amount based on the average cost of caring for patients with similar diagnoses in the past, regardless of whether the patient's care actually cost the hospital less, or more, to deliver.

[2] Skilled Nursing Facility Care

Medicare Part A provides payment for posthospital care in skilled nursing facilities (SNFs) for up to 100 days during each spell of illness. If Medicare coverage requirements are met, the patient is entitled to full coverage of the first 20 days of SNF care. From the 21st through the 100th day, Medicare pays for all covered services except for a daily coinsurance amount ($124 per day in 2007).

---

[58] Pub. L. No. 108-173 adding 1860D-1-1860D-42 of the Social Security Act, 42 U.S.C. §§1395w-101–1395w-151.

[59] 42 U.S.C. §1395x(b) and 42 C.F.R. §409.10-409.19 (inpatient hospital services covered); 42 U.S.C. §1395d(a) and 42 C.F.R. §409.61 (scope of benefit); 42 C.F.R. §409.82 (hospital deductible); 42 C.F.R. §409.83 (hospital coinsurance); 42 C.F.R. §409.60 (benefit period rules).

[60] 42 U.S.C. §1395ww(d).

The SNF patient will not be entitled to any Medicare coverage unless he or she was hospitalized for at least three days prior to the SNF admission and, generally, was admitted to the SNF within 30 days of the hospital discharge.[61]

Skilled nursing facility coverage includes the services generally available in a SNF: nursing care provided by registered professional nurses, bed and board, physical therapy, occupational therapy, speech therapy, social services, medications, supplies, equipment, and other services necessary for the patient to attain or maintain the highest practicable level of functioning. However, "convenience" items, such as a telephone, are not covered by Medicare.

There are certain requirements that must be met in order for a patient to receive Medicare coverage. These requirements include:

1. A physician must certify that the patient needs skilled nursing facility care;

2. The beneficiary must generally be admitted to the SNF within 30 days of a three-day qualifying hospital stay;

3. The beneficiary must require daily skilled nursing or rehabilitation; and

4. The care needed by the patient must, as a practical matter, be available only in a skilled nursing facility on an inpatient basis.

[3] Home Health Care

Medicare covers home health services in full, with no required deductible or copayments from the beneficiary. Services must be medically necessary and reasonable, and the following criteria must be met:

1. A physician has signed or will sign a plan of care.

2. The patient is homebound. This criterion is met if leaving home requires a considerable and taxing effort, which may be shown by the patient needing personal assistance, or the help of a wheelchair or crutches, etc. Occasional but infrequent "walks around the block" are allowable.

3. The patient needs or will need physical or speech therapy, *or* intermittent skilled nursing (from once a day for periods of 21 days at a time if there is a predictable end to the need for daily nursing care, to once every 60 days).

4. The home health care is provided by, or under arrangement with, a Medicare-certified provider.

---

[61] 42 U.S.C. §1395x(h) and 42 C.F.R. §409.20 (SNF services); 42 U.S.C. §1395d(a)(2)(A) and 42 C.F.R. §409.60 (scope of benefit); 42 U.S.C. §1395f(a)(2)(b) (physician certification requirement); 42 C.F.R. §409.35 (practical matter rule); 42 U.S.C. §1395x(i) (three-day qualifying hospital stay); 42 U.S.C. §1395x(i) (30-day rule); 42 C.F.R. §§409.30–409.34 (daily skilled care requirement).

If the triggering conditions described above are met, the beneficiary is entitled to Medicare coverage for home health services.[62] Home health services include:

- Part-time or intermittent nursing care provided by or under the supervision of a registered professional nurse;

- Physical, occupational, or speech therapy;

- Medical social services under the direction of a physician; and

- To the extent permitted in regulations, part-time or intermittent services of a home health aide.[63]

In addition to the coverage criteria described above:

1. For individuals who have Part A *and* Part B, payment is available under Part A for *only* 100 visits per spell of illness and *only* if the services are provided within 14 days of a three-day prior hospital stay or of a skilled nursing facility stay of any duration. This coverage is known as the postinstitutional home health benefit. The new home health spell of illness concept is similar to that which exists for hospital and skilled nursing facility care: it commences with the first day in which the beneficiary receives home health services and ends after the 60th consecutive day in which he or she is neither a hospital nor an SNF patient, nor provided home health services.

2. Payment is available under Part B for all services not covered under Part A, including those provided to individuals who do *not* meet the prior institutionalization requirement and those who have received coverage for the maximum 100 visits under Part A.

---

[62] 42 U.S.C. §1395x(m) and 42 C.F.R. §§409.40 *et seq.* (home health coverage and coverage criteria); 42 U.S.C. §§1395x(f)(a)(8), 1395n(a)(2)(f) (homebound criteria). Note: The Medicare, Medicaid, and SCHIP Benefits Improvement and Protection Act of 2000, Pub. L. No. 106-554 (Dec. 21, 2000), known as BIPA, amended the homebound definition to clarify that individuals who attend adult day centers or religious services should not be disqualified from Medicare home health coverage on grounds that they violate the homebound definition.

[63] Note: Good discharge planning is an important tool in obtaining proper home health and other posthospital services, including skilled nursing facility services and rehabilitation services. It is significantly underutilized as an advocacy tool. Discharge planning is available to Medicare beneficiaries and others as a condition of a hospital's participation in the Medicare program. Services should be more than a rudimentary search for the next nursing home bed or home health agency opening. *See* 42 U.S.C. §1395x(ee) (added to the Medicare Statute in OBRA '87); 42 C.F.R. §§482.43 *et seq.*, effective Jan. 12, 1995. Interpretive guidelines and survey procedures for hospital discharge planning are available in the Medicare State Operations Manual, CMS Publication 100-7, Appendix A, Section 482.43, <www.cms.gov/manuals/107>. *See also* Alfred J. Chiplin, Jr., *Breathing Life Into Discharge Planning,* 13 Elder L.J. 1, 1-83 (2005).

3. Individuals who *only* have Part A receive all coverage under that section of the Medicare program, with or without a prior institutionalization. Individuals who *only* have Part B receive all coverage under that section of the program.

4. The qualifying term "part time and intermittent," for purposes of defining the nursing services that will trigger coverage, is defined as nursing care that is provided as little as once every 60 days and as much as daily for predictable periods of 21 days at a time, with extensions in exceptional circumstances when the need for additional care is finite and predictable. Part-time or intermittent services, for purposes of coverage, are defined as skilled nursing and home health aide services furnished any number of days per week so long as they are furnished less than eight hours each day and 28 or fewer hours each week combined (or on a case-by-case basis, up to 35 hours per week combined).

5. Individuals who attend adult day centers or religious services should not be disqualified from Medicare home health coverage on grounds that they violate the homebound definition.[64] In addition, Congress in MMA created a two-year demonstration project in which some Medicare beneficiaries with chronic conditions who meet certain eligibility criteria will be deemed to be homebound for purposes of receiving home health services.[65]

6. The Secretary implemented a PPS for home health services on October 1, 2000. The financial incentives and disincentives under the PPS have led to reductions and terminations of care to some patients.

[4] Hospice Care

Medicare has provided coverage for hospice care since 1982. Hospice care is intended to provide palliative and supportive care for terminally ill people and their families rather than treatment for the underlying condition. Medicare covers two 90-day periods of hospice care and an unlimited number of additional periods of 60 days each.

To receive Medicare hospice coverage, a patient must elect affirmatively to enter hospice coverage and, as a consequence, out of most other Medicare coverage for treatment of the underlying terminal condition. The hospice care must generally be provided by, or under arrangement with, one Medicare-certified hospice program during each period.

To receive Medicare coverage for hospice care, the patient must be certified as terminally ill by the patient's physician and/or the hospice staff physician,[66] and

---

[64] The Medicare, Medicaid, and SCHIP Benefits Improvement and Protection Act of 2000 (Pub. L. No. 106-554 (Dec. 21, 2000)), known as BIPA.

[65] Pub. L. No. 108-173 702.

[66] Both the hospice physician and the patient's attending physician (if the patient has an attending physician) must certify that the patient is terminally ill for the first 90-day election period. For

the hospice care must be part of a written plan of treatment established by the attending physician and hospice medical professionals. If coverage conditions are met, Medicare is available for an array of services, including:

- Nursing care;

- Physician services;

- Counseling services for the patient and the family or other caretakers;

- Medical social services;

- Short-term inpatient care;

- Home health aides;

- Homemaker services;

- Medical supplies, equipment, appliances, and biologicals (including pain medication);

- Physical, occupational, and speech therapy.[67]

[B] Part B

Part B of Medicare provides coverage for a host of services for beneficiaries who are in non-institutionalized settings. Part B is optional. It is financed by premiums paid by individuals enrolled in the program and by general revenues from the federal government. Since 1973, individuals receiving Social Security retirement benefits, individuals receiving Social Security disability benefits for 24 months, and individuals otherwise entitled to Medicare Part A are automatically enrolled in Part B unless they decline coverage. Others must enroll in Part B by filing a request at the Social Security office during certain designated periods.

In 2007, the monthly premium will be $93.50. Starting in 2007 the Part B premium will be income-related, so that individuals with incomes of $80,000 or more and couples with incomes of $160,000 or more will pay higher Part B premiums. Participants often have this premium automatically deducted from their Social Security check. Part B also has an annual deductible ($131 in 2007). Each year, before Medicare pays anything, the patient must incur medical expenses sufficient to meet the deductible, based on Medicare's approved "reasonable

---

subsequent election periods, only one physician is required to certify that the patient is terminally ill. Pub. L. No. 105-33, 4443. Note: BIPA clarified that the certification regarding terminal illness of an individual shall be based on the attending physician's or medical director's *clinical* judgment regarding the normal course of the individual's illness. Pub. L. No. 106-554 332 (Dec. 21, 2000).

[67] 42 U.S.C. §1395x(dd) and 42 C.F.R. Pt. 418 (hospice benefit); 42 C.F.R. §418.22 (physician certification); 42 U.S.C. §1395d(d) (benefit periods); 42 C.F.R. §418.24(a) (hospice election rules).

charge," not on the provider's actual charge.[68] These figures are updated annually, effective April 1st of each year.

After the beneficiary meets the deductible, Part B will pay 80 percent of the reasonable charge for covered services, the reimbursement rate determined by Medicare; the beneficiary is responsible for the remaining 20 percent as coinsurance.[69] Unfortunately, the reasonable charge is often less than the provider's actual charge. If the provider agrees to "accept assignment," the provider agrees to accept Medicare's reasonable charge rate as payment in full, and the patient is only responsible for the remaining 20 percent.

If the provider does not accept assignment, the patient will be billed for a balance beyond the 20 percent coinsurance payment. There is, however, a ceiling on charges to Medicare beneficiaries even for providers who do not accept assignment. This ceiling is known as the "Limiting Charge," which is often higher than the Medicare reasonable charge but often less than the provider's actual charge, but can be no more than 115 percent above the Medicare reasonable charge.[70]

The major benefit under Part B is payment for physicians' services. In addition, durable medical equipment, outpatient therapy, diagnostic X-rays, and laboratory tests are covered. Congress has also mandated an increase in the home health services covered under Part B and added additional preventive benefits.[71]

The following is a partial list of items and services that can be covered under Part B:

- Physicians' services;

- Home health services;

- Services and supplies, including drugs and biologicals that cannot be self-administered, furnished incidental to physicians' services;

- Diagnostic X-ray tests, diagnostic laboratory tests, and other diagnostic tests;

- X-ray therapy, radium therapy, and radioactive isotope therapy;

---

[68] As a result of the MMA, the Part B deductible will increase yearly based on the yearly percentage increase in the monthly actuarial value of benefits paid out of the Part B trust fund. The income limits for determining the Part B premium will increase each year by the Consumer Price Index for urban consumers. Pub. L. No. 108-173 629, amending 42 U.S.C. §§1395l(b), 1395r, 1395w.

[69] Part B will only pay 50 percent (62.5 percent of the approved amount times 80 percent) of the reasonable charge for outpatient mental health treatment. However, diagnostic services such as psychological testing to establish a diagnosis, brief office visits to monitor or change prescriptions, and medical management furnished to someone with Alzheimer's disease or a related disorder are not subject to the additional payment limitation. 42 C.F.R. §410.155.

[70] 42 U.S.C. §1395w-4(g); *see* Garellick v. Sullivan, 987 F.2d 913 (2d Cir. 1993) (constitutionality of provision upheld), *cert. denied,* 510 U.S. 821, 114 S. Ct. 78, 126 L. Ed. 2d 47 (1993); *see also* Chiplin, *The Medicare Limiting Charge: An Issue of Implementation and Enforcement,* 26 Clearinghouse Rev. 167 (1992). (*See* further limiting charge discussion *infra,* 1.05[B][2].)

[71] 42 U.S.C. §§1395d *et seq.*

- Surgical dressings and splints, casts, and other devices used for fractures and dislocations;

- Durable medical equipment;

- Prosthetic devices;

- Braces, trusses, artificial limbs, and eyes;

- Ambulance services;

- Some outpatient and ambulatory surgical services;

- Some outpatient hospital services;

- Some physical therapy services;[72]

- Some occupational therapy;

- Some outpatient speech therapy;

- Comprehensive outpatient rehabilitation facility services;

- Rural health clinic services;

- Institutional and home dialysis services, supplies, and equipment;

- Ambulatory surgical center services;

- Antigens and blood-clotting factors;

- Influenza, pneumococcal, and hepatitis B vaccines;

- Some Health Maintenance Organization services;

- Some Pap smear screenings;

- Some mammography screenings;

- Some diabetes tests;

- Some other preventive services including colorectal, prostate cancer, and glaucoma screening, and some medical nutrition therapy;

- Qualified psychologist services;

- Therapeutic shoes for patients with severe diabetic foot disease.

Medicare Part B is fairly comprehensive but far from complete. Certain items and services are excluded from coverage. They include:

- Services that are not medically reasonable or necessary;

- Custodial care;

---

[72] Caps on the amount Medicare will pay for out-patient therapy services went into effect on January 1, 2006. In 2006, the combined annual limit for physical therapy and speech language pathology is $1760; the annual limit for occupational therapy is $1760. The 2007 caps were not available at the time this publication went to press.

- Personal comfort items and services;

- Care that does not meaningfully contribute to the treatment of illness, injury, or a malformed body member;

- Prescription drugs that do not require administration by a physician;

- Routine physical checkups;

- Eyeglasses or contact lenses in most cases;

- Eye examinations for the purpose of prescribing, fitting, or changing eyeglasses or contact lenses;

- Hearing aids and examinations for hearing aids;

- Immunizations except for pneumococcal and hepatitis B vaccine;

- Orthopedic shoes and other supportive devices for the foot unless intended as an instrumental part of a leg brace;

- Cosmetic surgery;

- Most dental services; and

- Routine foot care.

[1] Preventive Services

As a general rule, Medicare coverage is not available for preventive care services, checkups, comfort items, or respite care. However, since the late 1990s Congress has been adding preventive services to those few that already existed in the Medicare program (which included influenza, pneumococcal, and hepatitis B vaccines). These additional services include:

- An annual mammogram for women age 40 and over (Part B deductible does not apply).

- Annual Pap smears and pelvic exams for beneficiaries considered at high risk or following an abnormal Pap smear. For women not in these groups, coverage is for Pap smears and pelvic exams once every two years (deductible does not apply).

- Prostate cancer screening on an annual basis for men over age 50.

- Colorectal cancer screening tests for beneficiaries age 50 and older. Frequency and payment limits are to be determined by the Secretary. A formula for deductibles and co-pays is included in the legislation.

- Outpatient diabetes self-management training services, blood testing strips, and monitors.

- Bone mass measurement tests.

- Telehealth services when a beneficiary resides in a rural county designated as a health professional shortage area and where other criteria are met.

- Coverage of screening colonoscopy once every ten years or within four years of a screening flexible sigmoidoscopy for all persons who are *not* at high risk.

- Coverage of medical nutrition therapy services for patients with diabetes or kidney disease.

- New coverage for routine glaucoma screening for persons at risk for glaucoma.

Additional preventive benefits were added to Medicare by MMA (Public Law 108-173, December 8, 2003). These benefits include the following and became effective on January 1, 2005:[73]

- Coverage of an initial physical examination performed within the first six months of an individual's initial coverage under Part B. Note that this benefit is available only to individuals whose Part B coverage begins on or after January 1, 2005.

- Coverage of a blood test for early detection of cardiovascular disease including tests for cholesterol levels and other lipid or triglyceride levels for individuals determined to be at risk.

- Coverage of diabetes screening tests for the purpose of early detection in individuals who are considered to be at risk for diabetes.

- Coverage of intravenous immune globulin for the treatment of primary immune deficiency diseases in the home.

[2] Limits on Physician Charges

As discussed above, when an item or service is determined to be coverable under Medicare Part B, it is reimbursed at 80 percent of a payment rate approved by Medicare known as the "approved charge"; the patient is responsible for the remaining 20 percent. Unfortunately, the "approved" (or "reasonable") charge is often substantially less than the *actual* charge. The obvious result of this reimbursement system is that Medicare payment, even for items and services covered by Part B, is often inadequate. The patient is left with out-of-pocket expenses. When a physician accepts "assignment," he or she agrees to accept the Medicare-approved charge as full payment for the services provided. Medicare pays 80 percent of the approved charge. Either the patient or supplemental insurance pays the remaining 20 percent copayment. No further payment is due to the physician.

---

[73] Pub. L. No. 108-173 amending 42 U.S.C. §§1395x(s) 1395x(xx), 1395x(yy), 1395x(zz), 1395yy, 1395zz.

Often local senior centers, area agencies on aging, and Social Security offices have lists of physicians, other providers, and medical equipment suppliers who accept Medicare assignment. CMS provides information on its Medicare Web site at *www.medicare.gov*. Also, a few states require physicians and other Part B providers who serve Medicare patients to accept assignment via their own balanced billing statutes. Massachusetts, for example, requires physicians to accept assignment for all Medicare patients; Connecticut requires the acceptance of assignment for low- and moderate-income Medicare patients. New York and Pennsylvania also limit what physicians can charge Medicare patients.

When a physician does not accept assignment, he or she may "balance bill" the patient above the Medicare-approved charge. "Balance bill" refers to the physician's charge above the Medicare-approved rate. Federal law sets a limit known as the "limiting charge" on the amount a physician may balance bill. Since 1991 the limiting charge has been based upon a percentage of the Medicare approved charge for physician services.

Generally, a doctor who does not accept assignment may not charge a total of more than 115 percent of the Medicare-approved amount. The patient's Medicare Summary Notice (MSN), the written notice that is sent to patients after a Medicare claim is processed, will state the approved charge for the doctor's services. Usually, the patient can calculate the physician's limiting charge for the services described in the MSN by multiplying the Medicare-approved charge by 115 percent. Medicare's calculation of the limiting charge will be stated on the MSN.

For example, assume the patient goes to a doctor who does not accept assignment. The doctor's actual charge is $600, but the Medicare approved charge allows only $349.37. The doctor's total bill may not exceed $401.89 (115 percent × $349.47); this is the limiting charge. Medicare will pay $279.50 (80 percent of the $349.37 approved charge). The physician cannot charge the patient more than $122.39 ($401.89 - Medicare payment of $279.50). If the doctor bills above $401.89, he is billing above the limiting charge and is violating federal law.

In some instances, the limiting charge will be more or less than 115 percent of the approved charge. If this seems to be the case, or if other questions arise, you can obtain specific limiting charge information by calling the provider's Medicare carrier.

§1.06   MEDICARE SAVINGS PROGRAMS (MSP)

[A]   Qualified Medicare Beneficiary Program

States are required to pay the deductibles, coinsurance, and premiums for Medicare Parts A and B for certain low-income Medicare beneficiaries, under the Qualified Medicare Beneficiary Program (QMB).[74] These individuals can have incomes up to the federal poverty level, which is $816.67 per month for an

---

[74] 42 U.S.C. §1395d(p).

individual in 2006, and resources that are no more than twice the SSI resource level, in 2006.[75]

BBA '97 made modifications to the states' payment and cost-share obligations under the QMB program. It also allowed states to pay no more in deductibles, coinsurance, or copayments for Medicare cost sharing than its Medicaid program would have paid for services for its Medicaid recipients who are not eligible for QMB. These modifications were effective on August 5, 1997.[76] Since the BBA, many states have implemented legislation that limits these Medicare cost-sharing payments to Medicaid levels.

[B]   Specified Low Income Beneficiary Program (SLMB) and Qualified Individual Program (QI)

Under the Specified Low Income Medicare Beneficiary Program (SLMB), states must also cover Medicare Part B premiums *only* for persons of somewhat greater means than those who qualify for QMB. These are persons with incomes up to 120% of the federal poverty level, or $980 for an individual per month in 2006.[77]

Effective for premiums payable from January 1998 to December 2002, the BBA also established a block grant to states for payment of Part B premiums for individuals with income of at least 120 percent but less than 135 percent of the federal poverty level (Qualified Individual, or QI 1 program). This program was extended through September 30, 2005. The fate of the program after that time is unknown. Advocates should inquire about the status of the program after September 30, 2007. Each of the State Units on Aging and CMS should have this information.

Persons in the QI group cannot be otherwise eligible for Medicaid; the resource limit is twice the SSI resource limit. Note: the SLMB program remains an entitlement, while the BBA '97 block grant for QI 1 is to be allotted on a first-come, first-serve basis with the number of eligible individuals who can participate in the program being limited by each state's block grant allocation for the fiscal year. Individuals must apply each year, and enrollment is redetermined annually.[78]

§1.07   THE MEDICARE APPEALS PROCESS

Because of the size and complexity of the Medicare program and because of the desire to contain costs, Medicare coverage is often denied when it should be

---

[75] 42 U.S.C. §1396d(p)(1); 71 Fed. Reg. 3848 (Jan. 24, 2006). The new federal poverty levels are published in the *Federal Register* in January or February of each year, and are effective as of April 1st each year. Some states, such as Connecticut, apply state-specific Medicaid income disregard rules which may result in a higher income eligibility level. Check your state rules.

[76] Pub. L. No. 105-33, 4714, amending 42 U.S.C. §1396a(n).

[77] 42 U.S.C. §1396a(a)(10)(E)(iii); 71 Fed. Reg. 3848 (Jan. 24, 2006).

[78] Pub. L. No. 105-33, 4732, amending 1902(a)(10) of Social Security Act (42 U.S.C. §1396(a)(10)), and enacting Social Security Act 1933; *see also* §4732(c) of the BBA'97.

granted. Sometimes these denials are a result of errors; sometimes they are a result of policy that places cost containment concerns over the needs of individual beneficiaries. Whatever the underlying reasons for the denial, the Medicare program includes an appeals system that is designed, at least in theory, to reverse erroneous denials and to correct mistakes.[79] If the patient's attending physician feels the care in question is medically necessary and the care is not simply excluded from Medicare coverage (e.g., hearing aids, dental care,), the beneficiary should appeal. Changes to the appeals process that were enacted as part of BIPA[80] and the MMA[81] are now in effect. Unfortunately, these changes make the process less friendly to beneficiaries.

BIPA unified the appeals process for claims arising under Parts A and B, other than for claims for hospital services. The Medicare statute establishes different processes for claims arising under Part C and Part D through the reconsideration level of review. For the most part, once a claim reaches the Administrative Law Judge (ALJ) level of review and beyond, the process is the same regardless of whether the claim arises under Medicare Parts A, B, C, or D.

[A]   Traditional Medicare

[1]   Notice of Medicare Payment

Generally, official notice from Medicare must be obtained before a beneficiary has a right to appeal. The Medicare Summary Notice (MSN) constitutes the "initial determination" or written notice that briefly explains what Medicare will pay on a claim. The MSN is prepared by the Medicare contractor that reviews the claim.[82] Many claims are denied in whole or in part on the MSN due to insufficient information and mistakes. Determinations that find that the medical service was not medically necessary and is, therefore, not covered under Medicare should be closely examined. Errors are often made. If the claimant does not think Medicare is allowing a sufficient reimbursement amount, the claimant should also question the MSN.

It may be useful to telephone the contractor to question why Medicare benefits were denied. Often the claimant will discover that inadequate information or documentation was mailed to the contractor and that the coverage denial can be resolved by providing better documentation.

It is important to note that, for all Part A claims, the first notice Medicare beneficiaries should receive informing them that care will not be covered by Medicare is from the health care provider. This is also the case for most Part B

---

[79] See 42 U.S.C. §§1395ff et seq.; 42 C.F.R. §§405.900 et seq., 42 U.S.C. §§1395w-22(f), (g); 42 C.F.R. §422.560 et seq.; 42 U.S.C. §§1395w-104(f),(g), (h); 42 C.F.R. §§423.560 et seq.

[80] Pub. L. No. 106-554 (Dec. 21, 200).

[81] Pub. L. No. 108-173 (Dec. 8, 2003).

[82] Fiscal intermediaries review claims that arise under Part A and carriers review claims that arise under Part B.

services. Before they can charge a beneficiary, providers who participate in the Medicare program must first issue a written notice to the patient informing him or her that Medicare coverage will not be available. Providers have a financial incentive to issue denial notices because they may have to absorb the cost of the care they provide if they erroneously inform the beneficiary that the care will be covered but not if they erroneously deny coverage.

Notices from providers, however, do not form the basis for an appeal. The beneficiary must obtain a formal Medicare coverage determination or "initial determination" from the appropriate Medicare contractor.[83] Patients who receive denial notices from a provider must, therefore, request that a claim for payment be submitted to Medicare if they want to obtain an initial determination that can then be appealed. (In addition, the initial determination does sometimes grant coverage that was denied by the provider.) If the beneficiary or representative requests a provider to submit a claim to Medicare, the provider is required to do so.[84]

[2] Redeterminations

If the claimant remains dissatisfied with the initial determination as described in the MSN, a redetermination may be requested. The redetermination is the first formal appeal stage for Medicare Part A and Part B claims. The request for redetermination must be filed within 120 days of receipt of the MSN. The redetermination is performed by the entity that issued the initial determination denying benefits: the intermediary for Part A skilled nursing facility, home health, and hospice claims, the QIO for hospital claims, and the carrier for Part B claims. Generally, these appeals simply entail submitting a written request (forms are available on the CMS Web site at *www.medicare.gov*, but requests may also be made in writing without the form).[85] If at all possible, the claimant should attach a copy of the denial notice issued by the health care provider and a supporting letter and/or documentation from the treating physician to the redetermination request. (*Assistance from the attending physician is always the key to a successful appeal.*)[86] Be certain to keep copies of all appeal requests and all supporting data.

Although new regulations require that redetermination decisions be issued within 60 calendar days of receipt of the redetermination request,[87] in the past it has

---

[83] Medicare Claims Processing Manual, 100 Ch. 4, §40.7B; Sarrassat v. Bowen, No. C88-20161 (RPA) (N.D. Cal. 1989).

[84] Medicare Claims Processing Manual, 100 Ch. 1, §50.1.5. (CMS implementation of this provision has been spotty.)

[85] This level of appeal was known as "reconsideration" prior to implementation of the BIPA appeal changes.

[86] *See* Pilsums v. Harris, Medicare & Medicaid Guide (CCH) 30,908 (D. Conn. 1981).

[87] 42 C.F.R. §405.950(a). Note that the regulations extend this time frame if the provider or supplier, as well as the beneficiary, files an appeal. However, adherence to this time frame is not enforceable by the beneficiary.

not been unusual to wait many months for a decision from this first appeal stage. Unfortunately, it is also not unusual for meritorious claims to be denied at the redetermination stage. However, some of these decisions do result in additional benefits, and these steps are prerequisites to receiving a hearing.[88]

[3]   Reconsideration

BIPA created a new intermediate level of appeal, the "reconsideration," that beneficiaries must complete before receiving a hearing.[89] The reconsideration is a new level of review for Part A claims and replaces the carrier hearing for Part B claims. Reconsiderations are a paper review conducted by a new review entity that contracts with CMS, the Qualified Independent Contractor, or QIC. A beneficiary has 120 days after receipt of an unfavorable redetermination to request QIC review. The QIC must issue a decision within 60 days, with certain exceptions. If the QIC does not issue the decision in a timely manner, the beneficiary may request to escalate the case to an administrative law judge hearing. Regulations implementing the reconsideration review impose limitations on the submission of evidence on providers and suppliers, but not beneficiaries, who appeal to this level.[90] The reconsideration level of review became effective for redeterminations in Part A cases issued by fiscal intermediaries on or after May 1, 2005, and for redeterminations in Part B cases issued by carriers on or after January 1, 2006.[91] Beneficiaries may appeal an unfavorable reconsideration decision to an administrative law judge.

[4]   Where to File an Appeal Request

Note that many beneficiaries and their advocates have previously filed requests for an appeal with the Social Security Administration. However, the new regulations require beneficiaries to file a request for an appeal to the next level of review with the entity named in either the initial determination, redetermination, reconsideration, or administrative law judge decision.[92] In addition, the regulations set forth specific requirements for advocates who want to serve as appointed representatives and/or collect fees for their advocacy at the administrative law judge level and above.[93]

---

[88] 42 C.F.R. §§405.702–405.710, 466.83.

[89] Pub. L. No. 106-554, §521.

[90] 42 C.F.R. §§405-.960–405.978.

[91] 70 Fed. Reg. 11419 (Mar. 8, 2005), at 11425.

[92] 42 C.F.R. §§405.944, 405.964, 405.1014.

[93] 42 C.F.R. §405.910.

[5] Summary of Expedited Appeals Process

Effective July 2005, beneficiaries may seek expedited review of a skilled nursing facility, home health, hospice or comprehensive outpatient rehabilitation facility (CORF) services discharge or termination.[94] The provider must give the beneficiary a general, standardized notice at least two days in advance of the proposed end of the service. If the service is fewer than two days, or if the time between services is more than two days, then notice must be given by the next to last service. The notice describes the service, the date coverage ends, the beneficiary's financial liability for continued services, and how to file an appeal.

A beneficiary must request expedited review, orally or in writing, by noon of the next calendar day after receiving notice. At that time, the beneficiary is given a more specific notice that includes a detailed explanation of why services are being terminated, a description of any applicable Medicare coverage rules and information on how to obtain them, and other facts specific to the beneficiary's case. The beneficiary is not financially liable for continued services until the later of two days after receiving the notice or the termination date specified on the notice.

Expedited review is available in cases involving a discharge from the provider of services, or a termination of services where "a physician certifies that failure to continue the provision of such services is likely to place the individual's health at risk."[95] Services furnished by a residential provider, such as a hospital or a SNF, or a hospice, are discharges for which a doctor's certificate is not required. Services furnished by a "non-residential provider," such as home health services, are treated as a termination of services for which a doctor's certificate of significant health risk must be provided.[96] A reduction in service is not considered a termination or discharge for purposes of triggering expedited review.

Expedited review will be conducted by the QIO, which has 72 hours in which to make a decision. When the QIO receives the request for review, it must contact the provider, which then must supply the QIO with information supporting its determination by the close of the same business day. The QIO must solicit the views of the beneficiary and review the notice to determine if it meets CMS requirements. The beneficiary does not incur liability if the QIO decision is delayed because the provider did not get the necessary information to the reviewer in a timely manner.

If the QIO sustains the decision to terminate/discharge services, the beneficiary may request expedited reconsideration, orally or in writing, by noon of the calendar day following initial notification. The reconsideration will be

---

[94] 69 Fed. Reg. 69,264 (Nov. 26, 2004), adding 42 C.F.R. §§405.1200–405.1204, to implement 42 U.S.C. §1395ff(b)(1)(F).

[95] 42 U.S.C. §1395ff(b)(1)(F).

[96] 42 C.F.R. §405.1202(a).

conducted by the QIC, which must issue a decision within 72 hours of the request. If the QIC does not comply with the time frame, the beneficiary may escalate the case to the administrative law judge level.

Beneficiaries retain the right to utilize the standard appeals process rather than the new expedited process in all situations. A QIO may review an appeal from a beneficiary whose request is not timely filed, but the QIO does not have to adhere to the time frame for issuing a decision, and the limitation on liability does not apply.

[6]   Special Rules for Hospital Claims

Hospital inpatients denied Medicare during their stay may request an "expedited review" of a Medicare denial. These expedited requests must be decided by the QIO within three working days. Under previous regulations, a hospital inpatient who received a denial notice from the hospital and requested review immediately avoided being charged until the QIO issued an initial determination.[97] However, the new expedited appeals regulations protect from liability only those inpatients who did not know or could not reasonably have been expected to know that payment would not be made.[98]

A beneficiary may request reconsideration review of an unfavorable decision by the QIC. If the reconsideration decision is unsatisfactory and at least $200 remains in controversy, the beneficiary may request an ALJ hearing.[99] Hearing requests must be made within 60 days of receipt of the notice of the reconsideration decision. Late filing of a request for hearing may be accepted where good cause for the delay is shown. Examples of good cause include illness that prevents the beneficiary from making hearing requests on time; the loss of important records by fire or other accidental cause; and incorrect information given by Medicare concerning the requirements for a timely filing of a hearing request.[100] The hearing request should be made in writing and should be filed with the entity identified in the reconsideration notice.

If the hearing request is unsatisfactory, a beneficiary may request a review from the Medicare Appeals Council (MAC). The request must be made within 60 days of receipt of the hearing decision. If $2,000 remains in controversy after the hearing, the case may proceed into United States District Court.[101]

---

[97] 42 C.F.R. §412.42(c).

[98] 42 C.F.R. §405.1206(a), (f). The regulations implement an amendment made to 42 U.S.C. §1879(a)(2) by BIPA.

[99] 42 C.F.R. §§478.44, 478.46.

[100] 42 C.F.R. §4.05.1014 (c)(3); 43 C.F.R. §§405.942(b)(2), (3).

[101] 42 C.F.R. §§478.44, 478.46.

[B]   Appeal and Grievance Procedures in Medicare Part C Plans

[1]   Medicare Advantage Claims

Medicare Part C establishes a different appeals process for Medicare Advantage cases, including those from HMO, PPO, and PFFS plans (referred to here collectively as HMOs). In HMO cases, initial determinations are known as "organization determinations." Organization and reconsideration determinations are made by the HMO. If a reconsidered decision is denied in whole or in part, it is sent automatically to the Maximus Center for Health Dispute Resolution (Maximus CHDR), an external review organization hired by CMS to review Medicare HMO reconsidered decisions.[102]

In addition, HMOs are required to have internal grievance procedures.[103] They must provide information to members regarding this grievance process in the plan's written membership rules, along with timetables and information about the steps necessary to utilize the grievance process.[104] The grievance procedures are to be used in all cases that do not involve an "organization determination." For example, controversies about hours of service, location of facilities, or courtesy of personnel would go through the grievance process.[105]

HMOs must also inform enrollees of the appeals process in writing.[106] HMOs are required to provide access to QIO review on issues of hospital non-coverage;[107] to provide pre-termination review of home health, skilled nursing facility, and comprehensive outpatient rehabilitation facility (CORF) services;[108] to make expedited determinations with respect to emergency or urgently needed services;[109] to provide reconsideration review;[110] and to provide access to independent review outside the plan by an entity under contract with CMS for such review.[111]

If an unfavorable reconsideration determination is issued, whether through the expedited review process or within ordinary time frames, and the amount in

---

[102] 42 U.S.C. §1395w-22(f)-(g); 42 C.F.R. §§422.560–422.626 Note that MMA requires private insurance companies that offer a prescription drug plan under Part D to have grievance and appeals mechanisms that accord with the grievance and appeals mechanisms under Part C.

[103] 42 C.F.R. §§422.560, 422.564.

[104] 42 C.F.R. §422.111(b)(8).

[105] 42 C.F.R. §422.564(b).

[106] 42 C.F.R. §§422.111(b)(8), 422.562(a)(2). (Issues for appeal include coverage of emergency or urgently needed services, and denial or termination of other medical service, including specialist care and/or referrals.)

[107] 42 C.F.R. §422.620.

[108] 42.C.F.R. §422.624.

[109] 42 C.F.R. §422.570.

[110] 42 C.F.R. §§422.578, 422.580.

[111] 42 C.F.R. §422.592 (currently provided by the CHDR).

controversy in 2006 is $110 or more (figure for 2007 not available at press time), the enrollee has a right to a hearing before an ALJ.[112]

The written request for a hearing must be filed within 60 days of the date of the notice of the reconsideration determination. In HMO cases, the plan must be made a party to the hearing and subsequent levels of review.[113]

The following is a summary of the due process and grievance procedures required of Medicare Advantage plans:

1. Grievance Mechanism

   Each Medicare Advantage organization/plan must provide meaningful procedures for hearing and resolving grievances between the organization (including any entity or individual through which the organization/plan provides health care services) and its enrollees.[114]

2. Non-Expedited Appeals Process[115]

   A Medicare Advantage organization must have a procedure for making determinations regarding whether an individual enrolled with the plan is entitled to receive a health service under Medicare and the amount (if any) that the individual is required to pay with respect to the service. Decisions must be made on a timely basis.

   Determinations that deny coverage, in whole or in part, shall be in writing and shall include a statement in understandable language of the reasons for the denial and a description of the reconsideration and appeals process.

   If the organization makes a decision that is completely favorable to the beneficiary, the organization must issue the determination as expeditiously as the enrollee's health condition requires, but no later than 30 calendar days from the date it receives the request for a standard reconsideration.[116]

   The organization must provide for reconsideration of an adverse determination upon request by the enrollee involved. The reconsideration shall be within 30 days after the date of the receipt of the request for

---

[112] 42 U.S.C. §1395w-22(g)(5). Note that the new provisions concerning amount in controversy for administrative law judge hearings and judicial review also apply to Part C claims. 70 Fed. Reg. at 11423.

[113] *See* 42 C.F.R. §422.602(b), (c).

[114] 42 C.F.R. §422.564.

[115] *Id.* 42 C.F.R. §422.568 (standard time frames and notice requirements for organization determinations). The Medicare Advantage organization must notify the enrollee of its determination as expeditiously as the enrollee's health conditions require, but no later than 14 calendar days after the date the organization receives the request for a standard organization determination. This time period can be extended for a period of 14 days upon justification by the organization.

[116] 42 C.F.R. §422.590(a).

reconsideration.[117] A reconsideration relating to a determination to deny coverage based on a lack of medical necessity must be made only by a physician with appropriate expertise in the field of medicine at issue and who is other than a physician involved in the initial determination.

3.   Expedited Appeals Process[118]

The Medicare Advantage plan must maintain procedures for expediting organization determinations and reconsiderations when, upon request of an enrollee, the organization determines that the application of the normal time frame for making determinations or reconsiderations could seriously jeopardize the life or health of the enrollee or the enrollee's ability to regain maximum function. An enrollee or a physician may request expedited consideration orally or in writing. If the physician requests an expedited determination or reconsiderations, the expedited review is mandatory and commences right away.[119]

If the request is not made by or supported by a physician, it is within the discretion of the Medicare Advantage organization to grant the request for expedited determination or reconsideration.[120] If the Medicare Advantage organization denies a request for expedited determination or reconsideration, it must automatically transfer the request to the standard time frame and make the reconsideration determination within standard time frames.

If the organization expedites a request for reconsideration, it must complete its reconsideration and give the enrollee (and the physician involved, as appropriate) notice of its decision as expeditiously as the enrollee's health condition requires but no later than 72 hours after receiving the request.[121]

4.   Fast Track Review[122]

Effective January 1, 2004, a Medicare Advantage organization must provide an enrollee with notice at least two days in advance of termination of home health services, skilled nursing facility services, and therapy services in CORFs. The enrollee may request review by the QIO by noon of the day following receipt of the notice. The QIO then must request information from the plan, solicit the view of the enrollee, and issue a decision by close of business of the day after it receives the necessary information.

---

[117] The Medicare Advantage organization must make its reconsidered determination as expeditiously as the enrollee's health condition requires, but no later than 30 calendar days from the date it receives the request for a standard reconsideration. 42 C.F.R. §422.590(a)(1).

[118] 42 C.F.R. §§422.570–422.572.

[119] 42 C.F.R. §422.584.

[120] 42 C.F.R. §422.584(c)(2)(i).

[121] 42 C.F.R. §422.590(d).

[122] 42 C.F.R. §§422.624, 422.626.

5. Independent Review[123]

The Secretary contracts with an independent, outside entity known as the Maximus Center for Health Dispute Resolution (Maximus CHDR) to review and resolve in a timely manner reconsiderations that affirm the denial or coverage, in whole or in part. When the independent entity makes the reconsidered determination, it is responsible for mailing a notice of its reconsidered determination to the parties and for sending a copy to CMS.[124]

6. Appeal to ALJ and Federal District Court[125]

An enrollee with a Medicare Advantage plan who is dissatisfied with a CHDR determination may appeal to an administrative law judge using the same process as is used in traditional Medicare.

7. Quality Improvement Organization (QIO) Review: An Alternative Means of Appealing Hospital Denials[126]

An enrollee who wishes to appeal a determination by a Medicare Advantage plan or hospital that inpatient hospital care is no longer necessary may request immediate QIO review and may remain in the hospital without additional financial liability according to the following procedures:

The enrollee must submit the request for immediate review to the QIO, in writing or by telephone, by noon of the first working day after receipt of written notice that the Medicare Advantage plan or hospital has determined that the hospital stay is no longer necessary;

On the date of receipt of the request, the QIO must notify the Medicare Advantage plan that the enrollee has filed a request for immediate review; the organization must supply any information that the QIO requires to conduct its review, including medical records and other pertinent information; information is to be provided by telephone or in writing by the close of business of the first full working day immediately following the day the organization makes its request; the QIO must solicit the views of the enrollee with respect to the denial at issue;

Where the Medicare Advantage plan has authorized inpatient coverage of admission directly or by delegation, the organization continues to be financially responsible for the costs of the hospital stay when a timely appeal is filed until noon of the calendar day following the day the QIO notifies the enrollee of its review determination. If coverage of the hospital admission was never approved by the Medicare Advantage plan, the Medicare

---

[123] 42 C.F.R. §422.590(a).

[124] 42 C.F.R. §§422.600–422.616.

[125] 42 C.F.R. §422.622.

[126] 42 C.F.R. §422.622.

Advantage plan is liable for the hospital costs only if it is determined on appeal that the hospital stay should have been covered under the Medicare Advantage plan.

[C] Appeal and Grievance Procedures in Medicare Part D Plans

[1] Coverage Determination Process

As directed by Congress, the coverage determination and appeals process for Part D prescription drug plans[127] mirrors closely the process utilized for Medicare Part C, the Medicare Advantage program. The process begins when the prescription drug plan (PDP) or Medicare Advantage plan with prescription drug coverage (MA-PD) issues a coverage determination. The plan enrollee may request a redetermination by the drug plan of an unfavorable coverage determination and then a reconsideration by the Independent Review Entity (IRE) of an unfavorable redetermination. Following IRE review, the enrollee may appeal to an administrative law judge (ALJ), to the Medicare Appeals Council (MAC), and then to federal court. Expedited review is available if the Part C standards are met.

Plans must notify enrollees and the prescribing physician involved, as appropriate, of initial coverage determinations as expeditiously as the enrollee's health condition requires, but no later than 72 hours after receipt of the request. Plans must act on requests for expedited coverage determinations no later than 24 hours after receiving the request, and on expedited redeterminations within 72 hours.

Coverage determinations that trigger appeal rights include a decision not to pay for or provide a Part D drug because the drug is not on the formulary, is not medically necessary, is furnished by an out-of-network pharmacy, or is not a drug for which Medicare will pay under Part D. A denial of a request for prior authorization by the plan (i.e., the plan does not approve a physician's request to pay for a formulary drug for which the plan must first grant approval) is also a coverage determination. A coverage determination also includes the failure to provide a coverage determination in a timely manner when that delay would adversely affect the health of the enrollee, a decision concerning an exception request, and a decision on the amount of cost sharing for a drug.

[2] Exceptions Process

PDPs and MA-PDs must have an exceptions process in which enrollees can ask that a formulary drug be provided at a lower tier for cost sharing or that a non-formulary drug be covered by the plan. Because exception requests are coverage determinations and governed by the rules for coverage determinations, the plan

---

[127] 42 C.F.R. §§423.560–423.636.

must act within the time frame for standard coverage determinations (72 hours) and expedited coverage determinations (24 hours).

The plan may grant an exception request to change the cost-sharing tier (i.e., the amount the beneficiary pays as a copayment or as coinsurance) if it determines that the non-preferred drug is medically necessary, consistent with the physician's statement in support of the exception that the preferred drug would not be as effective or would have adverse consequences. In addition, the exceptions process must address situations where a formulary's tiering structure changes during the year and an enrollee is using a drug affected by the change. However, the plan does not have to cover non-preferred drugs that have a higher cost-sharing amount at the generic drug cost-sharing level if the plan maintains a separate tier dedicated to generic drugs. Also, if the plan maintains a formulary tier in which it places very high cost and unique items, such as genomic and biotech products, it may exclude the very high cost or unique drugs from its tiering exception process.

The plan may grant an exception request to cover a non-formulary drug whenever it determines that the drug is medically necessary, consistent with the physician's statement that formulary drugs would not be as effective or would have adverse consequences, and that the drug would be covered but for the fact that it is an off-formulary drug. Formulary use includes the application of cost utilization tools, such as a dose restriction, including the dosage form, that causes a particular Part D drug not to be covered for the number of doses prescribed, or a step therapy requirement that causes a particular Part D drug not to be covered until the requirements of the plan's coverage policy are met, or a therapeutic substitution requirement.

Although the regulations include some criteria for plans to consider when evaluating an exception request to change the tiered cost sharing or to pay for a non-formulary drug, each plan has the flexibility to establish its own criteria and to develop its own exception process. In addition, the regulations leave to a plan's discretion whether it will continue coverage after an exception has been granted into subsequent plan years.

[3] Appeals

The first level of appeal from an unfavorable coverage determination, including an unfavorable exception request, is a redetermination by the drug plan. The enrollee must file a request for a redetermination with the drug plan. Drug plans have 7 days in which to notify their enrollees of a standard redetermination decision. They have 72 hours to notify the enrollee of an expedited redetermination request.

An enrollee may request a reconsideration by the IRE of an unfavorable drug plan redetermination. The reconsideration request is filed with the IRE. The Part D regulations require the IRE to issue its reconsideration decision within the time frames for issuing a redetermination.

Note that the regulations provide for an automatic reconsideration review by the IRE if the Part D plan fails to issue either a timely coverage determination or redetermination. The regulations require a drug plan to forward the enrollee's request to the IRE within 24 hours if it does not act timely on the coverage determination or redetermination.[128]

[4] Notice

Plans must send written notice of a formulary change, including a change in cost-sharing tier placement, only to those enrollees who use an affected drug, at least 60 days in advance of the change. Notice must also be provided to CMS, state pharmacy assistance programs, pharmacies, and prescribing providers. The notice must include the name of the affected drug, whether the drug is being removed from the formulary or moved to another cost-sharing tier, the reason for the change, alternative drugs in the class, and the right to request an exception. Alternatively, the plan may give the enrollee a 60-day supply of the drug and the 60-day notice at the time the enrollee presents a prescription for an affected drug.

The PDP or MA-PD must provide notice of appeal rights for other coverage determinations. CMS does not consider the transaction at the pharmacy to be a coverage determination; thus, pharmacies have no obligation to provide individualized notice at the point of sale when coverage for a prescription is denied. Plans are required to arrange with their network pharmacies to post or distribute general notices instructing enrollees to contact their plan to obtain a coverage determination or to request an exception.

[D] Administrative Law Judge Hearings

As described above, a beneficiary who has received an unfavorable reconsideration decision for a claim under any part of Medicare may request an administrative law judge (ALJ) hearing. For all claims except hospital claims, in 2006 there must be at least $110 in controversy to proceed to an ALJ hearing; this amount may increase yearly.[129] Hospital claims may be appealed to an ALJ if $200 or more remains at issue. The request for hearing must be filed within 60 days of receipt of the reconsideration determination. The ALJ must issue a decision within 90 days of receipt of the appeal request, with certain exceptions.

The ALJ hearing has traditionally been the beneficiary's best chance to win Medicare coverage previously denied. ALJs have considered the beneficiary's right to Medicare coverage in accordance with the Medicare statute and regulations (in contrast to the less formal and more restrictive guidelines and directives used by

---

[128] 42 C.F.R. §§423.568(e), 423.590(c).

[129] Section 940 of the MMA requires that, starting in 2005, the amount in controversy for administrative law judge hearings and for judicial review be adjusted annually by the percentage increase in the medical care component of the consumer price index for urban consumers and be rounded to the nearest multiple of $10. The 2007 amounts were unavailable at the time of publication.

fiscal intermediaries, QIOs, and carriers at their decision levels). The different nature of the hearing evaluation has been reflected by the nationwide win rates in most cases. Appeals taken to ALJ hearings had been successful nationwide in about 70 percent of all cases. As described below, the ALJ process and standards changed in 2005 in ways contrary to the interests of beneficiaries. Nonetheless, ALJ hearings are still more likely to be successful than earlier appeals levels, Thus, it makes sense for an advocate to expend the greatest time and energy at the hearing stage where vigorous representation will often lead to satisfying results.

Previously, Medicare claims were heard by the same ALJs who reviewed Social Security claims. The Office of Medicare Hearings and Appeals (OMHA) in the Department of Health and Human Services was created in 2005, so that by January 1, 2006 all Medicare ALJ hearings are conducted by Medicare ALJs from OMHA. Instead of being located throughout the country, Medicare ALJs are housed in four offices, in Arlington, Virginia; Cleveland, Ohio; Irvine, California; and Miami, Florida.

For hearing requests filed on or after July 1, 2005, new rules create a presumption that all hearings will be conducted by video teleconference (VTC) where the technology is available. A beneficiary may request an in-person hearing, but that request is granted at the discretion of the ALJ, and granting the request automatically waives the 90-day time frame for decisions. Even if the beneficiary appears in person, other parties to the hearing may appear by VTC or by telephone. CMS may participate in an ALJ hearing as a party, with the right to submit evidence and cross-examine witnesses; CMS cannot examine and cross-examine witnesses if the beneficiary is unrepresented.

Further, and perhaps most significantly, although ALJs still will not be bound by less formal policy manuals and directives, they are required under the new rules to give them deference. If an ALJ decides not to follow a policy, the ALJ must explain in the decision why the policy is not being followed.

[E] Beyond ALJ: Medicare Appeals Council and United States District Court

If the ALJ decision is unsatisfactory and at least $110 (in 2006) ($200 in hospital cases)[130] remains in controversy, the case may be further appealed to the Medicare Appeals Council (MAC) of the United States Department of Health and Human Services. The MAC is the final administrative appeal review for all Medicare cases under Part A, Part B, Part C, and Part D. There is one Medicare Appeals Council for all Medicare cases. Cases are almost always decided on the record; the MAC may grant oral argument if it decides that the case raises important questions of policy or law or questions of fact that cannot be decided on the record. A request

---

[130] 42 C.F.R. §478.46 (amount in controversy for review of unfavorable ALJ decisions in hospital cases).

for MAC review must be filed within 60 days of receipt of the ALJ decision. Cases are sometimes won or remanded for new hearings. The MAC traditionally has taken a long time to issue decisions; new rules require decisions to be issued within 90 days of receipt of the appeal, with some exceptions.

Generally, a MAC decision is a prerequisite for proceeding with an individual Medicare appeal in federal court. The required amount in controversy for federal court appeals is also $1,090 in 2006 ($2,000 for hospital cases). Again, other than for hospital cases, these jurisdictional amounts will increase yearly; the 2007 rates were not available at press time. The complaint appealing a Medicare denial must be filed in federal court within 60 days of receipt of the MAC decision and must name the Secretary of the Department of Health and Human Services, in his or her official capacity, as defendant.[131]

[F]   Expedited Access to Judicial Review

Starting in May 2005, a party may request expedited access to judicial review (EAJR) in place of an ALJ hearing or MAC review. The party must show that there are no material facts in dispute. The party must also challenge the constitutionality of a statutory provision or the constitutionality or validity of a regulation or of a national coverage determination. After the party files a request for an ALJ hearing, the party may file a request for EAJR with the ALJ office. A determination on the request is made by a review entity consisting of up to three ALJs or members of the Departmental Appeals Board. If the review entity certifies the request, the party may file an appeal with federal district court within 60 days. If the request is denied, the case is returned to the ALJ hearing or MAC if a hearing has already been held.[132]

[G]   Challenges to Coverage Policies

A separate appeals process exists for beneficiaries who want to challenge the validity of a local coverage determination (LCD) or a national coverage determination (NCD) which sets rules concerning Medicare payment for a particular item or service.[133] Unlike the claims appeals process described above, a beneficiary does not have to receive a service or procedure before challenging the LCD or NCD governing the procedure as long as the beneficiary needs the service.

A beneficiary who needs but has not yet received the service may file an appeal with the Department Appeals Board (DAB) within 6 months of the treating physician's written statement indicating that the service is needed. A beneficiary

---

[131] If the defendant is not properly named, the plaintiff will be given 60 days to amend the complaint. 42 C.F.R. §405.1136(d).

[132] 42 C.F.R. §405.990.

[133] 42 C.F.R. §§426.100–426.587.

who has received the service must file an appeal with the DAB within 120 days of receipt of the initial determination. Someone who has received the service may appeal the claims denial at the same time as challenging the validity of the LCD or NCD used to deny the service. It is critical in both situations to include a statement from the doctor concerning the necessity of the service and other medical information to document why the LCD or NCD is no longer valid.

If the appeal involves a challenge to an LCD, it is conducted by an ALJ. The DAB conducts the review if the challenge involves an NCD. If the ALJ or the DAB upholds the appeal, the ALJ or the DAB may order the contractor to re-consider any claim filed by the beneficiary without application of the LCD or NCD in question.

§1.08   CONCLUSION

Unfair denials of Medicare coverage occur with surprising frequency. Because Medicare administrators and providers often use rules and procedures that improperly restrict coverage, patients are sometimes required to pay for care that should be covered by Medicare. In addition, the Medicare law is very complicated and errors are frequently made.

The appeal system was designed to find and correct mistakes. No matter what the service at issue, assistance from the patient's *attending physician is the key* to convincing those who make coverage decisions initially, and on appeal, that the care is in fact medically necessary and/or skilled and should be covered. If a claimant appeals a denial of Medicare coverage, he or she will not lose rights to other Medicare or Social Security benefits.

APPENDIX 1-1

2007 MEDICARE SUMMARY (Traditional Program)

Care Setting[134]	Coverage	Premium	Deductible	Coinsurance	Appeals
PART A		For Voluntary Enrollees Only $410/mo in 2007 if 29 or fewer quarters Soc. Sec. $226/mo in 2007 if 30 to 39 quarters Soc. Sec.			
HOSPITAL	90 days/spell of illness + 60 lifetime reserve days after deductible if medically necessary and reasonable		$992 per spell of illness	61st-90th day: $248/day 91st-150th day: $496/day	Redetermination by QIC Hearing by ALJ (if at least $200) HHS Medicare Appeals Council Federal Court (if at least $2,000)
SKILLED NURSING FACILITY	100 days if daily skilled care and if within 30 days of 3-day hospital stay			21st-100th day: $124/day in 2007	Reconsideration by QIC Hearing by ALJ (if at least $110) HHS Medicare Appeals Council Federal Court (if at least $1,090) (2007 amounts not yet available)

[134] On January 1, 2006, the Medicare prescription drug program began. Medicare Advantage (formerly Medicare+Choice and also known as Medicare Part C) is a set of financing systems including managed care plans.

2007 MEDICARE SUMMARY (Traditional Program) (continued)

Care Setting	Coverage	Premium	Deductible	Coinsurance	Appeals
HOME HEALTH (For individuals who *also* have Part B)	100 visits if homebound and need skilled care within 14 days of 3-day hospital stay or SNF stay of any duration				Reconsideration by QIC Hearing by ALJ (if at least $110) HHS Medicare Appeals Council Federal Court (if at least $1,090) (2007 amounts not yet available)
HOME HEALTH (For individuals who *only* have Part A)	Full coverage for undefined number of visits if homebound and need skilled care				Reconsideration by QIC Hearing by ALJ (if at least $110) HHS Medicare Appeals Council Federal Court (if at least $1,090) (2007 amounts not yet available)
HOSPICE	Two 90-day periods + unlimited 60-day periods if physician certifies and recertifies that patient is terminally ill and if elect palliative care only				Reconsideration by QIC Hearing by ALJ (if at least $110) HHS Medicare Appeals Council Federal Court (if at least $1,090) (2007 amounts not yet available)
PART B		$93.50/month in 2007 for individuals with incomes below $80,000	$131/year in 2007		

2007 MEDICARE SUMMARY (Traditional Program) (*continued*)

Care Setting	Coverage	Premium	Deductible	Coinsurance	Appeals
HOME HEALTH (If *only* have Part B *or* have used 100 Part A visits or did not meet institutionalization rules)	Full coverage for undefined number of visits if homebound and need skilled care		Deductible does *not* apply	(2007 amount not yet available)	
Physician Services Outpatient Services Therapy Services Durable Medical Equipment Prosthetic Devices Ambulance Services	80% of Medicare approved rate for covered services		$131/year in 2007	*Assigned Claims:* 20% of Medicare approved rate *Unassigned Claims:* 20% of approved rate + balance of actual charge up to an additional 15% of the approved charge	In 2006 Reconsideration by QIC ALJ Hearing (if at least $110 after Carrier Hearing) HHS Medicare Appeals Council Federal Court (if at least $1,090) (2007 amount not yet available)
Some Preventive Benefits (Including Flu Shots, Some Mammograms and Pap Smears, Bone Mass Tests, Prostate Screening, Diabetes Tests, etc.)	Some paid at 100%		Deductible waived for *some* preventive services		In 2006 Reconsideration by QIC ALJ Hearing HHS Medicare Appeals Council Federal Court (if at least $1,090) (2007 amount not yet available)

APPENDIX 1-2

TRADITIONAL MEDICARE APPEALS PROCESS

Level[135]	Decision Maker	Time Frame for Issuing Decision	Extension of Time Frame for Issuing Decision Available	Time Frame for Requesting Next Level of Appeal	Escalation
INITIAL	FI	w/in 30 days of receiving "clean" claim. §405.922		w/in 120 days of receipt of initial determination to request redetermination. §405.942(a)	No right to escalation
REDETERMINATION	FI	w/in 60 calendar days of receipt of request. §405.95(a)	If redetermination request filed untimely, time frame commences w/granting of "good cause." §405.942(b) If multiple timely requests filed, time frame is w/in 60 days of receipt of last request. §405.950(b)(1)&(2) If additional evidence submitted by party, time frame extended for 14 calendar day for each submission. §405.950()(3)	w/in 180 days of receipt of redetermination to request reconsideration. §405.962(a)	No right to escalation

135 70 Fed. Reg. 11420 *et seq.* (Mar. 8, 2005).

TRADITIONAL MEDICARE APPEALS PROCESS (continued)

Level	Decision Maker	Time Frame for Issuing Decision	Extension of Time Frame for Issuing Decision Available	Time Frame for Requesting Next Level of Appeal	Escalation
RECONSIDERATION	QIC NCDs binding on QIC. §405.968(a)(4) LCDs not binding on QIC but must give "substantial deference" to them in making decision. §405.968	w/in 60 days of receipt of request. §405.970(a)	Same as for redeterminations §405.970(b)	w/in 60 days of receipt of reconsideration to request ALJ. §405.1002(a)(1)	If time frame not met, have right to escalation. Must notify QIC in writing. §405.970(d) QIC has 5 days from receipt of escalation request to issue a decision or forward to ALJ. §405.970(d)(2)
ALJ	HHS ALJ NCDs binding on ALJ; LCDs not binding on ALJ but must give "substantial deference" to them in making decision. §405.968 (CMS may "participate" or be "party," unless appellant is unpresented	w/in 90 days of timely filing of ALJ request. §405.1016 (but requesting party may—by motion or stipulation—waive this time frame)	If ALJ request filed untimely, but "good cause" granted, time frame commences w/granting of "good cause." §405.1016(b) If ALJ request is escalated to ALJ from QIC, time frame for issuing decision is 180 days of timely filing of request. §405.1016(c) If CMS is a party and a party requests discovery,	Within 60 days of receipt of ALJ decision to request MAC appeal. §405.1102(a) [copy of request for MAC review must be sent by requestor to all parties]. §405.1105(a)	If time frame not met, have right to escalation to MAC. Must file request to escalate with ALJ in writing. §405.1104(a)(1) ALJ has 5 days from receipt of escalation request to issue a decision or forward to ALJ. Must file escalation request w/both ALJ and MAC and copy all

TRADITIONAL MEDICARE APPEALS PROCESS (*continued*)

Level	Decision Maker	Time Frame for Issuing Decision	Extension of Time Frame for Issuing Decision Available	Time Frame for Requesting Next Level of Appeal	Escalation
	beneficiary) §405.1000 §405.1010 §405.1012		time frame for issuing decision is tolled. §405.1016(d) If additional evidence submitted later than 10 days after receiving notice of hearing, period between when it should have been submitted and when received by ALJ is not counted toward adjudication deadline. §405.1018(b) If hearing is postponed at request of appellant, time between original hearing date and new hearing date not counted toward adjudication deadline. §405.1020(h)		parties. §405.1104(a)(2)

TRADITIONAL MEDICARE APPEALS PROCESS (continued)

Level	Decision Maker	Time Frame for Issuing Decision	Extension of Time Frame for Issuing Decision Available	Time Frame for Requesting Next Level of Appeal	Escalation
MAC	Medicare Appeals Council (MAC) (de novo review) §405.1108(a) (CMS may "participate" or be "party," unless appellant is unrepresented beneficiary)	w/in 90 days of timely filing of MAC request (MAC may issue decision or remand to ALJ). §405.1100(c)	If appellant fails to send copy of request to escalate from ALJ or request for MAC review to all parties, deadline tolls until all parties receive notice of the request for MAC review. §405.1106(b) Time frame tolled, if party asks to review evidence from the MAC and an opportunity to comment, beginning w/date MAC received request to review evidence through date comment received. §405.1118 Time frame tolled, if party requests to file brief, beginning w/date request to brief received through date brief filed. §405.1120	w/in 60 days of receipt of MAC decision, can request judicial review. §405.1102(a) (Also, can file w/in 60 days of receipt of MAC's notice that it cannot issue timely final action & cannot appeal ALJ dismissal to federal court which, according to regs, is not available. §405.1116)	If time frame not met, have right to escalation to federal court. §405.1132(a) Must file civil action w/in 60 days of receipt of MAC's notice that it cannot issue timely final action Cannot obtain judicial review of a dismissal of a claim. §405.1116

APPENDIX 1-3

2007 MEDICARE DEDUCTIBLE, COINSURANCE, AND PREMIUM AMOUNTS

PART A

Hospital

Deductible: $992.00

Coinsurance:

1st through 60th day: $0

61st through 90th day: $248.00/day

91st through 150th day: $496.00/day

Skilled Nursing Facility

Coinsurance:

1st through 20th day: $0

21st through 100th day: $124.00/day

Part A Premium (for voluntary enrollees only):

$410.00/month (if individual has 29 or fewer quarters of Social Security coverage)

$226.00/month (if individual has 30 to 39 quarters of Social Security coverage)

If uncertain of quarters, please call your local Social Security office.

PART B

Deductible: $131.00/year

Standard Premium: $93.50/month

CHAPTER 2

HOSPITAL COVERAGE

§2.01 INTRODUCTION

[A] Access to Covered Services

Access to Medicare hospital coverage, and the vital hospital care that coverage pays for, is a legal right crucial to the financial and physical well-being of millions of aged and disabled Americans. Part A of the Medicare program is financed by the Hospital Insurance Trust Fund, which in turn is funded through a mandatory Social Security payroll tax imposed on all wage earners.[1]

Although Medicare Part A is sometimes known as "hospital insurance," coverage is available under Part A for much more than services provided by a hospital. Of course, inpatient hospital services are covered under Part A, but Medicare Part A also provides coverage for skilled nursing facility (SNF) care, home health care, and hospice care.[2] The discussion in this chapter will first address overall eligibility for Medicare Part A, and then address obtaining Medicare coverage for inpatient hospital care, including Long-term Care Hospitals and Rehabilitation Hospitals.

[B] Medicare Administration

Section 1874A of the Social Security Act, gives the Secretary the authority to enter into contracts with an eligible entity to serve as a *Medicare administrative contractor* with respect to the performance of certain functions including determination of payment amounts and making payments, the development of local coverage determinations; beneficiary education and assistance; provider consultation, communication, education, and technical assistance; and other necessary functions, including functions concerning the Medicare Integrity Program. These functions were previously performed by entities known as "fiscal intermediaries" and "carriers." Section 1874A defines the appropriate Medicare administrative contractor as an entity that has a contract to perform one or more of the described functions in relation to an individual entitled to benefits under Part A or enrolled under Part B, or to a provider, supplier, or class of providers or suppliers. In addition, 42 U.S.C. §§1395h and 1395u specifically remove references to fiscal intermediaries and carriers, which, as noted, are now referred to as "contractors."

§2.02 ELIGIBILITY FOR MEDICARE HOSPITAL INSURANCE (PART A)

Medicare Part A provides basic protections against certain medical costs to persons age 65 or over who are eligible for retirement benefits under Title II of the

---

[1] Social Security Act 1817, 42 U.S.C. §1395i(a).

[2] 42 C.F.R. §406.2 (Scope).

Social Security Act (or would be eligible for such benefits if certain government employment were covered employment under Title II, or under the Railroad Retirement system); individuals under age 65 who have been entitled for not less than 24 months to benefits under Title II of the Social Security Act (or would have been so entitled if certain government employment were covered employment under Title II) or under the Railroad Retirement system on the basis of a disability;[3] and certain individuals who do not meet the requirements set out above but are medically determined to have end-stage renal disease (ESRD).[4]

Under the Medicare program, eligibility begins the first month in which an individual meets all the requirements, including application and enrollment.[5] The first month of entitlement is the first month for which the individual meets all the requirements for entitlement to Part A benefits.[6] An insured is an individual who has the number of quarters of coverage required for monthly Social Security benefits.[7] A quarter of coverage is a calendar quarter that is counted toward the number of covered quarters required for eligibility for monthly Social Security benefits; and a quarter is counted if during that quarter (or that calendar year) the individual earned a required minimum amount of money.[8]

Persons who are age 65 or over and certain persons under age 65, who do not meet the requirements for premium-free benefits, may obtain benefits by paying a premium.[9] Monthly premiums are promulgated each October, effective for the succeeding calendar year.[10]

---

[3] Section 115 of the Medicare, Medicaid, and SCHIP Benefits Improvement Protection Act of 2000 (BIPA), Pub. L. No. 106-554, amended 42 U.S.C. §426, to provide that for persons who have been medically determined to have amyotrophic lateral sclerosis (ALS), there shall be a waiting period of no longer than a month after disability has been established and that entitlement to benefits shall begin with the first month (rather than the 25th month) of entitlement. This amendment became effective July 1, 2001. *See also*, <http://www.cms.hhs.gov/publications/overview-medicare-medicaid/default3.asp>.

[4] Social Security Act 1811, 42 U.S.C. §1395c; 42 C.F.R. §406.13 (individual who has ESRD).

[5] 42 C.F.R. §406.3.

[6] *Id.*

[7] *Id.*

[8] *Id. See also* 20 C.F.R. Pt. 404, Subpt. B (determining quarters of coverage and minimum amounts necessary).

[9] 42 C.F.R. §406.5. For the requirements for premium hospital insurance, *see* 42 C.F.R. §406.20. Most people do not pay a monthly Part A premium either they or their spouse have 40 or more quarters of Medicare-covered employment. The Part A premium is $226 in 2007 ($216.00 in 2006) for enrollees who have 30-39 quarters of Medicare-covered employment. The Part A premium is $410 in 2007 ($393.00 in 2006) per month for those who are not otherwise eligible for premium-free hospital insurance and have less than 30 quarters of Medicare-covered employment. *See* <http://www.medicare.custhelp.com>.

[10] 42 C.F.R. §406.32(a). The procedure for determining the monthly premium amount is found at 42 C.F.R. §406.32(b)-(d); for collection of payments and payments due, *see* 42 C.F.R. §406.32(e), (f); and for group payment option, *see* 42 C.F.R. §406.32(g). Other premium rules are defined at §406.33 (determination of months to be counted for premium increase: enrollment) and §406.34 (determination of months to be counted for premium increase: reenrollment).

§2.03 APPLICATION OR ENROLLMENT FOR MEDICARE PART A

[A] Who Must File

Most Medicare beneficiaries are eligible for Medicare Part A as a result of being age 65 or older and entitled to monthly Social Security or Railroad Retirement cash benefits.[11] Persons eligible for benefits on this basis do not need to file an application for hospital insurance (Medicare Part A).[12]

An individual must file an application for Medicare Part A if he or she seeks entitlement on the basis of:

- Transition benefits;[13]

- Deemed entitlement to disabled widow's or widower's benefits;[14]

- A diagnosis of ESRD;[15]

- Eligibility for Social Security cash benefits if the individual has attained age 65 without applying for these benefits;[16] and

- Special provisions applicable to government employment.[17]

[B] Time Periods for Filing Application

An application is deemed filed, based on the transition periods or on ESRD as described above, in the first month of eligibility if it is filed not more than three months before the first month of eligibility and is retroactive to the first month of eligibility if filed within 12 months after the first month of eligibility.[18] Similarly, an application filed more than 12 months after the first month of eligibility is retroactive to the twelfth month before the month it is filed.[19]

---

[11] 42 C.F.R. §406.6.

[12] 42 C.F.R. §406.6(b).

[13] 42 C.F.R. §406.6(c)(1). *See* 42 C.F.R. §406.11 for discussion of transition benefits.

[14] 42 C.F.R. §406.6(c)(2). *See* 42 C.F.R. §406.12 for discussion of widow's and widower's benefits.

[15] 42 C.F.R. §406.6(c)(3). *See* 42 C.F.R. §406.13 for discussion of ESRD.

[16] 42 C.F.R. §406.6(c)(4). *See* 42 C.F.R. §406.10(a)(3) for discussion of eligibility based on this status.

[17] 42 C.F.R. §406.6(c)(5). *See* 42 C.F.R. §406.15 for discussion of provisions applicable to eligibility based on government employment.

[18] 42 C.F.R. §406.6(d)(1). *See* 42 C.F.R. §406.21(individual enrollment), §406.22 (effect of month of enrollment on entitlement). *See also* 42 C.F.R. §406.24 for a discussion of special enrollment period (SEP) applicable to group health plan (GHP) and large group health plan (LGHP) individuals; and *see* 42 C.F.R. §406.26 (enrollment under state buy-in).

[19] 42 C.F.R. §406.6(d)(1).

A valid application based on entitlement to widow's or widower's benefits is deemed filed if, before the first month in which the individual meets the conditions of eligibility, the conditions of eligibility are met before an initial determination, reconsideration, or hearing decision is made on the application.[20] An application, if validly filed within 12 months after the first month of eligibility, is deemed retroactive to that first month. If filed more than 12 months after the first month of eligibility, it is retroactive to the twelfth month before the month of filing.[21] A similar rule applies for persons eligible for Social Security benefits at or after age 65 for an application that is filed before the first month in which the individual meets all the eligibility conditions for that benefit.[22]

[C]   Forms and Where to File

Forms for applying for Medicare Part A benefits may be obtained by mail, free of charge, from the Centers for Medicare & Medicaid Services (CMS) or at any Social Security branch or district office.[23] In the alternative, an individual may use the application for monthly Social Security benefits to apply for Medicare entitlement if eligible for Medicare Part A at that time.[24]

§2.04   SCOPE OF BENEFITS—INPATIENT HOSPITAL COVERAGE BENEFIT PERIODS

[A]   In General

An individual insured under Medicare Part A is entitled to inpatient hospital or critical access hospital (CAH) services for up to 150 days during any spell of illness (or "benefit period"), minus one day for each day of such services in excess of 90 days, which were previously used during a prior spell of illness or benefit period.[25] (These days in excess of 90 days are known as "lifetime reserve days"). This inpatient hospital coverage is available to inpatients in an acute hospital or in a rehabilitation hospital. Coverage for inpatient psychiatric hospitals is somewhat different.[26]

In any benefit period, a Medicare beneficiary is entitled to 60 fully paid days of hospital care, subject only to an initial deductible amount per benefit period;

---

[20] 42 C.F.R. §406.6(d)(2).

[21] *Id.*

[22] 42 C.F.R. §406.6(d)(3).

[23] 42 C.F.R. §406.7.

[24] *Id.*

[25] Social Security Act 1812(a), 42 U.S.C. §1395d(a); 42 C.F.R. §409.61 (general limitations on amount of benefits), §409.82 (inpatient hospital deductible), §409.83 (inpatient hospital coinsurance).

[26] See **§2.04[C].**

after 60 days, a beneficiary must pay a daily coinsurance amount equal to one-fourth of the initial deductible; and after 90 days, the beneficiary is entitled to 60 "lifetime reserve" days, which may be used only once during the beneficiary's lifetime.[27] The initial deductible is $992; the daily coinsurance amount is $248 in 2007 for days 61 to 90 of a hospital stay; and the lifetime reserve day coinsurance amount in 2007 is $496 for days 91 to 150.[C1][28] The deductible and coinsurance amount and lifetime reserve day amount are adjusted each calendar year. Each adjustment is announced in the Federal Register, usually in October prior to the new calendar year.

[B] Benefit Period Explained

Example: Imagine that Mrs. Brown entered the hospital on January 1, 2007, and stayed for 200 days. Mrs. Brown returns home for 30 days before she is re-hospitalized. The Medicare hospital coverage available to Mrs. Brown may be described as follows: Mrs. Brown first pays the $992 deductible due before any Medicare coverage is paid. She then receives 60 days of hospital coverage without coinsurance. Mrs. Brown is next responsible for $248 of coinsurance per day between days 61 and 90. On day 91 Mrs. Brown begins to use her lifetime reserve days (assuming that she has not used any of these days in prior hospital stays). The lifetime reserve days require a daily coinsurance payment of $496 in 2007. After the lifetime reserve days are exhausted on the 150th day, Mrs. Brown will have exhausted her Medicare coverage for her current benefit period. When Mrs. Brown returns to the hospital after 30 days at home, she will be entitled to no additional Medicare coverage. As stated above, a beneficiary is entitled to a maximum of 150 days of hospital coverage in any one "spell of illness."[29] A spell of illness ends and a new spell of illness (with additional hospital coverage) becomes available only after the beneficiary has gone 60 consecutive days without receiving either an inpatient hospital level of care nor a SNF level of care.[30] A hospital or SNF level of care is one coverable by the Medicare program. Because Mrs. Brown was at home for only 30 days, she continues in the same spell of illness and her benefits remain exhausted.

It should also be noted that it is possible to have more than one benefit period in the same calendar year, requiring the payment of a new deductible and additional coinsurance.[31] This circumstance arises where a beneficiary has two separate hospitalizations in a year, and the first hospitalization is followed by a period of 60 consecutive days without receiving an inpatient hospital or SNF level of care.

---

[27] 42 C.F.R. §409.83 (inpatient hospital coinsurance), §409.60 (benefit period defined).

[28] *See* <http://www.medicare.custhelp.com>.

[29] 42 U.S.C. §1395d.

[30] Social Security Act 1861(a), 42 U.S.C. §1395x(a); 42 C.F.R. §409.60(b).

[31] 42 C.F.R. §409.80(a).

[C]   Inpatient Psychiatric Services

With respect to inpatient psychiatric hospital services, a beneficiary is entitled to a total of 190 days of inpatient care during his or her lifetime.[32] These 190 lifetime psychiatric inpatient days are in addition to the coverage available in acute and rehabilitation hospital settings, as discussed above.

Although an individual is entitled to 190 days of such care per lifetime, the individual is permitted to utilize only a maximum of 150 of these days in any given benefit period. Moreover, these 150 days are subject to the same deductible and coinsurance amounts that are applicable to care received in an acute or rehabilitation hospital setting.

> **Example:** If Mr. Jones entered a psychiatric hospital in 2007 with a full 190 lifetime days available to, he would be able to use only 150 of those days and would be required to pay the $992 deductible. In addition, commencing with the 61st day, he would be required to pay the $248 per day coinsurance and commencing with the 91st day, he would be required to pay the $496 per day coinsurance. Because he is permitted to use only 150 of his 190 lifetime psychiatric inpatient hospital days, the remaining 40 days of available coverage can be used only in a new benefit period, that is, only after he has gone 60 consecutive days without receiving an inpatient hospital or SNF level of care.

It also should be noted that if the individual was an inpatient in a psychiatric hospital on the first day of Medicare entitlement and for any of the 150 days immediately before the first day of Medicare entitlement, those days are subtracted from the 150 days that would otherwise be available in the initial benefit period for inpatient psychiatric services in a psychiatric or general hospital.[33] These subtracted days are, however, available to the individual in a subsequent benefit period. This reduction applies only if the hospital was participating in Medicare as a psychiatric hospital on the individual's first day of Medicare enrollment,[34] and only to the beneficiary's first benefit period.[35] Days spent in a general hospital before entitlements are not subtracted under this provision even if the stay was for diagnosis or treatment of mental illness.[36]

---

[32] 42 U.S.C. §1395d(b)(3); 42 C.F.R. §409.62.

[33] 42 C.F.R. §409 .63(a).

[34] 42 C.F.R. §409.63(a)(2).

[35] 42 C.F.R. §409.63(a)(3).

[36] 42 C.F.R. §409.63(b). *See also* set of examples explaining §409.63 reduction rule found at 42 C.F.R. §409.63(c), and *see* Legion v. Richardson, 354 F. Supp. 456 (S.D.N.Y.), *aff'd,* 414 U.S. 1058 (1973).

§2.05 MEDICARE-COVERED SERVICES

[A] In General

In order to fully understand Medicare inpatient hospital coverage, it is necessary to know the definition of certain terms used in the applicable statute and regulations. With respect to the provision of Medicare-covered services, "arrangements" include those arrangements that provide for Medicare payment for services delivered to Medicare beneficiaries; "covered" refers to services authorized for Medicare payment which meet Medicare coverage criteria as defined in the Medicare law and regulations;[37] "nominal charge provider" means a provider that furnishes services free of charge or at a nominal charge and is either a public provider or other provider that demonstrates to CMS's satisfaction that a significant portion of its patients are low income and requests that payment of its services be determined accordingly; "participating" refers to hospitals or other facilities that meet the conditions of participation and have in effect a Medicare provider agreement; a "qualified hospital" is one primarily engaged in providing, by or under the supervision of doctors of medicine or osteopathy, inpatient services for the diagnosis, treatment, and care or rehabilitation of persons who are sick, injured, or disabled, is not primarily engaged in providing skilled nursing care or related services, provides 24-hour nursing services, and is licensed in the United States, or in Canada or Mexico, for the purposes of furnishing non-emergency services to U.S. residents.[38]

[B] Covered Benefits

Covered benefits under Part A include the services, except for luxuries (such as a telephone or television), generally provided during a hospital or CAH hospital stay, including use of hospital facilities, room and board in a semiprivate room, nursing and related services, medical social services, operating and recovery room costs, drugs and medical supplies furnished in the hospital, certain diagnostic or therapeutic services, laboratory tests, radiological services billed by the hospital, rehabilitation services, and blood.[39] Inpatient hospital services generally do not

---

[37] Usually, Medicare coverage results in payment by Medicare for the services or items in question. However, some courts have distinguished Medicare coverage from Medicare payment. This is important to a beneficiary, because once Medicare coverage is established, the beneficiary is absolved of full financial responsibility for the items or services in question, regardless of whether the provider receives Medicare payment. *See, e.g.*, New York *ex rel.* Bodnar v. Secretary of HHS, 903 F.2d 122 (2d Cir. 1990).

[38] 42 C.F.R. §409.3.

[39] Social Security Act 1861(b), 42 U.S.C. §1395x(b); 42 C.F.R. §409.10 (included services), §409.11 (bed and board), §409.12 (nursing and related services), §409.13 (drugs and biologicals), §409.15 (services of interns and residents-in-training), §409.16 (other diagnostic or therapeutic services), §409.18 (services related to kidney transplantation), and §409.19 (services related to cardiac pacemakers and pacemaker leads).

include SNF-type care furnished by a hospital or a CAH that has a swing-bed approval, or any nursing-facility-type care that may be furnished as a Medicaid service under the Medicaid program.[40]

§2.06   COVERAGE CRITERIA EXPLAINED

[A]   Bed and Board

Except for applicable deductibles and coinsurance amounts, Medicare Part A covers in full bed and board and semiprivate (two to four beds) or ward (five or more beds) accommodations.[41] Private accommodations are similarly covered if the patient's treating physician concludes that the patient's condition requires isolation, or if the hospital or CAH hospital has no semiprivate or ward accommodations; or the semiprivate and ward accommodations of the hospital or CAH are fully occupied by other patients.[42] Medicare will continue to pay for private accommodations until the patient's condition no longer requires a private room or until semiprivate or ward accommodations are available.[43] The hospital is free to charge the patient the difference between the private room rate and the semiprivate or ward accommodations rate where the patient requests a private room absent a medical need for such.[44]

[B]   Nursing and Related Services

Medicare covers nursing and related services, use of hospital or CAH facilities, and medical social services as inpatient hospital or inpatient CAH services ordinarily furnished by the hospital for the care and treatment of inpatients.[45] Medicare, however, does not pay for private duty nurses or attendants.[46]

[C]   Drugs and Biologicals

Medicare pays for drugs and biologicals as inpatient hospital or inpatient CAH services if they represent a cost to the hospital, are ordinarily furnished by the hospital or CAH for the care and treatment of inpatients, and are furnished to an inpatient for use in the hospital or CAH.[47] In addition, Medicare will pay for a

---

[40] 42 C.F.R. §409.10(b).

[41] 42 C.F.R. §409.11(a).

[42] 42 C.F.R. §409.11(b).

[43] 42 C.F.R. §409.11(b)(2).

[44] 42 C.F.R. §409.11(b)(3).

[45] 42 C.F.R. §409.12(a).

[46] 42 C.F.R. §409.12(b).

[47] 42 C.F.R. §409.13(a).

limited supply of drugs for use outside the hospital or CAH if it is medically necessary to enable a beneficiary's departure from the hospital or CAH and required until the patient can obtain a continuing supply.[48]

[D] Services Furnished by an Intern or Resident-in-Training

Inpatient hospital services include the services of medical or surgical interns or residents-in-training.[49] Services must be provided through a teaching program approved by the Council on Medical Education of the American Medical Association or the Bureau of Professional Education of the American Osteopathic Association; a program approved by the Council on Dental Education of the American Dental Association; or a program approved by the Council on Podiatry Education of the American Podiatry Association.[50]

[E] Other Diagnostic or Therapeutic Items or Services

Diagnostic or therapeutic items or services are considered inpatient hospital or inpatient CAH services if furnished by the hospital or CAH, or others under arrangements made with the hospital or CAH; the billing for such services is performed as through the hospital or CAH; and the services are of the kind ordinarily furnished to inpatients either by the hospital or CAH or under arrangements made by the hospital.[51] Diagnostic services of independent clinical laboratories, furnished to Medicare inpatients under arrangements with a Medicare-participating hospital, are reimbursable under Medicare Part A.[52]

[F] Services Related to Kidney Transplantations

Medicare only pays for kidney transplantations performed in a Medicare-approved renal transplantation center.[53] Provided that the kidney is intended for an individual who has ESRD and is eligible for Medicare, Medicare payment is available for the evaluation or preparation of a potential or actual donor, for the donation of the kidney, or for postoperative recovery services directly related to the kidney donation.[54] The Medicare deductible and coinsurance requirements do not

---

[48] 42 C.F.R. §409.13(b).

[49] 42 C.F.R. §409.15(a).

[50] 42 C.F.R. §409.15(b), (c).

[51] 42 C.F.R. §409.16.

[52] 42 C.F.R. §482.27; CMS Pub. 100-02, Ch. 1, §50.3 (online manual system—<www.cms.hhs.gov>).

[53] 42 C.F.R. §409.18(a).

[54] 42 C.F.R. §409.18(b).

apply to any services furnished to an individual in connection with the donation of a kidney for transplant surgery.[55]

[G] Blood Services

With respect to blood, the patient must pay a deductible for the first three units of whole blood or units of packed red cells that a beneficiary receives during a calendar year as an inpatient of a hospital, CAH, or SNF, or on an outpatient basis under Medicare Part B.[56] A unit of packed red cells is treated as the equivalent of a unit of whole blood.[57] Generally, a provider may charge the patient its customary charge for any of the first three units.[58] The deductible does not apply to other blood components such as platelet, fibrinogen, plasma, gamma globulin, and serum albumin, or to the cost of storing and administering blood.[59] The beneficiary also has the option to arrange for the blood to be replaced rather than paying for it.[60]

The blood deductible is in addition to the inpatient hospital deductible and daily coinsurance.[61] The Part A blood deductible is reduced to the extent that the Part B blood deductible has been applied; for example, the beneficiary has received one unit under Medicare Part B.

The Medicare hospital benefit does not include coverage for physicians' services while in the hospital. Those services are covered under Medicare Part B.[62] The surgeon and anesthesiologist, for example, will bill the patient separately (the cost of physicians' services deemed reasonable and necessary would be covered under Part B of the Medicare program).

§2.07   LIMITATIONS ON PAYMENT FOR SERVICES

[A] Physician Certification and Payment Forms

Providers of Medicare services, including hospitals, must submit payment forms indicating that the services provided were medically necessary and appropriate. The forms for submitting a request for payment are promulgated by the Secretary and must be submitted for payment no later than the calendar year following the year in which such services are furnished. Services furnished in

---

[55] 42 C.F.R. §409.89.

[56] 42 U.S.C. §1395e(a)(2); 42 C.F.R. §409.87(a)(3).

[57] 42 C.F.R. §409.87(a)(2).

[58] 42 C.F.R. §409 .87(c).

[59] 42 C.F.R. §409.87(a)(4).

[60] 42 C.F.R. §409.87(b).

[61] 42 C.F.R. §409.87(a)(5).

[62] 42 U.S.C. §1395d; Social Security Act 1812(a)(1).

the last quarter of a calendar year, however, are deemed to have been delivered in the following calendar year.[63]

> **Example:** If a patient receives services in October 2006, those services will be viewed as having been delivered during the calendar year 2007 and, therefore, can properly be billed through the end of 2008. By contrast, services delivered in September 2006 could properly be billed only through the end of 2007.

The physician must certify that the inpatient hospital services that they provide over a period of time are required to be given on an inpatient basis for such individual's medical treatment, or that inpatient diagnostic study is medically required and such services are necessary for such purposes.[64] This certification is only to be furnished in such cases, and with such frequency and with supporting material as appropriate to the case involved, and as provided by the Secretary's regulations, the first such certification being furnished no later than the 20th day of the period in which services are being provided.[65] A similar certification is required for inpatient psychiatric hospital services.[66]

Physicians must also certify that dental services performed in the hospital setting, in connection with the care, treatment, filling, removal, or replacement of teeth or structures that directly support teeth, are such that the services must be performed in the hospital setting.[67] The certification must state that because of the underlying medical condition and clinical status of the patient, or the severity of the dental procedure, hospitalization is required.[68]

[B] Payment for Services Performed Outside the United States

Payment is available for inpatient hospital services furnished to Medicare beneficiaries in a hospital located outside the United States, or under arrangements with it, if such individual is a resident of the United States and such hospital is closer to, or substantially more accessible from, the residence of such individual than the nearest United States hospital adequately equipped to deal with and available to treat the beneficiary's illness or injury.[69]

---

[63] 42 C.F.R. §424.44.

[64] 42 U.S.C. §1395f(a)(2), (a)(3). *See also* 42 U.S.C. §1395f(a)(6) (physician certification where no utilization review committee findings have been made), §1395f(a)(8) with respect to inpatient critical access hospital services, requiring physician certification that the patient may reasonably be expected to be transferred to a hospital within 96 hours after admission to the critical access hospital.

[65] 42 U.S.C. §1395f(a)(3).

[66] 42 U.S.C. §1395f(a)(2)(A).

[67] 42 U.S.C. §1395f(a)(2)(D).

[68] *Id.*

[69] 42 U.S.C. §1395f(f).

§2.08   THE MEDICAL NECESSITY STANDARD
FOR INPATIENT HOSPITAL STAYS

[A]   In General

The substantive standard for Medicare coverage for general hospital services (also called acute hospital care) is one of "medical necessity." [70]A physician must certify that hospital "services are required to be given on an inpatient basis for such individual's medical treatment, or that inpatient diagnostic study is medically required. . . . "[71] The regulations provide that inpatient hospital care includes cases where a beneficiary needs a SNF level of care, but under Medicare criteria, a Medicare certified SNF-level bed is not available.[72] The Medicare statute requires that the beneficiary be "entitled to have payment made" for SNF care although remaining in the hospital awaiting an available SNF bed. Therefore, in addition to requiring a SNF level of care, a beneficiary must also have been covered by Medicare for at least three days during the hospital stay in question.[73] A patient must accept the first Medicare-certified bed available,[74] or lose continued Medicare inpatient hospital coverage. However, an offer of a non-certified bed may be rejected with no risk to continued inpatient hospital coverage.[75] In addition, the statute explicitly excludes from coverage any expenses incurred for items or services "not reasonable and necessary for the diagnosis or treatment of illness or injury or to improve the functioning of a malformed body member. . . . "[76]

> **Example:** Mrs. Smith sustains a fall and fractures her leg. Surgery is required to repair the fracture, and she is admitted to the hospital in order to receive such treatment. Close monitoring of her post-surgical condition is required because she has a history of peripheral vascular disease, venous thrombosis, and leg edema. Her treating physician has prescribed continuous intravenous anticoagulation therapy in order to prevent a stroke, and is unable to accurately discern whether the swelling in her leg is attributable to swelling relative to the fracture or to the venous thrombosis. During this entire time, the services

---

[70] 42 U.S.C. §1395f(a)(3).

[71] *Id.*

[72] 42 C.F.R. §412.42(c)(1); *see also* 42 C.F.R. §424.13(b).

[73] 42 U.S.C. §1395x(v)(1)(G)(i)(II I); *see also* 42 C.F.R. §409.30.

[74] Occasionally, the question arises as to how distant the SNF bed can be, in order for it to be deemed "available" to the patient. For example, can a patient be required to accept an SNF bed that is 300 miles from the patient's home? While there is no unequivocal answer to this question in the Medicare statute or regulations, Medicare policy does state that this requirement "is not defined to require a patient to be taken away from his family and transported over great distances." *See,* Medicare Intermediary Manual (CMS Pub. 13-1) §3421.1C. It does not appear that this provision has yet been transferred to the on-line Medicare Policy Manual system.

[75] 42 C.F.R. §412.42(c)(1); *see also* 42 C.F.R. §424.13(b).

[76] Social Security Act 1862(a)(1)(A), 42 U.S.C. §1395(a)(1)(A).

Mrs. Smith is receiving in the hospital could be performed only in a hospital, where 24-hour availability of a physician exists and the requisite close physician monitoring is available. Following resolution of these medical issues, Mrs. Smith's physician orders physical therapy five times per week and includes a statement that Mrs. Smith can be transferred to a SNF. However, no Medicare-certified SNF bed is immediately available. Under these circumstances, Mrs. Smith is still eligible to receive Medicare inpatient hospital coverage, because she needs a SNF level of care, but no Medicare-certified SNF bed is available to her. The days that Mrs. Smith spends in the hospital waiting for a Medicare certified SNF bed to become available are covered hospital days, subject to any applicable hospital coinsurance amounts, as well as the 150-day-per-benefit-period inpatient hospital limitation.

[B] Additional Requirements for Rehabilitation Hospitals

Medicare imposes additional coverage requirements for care received in rehabilitation hospitals.[77] Rehabilitation hospital care may be covered where it is provided in a freestanding rehabilitation hospital, or in a distinct rehabilitation unit of an acute care hospital. Effective January 1, 2002, inpatient rehabilitation hospitals and rehabilitation units are paid under a prospective payment system. Payments are made on the basis of prospectively determined rates and applied on a diagnosis-related group (DRG) basis.[78]

For a rehabilitation hospitalization to be covered, the following requirements must be satisfied:

- The physician must certify that the patient needs inpatient hospital rehabilitation;

- The hospital must be a Medicare-certified facility;

- The patient must require a relatively intense, multidisciplinary rehabilitation program provided by a coordinated team of physical therapists, occupational therapists, speech language pathologists, rehabilitation nurses, and/or training in rehabilitation medicine, which is evidenced by at least bi-weekly team meeting notes;

- The goal of the rehabilitation program must be to upgrade the patient's ability to function as independently as possible;

- The care must be reasonable and necessary, and not actually available at a lower level of care.[79]

---

[77] 42 C.F.R. §412.33(b).

[78] 42 C.F.R. §§412.600 *et seq.*

[79] 42 C.F.R. §412.23(v), §412.29; Medicare Hospital Manual 211. Medicare Benefit Policy Manual, Pub. 100-2, Ch. 1 §§110.1. *et seq. See* <http://www.cms.hhs.gov/manuals/102policy/bp102c01.pdf> (Medicare continues its process of moving from a paper-based manual system to

[C] Long-Term Care Hospitals

In general, Long-Term Care Hospitals (LTCHs) are defined in the Medicare law as hospitals that have an average inpatient length of stay greater than 25 days. They typically provide extended medical and rehabilitative care for patients with clinically complex conditions and for those who may suffer from multiple acute or chronic conditions. Services available in such facilities can include comprehensive rehabilitation, respiratory therapy, cancer treatment, head trauma treatment and pain management.[80]

To be eligible to receive payment under the prospect payment system for LTCHs, the facility must meet the criteria to be classified as a long-term care hospital[81] for exclusion from hospital inpatient prospective payment systems.[82] This condition of payment is subject to special payment provisions,[83] provisions on change in hospital status,[84] provisions related to hospitals within hospitals,[85] and satellite facilities.[86]

LTCHs may not charge beneficiaries for any covered services for which payment is made by Medicare, even if the hospital's costs of furnishing the service

---

an Internet system). Note that for many years the CMS interpreted "relatively intense" to mean that the patient had to require and receive at least three hours per day of physical and/or occupational therapy in order to qualify for Medicare coverage for hospital-level rehabilitation. This interpretation, found in CMS's Intermediary and Hospital Manuals, was found by the United States District Court to be an arbitrary rule of thumb that could not be used to deny coverage in Hooper v. Sullivan, *Medicare & Medicaid Guide* (CCH) 37,985 (D. Conn. 1989). In *Hooper*, the Secretary was ordered to revise the manual provisions to reflect the fact that Medicare determinations are to be made based on an individual assessment of each patient's needs and to prohibit denials based on the three-hour rule or any other rule of thumb. *See also* CMS Ruling 85-2, *Medicare & Medicaid Guide* (CCH) [1986-1 Transfer Binder] 34,817; *and see* New York *ex rel.* Holland v. Sullivan, 927 F.2d 57 (2d Cir. 1991); New York *ex rel.* Stein v. Secretary, Dep't of Health & Human Servs., 924 F.2d 431 (2d Cir. 1991); Probstein v. Sullivan, *Medicare & Medicaid Guide* (CCH) 41,423 (D. Conn. Jan. 5, 1993).

[80] *See* Section 123 of Public L. No. 106-113, the Balanced Budget Refinement Act of 1999 (BBRA), as amended by 307 of Public Law 106-554, the Medicare, Medicaid, and SCHIP Benefits Improvement and Protection Act of 2000 (BIPA). This provision directed the Secretary to develop and implement a per discharge, diagnosis-related group (DRG)-based prospective payment system (PPS) for LTCHs for cost-reporting periods beginning on or after October 1, 2002. The new system replaces the reasonable cost-based payment system over a five-year transition period through October 1, 2006. Regulations implementing PPS for LTCHs are located at 42 C.F.R. §§412.500–412.541. *See also* <http://www/cms/hhs/gov/providers/longterm/background.asp>. Citation and links to Long-Term Care Hospital PPS, federal regulations and notices, are available at <http://www.cms.hhs.gov/providers/longterm/frnotices.asp>.

[81] 42 C.F.R. §412.505; 42 C.F.R. §412.23(e).

[82] 42 C.F.R. §412.505; 42 C.F.R. §412.1(a)(1).

[83] 42 C.F.R. §412.505; 42 C.F.R. §412.22(c).

[84] 42 C.F.R. §412.505; 42 C.F.R. §412.22(d).

[85] 42 C.F.R. §412.505; 42 C.F.R. §412.22(e).

[86] 42 C.F.R. §412.505; 42 C.F.R. §412.22(h).

are greater than the Prospective Payment System (PPS) amount. The facility may charge the beneficiary only for the applicable deductible and coinsurance amounts.[87]

LTCHs must have an agreement with a Quality Improvement Organization (QIO) to provide ongoing review with respect to medical necessity, reasonableness, and appropriateness of hospital admissions and discharges; appropriateness of payments under outlier provisions; the validity of the hospital's diagnostic and procedural information; the completeness, adequacy, and quality of the services furnished by the hospital; and other medical or other practices with respect to beneficiaries or billing for services furnished to beneficiaries.[88]

§2.09 HOSPITAL PAYMENT

[A] Prospective Payment

A hospital must meet the conditions of Medicare participation under the Medicare Prospective Payment Service (PPS) for hospital services furnished to Medicare beneficiaries.[89] If a hospital fails to comply with these conditions, the CMS, which administers the Medicare program, may withhold Medicare payment, in full or in part, to the hospital until the hospital provides appropriate assurances of its compliance. Otherwise, CMS may terminate the hospital's provider agreement.[90]

Historically, prior to 1983, the Medicare program paid hospitals on a retrospective basis in an amount equal to the reasonable cost of covered services. In other words, Medicare paid a hospital what it cost the hospital to deliver the service involved. Effective October 1, 1983, however, Congress instituted a new financing structure called the PPS.[91]

[B] Diagnosis-Related Groups

The PPS applies to acute care and rehabilitation hospitals, as well as long term care hospitals, and to units in acute care hospitals that provide rehabilitation

---

[87] 42 C.F.R. §412.507. Applicable deductible and coinsurance amounts are discussed at 42 C.F.R. §§409.82, 409.83, and 409.87.

[88] 42 C.F.R. §412.508. QIOs, formerly known as Peer Review Organizations (PROs), are a creature of the Social Security Act, §§1151 et seq., 42 U.S.C §§1320c et seq., and provide certain quality and utilization review oversight with respect to a range of Medicare-covered services.

[89] 42 C.F.R. §412.40.

[90] 42 C.F.R. §412.40(b)(1), (2).

[91] 42 U.S.C. §1395ww(d). Note, generally, PPSs exist across a range of care settings, including hospitals, skilled nursing facilities, home health, hospice, and outpatient hospital services. CMS provides updating PPS rates, rules, and data on an ongoing basis. Discussion of PPS is generally incorporated as relevant to a particular care setting.

services.[92] Alcohol and drug treatment, psychiatric, and children's hospitals are not included in PPS, nor are units in acute care hospitals that provide alcohol and drug treatment, psychiatric, or pediatric services.[93]

PPS requires the payment of a prospectively determined amount for each Medicare discharge. All patient discharges are classified according to a list of Diagnosis-Related Groups (DRGs). The list includes approximately 490 DRGs. Each DRG is assigned a particular value based on the average cost of caring for patients with similar diagnoses in the past.[94]

The DRG for a stroke, for example, might be $6,000. For every patient discharged from a hospital after treatment for a stroke, the hospital would receive $6,000 in Medicare reimbursement even if the patient's care had actually cost the hospital less, or more, than $6,000 to deliver.

Only when a beneficiary has a medically necessary stay that is much longer or more expensive for the hospital than an average case covered by the appropriate DRG can the hospital receive additional Medicare coverage, called "outlier payments." The outlier payments amount to 60 percent of the average daily cost of caring for a patient with the diagnosis involved.[95] Because the hospital usually receives only the single predetermined DRG amount for a given hospital discharge, the hospital comes under severe pressure to discharge patients at the earliest possible time, thereby maximizing profit or minimizing loss.

[C] Limits on Charges to Beneficiaries

Hospitals may not charge a beneficiary for services that are paid for by Medicare, even if the hospital's cost of furnishing such services to the beneficiary is greater than the amount the hospital is paid under PPS.[96]

Under PPS, a hospital may charge a beneficiary for a covered stay, which includes at least one covered day, only for the following:

- Applicable deductible and coinsurance amounts;[97]

- Custodial care provided that is not part of medically necessary hospital services provided to the patient;[98]

- Items and services that are not medically necessary;[99]

---

[92] Regulations establishing a prospective payment system for rehabilitation hospitals have been issued by the CMS and became effective January 1, 2002. 42 C.F.R. §§412.600 *et seq.*

[93] 42 U.S.C. §1395ww(d)(1)(B); 42 C.F.R. §§412.20–412.32.

[94] 42 U.S.C. §1395ww(e).

[95] 42 C.F.R. §§412.80–412.84.

[96] 42 C.F.R. §412.42(a).

[97] *See* 42 C.F.R. §§409.82, 409.83, and 409.87.

[98] 42 C.F.R. §412.42(b)(2)(i). *See also* 42 C.F.R. §405.310(g).

[99] 42 C.F.R. §412.42(b)(2)(ii). *See also* 42 C.F.R. §405.310(k).

- Non-physician services furnished to hospital inpatients by other than the hospital or a provider or supplier under arrangements made by the hospital;[100]

- Items and services provided when a patient is not entitled to Medicare Part A benefits;[101] and

- Items and services provided after Medicare Part A benefits have been exhausted.[102]

[D] Inpatient Hospitalization No Longer Necessary

In addition, a hospital may charge a beneficiary for items and services provided after the hospital (acting directly or through its utilization review committee) has determined that the beneficiary no longer requires inpatient hospital care;[103] or where the attending physician agrees with the hospital determination in writing (for example, by issuing a written discharge order) that inpatient hospital services are no longer necessary.[104] Before a hospital can charge the beneficiary under these circumstances, the hospital must notify the beneficiary (or person acting on his or her behalf) in writing that:

- In the opinion of the hospital, and with the concurrence of the physician or the QIO,[105] the beneficiary no longer requires inpatient hospital care;

- Customary charges will be made for continued hospital care beyond the second day following the date of the notice;

---

[100] 42 C.F.R. §412.42(b)(2)(iii).

[101] 42 C.F.R. §412.42(b)(2)(iv). *See also* Subpart A of 408.

[102] 42 C.F.R. §412.42(b)(2)(v). *See also* 42 C.F.R. §409.61.

[103] 42 C.F.R. §412.42(c)(1), (2). Note, inpatient hospital care includes care where a beneficiary needs an SNF level of care and a Medicare-certified SNF bed is not available. *Id.* Occasionally, the question arises as to how distant the SNF bed can be, in order for it to be deemed "available" to the patient. For example, can a patient be required to accept an SNF bed that is 300 miles from the patient's home? While there is no unequivocal answer to this question in the Medicare statute or regulations, Medicare policy does state that this requirement "is not defined to require a patient to be taken away from his family and transported over great distances."

[104] 42 C.F.R. §412.42(c)(2). Note that if the hospital believes the patient no longer needs inpatient hospital care and is unable to get the agreement of the physician, the hospital may request immediate review by the appropriate QIO; concurrence by the QIO serves in lieu of the physician's agreement. *Id.*

[105] The QIO or intermediary may review any cases in which the hospital advises the beneficiary (or the person acting on the beneficiary's behalf) of the non-coverage of the services. The hospital must identify such cases to the QIO or intermediary in accordance with CMS instructions. 42 C.F.R. §412.42(g); *see also, generally*, Medicare Quality Improvement Organization Manual, Pub. 100, Ch. 10, §7-7000. A variety of procedural due process issues are raised with respect to when notice is given and the level of detail describing the medical rationale for discharge that is required in the notice (42 C.F.R. §412.42(c)(1)–(4)); *see also* 42 C.F.R. §§412.42–412.48, and timeframes (42 C.F.R. §478.32) for beneficiaries to pursue legal remedies. Advocates should look closely to see that rules on hospital discharge notices are strictly followed.

- The QIO will make a formal determination on the validity of the hospital's finding if the beneficiary remains in the hospital after he or she is liable for charges;

- The determination of the QIO made after the beneficiary received the purportedly non-covered services will be appealable by the hospital, the attending physician, or the beneficiary under the appeals procedures that apply to QIO determinations affecting Medicare Part A payment;

- The charges for continued payment will be invalid and refunded if collected by the hospital, to the extent that a finding is made that the beneficiary required continued care beyond the point indicated by the hospital.[106]

[E] Medically Unnecessary Diagnostic Procedures and Services

A hospital may charge a beneficiary for diagnostic procedures and studies and therapeutic procedures and courses of treatment (such as experimental procedures and treatments) that are excluded from coverage as medically unnecessary items and services.[107] This is true even when the beneficiary receives continued inpatient hospital care, if those services are furnished after the beneficiary (or person acting on his or her behalf) has acknowledged in writing that the hospital has informed him or her that the services are not considered reasonable and necessary under Medicare.[108] The written acknowledgment must state that the services are not considered reasonable and necessary; that customary charges will be made if the services are provided; that if the services are received, a formal determination on the validity of the hospital's finding is made by the intermediary or QIO, as appropriate; and that the determination is appealable by the hospital, the attending physician, or the beneficiary under the appeals procedure that applies to determinations affecting Medicare Part A payment.[109]

[F] Beneficiary Not Entitled to Medicare Part A
or Exhaustion of Part A Benefits

The hospital may charge the beneficiary its usual charges for non-covered items and services furnished on outlier days for which payment is denied because the beneficiary is not entitled to Medicare Part A or has exhausted benefits.[110] If payment is considered for outlier days, the entire stay is reviewed, and days up to the number of days in excess of the outlier threshold may be denied on the basis of

---

[106] 42 C.F.R. §412.42(c) (3)(i)-(v).

[107] 42 C.F.R. §412.42(d).

[108] Id.

[109] Id.

[110] 42 C.F.R. §412.42(e). Outlier days are defined in 42 C.F.R. §§412.82 and 412.84.

the beneficiary's not being entitled to Part A or having exhausted benefits.[111] Under this rule, the latest days will be denied first.[112]

[G] Private Rooms and Luxury Services

The hospital may also charge a beneficiary for the differential for a private room or other luxury service that is more expensive than is medically required and is furnished for the personal comfort of the beneficiary at his or her request (or the request of the person acting on his or her behalf).[113]

[H] Admission Denials

As described above, if Medicare coverage is granted, the hospital will generally receive a predetermined DRG amount. The QIO, which functions as a watchdog agency seeking to ensure that the hospital does not claim Medicare coverage for medically unnecessary care, will often retroactively deny coverage in certain types of cases. When such a retroactive denial occurs, the hospital loses the entire DRG payment. Moreover, because the hospital had, until the issuance of the QIO denial, considered the case to be covered by Medicare, it has not complied with the required denial notice process, and therefore may not charge the patient for the cost of care.[114] This danger of financial penalty is so extreme that hospitals are inhibited from admitting patients whose medical conditions resemble those of patients whose cases have been retroactively denied by the QIO in the past.

> **Example:** Many hospitals have received retroactive QIO denials for hospital care delivered to patients suffering from compression fractures of the spine. Although a substantial proportion of such patients do indeed require a hospital level of care, many QIOs arbitrarily deny such claims on the theory that they constitute "social" admissions for which hospital services are not really necessary. After being intimidated by the QIO, hospitals will often decline to admit spinal compression fracture patients to the hospital unless the patient agrees to accept personal financial liability for the cost of care. In effect, arbitrary denial practices by the QIO can force hospitals to deny access to care for classes of vulnerable and coverage-worthy patients.

[I] Loss of Access to Expensive Care

Even where the DRG amount is paid, the predetermined figure may be inadequate to compensate the hospital for the expense of essential, but expensive

---

[111] *Id.*

[112] *Id.*

[113] 42 C.F.R. §412.42(f).

[114] Social Security Act 1879, 42 U.S.C. §1395pp; 42 C.F.R. §§411.400–411.406.

technology, procedure, equipment, and services. Since the advent of PPS, beneficial but cost-increasing medical advances are occasionally assigned to DRGs that do not cover costs. These costs are not to be passed on to beneficiaries but absorbed in the DRG rates.[115] Note, however, Medicare does make provision for additional payment for certain extraordinary high-cost hospital stays and services.[116] Advocates need to remain vigilant about the effects of payment and access to service.

The question of the adequacy of PPS rates for purposes of diagnostic-related groups is ongoing. The focus is on the underlying cost assumptions in setting rates, on geographic variations in costs and wages, and on whether the appropriate national averages have been set for hospital wage levels. In response to these concerns, the Medicare program is continually adjusting and updating these rates.[117]

§2.10   UTILIZATION REVIEW AND QUALITY OF SERVICES

[A]   Hospital Utilization Review Committees

Each Medicare participating hospital must have a Utilization Review Committee (URC) that reviews services furnished by the hospital and members of its medical staff.

At least two members of the URC must be physicians. URC members are generally hospital medical and administrative staff with medical oversight responsibilities. They work closely with the respective QIOs in their geographic location. Before making a determination that an admission or continued stay is not medically necessary, the URC must consult a practitioner responsible for the care of the patient and afford that practitioner the opportunity to present his or her views. If the URC decides that coverage should be denied, written notification must be given within two days of its decision to the hospital, the patient, and the attending physician.[118] As a practical matter, hospitals tend to notify beneficiaries of the decision that a Medicare admission or continued stay is not medically necessary as soon as possible, usually on the day the determination has been made. This is so because the patient's liability for the cost of inpatient hospital care received does not begin until the patient has received notification in writing that Medicare coverage will be denied.[119] Once the beneficiary is notified of the determination of the URC, the beneficiary may exercise certain appeal rights, described at **§2.11.**

---

[115] *See* §§412.80 *et seq.*

[116] *See* §§412.87–412.88.

[117] *See* <http://www.cms.hhs.gov/medicare/ippsmain.asp>.

[118] 42 C.F.R. §482.30(d).

[119] Social Security Act 1879, 42 U.S.C. §1395 pp; 42 C.F.R. §§411.400-411.406. *See also* 42 C.F.R. §412.42.

[B] Quality Improvement Organizations

In 1982, as part of the Tax Equity and Fiscal Responsibility Act of 1982, Congress established the Peer Review Organizations (PROs), now called Quality Improvement Organizations (QIOs). This act established a peer review program to perform utilization and quality review of hospital services provided to Medicare beneficiaries.[120] Congress authorized the Secretary of the Department of Health and Human Services (HHS) to contract with private physician-controlled QIOs for each state or region of the country to carry out such utilization and quality review.

Each Medicare-participating hospital must have an agreement with a QIO for review of medical appropriateness and utilization of Medicare-covered services on an ongoing basis.[121] The QIO is to review the medical necessity, reasonableness, and appropriateness of hospital admissions and discharges; the appropriateness of inpatient care for which additional payment is sought under the outlier provisions; the validity of the hospital's diagnostic and procedural information; the completeness, adequacy, and quality of the services furnished in the hospital; and other medical or other practices related to beneficiaries or billing for services furnished to them.[122] QIOs have authority to deny Medicare payment for inappropriate or unnecessary services and to recommend that certain providers and physicians be excluded from the Medicare program because of their utilization patterns and practices.[123]

QIOs also have responsibility to monitor hospital performance under PPS. Specifically, QIOs are charged with reviewing and determining for payment purposes "the validity of diagnostic information provided by a hospital, the completeness, adequacy and quality of care provided, and the appropriateness of care for which additional payments are sought."[124]

[C] Hospital Discharge Planning as an Advocacy Tool

Federal law requires a discharge planning process for identifying and planning for the post-hospital care needs of Medicare patients.[125] The Secretary has developed guidelines and standards for the discharge planning process in order to ensure a timely and smooth transition to the most appropriate type of and setting for

---

[120] 42 U.S.C. §§1320c-1–1320c-12; *see also* http://www.cms.hhs.gov/manuals/downloads/qio110c05.pdf (quality of care review).

[121] 42 C.F.R. §412.44.

[122] *Id.*

[123] 42 U.S.C. §1320c-5(b)(1); 42 C.F.R. §412.48.

[124] Social Security Act 1866(a)(1)(F), 42 U.S.C. §1395cc(a)(1)(f).

[125] 42 U.S.C. §1395x(ee).

post-hospital or rehabilitative care. The guidelines and standards address the following:[126]

- The hospital must identify, at an early stage of hospitalization, those patients who are likely to suffer adverse health consequences upon discharge in the absence of adequate discharge planning.

- Hospitals must provide a discharge planning evaluation for patients identified under subparagraph (1) and for other patients upon the request of the patient, patient's representative, or patient's physician.

- Any discharge planning evaluation must be made on a timely basis to ensure that appropriate arrangements for post-hospital care will be made before discharge and to avoid unnecessary delays in discharge.

- A discharge planning evaluation must include an evaluation of a patient's likely need for appropriate post-hospital services and the availability of those services.

- The discharge planning evaluation must be included in the patient's medical record for use in establishing an appropriate discharge plan, and the results of the evaluation must be discussed with the patient (or the patient's representative).

- Upon the request of patient's physician, the hospital must arrange for the development and initial implementation of a discharge plan for the patient.

- Any discharge planning evaluation or discharge plan must be developed by, or under the supervision of, a registered professional nurse, social worker, or other appropriately qualified personnel.

Notice about this right is problematic. The only notice provided is a mention of discharge planning in the Medicare-required hospital notice that is given to Medicare patients on admission, a notice entitled "An Important Message from Medicare."[127] Unfortunately, neither the notice of appeal rights upon hospital discharge (when and if the hospital attempts to charge the patient privately for the cost of care involved)[128] nor the QIO determination notice[129] discusses discharge planning rights other than to say that the "hospital should arrange the services you will need after you leave the hospital." Thus, it is important that advocates work with discharge planners and physicians to ensure that discharge planning services are requested as discussed above.

---

[126] 42 C.F.R. §482.43 (Condition of Participation: Discharge Planning).

[127] Social Security Act 1866(a)(1)(M), 42 U.S.C. §1395cc(a)(1)(M); 42 C.F.R. §476.78(b)(3). A sampling of current notices reveals that some hospitals are including no mention of discharge planning.

[128] 42 C.F.R. §476.94 (Notice of QIO initial denial determination and changes as a result of a DRG).

[129] 42 C.F.R. §§478.40–478.42 (Beneficiary hearing rights).

The Secretary, however, has yet to establish an array of intermediate sanctions for the failure to provide discharge planning services. Advocates may wish to consider approaching the failure to provide discharge planning services as a violation of the Medicare conditions of participation and consider the sanctioning process available there, culminating in the ultimate sanction of a facility's losing its participation agreement.[130]

§2.11   APPEALING COVERAGE DENIALS

[A]   Overview of an Appeal for Inpatient Hospital Services

Usually, the first notice a Medicare beneficiary receives informing him or her that care will not be covered by Medicare is from the health care provider, in this case the hospital. As noted,[131] each hospital is required to have a utilization review committee, or "URC," which is charged with making preliminary determinations regarding Medicare coverage for hospital stays. The URC must make such decisions at the time of admission of a patient and, if it determines that Medicare coverage is not warranted, issue a written notice to the beneficiary or someone acting on his/her behalf ("admission denials"). Similarly, the URC must issue a written notice if it decides that Medicare coverage is no longer warranted, after the patient has been admitted and has received some coverage by Medicare ("continued stay denials").

Hospitals, as with all Medicare Part A providers, have a financial incentive to issue denial notices because they may have to absorb the cost of the care they provide if they erroneously inform the beneficiary that the care will be covered, but not if they erroneously deny coverage.[132]

In issuing a continued stay denial, a hospital must obtain the concurrence of the patient's treating physician before it can issue the written denial notice. If the treating physician does not concur, then the hospital cannot issue the written notice, but instead must refer the case to a Medicare contractor known as a Quality Improvement Organization (QIO),[133] which will review the medical records of the patient and decide whether Medicare coverage should continue or not. If the QIO decides that Medicare coverage should not continue, then the QIO itself issues a notice to the beneficiary. Note that no physician concurrence is required if the URC issues a Medicare denial at the time of the patient's admission to the hospital.

Because of this requirement for physician concurrence, the Medicare patient's treating physician is a key person in the coverage determination. The regulations require that the treating physician be given an opportunity to

---

[130] 42 C.F.R. Pt. 488 (Survey, Certification, and Enforcement Procedures).

[131] See §2.10[A].

[132] 42 U.S.C. §1395pp.

[133] See §2.11[B].

justify the medical necessity of hospital admissions or continued stays.[134] In practice, however, this often means that the treating M.D., or O.D., receives a telephone call informing him or her that a coverage denial is about to be issued in a given case. The treating physician may or may not attempt to convince the URC or QIO reviewer that coverage should be continued. In any event, the written record may not contain any notation beyond a terse statement that "the views of the attending physician were solicited."

As a practical matter, a beneficiary can appeal a denial of coverage of only those services actually received. Therefore, a beneficiary who is being informed that Medicare will not cover his or her stay upon admission must insist on admission anyway.[135] For a continuing hospital stay, the beneficiary must remain in the hospital in order to seek additional Medicare coverage through the appeals process.

Patients who receive denial notices from the hospital URC at the time of admission, or where a continued stay denial has been issued with the concurrence of the treating physician, must request that the case be submitted to the Medicare QIO for its review, if they want to obtain an initial determination that can then be appealed. (In addition, the QIO's initial determination does sometimes grant coverage that was denied by the hospital.) If the beneficiary or representative requests the hospital to submit a case to the Medicare QIO, the hospital is required to do so.

For a continuing stay denial, actual written concurrence by the attending physician with the denial determination is required before the hospital may issue a Medicare notice of non-coverage.[136] If the attending physician does not

---

[134] 42 C.F.R. §§412.42(c) and 482.30.

[135] 42 U.S.C. §1395ff(b) provides for a limited prior determination process regarding physician services determined by the Secretary to be subject to the process. Under the process, a participating physician who has permission from the patient or an individual who has received an advanced beneficiary notice (ABN) may ask the appropriate Medicare contractor for a determination of whether Medicare will pay for a service before actually receiving the service. *See also* Medicare Quality Improvement Organization Manual, Pub. 100-10, Ch. 7, §§7005 and 7015, that provide for inpatient hospital preadmission review.

[136] 42 C.F.R. §412.4 2(c)(2). The patient becomes financially responsible for the services provided beyond the second day following the date of the notice. *Id.* §412.42(c)(3)(ii). Increasingly, we are hearing that hospitals are only giving Medicare patients the hospital notice of non-coverage when the beneficiary requests it. This is contrary to regulations. Note, however, that in the context of Medicare Advantage (MA), the Medicare managed programs, CMS issued regulations, effective May 5, 2003, allowing MA hospitals to give an individualized notice of noncoverage only when the patient disagrees with the hospital's discharge decision. The preamble in these MA regulations implies that this is in accord with long-standing practice in issuing notices to hospital payments under the Traditional Medicare program. This is not the experience of Medicare advocates, however. *See* 42 C.F.R. §§422.620 *et seq.* (how enrollees of MA organizations must be notified of noncoverage of inpatient hospital care); *see also,* discussion of §422.620 in **Chapter 7** (Managed Care Chapter) of this handbook, *and* 42 C.F.R. §489.27 (Beneficiary Notice of Discharge Rights). *See also* Weichardt v. Thompson, C03-05490 VRW (N.D. Cal.), filed December 5, 2003.

The notice protections for hospitalized MA enrollees are likely to be expanded as the result of a settlement agreement in Weichardt v. Thompson, C.A. No. 03 5490 VRW (N.D. Cal. Settlement

concur, the URC may not issue a notice of non-coverage. Instead, it must refer the case to the QIO. The QIO will review the case and, if warranted, will issue a Medicare denial. This denial is the "initial determination."[137]

However, in those circumstances where the attending physician does concur with the URC's determination, the URC will issue a Medicare notice of non-coverage.[138] In such cases, the beneficiary has the right to request an expedited review by the QIO. If the patient requests QIO review before noon of the first working day after the denial notice was delivered to the patient, and the patient is still in the hospital, then:

1. The hospital must provide written records to the QIO by the close of that first working day and,

2. The QIO must issue a review decision within one full working day after the QIO received the review request and records.[139]

If the QIO upholds the denial of Medicare coverage by the hospital's URC, the denial is effective commencing with the third day following the date of the URC's original notice, and the beneficiary is required to pay for the services s/he received commencing with that date. If the beneficiary is dissatisfied with the initial determination, s/he may request a redetermination. Patient requests for redetermination about hospital services are filed with the QIO.[140] In hospital cases, the redetermination may be requested on an expedited basis.[141] This is followed by a request for a hearing before an ALJ (if at least $200 is in controversy), review by the Medicare Appeals Council (MAC), and finally judicial

---

Agreement, Oct. 28, 2005). Proposed regulations implementing this settlement have been published by the CMS. *See* Medicare Program; Notification Procedures for Hospital Discharges, 71 Fed. Reg. 17052-17062 (Apr. 5, 2006) (to be codified at 42 C.F.R. §§405.1205, 405.1206, 422.620, and 422.622, inter alia.) If adopted, the new system will include both a generic and a specific notice of discharge. The hospital will be required to deliver a generic notice of a discharge decision to the patient on the day before a planned discharge. This notice describes the process for immediate appeal of the discharge, and the financial consequences of the appeal options. 42 C.F.R. §422.620 (proposed). If a patient decides to request expedited appeal, the MA organization must deliver a second, detailed notice by the end of the day when appeal is requested. This notice sets out the factual and legal reasons why the MA believes hospital services are no longer covered. 42 C.F.R. §422.622(c) (proposed).

[137] 42 C.F.R. §412(c)(2).

[138] 42 C.F.R. §412.42(c)(2).

[139] 42 C.F.R. §476.94.

[140] A beneficiary has 120 days from the date of the initial determination to request a determination. *See* CMS Program Memorandum AB-02-111 (July 31, 2002), available at <www.cms.hhs.gov>. This Program Memorandum provision, of course, does not apply to expedited reconsideration requests. *See also* 42 C.F.R. §478.20(a), which CMS Program Memorandum AB 02-111 amends.

[141] 42 C.F.R. §§478.12(c) and 480.20(c).

review (if at least $2,000 is in controversy).[142,143] Appeal rights and procedures to the next level of appeal must be stated in each decision issued at each level of appeal. As the appeals process is in flux[144], the advocate should be certain to consult each decision to determine appeal rights to the next level of appeal.

[B] The QIO Reconsideration and Financial Liability for the Beneficiary

As noted, generally, a request for reconsideration must be filed within 120 days of receipt of the initial determination unless "good cause" can be shown. Hospital inpatients denied Medicare during their stay may also request an "expedited reconsideration" of a Medicare denial. These expedited requests must be decided by the QIO within three working days. Under previous regulations, a hospital inpatient who received a denial notice from the hospital and requested review immediately avoided being charged until the QIO issued an initial determination. However, the new expedited appeals regulations protect from liability only those inpatients who did not know or could not reasonably have been expected to know that payment would not be made. Thus, beneficiary financial liability may attach prior to the QIO's issuance of the initial determination.

[C] Appeals Arising Under Parts A and B of Medicare

New rules regarding Medicare appeals were published in the Federal Register on March 8, 2005, and are codified at Subpart G, of Part 405.[145] The rules establish a combined Part A and Part B appeals process. CMS's regulations implement the changes to the appeals process for Medicare Part A and Part B claims, and to implement changes to ALJ hearing process for all Medicare claims, including managed care claims and future prescription drug claims.[146]

In 2000, Congress enacted legislation designed to streamline and make uniform the appeals systems for claims arising under Parts A and B of Medicare. Although the new provisions were supposed to go into effect in 2002, the Centers for Medicare & Medicaid Services (CMS) only effectuated changes concerning the time for filing appeals from initial decisions and the reduced amount in controversy for hearings on Part B claims. Congress made additional changes to the appeals process in 2003, including authorizing the transfer of administrative law judges (ALJs) from the Social Security Administration (SSA) to the Department of Health and Human Services (HHS), and negating some of the earlier time savings by

---

[142] 42 C.F.R. §478.12.

[143] 42 C.F.R. §§478.18 and 478.32 (time limits for issuance of reconsideration decisions).

[144] *See* note 136, *supra*.

[145] *See* 42 C.F.R. §§405.701 *et seq.*

[146] 70 Fed. Reg. 11420 (Mar. 8, 2005).

extending the time in which contractors must complete their decisions.[147] The new rules regarding Medicare appeals incorporate these statutory changes.

Although the regulations contemplate that the new appeals process will fully apply to inpatient hospital appeals, to date it has only been applied to inpatient hospital appeals with respect to Administrative Law Judge appeals, Medicare Appeals Council appeals, and appeals into federal court. Thus, the initial determination and reconsideration issued by the QIO are generally followed directly by an appeal to an administrative law judge.

However, in some instances an individual may have failed to or chosen not to immediately appeal to the QIO, but continued to stay in the hospital and receive medical services. Under this scenario, the individual will ultimately receive a Medicare Summary Notice from a Medicare contractor indicating that the hospital services were denied coverage. In such instances, the individual may want to try to pursue an appeal under the new appeals system.

[D] Initial Determinations and Redeterminations

Under the scenario described above, the claims process begins when the Medicare contractor issues a Medicare Summary Notice, which is an initial determination of the claim submitted by the hospital. The regulations make clear that the initial determination, goes only to the beneficiary, even when the contractor is aware that the beneficiary has an appointed representative.[148] Someone who wants to appeal from the initial determination must submit a written, signed request for a redetermination within 120 days of the initial determination; the regulations assume the notice is received 5 days after the date of the notice.[149] Requests for redeterminations in this scenario must be filed with the Medicare contractor; beneficiaries can no longer file requests with Social Security offices.[150]

The regulations also allow, for the first time, hospital providers to request appeal of a denial of an initial determination, raising the possibility that both the beneficiary and the hospital will initiate the appeals process.[151] In such a case the QIO is required to consolidate the appeals.[152] The contractor has 60 days from receipt of the redetermination request to issue a decision.[153] If more than one party files a request, the time period runs from the date the last request is received.[154]

---

[147] *See* Pub. L. No.1008-173, 117 Stat. 2066 (Dec. 8, 2003).

[148] 42 C.F.R. §405.921 and 42 C.F.R. §405.910(i)(1); *see also*, CMS Program Memorandum AB-02-111 (July 31, 2002), available at <www.cms.hhs.gov>.

[149] 42 C.F.R. §40 5.942(a).

[150] 42 C.F.R. §405.944(a).

[151] 42 C.F.R. §405.940.

[152] 42 C.F.R. §405.944(c).

[153] 42 C.F.R. §405.950(a).

[154] 42 C.F.R. §405.950(b)(2).

For example, if a beneficiary files a redetermination request on day 1, but the hospital files on day 50, the 60-day time period for the contractor to act starts on day 50.

Unlike the initial determination, the notice of the redetermination will be sent to a beneficiary's appointed representative.[155] The notice will explain the facts, policies, and law relied upon in making the redetermination decision; the right to request a reconsideration decision and the process for doing so; and a statement of specific missing documents that must be submitted.[156] The notice will state that the hospital, but not beneficiaries[157] (unless they are represented by a provider), must submit all of their evidence at the next level of review in order for the evidence to be considered at any further stage of the appeals process. As a practical matter, the same notice is sent to beneficiaries and hospital providers, with a statement that evidentiary limitations do not apply to beneficiaries. However, in some instances the contractors and administrative law judges have confused this requirement. The advocate should be certain to point out to the adjudicator that a beneficiary is not required to submit all evidence until the administrative law judge level of appeal. In addition, contractors will not be required to send redetermination notices to multiple beneficiaries in overpayment cases brought by hospital providers if the beneficiary allegedly has no liability for the claim.[158] It is unclear how the contractor will determine in such cases whether the beneficiary has already paid for the services in question.

The regulations create a new reopening process to be used instead of the redetermination process to correct minor errors or omissions in initial determinations.[159] This process responds to a new section of the Medicare law that allows providers to correct minor mistakes without going through the appeals process. Re-openings can also be used at subsequent levels of review. Questions remain concerning the relationship of the new reopening process and the process for deciding remanded cases, as well as the ability of a contractor to reopen a decision in favor of the beneficiary.

[E] The QIC—Reconsideration Determinations

The 2000 law created a third level of review, the reconsideration. Reconsiderations will be conducted by a new group of Medicare contractors called Qualified Independent Contractors (QICs).[160] Beneficiaries and other parties to

---

[155] 42 C.F.R. §405.910(h)(2).

[156] 42 C.F.R. §405.956(b) and (c); §405.966(a).

[157] 42 C.F.R. §405.966(c).

[158] 42 C.F.R. §405.956(a)(2).

[159] 42 C.F.R. §§405.980 *et seq.*

[160] 42 C.F.R. §405.960. The jurisdiction of QICs over reconsideration determinations commenced on May 1, 2005, for all Part A determinations and those Part B determinations made by a QIO or fiscal

the redetermination have 180 days to request a reconsideration by filing a request at the location indicated on the redetermination notice.[161] Again, reconsiderations filed by beneficiaries and the hospital will be consolidated, and the time for issuing a decision runs from receipt of the last-filed appeal.[162]

Under the scenario described, starting May 1, 2005, appeals of redeterminations issued by the QIO in inpatient hospital cases will go to the QIC for a reconsideration determination, upon the filing of a request for reconsideration.[163]

The reconsideration level of review is a paper review; CMS states clearly in the preamble to the final regulations that QICs will not be conducting hearings. However, the QIC may solicit the view of the beneficiary.[164] As noted above, if hospital providers appeal from the QIO to the QIC, they are required to submit all of the evidence they want considered in the claim to the QIC. Evidence not submitted by the hospital to the QIC may be excluded at subsequent levels of review.[165] However, beneficiaries who appeal (except those who are represented by a provider) may present evidence at further levels of appeal.[166]

The QIC is supposed to complete its reconsideration within 60 days of the reconsideration request.[167] Again, the time frame runs from the last request filed if more than one party seeks reconsideration; the QIC must so notify a party who filed an earlier request.[168] The regulations do not indicate how QICs are supposed to document receipt or how beneficiaries are to know when the 60-day period ends. Although the statute allows a party to the reconsideration to ask for an extension of not more than 14 days for the QIC to conclude the reconsideration, the regulations add 14 days to the reconsideration time frame each time that additional evidence is submitted.[169]

In making its reconsideration determination, the QIC is bound by national coverage determinations (NCDs) promulgated by Medicare and CMS Rulings, as well as statute and regulations.[170] It is not bound by local coverage determinations made by Medicare contractors, nor by Medicare policy issued by CMS itself; however, the QIC must give "substantial deference" to these determinations

---

intermediary. The QIC's jurisdiction over Part B reconsideration determinations for all determination currently made by a Medicare Part B carrier will commence on January 1, 2006. 70 Fed. Reg. 11424–11426 (Mar. 8, 2005).

[161] 42 C.F.R. §405.962.

[162] 42 C.F.R. §405.964(c).

[163] 70 Fed. Reg. 11424–11426 (Mar. 8, 2005).

[164] 70 Fed. Reg. 11447–11478 (Mar. 8, 2005).

[165] 42 C.F.R. §405.966(a) and (c).

[166] 42 C.F.R. §405.966(c).

[167] 42 C.F.R. §405.970(a).

[168] 42 C.F.R. §405.970(b)(2).

[169] 42 C.F.R. §405.970(b)(3).

[170] 42 C.F.R. §405.1050(a)(4).

and policy in making its decision.[171] If the QIC declines to apply them, the QIC's decision must state the reason why they were not followed.[172]

[F] Escalation

The MMA introduced the concept of "escalation" into the Medicare appeals process. Commencing at the reconsideration level of appeal, if a decision is not rendered within a set time frame,[173] a party to the appeal may "escalate" the appeal to the next level. However, the interim final regulations set out many possible situations in which extensions of the time frame for the adjudicator to render its decision may occur.[174] Among these situations is the submission of additional evidence to the adjudicator by a party.

Generally, however, if a QIC does not issue a timely reconsideration decision (60 days from the date of its receipt of the request for reconsideration), the statute and regulations allow a party to request that the appeal be escalated to the next level of review, the ALJ level. The regulations give the QIC 5 days to either issue a decision or acknowledge the escalation request and send it to the ALJ level of review. The regulations indicate that an appeal escalated to the ALJ level must be completed within 180 days of receipt, rather than the statutorily mandated 90 days for ALJ decisions. Even at the ALJ level, however, additional extensions of the time frame for issuing a decision can occur.[175]

[G] Administrative Law Judge Appeals

Beneficiaries and other parties have 60 days from receipt of the reconsideration determination to file a request for an administrative law judge hearing.[176] As noted previously, whether an individual seeking redress from a denial of inpatient hospital coverage pursues an appeal through the QIO process, or pursues an appeal in response to a Medicare Summary Notice (MSN), the administrative law judge appeals level (and beyond) will be the same. The request for hearing must be filed at the address indicated on the reconsideration determination.[177] In addition,

---

[171] 42 C.F.R. §405.968(b)(1) and (2).

[172] 42 C.F.R. §405.968(b)(3).

[173] The timeframes are: 60 days for the QIC to render a reconsideration determination; 90 days for an ALJ to issue a hearing decision; 180 days for the Medicare Appeals Council (MAC) to issue its decision.

[174] 42 C.F.R. §§405.970(b) and 405.1002(a) [reconsideration level]; 42 C.F.R. §§405.1016 (a)–(d) and 405.1104 [administrative law judge level]; 42 C.F.R. §§405.1106(b) and 405.1132 [Medicare Appeals Council level].

[175] Id.

[176] Extension of this 60-day time frame may be granted upon a showing of good cause. 42 C.F.R. §405.1014(c).

[177] 42 C.F.R. §405.1014(b).

a party may escalate to the ALJ hearing from the QIC, when the QIC fails to issue a timely decision.[178] However, if an appeal is escalated to the ALJ, the 90-day time frame for deciding an ALJ appeal is automatically extended to 180 days, with the possibility for additional extensions beyond the 180 days.[179]

Many significant changes to the administrative law judge appeal level have been made.[180] Not the least of these significant changes is the transfer of jurisdiction for administrative law judge hearings from the Social Security Administration to the U.S. Department of Health and Human Services, a change which was mandated by the MMA. ALJs operate out of four locations: Miami; Cleveland; Irvine, California; and Falls Church, Virginia. These are the only hearing offices in which Medicare administrative law judges are housed.[181]

Under the regulations, in-person hearings are a thing of the past, except in "special or extraordinary circumstances."[182] Instead, beneficiaries will be offered a video teleconference (VTC) hearing, or if no VTC technology exists near the beneficiary, a telephone hearing.[183] The regulations do not spell out what constitutes a "special circumstance" that would justify an in-person hearing.[184] Even if such special circumstances are established, the in-person hearing will be afforded for the requestor's own testimony, but the entire hearing will not necessarily be in-person.[185] In addition, when an in-person hearing is requested and granted, the limited time frame for an ALJ to render his or her decision is deemed waived.[186]

Another important change is that CMS or its contractors may participate in or be made a party to the Administrative Law Judge hearings, with rights to submit "position papers" and present witnesses (if they are "participants") and the right to cross-examine other party's witnesses (if they are "parties").[187] An administrative law judge may seek to have CMS or its contractors participate or joined as parties, and CMS itself can request that it be a participant or party.[188] Under the

---

[178] 42 C.F.R. §40 5.1002(b)(1)–(3).

[179] 42 C.F.R. §405.1016(c). Among the bases for an extension are: CMS is a party and a party requests discovery against another party [42 C.F.R. §405.1016(d)]; submission of additional evidence by a party later than ten days after receiving a notice of hearing [42 C.F.R. §405.1018(b)]; a party's request for a copy of all or part of the administrative record [42 C.F.R. §405.1042(b)(2)]; and a granted request for postponement of the hearing [42 C.F.R. §405.1020(h)].

[180] 42 C.F.R. §§405.1004 *et seq.*

[181] *See* <www.cms.hhs.gov>.

[182] 42 C.F.R. §405.1020(b)(2).

[183] 42 C.F.R. §405.1020(b).

[184] The preamble to the interim final regulations discusses some circumstances which might warrant an in-person hearing. Among these is when the case "presents complex challenging or novel presentation issues" or based upon "the appellant's proximity to and ability to go to the local hearing office." 70 Fed. Reg. 11457 (Mar. 8, 2005).

[185] 42 C.F.R. §405.1020(c).

[186] 42 C.F.R. §405.1020(i)(4).

[187] 42 C.F.R. §§405.1010 (participants) and 405.1012 (parties).

[188] *Id.* and 42 C.F.R. §405.1010(a).

regulations, an ALJ must permit CMS or its contractors to participate or be joined as parties, if they so request.

A notice of the hearing must be given to all parties, the Medicare contractor and the QIC, advising them of the time and date for the hearing at least 20 days prior to the date of its scheduled date.[189] All of those receiving a notice of hearing are required to acknowledge whether they plan to attend the hearing or object to the proposed time and/or place of the hearing.[190] An objection to the time and/or place must be in writing and state the reasons for the objection.[191] If a party objects to the issues as stated in the notice of hearing, that party must notify the ALJ in writing no later than five days prior to the hearing of the objections, and send a copy of the objections to all other parties to the appeal.[192] The ALJ will make a decision with respect to the objections either in writing or at the hearing.[193]

Any new written evidence which a beneficiary wishes to submit must be submitted with the request for hearing or within 10 days prior to the scheduled date of the hearing.[194] Evidence may be submitted later than ten days prior to the hearing, but the time frame for the ALJ to issue his or her decision is tolled for the period between when the evidence was required to be submitted and when it was actually received.[195] Although providers are generally required to submit all their relevant evidence at the QIC level of appeal, they may submit additional evidence if they establish "good cause" for failing to do so earlier.[196] The ALJ must review the new evidence submitted by the provider and notify all parties whether it is excluded.[197]

Although generally the issues at the hearing will include all issues brought out at any prior level of appeal which were not decided in a party's favor, the ALJ may also include as an issue any portion of any prior determination that was decided favorably.[198] The parties must be notified of all issues before the hearing.[199] New issues may be raised at any time prior to the start of the hearing, if those new issues could have a material impact on the claims that are the subject of the request for hearing.[200]

---

[189] 42 C.F.R. §§405.1020(c) and 405.1022(a).

[190] 42 C.F.R. §405.1 200(c)(2).

[191] 42 C.F.R. §405.1020(e).

[192] 42 C.F.R. §405.1024 (a) and (b).

[193] 42 C.F.R. §405.1024(c).

[194] 42 C.F.R. §405.1018(a). Evidence may be submitted beyond this period, but it has the effect of tolling the time frame for the ALJ to render a decision. This provision does not apply to unrepresented beneficiaries. 42 C.F.R. §405.1018(d).

[195] 42 C.F.R. §405.1018(b).

[196] 42 C.F.R. §405.1018(c).

[197] 42 C.F.R. §405.1028(a)–(d).

[198] 42 C.F.R. §405.1032(a).

[199] 42 C.F.R. §405.1032.

[200] 42 C.F.R. §405.1032(b). Certain limitations apply to this. *See* 42 C.F.R. §405.980.

Discovery at the ALJ level of appeal is permissible only when CMS elects to be made a party to the hearing.[201] Discovery is permissible with respect to any matter that is relevant to the subject matter of the hearing, although the party from whom discovery is sought may raise objections based on the assertion that the material sought is privileged or otherwise protected.[202] Additionally, an ALJ may deny a request for discovery if s/he concludes that the discovery request is unreasonable, unduly burdensome or expensive, or otherwise inappropriate.[203] Discovery is limited. A party may request reasonable production of documents for inspection and copying, but depositions may not be taken unless the deponent agrees or the ALJ finds the proposed deposition is appropriate and necessary.[204] Similarly, requests for admissions and interrogatories are generally not permitted.[205]

The ALJ may hold a pre-hearing or a post-hearing conference, either at his or her own initiative or at the request of a party.[206] The ALJ must inform the parties of the time, place, and purpose of the conference at least seven calendar days prior to the conference date.[207] The ALJ may consider matters in addition to those stated on the notice of hearing, if the parties consent in writing.[208] A record of the hearing will be made, and the ALJ must issue an order stating all agreements and actions resulting from the conference.[209]

An administrative record, including marked exhibits, will be made.[210] Under the interim final regulations, a party may review the record at the hearing or, if a hearing is not held, at any time prior to the issuance of an ALJ decision.[211] However, given that hearings will most often not be held in-person, the regulations offer no explanation as to how such a review can be accomplished. A party may request and receive a copy of all or part of the record; however, the party can be asked to pay the costs of being provided the requested items.[212]

---

[201] 42 C.F.R. §405.1037(a).

[202] 42 C.F.R. §405.1037(a)(2).

[203] *Id.*

[204] 42 C.F.R. §405.1037(b)(1) and (2).

[205] 42 C.F.R. §405.103 7(b)(3).

[206] 42 C.F.R. §405.1040.

[207] 42 C.F.R. §405.1040(b).

[208] 42 C.F.R. §405.1040(c).

[209] *Id.* and §405.1404(d).

[210] 42 C.F.R. §405.1042. In practice, advocates have found that the exhibit lists are sometimes haphazardly assembled and often insufficiently detailed to permit understanding of the actual documents contained in the record. Since in-person hearings are extermely rare, advocates usually do not have access to the actual administrative record. If the exhibit list is ambiguous, it may be necessary to make a written request to the ALJ seeking a photocopy of the entire administrative record.

[211] 42 C.F.R. §405.1042(a)(3).

[212] 42 C.F.R. §405.1042(b)(1).

Once a hearing has been held,[213] the ALJ must issue a written decision that sets out findings of fact, conclusions of law, and the reasons for the decision.[214] The decision must be mailed to each party, the Medicare contractors, and the QIC.[215]

If an ALJ decision is not rendered within the appropriate time frame for the circumstances of the case, a party may escalate the appeal to the Medicare Appeals Council.[216] The request for escalation must be filed with the ALJ.[217] Once the request is received, the ALJ has five days to either issue a decision, remand the case to the QIC,[218] or notify the parties that a timely decision cannot be issued.[219] At that point, the QIC decision becomes the decision which the MAC will review.[220] In addition, the Medicare Appeals Council may, on its own initiative, remove a case from the ALJ and assume responsibility for holding a hearing and adjudicating the case itself.[221]

[H] Medicare Appeals Council Review

A party who is dissatisfied with an ALJ decision may request review by the Medicare Appeals Council (MAC).[222] A written request for MAC review must be filed with the MAC or the appropriate ALJ office.[223] The request must identify those parts of the ALJ decision (or other determination being appealed, if the case is before the MAC due to escalation) to which the party objects, and state the reasons for those objections.[224] Unless the appellant is an unrepresented beneficiary, the MAC will limit its review to those parts of the decision below specifically identified as objectionable in the request for review.

---

[213] Parties are free to waive their right to a hearing and have a decision issued solely on the administrative record. 42 C.F.R. §§405.1020(d) and 405.1038(b). In addition, an ALJ may, without holding a hearing, issue a decision that is fully favorable to the appellant(s) if the hearing record supports such a finding. 42 C.F.R. §405.1038(a).

[214] 42 C.F.R. §405.1046(a).

[215] Id.

[216] 42 C.F.R. §405.1104.

[217] 42 C.F.R. §405.1104(a)(1).

[218] 42 C.F.R. §§405.1104(a)(2) and 405.1 034.

[219] 42 C.F.R. §405.1104(b)(2) and (3).

[220] 42 C.F.R. §405.1104(b)(3).

[221] 42 C.F.R. §405.1050.

[222] The MAC may also exercise its "own motion" review. 42 C.F.R. §405.1110. This review can occur upon the MAC's own initiative or when a CMS (or any of its contractors) refers a case to the MAC that they think has been erroneously decided or the decision presents a broad policy or procedural issue that may affect the public interest. This, of course, gives CMS the ability to tightly control the decision-making process and its outcomes, even though the MMA requires the independence of administrative law judges.

[223] 42 C.F.R. §405.1112(a).

[224] 42 C.F.R. §405.1112(b).

If a party has requested review because s/he is dissatisfied with an ALJ decision, or has escalated an appeal from the ALJ to the MAC, the MAC will review *de novo* the decision below.[225] A party seeking MAC review does not have a right to a new hearing; however, the MAC, in its discretion, may conduct any additional proceedings, including holding a hearing.[226]

Generally, absent good cause,[227] no additional evidence may be introduced at the MAC level of appeal, unless the ALJ decision being reviewed decides a new issue that the parties were not afforded an opportunity to address before the ALJ.[228] However, a party to the MAC review which is before the MAC because of escalation may file a request for a subpoena of specified documents within 10 days of the request for escalation.[229]

The parties have the right to file briefs or other written statements with the MAC.[230] In addition, the MAC may request (but cannot require) CMS or its contractors to file a brief or position paper, if the MAC determines that it is necessary to resolve the issues in the case.[231] In some instances, the MAC may permit, or seek, oral argument on the appeal.[232]

The MAC may dispose of the case in a number of ways: it may remand the case to the ALJ;[233] it may dismiss the request for MAC review;[234] or it may issue a decision.[235] If the MAC fails to issue its decision within the required 90-day time frame from its receipt of the request for MAC review,[236] the appellant may request escalation to federal court.[237] If, upon filing of the escalation request and the lapse of the permissible time plus five additional days, the MAC is unable to issue a decision, remand, or dismissal, it must notify the appellant informing him or her that it is not able to do so.[238] A party may file an action in federal district court within 60 days after the date it receives this notification from the MAC.[239]

---

[225] 42 C.F.R. §405.1108.

[226] 42 C.F.R. §405.1108(a) and (d)(3).

[227] 42 C.F.R. §405.1122(c).

[228] 42 C.F.R. §405.1122(a).

[229] 42 C.F.R. §405.1122(d)(1)–(4).

[230] 42 C.F.R. §40 5.1120.

[231] *Id.*

[232] 42 C.F.R. §405.1124.

[233] 42 C.F.R. §405.1108(d)(3).

[234] 42 C.F.R. §405.1108(c) and (d)(4) and (5).

[235] 42 C.F.R. §405.1108(a) and (d)(1).

[236] 42 C.F.R. §405.1132. As with the other levels of appeal, the time frame for issuing a determination is subject to various extensions. *See*, for example, 42 C.F.R. §405.1114 [extension when party seeks evidence from the MAC]; 42 C.F.R. §405.1120 [extension when briefs are filed]; 42 C.F.R. §405.1122(e)(2)(ii) [stay upon issuance of subpoena].

[237] 42 C.F.R. §405.1132.

[238] 42 C.F.R. §405.1132(a)(2)

[239] 42 C.F.R. §405.1132(b).

[I] Judicial Review

A party to a MAC decision, who is dissatisfied with that decision, may obtain judicial review if the amount in controversy requirements are met.[240] The civil action must be filed within 60 days after receipt of notice of the MAC decision.[241] Provisions exist in the regulations for applying to the MAC for extension of the filing time.[242] The civil action must be filed in the district court for the judicial district in which the beneficiary resides or, if filed by a provider, in the judicial district where it has its principal place of business.[243] The Secretary of HHS in his or her official capacity is the proper defendant.[244] The standard of review for the court is whether the decision of the Secretary of HHS is supported by substantial evidence.[245]

In addition, Section 932 of the MMA modified 42 U.S.C. §1395ff(b) to create expedited access to the judicial review process whereby beneficiaries, providers, and suppliers can have expedited access to judicial review in certain appeals of Medicare Part A or Part B claims.[246] The new expedited appeals process also applies to provider contract disputes—primarily nursing home enforcement cases.[247] Expedited review is available when it is determined both that the Medicare Appeals Council (MAC) lacks authority to decide a question of law or regulation relevant to the case and that there is no material issue of fact in dispute.[248]

A beneficiary may file a request for expedited access to judicial review at the same time as, or after, filing a request for an ALJ hearing.[249] A review entity made up of three reviewers who are ALJs or members of the DAB has 60 days after receipt of the request to issue a written decision.[250] The review entity may request appropriate documents and materials from the beneficiary to support his or her contention that (1) no material issues of fact exist and (2) the MAC lacks authority to decide the relevant question of law or regulations.[251] If the review entity agrees with the beneficiary's request for expedited review, or if the review entity fails to act within 60 days of receipt of the request, the beneficiary skips ALJ and DAB review and may go directly to district court.[252] If the review entity finds against the

---

[240] 42 C.F.R. §405.1136.

[241] 42 C.F.R. §405.1130.

[242] 42 C.F.R. §405.1134.

[243] 42 C.F.R. §405.1136(b).

[244] 42 C.F.R. §405.1136(d).

[245] 42 C.F.R. §40 5.1136(f).

[246] 42 C.F.R. §405.990.

[247] 42 C.F.R. §405.906(a)–(c); §405.990(e).

[248] 42 C.F.R. §405.990(a)(2).

[249] 42 C.F.R. §405.990(d)(2).

[250] 42 C.F.R. §405.990(a)(1).

[251] 42 C.F.R. §405.990(c).

[252] 42 C.F.R. §405 .990(f)(4).

beneficiary, she has no further recourse and may not make another request for expedited review regarding the matter in dispute.[253]

[J] Appointments of Representatives and Attorneys' Fees

The interim final regulations also specify the elements of a proper appointment of representative, its duration, and rules about collection of fees for representing Medicare beneficiaries in an appeal of a Medicare denial.[254]

A valid appointment of representation form must:

- Be in writing and signed and dated by both the beneficiary and the representative.

- Authorize the representative to act on behalf of the beneficiary and authorize the adjudicator to release identifiable health information to the representative.

- Include an explanation of the purpose and scope of the representation.

- Include the name, phone number, and address for the beneficiary and the representative.

- Include the beneficiary's Medicare health insurance claim number.

- Include the representative's professional status or relationship to the beneficiary.

- Be filed with the entity processing the party's initial determination or appeal.[255]

If a form is defective, the representative will be given an opportunity to correct the defect. Otherwise, the representative will not have the authority to act on behalf of the beneficiary or to receive health information.[256]

The regulations limit the duration of the appointment of representation form to one year. A duly appointed representative may file multiple appeals on behalf of an individual beneficiary during the course of that year, but must submit a copy of the original appointment form with each additional appeal filed. Once an appointment of representation form has been filed in a case, the appointment lasts for the duration of the appeal unless it is revoked.[257]

The regulations prohibit an appointed representative from delegating the appointment to another person without the beneficiary's consent. Thus, a family member who already serves as an appointed representative cannot delegate that appointment to an advocate for purposes of pursing an appeal unless the beneficiary signs a written notice. A signed statement is not required where both the appointed and new representatives are attorneys (but not paralegals) in the same law firm or

---

[253] 42 C.F.R. §405.990(h)(3)(i).

[254] 42 C.F.R. §§405.910 and 405.912.

[255] 42 C.F.R. §405. 910(c).

[256] 42 C.F.R. §405.910(d).

[257] 42 C.F.R. §§405.910(e) and 405.912(e).

organization. When a beneficiary lacks the capacity to sign an appointment of representation form or form acknowledging delegation of the appointment, state law determines who has authority to authorize representation on his or her behalf.[258]

Under the new regulations, a beneficiary's appointed representative (but not a provider or supplier's representative) who wishes to charge a fee for services at the administrative law judge (ALJ) and Medicare Appeals Council (MAC) levels of review must obtain approval of the fee from the Secretary of the Department of Health and Human Services (HHS). The regulations also say that no award of fees or costs may be made against the Medicare trust fund, and that limitations on the amount of fees that apply in Social Security and SSI disability cases do not apply to Medicare appeals.[259]

The regulations do not contain any standard by which fee requests will be judged. However, the preamble indicates that guidelines for the application of Equal Access to Justice Act (EAJA) claims before HHS may be applicable to Medicare appeals.[260] The preamble further states that HHS will review the guidelines to determine whether they need to be changed in light of the new provision.[261]

The preamble justifies the policy change by saying that a change in the Medicare Act makes provisions concerning approval of fee arrangements from back awards of Social Security disability benefits applicable to Medicare appeals.[262] The preamble goes on to acknowledge, however, that, unlike Social Security cases, there is no back award of benefits from which attorneys can be paid, and that the limitation on Social Security attorneys' fees does not apply.[263]

[K] QIO Appeals for Denial of Hospital Services to Beneficiaries Enrolled in a Medicare Advantage Plan

The appeals system for beneficiaries enrolled in a Medicare Advantage plan is different, at least through the reconsideration level of appeal. The appeal rules for the ALJ level of appeal and beyond are the same as described above. Beneficiaries who receive Medicare-covered hospital services through Medicare Advantage plans (MA plans) are entitled to QIO review of denied, reduced, or terminated care. Included in these earlier regulations were the right to a grievance process for non-appealable complaints, time frames for each step in the appeals process, and the right to appeal hospital coverage determinations to the QIO, including expedited review.[264]

---

[258] 42 C.F.R. §405.911(l).

[259] 42 C.F.R. §405.910(f).

[260] 70 Fed. Reg. 11430 (Mar. 8, 2005).

[261] Id.

[262] 70 Fed. Reg. 11429 (Mar. 8, 2005).

[263] Id.

[264] 42 C.F.R. §§417.609, 417.617. The notice protections for hospitalized MA enrollees are likely to be expanded during 2006 as the result of a settlement agreement in Weichardt v. Thompson, C.A.

Prior to the enactment of the Medicare Advantage Program, managed care plans were required to provide procedural protections for beneficiaries, including meaningful grievance procedures and appeal rights.[265] These protections included the right to receive notice of an adverse "organization determination" regarding services or payment;[266] the right to an internal plan appeal (called a "reconsideration");[267] a final reconsidered determination by CMS;[268] and further review by an administrative law judge (if $100 or more is in controversy),[269] by the Departmental Appeals Board of the U.S. Department of Health and Human Services,[270] and by a federal district court (if $1,000 or more is in dispute).[271]

[L] Time Frames (Medicare Advantage)

All determinations and reconsiderations must be made "as expeditiously as the enrollee's health condition requires" but not to exceed a stated number of days.[272] Notice of organization determinations (initial decisions regarding the benefits an enrollee is entitled to receive) must be provided no later than 14 days after the initial request,[273] reduced from the previous 60-day limit. Expedited organization determinations must be made within 72 hours.[274] Reconsidered determinations must be issued no later than 30 calendar days from the request for a standard reconsideration,[275] reduced from the previous 60-day time limit. If the reconsideration is expedited, the deadline is 72 hours,[276] with

---

No. 03 5490 VRW (N.D.Cal. Settlement Agreement, Oct. 28, 2005). Proposed regulations implementing this settlement have been published by CMS. *See* Medicare Program; Notification Procedures for Hospital Discharges, 71 Fed. Reg. 17052–17062 (Apr. 5, 2006) (to be codified at 42 C.F.R. §§405.1205, 405.1206, 422.620, and 422.622, *inter alia*.) If adopted, the new system will include both a generic and a specific notice of discharge. The hospital will be required to deliver a generic notice of a discharge decision to the patient on the day before a planned discharge. This notice describes the process for immediate appeal of the discharge, and the financial consequences of the appeal options. 42 C.F.R. §422.620 (proposed). If a patient decides to request expedited appeal, the MA organization must deliver a second, detailed notice by the end of the day when appeal is requested. This notice sets out the factual and legal reasons why the MA believes hospital services are no longer covered. 42 C.F.R. §422.622(c) (proposed).

[265] 42 U.S.C. §1395(c)(5).

[266] 42 C.F.R. §§417.606–417. 610.

[267] 42 C.F.R. §417.614.

[268] 42 C.F.R. §417.620.

[269] 42 C.F.R. §417.630.

[270] 42 C.F.R. §417.634.

[271] 42 C.F.R. §417.636.

[272] *See, e.g.*, 42 C.F.R. §422.568, regarding organization determinations.

[273] 42 C.F.R. §422.568.

[274] 42 C.F.R. §422.572.

[275] 42 C.F.R. §422.590(a)(1).

[276] 42 C.F.R. §422.590(d)(1).

extensions up to 14 days upon enrollee or Medicare Advantage organization requests, and the delay is in the enrollee's interest.[277]

The regulations require CMS to contract with an independent outside entity to conduct a second level of review when the internal reconsideration remains, in whole or in part, adverse to the enrollee.[278] Review must be conducted as expeditiously as the enrollee's health condition requires, but the regulations do not specify a maximum time frame. Contractor deadlines are to be specified in the contract.[279]

[M]   Effectuation of Appeal Decisions (Medicare Advantage)

The regulations mandate that if an MA organization reverses its original determination, it must authorize or provide the service under dispute as expeditiously as the enrollee's health requires, but no later than 30 days after the beneficiary requests reconsideration.[280] If the original denial is reversed by the independent outside entity, the MA organization must comply within 60 days.[281] Inexplicably, there is no requirement for faster compliance if the appeal was expedited due to the enrollee's health condition.

[N]   Non-Coverage of Inpatient Hospital Care (Medicare Advantage)

Notice requirements are slightly different for persons in a hospital that is part of an HMO, Preferred Provider Organization (PPO), or private fee-for-service plan sponsored by an MA organization. The MA organization, or the hospital that has been delegated the authority to make the discharge decision, must provide the beneficiary with written notice of noncoverage, but only if and when the beneficiary disagrees with the discharge decision. Notice and appeal rights also arise if the MA organization, or the hospital that has been delegated the authority to make the discharge decision, is not discharging the individual but no longer intends to continue coverage of the inpatient stay.[282]

The CMS takes the position that the "Important Message from Medicare,"[283] a broad, general information notice that is given upon admission or shortly

---

[277] 42 C.F.R. §§422.572(b) and 422.590(d)(2).

[278] 42 C.F.R. §422.592.

[279] 42 C.F.R. §422.592(b).

[280] 42 C.F.R. §42 2.618(a). Reversals on a request for payment must be acted upon within 60 days. 42 C.F.R. §422.618(b).

[281] 42 C.F.R. §422.618(c).

[282] Revised 42 C.F.R. §422.620(a)(i) and (ii).

[283] On May 5, 2003, CMS issued a revised "Important Message From Medicare" that places more emphasis on discharge and appeal rights. CMS Transmittal No. 801, May 2, 2003 (available at <www.cms.hhs.gov>).

thereafter, is the only written notice that an inpatient will receive. If, upon being told that he or she is about to be discharged, the patient disagrees, he or she is to be given a notice of noncoverage with specific information about the basis of the hospital's discharge decision and about appeal rights. Therefore, as a practical matter, an enrollee who wishes to challenge a determination that the hospital stay is no longer necessary may need to remain in the hospital beyond the date on which Medicare non-coverage is slated to commence.

- An enrollee is entitled to coverage until at least noon of the day after the above notice is provided;[284]
- If QIO review is requested under §422.622 (requesting immediate QIO review of noncoverage of inpatient care), coverage is extended, and:

    The enrollee must submit a request for immediate review to the QIO that has an agreement with the hospital;

    The request must be in writing or by telephone;

    The request must be submitted by noon of the first working day after the patient receives written notice that the MCO hospital has determined that the hospital stay is no longer necessary; and

    The QIO must make a determination and notify the enrollee, or the hospital and the MA plan by the close of business of the first working day after it receives all necessary information from the hospital, or the organization, or both.

Before a notice of non-coverage is provided, the entity that makes the non-coverage/discharge determination must obtain the concurrence of the physician who is responsible for the enrollee's inpatient care.[285]

The written notice of non-coverage must be issued no later than the day before hospital coverage ends. The written notice must include the following elements:[286]

1. The reason why inpatient hospital care is no longer needed;

2. The effective date and time of the enrollee's liability for continued inpatient care;

3. The enrollee's appeal rights; and

4. Additional information specified by CMS.

---

[284] 42 C.F.R. §422.620(a)(2).

[285] 42 C.F.R. §422.620(b).

[286] *See* 42 C.F.R. §422.622(c).

[O] Grievances (Medicare Advantage)

MA organizations must have "meaningful procedures for timely hearing and resolution of grievances," which are complaints or disputes other than those involving organization determinations,[287] expressing dissatisfaction with any aspect of an MA organization or provider's operations, activities, or behaviors, regardless of whether remedial action is requested.

The regulation distinguishes between a grievance and appeal,[288] and requires MA organizations to inform beneficiaries whether their complaint is subject to the grievance procedure or the appeals procedure. It further distinguishes quality of care complaints,[289] and includes a process for expedited grievances,[290] requiring completion in 24 hours.

[P] Identifying Coverable Cases

Medicare claims for inpatient hospital care are suitable for Medicare coverage, and appeal if they have been denied, if they meet the following test:

The patient's condition must have been such that the care he required could only have been provided in a hospital, *or* he required an SNF level of care, and no SNF bed was actually available. (Note: An SNF level of care means that the patient required skilled services—from a physical therapist or a registered nurse, for example—on a daily basis.[291])

§2.12 DENIAL AND APPEAL PROCESS

Table 2-1 depicts the complex coverage determination and appeals process in Medicare hospital cases. The text that follows the chart describes the various steps in detail.

[A] Medicare Hospital Coverage Determination and Appeals Process

See Table 2-1.

---

[287] 42 C.F.R. §42 2.564.

[288] 42 C.F.R. §422.561.

[289] 42 C.F.R. §422.564.

[290] 42 C.F.R. §422.564(d)(1) and (2).

[291] *See* 42 C.F.R. §§409.30 *et seq.*

TABLE 2-1
MEDICARE PART A APPEALS
Hospital Care

Stage of Appeal:	Reconsideration Request	Hearing Request	Request for Dept. Appeals Board Review	Request for Judicial Review
Time Deadline for Filing Appeal:	60 Days After Receipt of "Notice of Medicare Claim Determination" (or within 3 Days if You Request an "Expedited Appeal")	60 Days After Receipt of "Reconsideration Determination"	60 Days After Receipt of "Hearing Decision"	60 Days After Receipt of "Appeals Board Decision"
Amount of Claim:	No Minimum	$200 Minimum*	$200 Minimum*	$2,000 Minimum
File Appeal Request With:	Quality Improvement Organization (QIO) or Local Social Security Office	Quality Improvement Organization (QIO) or Local Social Security Office (processed & forwarded to Social Security's Office of Hearings & Appeals)	U.S. Dept. of Health and Human Services	United States District Court
Appeal Reviewed & Decided By:	Quality Improvement Organization (QIO)	Administrative Law Judge from Social Security Departmental Office of Hearings and Appeals	U.S. Dept. of Health and Human Services Appeals Board	United States District Court
Time Deadline For Decision:	3 Days If Inpatient or Pre-Admission; 30 Days for All Others	None	None	None

*If the appeal is on a question of *entitlement* to Part A benefits, there is no minimum amount required.

[B] The Appeals Process in Operation

The determination and appeals process depicted in **Table 2-1** works like this:

1. The patient appears at the hospital seeking admission.

    Example: Mr. Brown and Mrs. Smith both are driven to the hospital by car. Mr. Brown, whose daughter takes him to the hospital, is having chest pains and has a history of a stroke and severe hypertension that is controlled by oral medications. By contrast, Mrs. Smith was found by a stranger wandering in the middle of a four-lane highway, dressed in a nightgown. Mrs. Smith, who lives alone, was incoherent and had a superficial wound on her leg. The stranger called the police, who took her to the hospital.

2. When confronted by a patient seeking admission, a hospital can choose one of these courses of action:

    a] The hospital may decide that the patient will be covered by Medicare, and admit the patient.

    b] The hospital may decide that Medicare coverage is not available but permit the patient to enter the hospital anyway. Under such circumstances, the hospital is required to issue the patient a notice of admission denial, informing the patient that the cost of hospital care will be the patient's responsibility. Written notice of noncoverage to the patient is necessary because the patient is not liable for the cost of care and may not be charged by the hospital until he or she has been given written notice that the services involved are not covered by the Medicare program.[292]

    c] Finally, the hospital may deny Medicare coverage and not admit the patient. Often the patient will balk at assuming responsibility for expensive care, or the hospital may simply refuse to allow the patient to enter. Usually no written Medicare denial notice is issued, and the patient has no right to appeal. An exception exists, however, where the QIO has a pre-procedure or preadmission review process in place. Although unusual, involvement of the QIO at the preadmission stage is good news for the advocate because appeal is possible. In such cases the QIO reviews the medical necessity or appropriateness of some or all of the Medicare admissions before they occur. If the QIO determines that Medicare coverage is not available, it issues an appealable initial determination notice to the beneficiary.[293]

    Example: Upon arriving at the hospital, Mr. Brown is examined in the emergency room, and admitted to the hospital. By contrast, Mrs. Smith is examined

---

[292] 42 C.F.R. §§411.404, 412. 42(c)(3)(ii); *see also* Social Security Act 1879, 42 U.S.C. §1395pp.

[293] Medicare Quality Improvement Organization Manual, Pub. 100-10, Ch. 7, §7101 2050(5)(A), (B).

and a determination is made that she does not need hospital care, but since she cannot be safely sent home, she will be admitted to the hospital. Mrs. Smith is given a written notice of Medicare noncoverage, and placed in one of the hospital's beds.

3. All patients actually admitted to the hospital must be given a special notice entitled "An Important Message from Medicare."[294] The mandatory notice is very explicit about a patient's rights while in the hospital. Most of the information in the "Important Message from Medicare" concerns the procedure to be followed when the hospital issues a continuing care denial of Medicare coverage. A continuing care denial occurs when the patient has been granted Medicare coverage on admission, but the hospital, usually acting through its URC, eventually determines that the patient no longer needs a hospital level of care.

> **Example:** After three days of tests, Mr. Brown is determined to require transfer to a nursing home. The hospital URC determines that he can be terminated from Medicare coverage because he no longer requires inpatient hospital care. A written continuing stay denial is issued to him.

4. Utilization review of a continuing stay often occurs because the stay is longer or more expensive than the average for that DRG. In such instances, the hospital may be motivated to avoid the financial loss represented by the gap between the DRG amount paid and the cost of the patient's care as the stay continues. Before issuing a determination that an admission or a continuing stay is not medically necessary, the URC must consult the attending physician and afford an opportunity to present his or her point of view.[295] Moreover, before a hospital may bill a patient for the cost of services rendered, however, the hospital must comply with a complex coverage determination, notice, and appeals process.

Federal regulations are quite specific concerning when a hospital may charge a Medicare-eligible patient for hospital services rendered. Generally, a hospital may not charge a beneficiary for any service for which payment is made by Medicare, even if the hospital's cost of furnishing services to the patient is greater than the amount the hospital is paid under PPS.[296] The hospital is always permitted to charge the patient the applicable deductible and coinsurance amounts. The hospital is not permitted to charge the patient for care excluded from Medicare coverage as custodial

---

[294] Social Security Act 1866(a)(1)(M), 42 U.S.C. §1395cc(a)(1)(M); 42 C.F.R. §466.78(b)(3); Medicare Quality Improvement Manual, Pub. 100-10, Ch. 7, §§7100-2000, 2005.

[295] 42 C.F.R. §482.30(d)(2).

[296] 42 C.F.R. §412.42(a).

care or medically unnecessary care[297] unless the following specific steps are followed:

The hospital must decide that the patient no longer requires inpatient hospital care. Inpatient hospital care includes cases where a beneficiary needs an SNF level of care, but, under Medicare criteria, an SNF level bed is not available.[298]

> **Example:** Mr. Brown receives three days of Medicare hospital coverage, following which a determination is made that he can be transferred to a nursing home. Transfer to a nursing home does not necessarily mean that Mr. Brown requires an SNF level of care under Medicare criteria. Therefore, an inquiry into the nature of the care that Mr. Brown requires will have to be made.

If the attending physician agrees with the hospital's determination in writing, the hospital may immediately issue a continuing care denial to the patient.[299] If the attending physician believes that a hospital level of care is still required, the hospital may request an immediate review of the case by the QIO. Concurrence by the QIO in the hospital's determination serves in lieu of the physician's agreement, and the denial notice may then be given to the patient.[300]

> **Example:** Mr. Brown's treating physician, who ordered that Mr. Brown could be discharged to a nursing home, agrees that he no longer requires a hospital level of care. Therefore, the hospital URC issues a denial notice to Mr. Brown.

The continuing care denial notice given the patient must inform the patient that customary charges will be assessed against the patient only *after the second day following the date of the notice.*[301] For example, if a patient receives a denial notice on Monday, the patient may not be charged for the cost of care until Thursday.

> **Example:** Mr. Brown was admitted to the hospital on Thursday and was determined to be suitable for nursing home placement on Saturday. The hospital URC, therefore, with Mr. Brown's physician's concurrence, issued a denial notice on Saturday. If Mr. Brown does nothing to appeal this denial, he could stay in the hospital, without incurring any financial liability, through Monday. He could be charged for his stay commencing on Tuesday.

---

[297] 42 C.F.R. §§411.400, 489.21(d)(1).

[298] 42 C.F.R. §412.42(c)(1).

[299] 42 C.F.R. §412.42(c)(2).

[300] *Id.*

[301] This limitation on charges to beneficiaries applies only where Medicare coverage was originally granted on admission, that is, where the patient's stay included at least one covered day. 42 C.F.R. §412.42(b).

For a case where coverage is denied on admission and no covered days whatsoever are granted, the hospital may not charge the patient for hospital care that is not medically necessary until the patient has been notified in writing that Medicare coverage is not available.[302] The notice must also inform the patient concerning the appeal rights described below.

Example: Mrs. Smith was given a denial notice immediately prior to her admission. The hospital would be able to charge her for her stay from the date of admission.

5. The right to appeal for a patient given a continuing care denial differs according to whether the attending physician has concurred with the URC's denial decision or whether the URC was required to obtain QIO approval of the proposed denial determination.[303]

If the attending physician has agreed with the hospital determination of noncoverage, the QIO has not yet been required to review the case. In this situation the patient is entitled to an expedited QIO review if the patient is still an inpatient in the hospital and requests an expedited review not later than noon of the first working day after the date the patient receives the URC denial notice.[304] The hospital is required to provide the QIO with a copy of the medical records by the close of business of such working day, and the QIO must issue a determination not later than one full working day after the date the QIO has received the request for expedited review and the medical records.[305] If the patient is no longer in the hospital, or fails to request an expedited determination by noon of the first working day after the notice of no coverage is received, the QIO is required to issue a review decision within 30 days of the request.

Example: Mr. Brown receives his continuing stay denial notice on Saturday. He must request an expedited review by the QIO by no later than noon on Monday, which he does. The QIO issues, and Mr. Brown receives, a decision that upholds the denial on Tuesday. The hospital may begin charging Mr. Brown for his stay on Tuesday. Under the Medicare regulations, an appeal to the QIO does not result in an extension of the hospital's inability to charge Mr. Brown, beyond two days after the original hospital URC notice was given to him, unless the QIO finds that, in fact, he required continued hospital care.[306] As can be seen, simply by requesting the expedited review, Mr. Brown has received an additional day of Medicare coverage in the hospital.

---

[302] 42 C.F.R. §411.404(b).

[303] 42 C.F.R. §412.42(c).

[304] Social Security Act 1154(e), 42 U.S.C. §1320c–3(c).

[305] *Id.*

[306] 42 C.F.R. §412.42(c)(3)(v).

If the patient's attending physician does not concur with the hospital's determination of noncoverage, the hospital must obtain the QIO's concurrence before it can bill the patient.[307] The QIO must give an opportunity to the provider and to the physician to discuss the merits of the case.[308] If the QIO concurs with the hospital's determination, the hospital is so informed by the QIO, and the hospital will issue a notice to the patient.[309] The QIO's concurrence constitutes an initial determination, and the QIO will also issue a notice to the patient.[310] In cases where the hospital has sought and received the QIO's agreement, the appropriate appeal is for reconsideration rather than review (because the QIO has already reviewed the case in such situations). If the beneficiary is still an inpatient when the QIO receives a request for reconsideration, the QIO must complete its determination and send a notice to the beneficiary within three working days after the QIO receives the reconsideration request.[311] If the beneficiary is no longer a hospital inpatient, the QIO must issue the reconsideration within 30 working days.[312]

It is unclear to what extent a hospital is required to notify the family members or legal representative of ill or incompetent patients. In one case the court found that the hospital had a duty to provide written, not oral, notice of the denial of Medicare coverage to the friend of an incompetent patient, where the hospital knew that the friend was acting on the patient's behalf.[313] In practice, hospitals usually attempt to notify both the patient and the relative or representative who has been acting on the patient's behalf.

> **Example:** Mrs. Smith arrived at the hospital in an incoherent state, yet the hospital delivered a denial notice to her. The notice would not be deemed effective if it could be shown that Mrs. Smith's medical condition prevented her from understanding the denial notice. As an alternative, the hospital could try to locate a family member willing and able to act on Mrs. Smith's behalf, and deliver the denial notice to the family member. As a further alternative, if state law permits, the hospital could go to a court of appropriate jurisdiction to petition for appointment of a conservator or guardian for Mrs. Smith. The conservator or guardian could then be given the denial notice.

6. The patient involved may appeal the QIO's initial determination by requesting a reconsideration.[314] Generally, a party who is dissatisfied must file a request

---

[307] 42 U.S.C. §1320c-3(e)(2); 42 C.F.R. §412.42(c)(2).

[308] 42 C.F.R. §466.93(b).

[309] 42 U.S.C. §1320c-3(e)(2); 42 C.F.R. §412.42(c)(2).

[310] 42 C.F.R. §466.83.

[311] 42 C.F.R. §478.32(a)(1).

[312] 42 C.F.R. §478.32(a)(3).

[313] Carpenter v. Secretary of HHS, Medicare & Medicaid Guide (CCH) 38,621 (D. Conn. June 21, 1990).

[314] 42 C.F.R. §466.83.

for reconsideration within 60 to 120 days after the receipt of the notice of an initial determination issued by the QIO.[315] If the beneficiary is still an inpatient in the hospital when the QIO receives the request for reconsideration, the QIO must complete its reconsideration determination and send written notice to the beneficiary within three working days after the QIO's receipt of the request for reconsideration.[316] The QIO must issue the reconsideration within 30 working days if the beneficiary is no longer an inpatient in the hospital.[317]

7. If the QIO reconsideration is unfavorable, the beneficiary may request a hearing before an administrative law judge of the US Dep't of Health and Human Services Office of Medicare Hearings and Appeals. The amount in controversy must be at least $200. The administrative hearing will be held by an ALJ of the Office of Medicare Hearings and Appeals. The hearing request must be filed within 60 days of receipt of the notice of the QIO reconsideration determination, unless the time is extended for good cause.[318] The request for reconsideration must be filed with the QIO.[319]

§2.13   HOW TO DEVELOP A WINNING APPEAL

While a denial of Medicare inpatient hospital coverage can occur for many reasons, frequently patients are denied coverage (1) in rehabilitation hospitals, (2) when, following at least three days of Medicare coverage in the hospital their condition improves, but they still require an SNF level of care after a hospital stay and no SNF bed is available, or (3) when the hospital determines that the patient requires admission for "social" reasons. The stated reason for denials of rehabilitation hospital care are often based upon the purported lack of intensity of the patient's rehabilitation program; the alleged absence of "sufficient" improvement in the patient's rehabilitation status; or a notion that the overall condition of the patient was such that the rehabilitation services could have been provided in an SNF, instead of a hospital. Denials of hospital coverage when an SNF bed is not available often occur because the hospital is simply unaware of the availability of continued Medicare coverage under such circumstances; or because the hospital improperly believes that, although a patient requires a nursing home placement, the patient's condition does not rise to the level of requiring SNF care. When faced with these bases for denials of Medicare coverage, the advocate must be prepared to thoroughly analyze the facts and the applicable Medicare coverage criteria.

---

[315] 42 C.F.R. §478.16. *But see also* CMS Program Memorandum AB 02-111 (July 31, 2002) which extends the time frame for requesting a reconsideration, under Medicare Part A, to 120 days from the date of the initial determination.

[316] 42 C.F.R. §478.20(a).

[317] 42 C.F.R. §478.32(a).

[318] 42 C.F.R. §478.42(b).

[319] Social Security Act 1861(ee), 42 U.S.C. §1395x(ee); 42 C.F.R. §482.43.

Denial of so-called social admissions (as in the previous example of Mrs. Smith) is often based upon the hospital's assessment that no other support system is available to the patient to assure the patient's overall safety, even though the patient—in the hospital's view—could properly receive medical treatment in some other setting. One argument that has been used successfully in such cases is that Medicare regulations require that care be provided to patients in the most economically feasible manner.[320] "Economically" is defined in the Medicare regulations as "provided at the least expensive, medically appropriate type of setting or care available."[321] Consequently, if it can be established that an inpatient hospital was the only medically appropriate type of setting or care available (and the simple fact that the patient was admitted to the hospital, rather than discharged home or sent to some other, less intensive care setting, is evidence of this fact), then the services received by the patient as a hospital inpatient are medically reasonable and necessary, in the absence of availability of any alternative care.

Of course, in any Medicare inpatient hospital appeal, as is usually the case in other areas of advocacy, effective analysis and factual development will greatly improve your chances of prevailing. Address these areas:

(1) Recognize an unfair coverage denial by comparing the facts of the case with the legal criteria of coverage. In acute hospital cases medical necessity is the amorphous standard. This is a two-part standard: (1) Is it medically necessary for the patient to be treated in a hospital[322] and (2) if the patient no longer requires treatment in the hospital and could be treated outside the hospital, does the patient need at least an SNF level of care, and is there no SNF bed available in a participating facility?[323]

(2) Build an alliance with the attending physician. The statute and regulations repeatedly require the involvement of the attending physician in the decision-making process. Physicians will typically feel divided loyalties. They do not want to see their hospital lose money, but they also want to protect their patients from unfair charges for care. It is the advocate's job to educate the physician concerning the legitimate rules of Medicare coverage and to encourage the physician to support the patient's claim by expressing an opinion, preferably in writing, that it is medically necessary for the patient to be treated in the hospital, or that the patient requires an SNF level of care and that no SNF bed in a participating facility is available. Often an explicit and detailed letter from the attending physician becomes the deciding factor in a successful Medicare appeal.

(3) Evaluate the medical record for skilled care. The degree and intensity of skill delivered to a patient is the central factor in determining what level of care the patient requires. If the patient requires a degree of skill and intensity of services

---

[320] 42 C.F.R. §1004.10.

[321] 42 C.F.R. §1004.1(b).

[322] 42 U.S.C. §1395f(a)(3).

[323] 42 C.F.R. §§412.42(c)(1) and 424.13(b).

* Now referred to as Quality Improvement Organization (QIO).

available only in a hospital, then it is medically necessary for the patient to be treated in a hospital. One benchmark, although not the exclusive one, is whether the beneficiary required the 24-hour availability of a physician. Such physician availability usually exists only in a hospital. If the patient requires daily skilled care in an institutional setting, then that patient requires an SNF level of care. The details found in the written medical record will often provide the evidence necessary to substantiate the patient's claim.

(4) Determine where you are in the process. You will notice that the coverage determination and appeals process is quite complex; your client's rights depend upon where in the process his or her claim happens to be. The advocate must gather all available notices and documentation to determine the present status of the appeal. Generally, it is in the patient's interest for an advocate to take action at the earliest possible time. For example, patients and their families often hear word of an impending continued care denial before a written notice is actually received. By encouraging the attending physician to support the claim at an early stage, an advocate can often delay or even prevent the issuance of the denial notice.

Hospital care is generally the most expensive care that a patient can receive. Because of the expense involved, denials of Medicare inpatient hospital coverage, or the threat of such a denial, can often lead patients to forgo necessary medical care. The result frequently can be a deteriorated and untreated state of health. The availability of advocacy on the patient's behalf, therefore, may mean the difference between the patient's receiving needed care or accepting and living with unnecessarily poor health. Hence, an advocate's role where Medicare hospital coverage is concerned is, first, to make sure the patient receives the care he or she requires, and second, to ensure that the patient is not charged for services that should be covered by Medicare.

As observed, economic considerations often override a purely medical perspective when it comes to access to Medicare-covered hospital care. However, a well-prepared advocate who is familiar with the Medicare inpatient hospital coverage criteria and the patient's medical condition and treatment can fight against this tide and ensure that the patient receives appropriate health care. By allying oneself with the patient in this way, the advocate may also influence and inform Medicare coverage determinations made in general by providers and, so, prevent future improper denials of Medicare coverage.

APPENDIX 2-1

Regional PRO Bulletin No. 90-39

DEPARTMENT OF HEALTH & HUMAN SERVICES

HEALTH CARE FINANCING ADMINISTRATION

Office of the Regional Administrator

Region 1
John F. Kennedy Federal Bldg.
Government Center
Boston, MA 02203

TO: Peer Review Organizations   DATE: August 14, 1990

FROM: Regional Administrator, Region I
Health Care Financing Administration

SUBJECT: Medicare Coverage for Hospital Patients Awaiting Skilled
Nursing Facility Placement

The purpose of this bulletin is to clarify continued Medicare coverage for hospital patients awaiting skilled nursing facility placement.[*]

Medicare covered "inpatient hospital care" includes cases in which a beneficiary no longer needs a hospital level of care but does need a skilled nursing facility level of care, and an SNF bed in a Medicare participating facility is not available in the patient's geographic area. In these instances, the patient continues to qualify for Medicare hospital coverage as long as he continues to need a skilled nursing facility level of care, as defined by the Medicare law and regulations.

It has come to our attention that Peer Review Organizations (PROs) and/or hospitals may not be reviewing consistently for the need and availability of skilled nursing facility care prior to denying these hospital patients continued Medicare coverage. Whenever a PRO or hospital is determining whether an inpatient hospital stay is medically necessary, an individualized assessment must be made of the patient's need for skilled nursing facility care. If the patient requires a skilled nursing facility level of care, the PRO or hospital must determine whether there is a bed available to the patient in a participating skilled nursing facility in the community or local geographic area (42 C.F.R. §424.13(b)(1), 42 C.F.R. §412.42(c)(1)).

---

[*] PROs are currently called Quality Improvement Organizations (QIOs).

If the PRO or hospital determines that the patient requires SNF care but no bed is available, it *must* find that the continued stay in the hospital is medically necessary. The patient's attending physician should be informed that it is her responsibility (with the assistance of the hospital's staff) to attempt regularly to place the patient in a local participating SNF. While the patient should cooperate with the SNF search and should not decline an appropriate bed, it is not her responsibility to find the bed.

Until such placement is made, or the patient declines placement in a Medicare certified SNF, or the patient no longer requires a skilled nursing facility level of care, the continued stay in the hospital is medically necessary and thus, covered by Medicare.

In making Medicare coverage determinations for inpatient hospital stays, PROs and hospitals must adhere to the instructions outlined above. To ensure uniform application of these rules and proper notice to patients, please send the attached notice and revised hospital notice of noncoverage to all hospital utilization review committees. We also request that PROs modify their initial denial determination letter to incorporate language that reflects the consideration of skilled nursing care and the availability of an SNF bed.

If you have questions regarding this bulletin, please contact Doris West, Chief, Medical Review Branch at (617) 565-1320.

Sidney C. Kaplan

Attachments

APPENDIX 2-2

TITLE 42—PUBLIC HEALTH

PART 412—PROSPECTIVE PAYMENT SYSTEMS FOR INPATIENT HOSPITAL SERVICES

Subpart A—General Provisions

Sec. 412.10   Changes in the DRG classification system.

(a) General rule. CMS issues changes in the DRG classification system in a Federal Register notice at least annually. Except as specified in paragraphs (c) and (d) of this section, the DRG changes are effective prospectively with discharges occurring on or after the same date the payment rates are effective.

(b) Basis for changes in the DRG classification system. All changes in the DRG classification system are made using the principles established for the DRG system. This means that cases are classified so each DRG is—

(1) Clinically coherent; and

(2) Embraces an acceptable range of resource consumption.

(c) Interim coverage changes—(1) Criteria. CMS makes interim changes to the DRG classification system during the Federal fiscal year to incorporate items and services newly covered under Medicare.

(2) Implementation and effective date. CMS issues interim coverage changes through its administrative issuance system and makes the change effective as soon as is administratively feasible.

(3) Publication for comment. CMS publishes any change made under paragraph (c)(1) of this section in the next annual notice of changes to the DRG classification system published in accordance with paragraph (a) of this section.

(d) Interim changes to correct omissions and inequities—(1) Criteria. CMS makes interim changes to the DRG classification system to correct a serious omission or inequity in the system only if failure to make the changes would have—

(i) A potentially substantial adverse impact on the health and safety of beneficiaries; or

(ii) A significant and unwarranted fiscal impact on hospitals or the Medicare program.

(2) Publication and effective date. CMS publishes these changes in the Federal Register in a final notice with comment period with a prospective effective date. The change is also published for public information in the next annual notice of changes to the DRG classification system published in accordance with paragraph (a) of this section.

(e) Review by ProPAC. Changes published annually in accordance with paragraph (a) of this section are subject to review and comment by ProPAC upon publication. Interim changes to the DRG classification system that are made in accordance with paragraphs (c) and (d) of this section are subject to review by ProPAC before implementation.

[50 FR 35688, Sept. 3, 1985, as amended at 51 FR 31496, Sept. 3, 1986; 57 FR 39820, Sept. 1, 1992]

***

Subpart B—Hospital Services Subject to and Excluded from the Prospective Payment Systems for Inpatient Operating Costs and Inpatient Capital-Related Costs

Sec. 412.20   Hospital services subject to the prospective payment systems.

(a) Except for services described in paragraphs (b), (c), and (d) of this section, all covered inpatient hospital services furnished to beneficiaries during subject cost reporting periods are paid under the prospective payment systems specified in Sec. 412.1(a)(1).

(b)(1) Effective for cost reporting periods beginning on or after January 1, 2002, covered inpatient hospital services furnished to Medicare beneficiaries by a rehabilitation hospital or rehabilitation unit that meet the conditions of Sec. 412.604 are paid under the prospective payment system described in subpart P of this part.

(2) CMS will not pay for services under Subpart P of this part if the services are paid for by a health maintenance organization (HMO) or competitive medical plan (CMP) that elects not to have CMS make payments to an inpatient rehabilitation facility for services, which are inpatient hospital services, furnished to the HMO's or CMP's Medicare enrollees, as provided under part 417 of this chapter.

(c) Effective for cost reporting periods beginning on or after October 1, 2002, covered inpatient hospital services furnished to Medicare beneficiaries by a long-term care hospital that meets the conditions for payment of Secs. 412.505 through 412.511 are paid under the prospective payment system described in subpart O of this part.

(d) Inpatient hospital services will not be paid under the prospective payment systems specified in Sec. 412.1(a)(1) under any of the following circumstances:

(1) The services are furnished by a hospital (or hospital unit) explicitly excluded from the prospective payment systems under Secs. 412.23, 412.25, 412.27, and 412.29.

(2) The services are emergency services furnished by a nonparticipating hospital in accordance with Sec. 424.103 of this chapter.

(3) The services are paid for by an HMO or competitive medical plan (CMP) that elects not to have CMS make payments directly to a hospital for inpatient hospital services furnished to the HMO's or CMP's Medicare enrollees, as provided in Sec. 417.240(d) and Sec. 417.586 of this chapter.

[50 FR 12741, Mar. 29, 1985, as amended at 53 FR 6648, Mar. 2, 1988; 57 FR 39820, Sept. 1, 1992; 59 FR 45400, Sept. 1, 1994; 66 FR 41386, Aug. 7, 2001; 67 FR 56048, Aug. 30, 2002; 68 FR 45698, Aug. 1, 2003]
***

Sec. 412.22   Excluded hospitals and hospital units: General rules.

(a) Criteria. Subject to the criteria set forth in paragraph (e) of this section, a hospital is excluded from the prospective payment systems specified in Sec. 412.1(a)(1) of this part if it meets the criteria for one or more of the excluded classifications described in Sec. 412.23. For purposes of this subpart, the term "hospital" includes a critical access hospital (CAH).

(b) Cost reimbursement. Except for those hospitals specified in paragraph (c) of this section, and Sec. 412.20(b), (c), and (d), all excluded hospitals (and excluded hospital units, as described in Sec. 412.23 through Sec. 412.29) are reimbursed under the cost reimbursement rules set forth in part 413 of this chapter, and are subject to the ceiling on the rate of hospital cost increases as specified in Sec. 413.40 of this chapter.

(c) Special payment provisions. The following classifications of hospitals are paid under special provisions and therefore are not generally subject to the cost reimbursement or prospective payment rules of this chapter.

(1) Veterans Administration hospitals.

(2) Hospitals reimbursed under State cost control systems approved under part 403 of this chapter.

(3) Hospitals reimbursed in accordance with demonstration projects authorized under section 402(a) of Public Law 90-248 (42 U.S.C. 1395b-1) or section 222(a) of Public Law 92-603 (42 U.S.C. 1395b-1 (note)).

(4) Nonparticipating hospitals furnishing emergency services to Medicare beneficiaries.

(d) Changes in hospitals' status. For purposes of exclusion from the prospective payment systems under this subpart, the status of each currently participating hospital (excluded or not excluded) is determined at the beginning of each cost reporting period and is effective for the entire cost reporting period. Any changes in the status of the hospital are made only at the start of a cost reporting period.

(e) Hospitals-within-hospitals. Except as provided in paragraph (f) of this section, a hospital that occupies space in a building also used by another hospital, or in one or more separate buildings located on the same campus as buildings used by another hospital, must meet the following criteria in order to be excluded from the prospective payment systems specified in Sec. 412.1(a)(1):

(1) Except as specified in paragraph (f) of this section, for cost reporting periods beginning on or after October 1, 1997—

(i) Separate governing body. The hospital has a governing body that is separate from the governing body of the hospital occupying space in the same building or on the same campus. The hospital's governing body is not under the control of the hospital occupying space in the same building or on the same campus, or of any third entity that controls both hospitals.

(ii) **Separate chief medical officer.** The hospital has a single chief medical officer who reports directly to the governing body and who is responsible for all medical staff activities of the hospital. The chief medical officer of the hospital is not employed by or under contract with either the hospital occupying space in the same building or on the same campus or any third entity that controls both hospitals.

(iii) **Separate medical staff.** The hospital has a medical staff that is separate from the medical staff of the hospital occupying space in the same building or on the same campus. The hospital's medical staff is directly accountable to the governing body for the quality of medical care provided in the hospital, and adopts and enforces by-laws governing medical staff activities, including criteria and procedures for recommending to the governing body the privileges to be granted to individual practitioners.

(iv) **Chief executive officer.** The hospital has a single chief executive officer through whom all administration authority flows, and who exercises control and surveillance over all administrative activities of the hospital. The chief executive officer is not employed by, or under contract with, either the hospital occupying space in the same building or on the same campus or any third entity that controls both hospitals.

(v) **Performance of basic hospital functions.** The hospital meets one of the following criteria:

(A) The hospital performs the basic functions specified in Sec. Sec. 482.21 through 482.27, 482.30, 482.42, 482.43, and 482.45 of this chapter through the use of employees or under contracts or other agreements with entities other than the hospital occupying space in the same building or on the same campus, or a third entity that controls both hospitals. Food and dietetic services and housekeeping, maintenance, and other services necessary to maintain a clean and safe physical environment could be obtained under contracts or other agreements with the hospital occupying space in the same building or on the same campus, or with a third entity that controls both hospitals.

(B) For the same period of at least 6 months used to determine compliance with the criterion regarding the age of patients in Sec. 412.23(d)(2) or the length-of-stay criterion in Sec. 412.23(e)(2), or for hospitals other than children's or long-term care hospitals, for a period of at least 6 months immediately preceding the first cost reporting period for which exclusion is sought, the cost of the services that the hospital obtains under contracts or other agreements with the hospital occupying space in the same building or on the same campus, or with a third entity that controls both hospitals, is no more than 15 percent of the hospital's total inpatient operating costs, as defined in Sec. 412.2(c). For purposes of this paragraph (e)(1)(v)(B), however, the costs of preadmission services are those specified under Sec. 413.40(c)(2) rather than those specified under Sec. 412.2(c)(5).

(C) For the same period of at least 6 months used to determine compliance with the criterion regarding the age of inpatients in Sec. 412.23(d)(2) or the length-of-stay criterion in Sec. 412.23(e)(2), or for hospitals other than children's or long-term care hospitals, for the period of at least 6 months immediately preceding the first cost reporting period for which exclusion is sought, the hospital has an inpatient population of whom at least 75 percent were referred to the hospital from a source other than another hospital occupying space in the same building or on the same campus.

(2) Effective for long-term care hospitals-within-hospitals for cost reporting periods beginning on or after October 1, 2004, the hospital must meet the governance and control requirements at paragraphs (e)(1)(i) through (e)(1)(iv) of this section.

(3) Notification of co-located status. A long-term care hospital that occupies space in a building used by another hospital, or in one or more entire buildings located on the same campus as buildings used by another hospital and that meets the criteria of paragraphs (e)(1) or (e)(2) of this section must notify its fiscal intermediary and CMS in writing of its co-location and identify by name, address, and Medicare provider number those hospital(s) with which it is co-located.

(f) Application for certain hospitals. If a hospital was excluded from the prospective payment systems under the provisions of this section on or before September 30, 1995, and at that time occupied space in a building also used by another hospital, or in one or more buildings located on the same campus as buildings used by another hospital, the criteria in paragraph (e) of this section do not apply to the hospital as long as the hospital either—

(1) Continues to operate under the same terms and conditions, including the number of beds and square footage considered to be part of the hospital for purposes of Medicare participation and payment in effect on September 30, 1995; or

(2) In the case of a hospital that changes the terms and conditions under which it operates after September 30, 1995, but before October 1, 2003, continues to operate under the same terms and conditions, including the number of beds and square footage considered to be part of the hospital for purposes of Medicare participation and payment in effect on September 30, 2003.

(g) Definition of control. For purposes of this section, control exists if an individual or an organization has the power, directly or indirectly, significantly to influence or direct the actions or policies of an organization or institution.

(h) Satellite facilities. (1) For purposes of paragraphs (h)(2) through (h)(4) of this section, a satellite facility is a part of a hospital that provides inpatient services in a building also used by another hospital, or in one or more entire buildings located on the same campus as buildings used by another hospital.

(2) Except as provided in paragraphs (h)(3), (h)(6), and (h)(7) of this section, effective for cost reporting periods beginning on or after October 1, 1999, a hospital that has a satellite facility must meet the following criteria in order to be excluded from the acute care hospital inpatient prospective payment systems for any period:

(i) In the case of a hospital (other than a children's hospital) that was excluded from the prospective payment systems for the most recent cost reporting period beginning before October 1, 1997, the hospital's number of State-licensed and Medicare-certified beds, including those at the satellite facilities, does not exceed the hospital's number of State-licensed and Medicare-certified beds on the last day of the hospital's last cost reporting period beginning before October 1, 1997.

(ii) The satellite facility independently complies with—

(A) For psychiatric hospitals, the requirements under Sec. 412.23(a);

(B) For rehabilitation hospitals, the requirements under Sec. 412.23(b)(2);

(C) For the children's hospitals, the requirements under Sec. 412.23(d)(2); or

(D) For long-term care hospitals, the requirements under Sec. Sec. 412.23(e)(1) through (e)(3)(i).

(iii) The satellite facility meets all of the following requirements:

(A) Effective for cost reporting periods beginning on or after October 1, 2002, it is not under the control of the governing body or chief executive officer of the hospital in which it is located, and it furnishes inpatient care through the use of medical personnel who are not under the control of the medical staff or chief medical officer of the hospital in which it is located.

(B) It maintains admission and discharge records that are separately identified from those of the hospital in which it is located and are readily available.

(C) It has beds that are physically separate from (that is, not commingled with) the beds of the hospital in which it is located.

(D) It is serviced by the same fiscal intermediary as the hospital of which it is a part.

(E) It is treated as a separate cost center of the hospital of which it is a part.

(F) For cost reporting and apportionment purposes, it uses an accounting system that properly allocates costs and maintains adequate statistical data to support the basis of allocation.

(G) It reports its costs on the cost report of the hospital of which it is a part, covering the same fiscal period and using the same method of apportionment as the hospital of which it is a part.

(3) Except as provided in paragraph (h)(4) of this section, the provisions of paragraph (h)(2) of this section do not apply to—

(i) Any hospital structured as a satellite facility on September 30, 1999, and excluded from the prospective payment systems on that date, to the extent the hospital continues operating under the same terms and conditions, including the number of beds and square footage considered, for purposes of Medicare participation and payment, to be part of the hospital, in effect on September 30, 1999; or

(ii) Any hospital excluded from the prospective payment systems under Sec. 412.23(e)(2)(ii).

(4) In applying the provisions of paragraph (h)(3) of this section, any hospital structured as a satellite facility on September 30, 1999, may increase or decrease the square footage of the satellite facility or may decrease the number of beds in the satellite facility if these changes are made necessary by relocation of a facility—

(i) To permit construction or renovation necessary for compliance with changes in Federal, State, or local law; or

(ii) Because of catastrophic events such as fires, floods, earthquakes, or tornadoes.

(5) Notification of co-located status. A satellite of a long-term care hospital that occupies space in a building used by another hospital, or in one or more entire buildings located on the same campus as buildings used by another hospital and that meets the criteria of paragraphs (h)(1) through (h)(4) of this section must notify its fiscal intermediary and CMS in writing of its co-location and identify by name, address, and Medicare provider number, those hospital(s) with which it is co-located.

(6) The provisions of paragraph (h)(2)(i) of this section do not apply to any long-term care hospital that is subject to the long-term care hospital prospective payment system under Subpart O of this subpart, effective for cost reporting periods occurring on or after October 1, 2002, and that elects to be paid based on 100 percent of the Federal prospective payment rate as specified in Sec. 412.533(c), beginning with the first cost reporting period following that election, or when the LTCH is fully transitioned to 100 percent of the Federal prospective rate, or to a new long-term care hospital, as defined in Sec. 412.23(e)(4).

(7) The provisions of paragraph (h)(2)(i) of this section do not apply to any inpatient rehabilitation facility that is subject to the inpatient rehabilitation facility prospective payment system under subpart P of this part, effective for cost reporting periods beginning on or after October 1, 2003.

[50 FR 12741, Mar. 29, 1985, as amended at 51 FR 34793, Sept. 30, 1986; 57 FR 39820, Sept. 1, 1994; 62 FR 46026, Aug. 29, 1997; 63 FR 26357, May 12, 1998; 64 FR 41540, July 30, 1999; 66 FR 41386, Aug. 7, 2001; 67 FR 50111, Aug. 1, 2002; 67 FR 56048, Aug. 30, 2002; 68 FR 10988, Mar. 7, 2003; 68 FR 34162, June 6, 2003; 68 FR 45469, Aug. 1, 2003; 69 FR 49240, Aug. 11, 2004; 69 FR 60252, Oct. 7, 2004; 69 FR 66976, Nov. 15, 2004; 70 FR 24222, May 6, 2005]
***

Sec. 412.23   Excluded hospitals: Classifications.

Hospitals that meet the requirements for the classifications set forth in this section are not reimbursed under the prospective payment systems specified in Sec. 412.1(a)(1):

(a) Psychiatric hospitals. A psychiatric hospital must—

(1) Meet the following requirements to be excluded from the prospective payment system as specified in Sec. 412.1(a)(1) and to be paid under the prospective payment system as specified in Sec. 412.1(a)(2) and in subpart N of this part;

(2) Be primarily engaged in providing, by or under the supervision of a psychiatrist, psychiatric services for the diagnosis and treatment of mentally ill persons; and

(3) Meet the conditions of participation for hospitals and special conditions of participation for psychiatric hospitals set forth in part 482 of this chapter.

(b) Rehabilitation hospitals. A rehabilitation hospital must meet the following requirements to be excluded from the prospective payment systems specified in Sec. 412.1(a)(1) and to be paid under the prospective payment system specified in Sec. 412.1(a)(3) and in Subpart P of this part:

(1) Have a provider agreement under part 489 of this chapter to participate as a hospital.

(2) Except in the case of a newly participating hospital seeking classification under this paragraph as a rehabilitation hospital for its first 12-month cost reporting period, as described in paragraph (b)(8) of this section, a hospital must show that during its most recent, consecutive, and appropriate 12-month time period (as defined by CMS or the fiscal intermediary), it served an inpatient population that meets the criteria under paragraph (b)(2)(i) or (b)(2)(ii) of this section.

(i) For cost reporting periods beginning on or after July 1, 2004 and before July 1, 2005, the hospital has served an inpatient population of whom at least 50 percent, and for cost reporting periods beginning on or after July 1, 2005 and before July 1, 2006, the hospital has served an inpatient population of whom at least 60 percent, and for cost reporting periods beginning on or after July 1, 2006 and before July 1, 2007, the hospital has served an inpatient population of whom at least 65 percent, required intensive rehabilitative services for treatment of one or more of the conditions specified at paragraph (b)(2)(iii) of this section. A patient with a comorbidity, as defined at Sec. 412.602, may be included in the inpatient population that counts towards the required applicable percentage if—

(A) The patient is admitted for inpatient rehabilitation for a condition that is not one of the conditions specified in paragraph (b)(2)(iii) of this section;

(B) The patient has a comorbidity that falls in one of the conditions specified in paragraph (b)(2)(iii) of this section; and

(C) The comorbidity has caused significant decline in functional ability in the individual such that, even in the absence of the admitting condition, the individual would require the intensive rehabilitation treatment that is unique to inpatient rehabilitation facilities paid under subpart P of this part and that cannot be appropriately performed in another care setting covered under this title.

(ii) For cost reporting periods beginning on or after July 1, 2007, the hospital has served an inpatient population of whom at least 75 percent required intensive rehabilitative services for treatment of one or more of the conditions specified in paragraph (b)(2)(iii) of this section. A patient with comorbidity as described in paragraph (b)(2)(i) is not included in the inpatient population that counts towards the required 75 percent.

(iii) List of conditions.

(A) Stroke.

(B) Spinal cord injury.

(C) Congenital deformity.

(D) Amputation.

(E) Major multiple trauma.

(F) Fracture of femur (hip fracture).

(G) Brain injury.

(H) Neurological disorders, including multiple sclerosis, motor neuron diseases, polyneuropathy, muscular dystrophy, and Parkinson's disease.

(I) Burns.

(J) Active, polyarticular rheumatoid arthritis, psoriatic arthritis, and seronegative arthropathies resulting in significant functional impairment of ambulation and other activities of daily living that have not improved after an appropriate, aggressive, and sustained course of outpatient therapy services or services in other less intensive rehabilitation settings immediately preceding the inpatient rehabilitation admission or that result from a systemic disease activation immediately before admission, but have the potential to improve with more intensive rehabilitation.

(K) Systemic vasculidities with joint inflammation, resulting in significant functional impairment of ambulation and other activities of daily living that have not improved after an appropriate, aggressive, and sustained course of outpatient therapy services or services in other less intensive rehabilitation settings immediately preceding the inpatient rehabilitation admission or that result from a systemic disease activation immediately before admission, but have the potential to improve with more intensive rehabilitation.

(L) Severe or advanced osteoarthritis (osteoarthrosis or degenerative joint disease) involving two or more major weight bearing joints (elbow, shoulders, hips, or knees, but not counting a joint with a prosthesis) with joint deformity and substantial loss of range of motion, atrophy of muscles surrounding the joint, significant functional impairment of ambulation and other activities of daily living that have not improved after the patient has participated in an appropriate, aggressive, and sustained course of outpatient therapy services or services in other less intensive rehabilitation settings immediately preceding the inpatient rehabilitation admission but have the potential to improve with more intensive rehabilitation. (A joint replaced by a prosthesis no longer is considered to have osteoarthritis, or other arthritis, even though this condition was the reason for the joint replacement.)

(M) Knee or hip joint replacement, or both, during an acute hospitalization immediately preceding the inpatient rehabilitation stay and also meet one or more of the following specific criteria:

(1) The patient underwent bilateral knee or bilateral hip joint replacement surgery during the acute hospital admission immediately preceding the IRF admission.

(2) The patient is extremely obese with a Body Mass Index of at least 50 at the time of admission to the IRF.

(3) The patient is age 85 or older at the time of admission to the IRF.

(3) Have in effect a preadmission screening procedure under which each prospective patient's condition and medical history are reviewed to determine whether the patient is likely to benefit significantly from an intensive inpatient hospital program or assessment.

(4) Ensure that the patients receive close medical supervision and furnish, through the use of qualified personnel, rehabilitation nursing, physical therapy, and occupational therapy, plus, as needed, speech therapy, social or psychological services, and orthotic and prosthetic services.

(5) Have a director of rehabilitation who—

(i) Provides services to the hospital and its inpatients on a full-time basis;

(ii) Is a doctor of medicine or osteopathy;

(iii) Is licensed under State law to practice medicine or surgery; and

(iv) Has had, after completing a one-year hospital internship, at least two years of training or experience in the medical-management of inpatients requiring rehabilitation services.

(6) Have a plan of treatment for each inpatient that is established, reviewed, and revised as needed by a physician in consultation with other professional personnel who provide services to the patient.

(7) Use a coordinated multidisciplinary team approach in the rehabilitation of each inpatient, as documented by periodic clinical entries made in the patient's medical record to note the patient's status in relationship to goal attainment, and that team conferences are held at least every two weeks to determine the appropriateness of treatment.

(8) A hospital that seeks classification under this paragraph as a rehabilitation hospital for the first full 12-month cost reporting period that occurs after it becomes a Medicare-participating hospital may provide a written certification that the inpatient population it intends to serve meets the requirements of paragraph (b)(2) of this section, instead of showing that it has treated that population during its most recent 12-month cost reporting period. The written certification is also effective for any cost reporting period of not less than one month and not more than 11 months occurring between the date the hospital began participating in Medicare and the start of the hospital's regular 12-month cost reporting period.

(9) For cost reporting periods beginning on or after October 1, 1991, if a hospital is excluded from the prospective payment systems specified in Sec. 412.1(a)(1) or is paid under the prospective payment system specified in Sec. 412.1(a)(3) for a cost reporting period under paragraph (b)(8) of this section, but the inpatient population it actually treated during that period does not meet the requirements of paragraph (b)(2) of this section, we adjust payments to the hospital retroactively in accordance with the provisions in Sec. 412.130.

(c) [Reserved]

(d) Children's hospitals. A children's hospital must—

(1) Have a provider agreement under part 489 of this chapter to participate as a hospital; and

(2) Be engaged in furnishing services to inpatients who are predominantly individuals under the age of 18.

(e) Long-term care hospitals. A long-term care hospital must meet the requirements of paragraph (e)(1) and (e)(2) of this section and, when applicable, the additional requirement of Sec. 412.22(e), to be excluded from the prospective payment system specified in Sec. 412.1(a)(1) and to be paid under the prospective payment system specified in Sec. 412.1(a)(4) and in Subpart O of this part.

(1) Provider agreements. The hospital must have a provider agreement under Part 489 of this chapter to participate as a hospital; and

(2) Average length of stay. (i) The hospital must have an average Medicare inpatient length of stay of greater than 25 days (which includes all covered and noncovered days of stay of Medicare patients) as calculated under paragraph (e)(3) of this section; or

(ii) For cost reporting periods beginning on or after August 5, 1997, a hospital that was first excluded from the prospective payment system under this section in 1986 meets the length of stay criterion if it has an average inpatient length of stay for all patients, including both Medicare and non-Medicare inpatients, of greater than 20 days and demonstrates that at least 80 percent of its annual Medicare inpatient discharges in the 12-month cost reporting period ending in fiscal year 1997 have a principal diagnosis that reflects a finding of neoplastic disease as defined in paragraph (f)(1)(iv) of this section.

(3) Calculation of average length of stay. (i) Subject to the provisions of paragraphs (e)(3)(ii) through (e)(3)(iv) of this section, the average Medicare inpatient length of stay specified under paragraph (e)(2)(i) of this section is calculated by dividing the total number of covered and noncovered days of stay of Medicare inpatients (less leave or pass days) by the number of total Medicare discharges for the hospital's most recent complete cost reporting period. Subject to the provisions of paragraphs (e)(3)(ii) through (e)(3)(iv) of this section, the average inpatient length of stay specified under paragraph (e)(2)(ii) of this section is calculated by dividing the total number of days for all patients, including both Medicare and non-Medicare inpatients (less leave or pass days) by the number of total discharges for the hospital's most recent complete cost reporting period.

(ii) Effective for cost reporting periods beginning on or after July 1, 2004, in calculating the hospital's average length of stay, if the days of a stay of an inpatient involves days of care furnished during two or more separate consecutive cost reporting periods, that is, an admission during one cost reporting period and a discharge during a future consecutive cost reporting period, the total number of days of the stay are considered to have occurred in the cost reporting period during which the inpatient was discharged. However, if after application of this provision, a hospital fails to meet the average length of stay specified under paragraphs (e)(2)(i) and (ii) of this section, Medicare will determine the hospital's average inpatient length of stay for cost reporting periods beginning on or after July 1, 2004, but before July 1, 2005, by dividing the applicable total days for Medicare inpatients under paragraph (e)(2)(i) of this section or the total days for all inpatients under paragraph (e)(2)(ii) of this section, during the cost reporting period when they occur, by the number of discharges occurring during the same cost reporting period.

(iii) If a change in a hospital's average length of stay specified under paragraph (e)(2)(i) or paragraph (e)(2)(ii) of this section is indicated, the calculation is made by the same method for the period of at least 5 months of the immediately preceding 6-month period.

(iv) If a hospital has undergone a change of ownership (as described in Sec. 489.18 of this chapter) at the start of a cost reporting period or at any time within the period of at least 5 months of the preceding 6-month period, the hospital may be excluded from the prospective payment system as a long-term care hospital for a cost reporting period if, for the period of at least 5 months of the 6 months immediately preceding the start of the period (including time before the change of ownership), the hospital has the required average length of stay, continuously operated as a hospital, and continuously participated as a hospital in Medicare.

(4) Rules applicable to new long-term care hospitals—(i) Definition. For purposes of payment under the long-term care hospital prospective payment system under subpart O of this part, a new long-term care hospital is a provider of inpatient hospital services that meets the qualifying criteria in paragraphs (e)(1) and (e)(2) of this section and, under present or previous ownership (or both), its first cost reporting period as a LTCH begins on or after October 1, 2002.

(ii) Satellite facilities and remote locations of hospitals seeking to become new long-term care hospitals. Except as specified in paragraph (e)(4)(iii) of this section, a satellite facility (as defined in Sec. 412.22(h)) or a remote location of a hospital (as defined in Sec. 413.65(a)(2) of this chapter) that voluntarily reorganizes as a separate Medicare participating hospital, with or without a concurrent change in ownership, and that seeks to qualify as a new long-term care hospital for Medicare payment purposes must demonstrate through documentation that it meets the average length of stay requirement as specified under paragraphs (e)(2)(i) or (e)(2)(ii) of this section based on discharges that occur on or after the effective date of its participation under Medicare as a separate hospital.

(iii) Provider-based facility or organization identified as a satellite facility and remote location of a hospital prior to July 1, 2003. Satellite facilities and remote locations of hospitals that became subject to the provider-based status rules under Sec. 413.65 as of July 1, 2003, that become separately participating hospitals, and that seek to qualify as long-term care hospitals for Medicare payment purposes may submit to the fiscal intermediary discharge data gathered during 5 months of the immediate 6 months preceding the facility's separation from the main hospital for calculation of the average length of stay specified under paragraph (e)(2)(i) or paragraph (e)(2)(ii) of this section.

(f) Cancer hospitals—(1) General rule. Except as provided in paragraph (f)(2) of this section, if a hospital meets the following criteria, it is classified as a cancer hospital and is excluded from the prospective payment systems beginning with its first cost reporting period beginning on or after October 1, 1989. A hospital classified after December 19, 1989, is excluded beginning with its first cost reporting period beginning after the date of its classification.

(i) It was recognized as a comprehensive cancer center or clinical cancer research center by the National Cancer Institute of the National Institutes of Health as of April 20, 1983.

(ii) It is classified on or before December 31, 1990, or, if on December 19, 1989, the hospital was located in a State operating a demonstration project under section 1814(b) of the Act, the classification is made on or before December 31, 1991.

(iii) It demonstrates that the entire facility is organized primarily for treatment of and research on cancer (that is, the facility is not a subunit of an acute general hospital or university-based medical center).

(iv) It shows that at least 50 percent of its total discharges have a principal diagnosis that reflects a finding of neoplastic disease.

(The principal diagnosis for this purpose is defined as the condition established after study to be chiefly responsible for occasioning the admission of the patient to the hospital. For the purposes of meeting this definition, only discharges with ICD-9-CM principal diagnosis codes of 140 through 239, V58.0, V58.1, V66.1, V66.2, or 990 will be considered to reflect neoplastic disease.)

(2) **Alternative.** A hospital that applied for and was denied, on or before December 31, 1990, classification as a cancer hospital under the criteria set forth in paragraph (f)(1) of this section is classified as a cancer hospital and is excluded from the prospective payment systems beginning with its first cost reporting period beginning on or after January 1, 1991, if it meets the criterion set forth in paragraph (f)(1)(i) of this section and the hospital is—

(i) Licensed for fewer than 50 acute care beds as of August 5, 1997;

(ii) Is located in a State that as of December 19, 1989, was not operating a demonstration project under section 1814(b) of the Act; and

(iii) Demonstrates that, for the 4-year period ending on December 31, 1996, at least 50 percent of its total discharges have a principal diagnosis that reflects a finding of neoplastic disease as defined in paragraph (f)(1)(iv) of this section.

(g) **Hospitals outside the 50 States, the District of Columbia, or Puerto Rico.** A hospital is excluded from the prospective payment systems if it is not located in one of the fifty States, the District of Columbia, or Puerto Rico.

(h) **Hospitals reimbursed under special arrangements.** A hospital must be excluded from prospective payment for inpatient hospital services if it is reimbursed under special arrangement as provided in Sec. 412.22(c).

(i) **Changes in classification of hospitals.** For purposes of exclusions from the prospective payment system, the classification of a hospital is effective for the hospital's entire cost reporting period. Any changes in the classification of a hospital are made only at the start of a cost reporting period.

[50 FR 12741, Mar. 29, 1985, as amended at 50 FR 35688, Sept. 3, 1985; 51 FR 22041, June 17, 1986; 51 FR 31496, Sept. 3, 1986; 52 FR 33057, Sept. 1, 1987; 55 FR 36068, Sept. 4, 1990; 55 FR 46887, Nov. 7, 1990; 56 FR 43240, Aug. 30, 1991; 57 FR 39820, Sept. 1, 1992; 59 FR 45396, Sept. 1, 1994; 60 FR 45846, Sept. 1, 1995; 62 FR 46026, Aug. 29, 1997; 66 FR 39933, Aug. 1, 2001; 66 FR 41386, Aug. 7, 2001; 67 FR 56048, Aug. 30, 2002; 68 FR 45469, Aug. 1, 2003; 69 FR 25720, May 7, 2004; 69 FR 25775, May 7, 2004; 69 FR 66976, Nov. 15, 2004]
***

Subpart C—Conditions for Payment Under the Prospective Payment Systems for Inpatient Operating Costs and Inpatient Capital-Related Costs

Sec. 412.42   Limitations on charges to beneficiaries.

(a) Prohibited charges. A hospital may not charge a beneficiary for any services for which payment is made by Medicare, even if the hospital's costs of furnishing services to that beneficiary are greater than the amount the hospital is paid under the prospective payment systems.

(b) Permitted charges—Stay covered. A hospital receiving payment under the prospective payment systems for a covered hospital stay (that is, a stay that includes at least one covered day) may charge the Medicare beneficiary or other person only for the following:

(1) The applicable deductible and coinsurance amounts under Sec. Sec. 409.82, 409.83, and 409.87 of this chapter.

(2) Noncovered items and services, furnished at any time during a covered stay, unless they are excluded from coverage only on the basis of the following:

(i) The exclusion of custodial care under Sec. 405.310(g) of this chapter (see paragraph (c) of this section for when charges may be made for custodial care).

(ii) The exclusion of medically unnecessary items and services under Sec. 405.310(k) of this chapter (see paragraphs (c) and (d) of this section for when charges may be made for medically unnecessary items and services).

(iii) The exclusion under Sec. 405.310(m) of this chapter of nonphysician services furnished to hospital inpatients by other than the hospital or a provider or supplier under arrangements made by the hospital.

(iv) The exclusion of items and services furnished when the patient is not entitled to Medicare Part A benefits under subpart A of part 406 of this chapter (see paragraph (e) of this section for when charges may be made for items and services furnished when the patient is not entitled to benefits).

(v) The exclusion of items and services furnished after Medicare Part A benefits are exhausted under Sec. 409.61 of this chapter (see paragraph (e) of this section for when charges may be made for items and services furnished after benefits are exhausted).

(c) Custodial care and medically unnecessary inpatient hospital care. A hospital may charge a beneficiary for services excluded from coverage on the basis of Sec. 411.15(g) of this chapter (custodial care) or Sec. 411.15(k) of this chapter (medically unnecessary services) and furnished by the hospital after all of the following conditions have been met:

(1) The hospital (acting directly or through its utilization review committee) determines that the beneficiary no longer requires inpatient hospital care. (The phrase "inpatient hospital care" includes cases where a beneficiary needs a SNF level of care, but, under Medicare criteria, a SNF-level bed is not available. This also means that a hospital may find that a patient awaiting SNF placement no

longer requires inpatient hospital care because either a SNF-level bed has become available or the patient no longer requires SNF-level care.)

(2) The attending physician agrees with the hospital's determination in writing (for example, by issuing a written discharge order). If the hospital believes that the beneficiary does not require inpatient hospital care but is unable to obtain the agreement of the physician, it may request an immediate review of the case by the QIO. Concurrence by the QIO in the hospital's determination will serve in lieu of the physician's agreement.

(3) The hospital (acting directly or through its utilization review committee) notifies the beneficiary (or person acting on his or her behalf) in writing that—

(i) In the hospital's opinion, and with the attending physician's concurrence or that of the QIO, the beneficiary no longer requires inpatient hospital care;

(ii) Customary charges will be made for continued hospital care beyond the second day following the date of the notice;

(iii) The QIO will make a formal determination on the validity of the hospital's finding if the beneficiary remains in the hospital after he or she is liable for charges;

(iv) The determination of the QIO made after the beneficiary received the purportedly noncovered services will be appealable by the hospital, the attending physician, or the beneficiary under the appeals procedures that apply to QIO determinations affecting Medicare Part A payment; and

(v) The charges for continued care will be invalid and refunded if collected by the hospital, to the extent that a finding is made that the beneficiary required continued care beyond the point indicated by the hospital.

(4) If the beneficiary remains in the hospital after the appropriate notification, and the hospital, the physician who concurred in the hospital determination on which the notice was based, or QIO subsequently finds that the beneficiary requires an acute level of inpatient hospital care, the hospital may not charge the beneficiary for continued care until the hospital once again determines that the beneficiary no longer requires inpatient care, secures concurrence, and notifies the beneficiary, as required in paragraphs (c)(1), (c)(2), and (c)(3) of this section.

(d) Medically unnecessary diagnostic and therapeutic services. A hospital may charge a beneficiary for diagnostic procedures and studies, and therapeutic procedures and courses of treatment (for example, experimental procedures) that are excluded from coverage under Sec. 405.310(k) of this chapter (medically unnecessary items and services), even though the beneficiary requires continued inpatient hospital care, if those services are furnished after the beneficiary (or the person acting on his or her behalf) has acknowledged in writing that the hospital (acting directly or through its utilization review committee and with the concurrence of the intermediary) has informed him or her as follows:

(1) In the hospital's opinion, which has been agreed to by the intermediary, the services to be furnished are not considered reasonable and necessary under Medicare.

(2) Customary charges will be made if he or she receives the services.

(3) If the beneficiary receives the services, a formal determination on the validity of the hospital's finding is made by the intermediary and, to the extent that the decision requires the exercise of medical judgment, the QIO.

(4) The determination is appealable by the hospital, the attending physician, or the beneficiary under the appeals procedure that applies to determinations affecting Medicare Part A payment.

(5) The charges for the services will be invalid and, to the extent collected, will be refunded by the hospital if the services are found to be covered by Medicare.

(e) Services furnished on days when the individual is not entitled to Medicare Part A benefits or has exhausted the available benefits. The hospital may charge the beneficiary its customary charges for noncovered items and services furnished on outlier days (as described in Subpart F of this part) for which payment is denied because the beneficiary is not entitled to Medicare Part A or his or her Medicare Part A benefits are exhausted.

(1) If payment is considered for outlier days, the entire stay is reviewed and days up to the number of days in excess of the outlier threshold may be denied on the basis of nonentitlement to Part A or exhaustion of benefits.

(2) In applying this rule, the latest days will be denied first.

(f) Differential for private room or other luxury services. The hospital may charge the beneficiary the customary charge differential for a private room or other luxury service that is more expensive than is medically required and is furnished for the personal comfort of the beneficiary at his or her request (or the request of the person acting on his or her behalf).

(g) Review. (1) The QIO or intermediary may review any cases in which the hospital advises the beneficiary (or the person acting on his or her behalf) of the noncoverage of the services in accordance with paragraph (c)(3) or (d) of this section.

(2) The hospital must identify such cases to the QIO or intermediary in accordance with CMS instructions.

[50 FR 12741, Mar. 29, 1985, as amended at 50 FR 35688, Sept. 3, 1985; 54 FR 41747, Oct. 11, 1989; 57 FR 39821, Sept. 1, 1992]
***

Subpart D—Basic Methodology for Determining Prospective Payment Federal Rates for Inpatient Operating Costs

Sec. 412.60   DRG classification and weighting factors.

(a) Diagnosis-related groups. CMS establishs a classification of inpatient hospital discharges by Diagnosis-Related Groups (DRGs).

(b) DRG weighting factors. CMS assigns, for each DRG, an appropriate weighting factor that reflects the estimated relative cost of hospital resources used with respect to discharges classified within that group compared to discharges classified within other groups.

(c) **Assignment of discharges to DRGs.** CMS establishs a methodology for classifying specific hospital discharges within DRGs which ensures that each hospital discharge is appropriately assigned to a single DRG based on essential data abstracted from the inpatient bill for that discharge.

(1) The classification of a particular discharge is based, as appropriate, on the patient's age, sex, principal diagnosis (that is, the diagnosis established after study to be chiefly responsible for causing the patient's admission to the hospital), secondary diagnoses, procedures performed, and discharge status.

(2) Each discharge is assigned to only one DRG (related, except as provided in paragraph (c)(3) of this section, to the patient's principal diagnosis) regardless of the number of conditions treated or services furnished during the patient's stay.

(3) When the discharge data submitted by a hospital show a surgical procedure unrelated to a patient's principal diagnosis, the bill is returned to the hospital for validation and reverification. CMS's DRG classification system provides a DRG, and an appropriate weighting factor, for the group of cases for which the unrelated diagnosis and procedure are confirmed.

(d) **Review of DRG assignment.** (1) A hospital has 60 days after the date of the notice of the initial assignment of a discharge to a DRG to request a review of that assignment. The hospital may submit additional information as a part of its request.

(2) The intermediary reviews the hospital's request and any additional information and decides whether a change in the DRG assignment is appropriate. If the intermediary decides that a higher-weighted DRG should be assigned, the case will be reviewed by the appropriate QIO as specified in Sec. 466.71(c)(2) of this chapter.

(3) Following the 60-day period described in paragraph (d)(1) of this section, the hospital may not submit additional information with respect to the DRG assignment or otherwise revise its claim.

(e) **Revision of DRG classification and weighting factors.** Beginning with discharges in fiscal year 1988, CMS adjusts the classifications and weighting factors established under paragraphs (a) and (b) of this section at least annually to reflect changes in treatment patterns, technology, and other factors that may change the relative use of hospital resources.

[50 FR 12741, Mar. 29, 1985, as amended at 52 FR 33057, Sept. 1, 1987; 57 FR 39821, Sept. 1, 1992; 59 FR 45397, Sept. 1, 1994]

CHAPTER 3

SKILLED NURSING FACILITY COVERAGE

§3.01 INTRODUCTION

The Medicare skilled nursing facility (SNF) benefit provides limited but valuable health care benefits for Medicare beneficiaries. It is, however, one of the most misunderstood areas of Medicare. Many people mistakenly believe that Medicare does not cover nursing home care at all. Others believe that Medicare covers long-term care. Still others realize there is limited coverage, but they do not understand that the level of care received (*e.g.*, skilled versus only custodial care) affects coverage.

Medicare coverage is available for up to 100 days per benefit period if the patient has had a qualifying three-day hospital stay and requires daily skilled care. If covered, the first 20 days are paid in full, and the patient must meet a copayment obligation for days 21 to 100.

§3.02 COVERAGE

Medicare will cover necessary post-hospital extended care services for up to 100 days.[1] Extended care services are defined in the statute as nursing care and rehabilitation provided to a Medicare beneficiary who is an inpatient in a SNF.[2] Such services must be provided daily, and the condition treated in the SNF must be one for which the patient received hospital services or a condition that arose at the SNF while the individual was being treated for a condition for which the hospital services were received.[3] Medicare covers the first 20 days in full; however, there is a copayment for the next 80 days. The daily copayment is equal to one-eighth of the hospital deductible amount.[4] Accordingly, for a 100-day stay in 2007, the patient would be responsible for $9,820 (80 coinsurance days × $124.00/day).

This is a significant amount of money, which either comes out of the beneficiary's pocket or is covered by a Medigap insurance policy.5 The beneficiary copayment obligation can present problems to Medicare beneficiaries. Although a patient's Medigap policy may cover the SNF copayment, the beneficiary must pay premiums for this private supplemental insurance coverage. Long-term care insurance policies are now offered in many states; however, these policies are generally medically underwritten, coverage may be limited, and premiums may be expensive.

Additional details regarding the skilled nursing facility coverage criteria are set forth in the Code of Federal Regulations promulgated by the Secretary

---

[1] 42 U.S.C. §1395d(a)(2)(A).

[2] 42 U.S.C. §1395x(h).

[3] 42 U.S.C. §1395f(a)(2)(B); 42 C.F.R. §409.31(b).

[4] 42 C.F.R. §409.85(a)(2).

of the Department of Health and Human Services.[5] The regulations also define covered skilled *nursing* services.[6] The regulations state, for example, that Medicare covers skilled nursing services of overall management and evaluation of a care plan, observation and assessment of a patient's changing condition, and patient education services.[7]

The regulations also state that Medicare coverage is available for *rehabilitation* services for the ongoing assessment of rehabilitation needs and potential, therapeutic exercises or activities, gait evaluation and training, range of motion exercises, *and* maintenance therapy.[8] Services may be considered skilled, and therefore coverable by Medicare, if they are necessary to *maintain* current status or to prevent further deterioration,[9] and if they must be provided by or under the supervision of a registered nurse or therapist.[10] The regulations explicitly state that in determining whether skilled rehabilitation services are required, the restoration potential of the individual is not dispositive.[11] These are particularly important sections of the regulations since those who administer the Medicare program regularly deny coverage on the grounds that the care or therapy required is "maintenance only" and that the patient's underlying condition will not improve.

§3.03   QUALIFYING CRITERIA

[A]   Basic Eligibility and Coverage

The following basic statutory requirements must be addressed when evaluating the availability of the Medicare Skilled Nursing Facility (SNF) benefit:

- Only admissions after a three-day hospital stay are covered;

- Ordinarily, post-hospital transfer to a skilled nursing facility must be made within 30 days after leaving the hospital;

- The patient must require daily skilled nursing and/or rehabilitation in order to qualify for coverage;

- The skilled services must be provided on a daily basis;

---

[5] 42 C.F.R. §§409.20 *et seq.*, 409.30, *et seq.* See also Centers for Medicare & Medicaid Servs., Medicare Benefit Policy Manual, CMS Pub., 100-2, Ch. 8, §§10, *et seq.*

[6] 42 C.F.R. §§409.21, 409.33(a), (b).

[7] 42 C.F.R. §§409.21, 409.33(a)(1)–(3). The regulations implementing a prospective payment system, a system based on resource utilization groups (RUGs), deleted these examples. (*See* preamble to May 12, 1998, regulations, 63 Fed. Reg. 26,284–26,285, noting an intent that the RUGs act as proxies for observation, assessment, management, and patient education.) In July 1999 these examples were reinstated into the regulations. 64 Fed. Reg. 41,670 (July 30, 1999); 42 C.F.R. §409.33(a)(1)–(3).

[8] 42 C.F.R. §409.33(c).

[9] 42 C.F.R. §§409.32(c), 409.33(c)(5).

[10] 42 C.F.R. §§409.32, 409.33(a), (b).

[11] 42 C.F.R. §409.32(c).

- Skilled care must be related to the condition for which the patient was hospitalized;
- A maximum of 100 days per spell of illness may be covered;
- As a practical matter, the care must be required on an inpatient basis.

[B] Three-Day Test

The Medicare statute limits coverage of skilled nursing facility stays to:

> . . . extended care services furnished an individual after transfer from a hospital in which he was a patient for not less than three consecutive days before his discharge from the hospital in connection with such transfer. For purposes of the preceding sentence, items and services shall be deemed to have been furnished to an individual after transfer from a hospital, and he shall be deemed to have been a patient in the hospital immediately before transfer therefrom, if he is admitted to the skilled nursing facility within 30 days after discharge from such hospital. . . . [12]

Accordingly, to qualify for coverage, a Medicare patient must first be an inpatient of a hospital for three days, and must be transferred to a Medicare-participating skilled nursing facility within 30 days of being discharged from the hospital.[13] The day of discharge does not count as one of the three qualifying days. When the patient is discharged on the fourth day, the advocate must make certain that the date the patient was taken to the hospital is the actual admission date.

Frequently the patient is taken to the hospital in an emergency situation and admitted through the hospital emergency room. However, hospitals often keep patients in the emergency room under observation for lengthy periods of time, even after a decision has been made to admit. Sometimes delays occur because hospital personnel have not had time to do the paperwork for admission. If an admission is logged in by hospital staff after midnight, the admission date is set as the next day.

In a case presenting these facts, one court has ruled that if the emergency room care constitutes one part of a course of treatment that continues after the formalities of admission are completed, time spent by the patient in the emergency room should count toward the required three-day hospital stay.[14]

---

[12] 42 U.S.C. §1395x(i).

[13] Id.; Medicare Benefit Policy Manual, Pub. 100-02, Ch. 8, §20.1.

[14] Jenkel v. Shalala, 845 F. Supp. 69 (D. Conn. 1994). Sometimes patients will be treated in the emergency room and never formally be admitted to the hospital, thus failing to satisfy the three-day prior hospitalization requirement and frustrating access to Medicare SNF coverage, and sometimes, access to services. If appropriate, advocates may wish to address this failure to admit (no hospitalization) issue as an aspect of "patient dumping." See, e.g., National Health Law Program, Protecting Residents Against Improper Discharge from Hospitals, 27 Clearinghouse Rev. 101 (1993). A similar problem is that of extremely short hospital stays—too short to meet the three-day prior hospitalization requirement.

For example, a patient admitted to the emergency room at 10:00 P.M. Monday, but not taken to her hospital room until 1:00 A.M. Tuesday morning, would be technically admitted on Tuesday. If the patient is discharged to a SNF on Thursday, he or she will not have met the qualifying three-day hospital stay requirement. In such a situation, the advocate should argue that the patient did actually enter the hospital on Monday, and stayed for three days, not including the day of discharge.[15] It would be patently inequitable for this beneficiary to forfeit SNF coverage when he or she *was* actually in the hospital for three days. Further, case law clearly indicates that the Medicare Act is to be broadly interpreted, *in favor* of the beneficiary.[16]

Recent litigation in the context of the three-day prior hospitalization requirement has focused on the failure of a Medicare-participating hospital to admit a beneficiary and bill Medicare for services provided to a beneficiary kept on a regular hospital floor and provided nursing and other services, but not "admitted" to the hospital. This status—"observation status"—has resulted in the patient's not qualifying for SNF care and having to pay privately, depleting all his or her resources, with no ability to get the matter before the Medicare agency for an initial determination of whether he or she was "admitted" to the hospital for Medicare purposes.[17]

A pending case, filed as a nationwide class action, challenges CMS's policy of refusing to count time spent in an emergency room or in observation status towards the three-day qualifying hospital stay.[18]

[C] Thirty-Day Test

The law provides that a patient must be admitted to the SNF within 30 days of discharge to the hospital.[19] The regulations and Medicare Benefit Policy Manual recognize limited exceptions to the 30-day rule. If it is not "medically appropriate" to begin the post-hospital SNF care within the 30-day period and if it is "medically predictable" at the time of discharge from the hospital that the beneficiary will need covered care in a "predeterminable time period," treatment may begin at a later date when it is medically appropriate to begin an active course of treatment or therapy.[20] For example, a patient recovering from a hip fracture will require skilled

---

[15] *See* Jenkel, *supra* note 14.

[16] Rosenburg v. Richardson, 538 F.2d 487, 490 (2d Cir. 1976).

[17] *See* Lormore v. Shalala, Civ. Action No. 3.00CV563 (D. Conn. Aug. 24, 2000) (dismissed by stipulation and remanded to fiscal intermediary).

[18] *See* Landers v. Leavitt, No. 3:04CV1988 JCH (D. Conn. Nov. 24, 2004). The court in it recent ruling deferred to the government's interpretation of the rule that conditions Medicare coverage for SNF care or spending at least three prior calendar days in the hospital. See, http://www.nysd. uscourts.gov/courtweb/public.htm, and go to *Landers v. Leavitt*; and on Westlaw at 2006 WL 2560297.

[19] 42 U.S.C. §1395x(i).

[20] 42 C.F.R. §409.30(b)(2); Medicare Benefit Policy Manual, Pub. 100-2, Ch. 8, §20.2.2.

therapy services. However, the patient may be non-weight-bearing during the 30-day period after discharge from the hospital. In this case, it would not be appropriate to begin therapy until the patient achieves a weight-bearing status and the fracture has had time to heal. The Medicare Benefit Policy Manual recognizes four to six weeks after hospital discharge as an appropriate and predictable time to begin therapy for a hip fracture.[21]

Even if the beneficiary with a hip fracture goes to a SNF, leaves after two days, and returns five weeks later for predictable rehabilitative care, both SNF stays are covered by Medicare.[22] Similarly, a beneficiary who is immediately admitted to a SNF following discharge from a hospital and receives *non-covered care* will get Mcdicare coverage at a later time if it was "medically predictable that covered SNF care would be required at a predeterminable time period."[23] The example in the Manual is a beneficiary whose leg is amputated who, after the stump is healed, requires daily skilled rehabilitative services to learn how to use a prosthesis.[24] The Manual further recognizes that if "complications" prevent initiation of deferred care—for example, the amputee's stump becomes infected—the SNF stay may be covered "even though care is not started within the usual anticipated time frame."[25]

However, if a beneficiary's medical needs are *not* predictable at the time of discharge from the hospital, admission to a SNF after 30 days will *not* fall within the exception to the 30-day rule.[26] The Manual's example is a beneficiary who receives covered care, but six weeks later, experiences an unexpected change in condition and again requires skilled care. The beneficiary's second need for skilled care is not covered by Medicare.[27]

The 30-day transfer requirement is also considered met if a beneficiary receiving covered SNF care "leaves a SNF and is readmitted to the same or any other participating SNF for further covered care within 30 days of the last covered skilled day."[28]

[D] Skilled Level-of-Care Requirement

Once a patient has established a qualifying hospital stay, Medicare payment for post-hospital extended care services will be available only when:

> . . . such services are or were required to be given because the individual needs
> or needed on a daily basis skilled nursing care (provided directly by or

---

[21] Medicare Benefit Policy Manual, Pub. 100-02, Ch. 8, §20.2.2.1.

[22] Medicare Benefit Policy Manual, Pub. 100-02, Ch. 8, §20.2.2.3, Example 1.

[23] Medicare Benefit Policy Manual, Pub. 100-02, Ch. 8, §20.2.2.3, Example 3.

[24] Medicare Benefit Policy Manual, Pub. 100-02, Ch. 8, §20.2.2.3, Example 2.

[25] Medicare Benefit Policy Manual, Pub. 100-02, Ch. 8, §20.2.2.4.

[26] Medicare Benefit Policy Manual, Pub. 100-02, Ch. 8, §20.2.2.2.

[27] Medicare Beneficiary Policy Manual, Pub. No. 100-02, Ch. 8, §20.2.2.3, Example 2.

[28] Medicare Benefit Policy Manual, Pub. 100-2, Ch. 8, §20.2.3.

requiring the supervision of skilled nursing personnel) or other skilled rehabilitation services, which as a practical matter can only be provided in a skilled nursing facility on an inpatient basis, for any of the conditions with respect to which he was receiving inpatient hospital services . . . prior to transfer to the skilled nursing facility. . . . [29]

These are four separate factors: services must reflect (1) skilled care; (2) that is required on a daily basis; (3) is provided, as a practical matter, only on an inpatient basis in a SNF; and (4) services must be reasonable and necessary. Analysis begins with whether the patient needs skilled care.[30]

A beneficiary admitted directly to a SNF after a three or more day hospital stay is presumed to meet the level of care for SNF coverage for the first five days if he or she is assigned to one of the upper 35 Resource Utilization Groups (RUG-III) identified under Medicare's prospective payment system for SNFs.[31] A beneficiary assigned to one of the lower 18 RUG-III categories may receive Medicare-covered care; an individual level of care determination must be made, "using existing administrative criteria and procedures."[32]

The Medicare program further defines a skilled nursing facility as an institution "primarily engaged in providing to patients (A) skilled nursing care and related services for patients who require medical or nursing care, or (B) rehabilitation services for the rehabilitation of injured, disabled, or sick persons."[33]

It is, therefore, necessary that a patient receive *skilled*, as opposed to *custodial*, care. Medicare will not reimburse any expenses when the level of care is only custodial.[34] However, custodial services are often provided in addition to skilled care. The key is that the patient require and receive skilled care on a daily basis and not just custodial care. If the skilled services are provided frequently, but not on a daily basis, Medicare coverage will not be available.

[1] Skilled Nursing or Rehabilitation Services

The regulations state the patient must require skilled nursing or rehabilitation services that are ordered by the attending physician.[35] The skilled services must be provided on a daily basis by, or furnished under the supervision of, skilled personnel.[36] "General supervision" "requires initial direction and periodic

---

[29] 42 U.S.C. §1395f(a)(2)(B).

[30] Medicare Beneficiary Policy Manual, Pub. 100-02, Ch. 8, §30.

[31] Medicare Benefit Policy Manual, Pub. 100-02, Ch. 8, §30.1. CMS annually publishes the RUGs categories that are subject to the presumption of SNF coverage.

[32] Medicare Benefit Policy Manual, Pub. 100-02, Ch. 8, §30.1.

[33] 42 U.S.C. §1395i-3(a)(1).

[34] 42 U.S.C. §1395y(a)(9).

[35] 42 C.F.R. §409.31(a)(1).

[36] 42 C.F.R. §409.31(a)(3), (b); Medicare Benefit Policy Manual, Pub. 100-02, Ch. 8, §30.2.1.

inspection of the actual activity," but not the physical presence of the supervisor whenever the assistant "is performing services."[37] In addition, the skilled services must be related to a condition for which the patient received inpatient hospital care or that arose at the SNF while the patient was being treated for such a condition.[38]

The inherent complexity of a service must be evaluated in the context of the patient's need for safe and effective service delivery.[39] Special medical complications may substantiate the need for skilled services that are not ordinarily required.[40] For example, while a qualified physical therapist is not usually required to give whirlpool baths, professional therapy services may be needed for a beneficiary whose condition "is complicated by circulatory deficiency, areas of desensitization, or open wounds."[41] Similarly, skilled management of unskilled services may justify the need for Medicare-covered care.[42] When rehabilitation services are the primary services supporting Medicare coverage, the key issue is whether the skills of a therapist are needed, not whether the patient has "potential for recovery."[43]

The regulations contain a list of examples of skilled nursing and rehabilitation services.[44] Some of the examples constitute skilled nursing care only if the services of a skilled or professional person are required. Other examples automatically constitute covered skilled nursing services. Skilled rehabilitation services are separately described. Advocates must evaluate the patient's medical records with these regulations in mind in order to identify the qualifying services and to document them for appeal.

The list of skilled *nursing* services may include the following when the skills of a technical or professional person are needed:[45]

- **Overall management and evaluation of care plan,**[46] Managing and evaluating a care plan constitutes skilled nursing services when skilled nursing personnel are required "to meet the patient's medical needs, promote recovery, and ensure medical safety."[47] Nonskilled services may require skilled management "when the condition of the beneficiary is such that there is an expectation that a change

---

[37] Medicare Benefit Policy Manual, Pub. 100-02, Ch. 8, §30.2.1, NOTE.

[38] 42 U.S.C. §1395f(a)(2)(B), §1395x(i); 42 C.F.R. §409.31(b)(2)(i), (ii) and 424.20.

[39] 42 C.F.R. §409.32(a).

[40] 42 C.F.R. §409.32(b).

[41] Medicare Benefit Policy Manual, Pub. 100-02, Ch. 8, §30.2.2 (second example).

[42] Medicare Benefit Policy Manual, Pub. 100-02, Ch. 8, §30.2.2 (third example, describing resident with multiple physical and mental impairments).

[43] Medicare Benefit Policy Manual, Pub. 100-02, Ch. 8 (first example).

[44] 42 C.F.R. §409.33. *See also* Medicare Benefit Policy Manual, Pub. 100-02, Ch. 8, §30.2 (Skilled Nursing and Skilled Rehabilitation Services).

[45] 42 C.F.R. §409.33(a). *See also* Medicare Benefit Policy Manual, Pub. 100-2, Ch. 8, §30.2.

[46] 42 C.F.R. §409.33(a)(1); Medicare Benefit Policy Manual, Pub. 100-02, Ch. 8, §30.2.3.1.

[47] 42 C.F.R. §409.33(a)(1)(i); Medicare Benefit Policy Manual, Pub. 100-02, Ch. 8, §30.2.3.1.

in condition is likely without that intervention."[48] The regulation's sole example and the Manual's first example find skilled personnel are necessary, based on the patient's condition, age, and immobility, which together create "a high potential for serious complications."[49] The second Manual example also supports a finding of skilled oversight based on the patient's immobility, confusion, and chest congestion, which create "high probability of relapse."[50] If the patient's record "clearly establishes that there was a likely potential for serious complications without skilled management, the intermediary will assume that skilled care was provided.[51]

- **Observation and assessment of the patient's changing condition**, if treatment may need to be modified, new medical procedures may need to be initiated, or the patient's treatment regimen needs to be stabilized.[52] The examples in the regulations and Manual illustrate the fact-specific nature of the inquiry.[53] Skilled observation is appropriate if there is a "reasonable probability" of a potential complication, even if the complication never develops.[54] The regulation and Manual also recognize that observation and assessment may be required for patients with primary or secondary psychiatric diagnoses, such as depression, anxiety, or agitation.[55]

- **Patient education services** to train and teach patients "self-maintenance" and "how to manage their treatment regimen."[56] The regulations provides two examples: a patient with a recent leg amputation, who needs skilled personnel to provide gait training and to teach care of the prothesis; and a newly diagnosed diabetic patient who needs skilled personnel to teach self-administration of insulin and foot-care precautions.[57] Additional examples in the Manual include teaching patients to self-administer medications, insulin injections, or medical gases; to perform self-catherization; and to self-administer gastrostomy feedings.[58]

---

[48] Medicare Benefit Policy Manual, Pub. 100-02, Ch. 8, §30.2.3.1.

[49] 42 C.F.R. §409.33(a)(1)(ii); Medicare Benefit Policy Manual, Pub. 100-02, Ch. 8, §30.2.3.1 (example 1).

[50] Medicare Benefit Policy Manual, Pub. 100-02, Ch. 8, §30.2.3. (example 2).

[51] Medicare Benefit Policy Manual, Pub. 100-02, Ch. 8, §30.2.3.1.

[52] 42 C.F.R. §409.33(a)(2); Medicare Benefit Policy Manual, Pub. 100-02, Ch. 8, §30.2.3.2.

[53] 42 C.F.R. §409.33(1)(2)(ii); Medicare Benefit Policy Manual, Pub. 100-02, Ch. 8, §30.232.

[54] Medicare Benefit Policy Manual, Pub. 100-02, Ch. 8, §30.2.3.1.

[55] 42 C.F.R. §409.33(a)(2)(ii); Medicare Benefit Policy Manual, Pub. 100-02, Ch. 8, §30.2.3.1.

[56] 42 C.F.R. §409.33(a)(3); Medicare Benefit Policy Manual, Pub. 100-02, Ch. 8, §30.2.3.3, respectively.

[57] 42 C.F.R. §409.33(a)(3)(ii).

[58] Medicare Benefit Policy Manual, Pub. 100-02, Ch. 8, §30.2.3.1.

The Manual describes as "questionable situations" those involving patients whose primary need is oral medication or who are "capable of independent ambulation, dressing, feeding, and hygiene."[59]

- If a patient is receiving one or more of the following skilled services on a daily basis, the requirement for receiving daily skilled care is met *per se*:[60]
- "Intravenous/intramuscular injections and intravenous feeding;"
- "Enteral feeding that comprises at least 26 percent of daily calorie requirements and provides at least 501 milliliters of fluid per day;"
- "Naso-pharyngeal and tracheostomy aspiration;"
- "Insertion, sterile irrigation, and replacement of suprapubic catheters;"
- "Application of dressings involving prescription medications and aseptic techniques;"
- "Treatment of extensive decubitus ulcers" (the Manual says stage 3 or worse) or "other widespread skin disorders;"
- "Heat treatments which have been specifically ordered by a physician as part of active treatment and which require observation by nurses to adequately evaluate the patient's progress;"
- "Initial phases of a regimen involving administration of medical gases;"
- "Rehabilitation nursing procedures, including the related teaching and adaptive aspects of nursing, that are part of active treatment—(e.g., the institution and supervision of bowel and bladder training programs);"
- The Manual adds "Care of a colostomy during the early post-operative period in the presence of associated complications" (justification and documentation in the medical record are required).[61]

Skilled physical therapy services must be related to "an active written treatment plan" and must require "the judgment, knowledge, and skills of a qualified physical therapist."[62] The services must be needed either to improve or to establish "a safe and effective maintenance program."[63] The services must also be considered specific and effective, under accepted standards of medical practice, as well as reasonable and necessary for the treatment of the patient's condition.[64] The Manual

---

[59] Medicare Benefit Policy Manual, Pub. 100-02, Ch. 8, §30.2.4.

[60] 42 C.F.R. §409.33(b). Medicare Benefit Policy Manual, Pub. 100-02, Ch. 8, §30.3.

[61] Medicare Benefit Policy Manual, Pub. 100-02, Ch. 8, §30.3.

[62] Medicare Benefit Policy Manual, Pub. 100-02, Ch. 8, §30.4.1.1.

[63] *Id.*

[64] *Id.*

cautions that many SNF patients require services that may be provided by supportive personnel, without the supervision of a physical therapist, and that these services are not covered by Medicare as skilled physical therapy.[65]

The regulations identify services that qualify as skilled rehabilitation services, with elaboration provided in the Manual:

• "Ongoing assessment of rehabilitation needs and potential."

• "Therapeutic exercises or activities" that require skilled personnel.

• "Gait evaluation and training" needed to "restore function in a patient whose ability to walk has been impaired by neurological, muscular, or skeletal abnormality." The Manual elaborates that while gait evaluation and training by a therapist is skilled physical therapy, activities of an aide ("repetitive exercises to improve gait, or to maintain strength and endurance, and assistive walking") are not.

• "Range of motion exercises." The Manual elaborates that range of motion *tests* are skilled physical therapy; range of motion *exercises* are not, unless they are part of active treatment. Passive range of motion is not skilled physical therapy.

• "Maintenance therapy" when the maintenance program must be designed and established by a therapist. The Manual says that establishing a maintenance program "intended to prevent or minimize deterioration caused by a medical condition" is a skilled service. As an example of covered maintenance therapy, the Manual describes determining the exercises required to maintain the present level of function for a patient with Parkinson's disease, including conducting an initial evaluation, designing a maintenance program, and instructing the patient or supportive personnel to carry out the maintenance program.

• Ultrasound, shortwave, and microwave diathermy treatments.

• "Hot packs, hydrocollator, infra-red treatments, paraffin baths, and whirlpool." Although these treatments do not ordinarily require skilled therapists, a patient's condition may support use of skilled therapy services.

• Speech pathologist or audiologist services.[66] (The Manual defines speech-language pathology and occupational therapy by reference to Inpatient Hospital Services in the Medicare Benefit Policy Manual.[67])

---

[65] *Id.*

[66] 42 C.F.R. §409.33(c); Medicare Benefit Policy Manual, Pub. 100-02, Ch. 8, §30.4.1.2.

[67] Medicare Benefit Policy Manual, Pub. 100-02, Ch. 8, §§30.4.2 and 30.4.3, respectively.

Except in certain circumstances,[68] personal care services do not qualify as skilled services:[69]

- "Administration of routine oral medication, eye drops and ointments." The Manual confirms that these are not skilled services, even if the patient is unable to self-administer these medications or state law requires a nurse to dispense them.

- "General maintenance care of colostomy and ileostomy."

- "Routine services to maintain satisfactory functioning of indwelling bladder catheters."

- "Changes of dressing for noninfected post-operative or chronic conditions."

- "Prophylactic and palliative skin care, including bathing and application of creams, or treatment of minor skin problems."

- Routine incontinence care.

- General maintenance of a plaster cast. The Manual notes that a patient with a preexisting skin or circulatory condition, or who needs traction adjusted, may require skilled services.

- Routine care of braces and similar devices.

- "Use of heat as a palliative and comfort measure" (e.g., whirlpool or hydrocollator).

- Routine administration of medical gases after a regimen of therapy has been established."

- "Assistance in dressing, eating, and going to the toilet."

- "Periodic turning and positioning in bed."

- "General supervision of exercises," including carrying out of repetitive exercises in a maintenance program.[70]

The regulations provide that the restoration potential of a patient is not the controlling factor in determining whether skilled care is necessary.[71] Skilled care may be necessary to preserve the patient's current status or to prevent further

---

[68] 42 C.F.R. §409.32(b) (exceptions allowing services usually viewed as nonskilled to be considered skilled); Medicare Benefit Policy Manual, Pub. 100-2, Ch. 8, §30.5 (non-skilled supportive or personal services).

[69] 42 C.F.R. §409.33(d)(1)-(13); Medicare Benefit Policy Manual, Pub. 100-02, Ch. 8, §30.5.

[70] Medicare Benefit Policy Manual, Pub. 100-02, Ch. 8, §30.5.

[71] 42 C.F.R. §409.32(c) ("The restoration potential of a patient is not the deciding factor in determining whether skilled services are needed."); Medicare Benefit Policy Manual, Pub. 100-2, Ch. 8, §30.2.

deterioration of the patient's medical condition.[72] Similarly, physical therapy to maintain the patient's present level of functioning may be a covered service when the skills and knowledge of a therapist are needed.[73]

Skilled nursing care is necessary when the patient's physical or mental condition requires management of the various aspects of a care plan to meet the patient's needs, promote recovery, and ensure medical safety: The regulations provide, "Those activities include the management of a plan involving a variety of personal care services only when, in light of the patient's condition, the aggregate of those services requires the involvement of technical or professional personnel."[74] Similarly, skilled nursing care may be essential to observe and assess the patient's condition when it is necessary to identify and evaluate the need for modification of treatment until the patient's condition is stabilized, and to ensure that it remains so. The SNF regulations contain examples of skilled services, which include overall management and evaluation of the patient's care plan and observation and assessment of the patient's changing condition.[75]

The regulations provide a specific example of a patient with congestive heart failure. Such a patient would require close nursing observation "to detect signs of decompensation, abnormal fluid balance, or adverse effects from medications."[76] Patients with acute psychological symptoms in addition to physical problems, such as depression, anxiety, or agitation, may require skilled nursing care to ensure safety of the patient and others.[77]

[2] Daily Skilled Services

To meet the definition of *daily,* skilled nursing care, or a combination of skilled nursing services and rehabilitation services, must be provided seven days per week.[78] Skilled rehabilitation services provided five days per week satisfy the daily requirement.[79]

The Medicare Benefit Policy Manual cautions against applying the "daily" requirement "too strictly," recognizing that the requirement may be met even when therapy is suspended in an "isolated break" for a day or two (for example, due to a resident's extreme fatigue).[80]

---

[72] 42 C.F.R. §409.32(c)

[73] 42 C.F.R. §409.33(c)(5).

[74] 42 C.F.R. §409.33(a)(1).

[75] 42 C.F.R. §409.33(a)(2)(ii).

[76] 42 C.F.R. §409.33(a)(2)(ii).

[77] 42 C.F.R. §409.33(a)(2)(ii).

[78] 42 C.F.R. §409.30 (basic requirements), §409.31 (skilled level of care requirement), §409.34 (definition of "daily").

[79] 42 C.F.R. §409.34(a)(2); Medicare Benefit Policy Manual, Pub. 100-02, Ch. 8, §30.6.

[80] Medicare Benefit Policy Manual, Pub. 100-02, Ch. 8, §30.6.

A temporary absence to attend "a special religious service, holiday meal, family occasion, going on a car ride, or for a trial visit home" is not by itself evidence that a beneficiary does not need skilled care.[81] The Manual cautions facilities against taking a "conservative approach" and notifying residents "that leaving the facility will result in denial of coverage."[82] Frequent or prolonged absences, however, may suggest that the beneficiary's care needs can be met outside a SNF.

The standard for establishing the practicality of inpatient SNF care is discussed in *Goodrich v. Bowen*.[83] This decision involved Medicare coverage of daily insulin injections for 17 SNF patients. The court appropriately noted that the patients received daily insulin injections and that the administration of subcutaneous injections was at that time presumed to be a skilled nursing service pursuant to the Medicare regulations.[84] *Goodrich* addressed the criteria for establishing "practical matter," discussing the availability and feasibility of using alternative services:

> the "practical matter" criteria requires [*sic*] an individual assessment of each claimant's overall condition and actual investigation into the availability and feasibility of alternatives to inpatient SNF care. It is not sufficient for the Secretary to look at only one aspect of a claimant's care such as the need for daily insulin injections. The Secretary must assess the need for skilled service along with the other services the claimant requires, both skilled and custodial, and then arrive at a determination of the "practical matter" requirement.[85]

[3] "Practical Matter" Test

Even if daily skilled services are medically necessary, Medicare coverage may still be denied unless the services "as a practical matter, can only be provided in a SNF, on an inpatient basis."[86] Whether skilled services must be provided only in a SNF, as a "practical matter," depends on "the availability and feasibility of using more economical alternative facilities or services are considered."[87]

---

[81] Medicare Benefit Policy Manual, Pub. 100-02, Ch. 8, §30.7.3 (Example).

[82] Medicare Benefit Policy Manual, Pub. 100-02, Ch. 8, §30.7.3.

[83] [1988 Transfer Binder] Medicare & Medicaid Guide (CCH) ¶37,241, at 17,950 (D. Conn. May 31, 1988).

[84] 42 C.F.R. §409.33(b)(1). *But see* 63 Fed. Reg. 26,284 (May 12, 1998), regarding insulin injections and the skilled care concept.

[85] *See* note 68.

[86] 42 C.F.R. §409.31(b)(3). *See also* 42 C.F.R. §409.35, Medicare Benefit Policy Manual, Pub. 100-2, Ch. 8, §30.7.

[87] 42 C.F.R. §409.35(a).

The "practical matter" test evaluates whether more economical services are *actually available* to *this* beneficiary.[88]

If the daily skilled services are not available on an outpatient basis where the beneficiary lives, the "practical matter" test is satisfied and inpatient care in a SNF is covered. However, in evaluating the availability of alternative care, the issue is the feasibility of the alternative care, not whether Medicare will pay for it. As a result, if a physical therapist could provide daily physical therapy to a patient, it is not relevant to the "practical matter" determination that the patient has exceeded the outpatient therapy cap or does not participate in Medicare Part B.[89]

If transportation to the outpatient services would pose "an excessive physical hardship" to the beneficiary or would be "less economical" or "less efficient or effective" than inpatient services in the SNF, the practical matter test is also satisfied.[90] "Less economical" is determined from the perspective of the health care delivery system. If getting services in a hospital outpatient department would require an ambulance ride and providing care in a SNF would be more economical, the "economy and efficiency" test is met. Similarly, "inordinate travel costs" to a patient's isolated residence also satisfy the "economy and efficiency" test.[91]

The patient's medical condition is critical to the practicality determination. If an alternative care setting would "adversely affect a patient's medical condition," SNF care is appropriate.[92] The Manual provides an example of "a 75-year old woman who has suffered a cerebrovascular accident and cannot climb stairs safely." If the patient lives on the second floor, which is accessible only by climbing a flight of stairs, she is eligible for SNF care, even when the physical and occupational therapy she needs is available one mile from her apartment. The Manual concludes, "because of her inability to negotiate the stairs, the daily skilled services she requires cannot, as a practical matter, be provided to the patient outside the SNF."[93]

Home care is not an alternative to SNF care if the patient does not have sufficient assistance at home from "capable and willing family" or others, such as a home health agency.[94]

As with the skilled care determination, the patient's total condition is important in assessing the practical matter standard. Here, however, the patient's custodial needs are as important as, or may be more important than, the need for skilled care.

In assessing the practicalities of providing the needed care at home, rather than in a SNF, relevant questions include: Are outpatient or home health care services actually available? Does the patient have access to such services even

---

[88] *Id.*

[89] Medicare Benefit Policy Manual, Pub. 100-02, Ch. 8, §30.7.1.

[90] Medicare Benefit Policy Manual, Pub. 100-02, Ch. 8, §30.7.

[91] Medicare Benefit Policy Manual, Pub. 100-02, Ch. 8, §30.7.2 (examples 1 and 2, respectively).

[92] Medicare Benefit Policy Manual, Pub. 100-02, Ch. 8, §30.7.3.

[93] Medicare Benefit Policy Manual, Pub. 100-02, Ch. 8, §30.7.3 (example).

[94] Medicare Benefit Policy Manual, Pub. 100-02, Ch. 8, §30.7, 30.7.1.

if they are available? Is the patient able to be maintained at home in order to receive the skilled outpatient or home health care services?

[E] The Benefit Period or "Spell of Illness"

Medicare covers a maximum of 100 days of SNF care during a benefit period, known as the "spell of illness."[95] A spell of illness begins the first day a Medicare beneficiary enters a hospital or skilled nursing facility and ends when he or she has been at less than a skilled level of care, or outside a hospital or SNF, for 60 consecutive days. It is theoretically possible for a beneficiary to have more than one spell of illness during a calendar year. However, the patient must remain outside a hospital or SNF for 60 consecutive days, or, if remaining in a nursing facility, must receive less than an SNF level of care for 60 consecutive days, in order to end a spell of illness.[96]

> **Example:** Mrs. Jones is admitted to the hospital and, after a four-day stay, is transferred to the SNF on March 25. Medicare coverage is granted for 100 days, through July 3. Mrs. Jones remains in the nursing home through August 28, but does not receive either daily skilled nursing or rehabilitation services. She is then readmitted to the hospital. Upon hospital discharge, she is readmitted to the SNF.

> Mrs. Jones will not be entitled to Medicare coverage for her second SNF admission because she did not have a "break" in her spell of illness and has already received 100 days of coverage during this spell of illness. (She went without receiving daily skilled care in a hospital or SNF for only 58 days, from July 3 to August 28.) Mrs. Jones would have to receive a custodial level of care in the SNF for 60 consecutive days and then require inpatient hospital care for at least three days, in order to qualify for further Medicare SNF coverage under a new spell of illness.

[F] Care in SNF Must Be Related to Condition for Which the Patient Was Hospitalized

To meet Medicare's level of care requirements, a patient must receive services either for a condition for which the patient received inpatient hospital services or for a condition that arose while the patient was receiving care in a SNF for a condition for which the patient received inpatient hospital services.[97] In other words, there must be some connection between the patient's condition during the

---

[95] 42 U.S.C. §1395d(a)(2)(A) and §1395x(a); 42 C.F.R. §409.60; *see* Mayburg v. Secretary of HHS, 740 F.2d 100 (1st Cir. 1984); Levi v. Heckler, 736 F.2d 848 (2d Cir. 1984).

[96] 42 C.F.R. §409.60(b); Medicare General Information, Eligibility, and Entitlement Manual, Pub. 100-01, Ch. 6, §10.4.4.

[97] 42 U.S.C. §1395f(a)(2)(B); 42 C.F.R. §409.31(b)(2)(i), (ii). *See also* Medicare Benefit Policy Manual, Pub. 100-02, Ch. 3, §§10.4.2, 10.4.3.2, 10.4.4.

qualifying hospital stay and subsequent SNF admission. A problem that occasionally arises is establishing that the SNF patient is receiving skilled care that is related to the patient's prior hospitalization. The problem most often encountered is a fact-finder's requiring that a SNF patient receive the exact services for the exact condition as provided in the hospital. Such an interpretation of the law is inappropriate and should be challenged.

In *Sowell v. Richardson,*[98] the court found that hospitalization was due to the patient's general physical condition. In *Hayner v. Weinberger,*[99] the court found that the patient's underlying condition was related to the condition subsequently treated at the SNF. Both courts found the patients eligible for Medicare coverage. In *Shepack v. Bowen,*[100] the court noted, "it is critical to ascertain the interrelationship between a claimant's various illnesses in order to determine if the condition for which a claimant received skilled nursing services in an SNF was a condition for which he or she received inpatient hospital services."[101] The court remanded the case to the ALJ to obtain further medical documentation. Upon rehearing, the ALJ found the services received at the SNF were for a condition previously treated at the hospital.

A district court liberally construed 42 C.F.R. §409.31(b)(2) in *Stefanko v. Secretary of HHS.*[102] The patient was treated in the hospital for a primary condition of a fractured knee and secondary conditions of congestive heart failure, diabetes, and kidney failure. The court found that treatment in the SNF of the surgical wound and insulin injections constituted skilled care for conditions that were treated in the hospital.

Practically speaking, an advocate should always collect documentation to establish that the SNF treatment was for a condition treated and/or diagnosed in the hospital. Document all of the conditions treated during the hospitalization. Treatment may consist of monitoring a cardiac or pulmonary condition. A diabetic experiencing unstable blood sugar levels while in the hospital may require careful monitoring. The patient may be generally weak or may present complexities due to multiple conditions that require skilled management.

§3.04   IDENTIFYING COVERABLE CASES

Medicare SNF claims are suitable for Medicare coverage, and appealable if they have been denied, if they meet the following criteria:

1. The patient must have been hospitalized for at least three days, and, in most cases, must have been admitted to the SNF within 30 days of hospital discharge.

---

[98] 319 F. Supp. 689, 692 (D.S.C. 1970).

[99] 382 F. Supp. 762, 765 (E.D.N.Y. 1974).

[100] No. N-85-157 (JAC) (D. Conn. Mar. 16, 1987).

[101] *Id.,* slip. op. at 11.

[102] Medicare & Medicaid Guide (CCH) ¶38,637 (D. Conn. Apr. 18, 1990).

2. A physician must certify that the patient needs SNF care.

3. The beneficiary must require "skilled nursing or skilled rehabilitation services, or both, on a daily basis." Skilled nursing and skilled rehabilitation services are those that require the skills of technical or professional personnel such as registered nurses, licensed practical nurses, physical therapists, and occupational therapists. In order to be deemed skilled, the service must be so inherently complex that it can be safely and effectively performed only by, or under the supervision of, professional or technical personnel.

4. The skilled nursing facility must be a Medicare certified facility.

Other Important Points

1. The restoration potential of a patient is not the deciding factor in determining whether skilled services are needed.

2. The management of a plan involving only a variety of "custodial" personal care services is skilled when, in light of the patient's condition, the aggregate of those services requires the involvement of skilled personnel.

3. The requirement that a patient receive "daily" skilled services will be met if skilled *rehabilitation* services are provided *five days* per week.

4. Examples of skilled services:
    a. Overall management and evaluation of care plan;
    b. Observation and assessment of the patient's changing condition;
    c. Levin tube and gastrostomy feedings;
    d. Ongoing assessment of rehabilitation needs and potential;
    e. Therapeutic exercises or activities;
    f. Gait evaluation and training.

5. The doctor is the patient's most importantly. If it appears that Medicare coverage will be denied, ask the doctor to help demonstrate that the standards described above are met.

6. If the nursing home issues a notice saying Medicare coverage is not available and the patient seems to satisfy the criteria above, ask the nursing home to submit a claim for a formal Medicare coverage determination. The nursing home must submit a claim at the patient's or representative's request; the patient is not required to pay until he or she receives a formal determination from Medicare.

7. Don't be satisfied with a Medicare determination unreasonably limiting coverage; appeal for the benefits the patient deserves. It will take some time, but you will probably win your case.

§3.05   SNF PROSPECTIVE PAYMENT SYSTEM AND RESOURCE UTILIZATION GROUPS (RUGS)

[A]   Prospective Payment System Mandated as of July 1, 1998

The Balanced Budget Act of 1997 mandated a prospective payment system for the Medicare SNF benefit.[103] The per diem rates cover all routine service, ancillary, and capital-related costs for Part A-covered stays.

The prospective payment system uses case-mix adjustments to relate payments to resident needs. The system accounts for the relative resource use of different types of patients, based on acuity, as determined by a patient classification system called Resource Utilization Groups (RUG-III). Each Medicare-coverable patient is placed into one of eight major classifications and then into one of 53 groups. (Originally and until Jan. 1, 2006, the PPS system used seven major classifications and 44 groups.) The classifications are mutually exclusive, meaning that every patient can be placed into one classification and no patient fits into more than one classification.[104]

The process of placing patients into the RUG-III classifications requires accurate and comprehensive information-gathering about a patient's characteristics and needs. A patient's RUG-III classification has implications for both reimbursement and Medicare coverage.

[B]   Impact on Nursing Home Reimbursement

The RUG classifications are hierarchical, with the higher categories providing greater reimbursement. The prospective reimbursement system was phased in over a three-year transition period. Depending upon when a facility's cost-reporting period ends, the phase-in began either October 1, 1998, or January 1, 1999.

[C]   The Eight Major RUG-III Categories

The eight major RUG-III categories, in hierarchical order based upon intensity of resource utilization, are:

1. Extensive Plus Rehabilitation (nine classifications)

2. Rehabilitation (14 classifications)

---

[103] Pub. L. No. 105-33, 4432(a) (Aug. 5, 1997), amending 1888 of the Social Security Act, by adding subsection (e), 42 U.S.C. §1395yy, effective on or after July 1, 1998.

[104] 63 Fed. Reg. 26,251 (May 12, 1998); 64 Fed. Reg. 41,643 (July 30, 1999); 65 Fed. Reg. 46,769 (July 31, 2000); 66 Fed. Reg. 39,561 (July 31, 2001); 67 Fed. Reg. 49,797 (July 31, 2002); 68 Fed. Reg. 46,035 (Aug. 4, 2003), 68 Fed. Reg. 55,882 (Sept. 29, 2003) (correction notice), 69 Fed. Reg. 45,775 (July 30, 2004); 70 Fed. Reg. 45,026 (Aug. 4, 2005).

3. Extensive Service (three classifications)

4. Special Care (three classifications)

5. Clinically Complex (six classifications)

6. Impaired Cognition (four classifications)

7. Behavior Only (four classifications)

8. Decreased Physical Function (10 classifications)

There are 35 RUG-III classifications within the first five major categories. A patient assigned to one of these categories following a qualifying hospital stay is presumed to meet a Medicare level of care during the first five-day assessment period.[105] The remaining 18 classifications are contained within the three lowest major RUG-III categories. A patient classified into one of these categories qualifies for Medicare coverage based upon the statutory and regulatory criteria for the SNF level of care.[106]

[D] Impact on Medicare Coverage: A Presumption of Medicare Coverage for "Upper 35"

One might assume that a Medicare beneficiary who is classified into one of the top 35 RUG-III categories would have an easy time with SNF placement. There are barriers to SNF admission, however, even for some beneficiaries in the top RUG-III categories. These barriers appear to be caused by the high cost to SNFs of caring for certain groups of individuals seeking SNF admission.

When the RUG-III system was first implemented, patients who met the SNF coverage criteria, but who nevertheless experienced difficulty gaining admission to a SNF, also commonly required:

• Kidney dialysis, with roundtrip ambulance transportation to a dialysis center three times a week; or

• Radiation therapy, with roundtrip ambulance transportation; or

• Fitting of a prosthesis; or

• Certain types of chemotherapy or other intravenous medications.

All of the costs of providing services needed by patients are covered by the SNF's Medicare prospective per diem rate. Many SNFs informally communicated

---

[105] Medicare Benefit Policy Manual, Pub. 100-02, Ch. 8, §30.1; 70 Fed. Reg. 45,025, at 45,045–45,046 (Aug. 4, 2005).

[106] These Medicare-covered groups may be redesignated on an annual basis, 63 Fed. Reg. 26,251, at 26,283 (May 12, 1998) (citing 42 C.F.R. §§409.31-.35 and Medicare manuals). Effective January 1, 2006, CMS designated 53 RUGs, with the upper 35 conferring a presumption of Medicare coverage, 70 Fed. Reg. 45,025, at 45,045-45,046 (Aug. 4, 2005).

a reluctance to accept individuals needing the services described above when Medicare is the apparent payment source, because of the costs involved. As a result, that individuals who had these needs encountered difficulties in obtaining SNF placement.[107]

In the Balanced Budget Refinement Act, effective April 1, 2000, Congress amended the Medicare statute in an effort to address these problems. Effective April 1, 2000, the cost of an ambulance ride to a hospital for the purpose of obtaining kidney dialysis or radiation therapy for cancer treatment was "unbundled" from the SNF's Medicare payment. As a result, the per diem RUG reimbursement for SNF patients needing ambulance transportation for these purposes was no longer required to pay for the ambulance in addition to the services provided in the SNF. Instead, the hospital could bill separately for these costs. Later statutory and regulatory revisions to the prospective payment system excluded additional services from the PPS rates. At present, services excluded from the SNF rate,[108] and separately billed to Medicare,[109] include:

- Certain cardiac catherizations;

- Certain computerized axial topography (CAT) scans;

- Certain magnetic resonance imaging (MRIs);

- Certain ambulatory surgeries involving the use of a hospital operating room;

- Certain radiation therapies;

- Certain antiographies, and lymphatic and venous procedures;

- Emergency services;

- Ambulance services when related to an excluded service within this list; and

- Ambulance transportation related to dialysis services.

The Medicare Prescription Drug, Improvement, and Modernization Act of 2003 provided for a temporary 128% increase in the PPS per diem for any SNF patient with Acquired Immune Deficiency Syndrome (AIDS).[110]

---

[107] The Office of Inspector General reported in September 2000 that Medicare beneficiaries were difficult to place in SNFs if they needed IV antibiotics or expensive drugs or if they were medically complex, needed a ventilator, had an infectious disease or needed isolation, had renal failure or needed dialysis, had behavior problems, or needed total parental feedings. OIG, *Medicare Beneficiary Access to Skilled Nursing Facilities*, OEI-02-0330, p. 7 (Sept. 2000). In July 2001, it found similar difficulties and also identified residents who had decubitus ulcers and needed wound care. OIG, *Medicare Beneficiary Access to Skilled Nursing Facilities*, OEI-02-01-00160, p. 7 (July 2001).

[108] Medicare Claims Processing Manual, Pub. 100-04, Ch. 6, §20.1.2.

[109] Medicare Benefit Policy Manual, Pub. 100-02, Ch. 8, §10.2.

[110] MMA §511, 42 U.S.C. §1395yy(e)(12).

Payment issues may be important to keep in mind when seeking benefits for SNF patients, especially for those who are not classified into one of the 35 RUG-III categories that carry a presumption of Medicare coverage.

§3.06 PROBLEM AREAS OF CONCERN FOR THE ADVOCATE

A comprehensive understanding of the Medicare statutes, regulations, and policy is a necessary foundation for the successful advocate. Having a working knowledge of the qualifying criteria and covered services, the decision-making process, important case law, and reimbursement pressures and incentives is also useful. It is also important to have a practical sense of Medicare SNF coverage and appeals. For example, cases in which the patient received physical therapy five times per week are almost always worthy of appeal.[111] Frequent problems that stand in the way of Medicare SNF coverage are addressed below.

[A] Skilled Versus Custodial Care

The crux of every Medicare SNF coverage determination is whether the patient was receiving a skilled level of care on a daily basis. The advocate should remember that the type of skilled care may be either nursing or rehabilitation services, or a combination of the two. Rehabilitation services include physical therapy, occupational therapy, and speech therapy. Importantly, rehabilitation services need only be provided five days per week to qualify as "daily," while nursing services, or a combination of nursing and therapy, must be provided seven days per week to meet the "daily" test.[112]

For example, a patient who receives physical therapy three days per week and occupational therapy two other days would be eligible for coverage. This patient has received skilled rehabilitation services five days per week. Similarly, a patient who receives physical therapy three days per week and skilled nursing care the other four days would be eligible for coverage. The key is that the patient is receiving skilled care each day of the week.

As noted previously, most Medicare SNF patients require custodial care in addition to daily skilled care. It is unusual to find an instance where a SNF patient does not require at least some nonskilled services. Frequently these patients are nonambulatory or semiambulatory. For example, a stroke patient will require physical therapy to learn how to walk again and to rebuild muscle strength. It is important for the advocate to be able to distinguish skilled care from custodial care. In fact the advocate will find that in meeting the practical-matter requirement for

---

[111] See, e.g., Fox v. Bowen, 656 F. Supp. 1236 (D. Conn. 1987).

[112] 42 C.F.R. §409.34. See also Medicare Benefit Policy Manual, Pub. 100-02, Ch. 8, §30.6.

inpatient coverage, it is often also necessary to establish that the needed custodial care can only be practically provided on an inpatient basis.[113]

In assessing whether care is skilled, the advocate should focus on the inherent complexity of the service. This line of analysis has been adopted by courts in making level of care determinations.[114] Courts have also noted that a common-sense, nontechnical consideration of the patient's condition as a whole must be made in determining the level of care.[115]

There is no definition of custodial care in the law. The regulations merely state that custodial care is care that does not meet the definition of SNF care.[116] As a general rule, custodial care is interpreted to be care that a layperson without any special skills or training can safely and effectively perform.[117]

The advocate must assess what actual services have been provided to the patient. The best way to analyze the level of care is to have a systematic approach and to review the medical record carefully. A checklist may be a valuable asset in evaluating level of care concerns:

• Is this a rehabilitation or nursing patient (or both)?

• What rehabilitation services have been provided (i.e., physical, occupational, or speech therapy)?

• Check the list of per se skilled therapy services.

• Is skilled development, management, and evaluation of the patient care plan required?

• Is skilled observation and assessment of the patient's changing or unstable condition required?

• What specific nursing services have been provided (e.g., injections, decubitus ulcer care, dressing changes)?

• Check the list of per se skilled nursing services.

• Are there any special medical complications that require the services of skilled personnel (e.g., multiple medications with potential adverse reactions, psychiatric components)?[118]

---

[113] The "practical matter" criterion of coverage requires that the beneficiary need care on an inpatient basis. 42 C.F.R. §409.35; Medicare Benefit Policy Manual, Pub. 100-02, Ch. 8, §30.7.

[114] Hurley v. Bowen, 857 F.2d 907, 911 (2d Cir. 1988); Hirsch v. Bowen, 655 F. Supp. 342, 344 (S.D.N.Y. 1987).

[115] Friedman v. Secretary of HHS, 819 F.2d 42, 45 (2d Cir. 1987); Pfalzgraf v. Shalala, 997 F. Supp. 360, 365 (W.D.N.Y. 1998); Landa v. Shalala, 900 F. Supp. 628, 635 (E.D.N.Y. 1995); Walsh v. Secretary of HHS, 636 F. Supp. 358, 360 (E.D.N.Y. 1986).

[116] 42 C.F.R. §411.15(g).

[117] Hirsch v. Bowen, 655 F. Supp. 342 (S.D.N.Y. 1987).

[118] 42 C.F.R. §409.33(a)(2); Medicare Benefit Policy Manual, Pub. 100-02, Ch. 8, §30.2.2.

- Have the services been provided by or under the supervision of certified skilled personnel?

- Is there sufficient documentary medical evidence to establish your position?

[B] Total Condition of the Patient

The courts have consistently taken the position that the patient's total condition must be taken into consideration, not merely each individual service provided.[119] In light of the move to SNF/PPS and its reliance on RUG-III, it is particularly important that advocates not lose sight of long-standing court developments with respect to legal standards for evaluating the level of care.

Courts have developed a number of principles that govern judicial review of final determinations of the Secretary regarding entitlement to benefits under the Act. In assessing the Medicare patient's total condition, the advocate should examine the record to determine the need for management and evaluation of the patient's care plan or observation and/or monitoring of the patient's medical condition.

[C] Management and Evaluation of the Patient Care Plan

SNF patients are entitled to Medicare coverage if they need and receive skilled observation, assessment, management of care plan, or patient education services, even if they do not require or receive specific nursing services such as injections or catheter irrigation, and even if they do not fall within the top 35 RUG-III categories.[120] Documentation to support coverage on these bases must be kept by the facility and should be found in the medical record, including the doctor's order, nurses' notes, and any medical assessment data that the SNF is required to keep for transmittal to the fiscal intermediaries for payment.[121]

Overall management and evaluation of a patient's care plan may involve skilled services, even when the individual services are not skilled. The need for skilled care may be inferred from the services provided, even when the skilled

---

[119] Pfalzgraf v. Shalala, 997 F. Supp. 360, 365 (W.D.N.Y. 1998); Yuknat v. Bowen, [1989 Transfer Binder] Medicare & Medicaid Guide (CCH) 37,822 (D. Conn. Mar. 31, 1989); Stearns v. Sullivan, [1989 Transfer Binder] Medicare & Medicaid Guide (CCH) 38,273 (D. Mass. Nov. 6, 1989); Perales v. Sullivan, [1989 Transfer Binder] Medicare & Medicaid Guide (CCH) 38,044 (S.D.N.Y. 1989); Scotto v. Bowen, [1989 Transfer Binder] Medicare & Medicaid Guide (CCH) 37,819 (E.D.N.Y. Sept. 18, 1989); Olson v. Bowen, [1988 Transfer Binder] Medicare & Medicaid Guide (CCH) 37,160 (W.D. Wis. May 31, 1988); Babula v. Secretary of HHS, 655 F. Supp. 1117 (W.D.N.Y. 1987); Hirsch v. Bowen, 655 F. Supp. 342 (S.D.N.Y. 1987); Israel v. Bowen, 669 F. Supp. 61 (W.D.N.Y. 1987); Gartmann v. Secretary of HHS, 633 F. Supp. 67 (E.D.N.Y. 1986); Howard v. Heckler, 618 F. Supp. 1333 (E.D.N.Y. 1985); Roth v. Secretary of HHS, 606 F. Supp. 636 (W.D.N.Y. 1985); Kuebler v. Secretary of HHS, 579 F. Supp. 1436 (E.D.N.Y. 1984).

[120] 42 C.F.R. §409.33(a)(1)-(3); Medicare Benefit Policy Manual, Pub. 100-02, Ch. 8, §30.2.3.

[121] See generally 42 C.F.R. §§413.343, 483.20.

planning and management activities are not specifically identified in the patient's clinical record.[122] One or more of the following nursing services may qualify a patient for Medicare coverage of his or her SNF stay:

- Skilled involvement to develop, manage, and evaluate a care plan formulated through physician orders;

- Skilled involvement to meet the patient's needs, promote recovery, and ensure medical safety when considering the patient's physical or mental condition;

- Skilled management of personal care services when the patient's condition and aggregate of services require technical or professional intervention;

- Skilled involvement to understand the relationship between services and evaluate the ultimate effect of one service on another;

- Skilled involvement required, even though each individual service is not considered skilled by itself;

- Skilled planning and management services not specifically articulated as such in the clinical record, if the patient's overall condition is documented as justifying the need for technical or professional services.[123]

Cases that rest solely on management and evaluation of the skilled service are among the most difficult to win because the standard is ambiguous and the qualifying factors are not easy to define. Certain factors are important in this type of case: age, number of medical conditions, mental impairment, patient safety, and actual professional staff involvement. An individual with medical problems involving vital organs and systems is more likely to require skilled management and evaluation.

The federal regulations are invaluable[124] and the Medicare Benefit Policy Manual[125] may be a valuable resource. Very often a case rests on the fact that skilled nursing personnel are involved in the development, management, and evaluation of the patient's care plan.

The Manual provides as an example "an aged patient with a history of diabetes mellitus and angina pectoris who is recovering from an open reduction of the neck of the femur." He requires skin care, appropriate medications, a diabetic diet, a therapeutic exercise program, and observation to identify signs of deterioration or complications. Although the individual services could be provided by non-skilled personnel, his age, condition, and immobility "create a high potential for serious complications" and justify skilled care until his treatment regimen is stabilized.[126]

---

[122] 42 C.F.R. §409.33(a)(1)(ii); Medicare Benefit Policy Manual, Pub. 100-02, Ch. 8, §30.2.3.1.

[123] *Id.*

[124] *See, e.g.,* 42 C.F.R. §409.33(a)(1).

[125] Medicare Benefit Policy Manual, Pub. 100-02, Ch. 8. *See* 30 *et seq.*

[126] Medicare Benefit Policy Manual, Pub. 100-02, Ch. 8, §30.2.3.1 (example 1).

The advocate should look closely at every aspect of the patient's condition, including the variety and intensity of services being performed by nursing personnel. The review should include the following steps:

- Checking the written care plan[127] and how plan elements are reflected in the ongoing medical assessment data.

- Checking whether the patient manifested behavioral symptoms of psychological or mental impairments and whether the patient had such a condition in addition to physical problems.

- Checking whether nursing intervention was necessary to ensure patient safety and promote recovery.

- Carefully assessing the aggregate of services in light of the patient's total condition. A patient may need assessment, observation, and other interventions relative to a refusal of medication and nutrition, and at the same time, require occupational therapy twice weekly as well as a variety of personal care services.

- Checking the interrelationship of services. One example is the frequent need for a nurse to assess the interaction of various medications taken simultaneously for different conditions.

Remember that several *per se* nonskilled services may require skilled management even if each service is nonskilled. Whenever there are multiple medical diagnoses and a great deal of nursing services, an argument may often be made for skilled management. A need for skilled management services may be established even without explicit clinical references to the planning and management services.[128]

Management and evaluation services are closely related to observation and assessment services.[129] Often a patient will require a combination of management and observation services. As a general tip, Medicare coverage is more likely to be granted when a patient requires skilled observation in addition to management of the care plan.

[D] Observation and Assessment of the Patient's Changing or Unstable Condition

Many SNF patients require skilled nursing monitoring of their overall medical condition.[130] An individual's condition may change, necessitating a

---

[127] 42 C.F.R. §483.20(k). Often the plan of care alone will not have sufficient information to be helpful. Physician's orders, medical treatment records, and nursing and/or therapy notes may contain additional and more specific proof that daily skilled care was needed and provided.

[128] Medicare Benefit Policy Manual, Pub. 100-02, Ch. 8, §30.2.3.1.

[129] Medicare Benefit Policy Manual, Pub. 100-02, Ch. 8, §30.2.3.2.

[130] 42 C.F.R. §409.33(a)(2); Medicare Benefit Policy Manual, Pub. 100-02, Ch. 8, §30.2.3.2.

change in the plan of care or additional medical interventions. Medicare covers such nursing care if it is required and if it can be established that the care was performed on a daily basis.

It is not the intent of the Medicare statute or regulations that frail or chronically ill persons deteriorate or suffer a medical setback in order to invoke Medicare coverage for skilled nursing observation and assessment. Rather, the risk of potential instability is sufficient to cover services that are needed to maintain a fragile person at the maximum medical and functional status.

The regulation and Manual give examples when observation and assessment constitute skilled services.[131] Stabilizing a patient's treatment regimen or observing a patient in an unstabilized post-operative period are examples.

An analysis of the record to determine the need for observation and assessment should demonstrate the following:

• Medical necessity was documented by physician orders and nursing or therapy notes;

• Skilled personnel were utilized to identify and evaluate the patient's needs;

• Modification of treatment was needed for additional medical procedures;

• Care was necessary until the patient's condition stabilized or to ensure the patient remained stable;

• There was a reasonable probability of a potential complication or further acute episode that required monitoring by skilled personnel (even if such complication or episode did not occur);

• Where applicable, acute psychological symptoms were present in addition to physical problems.

Remember that a SNF patient with acute psychological symptoms may not have the ability to cooperate with SNF personnel in the same way as others. For example, there may be an order for pain medication as needed. Due to psychological factors, the patient may not be able to express the need clearly. There may be nonverbal expressions or behaviors that require skilled interpretation and interventions. In addition, a patient may have an "as needed" order for medication for agitation or anxiety. It often requires the skill of a nurse to determine, after careful observation and assessment, when to administer medications pursuant to such an order.

[E] Patient Education

The third type of services that may be skilled are patient education services if technical or professional personnel are needed to teach a patient

---

[131] 42. C.F.R. §409.33(a)(2); Medicare Benefit Policy Manual, Pub. 100-02, Ch. 8, §30.2.3.2.

self-maintenance and how to manage his or her treatment regimen.[132] Illustrative examples include:

- Teaching self-administration of injectable medications;

- Teaching self-administration of a complex range of medications;

- "Teaching a newly-diagnosed diabetic to administer insulin injections, to prepare and follow a diabetic diet, and to observe foot-care precautions;"

- "Teaching self-administration of medical gases;"

- "Gait training and teaching of prothesis care for a patient who has had a recent leg amputation;"

- Teaching colostomy or ileostomy care;

- "Teaching patients how to perform self-catherization and self-administration of gastrostomy feedings;"

- "Teaching patients how to care for and maintain central venous lines, such as Hickman catheters;"

- "Teaching patients the use and care of braces, splints and orthotics, and any associated skin care;" and

- "Teaching patients the proper care of any specialized dressings or skin treatments."[133]

[F] Opinion of the Attending Physician

One critical issue, often present in SNF and other Medicare cases, is the question of how much weight should be given to various types of evidence. The most important evidentiary concept is that the opinion of an attending or treating physician should be given special consideration. This concept or rule of law was first developed in the context of Social Security disability cases.[134]

Most courts have held that the opinion of a Medicare attending physician is not binding. However, the preponderance of judicial authority has held that the opinion of an attending physician must be given great weight when there is no directly conflicting evidence.[135]

---

[132] 42 C.F.R. §409.33(a)(3); Medicare Benefit Policy Manual, Pub. 100-02, Ch. 8, §30.2.3.3.

[133] Medicare Benefit Policy Manual, Pub. 100-02, Ch. 8, §30.2.3.3.

[134] Schisler v. Heckler, 787 F.2d 76, 81-85 (2d Cir. 1986). *See also Schisler II*, 851 F.2d 43 (2d Cir. 1988). In response to the first two *Schisler* decisions, the Secretary of Health and Human Services promulgated regulations establishing an administrative treating physician rule. These regulations were upheld in the *Schisler III* decision, 3 F.3d 563 (2d Cir. 1993).

[135] *See, e.g.*, Hirsch v. Bowen, 655 F. Supp. 342 (S.D.N.Y. 1987); Israel v. Bowen, 669 F. Supp. 61 (W.D.N.Y. 1987); Gartmann v. Secretary of HHS, 633 F. Supp. 671 (E.D.N.Y. 1986); Walsh v.

The U.S. Court of Appeals for the Second Circuit has twice addressed the treating physician rule in the context of Medicare.[136] In response, HCFA (now CMS) issued a formal administrative ruling concerning the weight to be given a treating physician's opinion in determining hospital and SNF coverage.[137]

The ruling sets forth four specific points:

- No *presumptive* weight may be given to the opinion of a treating physician in determining the medical necessity of inpatient hospital or SNF services.

- The treating physician's opinion must be evaluated in the context of all the evidence contained in the administrative record.

- Treating physician certification is required for Medicare *payment*; however, *coverage* decisions are not based solely on physician certification.

- Coverage decisions are based upon objective medical information available from claims forms and, when necessary, the medical record, which includes the physician certification.

Although CMS's rule is consistent with the great weight that must be afforded to the opinion of the treating physician, a challenge arises when the attending physician's opinion is contradicted at hearings by a medical adviser who has been retained as a consultant by the administrative law judge.

Practice Tip: The advocate should cross-examine the medical adviser to establish that the medical adviser has not treated or even examined the patient. The medical adviser's opinion is totally derived from a review of the documentary medical evidence.

Courts have recognized that the opinion of a nontreating physician, based only upon review of medical records, should not be accorded as much evidentiary weight as the opinion of an attending physician.[138] In *Gartmann v. Secretary of HHS*,[139] the court found that the opinion of the medical adviser could not be

---

Secretary of HHS, 636 F. Supp. 358 (E.D.N.Y. 1986), *aff'd by* New York ex rel. Bodner, 903 F.2d 122 (2d Cir. 1990) (determination not binding on factfinder). *See also* Bodnar v. Secretary of HHS, [1989 Transfer Binder] Medicare & Medicaid Guide (CCH) ¶38,274 (N.D.N.Y. Aug. 1, 1989).

[136] New York ex rel. Holland v. Sullivan, 927 F.2d 57 (2d Cir. 1991); New York ex rel. Stein v. Sullivan, 924 F.2d 431 (2d Cir. 1991).

[137] HCFA Ruling, No. HCFA R93-1, [1993 Transfer Binder] Medicare & Medicaid Guide (CCH) 41,444 (May 18, 1993).

[138] Stenger v. Bowen, 692 F. Supp. 1474, 1476 (E.D.N.Y. 1988).

[139] 633 F. Supp. 674, 680 (E.D.N.Y. 1986).

considered substantial evidence to support a denial of coverage because it was not supported by the findings or opinions of the treating physician.

[G] Restoration Potential of the Rehabilitation Patient

Many Medicare beneficiaries receive SNF coverage as rehabilitation patients. Most of these patients receive physical therapy services. The regulations recognize rehabilitation services as skilled services, including cases in which *maintenance* therapy is required to be provided by skilled personnel.[140] Advocates find that Medicare intermediaries often erroneously require that a patient show significant rehabilitation potential and steady improvement in order to receive Medicare coverage. This is not the appropriate legal standard.

Medicare's policy and practice of denying coverage of SNF physical therapy services, based upon arbitrary rules of thumb without consideration of the patient's individual condition, was successfully challenged in *Fox v. Bowen*.[141] The court found that Medicare intermediaries were denying physical therapy coverage improperly based upon "arbitrary presumptions or rules of thumb," and included, *inter alia,* denying coverage for:

- Maintenance therapy;
- Non-weight-bearing therapy to fracture patients;
- Passive range-of-motion exercises;
- Patients able to ambulate 50 feet with supervision;
- Amputees not yet fitted with prostheses;
- Patients who require daily skilled physical therapy for a period over two weeks.[142]

The *Fox* ruling struck down these arbitrary rules of thumb and mandated that each patient's individual medical condition be carefully assessed to determine whether skilled physical therapy services are required. Implicit in this ruling is that coverage cannot be denied merely because an individual's restoration potential is not sufficient or because insufficient progress has been achieved. Such a blanket restriction is clearly arbitrary and contrary to the provisions of the Medicare regulations pertaining to restoration potential.

The regulations state explicitly, "The restoration potential of a patient is not the deciding factor in determining whether skilled services are needed. Even if full recovery or medical improvement is not possible, a patient may need skilled services

---

[140] 42 C.F.R. §409.33(c).

[141] 656 F. Supp. 1236 (D. Conn. 1987). This case was certified as a statewide class action in Connecticut; however, the ruling has affected Medicare coverage standards on the national level.

[142] 656 F. Supp. 1236, 1252.

to prevent further deterioration or preserve current capabilities."[143] The Skilled Nursing Facility Manual provides an example of a cancer patient with a terminal prognosis who nevertheless requires covered skilled services ("The fact that there is no potential for such a patient's recovery does not alter the character of the services and skills required for their performance.")[144] Even "when rehabilitation services are the primary services, the key issue is whether the skills of a therapist are needed. The deciding factor is not the patient's potential for recovery. . . ."[145]

[H] Noncertified Bed

In order for Medicare to pay for a skilled nursing facility stay, the patient must be in a bed that is certified for Medicare participation. Medicare will not cover skilled care if the patient is in a noncertified bed unless it can be shown that the placement was erroneous and the patient was not aware that he or she was in a noncertified bed or did not consent to the placement.[146] It is, therefore, necessary for the advocate to determine that the SNF is a Medicare-certified provider and that the patient is in a Medicare-certified bed.

The patient may inadvertently be placed in a non-Medicare-certified bed, but receive an SNF level of care. The law provides that when the sole reason for denial of Medicare coverage is an unintentional, inadvertent, or erroneous action concerning transfer to a noncertified bed, payment may be made.[147] This application of waiver of liability applies only when a patient has not consented to the transfer to a noncertified bed and the only reason for denial is the fact that the patient was in a noncertified bed.[148] It must be established that such a patient was eligible for and received daily skilled care.

§3.07   PRE-APPEALS ADVOCACY

[A] Overview

Like other areas of Medicare, coverage decisions are made at various levels, first by the provider, then by the administrative appeal system,[149] and, finally, by

---

[143] 42 C.F.R. §409.32(c).

[144] Skilled Nursing Facility Manual, §214.1.B (first example).

[145] Skilled Nursing Facility Manual, §214.1.B.

[146] 42 U.S.C. §1395pp(e); Medicare Claims Processing Manual, CMS Pub., 100-4, Ch. 30, §20; Hendry Convalescent Ctr. v. Harris, [1982 Transfer Binder] Medicare & Medicaid Guide (CCH) 31,934(A) (E.D. Mich. 1982); Wright v. Califano, [1979-1 Transfer Binder] Medicare & Medicaid Guide (CCH) 29,643.

[147] 42 U.S.C. §1395pp(e); Wright v. Califano, [1979-1 Transfer Binder] Medicare & Medicaid Guide (CCH) 29,643.

[148] Medicare Claims Processing Manual, CMS Pub., 100-4, Ch. 30, §§30.1 and 40.

[149] See §3.08.

the federal courts. The first decision regarding Medicare coverage is made by the SNF. A decision by the SNF is separate from a decision made by Medicare; only a formal Medicare decision triggers the appeals process. If a beneficiary requests that the SNF submit a claim to Medicare despite the facility's determination that Medicare will not cover the services, the facility must submit a claim.[150] A fiscal intermediary then issues a Medicare initial determination. Following the initial determination, an appeal can be taken to "redetermination" and "reconsideration," then on to an administrative law judge hearing, the Medicare Appeals Council, and finally, federal district court.

[B] The Importance of No-Payment or Demand Bill

SNFs submit consolidated bills to the intermediary for payment in accordance with CMS requirements.[151] It is important for beneficiaries and their advocates to understand that a bill must be submitted to the Medicare intermediary *even when* the SNF provider believes that services will not be covered. This procedure is referred to as "no-payment" or "demand" billing and was not changed by the consolidated billing process.[152] SNFs are required to submit such bills at the request of a beneficiary.[153] Furthermore, SNFs cannot bill the beneficiary until the Medicare intermediary issues a formal claim determination.[154] If the SNF does not submit a bill to the fiscal intermediary, however, the right to appeal is lost, because the fiscal intermediary would never make a Medicare initial determination from which an appeal may be taken.

Although it is the intermediary that performs the first official assessment of a patient's level of care, it has been the experience of beneficiaries that the intermediary often rubber-stamps the SNF provider denial.

[C] Waiver of Liability

A related issue involves the "waiver of liability" provision in the Medicare statute.[155] Pursuant to this provision, a beneficiary's financial liability for the cost of care not covered by Medicare may be waived under certain circumstances. In general, liability will be waived when it is found that the patient did not know, or have reason to know, that Medicare would not cover the services.[156]

---

[150] Sarrassat v. Sullivan, Medicare & Medicaid Guide (CCH) 38,504 (N.D. Cal. May 17, 1989).

[151] Pub. L. No. 105-33, 4432(b); Transmittal A-98-18.

[152] 42 C.F.R. §413.335.

[153] Medicare Claims Processing Manual, Pub. 100-04, Ch. 6, §10, Ch. 30, §70; Sarrassat v. Sullivan, Medicare & Medicaid Guide (CCH) 38,504, at 22,841 (N.D. Cal. May 17, 1989).

[154] Medicare Claims Processing Manual, Ch. 30, §70.6.13.

[155] 42 U.S.C. §1395pp.

[156] *Id.*

In order for liability to be waived, there must be a determination that Medicare will not cover the services, based upon a finding that the care was not medically reasonable and necessary or that it was custodial.[157] If both the patient and provider did not know or could not be reasonably expected to know that services would not be covered, then liability will rest with the Medicare program.[158]

In some instances, the patient is relieved of liability but the provider is not. Such a situation occurs, for example, when a provider has reason to know that Medicare will not cover the services because the provider has received denial notices for patients with similar medical conditions. In this situation, Medicare will indemnify the patient and make reimbursement to him or her for any amounts she paid to the provider during the period for which liability was waived. Medicare will then treat the payment to the provider as an overpayment and recoup the difference from later billings.[159]

[D]   Notice Issues

[1]   Function of the Notice

Notice plays a key role in determining waiver of liability issues, i.e., whether a patient knew or could be expected to know that Medicare would not cover the service. Medicare patients are not medical experts and can hardly be expected to know whether a service is medically necessary or what the difference is between skilled and custodial care. Accordingly, the patient must be notified ahead of time that Medicare will not cover the SNF services. Notice also informs a patient of his or her right to request a demand bill so that he or she can get an initial determination from the fiscal intermediary from which to file an appeal. CMS uses one notice to inform the beneficiary of both the potential liability if a claim is submitted to Medicare and Medicare determines non-coverage and the right to request a demand bill to initiate an appeal.

A SNF must give a beneficiary a notice if it intends to deny, reduce, or terminate Medicare Part A-covered services.[160]

[2]   Form of Notice

Although the statute is not specific about what notice is appropriate, the regulations provide that notice of noncoverage must be given to the patient in

---

[157] 42 U.S.C. §1395y(a)(1)(A), (9).

[158] 42 U.S.C. §1395pp(a)(2); 42 C.F.R. §411.400.

[159] 42 U.S.C. §1395pp(b); 42 C.F.R. §411.402.

[160] Medicare Claims Processing Manual, Pub. 100-04, Ch. 30, §70.2.3.1.

writing.[161] Generally, oral notice is not legally sufficient.[162] Thus, it is standard practice for a SNF to issue a written denial notice upon admission unless the provider is confident that Medicare will cover the services. Someone who is admitted as a Medicare patient will receive a written denial notice when the SNF believes Medicare will no longer pay for the care. If the reason for the non-coverage is statutory—either "medical necessity" (the services are "not reasonable and necessary") or level of care (the care is custodial, rather than skilled)—the SNF must use either the SNF Advance Beneficiary Notice (SNFABN)[163] or any of five denial letters.[164]

The notice must include an explanation in lay language[165] that the patient and his or her authorized representative "can comprehend"[166] and must be given to the patient or the patient's authorized representative[167] If the patient "is not capable of receiving the notice," the patient has not received "proper notice" and the facility may be financially responsible.[168]

A SNF using the model SNFABN form must give specific reasons in the "Because" section why it believes that Medicare payment will be denied.[169] The SNF's refusal to respond to inquiries from the patient or authorized representative about the notice and its meaning may result in the notice's invalidation.[170]

The CMS manual states that the SNFABN must meet its standards for cultural competency, clearly identify the particular item or service, and include the reasons why the SNF believes Medicare will not pay for the SNF stay.[171] The notice should not include abbreviations, diagnosis codes, or technical language. A SNFABN that

---

[161] 42 C.F.R. §411.404; Medicare Claims Processing Manual, Pub. 100-04, Ch. 30, §40.6.5.

[162] *See* Sarrassat v. Bowen, Medicare & Medicaid Guide (CCH) ¶38,504 (N.D. Cal. May 17, 1989), establishing that a beneficiary must receive a notice of noncoverage, including notice of the opportunity to request an appeal of the SNF's noncoverage determination and establishing that where the beneficiary requests an appeal, services continue through the issuance of the formal Medicare finding of noncoverage. *But see* HCFA Ruling 95-1 (Dec. 22, 1995); Medicare Claims Processing Manual, Pub. 100-04, Ch. 30, §§30.1 (establishing when beneficiary is on notice of noncoverage), 30-30.40.2 (presumption that beneficiary did not know services were not covered unless there is evidence of written notice to beneficiary). It should also be noted that often SNF staff will note on the written notice, included in the patient's record, that oral notice was provided over the telephone. These cases require close scrutiny.

[163] Form No. CMS-10055.

[164] The five denial notices are at <http://www.cms.hhs.gov/medicare/bni/ snf_denial_letters.pdf>. Medicare Coverage Policy Manual, ch. 30, §7.

[165] Medicare Claims Processing Manual, Pub. 100-04, Ch. 30, §70.3.1.

[166] Medicare Claims Processing Manual, Pub. 100-04, Ch. 30, §70.3.4. *See also* §70.3.5.

[167] Medicare Claims Processing Manual, Pub. 100-04, Ch. 30, §70.3.1.

[168] Medicare Claims Processing Manual, Pub. 100-04, Ch. 30, §70.3.4.

[169] Medicare Claims Processing Manual, Pub. 100-04, Ch. 30, §70.4.3.3.

[170] Medicare Claims Processing Manual, Pub. 100-04, Ch. 30, §70.4.3.4.

[171] Medicare Claims Processing Manual, Pub. 100-4, Ch. 30, §70.3.2.

a beneficiary cannot understand is defective and will not protect the SNF from financial liability.[172]

CMS has issued another notice for use with "Technical" denials, such as failure to meet the 3-day qualifying in-patient hospital stay or absence of days left in the benefit period.[173]

Another CMS form is used for expedited appeals.[174]

[3] SNF Billing Notices

CMS has established a new standard process requiring SNFs to submit bills to fiscal intermediaries for beneficiaries who "started a spell of illness under a SNF Part A benefit [on or after October 1, 2006] for every month of the related stay even though no benefits may be payable."[175] The bills are required when a beneficiary has exhausted his or her 100 day SNF benefit (*benefits exhaust*) and when a beneficiary no longer needs a Medicare-covered level of care but continues to reside in a Medicare-certified part of the SNF (*no payment*). When a SNF patient dropped to non-skilled care in a previous month, the SNF is allowed to submit a final discharge bill spanning multiple months through the month of discharge. CMS intends to use *benefits exhaust* and *no payment* bills to track beneficiaries' benefit periods and for purposes of national healthcare planning.

[E] Advocacy Tip

Waiver of the beneficiary's liability should always be considered by an advocate. In addressing a waiver issue, a sequential checklist may be helpful to the advocate:

• Was Medicare coverage denied upon admission or at a later date?

• Was the denial because the services were not skilled or because they were not reasonable and necessary?

• Was written notice given by the SNF provider?

• Who received the notice?

---

[172] Medicare Claims Processing Manual, Pub. 100-04, Ch. 30, §70.3.5.

[173] Notice of Exclusions from Medicare Benefits, Skilled Nursing Facility (NEMB-SNF), Form CMS-20014.

[174] Notice of Medicare Provider Non-Coverage, OMB No. 0938-0953. See **§3.08[C],** for discussion of expedited appeals.

[175] "Benefits Exhaust and No-Payment Billing Instructions for Medicare Fiscal Intermediaries (FIs) and Skilled Nursing Facilities (SNFs)," Medicare Claims Processing Manual, Pub. 100-04, Transmittal No. 930 (Apr. 28, 2006).

- Was the patient capable of understanding the notice (e.g., are there mental deficits or language barriers)?

- Was the notice mailed to a family member?

- When was the notice received?

When Medicare coverage is denied upon admission, the Medicare denial notice is one of many documents presented to the patient's representative on the day of admission. Consequently, people often do not remember receiving this notice. The advocate should seek a copy from the provider even if a family member does not remember receiving a notice. A copy might be found in the patient's file that is signed by the patient or family member. Review the notice to determine whether it complies with the forms approved by CMS.

§3.08 APPEALS

[A] Medicare Advantage

If the beneficiary has enrolled in a Medicare Advantage plan, Medicare Advantage appeal rights apply.[176]

[B] Appeals Process for Original Medicare

Interim final regulations implementing changes to the appeals process for Medicare Part A and Part B claims, and changes to ALJ hearing process for all Medicare claims, including managed care claims and future prescription drug claims, are effective for SNF appeals in 2005.[177]

[1] Initial Determinations and Redeterminations

As in the past, the claims process begins when the Medicare contractor (currently called a fiscal intermediary) issues an initial determination of a claim submitted by the SNF or, occasionally, by the beneficiary.[178] The regulations make clear that the initial determination, which will still be issued as the Medicare Summary Notice (MSN), goes only to the beneficiary, even when the contractor is aware that the beneficiary has an appointed representative.[179] Someone who wants to appeal from the initial determination must submit a written, signed request

---

[176] See §7.04[F].

[177] 70 Fed. Reg. 11420 (Mar. 8, 2005).

[178] 42 C.F.R. §§405.920, 405.921.

[179] 42 C.F.R. §405.921(a).

for a redetermination within 120 days of the initial determination;[180] the regulations assume the notice is received five days after the date of the notice. Requests for redeterminations must be filed with the office indicated on the MSN;[181] beneficiaries can no longer file requests with Social Security offices.

The regulations also, for the first time, allow SNFs to request appeal of a denial of an initial determination,[182] raising the possibility that both the beneficiary and the SNF will initiate the appeals process. In such a case, the contractor must consolidate the appeals. The contractor has 60 days from receipt of the redetermination request to issue a decision.[183] If more than one party files a request, the time period runs from the date the last request is received.[184] For example, if a beneficiary files a redetermination request on day 1, but the SNF files on day 50, the 60-day time period for the contractor to act starts on day 50.

Unlike the MSN, the notice of the redetermination will be sent to a beneficiary's appointed representative. The notice will explain the facts, policies, and law relied upon in making the redetermination decision; the right to request a reconsideration and the process for doing so; and a statement of specific missing documents that must be submitted. The notice will state that SNFs, but not beneficiaries (unless they are represented by a SNF), must submit all of their evidence at the next level of review in order for the evidence to be considered at any further stage of the appeals process.[185] It is unclear whether CMS will require contractors to send different notices to beneficiaries and SNFs, or whether CMS will include in the redetermination notice a statement that evidentiary limitations do not apply to beneficiaries. In addition, contractors will not be required to send redetermination notices to multiple beneficiaries in overpayment cases brought by SNFs if the beneficiary allegedly has no liability for the claim. It is unclear how the contractor will determine in such cases whether the beneficiary has already paid for the service in question.

The regulations create a new reopening process to be used instead of the redetermination process to correct minor errors or omissions in initial determinations.[186] This process responds to a new section of the Medicare law that allows SNFs to correct minor mistakes without going through the appeals process. Reopenings can also be used at subsequent levels of review. Questions remain concerning the relationship of the new reopening process and the process for deciding remanded cases, as well as the ability of a contractor to reopen a decision in favor of the beneficiary.

---

[180] 42 C.F.R. §405.942(a).

[181] 42 C.F.R. §405.944(a).

[182] 42 C.F.R. §405.906(a)(3).

[183] 42 C.F.R. §405.950(a).

[184] 42 C.F.R. §405.950(b)(2).

[185] 42 C.F.R. §405.956.

[186] 42 C.F.R. §405.980.

[2] Reconsiderations

A new third level of review, the reconsideration,[187] will be conducted by a new group of Medicare contractors called Qualified Independent Contractors (QICs). Beneficiaries and other parties to the redetermination have180 days to request a reconsideration by filing a request at the location indicated on the redetermination notice.[188] Again, reconsiderations filed by beneficiaries and the SNF will be consolidated, and the time for issuing a decision runs from receipt of the last-filed appeal.

Starting May 1, 2005, appeals of redeterminations by the fiscal intermediaries concerning SNF care go through the QIC reconsideration.

The reconsideration level of review is a paper review;[189] CMS states in the preamble to the final regulations that QICs will not be conducting hearings. However, the QIC is supposed to solicit the view of the beneficiary. As noted above, SNFs are required to submit all of the evidence they want considered in the claim to the QIC. Evidence not submitted may be excluded at subsequent levels of review.

The QIC is required to complete its reconsideration within 60 days of the reconsideration request.[190] Again, the time runs from the last request filed if more than one party seeks reconsideration; the QIC must so notify a party who filed an earlier request. The regulations do not indicate how QICs will document receipt or how beneficiaries will know when the 60-day period ends. Although the statute allows a party to the reconsideration to ask for an extension of not more than 14 days for the QIC to conclude the reconsideration, the regulations add 14 days to the reconsideration time frame each time that additional evidence is submitted.[191]

If a QIC does not issue a timely decision, the statute allows a party to request that the appeal be escalated to the next level of review, the ALJ level. The regulations give the QIC five days to either issue a decision or acknowledge the escalation request and send it to the ALJ level of review.[192] The regulations indicate that an appeal escalated to the ALJ level will be completed within 180 days of receipt, rather than the statutorily-mandated 90 days for ALJ decisions.

[3] ALJ Hearing and Beyond

If the reconsideration decision by the QIC is unsatisfactory and at least $100 remains in controversy in 2005, the beneficiary has 60 days in which to request an

---

[187] 42 C.F.R. §§405.960–.978.

[188] 42 C.F.R. §405.962(a).

[189] 42 C.F.R. §405.968(a)(1).

[190] 42 C.F.R. §405.970(a).

[191] 42 C.F.R. §405.970(b)(3).

[192] 42 C.F.R. §405.970(e)(2).

ALJ hearing.[193] The hearing request should be made in writing and should be filed with the entity identified in the reconsideration notice.[194] If the hearing request is unsatisfactory, a beneficiary may request a review from the Medicare Appeals Council (MAC).[195] The request must be made within 60 days of receipt of the hearing decision.[196] If $1,050 remains in controversy after the hearing, the case may proceed to a Federal District Court.[197]

[C] Expedited Appeals Process in Original Medicare

Effective July 2005, beneficiaries in original Medicare may seek expedited review of a SNF's discharge from care under Medicare Part A.[198] The SNF must give the beneficiary a general, standardized notice at least two days in advance of the proposed end of the service. If the service is fewer than two days, then notice must be given by the next-to-last service. The notice describes the service, the date coverage ends, the beneficiary's financial liability for continued services, and how to file an appeal.

A beneficiary must request expedited review, orally or in writing, by noon of the next calendar day after receiving notice. At that time, the beneficiary is given a more specific notice that includes a detailed explanation of why services are being terminated, a description of any applicable Medicare coverage rules and information on how to obtain them, and other facts specific to the beneficiary's case. The beneficiary is not financially liable for continued services until the later of two days after receiving the notice or the termination date specified in the notice.

Services furnished by a SNF are discharges for which a doctor's certificate is not required. A reduction in service where Medicare coverage continues is not considered a termination or discharge for purposes of triggering expedited review. If the reduction in service results in a loss of Medicare coverage, for example, the beneficiary no longer receives seven days of skilled nursing care or five days of rehabilitation services, expedited review may be available. In addition, if the SNF proposes to transfer the beneficiary to a non-Medicare certified part of the SNF, the beneficiary is entitled to notice and opportunity for a hearing under the Nursing Home Reform Law's transfer and discharge rules.[199]

---

[193] 42 C.F.R. §405.1014(b)(1). Section 940 of the MMA requires that, starting in 2005, the amount in controversy for administrative law judge hearings and for judicial review be adjusted annually by the percentage increase in the medical care component of the consumer price index for urban consumers and be rounded to the nearest multiple of $10. CMS announced that the 2005 amount is controversy for administrative law judge review remains $100. 70 Fed. Reg. at 11423.

[194] 42 C.F.R. §405.1014.

[195] 42 C.F.R. §§405.1100–.1130.

[196] 42 C.F.R. §405.1102(a).

[197] 42 C.F.R. §405.1136(a)(1).

[198] 42 C.F.R. §§405.1200–1204.

[199] 42 U.S.C. §§1395i-3(c)(2); 42 C.F.R. §483.12.

Expedited review will be conducted by the Quality Improvement Organization (QIO), which has 72 hours in which to make a decision. When the QIO receives the request for review, it must contact the provider, which then must supply the QIO with information supporting its determination by the close of the same business day. The QIO must solicit the views of the beneficiary and review the notice to determine if it meets CMS requirements. The beneficiary does not incur liability if the QIO decision is delayed because the provider did not get the necessary information to the reviewer in a timely manner.

If the QIO sustains the decision to terminate/discharge services, the beneficiary may request expedited reconsideration, orally or in writing, by noon of the calendar day following initial notification. The reconsideration will be conducted by the QIC, which must issue a decision within 72 hours of the request. If the QIC does not comply with the time frame, the beneficiary may escalate the case to the administrative law judge level.

Beneficiaries retain the right to utilize the standard appeals process rather than the new expedited process in all situations. A QIO may review an appeal from a beneficiary whose request is not timely filed, but the QIO does not have to adhere to the time frame for issuing a decision, and the limitation on liability does not apply.

[D] Which Cases to Appeal

The success of an appeal will be determined by the strength of the nursing and medical evidence, particularly the statements of treating physicians. In a meritorious case, the further an advocate pursues the appeals process, the more likely it is that a favorable decision can be obtained.

In assessing a case for appeal, review whether there are technical problems with the case (e.g., whether the patient was in a Medicare-certified bed, had a qualifying hospital stay, and was transferred to the SNF in a timely fashion). Next, determine if the case involves rehabilitation or skilled nursing care, or a combination of both. Cases with daily rehabilitation services, especially physical therapy, are generally good cases for appeal. Remember to make certain that the services are being provided by, or under the supervision of, a professional physical therapist.

When assessing a skilled nursing claim, determine whether the patient received daily *per se* nursing services as listed in the regulation. If not, take a closer look at the patient's total condition. A "total condition" case should be documented by sufficient daily nursing notes. If the nursing notes are sparse or skip days, it will be more difficult to establish daily monitoring or management.

It is common for a patient to receive physical therapy three times per week. A case may be worth appealing if skilled nursing services can be documented during the other four days. Remember that unless skilled rehabilitation therapy was provided five days per week, the skilled care must be provided seven *days* per week, not seven *times* each week (five days per week in rehabilitation therapy cases).

APPENDIX 3-1

REVIEWING SKILLED NURSING FACILITY MEDICAL RECORDS

Introduction

Medicare skilled nursing facility (SNF) case files contain several types of medical records. These are either typed or handwritten entries on various forms. Common medical records include hospital discharge summaries, SNF admission notes, physical examinations, physician orders, physician progress notes, daily nursing notes, medication charts, wound care charts, therapy evaluations, and therapy flow sheets (which could include physical, occupational, and speech therapy).

Hospital Discharge Summary

The hospital discharge summary is the first medical record that should be reviewed. It contains a great deal of valuable information, including the patient's diagnoses and treatment received in the hospital. The discharge summary also lists all diagnostic procedures and a brief medical history. The patient's age and a brief statement of the events that preceded hospitalization are usually included. Advocates should also look for any reference to future treatments to be performed at the SNF and for a listing of all discharge medications.

SNF Admission Notes

The next records to review are the SNF admission notes or physical examination forms. These are generally completed by nursing staff. Sometimes a full physical examination is done by the patient's treating physician. These records provide assessments pertaining to the patient's functional status upon admission, including vital sign data. Any functional or perceptual deficits are noted. Many forms include a body chart with specific references to skin problems or decubitus ulcers.

Physician's Orders

The physician's orders should be carefully reviewed. The initial admission orders may be handwritten. It is important to make every effort to decipher these orders because of the important information they contain. If penmanship is particularly bad, sometimes a magnifier may help. If necessary, a call to the doctor's office or review by another physician or a nurse may help in reading the writing and/or interpreting the abbreviations. The initial orders include the patient's primary and secondary diagnoses. Medications are listed with instructions for administration. For example, an order written "Inderal, PO, q.i.d." means the patient is taking Inderal, an antihypertensive medication, orally, four times daily. Note that some physicians will use the brand name (e.g., Inderal), while others may use the generic name (propranolol). An order written "Haldol, IM, prn" means the patient may be given intramuscular injections of Haldol on an as-needed basis. The *Physicians' Desk Reference* and *Mosby's Nursing Drug Reference* are useful reference materials in which to look up prescription drugs.

An important part of the orders is the physician certification for the required level of care. Most physician order sheets indicate whether the patient is certified for a SNF level of care. Orders are usually renewed every calendar month or 30 days. These orders are signed by the treating physician.

The physician's orders also include all other treatments and services provided to the patient. The orders indicate skilled services, such as physical therapy treatments, as well as orders for services that may not necessarily be considered a skilled service, such as the administration of over-the-counter (OTC) artificial tear drops. References such as the *Lippincott Manual of Nursing Practice* can assist the advocate in determining if the level of care performed is skilled nursing care. The orders may also include quality of life information such as whether a patient is allowed any alcoholic beverages or a leave of absence from the facility.

The file contains physician progress notes. This portion of the medical record may also contain notations from other specialities that see the patient; for example, a consultation with an ear, nose, and throat physician or a dietitian. Often the treating physician only goes to the facility one time per month to see the patient. An increase in frequency of visits may indicate the need for more skilled care by the patient, or that the patient's medical condition is deteriorating. The notes are very helpful to define the medical issues and to indicate the frequency with which the patient's medical condition required physician intervention. These notes are signed by the physician or whoever has examined the patient.

Nurses' Notes and Other Treatment Records

There are other areas of the medical file where information may be gleaned about the patient's specific treatments. These include flow sheets and drug and treatment records. The daily nursing notes are also extremely important. These clinical records reveal the day-to-day treatments as well as the patient's status. Some facilities keep better records than others and some nurses document patient care more thoroughly than others. First look to see if there are daily entries. Each entry is signed by the nurse on duty for the particular shift. Sometimes there may several days with no entry at all. A pattern of missing daily entries may indicate that the SNF felt the level of care was no longer skilled, which may or may not actually be the case. Unfortunately it is difficult to document observation and assessment or management of a care plan without detailed daily nursing notes.

Examining other documentation, such as wound care or medication sheets, may help substantiate daily skilled care.

A patient in a SNF may suffer from open skin ulcers, or decubitus ulcers. These indicate the general debility, loss of mobility, and compromised nutritional status of the patient. Specific treatments for this condition should be documented in the physician orders and nursing notes. There may also be a wound care chart or treatment record. This record has a diagram of the body showing the location of the ulcers or wounds. Entries in these records indicate the location, size, and depth of the wound. They also reveal whether there is any drainage from the wound and the "stage" of the wound. Skin ulcers are classified as stages I to IV, with stages indicating progressive degeneration of the wound. Stage I is inflammation or reddening of the skin. Stage IV is skin breakdown with deep tissue involvement and the presence of necrotic or dead tissue. Treatment progress is noted in these records.

Medication Charts

Medication charts document the daily administration of prescribed medications. These records reveal the drug, dose, and mode and frequency of administration. The original date of prescription, renewal date, and administration dates are noted. The administration of other treatments may also be noted. For example, daily decubitus ulcer care may be documented in the medication chart as opposed to a separate wound care chart, or a patient's bowel movements may be monitored through entries in the medication chart. There is usually a separate chart to document medication that is administered on an as-needed basis or medication that is withheld for any reason. Nurses' initials usually appear each time a medication is administered.

Therapy Records

Patients receiving therapy also have therapy evaluations and progress flow sheets. These are the most important records in cases that rely on daily physical therapy as the qualifying skilled service. The physical therapy evaluation also contains a patient care plan. The evaluation portion assesses the patient's need for rehabilitative physical therapy. The care plan portion addresses the patient's specific treatments. First, there is an assessment of the patient's functional problems. Then there is a listing of both short-term and long-term rehabilitation goals. The treatment plan sets forth the specific modality of treatment and frequency. This document is usually signed by both the registered physical therapist and the treating physician. The daily progress notes or flow sheet documents the treatments actually received by the patient. These records include the dates of services, mobility status, specific rehabilitation modalities, and patient endurance. Some records also have brief narrative notes concerning each treatment. These are signed or initialed by the treating physical therapist.

Nonskilled Services

Documentation of nonskilled services, such as care provided by certified nurse aides (CNAs), may be present in the record. The records may contain valuable information regarding the total condition of the patient, for example, input and output (I&O), pattern of bowel elimination, urinary incontinence, and mobility patterns. Their value should not be overlooked in supplementing the skilled nurse's notes.

Conclusion

A careful review and understanding of the beneficiary's medical records is key to a successful Medicare appeal. Once significant portions of the medical record are identified, be certain they are available to the ALJ or other decision-makers and that they become part of the formal Medicare appeal record.

APPENDIX 3-2

WORKSHEETS

1. Reviewing Skilled Nursing Facility Records

Documents Contained in a Skilled Nursing Facility Record:

- Hospital Discharge Summary (W-10)
- Skilled Nursing Facility Admission Notes
- Physician Orders
- Nurses' Notes & Other Treatment Records
- Medication Charts
- Therapy Records
- Nonskilled Services

2. Establishing Medical Necessity

- Review patient's demographics, e.g., age, gender
- Compare assistive devices, functional limitations, and activities permitted with patient's age, disability, and diagnoses
- Note complexity of diagnoses and conditions that interact with each other
- Group medications by classification, noting multiple drugs for the same diagnosis
- Look for new medications or changes in doses of existing medications
- New physician orders may indicate a change in patient's condition
- Note changes in vital signs
- Look for increases in frequency of visits by skilled staff, which may indicate deterioration of the patient or need for skilled observation
- Examine visit documentation for evidence of observation and assessment, management of a care plan, and patient education
- Review therapy narratives, ventilator settings, wound care charts, gastric tube feedings, and medical social worker records for changes in patient condition
- Wound care charts and diagrams show healing and treatment changes
- Compare therapeutic diets and fluid restrictions with patient's diagnoses, nutritional status, height, and weight
- Review nonskilled records for evidence of changes in patient's condition

3. Skilled Nursing Facility Review

Center Case No:

Date Reviewed:

Advocate:

Patient:

HIC#:

Provider:

Period at Issue:

Services at Issue/Delivered:

☐SN   ☐PT   ☐OT   ☐ST   ☐Other

Age:

Diagnoses:

1.

2.

3.

4.

Surgical Procedures:

1.

2.

Functional Limitations:

Activities Permitted:

Mental Status:

Therapeutic Diet:

Case No:

REASONABLENESS AND NECESSITY:

- ☐ Obs & Assess:
- ☐ Mgt of Care Plan:
- ☐ PT Teaching:

Skilled Nursing Services:

- ☐ IV or IM injections or IV feedings
- ☐ Enteral feedings (at least 26% of caloric requirements and at least 501 ml of fluid)
- ☐ Nasopharyngeal or tracheostomy aspiration
- ☐ Sterile insertion, irrigation, and replacement of catheters
- ☐ Dressings involving medications and aseptic technique
- ☐ Treatment of decubitus ulcers or widespread skin disorders
- ☐ Heat treatments ordered by MD
- ☐ Administration of medical gases
- ☐ Rehabilitation nursing

Therapy Services:

- ☐ Therapeutic exercises
- ☐ Gait evaluation & training
- ☐ ROM/Exercise
- ☐ Maintenance therapy
- ☐ Ultrasound, shortwave, and microwave therapy
- ☐ Hot pack, hydrocollator, infrared treatment, paraffin baths, and whirlpool
- ☐ Speech pathologist

Case No:

Number of Days Used:

Dates of Discontinuation of Therapy Services:

    ☐ PT_____
    ☐ OT_____
    ☐ ST_____

SNF Level of Care Required   ☐Yes   ☐No

Notice Issues:

Notice Adequate   ☐Yes   ☐No

    ☐ Unsigned Notice
    ☐ Telephone Notification Only
    ☐ No Evidence Notice Mailed/Received

Perceived issue for which claim may have been denied:

    ☐ No three-day qualifying hospital stay
    ☐ Not Reasonable and Necessary
    ☐ Non-Medicare—Certified Bed

Is documentation adequate to succeed on coverage appeal to ALJ?

    ☐ Yes
    ☐ No

If no, specify:_____

APPENDIX 3-3

IMPORTANT SECTIONS OF THE MEDICARE

BENEFIT POLICY MANUAL

Chapter 8—Coverage of Extended Care (SNF) Services Under Hospital Insurance

Skilled Nursing and Rehabilitation Definitions

30.2—Skilled Nursing and Rehabilitation Services
(Rev. 1, 10-01-03)
A3-3132.1, SNF-214.1

30.2.1—Skilled Services Defined
(Rev. 1, 10-01-03)
A3-3132.1.A, SNF-214.1.A

Skilled nursing and/or skilled rehabilitation services are those services, furnished pursuant to physician orders, that:

- Require the skills of qualified technical or professional health personnel such as registered nurses, licensed practical (vocational) nurses, physical therapists, occupational therapists, and speech pathologists or audiologists; and

- Must be provided directly by or under the general supervision of these skilled nursing or skilled rehabilitation personnel to assure the safety of the patient and to achieve the medically desired result.

NOTE: "General supervision" requires initial direction and periodic inspection of the actual activity. However, the supervisor need not always be physically present or on the premises when the assistant is performing services.

30.2.2.—Principles for Determining Whether a Service is Skilled
(Rev. 1, 10-01-03)
A3-3132.1.B, SNF-214.1.B

- If the inherent complexity of a service prescribed for a patient is such that it can be performed safely and/or effectively only by or under the general supervision of skilled nursing or skilled rehabilitation personnel, the service is a skilled service; e.g., the administration of intravenous feedings and intramuscular injections; the insertion of suprapubic catheters; and ultrasound, shortwave, and microwave therapy treatments.

- The intermediary considers the nature of the service and the skills required for safe and effective delivery of that service in deciding whether a service is a skilled service. While a patient's particular medical condition is a valid factor in deciding if skilled services are needed, a patient's diagnosis or prognosis should never be the sole factor in deciding that a service is not skilled.

EXAMPLE: When rehabilitation services are the primary services, the key issue is whether the skills of a therapist are needed. The deciding factor is not the patient's potential for recovery, but whether the services needed require the skills of a therapist or whether they can be provided by nonskilled personnel. (*See* §30.5.)

- A service that is ordinarily considered nonskilled could be considered a skilled service in cases in which, because of special medical complications, skilled nursing or skilled rehabilitation personnel are required to perform or supervise it or to observe the patient. In these cases, the complications and special services involved must be documented by physicians' orders and nursing or therapy notes.

EXAMPLE: Whirlpool baths do not ordinarily require the skills of a qualified physical therapist. However, the skills, knowledge, and judgment of a qualified physical therapist might be required where the patient's condition is complicated by circulatory deficiency, areas of desensitization, or open wounds.

- In determining whether services rendered in an SNF constitute covered care, it is necessary to determine whether individual services are skilled, and whether, in light of the patient's total condition, skilled management of the services provided is needed even though many or all of the specific services were unskilled.

EXAMPLE: An 81-year-old woman who is aphasic and confused, suffers from hemiplegia, congestive heart failure, and atrial fibrillation, has suffered a cerebrovascular accident, is incontinent, and has a Stage 1 decubitus ulcer, and is unable to communicate and make her needs known. Even though no specific service provided is skilled, the patient's condition requires daily skilled nursing involvement to manage a plan for the total care needed, to observe the patient's progress, and to evaluate the need for changes in the treatment plan.

- The importance of a particular service to an individual patient, or the frequency with which it must be performed, does not, by itself, make it a skilled service.

EXAMPLE: A primary need of a nonambulatory patient may be frequent changes of position in order to avoid development of decubitus ulcers. However, since such changing of position does not ordinarily require skilled nursing or skilled rehabilitation personnel, it would not constitute a skilled service, even though such services are obviously necessary.

- The possibility of adverse effects from the improper performance of an otherwise unskilled service does not make it a skilled service unless there is documentation to support the need for skilled nursing or skilled rehabilitation personnel. Although the act of turning a patient normally is not a skilled service, for some patients the skills of a nurse may be necessary to assure proper body alignment in order to avoid contractures and deformities. In all such cases, the reasons why skilled nursing or skilled rehabilitation personnel are essential must be documented in the patient's record.

30.2.3—Specific Examples of Some Skilled Nursing or Skilled Rehabilitation Services
(Rev. 1, 10-01-03)
A3-3132.1.C, SNF-214.1.C

30.2.3.1—Management and Evaluation of a Patient Care Plan
(Rev. 1, 10-01-03)
A3-3132.1.C.1, SNF-214.1.C.1

The development, management, and evaluation of a patient care plan, based on the physician's orders, constitute skilled nursing services when, in terms of the patient's physical or mental condition, these services require the involvement of skilled nursing personnel to meet the patient's medical needs, promote recovery, and ensure medical safety. However, the planning and management of a treatment plan that does not involve the furnishing of skilled services may not require skilled nursing personnel; e.g., a care plan for a patient with organic brain syndrome who requires only oral medication and a protective environment. The sum total of nonskilled would only add up to the need for skilled management and evaluation when the condition of the beneficiary is such that there is an expectation that a change in condition is likely without that intervention.

EXAMPLE 1: An aged patient with a history of diabetes mellitus and angina pectoris is recovering from an open reduction of the neck of the femur. He requires, among other services, careful skin care, appropriate oral medications, a diabetic diet, a therapeutic exercise program to preserve muscle tone and body condition, and observation to notice signs of deterioration in his condition or complications resulting from his restricted (but increasing) mobility. Although any of the required services could be performed by a properly instructed person, that person would not have the capability to understand the relationship among the services and their effect on each other. Since the nature of the patient's condition, his age, and his immobility create a high potential for serious complications, such an understanding is essential to assure the patient's recovery and safety. The management of this plan of care requires skilled nursing personnel until the patient's treatment regimen is essentially stabilized, even though the individual services involved are supportive in nature and do not require skilled nursing personnel.

EXAMPLE 2: An aged patient is recovering from pneumonia, is lethargic, is disoriented, has residual chest congestion, is confined to bed as a result of his debilitated condition, and requires restraints at times. To decrease the chest congestion, the physician has prescribed frequent changes in position, coughing, and deep breathing. While the residual chest congestion alone would not represent a high risk factor, the patient's immobility and confusion represent complicating factors which, when coupled with the chest congestion, could create high probability of a relapse. In this situation, skilled overseeing of the nonskilled services would be reasonable and necessary, pending the elimination of the chest congestion, to assure the patient's medical safety.

Skilled planning and management activities are not always specifically identified in the patient's clinical record. Therefore, if the patient's overall condition supports a finding that recovery and safety can be assured only if the total care, skilled or not, is planned and managed by skilled nursing personnel, the intermediary assumes that skilled management is being provided even though it is not readily discernible from the record. It makes the assumption only if the record as a whole clearly establishes that there was a likely potential for serious complications without skilled management.

30.2.3.2—Observation and Assessment of Patient's Condition (Rev. 1, 10-01-03) A3-3132.1.C.2, SNF-214.1.C.2

Observation and assessment are skilled services when the likelihood of change in a patient's condition requires skilled nursing or skilled rehabilitation personnel to identify and evaluate the patient's need for possible modification of treatment or initiation of additional medical procedures, until the patient's treatment regimen is essentially stabilized.

EXAMPLE 1: A patient with arteriosclerotic heart disease with congestive heart failure requires close observation by skilled nursing personnel for signs of decompensation, abnormal fluid balance, or adverse effects resulting from prescribed medication. Skilled observation is needed to determine whether the digitalis dosage should be reviewed or whether other therapeutic measures should be considered, until the patient's treatment regimen is essentially stabilized.

EXAMPLE 2: A patient has undergone peripheral vascular disease treatment including revascularization procedures (bypass) with open or necrotic areas of skin on the involved extremity. Skilled observation and monitoring of the vascular supply of the legs is required.

EXAMPLE 3: A patient has undergone hip surgery and has been transferred to an SNF. Skilled observation and monitoring of the patient for possible adverse reaction to the operative procedure, development of phlebitis, skin breakdown, or need for the administration of subcutaneous Heparin, is both reasonable and necessary.

EXAMPLE 4: A patient has been hospitalized following a heart attack, and following treatment but before mobilization, is transferred to the SNF. Because it is unknown whether exertion will exacerbate the heart disease, skilled observation is reasonable and necessary as mobilization is initiated, until the patient's treatment regimen is essentially stabilized.

EXAMPLE 5: A frail 85-year-old man was hospitalized for pneumonia. The infection was resolved, but the patient, who had previously maintained adequate nutrition, will not eat or eats poorly. The patient is transferred to an SNF for monitoring of fluid and nutrient intake, and assessment of the need for tube feeding and forced feeding if required. Observation and monitoring by skilled nursing personnel of the patient's oral intake is required to prevent dehydration.

If a patient was admitted for skilled observation but did not develop a further acute episode or complication, the skilled observation services still are covered so long as there was a reasonable probability for such a complication or further acute episode. "Reasonable probability" means that a potential complication or further acute episode was a likely possibility.

Skilled observation and assessment may also be required for patients whose primary condition and needs are psychiatric in nature or for patients who, in addition to their physical problems, have a secondary psychiatric diagnosis. These patients may exhibit acute psychological symptoms such as depression, anxiety, or agitation, which require skilled observation and assessment such as observing for indications of suicidal or hostile behavior. However, these conditions often require considerably more specialized, sophisticated nursing techniques and physician attention than is available in most participating SNFs. (SNFs that are primarily engaged in treating psychiatric disorders are precluded by law from participating in Medicare.) Therefore, these cases must be carefully documented.

30.2.3.3—Teaching and Training Activities
(Rev. 1, 10-01-03)
A3-3132.1.C.3, SNF-214.1.C.3

Teaching and training activities which require skilled nursing or skilled rehabilitation personnel to teach a patient how to manage his treatment regimen would constitute skilled services. Some examples are:

- Teaching self-administration of injectable medications or a complex range of medications;

- Teaching a newly diagnosed diabetic to administer insulin injections, to prepare and follow a diabetic diet, and to observe foot-care precautions;

- Teaching self-administration of medical gases to a patient;

- Gait training and teaching of prosthesis care for a patient who has had a recent leg amputation;

- Teaching patients how to care for a recent colostomy or ileostomy;

- Teaching patients how to perform self-catheterization and self- administration of gastrostomy feedings;

- Teaching patients how to care for and maintain central venous lines, such as Hickman catheters;

- Teaching patients the use and care of braces, splints and orthotics, and any associated skin care; and

- Teaching patients the proper care of any specialized dressings or skin treatments.

30.2.4—Questionable Situations
(Rev. 1, 10-01-03)
A3-3132.1.D, SNF-214.1.D

There must be specific evidence that daily skilled nursing or skilled rehabilitation services are required and received if:

- The primary service needed is oral medication; or

- The patient is capable of independent ambulation, dressing, feeding, and hygiene.

30.3—Direct Skilled Nursing Services to Patients
(Rev. 1, 10-01-03)
A3-3132.2, SNF-214.2

Some examples of direct skilled nursing services are:

- Intravenous, intramuscular, or intravenous feedings;

- Enteral feeding that comprises at least 26 percent of daily caloric requirements and provides at least 501 milliliters of fluid per day;

- Naso-pharyngeal and tracheotomy aspiration;

- Insertion, sterile irrigation, and replacement of catheters;

- Application of dressings involving prescription medications and aseptic techniques (*see* §30.5 for exception);

- Treatment of decubitus ulcers, of a severity rated at Stage 3 or worse, or a widespread skin disorder (*see* §30.5 for exception);

- Heat treatments which have been specifically ordered by a physician as part of active treatment and which require observation by skilled nursing personnel to evaluate the patient's progress adequately (*see* §30.5 for exception);

- Rehabilitation nursing procedures, including the related teaching and adaptive aspects of nursing, that are part of active treatment and require the presence of skilled nursing personnel; e.g., the institution and supervision of bowel and bladder training programs;

- Initial phases of a regimen involving administration of medical gases such as bronchodilator therapy; and

- Care of a colostomy during the early postoperative period in the presence of associated complications. The need for skilled nursing care during this period must be justified and documented in the patient's medical record.

30.4—Direct Skilled Rehabilitation Services to Patients
(Rev. 1, 10-01-03)
A3-3132.1.C, SNF-214.1.C

30.4.1—Skilled Physical Therapy
(Rev. 1, 10-01-03)
A3-3132.3A, SNF-214.3.A

30.4.1.1—General
(Rev. 1, 10-01-03)
A3-3132.3.A.1, SNF-214.3.A.1

Skilled physical therapy services must meet all of the following conditions:

- The services must be directly and specifically related to an active written treatment plan approved by the physician after any needed consultation with a qualified physical therapist;

- The services must be of a level of complexity and sophistication, or the condition of the patient must be of a nature that requires the judgment, knowledge, and skills of a qualified physical therapist;

- The services must be provided with the expectation, based on the assessment made by the physician of the patient's restoration potential, that the condition of the patient will improve materially in a reasonable and generally predictable period of time, or the services must be necessary for the establishment of a safe and effective maintenance program;

- The services must be considered under accepted standards of medical practice to be specific and effective treatment for the patient's condition; and

- The services must be reasonable and necessary for the treatment of the patient's condition; this includes the requirement that the amount, frequency, and duration of the services must be reasonable.

EXAMPLE 1: An 80-year-old, previously ambulatory, post-surgical patient has been bedbound for one week and, as a result, has developed muscle atrophy, orthostatic hypotension, joint stiffness, and lower extremity edema. To the extent that the patient requires a brief period of daily skilled physical therapy services to restore lost functions, those services are reasonable and necessary.

EXAMPLE 2: A patient with congestive heart failure also has diabetes and previously had both legs amputated above the knees. Consequently, the patient does not have a reasonable potential to achieve ambulation, but still requires daily skilled physical therapy to learn bed mobility and transferring skills, as well as functional activities at the wheelchair level. If the patient has a reasonable potential for achieving those functions in a reasonable period of time in view of the patient's total condition, the physical therapy services are reasonable and necessary.

If the expected results are insignificant in relation to the extent and duration of physical therapy services that would be required to achieve those results, the physical therapy would not be reasonable and necessary, and thus would not be covered skilled physical therapy services.

Many SNF inpatients do not require skilled physical therapy services but do require services, which are routine in nature. Those services can be performed by supportive personnel; e.g., aides or nursing personnel, without the supervision of a physical therapist. Such services, as well as services involving activities for the general good and welfare of patients (e.g., general exercises to promote overall fitness and flexibility and activities to provide diversion or general motivation) do not constitute skilled physical therapy.

30.4.1.2—Application of Guidelines
(Rev. 1, 10-01-03)
A3-3132.3.A.2, SNF-214.3.A.2

Some of the more common skilled physical therapy modalities and procedures are:

A—Assessment: The skills of a physical therapist are required for the ongoing assessment of a patient's rehabilitation needs and potential.

Skilled rehabilitation services concurrent with the management of a patient's care plan include tests and measurements of range of motion, strength, balance, coordination, endurance, and functional ability.

B—Therapeutic Exercises: Therapeutic exercises, which must be performed by or under the supervision of the qualified physical therapist, due either to the type of exercise employed or to the condition of the patient.

C—Gait Training: Gait evaluation and training furnished to a patient whose ability to walk has been impaired by neurological, muscular, or skeletal abnormality often require the skills of a qualified physical therapist.

Repetitious exercises to improve gait, or to maintain strength and endurance, and assistive walking are appropriately provided by supportive personnel, e.g., aides or nursing personnel, and do not require the skills of a physical therapist. Thus, such services are not skilled physical therapy.

D—Range of Motion: Only the qualified physical therapist may perform range of motion tests and, therefore, such **tests** are skilled physical therapy. Range of motion **exercises** constitute skilled physical therapy only if they are part of active treatment for a specific disease state which has resulted in a loss or restriction of mobility (as evidenced by physical therapy notes showing the degree of motion lost, the degree to be restored and the impact on mobility and/or function).

Range of motion exercises that are not related to the restoration of a specific loss of function often may be provided safely by supportive personnel, such as aides or nursing personnel, and may not require the skills of a physical therapist. Passive exercises to maintain range of motion in paralyzed extremities that can be carried out by aides or nursing personnel would not be considered skilled care.

E—Maintenance Therapy: The repetitive services required to maintain function sometimes involve the use of complex and sophisticated therapy procedures and, consequently, the judgment and skill of a physical therapist might be required for the safe and effective rendition of such services. (*See* §30.2.)The specialized knowledge and judgment of a qualified physical therapist may be required to establish a maintenance program intended to prevent or minimize deterioration caused by a medical condition, if the program is to be safely carried out by caregivers and the treatment goals of the physician are achieved. Establishing such a program is a skilled service.

EXAMPLE: A patient with Parkinson's disease may require the services of a physical therapist to determine the type of exercises that are required to maintain his present level of function. The initial evaluation of the patient's needs, the designing of a maintenance program which is appropriate to the capacity and tolerance of the patient and the treatment objectives of the physician, the instruction of the patient or supportive personnel (e.g., aides or nursing personnel) in the carrying out of the program, would constitute skilled physical therapy. While a patient is receiving a skilled physical therapy program, the physical therapist should regularly reevaluate the patient's condition and adjust any exercise program the patient is expected to carry out independently or with the aid of supportive personnel to maintain the function being restored. Consequently, by the time it is determined that no further restoration is possible, i.e., by the end of the last skilled session, the physical therapist will have already designed the maintenance program required and instructed the patient or supportive personnel in the carrying out of the program.

F—Ultrasound, Shortwave, and Microwave Diathermy Treatments: These modalities must always be performed by or under the supervision of a qualified physical therapist.

G—Hot Packs, Infra-Red Treatments, Paraffin Baths, and Whirlpool Baths: Heat treatments and baths of this type ordinarily do not require the skills of a qualified physical therapist. However, the skills, knowledge, and judgment of a qualified physical therapist might be required in the giving of such treatments or baths in a particular case, e.g., where the patient's condition is complicated by circulatory deficiency, areas of desensitization, open wounds, fractures, or other complications.

30.4.2—Speech Pathology
(Rev. 1, 10-01-03)
A3-3132.3.B, SNF-214.3.B

See the Medicare Benefit Policy Manual, Chapter 1, "Inpatient Hospital Services."

30.4.3—Occupational Therapy
(Rev. 1, 10-01-03)
A3-3132.3.C, SNF-214.3.C

See the Medicare Benefit Policy Manual, Chapter 1, "Inpatient Hospital Services."

30.5—Nonskilled Supportive or Personal Care Services
(Rev. 1, 10-01-03)
A3-3132.4, SNF-214.4

The following services are not skilled services unless rendered under circumstances detailed in §30.2:

• Administration of routine oral medications, eye drops, and ointments (the fact that patients cannot be relied upon to take such medications themselves or that State law requires all medications to be dispensed by a nurse to institutional patients would not change this service to a skilled service);

- General maintenance care of colostomy and ileostomy;

- Routine services to maintain satisfactory functioning of indwelling bladder catheters (this would include emptying and cleaning containers and clamping the tubing);

- Changes of dressings for uninfected post-operative or chronic conditions;

- Prophylactic and palliative skin care, including bathing and application of creams, or treatment of minor skin problems;

- Routine care of the incontinent patient, including use of diapers and protective sheets;

- General maintenance care in connection with a plaster cast (skilled supervision or observation may be required where the patient has a preexisting skin or circulatory condition or requires adjustment of traction);

- Routine care in connection with braces and similar devices;

- Use of heat as a palliative and comfort measure, such as whirlpool or steam pack;

- Routine administration of medical gases after a regimen of therapy has been established (i.e., administration of medical gases after the patient has been taught how to institute therapy);

- Assistance in dressing, eating, and going to the toilet;

- Periodic turning and positioning in bed; and

- General supervision of exercises, which have been taught to the patient and the performance of repetitious exercises that do not require skilled rehabilitation personnel for their performance. (This includes the actual carrying out of maintenance programs where the performances of repetitive exercises that may be required to maintain function do not necessitate a need for the involvement and services of skilled rehabilitation personnel. It also includes the carrying out of repetitive exercises to improve gait, maintain strength or endurance; passive exercises to maintain range of motion in paralyzed extremities which are not related to a specific loss of function; and assistive walking.) (*See* Medicare Benefit Policy Manual, Chapter 1, "Inpatient Hospital Services.")

30.6—Daily Skilled Services Defined
(Rev. 1, 10-01-03)
A3-3132.5, SNF-214.5

Skilled nursing services or skilled rehabilitation services (or a combination of these services) must be needed and provided on a "daily basis," i.e., on essentially a seven days a week basis. A patient whose inpatient stay is based solely on the need for skilled rehabilitation services would meet the "daily basis" requirement when they need and receive those services on at least five days a week. (If therapy services are provided less than five days a week, though, the "daily" requirement would not be met.)

This requirement should not be applied so strictly that it would not be met merely because there is an isolated break of a day or two during which no skilled rehabilitation services are furnished and discharge from the facility would not be practical.

EXAMPLE: A patient who normally requires skilled rehabilitation services on a daily basis may exhibit extreme fatigue, which results in suspending therapy sessions for a day or two. Coverage may continue for these days since discharge in such a case would not be practical.

In instances when a patient requires a skilled restorative nursing program to positively impact his functional well-being, the expectation is that the program be rendered at least six days a week. (Note that when a patient's skilled status is based on a restorative program, medical evidence must exist to justify the services. In most instances, it is expected that duration of a skilled restorative program last only a couple of weeks.)

30.7—Services Provided on an Inpatient Basis as a "Practical Matter" (Rev. 1, 10-01-03) A3-3132.6, SNF-214.6

In determining whether the daily skilled care needed by an individual can, as a "practical matter," only be provided in a SNF on an inpatient basis, the intermediary considers the individual's physical condition and the availability and feasibility of using more economical alternative facilities or services.

As a "practical matter," daily skilled services can be provided only in a SNF if they are not available on an outpatient basis in the area in which the individual resides or transportation to the closest facility would be:

• An excessive physical hardship;

• Less economical; or

• Less efficient or effective than an inpatient institutional setting.

The availability of capable and willing family or the feasibility of obtaining other assistance for the patient at home should be considered. Even though needed daily skilled services might be available on an outpatient or home care basis, as a practical matter, the care can be furnished only in the SNF if home care would be ineffective because the patient would have insufficient assistance at home to reside there safely.

EXAMPLE: A patient undergoing skilled physical therapy can walk only with supervision but has a reasonable potential to learn to walk independently with further training. Further daily skilled therapy is available on an outpatient or home care basis, but the patient would be at risk for further injury from falling, dehydration, or malnutrition because insufficient supervision and assistance could not be arranged for the patient in his home. In these circumstances, the physical therapy services as a practical matter can be provided effectively only in the inpatient setting.

30.7.1—The Availability of Alternative Facilities or Services (Rev. 1, 10-01-03) A3-3132.6.A, SNF-214.6.A

Alternative facilities or services may be available to a patient when health care providers such as home health agencies are utilized. These alternatives are not always available in all communities and even where they exist they may not be available when needed.

EXAMPLE: Where the residents of a rural community generally utilize the outpatient facilities of a hospital located some distance from the area, the hospital outpatient department constitutes an alternative source of care that is available to the community. Roads in winter, however, may be impassable for some periods of time and in special situations institutionalization might be needed.

In determining the availability of more economical care alternatives, the coverage or noncoverage of that alternative care is not a factor to be considered. Home health care for a patient who is not homebound, for example, may be an appropriate alternative in some cases. The fact that Medicare cannot cover such care is irrelevant.

The issue is feasibility and not whether coverage is provided in one setting and not provided in another. For instance, an individual in need of daily skilled physical therapy might be able to receive the services needed on a more economical basis from an independently practicing physical therapist. However, the fact that Medicare payment could not be made for the services because the $500 expense limitation applicable to the services of an independent physical therapist had been exceeded or because the patient was not enrolled in Part B, would not be a basis for determining that, as a practical matter, the needed care could only be provided in a SNF.

In determining the availability of alternate facilities or services, whether the patient or another resource can pay for the alternate services is not a factor to be considered.

30.7.2—Whether Available Alternatives Are More Economical in the Individual Case
(Rev. 1, 10-01-03)
A3-3132.6.B, SNF-214.6.B

If the intermediary determines that an alternative setting is available to provide the needed care, it considers whether the use of the alternative setting would actually be more economical in the individual case.

EXAMPLE 1: If a patient's condition requires daily transportation to the alternative source of care (e.g., a hospital outpatient department) by ambulance, it might be more economical from a health care delivery viewpoint to provide the needed care in the SNF setting.

EXAMPLE 2: If needed care could be provided in the home, but the patient's residence is so isolated that daily visits would entail inordinate travel costs, care in a SNF might be a more economical alternative.

30.7.3—Whether the Patient's Physical Condition Would Permit Utilization of an Available, More Economical Care Alternative
(Rev. 1, 10-01-03)
A3-3132.6.C, SNF-214.6.C

In determining the practicality of using more economical care alternatives, the intermediary considers the patient's medical condition. If the use of those alternatives would adversely affect the patient's medical condition, the intermediary concludes that as a practical matter the daily skilled services can only be provided by a SNF on an inpatient basis.

If the use of a care alternative involves transportation of the individual on a daily basis, the intermediary considers whether daily transportation would cause excessive physical hardship. Determinations on whether a patient's condition would be adversely affected if an available, more economical care alternative were utilized should not be based solely on the fact that the patient is nonambulatory. There are individuals confined to wheelchairs who, though nonambulatory, could be transported daily by automobile from their homes to alternative care sources without any adverse impact. Conversely, there are instances where an individual's condition would be adversely affected by daily transportation to a care facility, even though the individual is able to ambulate to some extent.

EXAMPLE: A 75-year-old woman has suffered a cerebrovascular accident and cannot climb stairs safely. The patient lives alone in a second-floor apartment accessible only by climbing a flight of stairs. She requires physical therapy and occupational therapy on alternate days, and they are available in a CORF one mile away from her apartment. However, because of her inability to negotiate the stairs, the daily skilled services she requires cannot, as a practical matter, be provided to the patient outside the SNF.

The "practical matter" criterion should never be interpreted so strictly that it results in the automatic denial of coverage for patients who have been meeting all of the SNF level of care requirements, but who have occasion to be away from the SNF for a brief period of time. While most beneficiaries requiring a SNF level of care find that they are unable to leave the facility, the fact that a patient is granted an outside pass or short leave of absence for the purpose of attending a special religious service, holiday meal, family occasion, going on a car ride, or for a trial visit home, is not, by itself evidence that the individual no longer needs to be in a SNF for the receipt of required skilled care. Where frequent or prolonged periods away from the SNF become possible, the intermediary may question whether the patient's care can, as a practical matter, only be furnished on an inpatient basis in a SNF. Decisions in these cases should be based on information reflecting the care needed and received by the patient while in the SNF and on the arrangements needed for the provision, if any, of this care during any absences. (*See* the Medicare Benefit Policy Manual, Chapter 3, "Duration of Covered Inpatient Services," §20.1.2, for counting inpatient days during a leave of absence.) A conservative approach to retain the presumption for limitation of liability may lead a facility to notify patients that leaving the facility will result in denial of coverage. Such a notice is not appropriate. If a SNF determines that covered care is no longer needed, the situation does not change whether the patient actually leaves the facility or not.

APPENDIX 3-4

TITLE 42—PUBLIC HEALTH
(CODE OF FEDERAL REGULATIONS):

PART 409—HOSPITAL INSURANCE BENEFITS

(Subpart C—Posthospital SNF Care)

Sec. 409.20 Coverage of services.

(a) Included services. Subject to the conditions and limitations set forth in this subpart and subpart D of this part, "posthospital SNF care" means the following services furnished to an inpatient of a participating SNF, or of a participating hospital or critical access hospital (CAH) that has a swing-bed approval:

(1) Nursing care provided by or under the supervision of a registered professional nurse.

(2) Bed and board in connection with the furnishing of that nursing care.

(3) Physical, occupational, or speech therapy.

(4) Medical social services.

(5) Drugs, biologicals, supplies, appliances, and equipment.

(6) Services furnished by a hospital with which the SNF has a transfer agreement in effect under Sec. 483.75(n) of this chapter.

(7) Other services that are generally provided by (or under arrangements made by) SNFs.

(b) Excluded services—(1) Services that are not considered inpatient hospital services. No service is included as posthospital SNF care if it would not be included as an inpatient hospital service under Secs. 409.11 through 409.18.

(2) Services not generally provided by (or under arrangements made by) SNFs. Except as specifically listed in Secs. 409.21 through 409.27, only those services generally provided by (or under arrangements made by) SNFs are considered as posthospital SNF care. For example, a type of medical or surgical procedure that is ordinarily performed only on an inpatient basis in a hospital is not included as "posthospital SNF care," because such procedures are not generally provided by (or under arrangements made by) SNFs.

(c) Terminology. In Secs. 409.22 through 409.36—

(1) The terms SNF and swing-bed hospital are used when the context applies to the particular facility.

(2) The term facility is used to mean both SNFs and swing-bed hospitals.

(3) The term "swing-bed hospital" includes a CAH with swing-bed approval under subpart F of part 485 of this chapter.

[48 FR 12541, Mar. 25, 1983, as amended at 50 FR 33033, Aug. 16, 1985; 58 FR 30667, May 26, 1993; 63 FR 26306, May 12, 1998; 64 FR 3648, Jan. 25, 1999; 64 FR 41681, July 30, 1999]

* * *

Sec. 409.21   Nursing care.

(a) **Basic rule.** Medicare pays for nursing care as posthospital SNF care when provided by or under the supervision of a registered professional nurse.

(b) **Exception.** Medicare does not pay for the services of a private duty nurse or attendant. An individual is not considered to be a private duty nurse or attendant if he or she is an SNF employee at the time the services are furnished.

[63 FR 26306, May 12, 1998]
* * *

Sec. 409.22   Bed and board.

(a) **Semiprivate and ward accommodations.** Except for applicable deductible and coinsurance amounts Medicare Part A pays in full for semiprivate (2 to 4 beds), or ward (5 or more beds) accommodations.

(b) **Private accommodations—(1) Conditions for payment in full.** Except for applicable coinsurance amounts, Medicare pays in full for a private room if—

(i) The patient's condition requires him to be isolated;

(ii) The SNF has no semiprivate or ward accommodations; or

(iii) The SNF semiprivate and ward accommodations are fully occupied by other patients, were so occupied at the time the patient was admitted to the SNF for treatment of a condition that required immediate inpatient SNF care, and have been so occupied during the interval.

(2) **Period of payment.** In the situations specified in paragraph (b)(1) (i) and (iii) of this section, Medicare pays for a private room until the patient's condition no longer requires isolation or until semiprivate or ward accommodations are available.

(3) **Conditions for patient's liability.** The facility may charge the patient the difference between its customary charge for the private room furnished and its most prevalent charge for a semiprivate room if:

(i) None of the conditions of paragraph (b)(1) of this section is met, and

(ii) The private room was requested by the patient or a member of the family who, at the time of request was informed what the charge would be.
* * *

Sec. 409.23   Physical, occupational, and speech therapy.

Medicare pays for physical, occupational, or speech therapy as posthospital SNF care if—

(a) It is furnished by the facility or under arrangements made by the facility, and

(b) Billing for the therapy is by or through the facility.
* * *

Sec. 409.24   Medical social services.

Medicare pays for medical social services as posthospital SNF care, including—

(a) Assessment of the social and emotional factors related to the beneficiary's illness, need for care, response to treatment, and adjustment to care in the facility;

(b) Case work services to assist in resolving social or emotional problems that may have an adverse effect on the beneficiary's ability to respond to treatment; and

(c) Assessment of the relationship of the beneficiary's medical and nursing requirements to his or her home situation, financial resources, and the community resources available upon discharge from facility care.

[63 FR 26306, May 12, 1998]
* * *

Sec. 409.25   Drugs, biologicals, supplies, appliances, and equipment.

(a) Drugs and biologicals. Except as specified in paragraph (b) of this section, Medicare pays for drugs and biologicals as posthospital SNF care only if—

(1) They represent a cost to the facility;

(2) They are ordinarily furnished by the facility for the care and treatment of inpatients; and

(3) They are furnished to an inpatient for use in the facility.

(b) Exception. Medicare pays for a limited supply of drugs for use outside the facility if it is medically necessary to facilitate the beneficiary's departure from the facility and required until he or she can obtain a continuing supply.

(c) Supplies, appliances, and equipment. Except as specified in paragraph (d) of this section, Medicare pays for supplies, appliances, and equipment as posthospital SNF care only if they are—

(1) Ordinarily furnished by the facility to inpatients; and

(2) Furnished to inpatients for use in the facility.

(d) Exception. Medicare pays for items to be used after the individual leaves the facility if—

(1) The item is one that the beneficiary must continue to use after leaving, such as a leg brace; or

(2) The item is necessary to permit or facilitate the beneficiary's departure from the facility and is required until he or she can obtain a continuing supply, for example, sterile dressings.

[63 FR 26307, May 12, 1998]
* * *

Sec. 409.26   Transfer agreement hospital services.

(a) Services furnished by an intern or a resident-in-training. Medicare pays for medical services that are furnished by an intern or a resident-in-training (under a hospital teaching program approved in accordance with the provisions of Sec. 409.15) as posthospital SNF care, if the intern or resident is in—

(1) A participating hospital with which the SNF has in effect an agreement under Sec. 483.75(n) of this chapter for the transfer of patients and exchange of medical records; or

(2) A hospital that has a swing-bed approval, and is furnishing services to an SNF-level inpatient of that hospital.

(b) Other diagnostic or therapeutic services. Medicare pays for other diagnostic or therapeutic services as posthospital SNF care if they are provided—

(1) By a participating hospital with which the SNF has in effect a transfer agreement as described in paragraph (a)(1) of this section; or

(2) By a hospital or a CAH that has a swing-bed approval, to its own SNF-level inpatient.

[63 FR 26307, May 12, 1998]

* * *

Sec. 409.27   Other services generally provided by (or under arrangements made by) SNFs.

In addition to those services specified in Secs. 409.21 through 409.26, Medicare pays as posthospital SNF care for such other diagnostic and therapeutic services as are generally provided by (or under arrangements made by) SNFs, including—

(a) Medical and other health services as described in subpart B of part 410 of this chapter, subject to any applicable limitations or exclusions contained in that subpart or in Sec. 409.20(b);

(b) Respiratory therapy services prescribed by a physician for the assessment, diagnostic evaluation, treatment, management, and monitoring of patients with deficiencies and abnormalities of cardiopulmonary function; and

(c) Transportation by ambulance that meets the general medical necessity requirements set forth in Sec. 410.40(d)(1) of this chapter.

[63 FR 26307, May 12, 1998, as amended at 64 FR 41681, July 30, 1999]

APPENDIX 3-5

TITLE 42—PUBLIC HEALTH
(CODE OF FEDERAL REGULATIONS)

PART 409—HOSPITAL INSURANCE BENEFITS

(Subpart D—Requirements For Coverage of Posthospital SNF Care)

Sec. 409.31   Level of care requirement.

(a) Definition. As used in this section, skilled nursing and skilled rehabilitation services means services that:

(1) Are ordered by a physician;

(2) Require the skills of technical or professional personnel such as registered nurses, licensed practical (vocational) nurses, physical therapists, occupational therapists, and speech pathologists or audiologists; and

(3) Are furnished directly by, or under the supervision of, such personnel.

(b) Specific conditions for meeting level of care requirements. (1) The beneficiary must require skilled nursing or skilled rehabilitation services, or both, on a daily basis.

(2) Those services must be furnished for a condition—(i) For which the beneficiary received inpatient hospital or inpatient CAH services; or

(ii) Which arose while the beneficiary was receiving care in a SNF or swing-bed hospital for a condition for which he or she received inpatient hospital or inpatient CAH services.

(3) The daily skilled services must be ones that, as a practical matter, can only be provided in a SNF, on an inpatient basis.

[48 FR 12541, Mar. 25, 1983, as amended at 58 FR 30666, May 26, 1993]
* * *

Sec. 409.32   Criteria for skilled services and the need for skilled services.

(a) To be considered a skilled service, the service must be so inherently complex that it can be safely and effectively performed only by, or under the supervision of, professional or technical personnel.

(b) A condition that does not ordinarily require skilled services may require them because of special medical complications. Under those circumstances, a service that is usually nonskilled (such as those listed in Sec. 409.33(d)) may be considered skilled because it must be performed or supervised by skilled nursing or rehabilitation personnel. For example, a plaster cast on a leg does not usually require skilled care. However, if the patient has a preexisting acute skin condition or needs traction, skilled personnel may be needed to adjust traction or watch for complications. In situations of this type, the complications, and the skilled services they require, must be documented by physicians' orders and nursing or therapy notes.

(c) The restoration potential of a patient is not the deciding factor in determining whether skilled services are needed. Even if full recovery or medical improvement is not possible, a patient may need skilled services to prevent further deterioration or preserve current capabilities. For example, a terminal cancer patient may need some of the skilled services described in Sec. 409.33.

[48 FR 12541, Mar. 25, 1983, as amended at 59 FR 65493, Dec. 20, 1994]
* * *

Sec. 409.33 Examples of skilled nursing and rehabilitation services.

(a) Services that could qualify as either skilled nursing or skilled rehabilitation services—(1) Overall management and evaluation of care plan. (i) When overall management and evaluation of care plan constitute skilled services. The development, management, and evaluation of a patient care plan based on the physician's orders constitute skilled services when, because of the patient's physical or mental condition, those activities require the involvement of technical or professional personnel in order to meet the patient's needs, promote recovery, and ensure medical safety. Those activities include the management of a plan involving a variety of personal care services only when, in light of the patient's condition, the aggregate of those services requires the involvement of technical or professional personnel.

(ii) Example. An aged patient with a history of diabetes mellitus and angina pectoris who is recovering from an open reduction of a fracture of the neck of the femur requires, among other services, careful skin care, appropriate oral medications, a diabetic diet, an exercise program to preserve muscle tone and body condition, and observation to detect signs of deterioration in his or her condition or complications resulting from restricted, but increasing, mobility. Although any of the required services could be performed by a properly instructed person, such a person would not have the ability to understand the relationship between the services and evaluate the ultimate effect of one service on the other. Since the nature of the patient's condition, age, and immobility create a high potential for serious complications, such an understanding is essential to ensure the patient's recovery and safety. Under these circumstances, the management of the plan of care would require the skills of a nurse even though the individual services are not skilled. Skilled planning and management activities are not always specifically identified in the patient's clinical record. Therefore, if the patient's overall condition supports a finding that recovery and safety can be ensured only if the total care is planned, managed, and evaluated by technical or professional personnel, it is appropriate to infer that skilled services are being provided.

(2) Observation and assessment of the patient's changing condition—(i) When observation and assessment constitute skilled services. Observation

and assessment constitute skilled services when the skills of a technical or professional person are required to identify and evaluate the patient's need for modification of treatment or for additional medical procedures until his or her condition is stabilized.

(ii) Examples. A patient with congestive heart failure may require continuous close observation to detect signs of decompensation, abnormal fluid balance, or adverse effects resulting from prescribed medication(s) that serve as indicators for adjusting therapeutic measures. Similarly, surgical patients transferred from a hospital to an SNF while in the complicated, unstabilized postoperative period, for example, after hip prosthesis or cataract surgery, may need continued close skilled monitoring for postoperative complications and adverse reaction. Patients who, in addition to their physical problems, exhibit acute psychological symptoms such as depression, anxiety, or agitation, may also require skilled observation and assessment by technical or professional personnel to ensure their safety or the safety of others, that is, to observe for indications of suicidal or hostile behavior. The need for services of this type must be documented by physicians' orders or nursing or therapy notes.

(3) Patient education services—(i) When patient education services constitute skilled services. Patient education services are skilled services if the use of technical or professional personnel is necessary to teach a patient self-maintenance.

(ii) Examples. A patient who has had a recent leg amputation needs skilled rehabilitation services provided by technical or professional personnel to provide gait training and to teach prosthesis care. Similarly, a patient newly diagnosed with diabetes requires instruction from technical or professional personnel to learn the self-administration of insulin or foot-care precautions.

(b) Services that qualify as skilled nursing services. (1) Intravenous or intramuscular injections and intravenous feeding.

(2) Enteral feeding that comprises at least 26% of daily calorie requirements and provides at least 501 milliliters of fluid per day.

(3) Nasopharyngeal and tracheostomy aspiration;

(4) Insertion and sterile irrigation and replacement of suprapubic catheters;

(5) Application of dressings involving prescription medications and aseptic techniques;

(6) Treatment of extensive decubitus ulcers or other widespread skin disorder;

(7) Heat treatments which have been specifically ordered by a physician as part of active treatment and which require observation by nurses to adequately evaluate the patient's progress;

(8) Initial phases of a regimen involving administration of medical gases;

(9) Rehabilitation nursing procedures, including the related teaching and adaptive aspects of nursing, that are part of active treatment, e.g., the institution and supervision of bowel and bladder training programs.

(c) Services that would qualify as skilled rehabilitation services.

(1) Ongoing assessment of rehabilitation needs and potential: Services concurrent with the management of a patient care plan, including tests and measurements of range of motion, strength, balance, coordination, endurance, functional ability, activities of daily living, perceptual deficits, speech and language or hearing disorders;

(2) Therapeutic exercises or activities: Therapeutic exercises or activities which, because of the type of exercises employed or the condition of the patient, must be performed by or under the supervision of a qualified physical therapist or occupational therapist to ensure the safety of the patient and the effectiveness of the treatment;

(3) Gait evaluation and training: Gait evaluation and training furnished to restore function in a patient whose ability to walk has been impaired by neurological, muscular, or skeletal abnormality;

(4) Range of motion exercises: Range of motion exercises which are part of the active treatment of a specific disease state which has resulted in a loss of, or restriction of, mobility (as evidenced by a therapist's notes showing the degree of motion lost and the degree to be restored);

(5) Maintenance therapy; Maintenance therapy, when the specialized knowledge and judgment of a qualified therapist is required to design and establish a maintenance program based on an initial evaluation and periodic reassessment of the patient's needs, and consistent with the patient's capacity and tolerance. For example, a patient with Parkinson's disease who has not been under a rehabilitation regimen may require the services of a qualified therapist to determine what type of exercises will contribute the most to the maintenance of his present level of functioning.

(6) Ultrasound, short-wave, and microwave therapy treatment by a qualified physical therapist;

(7) Hot pack hydrocollator, infrared treatments, paraffin baths, and whirlpool in particular cases where the patient's condition is complicated by circulatory deficiency, areas of desensitization, open wounds, fractures, or other complications, and the skills, knowledge, and judgment of a qualified physical therapist are required; and

(8) Services of a speech pathologist or audiologist when necessary for the restoration of function in speech or hearing.

(d) Personal care services. Personal care services which do not require the skills of qualified technical or professional personnel are not skilled services except under the circumstances specified in Sec. 409.32(b). Personal care services include, but are not limited to, the following:

(1) Administration of routine oral medications, eye drops, and ointments;

(2) General maintenance care of colostomy and ileostomy;

(3) Routine services to maintain satisfactory functioning of indwelling bladder catheters;

(4) Changes of dressings for noninfected postoperative or chronic conditions;

(5) Prophylactic and palliative skin care, including bathing and application of creams, or treatment of minor skin problems;

(6) Routine care of the incontinent patient, including use of diapers and protective sheets;

(7) General maintenance care in connection with a plaster cast;

(8) Routine care in connection with braces and similar devices;

(9) Use of heat as a palliative and comfort measure, such as whirlpool and hydrocollator;

(10) Routine administration of medical gases after a regimen of therapy has been established;

(11) Assistance in dressing, eating, and going to the toilet;

(12) Periodic turning and positioning in bed; and

(13) General supervision of exercises which have been taught to the patient; including the actual carrying out of maintenance programs, i.e., the performance of the repetitive exercises required to maintain function do [sic] not require the skills of a therapist and would not constitute skilled rehabilitation services (see paragraph (c) of this section). Similarly, repetitious exercises to improve gait, maintain strength, or endurance; passive exercises to maintain range of motion in paralyzed extremities, which are not related to a specific loss of function; and assistive walking do not constitute skilled rehabilitation services.

[48 FR 12541, Mar. 25, 1983, as amended at 63 FR 26307, May 12, 1998; 64 FR 41681, July 30, 1999]

APPENDIX 3-6

Notice of Exclusions from Medicare Benefits
Skilled Nursing Facility (NEMB-SNF)

Date of Notice:_____

NOTE: You need to make a choice about receiving these health care items or services.

It is not Medicare's opinion, but our opinion, that Medicare will not pay for the item(s) or service(s) described below. Medicare does not pay for all of your health care costs. Medicare only pays for covered items and services when Medicare rules are met. The fact that Medicare will not pay for a particular item or service does not mean that you should not receive it. There may be a good reason to receive it. Right now, in your case, **Medicare will not pay for –**

Items or Services:

We believe that Medicare will not pay, for the following reason. (See the reason checked off below.)

❏ No qualifying 3-day inpatient hospital stay.

❏ No days left in this benefit period.

❏ Care not ordered or certified by a physician.

❏ Daily skilled care not needed.

❏ SNF transfer requirement not met.

❏ Facility/Bed not certified by Medicare.

❏ Care not given by, nor supervised by, skilled nursing or rehabilitation staff.

❏ Items or services not furnished under arrangements by the skilled nursing facility.

❏ Other:_____

_____

The purpose of this notice is to help you make an informed choice about whether or not you want to receive these items or services, knowing that you will have to pay for them yourself or through other insurance that you may have. Before you make a decision about your options, you should **read this entire notice carefully.**

- Ask us to explain, if you don't understand why Medicare won't pay.
- Ask us how much these items or services will cost you (**Estimated Cost: $_____**).
  Your other insurance is:_____

PLEASE CHOOSE **ONE** OPTION. CHECK **ONE** BOX. **SIGN** AND **DATE** THIS NOTICE.

❏ **Option 1. YES** I want to receive these items or services and get an official Medicare decision about coverage. Please submit a claim, with any evidence supporting my need for these items or services, to Medicare for its official decision. I understand you will notify me when my claim is submitted and that you will not bill me for these items or services until Medicare makes its decision. If Medicare denies payment, I agree to be personally and fully responsible for payment. That is, I will pay personally, either out of pocket or through any other insurance that I have.

I understand that I can appeal if Medicare decides not to pay. Medicare will send me notice of its official decision not to pay that explains its decision in my case. That notice will explain how I can appeal Medicare's decision not to pay. If I do not hear from Medicare about its official coverage decision within 90 days, I can telephone Medicare at: (_____)_____. TTY/TDD: (_____)_____.

❏ **Option 2. YES** I want to receive these items or services. Do NOT submit a claim to Medicare. I agree to be fully and personally responsible for payment of any amount for which my other insurance will not pay. I realize I cannot appeal to Medicare.

❏ **Option 3. NO** I will not receive these items or services. I understand that you will not be able to submit a claim to Medicare and that I will not be able to appeal your opinion that Medicare won't pay.

Patient's Name	Medicare # (HICN)
Signature of the patient or of the authorized representative	Date

Form CMS-20014 (XX/2004)   OMB Exempt

SKILLED NURSING FACILITY'S NAME & ADDRESS
TELEPHONE NO. AND TTY/TDD NO.

Skilled Nursing Facility Advance Beneficiary Notice (SNFABN)

Date of Notice:_____

NOTE: You need to make a choice about receiving these health care items or services.

It is not Medicare's opinion, but our opinion, that Medicare will not pay for the item(s) or service(s) described below. Medicare does not pay for all of your health care costs. Medicare only pays for covered items and services when Medicare rules are met. The fact that Medicare may not pay for a particular item or service does not mean that you should not receive it. There may be a good reason to receive it. Right now, in your case, **Medicare probably will not pay for –**

Items or Services:

Because:

The purpose of this form is to help you make an informed choice about whether or not you want to receive these items or services, knowing that you might have to pay for them yourself. Before you make a decision about your options, you should **read this entire notice carefully.**
- Ask us to explain, if you don't understand why Medicare probably won't pay.
- Ask us how much these items or services will cost you (**Estimated Cost: $_____**), in case you have to pay for them yourself or through other insurance you may have. Your other insurance is:_____
- If in 90 days you have not gotten a decision on your claim, contact the Medicare contractor at: Address:_____
  _____ or at: Telephone: _____ TTY/TDD:_____ .
- If you receive these items or services, we will submit your claim for them to Medicare.

PLEASE CHOOSE **ONE** OPTION. CHECK **ONE** BOX. **DATE & SIGN** THIS NOTICE.

☐ **Option 1. YES. I want to receive these items or services.** I understand that Medicare will not decide whether to pay unless I receive these items or services. I understand you will notify me when my claim is submitted and that you will not bill me for these items or services until Medicare makes its decision. If Medicare denies payment, I agree to be personally and fully responsible for payment. That is, I will pay personally, either out of pocket or through any other insurance that I have. I understand that I can appeal Medicare's decision.

☐ **Option 2. NO. I will not receive these items or services.** I understand that you will not be able to submit a claim to Medicare and that I will not be able to appeal your opinion that Medicare won't pay. I understand that, in the case of any physician-ordered items or services, I should notify my doctor who ordered them that I did not receive them.

Patient's Name:_____ Medicare # (HICN):_____

_____

Date   Signature of the patient or of the authorized representative

Form No. CMS-10055

INTERMEDIARY DETERMINATION OF NONCOVERAGE

NAME OF SNF
ADDRESS
DATE

TO: NAME
     ADDRESS

RE: NAME OF BENEFICIARY
     HICN
     DATE OF ADMISSION

On (Date), the Medicare intermediary advised us that the services you receive will no longer qualify as covered under Medicare beginning (Date).

The Medicare intermediary will send you a formal determination as to the noncoverage of your stay after (Date). If you wish to appeal, the formal notice will contain information about how this can be done. The intermediary will inform you of the reason for denial and your appeal rights.

We regret that this may be your first notice of the noncoverage of services under Medicare. Our efforts to contact you earlier, in person or by telephone, were unsuccessful.

Please verify receipt of this notice by signing below.

    Sincerely yours,

_____
Signature of Administrative Officer

VERIFICATION OF RECEIPT OF NOTICE

A.   This acknowledges that I received this attached notice of noncoverage of services under Medicare on (date of receipt).

_____

(Signature of Beneficiary or Person
 acting on Beneficiary's behalf

B.   This is to confirm that you were advised of the noncoverage of the services under Medicare by telephone on (date of telephone contact).

_____

(Name of Beneficiary or
 Representative contacted)

_____

(Signature of Administrative Officer)

KEEP A COPY OF THIS FOR YOUR RECORDS

UR COMMITTEE DETERMINATION OF ADMISSION

NAME OF SNF
ADDRESS
DATE

TO: NAME
ADDRESS

RE: NAME OF BENEFICIARY
HICN
DATE OF ADMISSION

On (Date), our Utilization Review Committee reviewed your medical information available at the time of, or prior to your admission, and advised us that the services (you or beneficiary's name) needed do not meet the requirements for coverage under Medicare. The reason is:

(Insert specific reason the services were determined to be noncovered.)

This decision has not been made by Medicare. It represents the Utilization Review Committee's judgment that the services you needed did not meet Medicare payment requirements. Normally, under this situation, a bill is not submitted to Medicare. A bill will only be submitted to Medicare if you request us to submit one. Furthermore, if you want to appeal this decision you must request that a bill be submitted. If you request a bill be submitted, the Medicare intermediary will notify you of its determination. If you disagree with that determination you may file an appeal.

You must also request that a bill be submitted to Medicare if you have questions concerning your liability for payment for the services you received.

Under a provision of the Medicare law, you do not have to pay for noncovered services determined to be custodial care or not reasonable or necessary unless you had reason to know the services were noncovered. You are considered to know that these services were noncovered effective with the date of this notice.

We regret that this may be your first notice of the noncoverage of services under Medicare. Our efforts to contact you earlier in person or by telephone were unsuccessful.

Please check one of the boxes below to indicate whether or not you want your bill submitted to Medicare and sign the notice to verify receipt.

Sincerely yours,

_____
Signature of Administrative Officer

REQUEST FOR MEDICARE INTERMEDIARY REVIEW

/ /   A.   I want my bill submitted to the intermediary for a Medicare decision. You will be informed when the bill is submitted.

If you do not receive a formal Notice of Medicare Determination within 90 days of this request you should contact: (Name and address of intermediary).

/ /   B.   I do not want my bill submitted to the intermediary for a Medicare decision.

I understand that I do not have Medicare appeal rights if a bill is not submitted.

NOTE: You are not required to pay for services until a Medicare decision has been made.

VERIFICATION OF RECEIPT OF NOTICE

C.   This acknowledges that I received the notice of noncoverage of services under Medicare on (date of receipt).

_____
(Signature of Beneficiary or Person
 acting on Beneficiary's behalf)

D.   This is to confirm that you were advised of the noncoverage of the services under Medicare by telephone on (date of telephone contact).

_____
(Name of Beneficiary or
Representative contacted)

_____
(Signature of Administrative Officer)

KEEP A COPY OF THIS FOR YOUR RECORDS

UR COMMITTEE DETERMINATION ON CONTINUED STAY

NAME OF SNF
ADDRESS
DATE

TO: NAME
ADDRESS

RE: NAME OF BENEFICIARY
HICN
DATE OF ADMISSION

On (Date) our Utilization Review Committee reviewed your medical information and found that the services furnished (you or beneficiary's name) no longer qualified for payment by Medicare beginning (Date).

The reason for this is: (Insert specific reason services were determined to be noncovered).

This decision has not been made by Medicare. It represents the Utilization Review Committee's judgment that the services you needed no longer met Medicare payment requirements. A bill will be sent to Medicare for the covered services you received before (Date). Normally, the bill submitted to Medicare does not include services provided after this date. If you want to appeal this decision you must request that the bill submitted to Medicare include the services our URC determined to be noncovered. Medicare will notify you of its determination. If you disagree with that determination you may file an appeal.

Under a provision of the Medicare law, you do not have to pay for noncovered services determined to be custodial or not reasonable or necessary unless you had reason to know the services were noncovered. You are considered to know that these services were noncovered effective with the date of this notice.

We regret that this may be your first notice of the noncoverage of services under Medicare. Our efforts to contact you earlier in person or by telephone were unsuccessful.

Please check one of the boxes below to indicate whether or not you want the bill for services after (date) submitted to Medicare and sign the notice to verify receipt.

Sincerely yours,

_____
Signature of Administrative Officer

REQUEST FOR MEDICARE INTERMEDIARY REVIEW

/ /   A.   I want my bill for services I continue to receive to be submitted to the intermediary for a Medicare decision. You will be notified when the bill is submitted.

    If you do not receive a formal Notice of Medicare Determination within 90 days of this request you should contact: (Name and address of intermediary).

/ /   B.   I do not want my bill for services submitted to the intermediary for a Medicare decision.

    I understand that I do not have Medicare appeal rights if a bill is not submitted.

NOTE: You are not required to pay for services until a Medicare decision has been made.

VERIFICATION OF RECEIPT OF NOTICE

    C.   This acknowledges that I received this notice of noncoverage of services under Medicare on (date of receipt).

_____
(Signature of Beneficiary or Person
 acting on Beneficiary's behalf)

    D.   This is to confirm that you were advised of the noncoverage of the services under Medicare by telephone on (date of telephone contact).

_____
(Name of Beneficiary or
Representative contacted)

_____
    (Signature of Administrative Officer)

KEEP A COPY OF THIS FOR YOUR RECORDS

SNF DETERMINATION ON ADMISSION

NAME OF SNF
ADDRESS
DATE

TO: NAME
    ADDRESS

RE: NAME OF BENEFICIARY
    HICN
    DATE OF ADMISSION

On (Date), we reviewed your medical information available at the time of, or prior to your admission, and we believe that the services (you or beneficiary's name) needed did not meet the requirements for coverage under Medicare. The reason is:

(Insert specific reason services are determined to be noncovered.)

This decision has not been made by Medicare. It represents our judgment that the services you needed did not meet Medicare payment requirements. Normally, under this situation, a bill is not submitted to Medicare. A bill will only be submitted to Medicare if you request that a bill be submitted. Furthermore, if you want to appeal this decision, you must request that a bill be submitted. If you request that a bill be submitted, the Medicare intermediary will notify you of its determination. If you disagree with that determination, you may file an appeal.

Under a provision of the Medicare law, you do not have to pay for noncovered services determined to be custodial care or not reasonable or necessary unless you had reason to know the services were noncovered. You are considered to know that these services were noncovered effective with the date of this notice.

If you have questions concerning your liability for payment for services you received prior to the date of this notice, you must request that a bill be submitted to Medicare.

We regret that this may be your first notice of the noncoverage of services under Medicare. Our efforts to contact you earlier in person or by telephone were unsuccessful.

Please check one of the boxes below to indicate whether or not you want your bill submitted to Medicare and sign the notice to verify receipt.

Sincerely yours,

_____
Signature of Administrative Officer

REQUEST FOR MEDICARE INTERMEDIARY REVIEW

/ /   A.   I want my bill submitted to the intermediary for a Medicare decision. You will be informed when the bill is submitted.

If you do not receive a formal Notice of Medicare Determination within 90 days of this request you should contact: (Name and address of intermediary).

/ /   B.   I do not want my bill submitted to the intermediary for a Medicare decision.

I understand that I do not have Medicare appeal rights if no bill is submitted.

NOTE: You are not required to pay for services until a Medicare decision has been made.

VERIFICATION OF RECEIPT OF NOTICE

C.   This acknowledges that I received this notice of noncoverage of services under Medicare on (date of receipt).

_____
(Signature of Beneficiary or Person
 acting on Beneficiary's behalf)

D.   This is to confirm that you were advised of the noncoverage of the services under Medicare by telephone on (date of telephone contact).

_____
(Name of Beneficiary or Representative contacted)

_____
(Signature of Administrative Officer)

KEEP A COPY OF THIS FOR YOUR RECORDS

SNF DETERMINATION ON CONTINUED STAY

NAME OF SNF
ADDRESS
DATE

TO: NAME
     ADDRESS

RE: NAME OF BENEFICIARY
     HICN
     DATE OF ADMISSION

On (Date), we reviewed your medical information and found that the services furnished (you or beneficiary's name) no longer qualified as covered under Medicare beginning (Date).

The reason is: (Insert specific reason services are considered noncovered.)

This decision has not been made by Medicare. It represents our judgment that the services you needed no longer met Medicare payment requirements. A bill will be sent to Medicare for the services you received before (Date). Normally, the bill submitted to Medicare does not include services provided after this date. If you want to appeal this decision, you must request that the bill submitted to Medicare include the services we determined to be noncovered. Medicare will notify you of its determination. If you disagree with that determination you may file an appeal.

Under a provision of the Medicare law, you do not have to pay for noncovered services determined to be custodial care or not reasonable or necessary unless you had reason to know the services were noncovered. You are considered to know that these services were noncovered effective with the date of this notice.

We regret that this may be your first notice of the noncoverage of services under Medicare. Our efforts to contact you earlier in person or by telephone were unsuccessful.

Please check one of the boxes below to indicate whether or not you want your bill submitted to Medicare and sign the notice to verify receipt.

    Sincerely yours,

_____
    Signature of Administrative Officer

REQUEST FOR MEDICARE INTERMEDIARY REVIEW

/ /　A.　I want my bill for services I continue to receive to be submitted to the intermediary for a Medicare decision. You will be informed when the bill is submitted.

If you do not receive a formal Notice of Medicare Determination within 90 days of this request you should contact: (Name and address of intermediary).

/ /　B.　I do not want my bill for services I continue to need to be submitted to the intermediary for a Medicare decision.

　　I understand that I do not have Medicare appeal rights if a bill is not submitted.

NOTE:　You are not required to pay for services until a Medicare decision has been made.

VERIFICATION OF RECEIPT OF NOTICE

　　C.　This acknowledges that I received this notice of noncoverage of services under Medicare on (date of receipt).

_____

(Signature of Beneficiary or Person acting
　　　on Beneficiary's behalf)

　　D.　This is to confirm that you were advised of the noncoverage of the services under Medicare by telephone on (date of telephone contact).

_____

(Name of Beneficiary or Representative contacted)

_____

(Signature of Administrative Officer)

KEEP A COPY OF THIS FOR YOUR RECORDS

OMB Approval No. 0938-0953

{Insert logo here}
NOTICE OF MEDICARE PROVIDER NON-COVERAGE

Patient Name: **Medicare Number:**

THE EFFECTIVE DATE COVERAGE OF YOUR CURRENT {insert type} SERVICES WILL END: {insert effective date}

- Your provider has determined that Medicare probably will not pay for your current {insert type} services after the effective date indicated above.
- You may have to pay for any {insert type} services you receive after the above date.

YOUR RIGHT TO APPEAL THIS DECISION

- You have the right to an immediate, independent medical review (appeal), while your services continue, of the decision to end Medicare coverage of these services.

- If you choose to appeal, the independent reviewer will ask for your opinion and you should be available to answer questions or supply information. The reviewer will also look at your medical records and/or other relevant information. You do not have to prepare anything in writing, but you have the right to do so if you wish.

- If you choose to appeal, you and the independent reviewer will each receive a copy of the detailed explanation about why your coverage for services should not continue. You will receive this detailed notice only after you request an appeal.

- If you choose to appeal, and the independent reviewer agrees that services should no longer be covered after the effective date indicated above, Medicare will not pay for these services after that date.

- If you stop services no later than the effective date indicated above, you will avoid financial liability.

HOW TO ASK FOR AN IMMEDIATE APPEAL

- You must make your request to your Quality Improvement Organization (also known as a QIO). A QIO is the independent reviewer authorized by Medicare to review the decision to end these services.

- Your request for an immediate appeal should be made as soon as possible, but no later than noon of the day before the effective date indicated above.

- The QIO will notify you of its decision as soon as possible, generally by no later than two days after the effective date of this notice.

- Call your QIO at: {insert name and number of QIO} to appeal, or if you have questions.

See page 2 of this form for more information.

OTHER APPEAL RIGHTS:

- If you miss the deadline for filing an immediate appeal, you may still be able to file an appeal with a QIO, but the QIO will take more time to make its decision.

- Contact 1-800-MEDICARE (1-800-633-4227), or TTY/TDD: 1-877-486-2048 for more information about the appeals process.

ADDITIONAL INFORMATION (OPTIONAL)

Please sign below to indicate that you have received this notice.

I have been notified that coverage of my services will end on the effective date indicated on this notice and that I may appeal this decision by contacting my QIO.

Signature of Patient or Authorized Representative   **Date**

Form No. CMS-10123   Exp. Date 06/30/2008

According to the Paperwork Reduction Act of 1995, no persons are required to respond to a collection of information unless it displays a valid OMB control number. The valid OMB control number for this information collection is 0938-0953. The time required to prepare and distribute this collection is 5 minutes per notice, including the time to select the preprinted form, complete it and deliver it to the enrollee. If you have comments concerning the accuracy of the time estimates or suggestions for improving this form, please write to CMS, PRA Clearance Officer, 7500 Security Boulevard, Baltimore, Maryland 21244-1850.

CHAPTER 4

HOME HEALTH COVERAGE

§4.01   INTRODUCTION

The Medicare home health benefit is a crucial source of health care financing for Medicare beneficiaries struggling to live independently in the community. When properly implemented, the Medicare home health benefit can provide coverage for necessary services, even if the patient has a chronic condition and even if the services are expected to extend over a long period of time. Increasingly, these services are the central component of long-term care, and are not one service, but a constellation of skilled and non-skilled services that allows a Medicare beneficiary to remain at home.

When Medicare coverage is unfairly denied, beneficiaries may be unable to afford the home health care they need. Unable to live safely in the community, they may be forced to enter a nursing home. Vigorous advocacy can protect these patients' rights to coverage and care.

Starting in 1998, with the implementation of Balanced Budget Act of 1997 (BBA '97),[1] Medicare beneficiaries began experiencing increased uncertainty about the nature and extent of covered services under the Medicare home health benefit.[2] This was due in large part to significant changes in the Medicare reimbursement system for home care providers that were introduced at that time.[3]

Even though the Medicare home health care benefit was thrown into turmoil with the passage of the BBA '97, leading to inappropriate terminations, denials, and reductions of necessary home health services,[4] other aspects of the home health benefit remain unchanged, *e.g.*, services covered and approaches to advocacy. Thoughtful, informed advocacy continues to help beneficiaries obtain the Medicare coverage to which they are entitled for this important care.

§4.02   COVERAGE

[A]   Generally

The Medicare home health benefit is available under both Parts A and B. The substantive coverage criteria are identical regardless of whether the beneficiary

---

[1] *See* Pub. L. No. 105-33, Title IV, Subtitle G, 4601–4616 (Aug. 5, 1997) (Medicare Home Health Benefit), with significant home health care access limitations beginning in January 1998. *See* **§4.05.**

[2] Beginning in January 1998, there was an upswing in the denial, termination, and reduction of Medicare-covered home health care. Much of this was initially attributed to home health agency fears, misunderstandings, and concerns about changes in payment and reimbursement methods established by the Balanced Budget Act of 1997, Pub. L. No. 105-33 (Aug. 5, 1997).

[3] Beginning in January 1998, there was an upswing in the denial, termination, and reduction of Medicare-covered home health care. Much of this was initially attributed to home health agency fears, misunderstandings, and concerns about changes in payment and reimbursement methods established by the Balanced Budget Act of 1997, Pub. L. No. 105-33 (Aug. 5, 1997).

[4] *See* Pub. L. No. 105-33, Title IV, Subtitle G, 4601–4616 (Aug. 5, 1997) (Medicare Home Health Benefit), with significant home health care access limitations beginning in January 1998. See **§4.05.**

seeks coverage under Part A or Part B. As described below, however, pursuant to BBA '97, Part A coverage is sometimes limited to 100 visits and sometimes hinges on a prior hospital or skilled nursing facility stay.[5]

Medicare provides for coverage of home health services under Part A and Part B when the services are medically "reasonable and necessary," and when[6]

1. The individual is confined to his or her home (or "homebound");

2. The individual needs skilled nursing care on an intermittent basis, or physical or speech therapy or, in the case of an individual who has been furnished home health services based on such a need, but no longer needs such nursing care or therapy, the individual continues to need occupational therapy;

3. A plan for furnishing the services has been established and is periodically reviewed by a physician; and

4. Such services are furnished by, or under arrangement with, a Medicare certified home health agency (HHA).[7]

[B] Part A Coverage Criteria[8]

In addition to the coverage criteria described above, BBA '97 added a prior-institutionalization requirement, established a "home health spell of illness" benefit period, and created a 100-visit coverage limitation per spell of illness for most beneficiaries seeking coverage under Part A. These provisions were effective for services on or after January 1, 1998. Additional coverage for home care services that do not meet these Part A "prior-institutionalization" criteria and visit limitations is available under Part B for beneficiaries enrolled in both Part A and Part B. The prior-institutionalization requirement and 100-visit limitation do not apply to individuals enrolled only in Part A or only in Part B.[9]

[C] Home Health Spell of Illness Defined[10]

The BBA '97 created and defined several new concepts applicable to the Medicare home health care benefit:

---

[5] *See* **§4.05.**

[6] 42 U.S.C. §1395f(a)(2)(C); 42 C.F.R. §§409.42 *et seq.*

[7] 42 U.S.C. §1395x(m).

[8] 42 U.S.C. §1395d.

[9] *Id.*

[10] 42 U.S.C. §1395x.

1. *Post-institutional home health services.* Defined as home health services furnished to an individual:[11]

    After discharge from a hospital in which the individual was an inpatient for not less than three consecutive days before such discharge if such home health services were initiated within 14 days after the date of such discharge; or

    After discharge from a skilled nursing facility in which the individual was provided post-hospital extended care services if such home health services were initiated within 14 days after the date of such discharge.

2. *Home health spell of illness.* Defined as a period of consecutive days:

    Beginning with the first day (not included in a previous home health spell of illness):

    on which such individual is furnished post-institutional home health services; and which occurs in a month for which the individual is entitled to benefits under Part A, and

    Ending with the close of the first period of 60 consecutive days thereafter on each of which the individual is neither an inpatient of a hospital or rural primary care hospital, nor an inpatient of a skilled nursing facility, nor provided home health services.

3. For individuals who have both Part A and Part B, coverage is available under Part A for only 100 visits per spell of illness and only if the services are provided within 14 days of a prior hospital stay or a skilled nursing facility stay of any duration. (Additional services are available to these individuals under Part B.) The new home health spell of illness concept is similar to that which exists for hospital and skilled nursing facility care. It begins with the first day in which the beneficiary receives home health services and ends after the 60th consecutive day in which he or she is neither a hospital nor skilled nursing facility (SNF) patient, nor provided home health services.

4. Coverage is available under Part B for all services not covered under Part A, including those provided to individuals who do not meet the prior institutional requirement and those who have received coverage for the maximum 100 visits under Part A.

5. Individuals who *only* have Part A will receive all coverage under Part A, with or without a prior institutionalization. Individuals who *only* have Part B receive all coverage under that section of the program.

---

[11] 42 U.S.C. §1395x(tt)(1).

[D]   Home Health Services Described

If the triggering conditions described above are satisfied, the beneficiary is entitled to Medicare coverage for home health services. Home health services include:

1. Part-time or intermittent nursing care provided by or under the supervision of a registered professional nurse;

2. Physical, occupational, or speech therapy;

3. Medical social services under the direction of a physician; and

4. Part-time or intermittent services of a home health aide.[12]

In practice, the requirements that a patient is confined to his or her home (usually called the "homebound" rule); and needs intermittent skilled nursing care or physical or speech therapy, are of fundamental importance. Generally, if these preconditions can be met, the beneficiary will be able to establish eligibility for home health coverage.

§4.03   REQUIREMENTS FOR COVERAGE

[A]   The Homebound Rule

The requirement that a patient is homebound (confined to home) is described in detail in the Medicare statute as follows:

> an individual shall be considered to be "confined to his home" if the individual has a condition, due to an illness or injury, that restricts the ability of the individual to leave his or her home except with the assistance of another individual or the aid of a supportive device (such as crutches, a cane, a wheelchair, or a walker), or if the individual has a condition such that leaving his or her home is medically contraindicated. While an individual does not have to be bedridden to be considered "confined to his home," the condition of the individual should be such that there exists a normal inability to leave home, that leaving home requires a considerable and taxing effort by the individual, any absence of an individual from the home attributable to the need to receive healthcare treatment, including regular absences for the purpose of participating in therapeutic, psychosocial, or medical treatment in an adult day-care program that is licensed or certified

---

[12] 42 U.S.C. §1395x(m)(1)–(4).

by a State, or accredited, to furnish adult day-care services in the State shall not disqualify an individual from being considered to be "confined to his home." Any other absence of an individual from the home shall not so disqualify an individual if the absence is of infrequent or of relatively short duration. For purposes of the preceding sentence, any absence for the purpose of attending a religious service shall be deemed to be an absence of infrequent or short duration.[13]

As a careful reading will disclose, the statutory definition of homebound status is ambiguous. While the statute states, for example, that a patient is considered homebound if unable to leave home "except with the assistance of another individual or the aid of a supportive device," it also states that the "condition of the individual should be such that there exists a normal inability to leave home." The question, therefore, often arises whether a patient in a wheelchair is homebound if he leaves home in a wheelchair on a regular basis.[14] Advocates often find themselves quoting one section of the statute to support such a patient's homebound status, while Medicare decision makers attempt to justify denials with different language.

Changes to the Medicare statute enacted in 2000 clarify the threshold "homebound" criteria, making clear that individuals who attend adult day care services may also qualify for Medicare home health coverage.[15] While advocates have been widely successful in winning coverage on appeal for beneficiaries who attend day care, the law change creates the potential for coverage without appeal.

The *Medicare Benefit Policy Manual,*[16] Home Health Services chapter, provides examples of homebound patients and should be of use to advocates

---

[13] 42 U.S.C. §1395n(a)(F), as amended by the Medicare, Medicaid, and SCHIP Benefits Improvement and Protection Act of 2000 (BIPA), Pub. L. No. 106-554 (Dec. 21, 2000).

[14] The issue of how to evaluate whether a beneficiary is homebound, when the use of assistive devices or the assistance of another person allows a person to leave the home regularly, was litigated in O'Neal v. Shalala, No. 1:98CV01126 (D.D.C. filed May 6, 1998) (decision is pending). *See also* Dennis v. Shalala, 1994 WL 708166 (D. Vt. 1994) (infrequent trips to an adult day care program and to local supermarket held within the definition of homebound); Burgess v. Shalala, 1993 WL 327764 (D. Vt. 1993) (must consider both physical and mental effort of leaving home in determining homebound status); Labossiere v. Secretary of HHS, 1991 WL 531922 (D. Vt. 1991) (must show considerable and taxing effort in leaving the home, also must have strong evidentiary support of the nature of the assistance needed, including assistive devices); Pope v. Secretary of HHS, 1991 WL 236173 (D. Vt. 1991) (merely using a walker or wheelchair is not enough to trigger homebound status). The Medicare Prescription Drug Improvement and Modernization Act of 2003, Pub. L. 108-173, §702, authorized a demonstration project to study and clarify the definition of homebound. Titled "Medicare Home Health Demonstration," the project lasted 2 years. *See* <www.cms.hhs.gov/researchers/demos/homehealthindependence.asp for further information>.

[15] *See* Section 703 of the MMA, creating a three-year demonstration project in five states that will provide adult day care services as part of a home health plan of care.

[16] *See* <http://www.cms.hhs.gov/manuals/Downloads/bp102c07.pdf>.

attempting to establish homebound status. According to the manual, the following patients qualify as homebound:

- A beneficiary paralyzed from a stroke who is confined to a wheelchair or who requires the aid of crutches in order to walk;

- A beneficiary who is blind or senile and requires the assistance of another person in leaving his or her place of residence;

- A beneficiary who has lost the use of his or her upper extremities and, therefore, is unable to open doors, use handrails on stairways, etc., and, therefore, requires the assistance of another individual in leaving his or her place of residence;

- A patient with a psychiatric problem if the patient's illness is manifested in part by a refusal to leave his or her home environment or is of such a nature that it would not be considered safe for the patient to leave the home unattended, even if the patient has no physical limitations;[17] and

- A patient in the late stages of ALS or a neurodegenerative disability.

[B] Skilled Nursing Care on an Intermittent Basis, or Physical or Speech Therapy

[1] Generally

The second principal criterion for home health coverage under Medicare is the requirement that the patient need skilled nursing care on an intermittent basis or physical or speech therapy.[18] If the patient requires physical or speech therapy, the analysis is easy—the test is satisfied.[19] More often, however, an attempt to establish home health coverage is defeated by the beneficiary's inability to show a need for intermittent skilled nursing care; either the patient requires no skilled care, or the patient requires too much skilled nursing care, exceeding the intermittent level.[20]

---

[17] See note 13.

[18] 42 U.S.C. §1395f(a)(2)(C); Medicare Benefit Policy Manual, CMS Pub., 100-1, 4-30.3; id., 100-2, 7-30.4. CMS reorganized the paper manual into Internet-only manuals (IOMs) with a revision date of Oct. 1, 2003. The IOMs incorporate all applicable manual provisions for all health care providers. Manuals may be viewed at <http://www.cms.hhs.gov/manuals>.

[19] See note 15.

[20] In this context, the patient may require care that exceeds the part-time or intermittent requirement. Under this standard, a patient may receive skilled nursing and home health aide services furnished any number of days per week for less than eight hours per day and 28 or fewer hours each week (or, on a case-by-case basis, additional hours may be obtained with proper physician certification). Intermittent care is defined as skilled care needed or provided less than seven days a week, or less than eight hours a day for periods of 21 or fewer days. 42 U.S.C. §1395x(m) (effective Oct. 1, 1997). Note, the "part-time or intermittent" requirement must be met, as described above, in addition to the "intermittent" requirement. They are two interrelated requirements. Id.

[2] Defining Skilled Care

The *Medicare Benefit Policy Manual,* Home Health Services chapter defines skilled nursing services as those of a registered nurse or a licensed practical (vocational) nurse under the supervision of a registered nurse, necessary to treat the illness of a patient,[21] as defined in the regulations for SNFs.[22] Those regulations provide that a skilled service must be so inherently complex that it can be safely and effectively performed only by, or under the supervision of, professional or technical personnel,[23] and include numerous examples of skilled services, such as the management of wound care or the administration of intravenous medications.[24]

[3] CMS Medicare Benefit Policy Manual, Home Health Services, Chapter 7[25]

[a] Skilled Home Care

The *Medicare Benefit Policy Manual* defines skilled home health care in a way that parallels the skilled nursing facility regulations. The manual also provides numerous examples to help in determining whether patients require skilled care, including the following:[26]

1. A service that, by its nature, requires the skill of a licensed nurse to be provided safely and effectively continues to be a skilled service even if it is taught to the

---

[21] Medicare Benefit Policy Manual, CMS Pub., 100-2, 7-40.1.2 (skilled nursing care). *See also* "Skilled Nursing Care under the Medicare Home Care Benefit" (Apr. 7, 1998), a memorandum to all Regional Administrators and all Medical Directors in Regional Home Health Intermediaries (RHHIs), from the directors of CMS's Chronic Care Purchasing Policy Group, CHPP, and its Program Integrity Group M. This memorandum reiterates CMS's view that observation and assessment, management of a care plan, and patient education are covered skilled care services for Medicare home care patients.

[22] CMS has adopted, for purposes of defining skilled nursing in the home health care context, the skilled nursing examples and definitions contained in 42 C.F.R. §409.33, applicable to Medicare-certified skilled nursing facilities (SNFs). *See* 42 C.F.R. §409.44(b) (Dec. 20, 1994) (Home Health Agency Regulations) (effective Feb. 21, 1995). These regulations contain critical examples of skilled nursing services (§409.33(a)-(b)) and are relied upon extensively by home health care providers and beneficiaries. *See also* note 21.

[23] 42 C.F.R. §409.32(a) (skilled nursing facility regulations).

[24] 42 C.F.R. §409.33(a), (b) (skilled nursing facility regulations). The skilled services listed in the SNF regulations include overall management and evaluation of the patient's care plan, observation and assessment of the patient's changing condition, and patient education services, as well as specific skilled treatments such as injections, tube feedings, irrigation of an indwelling Foley catheter, changing a dressing on a wound, and suctioning a tracheotomy.

[25] <http://www.cms.hhs.gov/manuals/Downloads/bp102c07.pdf>.

[26] Medicare Benefit Policy Manual, CMS Pub. 100-2, §7-40.1.1.

patient, the patient's family, or other caregivers. For example, wound care is a skilled service, even when it is taught to a family member.[27]

2. A beneficiary's diagnosis should never be the sole factor in deciding that a service the beneficiary needs is either skilled or non-skilled.[28]

3. The determination whether a beneficiary needs skilled nursing care should be based solely upon the beneficiary's unique condition and individual needs, without regard to whether the illness or injury is acute, chronic, terminal, or stable.[29]

4. Observation and assessment of a patient's condition constitutes a skilled nursing service when the likelihood of change in the patient's condition requires skilled nursing personnel to identify and evaluate the patient's need for possible modification of a treatment or initiation of additional medical procedures until the beneficiary's treatment regimen is essentially stabilized.[30]

5. Skilled nursing visits for management and evaluation of the patient's care plan are also reasonable and necessary and covered under the Medicare program where underlying conditions or complications require that only a registered nurse can ensure that essential non-skilled care is achieving its purpose, for example, the services of a skilled nurse to oversee family care-giving efforts involving clients with multiple health problems.[31]

6. A service is not considered a skilled nursing service merely because it is performed by or under the direct supervision of the nurse. Where a service can be safely and effectively performed by the average non-medical person, this service cannot be regarded as skilled although a skilled nurse actually provides the service.[32]

[b] Intermittent Skilled Nursing Care

Although a need for skilled nursing care may be identified, if the patient does not also require skilled therapy, the question remains whether the patient needs *intermittent* skilled nursing care as required and defined by the statute. For many years, Medicare claims were routinely denied on the basis that the patient needed *more* than intermittent skilled nursing care. The meaning of the term "intermittent" was nowhere adequately described.

---

[27] *Id.* §40.1.1(3).
[28] *Id.* §40.1.1(4).
[29] *Id.*
[30] *Id.* §40.1.2.1.
[31] *Id.* §40.1.2.2.
[32] *Id.* §40.1.1(2).

On August 1, 1988, the United States District Court for the District of Columbia issued a decision clarifying this point.[33] This decision in *Duggan v. Bowen* establishes that intermittent means "less than daily."[34] In other words, a patient will need intermittent skilled care if he or she needs skilled care visits on six or fewer days per week. If the patient requires daily skilled care on a seven-day-per-week basis, however, the patient will be found to have violated the intermittent rule, and will be considered ineligible for continued home health coverage unless the patient can show that he or she will require daily skilled care for only a relatively short time (three weeks, for example), or that the need for daily skilled care will end at a certain predictable time in the future.[35]

Congress, in BBA '97, amended the Medicare statute for purposes of Section 1861(m) of the Social Security Act,[36] to define "part-time or intermittent services" as

> Skilled nursing and home health aide services furnished any number of days per week as long as they are furnished (combined) less than 8 hours each day and 28 or fewer hours each week (or subject to review on a case-by-case basis as to the need for care, less than 8 hours each day and 35 or fewer hours per week).[37]

In this amendment, Congress went on to define "intermittent" for purposes of Sections 1814(a)(2)(C)[38] and 1835(a)(2)(A)[39] of the Social Security Act as

> skilled nursing care that is either provided or needed on fewer than 7 days each week, or less than 8 hours of each day for periods of 21 days or less (with extensions in exceptional circumstances when the need for additional care is finite and predictable).[40]

Together, these BBA '97 amendments codified Health Care Financing Administration (HCFA, now CMS) manual standards and other internal guidelines, which have been used by providers and fiscal intermediaries for years to define the amount and frequency of home health nursing and aide services that are covered by Medicare.

---

[33] Duggan v. Bowen, 691 F. Supp. 1487 (D.D.C. 1988).

[34] 691 F. Supp. 1487, 1511.

[35] Medicare Benefit Policy Manual, CMS Pub. 100-2, §7-50.7.

[36] 42 U.S.C. §1395x(m).

[37] *Id.*

[38] *See* 42 U.S.C. §1395f(a) (conditions and limitations for payment).

[39] *See* 42 U.S.C. §1395n (payment of claims of providers of service).

[40] 42 U.S.C. §1395x(m). CMS policy has carved out a specific exception to this requirement for insulin-dependent diabetics who cannot self-administer insulin injections and for whom no one else can be found who is willing to inject the patient: that the need for daily skilled nursing services have a predictable and finite end is not required. *See* Medicare Benefit Policy Manual, CMS Pub., 100-2, §7-40.1.2.4.A.2.

[4]   Skilled Therapy

A patient's need for physical therapy services will, assuming the patient is homebound, trigger home health coverage even where the patient does not require skilled nursing services. In order to qualify, therapy must be skilled. The *Medicare Benefit Policy Manual,* Home Health Services chapter provides that the service of a physical, speech, or occupational therapist is a skilled therapy service if the inherent complexity of the service is such that it can be performed safely and/or effectively only by or under the supervision of a skilled therapist.[41] To be considered reasonable and necessary, the therapy must be consistent with the nature and severity of the illness or injury and the beneficiary's particular needs. The amount, frequency, and duration of the services must be reasonable, and the services must be considered, under accepted standards of medical practice, to be specific and effective treatment for the patient's condition.[42]

Many Medicare denials are based on the lack of expectation of a significant improvement in the patient's condition within a reasonable and predictable period of time. However, "restoration potential" is *not* required by law and a maintenance program *can* be covered if skilled services are necessary to prevent further deterioration or preserve current capabilities. This *includes* visits by the therapist to provide or supervise a maintenance program.[43]

The following types of skilled therapy are covered by the Medicare home health benefit:

1. Assessment by a physical therapist to determine a beneficiary's rehabilitation needs and potential, or to develop and implement a physical therapy program;[44]

2. Therapeutic exercises that must be taught by or under the supervision of a qualified physical therapist to ensure the safety of the beneficiary and the effectiveness of the treatment;[45]

3. Gait training furnished a beneficiary whose ability to walk has been impaired by neurological, muscular, or skeletal abnormality;[46]

4. Range of motion tests, and range of motion exercises, if they are part of an active treatment for a specific disease, illness, or injury that has resulted in a loss or restriction of mobility.[47]

---

[41] Medicare Benefit Policy Manual, CMS Pub. 100-2, §7-40.2.1.a and b.

[42] *Id.*

[43] 42 C.F.R. §409.44(c)(2)(iii); Medicare Benefit Policy Manual, CMS Pub.100-2, §7-40.2.1.C, §40.2.2.E.

[44] Medicare Benefit Policy Manual, CMS Pub. 100-2, §7-40.2.2.A.

[45] *Id.* §40.2.2.B.

[46] *Id.* §40.2.2.C.

[47] *Id.* §40.2.2.D.

[C] Part-Time or Intermittent Services

Once a patient has satisfied the homebound and established a need for skilled nursing care on an intermittent basis, or physical or speech therapy, home health coverage under Medicare is available for the therapy *and* for part-time or intermittent services of a home health aide or nurse. As discussed above, intermittent services are services delivered less than daily, that is, fewer than seven days per week. Part-time services are services delivered fewer than eight hours per day.[48]

Reading the part-time and intermittent standards together, a patient *should* be able to obtain coverage for home health aide or nursing service seven days a week but fewer than eight hours each day (part-time services), or six or fewer times a week for as many as 24 hours per day (intermittent services). In practice, however, do not assume the availability of this heavy degree of coverage on an ongoing basis. Current law and Medicare guidelines provide that coverage may be available for up to 28 hours of aide and nurse services combined each week without the necessity of special documentation. Coverage is available for aide and nurse services totaling as many as 35 hours per week if additional medical justification is shown.[49] Thus, even using the government's own guidelines, application of the part-time or intermittent rule should allow for very extensive coverage of home health nursing and aide services.

Advocates should also be aware that although Medicare home health coverage *should* be available for extended periods of care, the Medicare reimbursement system works to discourage the actual delivery of long periods of care. Fearing inadequate reimbursement, home health agencies may resist serving patients who require long-term care, or numerous, or extended visits. Excuses used may include that care is "chronic" or staff shortages exist. It is, therefore, particularly important to note that both the federal regulations and the CMS manual state that Medicare coverage *is* available even if the patient's care is to last over a long period of time.[50]

§4.04 CHRONIC, STABLE, AND MAINTENANCE-LEVEL PATIENTS

Fiscal intermediaries routinely deny home health coverage to patients deemed chronic, stable, in need of care to "maintain" their conditions, or who otherwise are not getting better or worse at a rapid pace. As a legal matter, however, Medicare coverage *is* available when individuals are confined to home and need intermittent nursing care or physical or speech therapy *even* if the patient

---

[48] Duggan v. Bowen, 691 F. Supp. 1487, 1511 (D.D.C. 1988).

[49] Medicare Benefit Policy Manual, CMS Pub. 100-2, §7-50.7.

[50] 42 C.F.R. §409.44(b)(3)(iii); Medicare Benefit Policy Manual, CMS Pub., 100-2, §7-40.1.1. In the preamble to the final home health prospective payment regulations CMS stated, "In order to address the needs of longer stay patients we are not limiting the number of 60-day episode recertifications permitted in a given fiscal year assuming a patient remains eligible for the Medicare home health benefit," 65 Fed. Reg. 41,128, 41,140 (July 3, 2000). *See* §4.05[D].

is chronically ill and the care is needed over an extended period of time. The fiscal intermediary's own manual makes it clear that Medicare coverage may be available in such cases and that

> [t]he determination of whether a beneficiary needs skilled nursing care should be based solely upon the beneficiary's unique condition and individual needs, without regard to whether the illness or injury is acute, chronic, terminal or expected to extend over a long period of time. In addition, skilled care may, dependent upon the unique condition of the beneficiary, continue to be necessary for a beneficiary whose condition is stable.[51]

Section 40.1.2.2 of Chapter 7 of the Medicare Benefit Policy Manual, CMS Pub. 100-2 makes it clear that management and evaluation of a patient's plan of care will be considered skilled nursing in certain circumstances:

> Skilled nursing visits for management and evaluation of the patient's care plan are also reasonable and necessary where underlying conditions or complications require that only a registered nurse can ensure that essential non-skilled care is achieving its purpose. For skilled nursing care to be reasonable and necessary for management and evaluation of the beneficiary's plan of care, the complexity of the necessary unskilled services which are a necessary part of the medical treatment must require the involvement of skilled nursing personnel to promote the patient's recovery and medical safety in view of the beneficiary's overall condition.[52]

The federal regulations reiterate this important concept:

> The determination of whether skilled nursing care is reasonable and necessary must be based solely upon the beneficiary's unique condition and individual needs, without regard to whether the illness or injury is acute, chronic, terminal, or expected to last a long time.[53]

As enunciated by these sections of the Medicare Act, federal regulations, and CMS guidelines, individuals with chronic conditions can be entitled to Medicare coverage, even if the care they need will continue for long periods of time. Restoration should not be the decisive factor in determining entitlement to coverage.[54]

Furthermore, the United States District Court for the District of Connecticut ruled in *Fox v. Thompson (sub nom. Fox v. Bowen)*,[55] a federal class action concerning Medicare coverage for skilled nursing facility care, that the Secretary

---

[51] Medicare Benefit Policy Manual, CMS Pub. 100-2, §7-40.1.1.

[52] *Id.* §40.1.2.2.

[53] 42 C.F.R. §409.44(b)(3)(iii).

[54] 42 C.F.R. §409.32, incorporated into the home health regulations at 42 C.F.R. §409.44(b).

[55] 656 F. Supp. 1236 (D. Conn. 1986).

of Health and Human Services (HHS) shall not deny Medicare coverage on the basis of "arbitrary rules of thumb." Instead, as the court ruled in *Fox*, each claimant should receive an individualized assessment of his or her need for care based on the facts and circumstances of the claimant's particular case. A particular patient with multiple sclerosis, for example, may well be homebound, require intermittent skilled nursing and/or therapy, and qualify for Medicare coverage, even though the underlying medical condition will remain.[56]

Unfortunately, home health agencies are often convinced that Medicare coverage is unavailable for patients who will not recover and for those in need of maintenance physical therapy. In order to avoid the financial penalties associated with a claim submission that will be denied by the fiscal intermediary, many agencies deny coverage in these cases themselves and decline to submit a claim unless the patient insists. Since agencies usually rely upon the CMS manual, it is particularly important to note supportive sections of the manual, and to instruct the provider that the federal regulations are clear that coverage is available even if the patient is unlikely to improve and even when the care is needed to maintain his or her condition.

§4.05 PROSPECTIVE PAYMENT SYSTEM FOR HOME HEALTH SERVICES

BBA '97 added a requirement to the Medicare statute that all costs for Medicare home health services be reimbursed under a prospective payment system (PPS).[57] Final regulations to implement home health PPS were published in the Federal Register on July 3, 2000,[58] and the Centers for Medicare and Medicaid Assistance (CMS) began paying home health agencies under PPS on October 1, 2000.

[A] What Is PPS?

PPS is a payment system; it does not change eligibility and coverage criteria for Medicare home health benefits. Under the new system, Medicare pays a fixed rate to HHAs for the services they provide a beneficiary during a 60-day episode of care.[59] PPS covers all home health services and non-routine medical supplies

---

[56] Smith v. Shalala, 855 F. Supp. 658 (D. Vt. 1994); Bergeron v. Shalala, 855 F. Supp. 665 (D. Vt. 1994).

[57] *See* 42 U.S.C. §1395ff.

[58] 65 Fed. Reg. 41,128 (July 3, 2000).

[59] 42 C.F.R. §§409.43(f), 424.22(b), 484.205(a). Before PPS, a home health plan of care had to be reviewed every 62 days.

including outpatient physical therapy. PPS does not cover the cost of durable medical equipment (DME) or certain osteoporosis drugs, which are reimbursed separately.[60]

[B] Determining the Amount of Payment

Effective July 19, 1999, a home health agency must use the Outcome and Assessment Information Set (OASIS) to perform an assessment of each new patient before care is provided.[61] Information from the new assessment helps determine the appropriate payment amount under PPS for each patient. First, CMS determines a national prospective 60-day episode payment rate. The rate is then adjusted by two factors: (1) a wage index appropriate for the area in which the beneficiary receives the services, and (2) a case-mix adjuster consisting of selected data elements from OASIS plus an additional data element measuring therapy services.[62] The PPS rate varies, depending upon the patient's clinical condition, functional status, and service needs.

A patient is reassessed at the end of each 60-day episode of care to ensure proper payment. The reassessment also helps determine the proper payment amount for the next episode of care if more services are needed.

If a patient's care needs change substantially during the 60-day episode of care,[63] or if the patient's care plan is completed earlier than expected,[64] CMS may change the amount of payment. CMS may also make an additional payment if the actual costs of providing services are much greater than anticipated.[65] If the patient requires four or fewer home health visits, CMS makes a low-utilization payment adjustment (LUPA), and the agency is paid on a per visit amount that changes depending on the service provided.[66]

---

[60] 42 C.F.R. §§409.100(a), 410.150(b)(19), 413.1(h).

[61] 64 Fed. Reg. 32,984 (June 18, 1999). OASIS is a group of data elements developed under a contract for CMS to assess each home health care patient and to measure patient outcomes.

[62] 42 C.F.R. §§484.210, 484.215, 484.220, 484.250. The PPS rate is generally more for a beneficiary who needs at least eight hours, or ten visits, of therapy services.

[63] A significant change in condition (SCIC) adjustment is made if a new OASIS adjustment shows the beneficiary has a significant change in condition not anticipated in the original plan of care and the doctor certifies the new plan of care. 42 C.F.R. §§484.205(e), 484.237.

[64] If a beneficiary changes agencies in the middle of a 60-day episode, or if a beneficiary is discharged after reaching her goals and then returns to the same agency during the 60-day period, the agency will receive a partial episode payment (PEP) adjustment. The agency will be paid the prorated PPS amount based on the number of days services were provided during the 60-day episode. 42 C.F.R. §§484.205(d), 484.235.

[65] An agency may receive an outlier payment in addition to the PPS amount if the imputed cost of the 60-day episode exceeds 113 percent of the payment amount. 42 C.F.R. §§484.205(f), 484.40.

[66] 42 C.F.R. §§484.205(c), 484.230.

[C] The Claims Process

The claim submission process differs under PPS from the old fee-for-service process. PPS provides for split percentage payments.[67] At the beginning of an episode of care, the home health agency submits to the Medicare contractor a request for anticipated payment (RAP) for the initial percentage payment. The initial payment is 60 percent of the total PPS amount for new patients and 50 percent for ongoing patients.[68] At the end of the episode the agency submits a request for the residual final payment, and is paid the remaining amount.

The initial request for payment does not constitute a Medicare claim.[69] Medicare will only pay for home health services if there is a signed doctor's certificate.[70] Under the final PPS rules, the RAP may be submitted without a care plan signed by a doctor. The request for payment may be based on a signed doctor's referral prescribing detailed orders or on verbal doctor's orders that are recorded in the plan of care, that include a description of the patient's condition and services to be provided, that are attested to by the nurse or therapist responsible for the care, and that are included in a plan of care that is submitted to the doctor.[71] The care plan must be signed and dated by the doctor before the claim for each episode is submitted for the final percentage PPS payment.[72]

[D] Issues Under PPS

Under PPS, home health agencies are paid based on the medical and service needs of each particular beneficiary. Nevertheless, some beneficiaries who otherwise meet the eligibility criteria for Medicare home health benefits report problems in getting services or in getting the level of services prescribed by their doctors. Beneficiaries reporting problems include people with chronic conditions and those who use a large amount of non-routine medical supplies. Problems in getting services or supplies may arise where the agency does not believe the PPS rate adequately covers its costs. Thus, though PPS is ostensibly only a payment system, it may deter some home health agencies from serving certain beneficiaries. Advocates should continue to watch PPS closely to ensure that PPS does not

---

[67] 42 C.F.R. §484.205(b)(1), (2).

[68] 42 C.F.R. §484.205(b).

[69] Although the initial request for payment is not a claim for Medicare purposes, it is a claim for enforcement purposes. 42 C.F.R. §409.43(c)(2).

[70] 42 C.F.R. §424.22.

[71] 42 C.F.R. §409.43(c)(1).

[72] 42 C.F.R. §409.43(c)(3).

generate the same adverse consequences as generated by the interim payment system (IPS) in effect from 1998 through September 2000.[73]

§4.06   CLAIMS SUBMISSION, DETERMINATION, AND APPEAL

[A]   Generally

The home health claims submission process is complex and its reimbursement system seriously impedes the granting of appropriate coverage. The sections that follow describe the procedure in detail.

[B]   Medicare Home Health Claims Submission and Appeals Process

[1]   Medicare Advantage

In the event that the home health beneficiary has enrolled in a Medicare Advantage plan, then the beneficiary will be afforded the Medicare Advantage appeal rights.[74]

[2]   Appeals Arising Under Parts A and B of Medicare

Rules regarding Medicare appeals were published in the *Federal Register* on March 8, 2005 and codified at Subpart G, of Part 405.[75] The rules establish a combined Part A and Part B appeals process. CMS' regulations implement the changes to the appeals process for Medicare Part A and Part B claims and implement changes to ALJ hearing process for all Medicare claims, including managed care claims and prescription drug claims.[76]

The rules implement Medicare legislation enacted in 2000 designed to streamline and make uniform the appeals systems for claims arising under Parts A and B of Medicare. Although these provisions were supposed to go into effect in 2002, the Centers for Medicare & Medicaid Services (CMS) only effectuated changes concerning the time for filing appeals from initial decisions and the reduced amount in controversy for hearings on Part B claims. Congress made additional changes to the appeals process in 2003, including authorizing the transfer of administrative law judges (ALJs) from the Social Security Administration (SSA)

---

[73] BBA created an IPS for reimbursement to be used until PPS was effectuated. Its cap on reimbursement to HHAs caused HHAs to reduce care to patients and, in many instances, to terminate services or deny admission to patients because of their diagnosis or care needs. *See, e.g.*, Winkler v. Interim Healthcare, Inc., 36 F. Supp. 2d 1026 (D. Tenn. 1999).

[74] *See* §7.04 [F].

[75] *See* 42 C.F.R. §§405.701 *et seq.*

[76] 70 Fed. Reg. 11,420 (Mar. 8, 2005).

to the Department of Health and Human Services (HHS), and negating some of the earlier time savings by extending the time in which contractors must complete their decisions.

[3]   Initial Determinations and Redeterminations

As in the past, the claims process begins when the Medicare contractor (currently called a fiscal intermediary) issues an initial determination of a claim submitted by the home health provider or, occasionally, by the beneficiary. The regulations make clear that the initial determination, which will still be issued as the Medicare Summary Notice (MSN), goes only to the beneficiary, even when the contractor is aware that the beneficiary has an appointed representative. Someone who wants to appeal from the initial determination must submit a written, signed request for a redetermination within 120 days of the initial determination; the regulations assume the notice is received 5 days after the date of the notice. Requests for redeterminations must be filed with the office indicated on the MSN; beneficiaries can no longer file requests with Social Security offices.

The regulations also, for the first time, allow home health providers to request appeal of a denial of an initial determination, raising the possibility that both the beneficiary and the provider or supplier will initiate the appeals process. In such a case the contractor must consolidate the appeals. The contractor has 60 days from receipt of the redetermination request to issue a decision. If more than one party files a request, the time period runs from the date the last request is received. If, for example, a beneficiary files a redetermination request on day 1, but the home health provider files on day 50, the 60-day time period for the contractor to act starts on day 50.

Unlike the MSN, the notice of the redetermination is sent to a beneficiary's appointed representative. The notice explains the facts, policies and, law relied upon in making the redetermination decision; the right to request a reconsideration and the process for doing so; and a statement of specific missing documents that must be submitted. The notice will state that home health providers, but not beneficiaries (unless they are represented by a provider), must submit all of their evidence at the next level of review in order for the evidence to be considered at any further stage of the appeals process. It is unclear whether CMS will require contractors to send different notices to beneficiaries and home health providers, or whether CMS will include in the redetermination notice a statement that evidentiary limitations do not apply to beneficiaries. In addition, contractors will not be required to send redetermination notices to multiple beneficiaries in overpayment cases brought by home health providers if the beneficiary allegedly has no liability for the claim. It is unclear how the contractor will determine in such cases whether the beneficiary has already paid for the service in question.

The regulations create a new reopening process to be used instead of the redetermination process to correct minor errors or omissions in initial determinations. This process responds to a new section of the Medicare law that allows home health providers to correct minor mistakes without going through the appeals process. Re-openings can also be used at subsequent levels of review. Questions remain concerning the relationship of the new reopening process and the process for deciding remanded cases, as well as the ability of a contractor to reopen a decision in favor of the beneficiary.

[4] Reconsideration

The 2000 law created a third level of review, the reconsideration. Reconsiderations will be conducted by a new group of Medicare contractors called Qualified Independent Contractors (QICs). Beneficiaries and other parties to the redetermination have 180 days to request a reconsideration determination by filing a request at the location indicated on the redetermination notice. Again, reconsiderations filed by beneficiaries and the home health provider will be consolidated, and the time for issuing a decision runs from receipt of the last-filed appeal.

Starting May 1, 2005, appeals of redeterminations by the fiscal intermediaries, concerning home health care, go through the QIC reconsideration.

The reconsideration level of review is a paper review; CMS states clearly in the preamble to the final regulations that QICs will not be conducting hearings. However, the QIC is supposed to solicit the view of the beneficiary. As noted above, home health providers are required to submit all of the evidence they want considered in the claim to the QIC. Evidence not submitted may be excluded at subsequent levels of review.

The QIC is supposed to complete its reconsideration within 60 days of the reconsideration request. Again, the time frame runs from the last request filed if more than one party seeks reconsideration; the QIC must so notify a party who filed an earlier request. The regulations do not indicate how QICs are supposed to document receipt or how beneficiaries are to know when the 60-day period ends. Although the statute allows a party to the reconsideration to ask for an extension of not more than 14 days for the QIC to conclude the reconsideration, the regulations add 14 days to the reconsideration time frame each time that additional evidence is submitted.

If a QIC does not issue a timely decision, the statute allows a party to request that the appeal be escalated to the next level of review, the ALJ level. The regulations give the QIC 5 days to either issue a decision or acknowledge the escalation request and send it to the ALJ level of review. Under the regulations, an appeal escalated to the ALJ level will be completed within 180 days of receipt, rather than the statutorily mandated 90 days for ALJ decisions.

[C]   Summary of Expedited Appeals Process

Effective July 2005, beneficiaries may seek expedited review of a home health service appeal.[77] The provider must give the beneficiary a general, standardized notice at least two days in advance of the proposed end of the service. If the service is fewer than two days, or if the time between services is more than two days, then notice must be given by the next to last service. The notice describes the service, the date coverage ends, the beneficiary's financial liability for continued services, and how to file an appeal.

A beneficiary must request expedited review, orally or in writing, by noon of the next calendar day after receiving notice. At that time, the beneficiary is given a more specific notice that includes a detailed explanation of why services are being terminated, a description of any applicable Medicare coverage rules and information on how to obtain them, and other facts specific to the beneficiary's case. The beneficiary is not financially liable for continued services until the later of two days after receiving the notice or the termination date specified on the notice.

Expedited review is available in cases involving a discharge from the provider of services, or a termination of services where "a physician certifies that failure to continue the provision of such services is likely to place the individual's health at risk."[78] Home health services are treated as a termination of services for which a doctor's certificate of significant health risk must be provided.[79] A reduction in service is not considered a termination or discharger for purposes of triggering expedited review.

Expedited review is conducted by the QIO, which has 72 hours in which to make a decision. When the QIO receives the request for review, it must contact the provider, which then must supply the QIO with information supporting its determination by the close of the same business day. The QIO must solicit the views of the beneficiary and review the notice to determine if it meets CMS requirements. The beneficiary does not incur liability if the QIO decision is delayed because the provider did not get the necessary information to the reviewer in a timely manner.

If the QIO sustains the decision to termination/discharge services, the beneficiary may request expedited reconsideration, orally or in writing, by noon of the calendar day following initial notification. The reconsideration will be conducted by the QIC, which must issue a decision within 72 hours of the request. If the QIC does not comply with the time frame, the beneficiary may escalate the case to the administrative law judge level.

Beneficiaries retain the right to utilize the standard appeals process rather than the new expedited process in all situations. A QIO may review an appeal from

---

[77] 69 Fed. Reg. 69,264 (Nov. 26, 2004), adding 42 C.F.R. §§405.1200–405.1204, to implement 42 U.S.C. §1395ff(b)(1)(F).

[78] 42 U.S.C. §1395ff(b)(1)(F).

[79] 42 C.F.R. §405.1202(a).

a beneficiary when the request is not timely filed, but the QIO does not have to adhere to the otherwise applicable time frame for issuing a decision, and the limitation on liability does not apply.

[D] Claims Development and Submission

When a beneficiary desires Medicare home health coverage, the beneficiary must contact a home health agency certified by Medicare, present to the home health agency a physician's order for care, and request Medicare-covered services. Typically, the agency will evaluate the patient and determine whether coverage will be available for the needed care (including developing the plan of care which must be approved by the patient's physician), and determine the home health resource group (HHRG) to which the patient will be assigned under PPS. If the agency believes coverage will be granted by the fiscal intermediary (the entity, usually an insurance company, acting as Medicare's agent), the agency will submit a request for anticipated payment (RAP) for the first part of its payment under PPS. The agency will deliver the services and then submit a claim for coverage to the fiscal intermediary at the end of the 60-day episode to receive the final PPS payment.[80] The claims are usually submitted at two-month intervals.

[E] Notice and Appeal Rights in Home Health Care

The Medicare statute requires home health agencies, as a condition of participation, to protect and promote the following for each individual under its care:[81]

(1) The right to be fully informed in advance about the care and treatment to be provided by the agency, to be fully informed in advance of any changes in the care or treatment to be provided by the agency that may affect the individual's well-being, and (except with respect to an individual adjudged incompetent) to participate in planning care and treatment or changes in care or treatment.

(2) The right to be fully informed orally and in writing (in advance of coming under the care of the agency) of—

  1. . . . (iv) any change in the charges or items described in clause (i), (ii), or (iii) [services not covered by Medicare].

(3) The right to be fully informed in writing (in advance of coming under the care of the agency) of the individual's rights and obligations under this title.

Medicare regulations also require home health agencies to give their patients written and oral notice called home health advanced beneficiary notice (HHABN)

---

[80] 42 C.F.R. §§409.43, 424.33.

[81] 42 U.S.C. §1395bbb(a)(1).

concerning when Medicare will pay for services initially as well as when there is a change in expectations of Medicare payment for services.[82] In addition, the *Medicare Benefit Policy Manual, CMS Pub. 100-4,* requires home health agencies to give their patients notice when the agencies deem services not covered.[83] Note, however, the Manual does not require agencies to notify such patients that they can demand that a claim be submitted to Medicare, but does require the agencies to submit such claims if the patients learn on their own about the demand bill process.[84]

Unfortunately, these notice provisions are not monitored and enforced by CMS, and consequently home health agencies have failed to provide patients with notice of denials, reductions, or terminations of care. As a result, beneficiaries often lack information about appeal rights, including where to file, what to file, or how best to supplement one's record in support of a claim for coverage.[85] Effective March 1, 2001, home health agencies must use a model notice whenever a triggering event defined by CMS occurs. Note: *Lutwin (Healey)* requires notice in all situations where services are denied, reduced, or terminated. Issues involving CMS's monitoring and enforcement of the notice requirement are being resolved in large part through CMS' new Transmittal No. 1025 (Medicare Claims Processing).[86]

Although theoretically there is a procedure for appealing Medicare home health terminations and reductions, several characteristics of its design render it useless for most beneficiaries. First, appeal is only permitted with respect to services actually received; second, most home health agencies will not provide services after a reduction or termination; third, agencies that agree to provide services only do so if the beneficiary pays for the services pending appeal, which most beneficiaries cannot afford; and fourth, the appeal process itself is so slow that decisions come long after the need for services.

[F] Liability Protections

The liability of the patient for the cost of care is waived until he or she is informed in writing, by issuance of the HHABN, that coverage is not available.

---

[82] 42 C.F.R. §484.10(1), (2).

[83] Medicare Benefit Policy Manual, Pub. 100-4, §10-50.

[84] Lutwin (Healey) v. Thompson, 361 F.3d 146 (2d Cir. 2004) requires notice to beneficiaries whenever home health care is denied, reduced, or terminated. For latest developments, it is best to consult CMS's notice initiative page periodically. The key notion here is that the beneficiary is provided the medical and factual basis for a termination of services and the steps to take in order to challenge such terminations. *See* http://www.cms.hhs.gov/BNI

[85] Program Memorandum A-01-30 (Feb. 28, 2001), reissued as Program Memorandum A-02-017 (Feb. 26, 2002); Program Memorandum A-01-05 (Jan. 16, 2001), reissued as Program Memorandum A-02-018 (Feb. 26, 2002); Healey v. Thompson, 186 F. Supp. 2d 105 (D. Conn. 2001).

[86] Lutwin (Healey) v. Thompson, 361 F.3d (2d Cir. 2004).

Situations exist where PPS payment has been made for the full episode. Should additional coverage be granted, for example, additional home health aide hours, but care does not increase to outlier criteria, the HHA would not receive additional payment. But they cannot charge the beneficiary for the additional cost of care.

Whenever the home health agency submits a claim to the Medicare contractor, it risks a financial penalty. If the intermediary determines that the services involved should not be covered, it issues an initial determination denying the claim. The home health agency may not charge the patient for the cost of services delivered until the patient is informed in writing that Medicare coverage is denied.[87] Thus, the agency is forced to absorb the cost of the care involved.

If the home health agency believes that coverage will be denied by the contractor, or when the agency is unsure whether coverage will be granted, it will generally seek to avoid submitting a claim in order to escape any possible financial penalty. The agency may be found liable if it failed to issue a notice or issued a defective notice. Although the beneficiary has a right to insist that a claim be submitted even where the home health agency believes coverage will be denied (called a "demand bill"), often the agency will seek to discourage the patient from requiring such a no-payment claim submission because, under some circumstances, the agency may be penalized if the contractor determines that a claim should have been deemed covered initially by the agency.[88]

In many cases, this system results in a complete loss of care as well as the loss of the right to appeal. When the agency is afraid to claim coverage from the contractor, the agency usually will not deliver home health services unless the patient agrees to pay for them. If the patient is unable to afford the expensive home health care involved, the care will not be delivered even though Medicare coverage should have been granted, and could have been won on appeal had the care been delivered and a claim submitted. (Remember, the contractor will not make an initial determination on a claim until after the services involved have been rendered.)

Inappropriate restrictions on Medicare coverage can result in the complete loss of home health care, or can mean that the patient will receive less care than he or she actually needs. Ultimately, the Medicare program may pay less home health coverage, but at the cost of increased disability, patient indigence, and unnecessary institutionalization.

§4.07   THE ROLE OF ADVOCACY

Advocacy in the home health arena, as in other Medicare areas, is often the key to the individual's ability to "access" services. Good advocacy allows people to be heard. It focuses on the important questions of whether the circumstances of a

---

[87] 42 C.F.R. §§411.400–411.406.

[88] Medicare Part A Intermediary Manual 3439.3 (CMS Pub. 13-3). *See* **Appendix 4-1.**

particular individual have been given full consideration with respect to coverage and services.

Effective advocates can include Medicare beneficiaries themselves as well as lawyers, paralegals, family members, and friends acting on the beneficiary's behalf. Effectiveness is grounded in good information about the Medicare program and in a keen appreciation of, and insistence upon, the right to be heard when services are denied, reduced, or terminated.

Advocates should develop a working knowledge of the Medicare benefit, and a good and supportive relationship with health care providers. This will ensure a broad knowledge base for advocates about the law and the relevant medical facts that must be demonstrated in order to prove eligibility for coverage and services. At the same time, this activity on behalf of a beneficiary will often educate medical providers about the basic legal requirements for Medicare coverage. This synergy is essential to effective advocacy.

§4.08   HOW TO DEVELOP A WINNING APPEAL

[A]   Sequential Approach to Case Development

Advocacy can make a crucial difference to your client's chance of success on appeal. The following approach is suggested:

1. Ascertain whether the home health agency involved is certified to participate in the Medicare program.

2. Determine whether your client is homebound and whether he or she requires intermittent skilled nursing services or physical or speech therapy. You must also ascertain whether the care billed to the Medicare program qualifies as part-time or intermittent nursing, or aide services.

   Ensure that the home health care your client needs is delivered. The fiscal intermediary will not issue an initial determination except where a claim for payment is submitted by a certified home health agency for the cost of home health services already rendered. Unfortunately, unfair Medicare coverage denials often have an unappealable prospective effect. The agency decides that services will henceforth not be covered by the fiscal intermediary, and declines to deliver the care unless payment is forthcoming. If the patient cannot pay for the care, the care will not be delivered; a claim will not be submitted, and the patient will not be able to challenge the unfair coverage denial. Accordingly, it is the advocate's first duty to make sure that care is rendered. Here are three ways to obtain an appealable initial determination:

   If your client has funds sufficient to cover the cost involved, or if other public or private funds are available, urge him or her to consider paying for the care and then to file an appeal for Medicare coverage. This approach is often fruitful where there is a strong medical basis for coverage.

If your client is unable to afford the care involved, attempt to convince the home health agency to "carry" the case. That is, try to persuade the agency to deliver the care without receiving payment in advance while the claim and appeals process proceed. Your client may be required to assume liability for the cost of services in writing should Medicare coverage be denied.

Finally, you may be able to persuade the home health agency to take a chance on the claim. Especially if you can demonstrate a successful record in appeals of similar cases, the home health agency may be willing to deliver the care without assurance of payment in expectation that your appeal will prove successful.

3. Provide the home health agency with copies of relevant, supporting language from the federal regulations and CMS manual.

4. Request *in writing* that the home health agency submit a claim to Medicare for all the services ordered by the patient's physician that are coverable by Medicare.

5. Solicit the written opinion of the attending physician. For care already initiated by the agency, the attending physician will have been required to sign a certification and plan-of-treatment form. You should obtain a copy of this document for review and for submission with your appeal if it is helpful.

It will further help the case, however, to obtain a more elaborate letter from the physician emphasizing the patient's homebound status, the need for skilled care, and the medical necessity of both the skilled care and the home health aide and other services that will be billed to the Medicare program. A persuasive attending physician's letter will encourage the contractor to grant the claim at the initial determination level, thereby avoiding the need for further appeal. If you must appeal to the reconsideration or administrative law judge hearing levels, a strong and detailed attending physician's letter will often be the key to coverage in most cases.

[B] The Patient's Care Plan as an Advocacy Tool

[1] Plan-of-Care Requirements

A plan of care is a prerequisite for Medicare coverage for home health services. The plan of care must include physician's orders as well as drug treatments and frequency, and should explain the interrelationship of other medical/ social services that the particular patient might receive, including physical therapy, or speech therapy.[89] It must be signed and dated by a physician.[90]

---

[89] 42 C.F.R. §§409.43 *et seq.*

[90] *See* 42 C.F.R. §424.22(d) (the certifying physician may not have a significant ownership interest in the Home Health Agency (HHA) as defined in §424.22(d)(2)-(4), a 5 percent or more ownership interest, or financial or contractual relationship).

[2] Physician Attestation Required

The plan of care must be signed by the physician before the bill for services is submitted, and any changes in the plan must be signed and dated by the physician.[91] Orders for "as needed" services or "PRN" services must be accompanied by a description of the medical signs and symptoms that would occasion such visits and a specific number of visits that can be made under that order before an additional physician's order would have to be obtained,[92] including oral orders.[93]

[3] Plan of Care as Advocacy Tool

In some instances, HHAs, without consulting with attending physicians and obtaining their consent, are notifying patients at the end of a plan-of-care period that home health services will no longer be provided. Advocates should therefore pay particular attention to both the plan of care document *and* the process of its development to ensure that the physician is responsible for the plan and supports its contents. This approach may be helpful in avoiding a termination of services initiated by the home health agency. Such terminations are particularly prevalent when the patient needs costly care or care that will be required for a long period of time.

[4] Continuing Need for Care

Advocates must demonstrate that the beneficiary continues to meet Medicare home health criteria, including the need for skilled care services. The plan of care should include as much detail as possible, supporting the need for the specific services to be continued.

[5] Termination of the Plan of Care

Federal regulations provide that a plan of care is considered terminated if the beneficiary does not receive at least one covered skilled nursing, physical therapy, speech-language pathology service, or occupational therapy visit in a 60-day period, unless the physician documents that the interval without such care is appropriate.[94] Medicare regulation and manual provisions anticipate at least a minimal process for recertification,[95] to the extent that the physician is given an opportunity

---

[91] 42 C.F.R. §409.33(c). Under PPS, a signed plan of care is submitted at the end of the 60-day episode of care, and not with the initial request for anticipated payment.

[92] 42 C.F.R. §409.43(b).

[93] 42 C.F.R. §409.43(d).

[94] 42 C.F.R. §409.43(f).

[95] 42 C.F.R. §424.22(b) (recertification).

to review the plan of care, every 60 days, and sign a new care plan if services are needed.[96]

[6] Cycle for Plan Review

The plan of care should be reviewed by the physician in consultation with the professional staff of the HHA at least every 60 days under PPS. Each such review is to be signed and dated by the physician.[97] As discussed above, termination of a plan of care is often a tricky issue, especially as HHAs seek to divest themselves of their heavy care patients. Again, be sure that the patient's attending physician is in charge of the plan of care, supports its contents, and approves of any discharge from home care.

[C] Identifying Coverable Home Health Cases

The following list can be used as a quick reference aid to help identify coverable home health claims.

[1] Coverage Criteria

Home health claims are suitable for Medicare coverage, and appeal if they have been denied, if they meet the following criteria:

1. A physician has signed or will sign a plan of care.

2. The patient is or will be homebound. This criterion is met if leaving home requires a considerable and taxing effort which may be shown by the patient needing personal assistance, or the help of a wheelchair or crutches, etc. Occasional but infrequent "walks around the block" are allowable.

3. The patient needs or will need skilled nursing care on an intermittent basis (from as much as every day for recurring periods of 21 days—if there is a predictable end to the need for daily care—to as little as once every 60 days) or physical or speech therapy.

4. The care must be provided by, or under arrangements with, a Medicare certified provider.

---

[96] *Id.*

[97] 42 C.F.R. §409.43(e). *See* the CMS Web site for its Notice Initiative for ongoing updates to notices in the home health arena. <http://www.cms.hhs.gov/medicare/bni/ default.asp>.

*Remember: If nursing, physical therapy, or speech therapy was needed originally, but ends, continued occupational therapy will allow Medicare home health coverage to continue.

[2] Coverable Home Health Services

If the triggering conditions described above are met, the beneficiary is entitled to Medicare coverage for home health services. There is no coinsurance or deductible. Home health services include:

- Part-time or intermittent nursing care provided by or under the supervision of a registered professional nurse;
- Physical, occupational, or speech therapy;
- Medical social services under the direction of a physician; and
- To the extent permitted in regulations, part-time or intermittent services of a home health aide.

[3] Additional Hints

- Medicare coverage should not be denied simply because the patient's condition is "chronic" or "stable." "Restorative potential" is not necessary.
- Resist arbitrary caps on coverage imposed by the intermediary. For example, do not accept provider or intermediary assertions that aide services in excess of one visit per day are not covered, or that daily nursing visits can never be covered.
- There is no legal limit to the duration of the Medicare home health benefit. Medicare coverage is available for necessary home care even if it is to extend over a long period of time.
- The doctor is the patient's most important ally. If it appears that Medicare coverage will be denied, ask the doctor to help demonstrate that the standards above are met. Home care services should not be ended or reduced unless this has been ordered by the doctor.
- In order to be able to appeal a Medicare denial, the home health agency must have filed a Medicare claim for the patient's care. You should request, in writing, that the home health agency file a Medicare claim even if the agency told you that Medicare will deny coverage.

APPENDIX 4-1

CMS PROGRAM MEMORANDUM, TRANSMITTAL A-01-21
(FEB. 6, 2001)

Program Memorandum **Intermediaries**	Department of Health and Human Services (DHHS) HEALTH CARE FINANCING ADMINISTRATION (HCFA)

Transmittal A-01-21	**Date: FEBRUARY 6,2001**

SUBJECT: **Clarification of the Homebound Definition Under the Medicare Home Health Benefit**

Background

Section 507 of the Beneficiary Improvement and Protection Act (BIPA) amends the Social Security Act (the Act (§§1814(a) and 1835(a)); (42 U.S.C. 1395f(a) and 1395n(a)), which establish the homebound requirement under the Medicare home health benefit. The statutory language of the homebound definition is amended as follows:

(A) In the last sentence, by striking, "and that absences of the individual from home are infrequent or of relatively short duration, or are attributable to the need to receive medical treatment," and

(B) By adding at the end the following new sentences: "Any absence of an individual from the home attributable to the need to receive health care treatment, including regular absences for the purpose of participating in therapeutic, psychosocial, or medical treatment in an adult day-care program that is licensed or certified by a State, or accredited, to furnish adult day-care services in the State shall not disqualify an individual from being considered to be confined to his home. Any other absence of an individual from the home shall not so disqualify an individual if the absence is of infrequent or of relatively short duration. For purposes of the preceding sentence, any absence for the purpose of attending a religious service shall be deemed to be an absence of infrequent or short duration."

The amendments made to the Act (§§1814(a); and 1835(a)); (42 U.S.C. 1395n(a)), apply to home health services furnished on or after December 21, 2000 (the enactment date of BIPA).

Discussion

This Program Memorandum (PM) provides clarification of the homebound statutory eligibility requirement applicable to the Medicare home health benefit now that it has been amended by BIPA.

Sections 1814 and 1835 of the Act and §1395 of the U.S.C. establish the homebound/confined to the home definition under the Medicare home health benefit. Section 507 of BIPA clarifies the statutory definition of homebound/confined to the home for purposes of eligibility under the Medicare home health benefit. To qualify for the Medicare home health benefit, §§1814(a)(2)(C)and 1835(a)(2)(A) of the Act require a Medicare beneficiary to be confined to the home, under the care of a physician, receiving services under a plan of care established and periodically reviewed by a physician, be in need of skilled nursing care on an intermittent basis (other than solely venipuncture), or physical therapy or speech-language pathology or have a continuing need for occupational therapy.

Sections 1814 and 1835 of the Act sets forth the conditions and limitations on payment for home health services. Physician certification that the beneficiary is confined to his home is an eligibility requirement for all home health services.

The new provision expands the list of circumstances in which absences from the home would be consistent with a determination that the patient is "confined to the home" or "homebound" for Medicare purposes, it does not change the existing homebound guidelines beyond the two specific provisions below. The new provisions include:

- Any absence of an individual from the home attributable to the need to receive health care treatment, including regular absences for the purpose of participating in therapeutic, psychosocial, or medical treatment in an adult day-care program that is licensed or certified by a State, or accredited, to furnish adult day care services in the State shall not negate the beneficiary's homebound status for purposes of eligibility.

- Any absence for religious service is deemed to be an absence of infrequent or short duration and thus does not negate the homebound status of the beneficiary.

This new statutory provision does not imply that Medicare coverage has been expanded to include adult day care services.

Implementation

The new statutory provisions replace the eligibility requirements which have been used in the course of medical review. Accordingly, replace the previous definition of "confined to the home" in your medical review guidelines with the new provisions contained in this PM. This material will subsequently be incorporated into HCFA manuals and program regulations.

Home health agencies (HHAs) enrolling patients eligible for these new provisions are responsible for demonstrating the adult day care center is licensed or certified/accredited as part of determining whether the patient is homebound for purposes of Medicare eligibility. Examples of information that could demonstrate licensure or certification/accreditation include: the license/certificate of accreditation number of the adult day care center and the effective date of the license/certificate of accreditation and the name of the authority responsible for the license/certificate or accreditation of the adult day care center.

Inform HHAs of this statutory clarification of current Medicare policy. The contents of this PM should be published in the next regularly scheduled edition of your bulletin or newsletter and should also be posted on your web-site for HHAs.

These instructions should be implemented within your current operating budget.

The *effective date* for this PM is December 21, 2000.

The *implementation date* is February 6, 2001.

The discard date for this PM is February 6, 2002.

If you have any questions, contact: Kathy Walch (410) 786-7970.

APPENDIX 4-2

HOME HEALTH CARE HEARING CHECKLIST

(Compiled by the Center for Medicare Advocacy, Inc.)

This checklist will help you make sure that the evidence you have gathered is sufficient to demonstrate that the patient involved is entitled to Medicare home health coverage. Each of the essential points you must prove is listed. Underneath each point you will find a description of the documents or other evidence which will help you meet the legal requirement involved.

		YES	NO
1.	The claimant is enrolled in the Medicare program.	[ ]	[ ]
	Look for the claimant's Medicare number which can be found on the Medicare enrollment card.	[ ]	[ ]
2.	The patient is confined to his or her home.	[ ]	[ ]

Look for documentation or testimony that the patient has a normal inability to leave his or her home without difficulty. The requirement is met if the beneficiary must be assisted by another person, or requires the help of an assistive device such as a cane or wheelchair in order to leave the home.

3.	The patient is under the care of a physician.	[ ]	[ ]

Look for:

(a) physician's order for home health services;

(b) physician's statement or Attending Physician Report.

4.	The beneficiary needs skilled nursing care on an intermittent basis or physical or speech therapy.	[ ]	[ ]

Look for:

(a) documentation or testimony that it is medically necessary that the patient receive skilled care at least once every 60 days;

(b) physician's testimony or written statement that intermittent skilled care is medically necessary is the best evidence of this requirement (Attending Physician's Report, etc.);

(c) nurse or therapist notes.

5. The beneficiary needs home health aide care,   [ ]   [ ]
    occupational therapy, or other home medical
    services (if you are seeking Medicare coverage for
    these services.)*

    Look for:

    (a) physician's testimony or written statement that home health aide or other care is medically necessary is the best evidence of this requirement (Attending Physician's Report, etc.);

    (b) home health aide notes, therapist, medical social service provider notes.

APPENDIX 4-3

ATTENDING PHYSICIAN REPORT—HOME HEALTH CARE

(Compiled by the Center for Medicare Advocacy, Inc.)

Patient: HIC#

Provider: Period At Issue:

Physician:

PLEASE RESPOND TO THE FOLLOWING QUESTIONS BY CHECKING THE APPROPRIATE RESPONSES AND ELABORATING WHERE INDICATED. BE SURE YOUR RESPONSES REFER TO THE TIME PERIOD ENTERED ABOVE.

1. Were you an attending physician to this patient during the period at issue described above? _____Yes _____No

2. Please indicate whether the patient required any of the following services during the period at issue: _____Yes _____ No

    (a) Skilled Nursing

    If yes, please specify type(s): _____

    _____

    _____

    (b) Skilled Physical Therapy _____Yes _____ No

    If yes, please specify type(s): _____]

    _____

    _____

    (c) Skilled Speech Therapy _____Yes _____ No

    If yes, please specify type(s): _____

    _____

    _____

    (d) Occupational Therapy _____Yes _____ No

    (e) Home Health Aides _____Yes _____ No

    (f) Medical Social Services _____Yes _____ No

(g) Durable Medical Equipment   _____Yes   _____ No

(h) Medical Supplies   _____Yes   _____ No

(i) Other (please specify): _____

3. During the time period at issue, was the patient
    confined to his/her home? (The individual had a
    condition that restricted the ability of the individual
    to leave his or her home except with the assistance of
    another individual or the aid of a supportive device, or
    the individual had a condition such that leaving his
    or her home was contraindicated.)   _____Yes   _____ No

    Comment: _____

    _____

    _____

4. Was the skilled nursing which the patient
    required, needed on an "intermittent" basis (from
    once a day for a predictable period of time to
    once every 60 days)   _____Yes   _____ No

    Comment: _____

    _____

    _____

5. Did the patient require the services of a "part-time"
    (less than 8 hours per day) or "intermittent" home
    health aide in addition to the skilled nursing
    and/or rehabilitative services?   _____Yes   _____ No

    Comment: _____

    _____

    _____

6. Please respond to the following:

   (a) Did the patient have special medical
      complications that required the professional
      or technical administration of services which
      are generally considered nonskilled? _____Yes _____ No

   If yes, please elaborate: _____

_____

_____

   (b) Did the patient's overall management and care
      plan require technical or professional personnel
      to assure recovery and/or safety? _____Yes _____ No

   (c) Was the patient's condition such that technical
      or professional personnel were needed to
      properly *observe* and possibly *modify* treatment? _____Yes _____ No

   (d) Was the use of technical or professional _____ No
      personnel necessary to teach the patient
      self-maintenance? _____Yes

FURTHUR REMARKS: _____

_____

_____

_____

_____

_____

Date   Signature of Physician

THANK YOU FOR YOUR TIME AND CONSIDERATION IN COMPLETING THIS REPORT.

APPENDIX 4-4

IMPORTANT SELECTIONS FROM THE

CMS MEDICARE BENEFIT POLICY MANUAL,

PUB. 100-2

(Compiled by the Center for Medicare Advocacy, Inc.)

A finding that care is not reasonable and necessary must be based on information provided on the forms and in the medical record with respect to the unique medical condition of the individual beneficiary. *That is, a coverage denial may not be based solely on the reviewer's general inferences about patients with similar diagnoses or on data related to utilization generally, but must be based upon objective clinical evidence regarding the patient's individual need for care.*

20.3 *Use of Utilization Screens and "Rules of Thumb."* —Medicare recognizes that determinations of whether home health services are reasonable and necessary must be based on an assessment of each beneficiary's individual care needs. Therefore, denial of services based on numerical utilization screens, diagnostic screens, diagnosis or specific treatment norms is not appropriate.

40.1.1—The determination of whether a beneficiary needs skilled nursing care should be based solely upon the beneficiary's unique condition and individual needs, without regard to whether the illness or injury is acute, chronic, terminal or expected to extend over a long period of time. In addition, skilled care may, dependent upon the unique condition of the beneficiary, continue to be necessary for beneficiaries whose condition is stable.

40.1.2 *Management and Evaluation of a Patient Care Plan.*—Skilled nursing visits for management and evaluation of the patient's care plan are also reasonable and necessary where underlying conditions or complications require that only a registered nurse can ensure that essential nonskilled care is achieving its purpose. For skilled nursing care to be reasonable and necessary for management and evaluation of the beneficiary's plan of care, the complexity of the necessary unskilled services which are a necessary part of the medical treatment must require the involvement of skilled nursing personnel to promote the patient's recovery and medical safety in view of the beneficiary's overall condition.

40.2   *Skilled Therapy Services.*—

40.2.1. *General Principles Governing Reasonable and Necessary Physical Therapy, Speech-Language Pathology Services, and Occupational Therapy.*—

The service of a physical, speech-language pathologist or occupational therapist is a skilled therapy service if the inherent complexity of the service is such that it can be performed safely and/or effectively only by or under the general supervision of a skilled therapist. To be covered, the skilled services must also be reasonable and necessary to the treatment of the patient's illness or injury or to the restoration or maintenance of function affected by the patient's illness or injury. It is necessary to determine whether individual therapy services are skilled and whether, in view of the patient's overall condition, skilled management of the services provided is needed although many or all of the specific services needed to treat the illness or injury do not require the skills of a therapist.

The development, implementation, management and evaluation of a patient care plan based on the physician's orders constitute skilled therapy services when, because of the patient's condition, those activities require the involvement of a skilled therapist to meet the patient's needs, promote recovery and ensure medical safety. Where the skills of a therapist are needed to manage and periodically reevaluate the appropriateness of a maintenance program because of an identified danger to the patient, such services would be covered even if the skills of a therapist are not needed to carry out the activities performed as part of the maintenance program.

While a patient's particular medical condition is a valid factor in deciding if skilled therapy services are needed, the diagnosis or prognosis should never be the sole factor in deciding that a service is or is not skilled. The key issue is whether the skills of a therapist are needed to treat the illness or injury, or whether the services can be carried out by nonskilled personnel.

A service that is ordinarily considered nonskilled could be considered a skilled therapy service in cases in which there is clear documentation that, because of special medical complications, skilled rehabilitation personnel are required to perform or supervise the service or to observe the patient. However, the importance of a particular service to a patient or the frequency with which it must be performed does not, by itself, make a nonskilled service into a skilled service.

The skilled therapy services must be reasonable and necessary to the treatment of the patient's illness or injury within the context of the patient's unique medical condition. To be considered reasonable and necessary for the treatment of the illness or injury:

    a. The services must be consistent with the nature and severity of the illness or injury, the patient's particular medical needs, including the requirement that the amount, frequency and duration of the services must be reasonable;

b. The services must be considered, under accepted standards of medical practice, to be specific, safe, and effective treatment for the patient's condition; and

c. The services must be provided with the expectation, based on the assessment made by the physician of the patient's rehabilitation potential, that the condition of the patient will improve materially in a reasonable and generally predictable period of time; or the services are necessary to the establishment of a safe and effective maintenance program.

Services involving activities for the general welfare of any patient, e.g., general exercises to promote overall fitness or flexibility and activities to provide diversion or general motivation, do not constitute skilled therapy. Nonskilled individuals without the supervision of a therapist can perform these services.

Services of skilled therapists for the purpose of teaching the patient, family or caregivers necessary techniques, exercises or precautions are covered to the extent that they are reasonable and necessary to treat illness or injury. However, visits made by skilled therapists to a patient's home solely to train other HHA staff (e.g., home health aides) are not billable as visits since the HHA is responsible for ensuring that its staff is properly trained to perform any service it furnishes. The cost of a skilled therapist's visit for the purpose of training HHA staff is an administrative cost to the agency.

Example: A patient with a diagnosis of multiple sclerosis has recently been discharged from the hospital following an exacerbation of her condition that has left her wheelchair bound and, for the first time, without any expectation of achieving ambulation again. The physician has ordered physical therapy to select the proper wheelchair for her long term use, to teach safe use of the wheelchair, and safe transfer techniques to the patient and family. Physical therapy would be reasonable and necessary to evaluate the patient's overall needs, to make the selection of the proper wheelchair and to teach the patient and family safe use of the wheelchair and proper transfer techniques.

26. e The amount, frequency, and duration of the services must be reasonable.

40.2.2. *Application of the Principles to Physical Therapy Services.*—The following discussion of skilled physical therapy services applies the principles in 40.2 to specific physical therapy services about which questions are most frequently raised.

A. *Assessment.*—The skills of a physical therapist to assess a patient's rehabilitation needs and potential or to develop and/or implement a physical therapy program are covered when they are reasonable and necessary because of the patient's condition. Skilled rehabilitation services concurrent with the management of a patient's care plan include objective tests and measurements such as, but not limited to, range of motion, strength, balance, coordination, endurance or functional ability.

B. *Therapeutic Exercises.*—Therapeutic exercises which must be performed by or under the supervision of the qualified physical therapist to ensure the safety of the patient and effectiveness of the treatment, due either to the type of exercise employed or to the condition of the patient, constitute skilled physical therapy.

C. *Gait Training.*—Gait evaluation and training furnished to a patient whose ability to walk has been impaired by neurological, muscular or skeletal abnormality require the skills of a qualified physical therapist and constitute skilled physical therapy and are considered reasonable and necessary if training can be expected to improve materially the patient's ability to walk.

Gait evaluation and training that is furnished to a patient whose ability to walk has been impaired by a condition other than a neurological, muscular or skeletal abnormality would nevertheless be covered where physical therapy is reasonable and necessary to restore the lost function.

Example 1: A physician has ordered gait evaluation and training for a patient whose gait has been materially impaired by scar tissue resulting from burns. Physical therapy services to evaluate the patient's gait, establish a gait training program, and provide the skilled services necessary to implement the program would be covered.

Example 2: A patient who has had a total hip replacement is ambulatory but demonstrates weakness and is unable to climb stairs safely. Physical therapy would be reasonable and necessary to teach the patient to safely climb and descend stairs.

Repetitive exercises to improve gait, or to maintain strength and endurance and assistive walking are appropriately provided by nonskilled persons and ordinarily do not require the skills of a physical therapist. Where such services are performed by a physical therapist as part of the initial design and establishment of a safe and effective maintenance program, the services would, to the extent that they are reasonable and necessary, be covered.

Example 3: A patient who has received gait training has reached his maximum restoration potential and the physical therapist is teaching the patient and family how to perform safely the activities that are a part of a maintenance program. The visits by the physical therapist to demonstrate and teach the activities (which by themselves do not require the skills of a therapist) would be covered since they are needed to establish the program.

D. *Range of Motion.*—Only a qualified physical therapist may perform range of motion tests and, therefore, such tests are skilled physical therapy.

Range of motion exercises constitute skilled physical therapy only if they are part of an active treatment for a specific disease state, illness, or injury that has resulted in a loss or restriction of mobility (as evidenced by physical therapy notes showing the degree of motion lost and the degree to be restored). Range of motion exercises unrelated to the restoration of a specific loss of function often may be provided safely and effectively by nonskilled individuals. Passive exercises to maintain range of motion in paralyzed extremities that can be carried out by nonskilled persons do not constitute skilled physical therapy.

However, as indicated in §40.2, where there is clear documentation that, because of special medical complications (e.g., susceptible to pathological bone fractures), the skills of a therapist are needed to provide services that ordinarily do not need the skills of a therapist, then the services would be covered.

APPENDIX 4-5

TITLE 42—PUBLIC HEALTH
(CODE OF FEDERAL REGULATIONS)

PART 409—HOSPITAL INSURANCE BENEFITS

Subpart E—Home Health Services Under Hospital Insurance

Sec. 409.44 Skilled services reqirements.

(a) **General.** The intermediary's decision on whether care is reasonable and necessary is based on information provided on the forms and in the medical record concerning the unique medical condition of the individual beneficiary. A coverage denial is not made solely on the basis of the reviewer's general inferences about patients with similar diagnoses or on data related to utilization generally but is based upon objective clinical evidence regarding the beneficiary's individual need for care.

(b) **Skilled nursing care.** (1) Skilled nursing care consists of those services that must, under State law, be performed by a registered nurse, or practical (vocational) nurse, as defined in Sec. 484.4 of this chapter, and meet the criteria for skilled nursing services specified in Sec. 409.32. *See* Sec. 409.33(a) and (b) for a description of skilled nursing services and examples of them.

(i) In determining whether a service requires the skill of a licensed nurse, consideration must be given to the inherent complexity of the service, the condition of the beneficiary, and accepted standards of medical and nursing practice.

(ii) If the nature of a service is such that it can safely and effectively be performed by the average nonmedical person without direct supervision of a licensed nurse, the service cannot be regarded as a skilled nursing service.

(iii) The fact that a skilled nursing service can be or is taught to the beneficiary or to the beneficiary's family or friends does not negate the skilled aspect of the service when performed by the nurse.

(iv) If the service could be performed by the average nonmedical person, the absence of a competent person to perform it does not cause it to be a skilled nursing service.

(2) The skilled nursing care must be provided on a part-time or intermittent basis.

(3) The skilled nursing services must be reasonable and necessary for the treatment of the illness or injury.

(i) To be considered reasonable and necessary, the services must be consistent with the nature and severity of the beneficiary's illness or injury, his or her particular medical needs, and accepted standards of medical and nursing practice.

(ii) The skilled nursing care provided to the beneficiary must be reasonable within the context of the beneficiary's condition.

(iii) The determination of whether skilled nursing care is reasonable and necessary must be based solely upon the beneficiary's unique condition and individual needs, without regard to whether the illness or injury is acute, chronic, terminal, or expected to last a long time.

(c) Physical therapy, speech-language pathology services, and occupational therapy. To be covered, physical therapy, speech-language pathology services, and occupational therapy must satisfy the criteria in paragraphs (c)(1) through (4) of this section. Occupational therapy services initially qualify for home health coverage only if they are part of a plan of care that also includes intermittent skilled nursing care, physical therapy, or speech-language pathology services as follows:

(1) Speech-language pathology services and physical or occupational therapy services must relate directly and specifically to a treatment regimen (established by the physician, after any needed consultation with the qualified therapist) that is designed to treat the beneficiary's illness or injury. Services related to activities for the general physical welfare of beneficiaries (for example, exercises to promote overall fitness) do not constitute physical therapy, occupational therapy, or speech-language pathology services for Medicare purposes.

(2) Physical and occupational therapy and speech-language pathology services must be reasonable and necessary. To be considered reasonable and necessary, the following conditions must be met:

(i) The services must be considered under accepted standards of medical practice to be a specific, safe, and effective treatment for the beneficiary's condition.

(ii) The services must be of such a level of complexity and sophistication or the condition of the beneficiary must be such that the services required can safely and effectively be performed only by a qualified physical therapist or by a qualified physical therapy assistant under the supervision of a qualified physical therapist, by a qualified speech-language pathologist, or by a qualified occupational therapist or a qualified occupational therapy assistant under the supervision of a qualified occupational therapist (as defined in Sec. 484.4 of this chapter). Services that do not require the performance or supervision of a physical therapist or an occupational therapist are not considered reasonable or necessary physical therapy or occupational therapy services, even if they are performed by or supervised by a physical therapist or occupational therapist. Services that do not require the skills of a speech-language pathologist are not considered to be reasonable and necessary speech-language pathology services even if they are performed by or supervised by a speech-language pathologist.

(iii) There must be an expectation that the beneficiary's condition will improve materially in a reasonable (and generally predictable) period of time based on the physician's assessment of the beneficiary's restoration potential and unique medical condition, or the services must be necessary to establish a safe and effective maintenance program required in connection with a specific disease, or the skills of a therapist must be necessary to perform a safe and effective maintenance program. If the services are for the establishment of a maintenance program, they may include the design of the program, the instruction of the beneficiary, family, or home health aides, and the necessary infrequent reevaluations of the beneficiary and the program to the degree that the specialized knowledge and judgment of a physical therapist, speech-language pathologist, or occupational therapist is required.

(iv) The amount, frequency, and duration of the services must be reasonable.

[59 FR 65494, Dec. 20, 1994]

* * *

Sec. 409.45 Dependent services requirements.

(a) **General.** Services discussed in paragraphs (b) through (g) of this section may be covered only if the beneficiary needs skilled nursing care on an intermittent basis, as described in Sec. 409.44(b); physical therapy or speech-language pathology services as described in Sec. 409.44(c); or has a continuing need for occupational therapy services as described in Sec. 409.44(c) if the beneficiary's eligibility for home health services has been established by virtue of a prior need for intermittent skilled nursing care, speech-language pathology services, or physical therapy in the current or prior certification period; and otherwise meets the qualifying criteria (confined to the home, under the care of a physician, in need of skilled services, and under a plan of care) specified in Sec. 409.42. Home health coverage is not available for services furnished to a beneficiary who is no longer in need of one of the qualifying skilled services specified in this paragraph. Therefore, dependent services furnished after the final qualifying skilled service are not covered, except when the dependent service was not followed by a qualifying skilled service as a result of the unexpected inpatient admission or death of the beneficiary, or due to some other unanticipated event.

(b) **Home health aide services.** To be covered, home health aide services must meet each of the following **requirements**:

(1) The reason for the visits by the home health aide must be to provide hands-on personal care to the beneficiary or services that are needed to maintain the beneficiary's health or to facilitate treatment of the beneficiary's illness or injury. The physician's order must indicate the frequency of the home health aide services required by the beneficiary. These services may include but are not limited to:

(i) Personal care services such as bathing, dressing, grooming, caring for hair, nail and oral hygiene that are needed to facilitate treatment or to prevent deterioration of the beneficiary's health, changing the bed linens of an incontinent beneficiary, shaving, deodorant application, skin care with lotions and/or powder, foot care, ear care, feeding, assistance with elimination (including enemas unless the skills of a licensed nurse are required due to the beneficiary's condition, routine catheter care, and routine colostomy care), assistance with ambulation, changing position in bed, and assistance with transfers.

(ii) Simple dressing changes that do not require the skills of a licensed nurse.

(iii) Assistance with medications that are ordinarily self-administered and that do not require the skills of a licensed nurse to be provided safely and effectively.

(iv) Assistance with activities that are directly supportive of skilled therapy services but do not require the skills of a therapist to be safely and effectively performed, such as routine maintenance exercises and repetitive practice of functional communication skills to support speech-language pathology services.

(v) Routine care of prosthetic and orthotic devices.

27.(2) The services to be provided by the home health aide must be—

28.(i) Ordered by a physician in the plan of care; and

29.(ii) Provided by the home health aide on a part-time or intermittent basis.

30.(3) The services provided by the home health aide must be reasonable and necessary. To be considered reasonable and necessary, the services must—

(i) Meet the requirement for home health aide services in paragraph (b)(1) of this section;

(ii) Be of a type the beneficiary cannot perform for himself or herself; and

(iii) Be of a type that there is no able or willing caregiver to provide, or, if there is a potential caregiver, the beneficiary is unwilling to use the services of that individual.

31. (4) The home health aide also may perform services incidental to a visit that was for the provision of care as described in paragraphs (b)(3)(i) through (iii) of this section. For example, these incidental services may include changing bed linens, personal laundry, or preparing a light meal.

C. Medical social services. Medical social services may be covered if the following requirements are met:

32. (1) The services are ordered by a physician and included in the plan of care.

(2)(i) The services are necessary to resolve social or emotional problems that are expected to be an impediment to the effective treatment of the beneficiary's medical condition or to his or her rate of recovery.

(ii) If these services are furnished to a beneficiary's family member or caregiver, they are furnished on a short-term basis and it can be demonstrated that the service is necessary to resolve a clear and direct impediment to the effective treatment of the beneficiary's medical condition or to his or her rate of recovery.

(3) The frequency and nature of the medical social services are reasonable and necessary to the treatment of the beneficiary's condition.

(4) The medical social services are furnished by a qualified social worker or qualified social work assistant under the supervision of a social worker as defined in Sec. 484.4 of this chapter.

(5) The services needed to resolve the problems that are impeding the beneficiary's recovery require the skills of a social worker or a social work assistant under the supervision of a social worker to be performed safely and effectively.

(d) **Occupational therapy.** Occupational therapy services that are not qualifying services under Sec. 409.44(c) are nevertheless covered as dependent services if the requirements of Sec. 409.44(c)(2)(i) through (iv), as to reasonableness and necessity, are met.

(e) **Durable medical equipment.** Durable medical equipment in accordance with Sec. 410.38 of this chapter, which describes the scope and conditions of payment for durable medical equipment under Part B, may be covered under the home health benefit as either a Part A or Part B service. Durable medical equipment furnished by an HHA as a home health service is always covered by Part A if the beneficiary is entitled to Part A.

(f) **Medical supplies.** Medical supplies (including catheters, catheter supplies, ostomy bags, and supplies relating to ostomy care but excluding drugs and biologicals) may be covered as a home health benefit. For medical supplies to be covered as a Medicare home health benefit, the medical supplies must be needed to treat the beneficiary's illness or injury that occasioned the home health care.

(g) **Intern and resident services.** The medical services of interns and residents in training under an approved hospital teaching program are covered if the services are ordered by the physician who is responsible for the plan of care and the HHA is affiliated with or under the common control of the hospital furnishing the medical services. Approved means—

(1) Approved by the Accreditation Council for Graduate Medical Education;

(2) In the case of an osteopathic hospital, approved by the Committee on Hospitals of the Bureau of Professional Education of the American Osteopathic Association;

(3) In the case of an intern or resident-in-training in the field of dentistry, approved by the Council on Dental Education of the American Dental Association; or

(4) In the case of an intern or resident-in-training in the field of podiatry, approved by the Council on Podiatric Medical Education of the American Podiatric Medical Association.

[59 FR 65495, Dec. 20, 1994; 60 FR 39122, 39123, Aug. 1, 1995]

APPENDIX 4-6

MEDICARE BENEFIT POLICY MANUAL

CMS PUB. 100-2

CH. 7—COVERAGE OF SERVICES

20. COVERAGE OF SERVICES 04-96

20.1 Reasonable and Necessary Services.—

20.1.1. Background.—In enacting the Medicare program, Congress recognized that the physician would play an important role in determining utilization of services. The law requires that payment may be made only if a physician certifies the need for services and establishes a plan of care. The Secretary is responsible for ensuring that the claimed services are covered by Medicare, including determining whether they are "reasonable and necessary."

20.1.2. Determination of Coverage.—The intermediary's decision on whether care is reasonable and necessary is based on information reflected in the home health plan of care (CMS 485), and the OASIS as required by 42 C.F.R. 484.55 or a medical record of the individual patient. A coverage denial is not made solely on the basis of the reviewer's general inferences about patients with similar diagnoses or on data related to utilization generally, but is based upon objective clinical evidence regarding the patient's individual need for care.

* * *

20.3 Use of Utilization Screens and "Rules of Thumb."—
Medicare recognizes that determinations of whether home health services are reasonable and necessary must be based on an assessment of each patient's individual care needs. Therefore, denial of services based on numerical utilization screens, diagnostic screens, diagnosis or specific treatment norms is not appropriate.

* * *

40.1 COVERAGE OF SERVICES 04-96

40.1.1 General Principles Governing Reasonable and Necessary Skilled Nursing Care.—

4. The skilled nursing service must be reasonable and necessary to the diagnosis and treatment of the patient's illness or injury within the context of the patient's unique medical condition. To be considered reasonable and necessary

for the diagnosis or treatment of the patient's illness or injury, the services must be consistent with the nature and severity of the illness or injury, his or her particular medical needs, and accepted standards of medical and nursing practice. A patient's overall medical condition is a valid factor in deciding whether skilled services are needed. A patient's diagnosis should never be the sole factor in deciding that a service the patient needs is either skilled or unskilled.

The determination of whether the services are reasonable and necessary should be made in consideration that a physician has determined that the services ordered are reasonable and necessary. The services must, therefore, be viewed from the perspective of the condition of the patient when the services were ordered and what was, at that time, reasonably expected to be appropriate treatment for the illness or injury throughout the certification period.

> **Example 1:** A physician has ordered skilled nursing visits for a patient with a hairline fracture of the hip. In the absence of any underlying medical condition or illness, nursing visits would not be reasonable and necessary for treatment of the patient's hip injury.

> **Example 2:** A physician has ordered skilled nursing visits for injections of insulin and teaching of self-administration and self-management of the medication regimen for a patient with diabetes mellitus. Insulin has been shown to be a safe and effective treatment for diabetes mellitus, and therefore, the skilled nursing visits for the injections and teaching self-administration and management of the treatment regimen would be reasonable and necessary.

The determination of whether a patient needs skilled nursing care should be based solely upon the patient's unique condition and individual needs, without regard to whether the illness or injury is acute, chronic, terminal or expected to extend over a long period of time. In addition, skilled care may, dependent upon the unique condition of the patient, continue to be necessary for patients whose condition is stable.

14.6 Rev. 277
* * *

40.1.2 Application of the Principles to Skilled Nursing Services.—The following discussion of skilled nursing services applies the foregoing principles to specific skilled nursing services about which questions are most frequently raised.

40.1.2.1. Observation and Assessment of Patient's Condition When Only the Specialized Skills of a Medical Professional Can Determine a Patient's Status.—Observation and assessment of the patient's condition by a licensed nurse are reasonable and necessary skilled services when the likelihood of change in a patient's condition requires skilled nursing personnel to identify and evaluate the patient's need for possible modification of treatment or initiation of additional medical procedures until the patient's treatment regimen is essentially stabilized. Where a patient was admitted to home health care for skilled observation because there was a reasonable potential of a complication or further acute episode, but did not develop a further acute episode or complication, the skilled observation services are still covered for 3 weeks or as long as there remains a reasonable potential for such a complication or further acute episode.

Information from the patient's medical history may support the likelihood of a future complication or acute episode and, therefore, may justify the need for continued skilled observation and assessment beyond the three-week period. Moreover, such indications as abnormal/fluctuating vital signs, weight changes, edema, symptoms of drug toxicity, abnormal/fluctuating laboratory values, and respiratory changes on auscultation may justify skilled observation and assessment. Where these indications are such that it is likely that skilled observation and assessment by a nurse will result in changes to the treatment of the patient, then the services would be covered. There are cases where patients who are stable continue to require skilled observation and assessment. . . . However, observation and assessment by a nurse is not reasonable and necessary to the treatment of the illness or injury where these indications are part of a longstanding pattern of the patient's condition, and there is no attempt to change the treatment to resolve them.

> **Example 1:** A patient with arteriosclerotic heart disease with congestive heart failure requires close observation by skilled nursing personnel for signs of decompensation or adverse effects resulting from prescribed medication. Skilled observation is needed to determine whether the drug regimen should be modified or whether other therapeutic measures should be considered until the patient's treatment regimen is essentially stabilized.

> **Example 2:** A patient has undergone peripheral vascular disease treatment including a revascularization procedure (bypass). The incision area is showing signs of potential infection (e.g., heat, redness, swelling, drainage) and the patient has elevated body temperature. Skilled observation and monitoring of the vascular supply of the legs and the incision site is required until the signs of potential infection have abated and there is no longer a reasonable potential of infection.

> **Example 3:** A patient was hospitalized following a heart attack and, following treatment but before mobilization, is discharged home. Because it is not known whether exertion will exacerbate the heart disease, skilled observation is reasonable and necessary as mobilization is initiated until the patient's treatment regimen is essentially stabilized.

> **Example 4:** A frail 85-year-old man was hospitalized for pneumonia. The infection was resolved, but the patient, who had previously maintained adequate nutrition, will not eat or eats poorly. The patient is discharged to the HHA for monitoring of fluid and nutrient intake, and assessment of the need for

tube feeding. Observation and monitoring by licensed nurses of the patient's oral intake, output and hydration status is required to determine what further treatment or other intervention is needed.

Example 5: A patient with glaucoma and a cardiac condition has a cataract extraction. Because of the interaction between the eye drops for the glaucoma and cataracts and the beta blocker for the cardiac condition, the patient is at risk for serious cardiac arrhythmias. Skilled observation and monitoring of the drug actions is reasonable and necessary until the patient's condition is stabilized.

Example 6: A patient with hypertension suffered dizziness and weakness. The physician found that the blood pressure was too low and discontinued the hypertension medication. Skilled observation and monitoring of the patient's blood pressure and medication regimen is required until the blood pressure remains stable and in a safe range.

40.1.2.2. Management and Evaluation of a Patient Care Plan.—Skilled nursing visits for management and evaluation of the patient's care plan are also reasonable and necessary where underlying conditions or complications require that only a registered nurse can ensure that essential nonskilled care is achieving its purpose. For skilled nursing care to be reasonable and necessary for management and evaluation of the patient's plan of care, the complexity of the necessary unskilled services that are a necessary part of the medical treatment must require the involvement of licensed nurses to promote the patient's recovery and medical safety in view of the patient's overall condition.

40.1.2.3. Teaching and Training Activities.—Patient education services are skilled services if the use of technical or professional personnel is necessary to teach a patient self-maintenance. For example, a patient who has had a recent leg amputation needs skilled rehabilitation services provided by technical or professional personnel to provide gait training and to teach prosthesis care. Likewise, a patient newly diagnosed with diabetes requires instruction from technical or professional personnel to learn the self-administration of insulin or foot-care precautions, etc.

APPENDIX 4-7

TRANSMITTAL 1025, HOME HEALTH BENEFICIARY NOTICE
(CHANGE REQUEST NO. 5009)

CMS Manual System	Department of Health & Human Services (DHHS)
Pub 100-04 Medicare Claims Processing	Centers for Medicare & Medicaid Services (CMS)
Transmittal 1025	Date: AUGUST 11, 2006
	Change Request 5009

NOTE: This transmittal is being re-communicated to correct the Effective and Implementation dates in the manual instruction only, which were erroneously input as 08-01-06 instead of 09-01-06 as stated on the transmittal page. This transmittal will retain the original Transmittal number and issue date. All other material remains the same.

Subject: Revised Home Health Advance Beneficiary Notice

I. SUMMARY OF CHANGES: This transmittal implements the revised HHABN and instructions. Chapter 30, section 60 and its subsections are being revised, incorporating previously released information from section 60 with new information.

New/Revised Material
Effective Date: September 1. 2006
Implementation Date: September 1. 2006

Disclaimer for manual changes only: The revision date and transmittal number apply only to red italicized material. Any other material was previously published and remains unchanged. However, if this revision contains a table of contents, you will receive the new/revised information only, and not the entire table of contents.

II. CHANGES IN MANUAL INSTRUCTIONS: (N/A if manual is not updated)
R=REVISED, N=NEW, D=DELETED

R/N/D	CHAPTER/SECTION/SUBSECTION/TITLE
R	10/50/Beneficiary-Driven Demand Billing HH PPS
R	10/60/No Payment Billing
R	30/50/50.8.2/ABNs for Part B Services Furnished in a Skilled Nursing Facility (SNF)
D	30/50/50.8.3/ABNs for Part B Services Furnished in a Skilled Nursing Facility (SNF)
R	30/60/60.1/Background on the HHABN
D	30/60/60.1.1/Approved Standard Forms
D	30/60/60.1.2/User-Customizable Sections
D	30/60/60.1.3/Where to Obtain the HHABN Forms

D	30/60/60.1.4/OMB Burden Notice for Form CMS-R-296
R	30/60/60.2/Scope of the HHABN
D	30/60/60.2.1/Expectation of Denial
D	30/60/60.2.2/Situations In Which HHABN Is Not Given
D	30/60/60.2.2.1/Categorical Exclusions
D	30/60/60.2.2.2/Technical Exclusions
D	30/60/60.2.2.3/Services Not Under HHA PPS
D	30/60/60.2.2.4/When Home Health Services Will Not Be Furnished
D	30/60/60.2.2.5/M+C Enrollees and Non-Medicare Patients
D	30/60/60.2.3/Situations in Which HHABN Should Be Given
D	30/60/60.2.3.1/Triggering Events
D	30/60/60.2.3.2/Dual-Eligibles
D	30/60/60.2.3.3/Medicare as Sole Payer
D	30/60/60.2.4/Routine HHABN Prohibition
D	30/60/60.2.5/To Whom an HHABN Should Be Given
R	30/60/60.3/HHABN Triggering Events
D	30/60/60.3.1/Delivery Must Meet Advance Beneficiary Notice Standards
D	30/60/60.3.2/HHABN Specific Delivery Issues
D	30/60/60.3.3/Timely Delivery
D	30/60/60.3.4/Actual Receipt of Notice Required
D	30/60/60.3.5/Understandability and Comprehensibility of Notice
R	30/60/60.4/Completing the HHABN
D	30/60/60.4.1/General Rules
D	30/60/60.4.2/Header of HHABN
D	30/60/60.4.3/Body of HHABN
D	30/60/60.4.4/Option Boxes
R	30/60/60.5/Special Issues Associated with the HHABN
R	30/60/60.6/Effective Delivery/Effective HHABNs
R	30/60/60.6.1/Defective HHABNs
D	30/60/60.6.2/Acceptance of Rejection of the HHABN
D	30/60/60.6.3/Effective of HHABN on Beneficiary
D	30/60/60.6.4/Financial Liability
D	30/60/60.6.5/Limitation on Liability

D	30/60/60.6.6/Home Care Not Ordered by Physicians
D	30/60/60.6.7/Regulatory Requirements
D	30/60/60.6.8/Standards
D	30/60/60.6.9/Effect of Furnishing HHABNs and Collections From Beneficiary
D	30/60/60.6.9.1/Effective Notice
D	30/60/60.6.9.2/Defective Notice
D	30/60/60.6.9.3/Collection From Beneficiary
D	30/60/60.6.9.4/Unbundling Prohibition
N	30/60/60.7/Collection of Funds and Liability Related to the HHABN
N	30/60/60.8/Revision, Re-issuance and Retention of the HHABN
R	30/90/Form CMS-20007 - Notice of Exclusions From Medicare Benefits (NEMBs)
R	30/90/90.1.1/Using NEMBs With Categorical Denials
R	30/90/90.1.2/Using NEMBs With Technical Denials

III. FUNDING:

No additional funding will be provided by CMS; contractor activities are to be carried out within their FY 2006 operating budgets.

IV. ATTACHMENTS:

Business Requirements

Manual Instruction

*Unless otherwise specified, the effective date is the date of service.

Attachment - Business Requirements

Pub. 100-04	Transmittal: 1025	Date: August 11, 2006	Change Request 5009

NOTE: This transmittal is being re-communicated to correct the Effective and Implementation dates in the manual instruction only, which were erroneously input as 08-01-06 instead of 09-01-06 as stated on the transmittal page. This transmittal will retain the original Transmittal number and issue date. All other material remains the same.

SUBJECT: Revised Home Health Advance Beneficiary Notice (HHABN)

I.   GENERAL INFORMATION

A.   Background: HHABNs have been required since 2002 to inform beneficiaries in Original Medicare about possible noncovered charges when limitation of liability applies. CMS was directed, however, by a Federal court decision to revise this notice and its instructions to encompass broader notification requirements codified under the Conditions of Participation (COPs) for Home Health Agencies (HHAs).

B.   Policy: Section 1879 of the Social Security Act (the Act) protects beneficiaries from payment liability in certain situations unless they are notified of their potential liability in advance. The COPs for HHAs at §1891 of the Act require general notification of changes in charges and care.

II.   BUSINESS REQUIREMENTS

"Shall" denotes a mandatory requirement
"Should" denotes an optional requirement

Requirement Number	Requirements	Responsibility ("X" indicates the columns that apply)								
		FI	RHHI	Carrier	DMERC	Shared System Maintainers				Other
						FISS	MCS	VMS	CWF	
5009.1	Regional Home Health Intermediaries (RHHIs) shall take any actions necessary to implement the attached instructions, primarily by assisting HHAs in understanding their responsibilities. [Note this instruction updates policy previously implemented by Joint Signature Memorandum, JSM-06299, Revised Home health Advance Beneficiary Notice and Instructions for Immediate Release, dated February 17, 2006].	X								

Requirement Number	Requirements	Responsibility ("X" indicates the columns that apply)								
		F I	R H H I	C a r r i e r	D M E R C	Shared System Maintainers				Other
						F I S S	M C S	V M S	C W F	
5009.1.1	RHHIs shall remove the JSM instructions mentioned above from their Web sites on the HHABN that are dated once this CR is effective.		X							

III. PROVIDER EDUCATION

Requirement Number	Requirements	Responsibility ("X" indicates the columns that apply)								
		F I	R H H I	C a r r i e r	D M E R C	Shared System Maintainers				Other
						F I S S	M C S	V M S	C W F	
5009.2	A provider education article related to this instruction will be available at www.cms.hhs.gov/MLNMattersArticles shortly after the CR is released. You will receive notification of the article release via the established "medlearn matters" listserv. Contractors shall post this article, or a direct link to this article, on their Web site and include information about it in a listserv message within 1 week of the availability of the provider education article. In addition, the provider education article shall be included in your next regularly scheduled bulletin and incorporated into any educational events on this topic. Contractors are free to supplement Medlearn Matters articles with localized information that would benefit their provider community in billing and administering the Medicare program correctly.	X								

IV. SUPPORTING INFORMATION AND POSSIBLE DESIGN CONSIDERATIONS

A. Other Instructions: N/A

X-Ref Requirement #	Instructions

B. Design Considerations: N/A

X-Ref Requirement #	Recommendation for Medicare System Requirements

C. Interfaces: N/A

D. Contractor Financial Reporting /Workload Impact: The HHABN is an existing requirement primarily executed by HHAs. Though expanded in scope with this instruction, HHABN policy is simplified in other ways and should not have any impact on RHHI workload beyond short-term educational demands. Note the most recent year of data available shows that less than 4 percent of home health claims are linked to HHABNs.

E. Dependencies: None.

F. Testing Considerations: None, this is a non-systems instruction.

V. SCHEDULE, CONTACTS, AND FUNDING

Effective Date*: September 1, 2006 **Implementation Date:** September 1, 2006 **Pre-Implementation Contact(s):** Elizabeth Carmody, elizabeth.carmody@cms.hhs.gov, 410-786-7533 **Post-Implementation Contact(s):** Appropriate Regional Office	**No additional funding will be provided by CMS; contractor activities are to be carried out within their FY 2006 operating budgets.**

*Unless otherwise specified, the effective date is the date of service.

50 - Beneficiary-Driven Demand Billing Under HH PPS
(Rev. 1025, Issued: 08-11-06; Effective/Implementation Dates: 09-01-06)

Demand billing is a procedure through which beneficiaries can request Medicare payment for services that: (1) their HHAs advised them were not medically reasonable and necessary, or that (2) they failed to meet the homebound, intermittent or noncustodial care requirements, and therefore would not be reimbursed if billed. The HHA must inform the beneficiary of this assessment in a Home Health Advance Beneficiary Notice (HHABN), Form CMS-R-296, which also must be signed by the beneficiary or appropriate representative. *Instructions for the HHABN are found in Chapter 30 of this manual, §60.*

Beneficiaries pay out of pocket or third party payers cover the services in question, but HHAs in return, upon request of the beneficiary, are required to bill Medicare for the disputed services. If, after its review, Medicare decides some or all the disputed services received on the "demand bill" are covered and pays for them, the HHA would refund the previously collected funds for these services. If the Medicare determination upholds the HHA's judgment that the services were not medically reasonable and necessary, or that the beneficiary failed to meet the homebound or intermittent care requirements, the HHA keeps the funds collected, unless the Regional Home Health Intermediary (RHHI) determines the HHABN notification was not properly executed, or some other factor changed liability for payment of the disputed services back to the HHA.

The Medicare payment unit for home care under the home health prospective payment system (HH PPS) is an episode of care, usually 60 days in length. In order to be eligible for episode payment, Medicare beneficiaries must be: (1) under a physician plan of care, and (2) at least one service must have been provided to the beneficiary, so that a request for anticipated payment (RAP) can be sent to Medicare and create a record of an episode in Medicare claims processing systems. Therefore, demand billing *under HH PPS* must conform to ALL of the following criteria:

- Situations in which disputed services are called for under a plan of care, but the HHA believes the services do not meet Medicare criteria for coverage;

- Claims sent to Medicare with TOB 32X and 33X; and

- Episodes on record in Medicare claims processing systems (at least one service in episode).

A - Interval of Billing

Under HH PPS, the interval of billing *is* standard. At most, a RAP and a claim *are* billed for each episode. Providers may submit a RAP after the delivery of the first service in the 60-day episode, and they must submit a claim either after discharge or after the end of the 60-day episode. This *does* not change in demand bill situations, so that only the claim at the end of the episode is the demand bill.

B - Timeliness of Billing

The CMS requests that HHAs submit demand bills promptly. Timely filing requirements were not changed by HH PPS (see Chapter 1 for information on timely filing). CMS has defined "promptly" for HH PPS to mean submission at the end of the episode in question. The beneficiary must also be given either a copy of the claim or a written statement of the date the claim was submitted. HH PPS provides a new incentive to be prompt in filing claims, since RAP payments *are* automatically recouped against other payments if the claim for a given episode does not follow the RAP in the later of: (1) 120 days from the start of the episode; or (2) 60 days from the payment date of the RAP. The RAP must be re-billed once payment has been recouped if the claim is to be billed unless the claim is a no-RAP LUPA as described in §40.3.

C - Claim Requirements

Original HH PPS claims are submitted with TOB 329 in form locator (FL) 4, and provide all other information required on that claim for the HH PPS episode, including all visit-specific detail for the entire episode (the HHA must NOT use 3X0). When such claims also serve as demand bills, the following information must **also** be provided: condition code "20" in FL 24-30; and the services in dispute shown as noncovered (FL 48) line items. Demand Bills may be submitted with all noncovered charges. Provision of this additional information assures medical review of the demand bill. HH PPS adjustment bills, TOB 327, may also be submitted but must have been preceded by the submission of a 329 claim for the same episode. RAPs are not submitted as demand bills, but must be submitted for any episode for which a demand bill will be submitted. Such RAPs should not use condition code 20, only the claim of the episode uses this code.

Cases may arise in which the services in dispute are visits for which an HHA has physician's orders, but the duration of the visits exceeds Medicare coverage limits. However, the portion of these visits that is not covered by Medicare may be covered by another payer (e.g., an 8 hour home health aide visit in which the first 2 hours may be covered by Medicare and the remaining 6 hours may be covered by other insurance). In such cases, HHAs must submit these visits on demand bills as a single line item, representing the portion potentially covered by Medicare with a covered charge amount and the portion to be submitted for consideration by other insurance with a noncovered charge amount on the same line. Units reported on this line item should represent the entire elapsed time of the visit (the sum of the covered and noncovered portions), represented in 15 minute increments.

D - Favorable Determinations and Medicare Payment

Results of Medicare determinations favorable to the party requesting the demand bill will not necessarily result in increased Medicare payment. In such cases, and even if a favorable determination is made but payment does not change, HHAs will still refund any monies collected from beneficiaries or other payers for services previously thought not medically necessary under Medicare. Medicare payment will change only with the addition of covered visits if one or more of the following conditions apply:

- An increase in the number of therapy visits results in meeting the therapy threshold for an episode in which the therapy threshold was not previously met - in such cases, the payment group of the episode would be changed by the RHHI in medical review;

- An increase in the number of overall visits that either:

   1. Changes payment from a low-utilization payment adjustment to a full episode; or

   2. Results in the episode meeting the threshold for outlier payment (it is highly unlikely both things occur for the same episode).

- A favorable ruling on a demand bill adds days to:

   3. An episode that received a partial episode payment (PEP) adjustment, or

   4. A period within an episode that received a significant change in condition (SCIC) adjustment.

If a favorable determination is made, RHHIs will assure pricing of the claim occurs after medical review so that claims also serving as demand bills receive appropriate payment.

E - Appeals

Appeal of Medicare determinations made on HH PPS claims also serving as demand bills is accomplished by appealing the HH PPS claim. Such appeals are done in accordance with regulations stipulating appeals rights for Medicare home health claims. HH PPS RAPs do not have appeal rights; rather, appeals rights are tied to the claims that represent all services delivered for the entire episode unit of payment.

F – Specific Demand Billing Scenarios

1. Independent Assessment. Billing questions relative to the HHABN and home health assessments have persisted. With regard to payment liability for the assessment itself, the assessment is a non-covered service that is not a Medicare benefit and is never separately payable by Medicare. In all *such* cases, a choice remains: The provider may or may not decide to hold the beneficiary liable, and Medicare cannot specify which is appropriate because the service at issue is outside Medicare's scope.

If a decision is made to hold a beneficiary liable for just the assessment, CMS believes providers must be in compliance with the home health Conditions of Participation (COPs), as follows:

484.10.e (1) The patient has the right to be advised, before care is initiated, of the extent to which payment for the HHA services may be expected from Medicare or other sources, and the extent to which payment may be required from the patient. Before care is initiated, the HHA must inform the patient, orally and in writing, of: (i) The extent to which payment may be expected from Medicare, Medicaid or any other Federally funded or aided program known to the HHA; (ii) The charges for services that will not be covered by Medicare; and (iii) The charges that the individual has to pay.

Therefore, while no notice may be required if the provider chooses to be liable, the conditions state a notice is required if the beneficiary is to be held liable, and must be delivered prior to the service in question. HHABN*s can* be used for this purpose.

2. **Billing in Excess of the Benefit.** In some states, the Medicaid program will cover more hours of care in a week than the Medicare benefit. Therefore, *an* HHA may be billing hours/visits in excess of the benefit during a Medicare home health episode for a dually eligible beneficiary. Since the care delivered in excess of the benefit is not part of the benefit, and does not affect the amount of Medicare's prospectively set payment, there is no dispute as to liability, and *an* HHABN is not required unless a triggering event occurs; that is, care in excess of the benefit is not a triggering event in and of itself requiring an HHABN. Billing services in excess of the benefit is discussed in C in this section.

3. **One-Visit Episodes.** Since intermittent skilled nursing care is a requirement of the Medicare home health benefit, questions often arise as to the billing of one-visit episodes. Medicare claims systems will process such billings, but these billings should only be done when some factor potentially justifies the medical necessity of the service relative to the benefit.

Many of these cases do not even need to be demand billed, because coverage is not in doubt, since physician orders called for delivery of the benefit. When the beneficiary dies after only one visit is a clear-cut example. When physician orders called for additional services, but the beneficiary died before more services could be delivered, the delivery of only one visit is covered. The death is clearly indicated on the claim with use of patient status code 20. Other cases in which orders clearly called for additional services, but circumstances prevented delivery of more than one service by the HHA, are also appropriately billed to Medicare in the same fashion.

There may be rare cases where, even though orders do not clearly indicate the need for additional services, the HHA feels delivery of the service is medically justified by Medicare's standard, and should be covered. In such situations, when doubt exists, *an* HHA should still give the beneficiary *an* HHABN if a triggering event has occurred, explaining Medicare may not cover the service, and then demand bill the service in question.

No billing is required when there is no dispute that the one service called for on the order does not meet the requirements for the Medicare home health benefit, or is not medically necessary. However, there are options for billing these non-covered services as discussed in Chapter 1 of this manual, Section 60. Note the COPs may require notification in this situation if the beneficiary is to be held liable, as discussed in 1. immediately above.

60 - No Payment Billing
(Rev. 1025, Issued: 08-11-06; Effective/Implementation Dates: 09-01-06)

No-Payment Billing and Receipt of Denial Notices Under HH PPS

Claims for homebound Medicare beneficiaries under a physician plan of care and electing fee-for-service coverage are reimbursed under HH PPS. *Under HH PPS,* home health agencies may continue to seek denials for entire claims from Medicare in cases where a provider knows all services will not be covered by Medicare. Such denials are usually sought because of the requirements of other payers for providers to obtain Medicare denial notices before they will consider providing additional payment. Such claims are often referred to as no-payment or no-pay bills, or denial notices.

A - Submission and Processing

In order to submit a no-payment bill to Medicare under HH PPS, providers must use TOB 3x0 in Form Locator (FL) 4, and condition code 21 in FL 24-30 of the Form CMS-1450 claim form. The statement dates on the claim, FL 6, should conform to the billing period they plan to submit to the other payer, insuring that no future date is reported. Providers must also key in the charge for each line item on the claim as a non-covered charge in FL 48 of each line. In order for these claims to process through the subsequent HH PPS edits in the system, providers are instructed to submit a 0023 revenue line and OASIS Matching Key on the claim. If no OASIS assessment was done, report the lowest weighted HIPPS code (HAEJ1) as a proxy, *an* 18-digit string of the number 1, "111111111111111111", for the OASIS Claim-Matching-Key in FL 63, and meet other minimum Medicare requirements for processing RAPs. If an OASIS assessment was done, the actual HIPPS code and Matching-Key output should be used. Medicare standard systems will bypass the edit that requires a matching RAP on history for these claims, then continue to process them as no-pay bills. Standard systems also ensure that a matching RAP has not been paid for that billing period. FL 20, source of admission, and treatment authorization codes, FL 63, *are* unprotected for non-pay bills.

B - Simultaneous Covered and Non-Covered Services

In some cases, providers may need to obtain a Medicare denial notice for non-covered services delivered in the same period as covered services that are part of an HH PPS episode. In such cases, the provider should submit a non-payment bill according to the instructions above for the non-covered services alone, AND submit the appropriate HH PPS RAP and claim for the episode. If the episode billed through the RAP and claim is 60 days in length, the period billed under the non-payment bill should be the same.

Medicare standard systems and the CWF will allow such duplicate claims to process when all services on the claim are non-covered.

C - Custodial Care under HH PPS, or Termination of the Benefit during an Episode Period

In certain cases, CMS allows the use of no payment claims in association with *an* HHABN involving custodial care and termination of a benefit during an episode period. This does not apply to cases in which a determination is being requested as to the beneficiary's homebound status at the beginning of an episode; there *an HHABN* must be used *assuming* a triggering event occurs *(i.e., the initiation of completely noncovered care)*. However, in cases where the HH plan of care prescribes only custodial care, or if the benefit has terminated during a *previous* episode period, and the physician, beneficiary, and provider are all in agreement the benefit has terminated or does not apply, home health agencies (HHAs) can use:

1. The HHABN for notification of the beneficiary, *using* Option *Box 1 language, with the beneficiary selecting the third checkbox indicating both services and billing is desired, and then also the following checkbox for Medicare billing* on that *notice*, and,

2. A condition code 21 no-payment claim to bill all subsequent services.

NOTE: Providers can never pre-select *HH*ABN options for beneficiaries, in accordance with existing *liability notice* policy. In each case, the beneficiary must be consulted as to the option they want to select. The *HH*ABN options presented relative to specific billing scenarios above, and in the rest of the document, are only illustrations and in no way authorization for pre-empting a beneficiary's right to choose a specific option.

Medicare Claims Processing Manual

Chapter 30 - Financial Liability Protections

Table of Contents

(Rev. 1025, 08-11-06)

50.8.2 - *ABNs for Part B Services Furnished in a Skilled Nursing Facility (SNF)*
(Rev. 1025, Issued: 08-11-06; Effective/Implementation Dates: 09-01-06)

Insofar as payment may be made under Part B for certain items and services when furnished by a participating SNF (either directly or under arrangements) to an inpatient of the SNF, if payment for these services cannot be made under Part A (e.g., the beneficiary has exhausted his/her allowed days of inpatient SNF coverage under Part A in his/her current spell of illness or was determined to be receiving a noncovered level of care, or the 3-day prior hospitalization or the transfer requirement is not met), the instructions in §50.1 - §50.7 and §150 are applicable with respect to such Part B claims.

60.1 - Background on the HHABN
(Rev. 1025, Issued: 08-11-06; Effective/Implementation Dates: 09-01-06)

Since 2002, home health agencies (HHAs) have issued one-page HHABNs related to the absence or cessation of Medicare coverage when a beneficiary had liability protection under §1879 of the Social Security Act (the Act; see 60.2 H. below). This section also takes into account not only notification responsibilities under §1879, but also those under §1891 of the Act, the Conditions of Participation (COPs) for HHAs, in accordance with the 2nd Circuit's decision in LUTWIN V. THOMPSON. In particular, HHABNs are required more frequently for reductions and terminations. For example:

- *HHABNs are required more frequently for changes in noncovered home care;*

- *HHABNs are now required in some situations where qualifying requirements for Medicare benefits are not being met, such as when there is a lack of physician orders for further home care; and*

- *HHABNs are required in a larger number of circumstances where covered care is reduced or terminated.*

These HHABN instructions also take into account expedited determination notice requirements, which were implemented in 2005. As detailed below (see 60.2 B), the HHABN and expedited determination notices are now the only two types of notices an HHA will need to use to convey liability to beneficiaries.

60.2 - Scope of the HHABN
(Rev. 1025, Issued: 08-11-06; Effective/Implementation Dates: 09-01-06)

A. Statutory Authorization for HHABN

The requirement to give an HHABN is based on §1879 of the Act with its financial liability protections, and §1891, the COPs for HHAs (the COPs are further implemented through Title 42 of the Code of Federal Regulations (CFR), Part 484.) In particular, relative to written notification, §1891(a)(1)(E) stipulates that beneficiaries have:

> *'The right to be fully informed orally and in writing (in advance of coming under the care of the [home health] agency) of --*
>
> *(i)   all items and services furnished by (or under arrangement with) the agency for which payment may be made under this title,*
>
> *(ii)   the coverage available for such items and services under this title, title XIX or any other Federal program of which the agency is reasonably aware,*

(iii)   any charges for items and services not covered under this title and any charges the individual may have to pay with respect to items and services furnished by (or under arrangement with) the agency, and

(iv)   any changes in the charges or items and services described in clause (i), (ii) or (iii)."

The following chart summarizes the notice requirements under §1879 and §1891, which can also vary based on whether the home health benefit is at issue or if other care delivered by HHAs is involved (see 60.2 E below). Note CMS has designated the HHABN as the standard notification vehicle in all these cases:

Overview of HHABN Statutory Authorization

HHABN Requirement	HH Benefit	HHA Services "Outside the HH Benefit*"
§1891 Notification of Plan of Care (POC) Reductions and Terminations	Required	Not Required
§1879 Liability Notification for a Defined Medicare Benefit	Required	Required
Liability Notification for Care that is Not a Defined Medicare Benefit	Not Applicable	Voluntary

* For definition, see 60.2 E below

B. HHABNs and Other Liability Notices

Since 2006, the HHABN has a broader scope that makes some other liability-related notices formerly used by HHAs unnecessary. Subsequently, HHAs no longer use:

- The general ABN (CMS-R-131) for Part B non-covered items/services outside the home health benefit-- HHAs use the HHABN for all benefits.

- The voluntary notices, Notice of Exclusion from Medicare Benefits (NEMB) or the NEMB-Home Health Agency (NEMB-HHA), for noncovered care outside the definition of a Medicare benefit -- HHAs use the HHABN for voluntary as well as mandatory liability notification.

Along with the HHABN, HHAs must use expedited determinations notices when required. [In short, expedited determination notices are given to beneficiaries before the termination of all Medicare covered services, so they are alerted to their right to obtain an independent, immediate review by a Quality Improvement Organization (QIO) of the decision to end coverage. For Original (Fee-For-Service, "FFS") Medicare, the first or Generic Expedited Determination Notice is entitled, "Notice of Medicare Provider Non-Coverage," Form Number CMS-10123, and the second or detailed notice is called the

"Detailed Explanation of Non-Coverage," Form Number CMS-1024.] Links for "FFS HHABN" and "FFS ED Notices" are links found on CMS Web site at:

http://www.cms.hhs.gov/BNI/

Instructions for the expedited notices, like the HHABN, will ultimately be placed in this chapter (a new and independent section), since this chapter is the primary source of guidance on all such notices used in Original Medicare.

C. HHABN Issuers and Recipients

Only HHAs, no other types of Medicare providers, issue the HHABN. *HHAs issue HHABNs only for services that they bill or furnish, not for items or services that beneficiaries under their care may permissibly obtain from other sources (note this policy generally applies to all financial liability protection notices that are used to meet the requirements of §1879 of the Act).*

An example is when durable medical equipment (DME) suppliers, and not HHAs, are providing equipment to beneficiaries receiving home care. In such cases, it is the supplier's responsibility, as the entity billing the equipment, not the HHA's, to notify the beneficiary of potentially noncovered items they may deliver. Suppliers use the general ABN and follow the instructions for this notice found elsewhere in this chapter. Another example is when an HHA has an intravenous infusion division, but a pharmacy provides medications to be infused and bills the patient's drug benefit directly. Here the pharmacy does the billing, and therefore would have any applicable notification responsibility. (Note there is no ABN-type notification requirement for Medicare Part D, only potentially for drugs provided under Part B (of Original Medicare)).

Regarding beneficiaries receiving the HHABN, §1879 financial liability protection notices like the HHABN continue to be used solely for beneficiaries enrolled in Original Medicare, as §1879 of the Act applies only to Parts A and/or B of the Program. **HHABNs are not used in Medicare managed care.** *When a beneficiary transitions to Medicare managed care from Original Medicare during a home health episode, no HHABN is required assuming there is no potential liability for payment or need to provide notification of changes in care. In this case, the beneficiary is still receiving the same basic Medicare covered care, just the type of Medicare "plan" is changing from Original Medicare to managed care (i.e., Medicare Advantage).*

> **NOTE:** *In the instructions in this section, the term "beneficiary" is used either to mean the beneficiary or the beneficiary's authorized representative, as applicable. Therefore, these instructions apply whether the HHA gives the HHABN to a beneficiary or an authorized representative. For more information on authorized representatives, see this chapter, §40.3.5 and §40.3.4.3. Note an authorized representative can sign and date an HHABN without further annotation when properly designated.*

HHAs should contact their Regional Home Intermediary (RHHI) if they have questions on the HHABN or related instructions, since RHHIs administer home health benefits for Original Medicare. Beneficiaries may be directed to call 1-800-MEDICARE.

D. Effect of Other Insurers/Payers

If a beneficiary is eligible for both Original Medicare and Medicaid (a "dual eligible"), or if Original Medicare and another insurance program or payer, HHABN requirements are modified when a triggering event occurs (see 60.3 below for discussion of triggering events). For example, when a beneficiary is a dual eligible, and is receiving services that are covered only under Medicaid-- so that from Medicare's perspective, all care is noncovered-- an HHABN has to be issued only at the initiation of this noncovered care. Therefore, there would be no need for delivery of other HHABNs at subsequent triggering events, such as reductions in care, as long as coverage remained the same and the HHABN given at initiation was still effective. No additional HHABN would need to be given, unless: (1) the beneficiary again became eligible for Medicare coverage and a triggering event occurred, or (2) continuous treatment lasted for more than a year.

The same principle applies for beneficiaries who have Medicare and additional health insurance or payers other than Medicaid, when the other insurance or payer provides coverage and Medicare does not. Other payers can include: waiver programs, Office on Aging funds, community agencies (e.g., Easter Seals) and grants. However, if there is secondary or any subsequent Medicare coverage, HHABNs must again be issued at all triggering events.

> **NOTE:** *When Medicare beneficiaries have no coverage in addition to Medicare, HHAs must provide HHABNs at all triggering events, whether care is covered or noncovered.*

Regarding timing of notification in cases when periods of Medicare covered and other payer/insurer covered care overlap, there is some flexibility. A common example is "split billing" nursing hours paid by Medicaid above those allowed by Medicare in keeping with its coverage policy on intermittent need. If an HHABN was given prior to/at the beginning of the period, such as a recertification period, where split billing was to be done, and explicitly described the care only Medicaid covers, another HHABN would not have to be given just because Medicare coverage ended after that point, assuming the previously given HHABN was still effective (see 60.6). However, the HHA could instead choose to wait to issue the HHABN for the ongoing noncovered care until Medicare coverage was ending-- HHAs can determine which approach will lead to the most effective communication with each individual beneficiary they serve. Note, however, expedited determination notices must be issued when termination of Medicare coverage occurs, in accordance with requirements for this distinct appeal right.

E. Use of HHABNs for All Home Health Services

Since 2006, HHABNs are used both within and outside of the Medicare home health benefit. If HHAs are administering home health plans of care, related items and services are considered delivered under the home health benefit. Examples of services outside the home health benefit include equipment delivered when HHAs are acting as durable medical equipment suppliers, or possibly when administering therapy to non-homebound beneficiaries under a therapy, not home health, plan of care.

In terms of billing, this distinction is drawn by the type of bill: care that is part of the home health benefit is billed with either a 32X or 33X, care outside the home health benefit is billed with 34X. For the HHABN, items or services within and outside of the home health benefit are defined in the same way as they are in billing. Note that:

- *Any Medicare benefit can be either covered or noncovered, depending on individual circumstances involved; and*

- *Generally the term "care outside the benefit" includes: (1) benefits other than the one under consideration (in this section, home health), and (2) items or services that are never-covered as Medicare benefits (see F. immediately below for more on noncovered care).*

   NOTE: *There are differences in when the HHABN has to be issued based on whether care is, or is not, provided under the home health benefit (see 60.3 below).*

F. Noncovered Services

Generally, coverage equates with payment. Covered services are those which Medicare pays in accordance with its established policies, and in Medicare manuals the term "covered" most often means usually or potentially covered under Medicare policy.

Conversely, if a service is "noncovered" in Medicare, this usually means Medicare normally is not expected to or will not pay. Lack of eligibility for a benefit, such as failure to meet the homebound criterion for Medicare to cover home care, is an example of noncoverage due to coverage/payment policy. (Note that while such policy is often the reason payment is not expected, there are other reasons, such as a beneficiary's lack of eligibility for a Part of Medicare, that are different from lack of eligibility for a specific benefit like home health).

There are two basic types of noncovered services under policy as described above:

- ***Never-Covered Care.*** *Items or services that Medicare never covers, such as: (1) defined exclusions like routine foot care cited under §1862(a)(13)(C) of the Act, or (2) care that is not described as covered either in broad categories under Title 18 of the Act (the authorizing statute for Medicare), or in more specific national or local Medicare coverage decisions. Examples of such services which HHAs* *deliver include: telemonitoring of health status, geriatric alcohol prevention programs.*

• **Usually Covered Care.** *Items or services that Medicare* **usually covers,** *but are denied in individual cases for specific reasons, such as when the service in question is considered not reasonable and necessary in a particular case.*

Never-Covered Care -- Home Health Benefit. *Preliminary guidance on the HHABN in 2006 stated that "never-covered" services, when included on the home health plan of care, must be treated like other on the plan in terms of HHABN notification. However, this instruction clarifies that the COPs for HHAs do not require notification for such never-covered care, even when described on home health care plans, as long as there are no charges to the beneficiary. That is, consistent with §1891(a)(1)(E)(iii)-(iv), which focus on charges: notice only has to be given when items and services never-covered under this title are provided to beneficiaries AND the beneficiary is charged for that care.* **If there are no charges, there is no notification requirement.**

Never-Covered Care -- Outside the Home Health Benefit. *Never-covered services that are either benefits other than home health or cannot be categorized as a Medicare benefit at all are not subject to HHABN notification requirements as discussed above relative to the home health benefit. Such care is not required to be administered under home health plans of care, and is not necessarily concurrent with Medicare covered home care. The HHABN may not be required even if HHAs charge for this care, as long as there is no beneficiary liability as recognized under §1879 of the Act (see H. immediately below).* **If §1879 does not apply to care outside the benefit, use of the HHABN is voluntary.**

Usually Covered Care (Noncovered in an Individual Case). *In contrast to never-covered services, note that §1891(a)(1)(E)(i)-(ii) require notification for "all items and services furnished... for which payment may be made under this title." These sections do not reference charges, and set a higher notification standard when care "may" be covered (paid) by Medicare (i.e., this care is not "never-covered" because it can be covered in certain cases). HHABN notification is required when such noncovered items or services are on home health plans of care and reduced or terminated, whether or not there are charges. Again, there is no parallel notification requirement for care outside the home health benefit not administered under home health care plans.*

G. Bundled Payment

For home health, the primary example of bundled payment is the 60-day episode under the home health prospective payment system. This is a global payment for all Medicare covered home care needed in the 60 day episode; it is not based on individual items and services. (Note there are a few exceptions, since separate payment is made for DME osteoporosis drugs provided under the benefit during the episode.)

NOTE: *Items and services that Medicare never covers, as opposed to service Medicare usually covers but may not in an individual case (for reasons such as a lack of* *medical necessity, see F. immediately above), are not considered part of the bundled home health prospective payment. Never-covered care is not within the definition of any Medicare benefit. Examples of never-covered care specific to the home health benefit include: care provided to beneficiaries who are not homebound, telemonitoring, and full-time skilled nursing care.*

Initiation. *HHABNs are not required at initiation of bundled care since the related payment is for any related services that are potentially covered as part of the home health benefit. This is consistent with ongoing financial liability protection policy, which states such notices cannot be used, in effect, to double charge by collecting funds from a beneficiary for care Medicare has already covered in a bundle (see 50.7.7.6 in this chapter on bundled payment; and note Chapter 7 in Pub.100-02, the Medicare Benefit Policy Manual, describes the home health benefit in detail--this manual is 100-04 in the same series).*

> **NOTE:** *If an HHABN was not given at admission/start of care because an HHA was delivering covered and noncovered care in the same bundled payment, and subsequently care continued and became completely noncovered, then an HHABN would have to be issued (see F. above, and 60.3 C. below).*

Reductions. *After initiation, for care considered within a bundle, HHAs must issue HHABNs if during the 60-day episode reductions occur in care that Medicare usually covers. This assures that the beneficiary is aware of these changes as required under the COPs. Such notification is required even if there is no additional liability for the beneficiary (i.e., because the 60-day payment remains the same despite the change, or the payment group changes but the beneficiary still has no liability).*

Terminations. *For terminations of bundled care under the home health benefit, HHABNs are not required, since expedited determination notices fulfill notification requirements. An HHABN is only required if: (1) expedited determination notification requirements do not apply; and/or (2) completely noncovered care continues after coverage ends (see 60.3 below).*

H. Limitation of Liability

Home Health Benefit. *Historically, CMS has required HHABNs only in those specific situations where "limitation on liability" (LOL) protection was afforded under §1879 of the Act for items(s) and/or service(s) ordered by physicians that HHAs believed Medicare would not cover. Prior to 2006, CMS also only required that HHABNs be issued for care that was part of the home health benefit.*

Under these instructions, HHAs continue to use the HHABN in these circumstances, that is, in order to charge beneficiaries for home care presumed to be noncovered, assuming beneficiaries make choices to receive such care and accept liability. The chart below lists anticipated denial reasons where §1879 protections apply.

Application of LOL for the HH Benefit

Citation from the Act	Brief Description of Situation	Explanation
§1862(a)(1)(A)	Care is not reasonable and necessary	Medicare does not pay for such care
§1862(a)(9)	Custodial care is the only care delivered	Medicare does not usually pay for such care, except for some hospice services
§1879(g)(1)(A)	Beneficiary is not homebound	Medicare requires that a beneficiary cannot leave home (with certain exceptions) in order to cover services under the home health benefit
§1879(g)(1)(B)	Beneficiary does not need full time skilled nursing care	Medicare requires an intermittent need in order to cover such services under the home health benefit

Another change in HHABN policy is that HHABNs are not only required in situations where LOL protection is available regardless of financial liability. This is necessary to meet HHA notification requirements under §1891 of the Act (see A. immediately above).

Outside the Home Health Benefit. *With HHABNs given for care outside the home health benefit, the usual reason for presumed noncoverage will be under §1862(a)(1)(A) of the Act, namely that care is not reasonable and necessary. Note that the required frequency of notification for such care has not changed, only the particular notice employed (see 60.2 above, particularly B. and E.).*

60.3 - HHABN Triggering Events
(Rev. 1025, Issued: 08-11-06; Effective/Implementation Dates: 09-01-06)

Generally, HHAs are required to issue HHABNs whenever they believe they are about to deliver noncovered item(s) and/or service(s) at three points in time, called "triggering events":

Definition of Triggering Events

EVENT	DESCRIPTION
A. Initiation	When an HHA expects that Medicare will not cover any item(s) and/or service(s) delivered under a planned course of treatment from the start of a spell of illness, OR before the delivery of one-time item(s) and/or service(s) that Medicare is not expected to cover.
B. Reduction	When an HHA reduces or stops some item(s) and/or service(s) during a spell of illness, while continuing others, including when one home

	health discipline ends but others continue, independent of Medicare coverage.
C. Termination	*When an HHA ends delivery of either all Medicare-covered care, or all care in total.*

NOTE:

- *See A., B. and C. immediately below for more information on each triggering event.*

- *See D. below for certain limited exceptions for the home health benefit when an HHABN is not required even though a triggering event may have occurred.*

Home Health Benefit. *HHAs must issue HHABNs at triggering events when either §1879 or §1891 of the Act apply (see 60.2 A. and H. above), as summarized in the following charts:*

TABLE A - Triggering Events For the HH Benefit: §1879 or §1891 Applies

Application:	Medicare COVERED CARE
Population:	All Beneficiaries
Initiations	Not Required
Reductions	HHABN
Terminations for Coverage Reasons*	Generic Expedited Determination Notice**
Terminations not based on Coverage*	HHABN

* For definition, see C. below.
**HHABNs are also given ONLY if noncovered care continues after coverage ends. See C. below on terminations.

TABLE B - Triggering Events For the HH Benefit: §1879 or §1891 Applies

Application:	Medicare NONCOVERED CARE	
Population:	Beneficiaries with other coverage (i.e., Medicaid)	Beneficiaries with no other coverage
Initiations*	HHABN	HHABN
Reductions	Not Required	HHABN
Terminations**	Not Required	HHABN

* Of completely noncovered care, see C. below.
** In contrast to Table A above, there are no expedited determination requirements when care is noncovered.

Outside the Home Health Benefit. *HHAs must issue HHABNs for triggering events only when required under §1879 (see 60.2 H. above), summarized as follows:*

TABLE A - Triggering Events Outside the HH Benefit - §1879 Applies

Application:	Medicare COVERED CARE
Population:	All Beneficiaries
Initiations	Not Required
Reductions	HHABN
Terminations for Coverage Reasons*	Generic Expedited Determination Notice** and/or HHABN
Terminations not based on Coverage*	Not Required

* For definition see discussion in C. below on terminations.

** Expedited determinations are only required at the end of a planned course of covered treatment usually delivered over the course of time, such as when administering a therapy plan of care, and are not used for one-time or sporadic item(s) or service(s). (Note one-time items or services are classified as initiations, not terminations (see A. below).) HHABNs are also given ONLY if noncovered care continues after coverage ends. When expedited determination notices are not required, the HHABN is required only if LOL applies (see 60.2 H).

TABLE B - Triggering Events Outside the HH Benefit - §1879 Applies

Application:	Medicare NONCOVERED CARE	
Population:	Beneficiaries with other coverage (i.e., Medicaid)	Beneficiaries with no other coverage
Initiations*	HHABN	HHABN
Reductions	Not Required	Not Required
Terminations **	Not Required	Not Required

* Of completely noncovered care, see C. below.

** In contrast to Table A above, there are no expedited determination requirements when care is noncovered.

NOTE:

- When §1879 does not apply and care is outside the home health benefit, such as care that is part of another Medicare benefit, notification of liability with the HHABN is voluntary, not required.

- These notice delivery rules are unique for HHAs. HHAs that also operate as hospices or other types of Medicare providers or suppliers (under separate provider or supplier identification numbers), should NOT assume these requirements are applicable to other types of providers.

- **For ongoing continuous (long-term) noncovered care exceeding a year in duration,** another HHABN must be given as each new year begins, assuming coverage remains the same and therefore HHABN requirements still apply. This is in keeping with standing Medicare liability notice practices that serve to confirm both beneficiary retention of coverage information and that coverage status is in fact unchanged (see 50.7.1 in this chapter).

> ▪ *See 60.4 G.2.b below for a summary of triggering events further broken down by which option box language is used on the HHABN.*

A. Initiations

With respect to the initial assessment of a beneficiary, prior to admission (i.e., start of care), no notification is required if the HHA only assessed the beneficiary, did not admit him/her, and did not charge for the assessment. However, if an HHA charges for an assessment, the HHA must provide notice to the beneficiary before charging for the service as cited in Chapter 10 of this manual (50 F).

In their admission processes for home care, HHAs provide information on covered and noncovered charges as required under the COPs for HHAs. CMS does not mandate that a standardized notice format, like the HHABN, be used in the admission process when covered care is to be delivered. The HHABN is only issued to a beneficiary at initiation when care is completely noncovered by Medicare. If there is delivery of some noncovered care from initiation, such as when there is a noncovered part of bundled care that is covered as a whole (see 60.2 G. above), an HHABN is not required. Another example of HHABNs not being required at initiation is when Medicare covered nursing hours will be provided up to the Medicare limit, and hours beyond that limit will also be provided and paid by Medicaid for a dually eligible beneficiary.

Initiation of completely noncovered care is usually a triggering event for all beneficiaries for all benefits (the exception is care outside the home health benefit when LOL does not apply, see 60.2 H above). Relative to the home health benefit, if another payer or insurer provides coverage after that point while that beneficiary remains ineligible for coverage under Medicare, HHAs do not need to issue HHABNs for subsequent triggering events for up to a year (see 60.2 D. above). For other benefits, HHAs are not required to issue HHABNs for other triggering events after initiation when care remains completely noncovered.

One-Time Items/Services. *Neither HHABNs nor expedited determination notices are necessary for one-time treatments not covered by Medicare where there is no beneficiary liability. If, however, the beneficiary is charged, the HHABN may be required. Any one-time care (that which is provided and completed in a single encounter) is considered an initiation in terms of triggering events, since such care cannot be reduced or terminated over time.*

Under the home health benefit, one-time services are uncommon, such as episodes that are truncated to one visit because of a beneficiary's death. In such cases, HHABNs would not have been required since services at delivery would have been presumed to be covered. If an HHA knowingly plans to provide a potentially noncovered one-time service or item, under the home health benefit (including related assessments), an HHABN must be issued unless: (1) there are no charges to the beneficiary, or (2) a recognized exception applies (see D below). If a one-time service is provided under another Medicare benefit, such as when HHAs provide DME as suppliers under Part B,

HHABNs are only required when the item supplied is not believed to be reasonable or necessary for treatment (LOL applies, see 60.2 H. above).

B. Reductions

Reductions and terminations are sometimes confused, but in the case of reductions, HHAs must be discontinuing some, but not all, care. For example, reductions may include cases where one type of care ends but other type(s) continue, such as the end of one discipline under the home health benefit (skilled nursing) while another (physical therapy) continues.

For most beneficiaries receiving the home health benefit, HHABNs are required for reductions whether or not the care that is ending (the reduction) or the care that continues afterward is covered by Medicare, unless an explicit exception applies (see D. below). Only beneficiaries that are receiving completely noncovered care under Medicare that is covered through another payer or insurer are excepted (see 60.2 D above and the 2 Table Bs at the beginning of this section, as well as D. below). Outside the home health benefit, HHAs are only required to issue HHABNs when Medicare covered care is being reduced and LOL applies (see 60.2 H. above).

C. Terminations

Termination is the complete cessation of all item(s) and/or service(s) at the end of a course of treatment, as opposed to reductions, where only some care ends. Particularly because of expedited determination notice requirements effective July 2005, HHABNs are not always required at termination of home care.

The HHABN and generic expedited notices address different things: the generic notice gives information on the right to a quick decision from a QIO affirming or disputing the end of all covered care. The right to an expedited determination only applies when coverage for a course of treatment under certain Medicare benefits is terminated for Medicare coverage reasons (see "Reasons for Termination" below). Instructions for expedited determinations are in Transmittal 594, CR 3903 dated June 24, 2005 (which will be added to this chapter in the future). Home health and therapy (i.e., administered under a therapy, not home health, plan of care) would likely be the only benefits HHAs provide to which the expedited right applies. In contrast to expedited determination notices, the HHABN provides information on potential liability for care that would be delivered after coverage ends, and on claim-related appeal rights.

Beneficiaries must receive notice for ANY terminations of home care. *For the purposes of the COPs for HHAs, either an expedited determination notice or an HHABN can fulfill this requirement. If §1879 requirements also apply (i.e., noncovered care for which the beneficiary may be liable will continue after termination of coverage), the HHABN must also be provided. A generic expedited determination notice must be issued at termination if: (1) the reason care is ending is related to Medicare coverage policy, and (2) noncovered care will not continue after coverage ends.*

Reasons for Termination. *Regarding (1) in the paragraph above, common examples of care ending for Medicare coverage reasons for the home health benefit are lack of a physician order or a beneficiary no longer being homebound. Outside the home health benefit, lack of orders is also a common reason for noncoverage of other benefits.*

Expedited determination notices are required in these situations. *Terminations not related to coverage policy are likely when HHAs decide to stop providing some or all care for their own financial and/or other reasons, regardless of Medicare policy or coverage. For example, this could occur due to the availability of staffing, closure of the HHA or concerns for staff safety in a beneficiary home. It could also be a situation such as a termination of an HHA's provider agreement with Medicare, which though not necessarily the HHA's choice, still does not affect a given beneficiary's eligibility for Medicare covered home care, nor is such a termination based on Medicare coverage policy.*

NOTE: *As with other triggering events, exceptions to HHABN notification requirements may apply (see D. immediately below).*

Dual Eligible Example. *If a dually eligible beneficiary who has been receiving home care services under Medicare ceases to be homebound, the payer/insurer becomes Medicaid. Since triggering event definitions are written in the context of Medicare coverage, an expedited determination notice is given because Medicare coverage is terminating, but since Medicare noncovered (Medicaid covered) care will be continuing from that point forward, an HHABN is issued too because of the initiation of noncovered care from Medicare's perspective. Medicare requires that its beneficiaries be informed of potential liability in advance of actually incurring that liability (i.e., receiving the noncovered care), when LOL applies (see 60.2 H. above), even if another payer/insurer exists and is likely to provide coverage (see 60.2 D above and D. below).*

D. Exceptions to HHABN Notification Requirements

HHABN notification requirements for care outside the home health benefit are much smaller in scope than requirements than when the home health benefit is being delivered (see the tables at the beginning of this section for illustration of this point). Therefore, the following exceptions in the table below were developed to apply only to the home health benefit. (Note that for services "outside the home health benefit" (see 60.2 E. for definition), HHABNs would not be required in any of the cases listed below, with the possible exception of meeting patient goals if noncovered care continued thereafter and LOL applied (see 60.2 H above and 14. in the table below)).

Table of Exceptions to HHABN Notification Requirements - HH Benefit

#	EXCEPTION	APPLICATION	DESCRIPTION
1	Increases in Care	General	Any increases whether under the original plan of care (POC) or subsequent orders (includes noncovered care simultaneous to but exceeding Medicare coverage, i.e., private duty nurses, other payer/insurer coverage).
2	Transfers	General	Transfers to other covered care, i.e., another home health agency or another type of Medicare provider (includes worsening patients needing hospitalization, until such time as the patient returns to the HHA's care).
3	Emergency or Unplanned Situations	General	Emergencies or unplanned situations beyond the HHA's control (i.e., natural disasters, staff member illnesses or transportation failures).
4	Changes in Caregiver or Personnel	General	Any changes in HHA caregivers or personnel as decided by the HHA.
5	Changes in Arrival or Departure Time	General	Any changes in expected arrival or departure time for HHA staff as determined by the HHA.
6	Changes in Brand	General	Any changes in brand of product, i.e., the same item produced by a different manufacturer as determined by the HHA.
7	Free Care Never-covered by Medicare*	General	Care that is never-covered by Medicare under any circumstances and for which the HHA will not charge the beneficiary.
8	Free Initial Assessment (never-covered by Medicare)**	Initiation	Initial assessments (in cases where beneficiaries are not admitted) for which HHAs do not charge.
9	Noncovered Parts of a Covered Bundled Payment***	Initiation	Noncovered item(s)/service(s) that are part of care covered in total under a Medicare bundled payment (i.e., HH PPS episode payment).
10	Length of Visit/Care	Reductions	Any change in the duration of services included in the POC and communicated to the beneficiary by the HHA, i.e., shorter therapy sessions as health status improves, perhaps going from an hour to 45 minutes.

#	*EXCEPTION*	*APPLICATION*	*DESCRIPTION*
11	*Lessening the Number of Items or Services*	*Reductions*	*Only applicable to reductions anticipated in the POC and communicated by the HHA to the beneficiary (see 1. and 2. below table for further discussion).*
12	*Changes in Services within a Discipline*	*Reduction*	*Changes in the mix of services delivered in a specific discipline (i.e., skilled nursing) with no decrease in frequency with which that discipline is delivered (see 3. below table for examples).*
13	*Changes in Modality of Care Resulting in Use of Different Supplies*	*Reduction*	*Changes in the modality affecting supplies employed as part of specific treatment (i.e., wound care) with no decrease in the frequency with which those supplies are provided (see 4. below table for examples).*
14	*Patient Goals Met*	*Terminations*	*All care (every discipline) ending with all patient goals met and/or physician orders completed **(note an expedited determination notice must still be given in this case).***
15	*Beneficiary Choice*	*Reduction or Termination*	*Changes in care that are the beneficiary's decision and are documented in the medical record.*
16	*Exclusive Coverage under Other Payer/Insurer*****	*Reduction or Termination*	*When there is no applicable Medicare coverage but another payer/insurer will cover the beneficiary's care.*

* See 60.2 F (above).
** See A. immediately above.
*** See 60.2 G.
**** See 60.2 D.

1. Ranges in Orders ("11" in chart above)

Section 30.2.2 of Chapter 7 of Pub. 100-02, Medicare Benefit Policy Manual, allows the use of ranges when physicians write home health care orders. An example of orders given in ranges is: "therapy 2–3 times per week for 3 weeks", as opposed to more prescriptive orders allowing HHAs less flexibility in judging patient progress (as well as making revisions in orders more likely): "3 visits a week for 2 weeks, 2 visits the final week". Since the purpose of the HHABN is to keep the beneficiary informed of specific changes in the POC, the use of ranges on HHABNs is not permitted. That is, language on the HHABN cannot be open-ended as to when a specific change described would occur, particularly if listing a number of potential future changes in a range that is not projected to occur at specific points in time or with the achievement of specific goals (see 2. immediately below).

2. Advance Notification ("11" in chart above)

Some HHAs do not believe they can accurately inform beneficiaries of specific timeframes based on the POC developed from physician orders, because they cannot guarantee that patient's progress will conform to such plans. Other HHAs do feel comfortable advising their beneficiaries in advance, perhaps as part of reviewing the plan of care for the upcoming 60-day episode. **If an HHA is comfortable giving advance notice of all triggering events anticipated in the POC, such notice can be given before the period begins or prior to the first triggering event.** *Another HHABN would then not have to be given in that period as long as treatment did in fact conform to expectations. However, if patient progress was not what was anticipated, or if a change in orders occurred, or for any other reason the previous HHABN no longer captured all reductions/terminations for the period, another HHABN would be required. Alternatively, an HHABN could be provided in advance of each triggering event. There is no mandate to take one approach over the other.*

NOTE:

- *When a certain type of service/home health discipline is close to ending, HHAs can use an endpoint describing when specific goals are met. This assumes the HHA either describes the actual goal on the HHABN ("you can transfer from bed to a chair independently") or fully explains verbally what the term "goals met" (if used on the HHABN) means to the affected beneficiary-- the medical record would also make clear the goal at issue had been discussed with the beneficiary. However, if physician orders exist for specific frequencies of care, this approach cannot be used as an alternative to what is specified in the order.*

- *Sometimes the statement is made that any change in a physician order, and subsequently, the home health POC, requires an HHABN be provided. Given the nature of the home health benefit, services are usually decreasing as a patient improves; thus, subsequent orders would likely be for a reduced number of services. However, new orders can still have one of four possible results: stopping care altogether, reducing care (the most common by far), maintaining care at the same level, or increasing care. Of these possibilities, it is only when reductions or terminations occur that HHABNs may be required.*

3. Use of the HHABN within Home Health Disciplines ("12" in chart above)

Regarding item(s) or service(s) provided within the scope of a single one of the six home health disciplines (see Chapter 7 of Pub. 100-02, Medicare Benefit Policy Manual for basic information on this benefit), an HHABN is only required when the frequency of that discipline is reduced, such as from 3 to 2 visits a week.

EXAMPLES:

- *A beneficiary is receiving several skilled nursing services during visits that are scheduled 3 times a week. One service within that discipline, a Protime draw 1 time a week, is discontinued. Other skilled nursing services (wound care and education) continue, such that skilled nursing visits continue to occur 3 times per week. No HHABN is required when the Protime draws are discontinued, only when skilled nursing is reduced in frequency.*

- *A beneficiary is receiving physical therapy 3 times a week. The therapist changes the beneficiary from a walker to a cane while continuing to visit at the same frequency. No HHABN is required.*

4. Use of the HHABN when Changes in Modality Affect Supplies ("13" in chart above)

When an HHA is providing multiple supplies for complex treatments such as wound care, HHABNs are not required if there is a change in the modality of this treatment, only when supplies are reduced.

EXAMPLES:

- *Specific wound care products like Mesalt and Alldress are stopped, and a Hydrogel pad is started. Since this represents a change in the modality (or intervention), not a reduction, no HHABN is necessary. However, if the frequency of the provision of wound care supplies was reduced, such as from 3 to 2 times a week, an HHABN would be required.*

- *A beneficiary is receiving just skilled nursing care and supplies for wound care. Once the beneficiary learns to do his own wound care, the frequency of skilled nursing visits decreases, and an HHABN is required for this service reduction (although the provision of wound care supplies may stay the same for a time). As the wound continues to heal and the beneficiary is performing wound care less often, at the point fewer supplies are needed, an HHABN is required for that subsequent reduction in the frequency of supplies.*

60.4 - Completing the HHABN
(Rev. 1025, Issued: 08-11-06; Effective/Implementation Dates: 09-01-06)

A. Notices

HHABNs are available at:

http://www.cms.hhs.gov/BNI/

The notice is available in English and Spanish, and in PDF and Word formats, under a dedicated link on the top left-hand margin: "FFS HHABN".

The HHABN is the Office of Management and Budget (OMB) approved standard notice for use by Medicare HHAs to: (1) advise Medicare beneficiaries of potential liability for noncovered item(s) and/or service(s) they deliver, allowing such HHAs to collect payment up-front from beneficiaries in such cases, and (2) inform beneficiaries of changes in the POC when required by the COPs for HHAs. HHAs are strongly advised to use the approved standard notice, as failure to use this notice could result in improper notification (see 60.6 below).

B. Choosing the Correct Language Version

HHAs should choose the appropriate version of the HHABN based on the language the beneficiary best understands. When Spanish-language HHABNs are used, the HHA should make insertions on the notice in Spanish. If this is impossible, additional steps need to be taken to ensure that the beneficiary comprehends the content of the notice.

C. Compliance with Paperwork Reduction Act of 1995

Consistent with the Paperwork Reduction Act of 1995, the valid OMB control number for this information collection appearing on the HHABN is 0938-0781. The estimated time required to complete this information collection ranges from 4 to 18 minutes for a single notice, depending on the option box language used (see F. 2 immediately below). This includes the time to prepare the notice, review it with the beneficiary and obtain beneficiary choices and signature.

Commenters may send comments concerning the accuracy of the time estimate(s) or suggestions for improving this notice to:

> *Centers for Medicare & Medicaid Services*
> *Attn: Reports Clearance Officer*
> *Room C4-26-05*
> *7500 Security Boulevard*
> *Baltimore, Maryland 21244-1850*

D. Effective Dates

HHABNs are effective as of the OMB approval date given at the bottom of each notice. The routine approval is for 3-year use. HHAs are expected to exclusively employ the effective version of the HHABN.

E. Ongoing Care Situations

Generally, the HHABN version that should be used is the one effective when the triggering event requiring notification occurs, such as a reduction or termination in care. For prior admissions, specifically noncovered admissions when HHABNs are required at initiation of care, there is no need to re-notify beneficiaries who have received prior HHABN versions just because a new version has become effective.

F. General Notice Requirements

The following are the general instructions HHAs must follow in preparing an HHABN:

1. Number of Copies: A minimum of two copies, including the original, must be made so the beneficiary and HHA each have one.

2. Reproduction: HHAs may reproduce the HHABN by using self-carbonizing paper, photocopying the HHABN, or using another appropriate method. All reproductions must conform to applicable instructions.

3. Length and Page Size: The HHABN must NOT exceed one page in length. The HHABN is designed as a letter-sized form. If necessary, it may be expanded to a legal-sized page to accommodate information HHAs insert in the notice, such as the HHA's name, list of item(s) and/or service(s) that will no longer be provided, and cost information.

4. Contrast of Paper and Print: A visually high-contrast combination of dark ink on a pale background must be used. Do not use reversed print (e.g., white on black), or block-shade (highlight) notice text.

5. Modification: The HHABN may not be modified, except as specifically allowed by these instructions.

6. Font: The HHABN must meet the following requirements in order to facilitate beneficiary understanding:

    a. Font Type: To the greatest extent practicable, the fonts as they appear in the HHABN downloaded from either RHHI or CMS Web site should be used. Any changes in the font type should be based solely on software and/or hardware limitations of the HHA. Examples of easily readable alternative fonts include: Arial, Arial Narrow, Times New Roman, and Courier.

    b. Font Effect/Style: Any changes to the font, such as italics, embossing, bold, etc., should not be used since they can make the HHABN more difficult to read.

    c. Font Size: The font size generally should be 12 point. Titles should be 18 point, but insertions in blanks of the HHABN can be as small as 10 point if needed.

    d. Insertions in Blanks: Information inserted by HHAs in the blank spaces on the HHABN may be typed or legibly hand-written.

7. Customization: HHAs are permitted to do some customization of HHABNs, such as pre-printing agency-specific information to promote efficiency and to ensure clarity for beneficiaries. Guidelines for customization are:

a. *HHAs may have multiple versions of the HHABN specialized to common treatment scenarios, using all the required language and formatting of the HHABN, but with pre-printed language in its blanks.*

b. *HHAs may print different versions of HHABNs on different color paper to easily differentiate the versions, but in all cases high-contrast combinations of light paper and dark font color should be used.*

c. *HHAs may also differentiate versions of their HHABNs by adding letters or numbers in the header area.*

d. *Maintaining underlining in the blank spaces is not required.*

e. *Information in blanks that is constant can be pre-printed, such as the HHA's name, or Medicare's telephone (1-800-MEDICARE or 1-800-633-4227) and/or TTY (1-877-486-2048) numbers. Note the TTY phone number only needs to be entered when appropriate and based on the needs of beneficiaries.*

f. *If pre-printed multiple options are used describing the items or services and reasons for noncoverage, the beneficiary should only see information applicable to his/her case clearly indicated in each blank or checked off in a checkbox.*

g. *Checkboxes for disciplines, if used to describe item(s) and/or service(s), must still allow for explanation of what is changing; for example: "☐ Physical Therapy: Reduced to 2 times per week." Just checking off a discipline without an explanation could render the notice invalid.*

h. *HHAs should have available HHABNs without pre-printed information on hand for staff to use in unusual cases that do not conform to pre-printed language for items or services or reasons for noncoverage.*

   NOTE:

   - *HHAs must exercise caution before adding any customizations beyond these guidelines, since changing HHABNs too much could result in invalid notice and provider liability for noncovered charges. Medicare's liability notice policy generally bases validity determination on two factors: effective delivery and beneficiary comprehension (see 60.6 below).*

   - *Medicare does not validate adaptations of the HHABN made by individual HHAs. Validity judgments are generally made by RHHIs, usually when reviewing HHABN-related claims.*

G. Completing Sections of the HHABN

The new HHABN continues to be a one-page notice, composed of four sections:

- *Header Section*
- *Body Section*
- *Option Boxes*
- *Signature/Date Section*

The HHABN file contains four pages. The first page is instructional and never distributed to beneficiaries-- it is marked "SAMPLE" in the bottom right corner. It has instructions for filling in the blanks and boxes in the notice. To differentiate the instructions from the actual notice text, the instructions are printed in a different font in the appropriate blanks.

The next three pages are "ready to use" HHABNs. The second page is an HHABN with Option Box 1 text placed into the boxed area of the notice-- it is marked "OPTION BOX 1" in the bottom right corner. The third page is an HHABN with Option Box 2 text in the boxed area-- it is marked "OPTION BOX 2" in the bottom right corner. The last page is also a blank HHABN, with Option Box 3 text in the boxed area -- it is marked "OPTION BOX 3" in the bottom right corner. See section 2.b below on which option box to use.

1. The Header Section

HHAs are permitted to customize the header section of the HHABN. The header section is above the title of the notice, "Home Health Advance Beneficiary Notice," which appears in larger point font size at the top of the page.

After downloading the notice from a RHHI/CMS Web site, HHAs may add identifying information, including the HHA's name, logo, and billing address. At a minimum, information allowing the beneficiary to contact the HHA must appear, including the provider's name and address (telephone number is given elsewhere on the notice).

2. The Body Section and Option Boxes

a. Instructions for the Body Section

The body section of the HHABN is below the header and above the option boxes. The HHA starts by inserting standard information into the following two blanks in this section:

> **Step 1:** *The HHA inserts its name in the blank space provided in the sentence beginning: "WE, _____, YOUR HOME HEALTH AGENCY,. . .". Since the entry in the "Step 1" blank is the same no matter what option box is used, the name can be pre-printed in the notice.*

Step 2: *In the next blank beginning:* "ARE LETTING YOU KNOW THAT
WE_____", *the HHA inserts the appropriate phrase, depending on
which option box is used (see b. immediately below).*

Step 3: *The HHA must describe on the blank lines immediately after:* "WITH THE
FOLLOWING ITEMS AND/OR SERVICES:_____..." *the item(s) and/or
service(s) anticipated to be noncovered that are the reason for issuing the
HHABN.*

Regarding Step 3:

- *The HHA should describe either the items or services that: (1) Medicare will no
  longer cover but may still be provided by the HHA (this applies only when Option
  Box 1 is used, see b. immediately below), (2) the applicable reduction in items or
  services, or (3) the termination of all Medicare-covered care.*

- *General descriptions of multi-faceted services or supplies are permitted. For
  example, "wound care supplies" would be a sufficient description of a group of items
  used to provide this care. An itemized list of each supply is not required.*

- *The HHABN should be used to describe reductions in either supplies or services.
  This is even true for care, like wound care, where delivery of supplies and services is
  highly integrated. Thus, notice would still be required if frequency of services was
  reduced although level of supplies remained constant. The converse would also be
  true, i.e., services remain constant and the level of supplies is decreased.*

- *When a reduction occurs, enough additional information must be included so that the
  beneficiary understands the nature of the reduction. For example, entering "wound
  care supplies weekly (now to be provided monthly)" would be appropriate to describe
  a decrease in frequency for this category of supplies, whereas just writing "wound
  care supplies" would not be sufficient in this particular case.*

- *Changes in the modality or interventions that are part of a service like wound care
  are not considered reductions. Again, if the frequency of the service is reduced, an
  HHABN would be required. (See 60.3, D.4 above.)*

- *AN HHA may add date information in the blank where items and/or services are
  described on the HHABN to help a beneficiary better understand when noncoverage
  begins. Note however that policy on timely HHABN delivery remains the same:* **the
  HHABN has to be issued before the care in question is provided, so that the
  beneficiary can make an informed choice on accepting responsibility for payment
  when payment is at issue.** *The time frame for how far before giving the notice is
  flexible, though notification must occur with enough advance that the beneficiary has
  time to make an informed choice.*

Step 4: *After the word: "*BECAUSE:_____...*" the HHA must describe why the item(s) and/or service(s) listed are expected not to be covered by Medicare, or will no longer be provided by the HHA.*

Regarding Step 4:

- *The reasons provided must be in plain language that allows the beneficiary to understand why the notice is being given and enables the beneficiary to make an informed choice about accepting financial liability (when applicable). The information must convey more than simply that care is "not reasonable or necessary." A large amount of text is not required, nor is a citation to an actual policy document.*

- *The level of detail in the reason given should at a minimum be similar to that found in a Medicare Summary Notice (MSN) message. For example, a Step 4 entry could be: "you are no longer homebound" or, even more consistent with the related MSN message: "you can now leave your home unaided." Both phrases are simply worded examples of concise yet complete explanations of a common yet specific reason why, according to Medicare policy, the home health benefit may not be covered for an improving individual. If needed, supplemental explanations should be provided verbally when delivering the notice.*

- *If multiple item(s) and/or service(s) are listed by the HHA in Step 3, and different reasons exist for including each item or service on the HHABN, the HHA is responsible for providing sufficient information in Step 4 to allow the beneficiary to understand each reason specifically associated with each item or service listed.*

Step 5: *In the paragraph beginning: "*IF YOU HAVE QUESTIONS . . .*", the HHA must enter its own telephone number, and/or provide a TTY number, or directions for using another telecommunication system for speech or hearing impaired beneficiaries when appropriate.*

b. Use of the Option Boxes

There are three choices of option box language, and each can be linked to specific statutory authority:

Authority Supporting HHABN Option Boxes

Application	HH Benefit	Outside HH Benefit*
§1879 Liability Notice given prior to care to alert the beneficiary of potential liability for Medicare benefit	*HHABN – Option Box 1*	*HHABN – Option Box 1*
§1891 COP-Required Notice alerting beneficiaries to changes in care, specifically occurring because the HHA will no longer provide services for their own business or financial reasons	*HHABN – Option Box 2*	*None Required*

Application	HH Benefit	Outside HH Benefit*
§1891 COP-Required Notice alerting beneficiaries of changes in the POC based on physician orders	HHABN – Option Box 3	None Required
Voluntary Notice alerting beneficiaries of potential financial liability for care that is not part of a defined Medicare benefit** or when not otherwise required by LOL policy (i.e., formerly NEMB or NEMB-HHA was used)	Not Applicable	Voluntary use of HHABN - Option Box 1

* See 60.2 E. above for definition.
** See 60.2 E. and F.

The appropriate option box is placed in the middle of the HHABN between the Body and Signature and Date sections. An overview of option box use is provided in the following chart based on context of use (rather than supporting authority).

General Summary of Option Box Use

Option Box	Possible Beneficiary Liability	Assessments without Admission	Home Health Benefit Use	Other Medicare Benefit Use*	Care Not a Medicare Benefit*	Contains Billing Information
1	Must use	Use if charging beneficiary	Yes	Yes	Voluntary use	Yes
2	Can't use	Voluntary use if not charging	Yes	No	No	No
3	Can't use	Can't use	Yes	No	No	No

* See 60.2 E. and F.

Note with regard to triggering events and the option boxes:

- Only Option Box 1 HHABNs are given with generic expedited determination notices when potential liability for noncovered care exists after coverage.

- Multiple instances of a single triggering event may be described on a single HHABN, assuming that HHABN is appropriate to each event.

EXAMPLES:

- Two reductions happening simultaneously both due to changes in the physician order can both be described on a single Option Box 3 HHABN (i.e., goals being met for one discipline -- physical therapy -- and a reduction in skilled nursing care).

- Less common cases where multiple different triggering events occur simultaneously may require separate HHABNs, such as with an initiation of completely new noncovered care (and for which the beneficiary may be liable), and a reduction in ongoing covered care due to physician orders (with *no liability). **Option Box 1 must be used any time there is liability**, Option Box 3 could be used for the reduction related to orders. If such events were combined on a single Option Box 1 HHABN, the HHA would still have to assure the beneficiary understood which event entailed potential liability (and which did not).*

The following chart summarizes the circumstances in which each option box should be used.

Triggering Event	Option Box 1	Option Box 2	Option Box 3
INITIATIONS			
Initiations of Entirely **Noncovered** Treatment, Any Medicare Benefit, when §1879 LOL* Applies	Yes	No	No
One-time **Noncovered** Items/Services, Beneficiary Liable, Any Medicare Benefit, §1879 LOL* Applies	Yes	No	No
One-time **Noncovered** Items/Services, §1879 LOL* Does **Not** Apply **and/or** Not a Medicare Benefit	Voluntary	No	No
REDUCTIONS			
Any Reduction for HHA Reasons (Unrelated to Coverage)**, No Beneficiary Liability, HH Benefit	No	Yes	No
Any Reduction by Physician Order, No Beneficiary Liability, HH Benefit	No	No	Yes
Any Other Reductions, HH Benefit	Yes	No	No
Other **Covered** Care Reductions, Other Medicare Benefits, §1879 LOL* Applies	Yes	No	No
Any Other Reductions (Outside HH Benefit)***	Voluntary	No	No
TERMINATIONS			
Any Termination for HHA Reasons (Unrelated to Coverage)**, No Beneficiary Liability, HH Benefit	No	Yes	No
Covered Care Termination for Coverage Reasons (Including Physician Orders), HH Benefit	Yes****	No	No
Covered Care Termination for Coverage Reasons (Including Physician Orders), Any Medicare Benefit Subject to Expedited Determinations (i.e., therapy delivered by HHAs under a therapy plan of care)	Yes****	No	No

Any Other Terminations (services not subject to Expedited Determinations or §1879 LOL)	Not Required	No	No

* See 60.2 H for definition.
** See 60.3 C for definition.
*** See 60.2 E for definition.
**** Expedited Determination Notice MUST be given, and HHABN is also needed **only** when noncovered care continues after coverage ends.

Instructions specific to each option box follow.

i. Instructions for Option Box 1

Option Box 1 is used in any of the following situations (see the charts earlier in this section for guidance on when to use this option box for different triggering events.):

- A beneficiary faces potential liability/will be receiving noncovered care/will be charged.

- A beneficiary wants a claim filed for potentially noncovered care the HHA provides.

- The care at issue is outside the Medicare home health benefit.

- A beneficiary will be charged for an assessment although not admitted to care.

- Any circumstance that may arise for which neither Option Box 2 nor 3 is appropriate.

If Option Box 1 is being used, HHAs should insert the most appropriate of the following phrases in the Step 2 blank in the body of the HHABN:

- "will not provide you (if choosing Box 1 below)"
- "will no longer provide you (if choosing Box 1 below)"
- "believe Medicare will not provide you"
- "believe Medicare will no longer provide you"

The text insertion for Option Box 1 is in quotation marks below:

Option Box 1 Text

"The estimated cost of the items and/or services listed above is $_____

_____. If you have other insurance, please see #3 below.

You have three options available to you. You must choose only one of these options by checking the box next to the option and then signing below:

□ 1. *I don't want the items and/or services listed above. I understand that I won't be billed and that I have no appeal rights since I will not receive those items and/or services.*

□ 2. *I want the items and/or services listed above, and I agree to pay myself since I don't want a claim submitted to Medicare or any other insurance I have. I understand that I have no appeal rights since a claim won't be submitted to Medicare.*

□ 3. *I want the items and/or services listed above, and I agree to pay for the items and/or services myself if Medicare or my other insurance doesn't pay. Send the claim to:*

(Please check one or both boxes):
□ *Medicare*
□ *My other insurance.* _____

Please note: If you select option 3 and a claim is submitted to Medicare, you will get a Medicare Summary Notice (MSN) showing Medicare's official payment decision. If the MSN indicates that Medicare won't pay all or part of your claim, you may appeal Medicare's decision by following the appeal procedures in the MSN. If you don't receive an MSN for your claim, you can call Medicare at: (___) _____. TTY: (___) _____. You may have to pay the full cost at the time you get the items and/or services. If Medicare or your other insurance decides to pay for all or part of the items and/or services that you have already paid for, you should receive a refund for the appropriate amount.

By signing below, I understand that I received this notice because this Home Health Agency believes Medicare will not pay for the items/services listed, and so I chose the option checked above."

Step 1: *The HHA must provide an estimate of the total cost of the items and/or services listed in the first blank in this option box. Since one or multiple items and services could be at issue, the HHA must enter a total cost that reflects each item or service as clearly as possible, including information on the period of time involved when appropriate (i.e., not a one-time service). For example:*

- *"$400 in total for 4 weekly nursing visits in 1/06"*

- *"$210 in total for 3 physical therapy visits 1/3-17/06, $50 for medical equipment" (Specific pieces of durable medical equipment [DME] should be identified as space allows.)*

NOTE:

- *The cost estimate is meant to give the beneficiary an idea of what costs would be if he/she paid out of pocket, not what the beneficiary may actually have to pay given other coverage. The fact that other insurance might pay appears next in the*

HHABN after the cost estimate; thus, HHAs will inform beneficiaries of cases where other insurance will cover costs.

- *The HHA must provide a reasonably good faith estimate of the total cost sufficient to assist the beneficiary in making a decision to accept or decline potential financial responsibility.*

- *The estimated cost reported on the HHABN may be $0 if, for example, an HHA chooses not to charge a beneficiary, or if bundled payments with no beneficiary liability are involved.*

- *Since it may not be possible for HHAs to project all possible costs for future periods into one blank, a proxy like average daily cost can be given. For example, if an average day involves a skilled nursing visit, an average visit charge or private fee charge master amount for this service could be used to give a daily cost, noting when possible the duration over which continuing care could be expected. The use of "posted charges" is also acceptable in making an estimate.*

- *If an HHA bills for the administration of drugs in cases where it believes that this service will not be covered, although it is usually Medicare covered, the HHA would have to give an HHABN for that specific service if the HHA planned to charge for it, but would not have to include the actual drug in estimated costs if supplied and billed by another entity (i.e., a pharmacy).*

- *The HHA must annotate the amount the beneficiary may have to pay if he/she later chooses to receive only certain items or services of those listed on the HHABN instead of everything originally listed.*

- *Abbreviations can be used due to the limited space available for cost estimates. Abbreviations generally should still be avoided, but are permitted in this space and overall are more acceptable if spelled out elsewhere on the notice (such as where the care at issue is described). If used, abbreviations would be part of what an HHA must cover verbally to assure the beneficiary comprehends the HHABN.*

Step 2: (Check Boxes and the Related Insurance Blank): *The two sets of check boxes-- the first concerning the beneficiary's desire to get the items or services at issue and numbered 1-3, and the second under Check Box 3 indicating whether Medicare and/or another insurer, i.e., Medicaid for dual eligibles and Medigap insurance for those with such policies, should be billed--are NEVER completed in advance (see 60.6). However, the HHA may fill in the blank naming the other insurance in advance when it is familiar with the coverage of a beneficiary, such as for an established patient. At a minimum, HHAs must identify all Federal government-funded insurance they are aware the beneficiary may have that could provide coverage.*

Step 3: *In the space provided in the "PLEASE NOTE:" section of Option Box 1, the HHA must provide the Medicare phone number and the TTY telephone. The phone number is 1-800-MEDICARE (or 1-800-633-4227), and the TTY number is: 1-877-486-2048. These numbers may be pre-printed when the HHA prepares the HHABN.*

ii. Instructions for Option Box 2

Option Box 2 is used when an HHA decides to stop providing some or all care for its own financial and/or other reasons, regardless of Medicare policy or coverage. *Examples of such reasons include: the lack of availability of staffing, closure of the HHA or safety concerns in a beneficiary home. (See the charts earlier in this section for guidance on when to use this option box for different triggering events.) Generally, this language can be used only when:*

- *There is no beneficiary liability.*

- *There is no further delivery of the care described in the body of the HHA (that is, a reduction or termination with no ensuing care of the type described, not a change from covered to noncovered care, such as when Medicare stops paying but care continues).*

- *There is no related claim (that is, there is no ensuing care described that could be billed later).*

Option Box 2 could seem appropriate in similar cases when benefits other than home health are involved. However, notification is not required in these cases, and additionally, the wording of this option box references home care. Note that an HHA may issue HHABNs with Option Box 2 language voluntarily to provide notice that it will not charge nor admit a beneficiary after an assessment is done.

Steps for Completion. *If Option Box 2 is used, HHAs should insert the following phrase in the Step 2 blank in the body of the HHABN:*

"will no longer provide you"

The HHA would fill out the rest of the body of the HHABN as described above. Unlike for Option Box 1, however, there is no information to complete in Option Box 2 itself, as shown below:

Option Box 2

"By signing below, I understand that I received this notice because this Home Health Agency decided to stop providing the items and/or services listed above. The Agency's decision doesn't change my Medicare coverage or other health insurance coverage. I can't appeal to Medicare since this Home Health Agency won't provide me with any more items and/or services; however, I can try to get the items and/or services from another Home Health Agency.

Please note that there are many different ways to find another Home Health Agency, including by contacting your doctor who originally ordered home care. You may then ask the new Home Health Agency to bill Medicare or your other insurance for items and/or services you receive from them."

iii. Instructions for Option Box 3

Option Box 3 is used when the HHA stops providing, or reduces the frequency of, certain items and/or services due to lack of a physician order, but other care continues. That is, this option box is only used with reductions. *(See 60.3 regarding definition of triggering events, and clarification of the difference between a reduction and termination of all care; note the charts earlier in this section provide guidance on which option box to use with different triggering events.) Thus, Option Box 3 is appropriate when:*

- *There is no beneficiary liability.*

- *There is no further delivery of the care described in the body of the HHA (that is, the reduction entails no ensuing care of the type described, as opposed to a reduction in coverage where particular items/services change from Medicare covered to noncovered, and delivery of care continues thereafter).*

- *There is no related claim (there is no ensuing care described that could be billed later).*

Option Box 3 could seem appropriate in cases when benefits other than home health are involved and affected by similar changes in physician orders. However, notification is not required in these cases, and additionally the wording of this option box references home care.

Steps for Completion. *If Option Box 3 is used, HHAs should insert the following phrase in the Step 2 blank in the body of the HHABN:*

"will no longer provide you"

The HHA would fill out the rest of the body of the HHABN as described above.

> **NOTE:** *An HHA may substitute the phrase "will reduce" or "will stop" for this language-- and delete the following word "WITH" from the notice-- if it believes this phrasing will lead to clearer communications with beneficiaries.*

There is no information to complete in Option Box 3 itself, as shown below:

Option Box 3

"By signing below, I understand that I received this notice because my doctor has changed my orders and so my home health plan of care is changing. This home health agency has explained to me that they cannot provide home care without a doctor's order."

3. The Signature and Date Section

Once the beneficiary has reviewed and understands the information contained in the HHABN, the HHA must request that the beneficiary complete all four blanks in the boxed Signature and Date Section at the bottom of the HHABN. The four blanks are:

- **Patient's Name:** *The beneficiary's full name should be inserted in the blank.*

- **Medicare # (HICN):** *The beneficiary's Medicare health insurance claim number should be inserted in the blank.*

- **Signature:** *The beneficiary must personally sign the HHABN.*

- **Date:** *The beneficiary must personally enter the date that the HHABN was completed.*

  NOTE: *The HHA may complete the first two blanks to assist the beneficiary.*

4. Other Considerations During Completion

a. Requests for Additional Information. *If while completing the HHABN the beneficiary requests additional information, the HHA must respond timely, accurately, and completely to the information request. See 60.6 for other requirements for effective delivery.*

b. Refusal to Complete or Sign. *If the beneficiary refuses to choose an option, where applicable, and/or refuses to sign the HHABN, the HHA should annotate its copy of the HHABN, indicating the refusal to sign and individuals present. The HHA must still provide a copy of the annotated HHABN to the beneficiary. The HHA must keep the original version of the annotated HHABN.*

Whether item(s) and/or service(s) will be provided or not when the beneficiary has refused to sign (or not expressly agreed to be responsible for payment) must be decided by the HHA. If under these circumstances the HHA decides to provide the care in question, the HHA should have a second person witness the provision of the HHABN and the beneficiary's refusal to sign/select an option by making an annotation on the HHABN indicating that he/she witnessed this event. The witness must then sign and date next to his/her annotation. Where there is only one person on site, the second witness may be contacted by telephone and may sign the HHABN annotation at a later time. The unused patient signature line on the HHABN may be used for such an annotation; writing in the margins of the notice also is permissible. An HHA is not obligated to provide noncovered care when a beneficiary refuses to accept liability (See 40.3.4.6 in this chapter).

c. Beneficiary Changes His/Her Mind. *If a beneficiary chooses a particular option and later changes his/her mind, where possible, the HHA should present the previously completed HHABN to the beneficiary and request that the beneficiary annotate the original HHABN to show and date the beneficiary's current choice. In those situations where the HHA is unable to present the HHABN to the beneficiary in person, the HHA may annotate the beneficiary's current intent on the notice and immediately forward a copy to the beneficiary. In either situation, a copy of the revised HHABN must be provided to the beneficiary within 30 calendar days.*

> ***NOTE:*** *For requirements after completion, such as retention, see 60.8 below.*

60.5 - Special Issues Associated with the HHABN
(Rev. 1025, Issued: 08-11-06; Effective/Implementation Dates: 09-01-06)

A. Option Selection for Dual Eligibles.

As discussed above, HHAs must use Option Box 1 whenever there is potential beneficiary financial liability. Some States have also established specific HHABN rules involving situations where "dual eligibles" (Medicaid recipients who are also Medicare beneficiaries) would face liability that would be covered by Medicaid. In those cases, such States insist that HHABNs be completed to select the third checkbox in Option Box 1 language (referred to here as "Option 3"), and subsequently that the choice to bill Medicare is also indicated. (Medicaid has the authority to make this assertion under Title XIX of the Act, where Medicaid is recognized as the "payer of last resort", meaning other Federal programs like Medicare (Title XVIII) must pay in accordance with their own policies before Medicaid picks up any remaining charges.)

Medicare HHAs serving dual eligibles need to comply with State policy on HHABNs when it exists. (In the absence of explicit guidance from a State, dual eligibiles may select whatever HHABN choice they want.) However, the State rules apply only when Medicaid will be billed. If Medicaid will not be billed (because the dual eligible makes a choice on the HHABN either not to receive any care at all, or to exercise the right to self-pay), the Medicaid requirement would not apply. (This is consistent with policy that the mandatory billing provisions of §1848(g) of the Act* do not apply when a beneficiary self-pays.)

Normally, an HHA may choose the method of billing it feels is most appropriate in association with a beneficiary's choices on a specific HHABN (though HHAs must always bill Medicare as directed by a beneficiary when he/she expresses a preference). The choices for billing related to HHABNs are: a "demand bill" if detailed review of the HHABN coverage assumption represented on the claim is sought, or a "no-payment bill" in cases where noncoverage is not in doubt and a denial is sought for reasons such as facilitating consideration by a subsequent payer (see Chapters 1 and 10 in this manual for billing information pertinent to HHAs). However, beyond which HHABN option to choose as discussed above, some States have also specified the type of Medicare billing to be done related to the HHABN, requiring that a demand bill be filed instead of a no-payment claim. Note in such cases, if the HHABN and related demand bill do not appear to be consistent, specifically because the beneficiary has not selected Option 3 and did not specify that Medicare be billed, RHHIs will still process the associated claim, not acting to "return to provider" (RTP) as would be done with other potential administrative errors. (Note that if needed, the intermediary can confirm whether the beneficiary is dual eligible by reviewing the MDS/OASIS items that indicate payer source.)

[*Mandatory claim submission applies when Medicare payment may be sought, and it is a requirement for providers or suppliers in such cases to file claims for services that are or may be covered under Part B (i.e., care outside the home health benefit, see 60.2 E). This includes situations where the provider or supplier believes claims might be denied due to lack of medical necessity. Generally, the only exceptions to mandatory submission are: (1) when a physician or practitioner opts out of Medicare, (2) when a beneficiary does not authorize the physician or supplier to submit the claim (i.e., is receiving a service and accepting personal responsibility for payment), and (3) when a physician or supplier provides care for free. Medicare would not make a payment in any one of these situations. Note that when a State Medicaid program insists Medicare billing be done for dually eligible beneficiaries, the beneficiary still has the right to self-pay and demand no claim be filed. In such cases, neither Medicare nor Medicaid payment would be sought.]

B. Effect of Expedited Determinations

If a decision is made on a beneficiary request for an expedited determination (see 60.3 C) or reconsideration that contradicts the expectation on coverage made on an HHABN, the HHABN becomes moot for any period of overlap. For example, if an expedited determination finds that 3 days of care listed on an HHABN as noncovered are covered, the HHABN is moot and the Medicare program, not the beneficiary, will pay for that care. In general, decisions made under expedited review are official Medicare determinations that supersede provider projections on coverage made on HHABNs. Specifically, if an HHABN anticipated that a beneficiary would be liable, but a later decision under the expedited process found the provider liable, the provider would be liable and the HHABN moot. HHAs should annotate HHABNs that have become moot in such cases, noting the subsequent expedited determination. Note that the processing of claims related to a decision made under the expedited determination process must conform to that official Medicare decision.

60.6 - Effective Delivery/Effective HHABNs
(Rev. 1025, Issued: 08-11-06; Effective/Implementation Dates: 09-01-06)

As discussed earlier in this chapter, HHABNs are required in specific circumstances (see 60.3 in particular). When an HHABN is required, the delivery of an HHABN must be effective, or notification may not be deemed valid for purposes of assigning liability to a beneficiary. In order for delivery of an HHABN to be considered effective:

- *The HHABN must be delivered to the beneficiary in person whenever possible. However, Medicare's notice policy allows for cases where this may not be possible. For example, notice may instead be given timely by telephone or email and followed up by mail. If e-mail is used, statutory privacy requirements under the Health Insurance Portability and Accountability Act (HIPAA) are met (i.e., not transmitting any personal identifiers such as social security numbers or HICNs). Instructions on ABN telephone notice are found in this chapter, 40.3.4.2 (these general instructions are also applicable to HHABNs).*

- *When delivering HHABNs to beneficiaries, HHAs are required to explain the entire notice and its content, and answer all beneficiary questions orally to the best of their ability. HHAs must make every effort to ensure that beneficiaries understand the entire HHABN prior to signing it.*

- *The HHABN must be received by the beneficiary prior to the beneficiary receiving the item(s) and/or service(s) at issue. This should be far enough in advance to give the beneficiary time to make an informed choice, but not so far in advance as to cause confusion about what care is described by the HHABN.*

  o *Some allowance is made for "immediate" delivery prior to furnishing the care at issue when unforeseen circumstances arise. This should be avoided whenever possible, but is permissible as long as the beneficiary still can make an informed choice.*

- *The HHABN must convey the HHA's genuine doubt regarding the likelihood that Medicare may not pay for the listed item(s) and/or service(s), the reason(s) the HHA expects that Medicare may not pay for each listed item or service, the estimated cost for each item and/or service, and the beneficiary's options.*

- *The HHABN must be signed by the beneficiary, unless an appropriate reason for the lack of signature is recorded on the HHABN, such as a properly annotated signature refusal.*

  o *If the beneficiary is physically unable to sign the HHABN, but is fully capable of understanding the notice, so that there is no need for an authorized representative, the beneficiary may allow the HHA to annotate the HHABN on his/her behalf regarding this circumstance. For example, a fully cognizant beneficiary with two broken hands may allow an HHA staff person to sign and date the notice in the presence of and under the direction of the beneficiary, inserting the beneficiary's name along with his/her own name, i.e., "John Smith, Shiny HHA, signing for Jane Doe." Such signatures should be witnessed by a second person whenever possible. Further, the medical record should support the beneficiary's inability to write in the applicable time period.*

- *In general, an HHABN remains effective for the predicted denial it communicates to the beneficiary as long as no other triggering event occurs (see 60.3 above on triggering events and exceptions, see 60.5 B and 60.7 D for conditions where HHABNs become moot). HHABNs can at most describe care given over a single year. If a new triggering event does occur, or if care stretches into another year, then another HHABN must be given.*

- *Upon appeal of a related claim, a previously furnished HHABN may serve as acceptable evidence of knowledge that care would not have been covered (i.e., the HHABN cited similar or reasonably comparable item(s) and/or service(s) for which a similar denial was expected). A denial of a claim for such care received not more than 1 year previously may also be acceptable evidence of knowledge a similar denial would be likely. Still, HHAs are advised to provide an HHABN every time it is required, and not rely on a retrospective interpretation of evidence to determine liability.*

Regarding notice delivery in general, subcontractors may deliver HHABNs under the direction of a primary HHA. Note however that overall notification responsibility, including effective delivery, always rests with the primary HHA. If however a patient chooses to acquire care from another HHA following care delivered by a previous HHA, the previous HHA is never responsible for providing HHABNs for future triggering events that occur under the care of the "new" HHA. HHAs are always only responsible for providing HHABNs associated with the care that they themselves provide.

Further, if a vendor other than an HHA provides services to a beneficiary receiving home care, it is the vendor that is responsible for providing liability notification to the beneficiary, when required, for the care that vendor furnishes and bills. An example is when a supplier of DME directly supplies equipment to a beneficiary.

60.6.1 - Defective HHABNs
(Rev. 1025, Issued: 08-11-06; Effective/Implementation Dates: 09-01-06)

The following are examples of defective notice that may result in beneficiaries being protected from liability under §1879 of the Act. In such cases, HHAs cannot collect the cost of noncovered item(s) and/or service(s) from beneficiaries.

Failure to Use the Standard Notice. *HHAs are strongly encouraged to use the OMB-approved HHABN notice format, consistent with these instructions. HHAs should not alter the standard notice in any way not expressly permitted in these instructions. Failure to use the approved HHABN greatly increases the possibility of an invalid notification.*

Unintelligible Notice. *Notice will be considered defective if the HHABN is unreadable, illegible, incomprehensible, or it can be demonstrated that the beneficiary did not understand the notice due to particular circumstances that were within the HHA's control, i.e., failure to use plain language.*

Unable to Give Consent. Notice may be ruled defective if given when the beneficiary cannot give informed consent, such as during a medical emergency or health crisis, especially if the notice could have been delivered by the HHA at another point in time.

Coercion. Notice may be found defective if the HHA is judged to have forced the beneficiary to complete the HHABN in a certain way, such as by forcing the selection of a given checkbox option in Option Box 1, or if the HHA intentionally misled the beneficiary during completion of the notice.

Routine Notice. Notice may be found defective if the HHA routinely gives the HHABN for all items(s) and/or service(s) the HHA provides, disregarding whether or not the HHABN is required.

Last Minute or Untimely Notice. Last minute notification does not allow the beneficiary time to make an informed decision regarding his/her healthcare options. HHABNs given at the last minute may be found defective. HHABNs are also ineffective if given too far in advance of item(s) and/or service(s) at issue, or after the delivery of such care.

Notice Given More than 1 Year Prior. HHABNs are considered effective for no more than 1 year. HHABNs given for services for a period of over a year will be found defective for the period of time exceeding 1 year.

Generic HHABNs. Generic HHABNs that do not provide sufficient specificity in order for the beneficiary to make an informed decision regarding his/her healthcare are considered defective. For example, HHABNs that do no more than state that Medicare denial of payment is possible, that the HHA never knows whether Medicare will deny payment, or that the HHA never knows the policy of other applicable insurers will be deemed too generic in order to properly notify the beneficiary.

Blanket HHABNs. Blanket HHABNs are given to beneficiaries for all or too broad of a range of item(s) and/or service(s). Therefore, these notices are defective because they do not provide sufficient information for the beneficiary to make an informed decision regarding his/her healthcare options.

Signed Blank HHABNs. An HHA is prohibited from obtaining beneficiary signatures on blank HHABNs, i.e., HHABNs that contain no information regarding item(s) and/or service(s) and the reasons for issuing the notice. A beneficiary's signature must not be obtained until after the HHABN is delivered.

Advance Completion of Information Completed by the Beneficiary. An HHABN may be deemed invalid if an HHA checks off boxes in Option Box 1 before delivering the HHABN to the beneficiary.

Failure to Include Valid Information. An HHABN may be deemed invalid because the HHA fails to include key information in the HHABN. The inclusion of erroneous information will also be treated in the same manner. As examples, the failure to list *significant item(s) and/or service(s) or the failure to provide an estimate of the total actual cost of each item or service may result in the HHABN being deemed defective.*

> ***NOTE:*** *With regard to the estimated cost, an amount that is different from the final actual cost does not invalidate the HHABN, as long as the amounts on the notice represent a good faith attempt to estimate costs for all the item(s) and/or service(s) for which the beneficiary may be liable.*

Failure to Ensure Comprehension of the HHABN. *An HHABN may be deemed defective if the HHA does not make best efforts and take appropriate steps to ensure that the beneficiary understands the information contained in the HHABN. It is not acceptable to hand the beneficiary the notice and have him/her sign it with no oral review of the notice. Failing to select a checkbox in Option Box 1 language, or selecting multiple checkboxes when a choice of one is indicated on the HHABN, will be seen as a lack of comprehension deeming the HHABN defective.*

A. Special Exceptions to Defective Notice

Services Which Are Always Denied for Medical Necessity. *In any case where a national Medicare coverage determination provides that a particular item or service is neither covered nor reasonable and necessary, an HHABN that gives as the reason for expecting denial that: "Medicare never pays for this item/service under written national policy" may be routinely given to beneficiaries, and no claim need be submitted to Medicare unless the beneficiary requests that a claim be submitted. This exception also applies codified local Medicare coverage policy.*

Experimental Items and Services. *Any item or service which Medicare considers to be experimental (e.g., "Research Use Only" and "Investigational Use Only" laboratory tests) is denied as not reasonable and necessary under §1862(a)(1) of the Act because Medicare has judged that it has not been proven to be safe and effective. The beneficiary may be given an HHABN that specifies as the reason for expecting denial as: "Medicare does not pay for services which it considers to be experimental/for research use." Alternatively, more specific language with respect to Medicare coverage for clinical trials may be substituted as necessary as the reason for expecting that Medicare will deny the claim.*

Frequency Limited Items and Services. *Some items or services furnished have established statutory or regulatory frequency limitations on Medicare coverage, or frequency limitations on coverage on the basis of a national coverage decision or on the basis of the contractor's local medical review policy. Since all or virtually all beneficiaries may be at risk of having their claims denied in those circumstances, the HHA may routinely give HHABNs to beneficiaries in such cases. In issuing the HHABN, the HHA must state the frequency limitation as the HHABN's reason for expecting denial (e.g., "Medicare does not usually pay for a flu shot more than once a year").*

Repetitive or Extended Notices. *A single HHABN covering an extended course of treatment is acceptable provided that the HHABN identifies every item and/or service for which the HHA believes Medicare will not pay. Item(s) and/or service(s) that are provided on a regularly scheduled basis may be considered an extended course of treatment; and a single HHABN may suffice as long as all other applicable notification requirements are fulfilled. If, however, as the extended course of treatment progresses, and additional items or services are to be furnished, which Medicare or other applicable insurers will not cover, the HHA must separately notify the beneficiary by issuing another HHABN.*

60.7 - Collection of Funds and Liability Related to the HHABN
(Rev. 1025, Issued: 08-11-06; Effective/Implementation Dates: 09-01-06)

A. Collection of Funds and Beneficiary Liability

A beneficiary's agreement to be responsible for payment on an HHABN means that the beneficiary agrees to pay for expenses out-of-pocket or through any other insurance other than Medicare that the beneficiary may have. The HHA may bill and collect funds from the beneficiary for noncovered item(s) and/or service(s) at the time of delivery of such HHABNs, unless prohibited from collecting in advance of the Medicare payment determination by other applicable Medicare policy, State or local law. Note there is no general Medicare policy affecting timing of such collection by HHAs.

When delivery of an HHABN is effective and Medicare ultimately denies payment of the related claim, the HHA retains the funds collected from the beneficiary. However, if Medicare subsequently pays all or part of the claim for item(s) and/or service(s) previously paid for by the beneficiary to the HHA, the HHA must refund the beneficiary the proper amount. Medicare regulations require prompt payment of refunds to beneficiaries when Medicare provides payment.

When the beneficiary has insurance other than Medicare, and payment is subsequently received from that source, the HHA similarly should refund any previously collected amounts to the beneficiary consistent with the other insurer's payment. Note, however, that Medicare laws or regulations concerning the handling of incorrect collections do not provide for Medicare to ensure that prompt refunds occur when payment is made by another insurer or payer, referred to on the HHABN as "my other insurance." This is true even for the home health benefit and despite the incorporation of the home health COPs in HHABN requirements. Medicare would not have a claim to those monies or be able to act on behalf of the beneficiary in these cases, and Medicare may be unaware of such incorrect collections.

B. Financial Liability for Providers

HHAs may be held financially liable for the cost of item(s) and/or service(s) in situations where the HHA fails to issue an HHABN when required or issues a defective HHABN, since the beneficiary may be afforded liability protection under §1879 (see 60.2 H).

When a beneficiary does have liability protection and proper notification has not occurred, HHAs are precluded from collecting funds from the beneficiary, and will be required to make prompt refunds to the beneficiary (if funds were previously collected), or face possible sanctions for failure to do so. HHAs will be held financially liable if unable to demonstrate that they did not know or could not reasonably have been expected to know either that Medicare would not make payment, or that the care in question was noncovered and liability protection applied.

C. Unbundling Prohibition and Shifting of Financial Liability

*In issuing HHABNs, HHAs may not use these notices to shift financial liability to a beneficiary when full payment is made through bundled payments (see 60.2 G.); that is, where the beneficiary would otherwise not be financially liable for payment for the service because Medicare made full payment for a bundled group of items and/or services. **Using HHABNs to collect from beneficiaries where full payment is made on a bundled basis would constitute double billing.** An HHABN may be used, however, for any part of the cost of care that is specifically excluded from the Medicare bundled payment.*

D. Effect of Initial Payment Determinations on Liability

An HHABN informs a beneficiary of his/her HHA's expectation with regard to Medicare coverage. If the care described on the HHABN is provided, Medicare makes an actual payment determination on the item(s) and/or service(s) at issue when adjudicating the related claim. Such adjudications may uphold the provider's expectation, in which case the beneficiary will remain liable for payment if agreeing to accept this liability based on a valid HHABN. However, adjudication may not conform to the provider's expectation, in which case the decision made on the claim supersedes the expectation given on the HHABN. That is, Medicare may cover and pay for care despite the HHA's expectation, or deny the claims and find the provider liable. In such cases, if the HHA collected funds from the beneficiary, the HHA must refund promptly the beneficiary for the appropriate amount.

60.8 - Revision, Re-issuance and Retention of HHABN
(Rev. 1025, Issued: 08-11-06; Effective/Implementation Dates: 09-01-06)

A. Requirements for Retention after Completion

The HHA keeps the original version of the completed HHABN, whether annotated or signed, in the beneficiary's record. The primary HHA must retain the HHABN if a subcontractor is used. The beneficiary receives a copy of the completed HHABN.

An HHABN, once signed by the beneficiary, may not be modified or revised. Annotations are only made as permitted under these instructions. When a beneficiary must be notified of new information beyond the scope of the original notice with or without annotations, a new HHABN must be given.

Applicable retention periods are discussed in Chapter 1 of this manual, §110. In general, this is 5 years from discharge when there are no other applicable requirements under State law. Retention is required even if the beneficiary refused to choose an option or sign the notice, and even when no care was ultimately provided to the beneficiary.

B. Beneficiary and Related Party Requests for Copy of the HHABN

HHAs are required to provide a copy of an HHABN not only to a beneficiary but also to the beneficiary's subrogees if a copy is requested during the applicable claim timely filing period. Timely filing periods are described in this manual, Chapter 1, §70. The most common example of a subrogee is a State acting on behalf of a beneficiary with dual Medicare and Medicaid eligibility.

C. Request for Copies by RHHIs/Approved Governmental Agents

HHAs are not required to routinely submit copies of HHABNs to their Medicare RHHIs. However, copies must be supplied upon the request of an RHHI, QIO or other approved CMS administrative agent, or directly to CMS Central or Regional Offices when specified. Such requests may be made in relation to medical review of a claim, statute requirement, court case or Federal oversight agency request (i.e., Office of Inspector General). Medicare or its agents may also request HHAs to report on their HHABNs separate from providing copies (such as counting the number of HHABNs provided in a year by type of checkbox or Option Box language, in order for Medicare to meet applicable reporting requirements under statute).

90 - Form CMS-20007 - Notices of Exclusions From Medicare Benefits (NEMBs)

(Rev. 1025, Issued: 08-11-06; Effective/Implementation Dates: 09-01-06)

> NOTE: *HHAs do not use the NEMB.*

For all expected denials of Medicare payments for items and services for which an ABN is not used because neither LOL nor RR applies, the Notice Of Exclusions From Medicare Benefits (NEMB) Form CMS-20007 may be used to advise beneficiaries, before items or services that are not Medicare benefits are furnished, that Medicare will not pay for them. NEMBs allow beneficiaries to make informed consumer decisions about receiving items or services for which they must pay out-of-pocket and to be more active participants in their own health care treatment decisions. The NEMB may be used, on an entirely voluntary basis, by physicians, practitioners, suppliers and providers to advise their Medicare patients of the services that Medicare never covers, for which it is not appropriate to use ABNs. The NEMB Form CMS-20007 is available online in English and Spanish at the CMS Beneficiary Notices Initiative (BNI) Web page at:

http://www.cms.hhs.gov/*BNI*/

Physicians, practitioners, suppliers and providers may use notices of their own design rather than the NEMB form. Some professional associations, with the assistance and approval of CMS, have developed service-specific NEMB type notices to advise Medicare beneficiaries of the limits of Medicare coverage for certain items and services. Those service-specific notices, which are not government notices but proprietary notices of the authoring associations, are also available in PDF format at the BNI and ABN links given above.

90.1.1 - Using NEMBs With Categorical Denials

(Rev. 1025, Issued: 08-11-06; Effective/Implementation Dates: 09-01-06)

> NOTE: *HHAs do not use the NEMB.*

Physicians, practitioners, suppliers and providers prepare and deliver to *Medicare beneficiaries, or people acting on their behalves, NEMBs* when it is known that Medicare will not pay for, or will not continue to pay for, items or services on the basis of any categorical statutory exclusion listed in the third box on *this notice. In these cases, notification is voluntary.*

In these cases, insert a mark in check-off box number 2. an NEMB IS NOT used for either of the following two categorical exclusions that trigger statutory protections:

- The service may be denied as "not reasonable and necessary" ("medical necessity") - §1862(a)(1) of the Act; or

- The service may be denied as "custodial care" - §1862(a)(9) of the Act.

90.1.2 - Using NEMBs With Technical Denials
(Rev. 1025, Issued: 08-11-06; Effective/Implementation Dates: 09-01-06)

> NOTE: *HHAs do not use the NEMB.*

Physicians, practitioners, suppliers and providers may prepare and deliver to *Medicare beneficiaries, or people acting on their behalves, NEMBs* when it is known that Medicare will not pay for, or will not continue to pay for, items or services on the basis of any technical statutory exclusion. *That is, NEMBs may be given for any failure to meet completely the statutory definition of a Medicare benefit. In these cases, notification is voluntary.*

In these cases, insert a mark in check-off box number 1 in the second box on the form. A*n* NEMB **IS NOT** used for any of the following *four* technical exclusions that trigger statutory protections:

- The patient in hospice is found not to be terminally ill – §1861(dd)(3)(A) of the Act;

- The patient received a prohibited telephone solicitation ("cold call") in the case of medical equipment & supplies - §1834(a)(17)FIRST(B) of the Act;

- The supplier does not have a supplier number, in the case of medical equipment & supplies denials - §1834(j)(1) of the Act; or

- The supplier has not obtained a required advance coverage determination in the case of medical equipment & supplies denials – §1834(a)(15) of the Act.

CHAPTER 5

HOSPICE COVERAGE

§5.01 INTRODUCTION

The Medicare Hospice benefit[1] is different from all other Medicare benefits in that it does not provide for the curative treatment of illness or injury;[2] rather it is designed for the palliation and management of terminal illness.[3] One can receive hospice benefits under Medicare only after specifically opting into the hospice benefit and thereby opting out of Medicare coverage for services related to the terminal illness. Electing hospice care, however, does *not* mean that all curative treatment is waived. Beneficiaries who elect the Medicare hospice benefit may still receive Medicare coverage for medically reasonable and necessary treatment for diagnoses unrelated to their terminal illness.[4]

Medicare Advantage plans may provide, but are not required to provide, hospice services to Medicare beneficiaries.[5] Those Medicare beneficiaries enrolled in a Medicare Advantage plan must, like other Medicare beneficiaries, opt into the hospice benefit.[6] If the Medicare Advantage plan offers hospice coverage, then the hospice care will be provided through the Medicare Advantage plan. If the Medicare Advantage plan does not offer hospice coverage, then the beneficiary may elect hospice care, which will be covered under traditional Medicare. If the beneficiary elects hospice coverage through traditional Medicare, his or her enrollment in the Medicare Advantage plan will continue with respect to all services not provided by the hospice agency.[7] In other words, the beneficiary still will continue to be eligible for all benefits that are offered by the Medicare Advantage plan for services unrelated to the terminal illness.

Medicare hospice care must be provided by a Medicare-certified hospice program. The hospice must meet various conditions of participation in order to become Medicare-certified. Hospice care can be provided by both freestanding hospices and hospice home care programs. Both can provide services in a beneficiary's home; however, a freestanding hospice provides inpatient care directly, whereas a home-based hospice program provides inpatient services by arrangement with other institutions. These "other institutions" must meet specific standards regarding 24-hour nursing services[8] and patient areas.[9] The services required to be provided to a Medicare hospice beneficiary, however, are the same for both freestanding hospices and home-based hospice programs.[10]

---

[1] 42 U.S.C. §1395x(dd).

[2] 42 U.S.C. §1395y(a)(1)(A).

[3] 42 U.S.C. §1395y(a)(1)(C).

[4] 42 C.F.R. §418.24.

[5] 42 C.F.R. §§422.101, 422.266.

[6] *Id.*

[7] 42 C.F.R. §§422.266(b), 418.24.

[8] 42 C.F.R. §418.100(a).

[9] 42 C.F.R. §418.100(e).

[10] *See* §5.09.

§5.02   ELIGIBILITY

The Medicare hospice benefit is provided under Part A of the Medicare program. Therefore, in order to be eligible for Medicare hospice, one must be enrolled in Medicare Part A. In addition, prior to receiving Medicare hospice care, the beneficiary must be certified by the hospice physician and the individual's attending physician as terminally ill.[11] The certification is based on the physician's clinical judgment regarding the normal course of the individual's illness. The certification must specify that the individual's prognosis is for a life expectancy of six months or less if the terminal illness runs its normal course.[12] Clinical information and other documentation that support the medical prognosis must be filed in the medical record with the written certification.[13] Initially the clinical information may be provided verbally, and must be filed in the hospice medical record and included as part of the hospice's eligibility assessment.[14] The certification is filed with the hospice.[15]

§5.03   ELECTION OF THE HOSPICE BENEFIT

An election to receive hospice care is made by filing an election statement with a hospice of choice.[16] An election statement may be filed by either the beneficiary or his or her legal representative.[17] Once a beneficiary has elected to receive the hospice benefit, he or she waives all rights to Medicare payment for services that are *related to the treatment of the terminal condition or a related condition* except for services provided by the designated hospice or by another provider under arrangements made by the designated hospice, or by the individual's attending physician.[18] The advocate should emphasize this point to the

---

[11] 42 C.F.R. §418.24(c). Sources of certification. (1) For the initial 90-day period, the hospice must obtain written certification statements . . . from (i) The medical director of the hospice or the physician member of the hospice interdisciplinary group; and (ii) The individual's attending physician if the individual has an attending physician. (2) For subsequent periods, the only requirement is certification by one of the physicians listed in paragraph(c)(1)(i) of this section.

[12] 42 C.F.R. §418.22(b)(1). *Also see* **Appendix 5-1, HCFA Program Memorandum, Transmittal AB-01-99 (Jan. 24, 2001),** which emphasizes that the certification is based on clinical judgment regarding the normal course of illness and that making medical prognostication of life expectancy is not always exact.

[13] 42 C.F.R. §418.22(b)(2).

[14] *Id.*

[15] 42 C.F.R. §418.22.

[16] 42 C.F.R. §418.24.

[17] *Id.*

[18] This is only the case if the attending physician is not an employee of the designated hospice or receiving compensation from the hospice for the provided services. 42 C.F.R. §418.24(d)(2)(iii). Furthermore, the Medicare Hospice Manual limits such services to the personal professional services of the attending physician. In other words, the costs for services such as labs or X-rays must be

beneficiary, as the beneficiary may not fully understand the ramifications of a hospice election.

The election statement itself must:

- Identify the hospice that will provide the beneficiary's care;

- Contain an acknowledgment by the individual that he or she has been given a full understanding of the palliative rather than the curative nature of hospice care as it relates to the individual's terminal illness;

- Contain an acknowledgment that the beneficiary, in electing hospice care, understands that he or she is waiving certain other Medicare services;

- State the effective date of the election, which in no event can be prior to the date of the election statement;[19] and

- Be signed by the beneficiary or his or her legal representative.[20]

An individual may elect to receive hospice care during one or more of the following election periods: an initial 90-day period; a subsequent 90-day period; or an unlimited number of subsequent periods.[21] At the start of each new benefit period, the attending physician and/or hospice physician[22] must make a written certification that the beneficiary is terminally ill.[23]

An election to receive hospice care will be considered to continue through the initial election period and through the subsequent election periods without a break in care, as long as the individual remains in the care of the hospice; does not revoke the election; and is not discharged from the hospice.[24] At the start of each new benefit period, the attending physician and/or hospice physician[25] must make a written certification that the beneficiary is terminally ill.[26]

---

provided under arrangements with the hospice and will not be reimbursed by Medicare if independently ordered by the attending physician. Medicare Claims Processing Manual, Pub. 100-4, Ch. 11, §40.1.3.

[19] 42 C.F.R. §418.24.

[20] *Id.*

[21] 42 C.F.R. §418.21.

[22] 42 C.F.R. §418.22(c). *"Sources of Certification."* (1) For the initial 90-day period, the hospice must obtain written certification statements . . . from (i) The medical director of the hospice or the physician member of the hospice interdisciplinary group; and (ii) The individual's attending physician if the individual has an attending physician. (2) For subsequent periods, the only requirement is certification by one of the physicians listed in paragraph (c)(1)(i) of this section.

[23] *See* note 12.

[24] *See* note 11.

[25] 42 C.F.R. §418.22(c)(2).

[26] *Id.*

§5.04   WHO MAY MAKE AN ELECTION FOR HOSPICE CARE

[A] Generally

Medicare beneficiaries may elect hospice care for palliative treatment of a terminal illness.[27] Problems may arise when persons lack the mental capacity to make an election.

[B] Incapacitated Persons

Ideally, an election of the hospice benefit will be made by the patient. However, sometimes a patient may be so incapacitated that he or she is unable to make the election.

A threshold issue, therefore, is how an election may be made for an incapacitated patient. Medicare regulations provide that an election may be filed by either the beneficiary or the beneficiary's representative. For this purpose, a representative means a person who is, because of the beneficiary's mental or physical incapacity, authorized in accordance with state law to execute or revoke an election for hospice care or terminate medical care on behalf of the terminally ill individual.[28]

Virtually all states have guardianship or conservatorship statutes. These generally allow a court to adjudicate a person incompetent and to appoint some other person to make decisions on the incompetent person's behalf. If a hospice election is desired and a guardian or conservator has been appointed, then the guardian or conservator might be authorized to make the election. The advocate should be certain to ascertain from the court's order what powers have been granted to the guardian or conservator by the court.

Not all guardians or conservators are empowered to make medical decisions on behalf of the incapacitated person. If the court order does not grant decision-making authority for medical treatment decisions, it may be necessary to petition the court for an additional grant of this power. If no guardian or conservator at all has been appointed and the patient is incapacitated, consideration may have to be given to having a guardian or conservator appointed. Since the applicable laws vary from state to state, the advocate should become familiar with the legal bases and procedural requirements for appointment of guardians or conservators in his or her state, as well as the powers that can be granted to a guardian or conservator.[29] Some states have adopted durable power of attorney statutes.

---

[27] 42 C.F.R. §418.24.

[28] 42 C.F.R. §418.3.

[29] For further discussion of these and related issues, *see* F. Rozovsky, Consent to Treatment: A Practical Guide (Aspen Publishers, 2d ed. 1997); *Medical Treatment for the Elderly and Disabled*, 23 Clearinghouse Rev. 1154 (1990). *See also* Alfred J. Chiplin, Jr., Vicki Gottlich, Naomi Karp, and Erica Wood, *Choice, Quality, Appeals Rights, and Surrogate Decision Making: A Medicare+Choice Primer*, 32 Clearinghouse Rev. 327, 334-36 (Nov.-Dec. 1998) (discussing incapacity and enrollment issues).

Finally, in some states, laws exist that permit next of kin to consent to medical treatment when the patient becomes incompetent. These laws, known as family consent statutes, also vary from state to state, and the advocate should explore whether such laws exist in his or her state and what the precise provisions of those laws are.[30]

§5.05 HOSPICE ADMISSION

The hospice admits a patient only on the recommendation of the hospice medical director in consultation with, or input from, the patient's attending physician.[31] In reaching a decision to certify that the patient is terminally ill, the hospice medical director must consider at least the following information: diagnosis of the terminal condition of the patient; other health conditions, whether related or unrelated to the terminal condition; and current clinically relevant information supporting all diagnoses.[32]

§5.06 HOSPICE REVOCATION

An individual or legal representative may revoke the election of hospice care at any time during the period in question.[33] To revoke the election of hospice care, the individual or legal representative must file a statement with the hospice that includes the following information:

- The signature of the beneficiary or legal representative; and

- The date of revocation (which cannot be earlier than the date upon which the revocation is made).[34]

Upon revocation, the beneficiary is no longer covered under Medicare for hospice care;[35] resumes Medicare coverage for benefits previously waived;[36] and may at any time elect to receive hospice coverage for any other hospice election periods that he or she is eligible to receive.[37]

As a practical matter, each hospice will have designed and printed its own election and revocation statements for the use of the beneficiary. The patient or advocate should contact the hospice for such forms.

---

[30] *See* F. Rozovsky, Consent to Treatment: A Practical Guide, §10.9 (Aspen Publishers, 2d ed. 1997).

[31] 42 C.F.R. §418.25(a).

[32] 42 C.F.R. §418.25(b).

[33] 42 C.F.R. §418.28.

[34] 42 C.F.R. §418.28(b)(2).

[35] 42 C.F.R. §418.28(c)(1).

[36] 42 C.F.R. §418.28(c)(2).

[37] 42 C.F.R. §418.28(c)(3).

§5.07   HOSPICE DISCHARGE

As hospice may discharge a patient if: the patient moves out of the hospice's service area or transfers to another hospice; the hospice determines that the patient is no longer terminally ill; or the hospice determines that the patient's or other person's in the patient's home behavior is disruptive, abusive, or uncooperative to the extent that delivery of care to the patient or the ability of the hospice to operate effectively is seriously impaired.[38]

The hospice must do the following before it seeks to discharge a patient for cause:

- Advise the patient that a discharge for cause is being considered;

- Make a serious effort to resolve the problem(s) presented by the patient's behavior or situation;

- Ascertain that the patient's proposed discharge is not due to the patient's use of necessary hospice services; and

- Document the problem(s) and efforts made to resolve the problem(s) and enter this documentation into its medical record.[39]

Prior to discharging a patient, the hospice must obtain a written physician's discharge order from the hospice medical director.[40] If a patient has an attending physician involved in his or her care, this physician should be consulted before discharge and his or her review and decision included in the discharge note.[41]

An individual, upon discharge from the hospice during a particular election period for reasons other than immediate transfer to another hospice: is no longer covered under Medicare for hospice care; resumes previously waived Medicare coverage;[42] and may at any time elect to receive hospice care if he or she is again eligible to receive the benefit.[43]

---

[38] 42 C.F.R. §418.26(a).

[39] *Id. Also see* Medicare Benefit Policy Manual, Pub. 100-2, Ch. 9, §20.2.1, "There may be extraordinary circumstances in which a hospice would be unable to continue to provide hospice care to a patient. These situations include issues where patient safety or hospice staff safety is compromised. The hospice must make every effort to resolve these problems satisfactorily before it considers discharge an option. All efforts by the hospice to resolve the problem(s) must be documented in detail in the patient's clinical record and the hospice must notify the fiscal intermediary and State Survey Agency of the circumstances surrounding the impending discharge. The hospice may also need to make referrals to other relevant state/community agencies (i.e., Adult Protective Services) as appropriate."

[40] 42 C.F.R. §418.26(b).

[41] *Id.*

[42] *See* §5.01.

[43] 42 C.F.R. §418.26(c).

Hospice programs must have in place a discharge planning process that takes into account the prospect that a patient's condition might stabilize or otherwise change such that the patient cannot continue to be certified as terminally ill.[44] The discharge planning process must include planning for any necessary family counseling, patient education, or other services before the patient is discharged because he or she is no longer terminally ill.[45]

Prior to a patient's discharge, the hospice must issue a standardized termination notice.[46] This notice must indicate that Medicare coverage for hospice care is ending, the date coverage ends, the beneficiary's financial liability for continued service, and how to appeal the discharge.[47] This generic notice is the first step in the expedited appeals process which guarantees Medicare beneficiaries review of their cases within 72 hours of request.[48]

§5.08   CHANGING THE HOSPICE THAT IS PROVIDING CARE

A beneficiary may change, once each election period, the designation of the particular hospice from which the care will be received. The change of the designated hospice is not a revocation of the election of hospice benefits. In order to change the designated hospice, the beneficiary or representative must file, with both the hospice from which the beneficiary has been receiving care and the new hospice from which the beneficiary will be receiving care, a signed statement indicating the name of each hospice and the effective date of the change.[49]

Note that such a change may be made only once during each election period. If an additional change were desired, the beneficiary would have to completely revoke the hospice coverage and then reelect hospice coverage using a new election period.

§5.09   SERVICES PROVIDED UNDER THE HOSPICE BENEFIT

The Medicare hospice benefit covers the following services:

- Nursing services provided by or under the supervision of a registered nurse;

- Medical social services provided by a social worker under the direction of a physician;

---

[44] 42 C.F.R. §418.26(d)(1).

[45] 42 C.F.R. §418.26(d)(2).

[46] 42 C.F.R. §405.1200.

[47] *Id.*

[48] 70 Fed. Reg. 11,419 (Mar. 8, 2005), 42 C.F.R. §405.1202. *See also*, **§§1.07 [A][1] and 5.11[G].**

[49] 42 C.F.R. §418.30.

- Physician's services;

- Counseling services provided to the terminally ill individual and the family members or other persons caring for the individual at home;

- Short-term inpatient care provided in a participating hospice inpatient unit or in a participating hospital or skilled nursing facility;

- Medical appliances and supplies, including drugs and biologicals;

- Home health aide services;

- Homemaker services;

- Physical therapy, occupational therapy, and speech-language pathology services provided for purposes of symptom control or to enable the patient to maintain activities of daily living and basic functional skills.[50]

- Any other service that is specified in the patient's plan of care as reasonable and necessary for the palliation and management of the patient's terminal illness and related conditions and for which payment may otherwise be made under Medicare.[51]

Any services that are to be provided to a Medicare hospice patient must be included in a written plan of care established by the hospice interdisciplinary group.[52] The plan must include an assessment of the patient's needs and must identify the services (including the management of discomfort and symptom relief) to be provided, and must state in detail the scope and frequency of services needed to meet the patient's and caregiver's needs.[53] The plan must also specify the drugs and biologicals that will be administered to the patient and designate the persons authorized to administer each.[54] The written plan of care must be reviewed and updated at intervals specified in the plan itself, and the hospice must document these reviews and updates.[55]

In the regulations, nursing services, medical social services, physician services, and counseling services are referred to as core services.[56] Generally, these

---

[50] 42 C.F.R. §418.202.

[51] 42 C.F.R. §418.202. Effective April 1, 1998.

[52] 42 C.F.R. §418.58. *See* also 42 C.F.R. §418.68. Each hospice must establish an interdisciplinary group composed of individuals who provide or supervise the care and services offered by the hospice. The interdisciplinary group must include at least a physician, a registered nurse, a social worker, and a pastor or other counselor. The group is responsible, in addition to establishing the written care plan, for provision or supervision of the hospice care and services and for periodic review and updating of the plan of care for each individual receiving hospice care, as well as establishing policies governing the day-to-day provision of hospice care and services.

[53] 42 C.F.R. §418.58.

[54] 42 C.F.R. §418.96.

[55] 42 C.F.R. §418.58(b).

[56] 42 C.F.R. §418.80.

must be provided directly by hospice employees, as opposed to being provided by independent practitioners or other facilities under arrangements with the hospice. A waiver of this requirement for nursing services may be granted to hospices located in non-urban areas.[57] Noncore services may be provided either directly by hospice employees or by other personnel under arrangements made by the hospice.[58]

[A] Nursing Care

Nursing care, to be covered under the hospice benefit, must be provided by, or under the supervision of, a registered nurse.[59] The nurses' services must be directed to ensure that the nursing needs of the patient are met and must be provided in accordance with recognized standards of practice.[60]

Nursing care may be provided on a continuous basis for as much as 24 hours a day *during periods of crisis* as necessary to maintain an individual at home. A period of crisis is one in which the patient requires continuous care to achieve palliation or management of acute medical symptoms.[61]

[B] Bereavement Counseling

Though not reimbursed by Medicare, bereavement counseling is a required hospice service.[62] Each Medicare-certified hospice provider must have an organized program for the provision of bereavement services under the supervision of a qualified professional. The plan of care for these services should reflect family needs as well as a clear delineation of services to be provided and the frequency of service delivery (up to one year following the death of the patient).[63]

[C] Short-Term General Inpatient Care

Short-term general inpatient care must be made available by the hospice for pain control and symptom management. These services may be provided only in a Medicare- or Medicaid-certified hospice, hospital, or skilled nursing facility[64] meeting certain staffing requirements and physical plant standards.[65] While

---

[57] 42 C.F.R. §418.83.

[58] 42 C.F.R. §418.90.

[59] 42 C.F.R. §418.202.

[60] 42 C.F.R. §418.82.

[61] 42 C.F.R. §418.204(a).

[62] 42 C.F.R. §418.204(c).

[63] 42 C.F.R. §418.88(a).

[64] 42 C.F.R. §418.98(a).

[65] *Id.*

there is no limit on the number of days for which an individual hospice patient may receive general inpatient care, hospices themselves are limited in the number of general inpatient days per year they may provide to all Medicare hospice beneficiaries. This limitation applies to both freestanding and community-based hospice programs.[66] The practical effect of this limitation on the hospice is that a hospice may be inclined to limit the number of inpatient days an individual receives in order to comply with the overall limit placed on it. When an individual is at a general inpatient level of care, the hospice benefit pays for both the beneficiary's hospice care, and the beneficiary's room and board.

As an aside, the Medicare Benefit Policy Manual states that general inpatient care is covered under the Medicare hospice benefit in the event that skilled nursing care is needed by the patient because his or her home support has "broken down."[67] The manual also lists the following as examples of circumstances in which general inpatient care is appropriate: medication adjustment; observation; other stabilizing treatment, such as psychosocial monitoring; or a patient whose family is unwilling to permit needed care to be furnished in the home.[68]

As there is no copayment or limit on available general inpatient days per patient, when appropriate, it may behoove the hospice beneficiary to receive his or her inpatient care under the general inpatient level of care rather than the respite level of care (respite care is discussed in the next section). However, it should be noted that hospice inpatient care in a skilled nursing facility serves to prolong current benefit periods for general Medicare hospital and skilled nursing facility (SNF) benefits.[69] On the other hand, if a hospice patient receives general inpatient care for three or more days, and then revokes the hospice benefit, then the three-day stay in the inpatient facility (although not necessarily the same as a hospital level of care in terms of kind of care provided) would qualify the beneficiary for covered skilled nursing facility services.[70] In other words, the three-day general inpatient hospice stay is considered, for purposes of obtaining Medicare coverage of skilled nursing facility care, to be the equivalent of a three-day qualifying hospital stay.

---

[66] 42 C.F.R. §418.98(c).

[67] "General inpatient care may be required for procedures necessary for pain control or acute or chronic symptom management that cannot feasibly be provided in other settings. Skilled nursing care may be needed by a patient whose home support has broken down if this breakdown makes it no longer feasible to furnish care in the home setting." Medicare Benefit Policy Manual, Pub. 100-2, Ch. 9, §40.1.5.

[68] *Id.*

[69] *Id.* This is significant in the event the beneficiary should decide to revoke the hospice benefit. It means that each day spent at a general inpatient level of care would be categorized at a skilled level of care for purposes of calculating benefit periods. Medicare coverage is only available for 100 days of skilled nursing facility care within a benefit period. A benefit period does not end until there is a 60-day break from inpatient skilled care. See **§3.03[F]**.

[70] Medicare Benefit Policy Manual, Pub. 100-2, Ch. 9, §40.1.5.

[D] Inpatient Care for Respite Purposes

Inpatient care for respite purposes is provided to the hospice patient when necessary to relieve the beneficiary's caregiver(s).[71] Respite care may be provided only on an occasional basis and is limited to no more than five consecutive days at a time.[72] The respite care must be provided in a Medicare or Medicaid certified freestanding hospice, hospital, skilled nursing facility, or intermediate care facility.[73] While the beneficiary is at a respite level of care, the hospice benefit pays for both the beneficiary's medical care and the beneficiary's room and board. There is a coinsurance amount that the hospice agency may require the patient to pay if respite services are received. The daily coinsurance amount for respite care can be no more than five percent of the payment made by the Centers for Medicare and Medicaid Services (CMS) for a respite day. The actual amount will vary from hospice to hospice. However, in no event may the total amount of the coinsurance exceed the inpatient hospital deductible in effect in the year in which the hospice benefit was elected. In 2007, this amount is $992. The coinsurance is payable for each coinsurance period. A coinsurance period begins on the first day an election is effective and ends with the close of the first period of 14 consecutive days on each of which an election is not in effect for the beneficiary.[74] So for example, if the patient elected 210 consecutive days of hospice coverage, the patient would be required to pay the respite coinsurance up to the maximum only once.

[E] Residents of Skilled Nursing Facilities and Nursing Facilities

Some skilled nursing facilities (SNFs) or nursing facilities (NF) have written agreements with Medicare hospice programs under which their residents may receive hospice care within the facilities. Under these agreements, the hospice takes full responsibility for the professional management of the individual's hospice care, and the facility remains responsible for the provision of room and board.[75] Where there is a source to pay for the residential care (usually private pay, long-term nursing facility insurance, or Medicaid) and where there is a contract between the facility and a Medicare certified hospice, the Medicare beneficiary who resides in such a facility may elect the hospice benefit.[76] In other words, when a beneficiary is at a routine level of care and is receiving

---

[71] 42 C.F.R. §418.204(b)(1).

[72] 42 C.F.R. §418.204(b)(2).

[73] 42 C.F.R. §418.98.

[74] 42 C.F.R. §418.400(b).

[75] Room and board services include the performance of personal care services, assistance of daily living, socializing activities, administration of medication, maintaining the cleanliness of a resident's room, and supervising and assisting in the use of durable medical equipment and prescribed therapies. Medicare Benefit Policy Manual, Pub. 100-2, Ch. 9, §20.3.

[76] *Id.*

hospice care while residing in a nursing home, the hospice benefit will pay for the beneficiary's hospice care, but not for the beneficiary's room and board.

Alternatively, it is possible for an individual to receive both Medicare-covered skilled nursing facility care and Medicare-covered hospice care.[77] For this to occur, the Medicare skilled nursing facility care must be for a condition unrelated to the terminal condition. For instance, if a Medicare beneficiary who has elected hospice falls and breaks a hip, has a three-day qualifying hospital stay,[78] and then is transferred to a skilled nursing facility, so long as the broken hip is not related to the beneficiary's underlying terminal illness, then the beneficiary may continue to receive Medicare-covered hospice care for the terminal illness, while also receiving Medicare-covered skilled nursing facility care for the broken hip. This is significant because Medicare-covered skilled nursing facility inpatient care includes payment for room and board.

[F]   Medical Appliances and Supplies

Medical appliances and supplies must be provided as needed for the palliation and management of the terminal illness and related conditions.[79] It should be noted that the definition of medical appliances and supplies extends to durable medical equipment and *self-help and personal comfort items* related to the palliation or management of the patient's terminal illness.[80]

[G]   Drugs and Biologicals

"Medications needed for palliative purposes" are covered under the hospice benefit.[81] This means that all medications used for symptom control (e.g., pain management; nausea; constipation) are covered under the hospice benefit. For each medication provided while the beneficiary is not an inpatient, the hospice program may charge the beneficiary a coinsurance payment.[82] This coinsurance cannot exceed $5.00.[83]

[H]   Home Health Aide and Homemaker Services

Home health aide and homemaker services must be available and adequate in frequency to meet the needs of the patient.[84] There is, therefore, no limit on the

---

[77] *Id.*

[78] 42 U.S.C. §1395x(i). *See also* **§3.03**.

[79] 42 C.F.R. §418.96.

[80] Medicare Benefit Policy Manual, Pub. 100-2, Ch. 9, §40.1.6.

[81] 42 C.F.R. §418.202(f).

[82] 42 C.F.R. §418.400.

[83] 42 C.F.R. §418.400(a).

[84] 42 C.F.R. §§418.94, 418.50(b)(2), 418.202.

amount of these services that can be received, so long as the services are reasonable and necessary for the palliation and management of the terminal condition. A registered nurse must visit the patient's home at least every two weeks when aide services are being provided. The visit must include an assessment of the aide services.[85] Written instructions for the patient's care must be prepared by the registered nurse.[86] Home health aides, unlike homemakers, are required to have 75 hours of training, with at least 16 hours devoted to supervised practical training. In addition, they must receive competency evaluations at least once every 12 months.[87]

Home health aides provide a variety of personal care services. Routine services to maintain satisfactory functioning of indwelling bladder catheter, changes of dressings for non-infected postoperative or chronic conditions, and assistance in dressing, eating, or going to the toilet are all examples of personal care services.[88] Aides may also perform household services to maintain a safe and sanitary environment in areas of the home used by the patient, such as changing the bed or light cleaning or essential laundering.[89] Similarly, homemaker services may include assistance in personal care, maintenance of a safe and healthy environment, and services to enable the patient to carry out the treatment plan.[90]

While the beneficiary is at a continuous level of care,[91] that is, during a period of crisis, home health aide and homemaker services may be provided to supplement nursing services.[92] However, care provided during such a period of crisis must be predominately nursing care.[93]

§5.10 DEDUCTIBLES AND COINSURANCE FOR NON-HOSPICE CARE

The hospice patient is liable for coinsurance amounts only for respite care and drugs and biologicals (*see supra*, §5.09[D] and §5.09[G]). No other services *provided by the hospice* for the palliation and management of the patient's terminal illness may be billed to the patient.

If while on hospice, the patient receives medical care for conditions not related to his or her terminal condition, then she will be liable for the standard Medicare deductibles and coinsurance payments related to that care. Examples of

---

[85] 42 C.F.R. §418.94(a).

[86] 42 C.F.R. §418.94(b).

[87] 42 C.F.R. §484.36.

[88] For other examples, *see* 42 C.F.R. §409.33(d).

[89] 42 C.F.R. §418.202(g).

[90] *Id.*

[91] There are four payment levels for hospice care: routine home care; continuous home care; inpatient respite care; and general inpatient care. 42 C.F.R. §418.302. During a period of crisis, the hospice may bill Medicare at an hourly rate for continuous home care for at least eight hours and for as many as twenty-four hours. *Id. See also* **§5.09[A].**

[92] 42 C.F.R. §418.204(a).

[93] *Id.*

services not considered hospice care and consequently subject to these various charges include services furnished before or after a hospice election; services of the individual's attending physician, if the attending physician is not an employee of or working under arrangements with the hospice; and Medicare services received for the treatment of an illness or injury not related to the individual's terminal condition.[94]

§5.11   THE APPEALS PROCESS

Hospice patients are afforded the same appeal rights as those granted to other recipients of services under Part A of Medicare.[95]

As a practical matter, denials of coverage for hospice care seem to occur with much less frequency than denials of coverage to patients receiving care in other settings. This may be partially due to the limited number of beneficiaries who are deemed to be terminally ill or to the limited number of terminally ill patients who elect hospice coverage.

[A]   Coding Problems

Frequently Medicare beneficiaries who have elected the Medicare hospice benefit, inappropriately receive coverage denials for care they received that was not related to the terminal illness. These denials are often caused by inappropriate coding by the medical care provider's billing office and can usually be remedied without a Medicare appeal. However, in the event that the provider's billing office is not cooperative and refuses to re-bill or if Medicare continues to deny the claim despite the fact that the provider has billed correctly, these claims should be appealed. As was discussed above, upon electing hospice, one does not waive all rights to Medicare coverage, only some of those rights related to the terminal illness.[96]

[B]   Billing Errors

Another source of inappropriate denials also occurs through billing error. Hospices frequently have contractual relationships with other entities for the provision of care related to the terminal illness.[97] For instance, a hospice may have a contractual relationship with a durable medical equipment (DME) provider for the provision of items such as wheelchairs and hospital beds. These contracts

---

[94] 42 C.F.R. §418.402.

[95] See §1.07.

[96] See §5.01.

[97] Medicare Benefit Policy Manual, Pub. 100-2, Ch. 9, §40.4.

specify that the providers of services and goods are to bill the hospice for the services and goods provided. In other words, they are not to bill Medicare and they are not to bill the beneficiary. However, sometimes through billing error, the contracted provider will bill Medicare rather than the hospice. This will result in a Medicare denial. Should this occur, the hospice should be contacted and asked to remedy the problem. If the hospice is unwilling or unable to remedy the problem, then the denial should be appealed.

In the event that the hospice has arranged for the beneficiary to receive care for the terminal illness from another provider, but has failed to arrange a billing contract for that purpose, the provider will probably bill Medicare for the care in question. Should this happen, a denial of coverage will probably be issued. Under these circumstances, the beneficiary's liability should be waived[98] because he or she had no way of knowing that the care in question would not be covered. If this is not indicated on the initial determination, and instead the beneficiary is held financially liable for the care, the denial should be appealed. Beneficiaries, however, must remember, that upon electing hospice, they waive their rights to Medicare coverage for treatment of the terminal illness that is not provided by their attending physician, the hospice, or under arrangement with the hospice.[99] Should beneficiaries seek out care for their terminal illness from non-hospice providers, their care will not be covered by Medicare, and they may ultimately be held financially responsible.

[C] Terminal Status

Because Medicare coverage of hospice care hinges almost exclusively on whether or not the beneficiary had a life expectancy of six months or less,[100] nontechnical denials of hospice coverage are most likely made based on a finding that the beneficiary's life expectancy was not six months or less. In pursuing a hospice appeal of such a denial, the advocate should attempt to obtain an explicit and detailed letter from the patient's attending physician, listing specific clinical findings and other documentation supporting the beneficiary's limited life expectancy. This letter often can be the pivotal factor in achieving a successful result. In addition, the advocate should closely examine the medical record for notations indicating that the beneficiary was terminally ill with a limited life-expectancy. Doctors' orders, nurses' notes, and the written care plan[101] established for the

---

[98] 42 U.S.C. §1395pp(g); *see also*, Medicare Benefit Policy Manual, Pub. 100-2, Ch. 9, §50 and **§5.11[D]**.

[99] *See* **§5.01.**

[100] *See* **§5.02.**

[101] 42 C.F.R. §418.58. "A written plan of care must be established and maintained for each individual admitted to a hospice program, and the care provided to an individual must be in accordance with that plan."

patient will often be useful sources of evidence to support a claim for Medicare coverage. Any notes of the hospice's interdisciplinary group regarding the patient's care will also prove helpful.[102]

[D]   Waiver of Liability

Section 1879 of the Social Security Act provides protections from liability for charges for claims denied by Medicare for services provided to beneficiaries who were not aware that the services would not be covered by Medicare. On August 5, 1997, the limitation of liability was extended to Medicare hospice coverage via Section 1879(g) of the Act.[103]

[E]   Demand Bills

Prior to providing care to a non-terminal beneficiary, in order to avoid financial liability for the care, the hospice must notify the beneficiary that the care will not be covered by Medicare. In the event that the beneficiary believes that the hospice's determination is incorrect, he or she may request a *demand bill*. This should be done in writing. In the event that no demand bill is requested, then no bill will be submitted to Medicare, and thus the beneficiary will have no right to a Medicare appeal. Once the hospice provider receives the demand bill, it should submit the bill to the Medicare contractor for an initial determination.[104]

[F]   Standard Appeals

The Medicare contractor, upon receiving the claim, will review the medical evidence and issue an initial determination indicating whether or not the hospice care is covered by Medicare.[105] After this determination, a notice of initial determination will be sent to the beneficiary's last known address.[106] The notice must be written in a manner calculated to be understood by the beneficiary.[107] It must contain:

• The reasons for the determination, including whether a local medical review policy, a local coverage determination, or a national coverage determination was applied;

---

[102] 42 C.F.R. §418.68. "The hospice must designate an interdisciplinary group or groups composed of individuals who provide or supervise the care and services offered by the hospice."

[103] *See* note 100.

[104] Medicare Claims Processing Manual, Pub. 100-4, Ch. 11, §30.3.

[105] 42 C.F.R. §405.921.

[106] 42 C.F.R. §405.921(a)(1).

[107] *Id.*

- Procedures for obtaining additional information concerning the contractor's determination, such as a specific provision of a policy, manual, law or regulation used in making the determination;

- Information on the right to a redetermination if the beneficiary is dissatisfied with the outcome of the initial determination and instructions on how to request a redetermination; and

- Any other requirements specified by the Centers for Medicare & Medicaid Services.[108]

If the patient receives a full denial, a partial denial, or a denial, but his or her liability is waived, the patient may wish to appeal. An initial determination that denies coverage but waives the patient's liability should be appealed because if, in the future, the patient receives the same or similar care, the patient may be deemed to know that such care is not covered (by virtue of the prior denial), and the patient would then be held liable for payment.[109]

[G] Expedited Appeals

In the event that the hospice program intends to discharge a beneficiary because it believes that he or she is no longer terminally ill, it must first give the beneficiary a standardized termination notice.[110] The standardized termination notices are designed to inform beneficiaries that they are being discharged from hospice care and that they have a right to an expedited appeal.[111] A beneficiary who wishes to exercise the right to an expedited appeal must submit a request for a determination to the Quality Improvement Organization (QIO) in the State in which the beneficiary is receiving services, in writing or by telephone, by no later than noon of the calendar day following receipt of the provider's notice of termination.[112] No later than 72 hours after receipt of the request for an expedited review, the QIO must notify the beneficiary, beneficiary's physician, and the hospice program of its determination whether termination of Medicare coverage is the correct decision, either on the basis of medical necessity or based on other Medicare coverage policies.[113]

[H] Holistic Mission

Advocates should remember that Medicare-certified hospices have a legal duty and a philosophical mandate requiring them to provide holistic care to the

---

[108] 42 C.F.R. §405.921(a)(2).

[109] 42 C.F.R. §§405.710, 405.711.

[110] 42 C.F.R. §411.404.

[111] *Id. Also see* **§1.07**.

[112] 42 C.F.R. §405.1202(b).

[113] 42 C.F.R. §405.1202(e)(6).

patient and caregiver(s). This holistic care should enable the hospice family to focus on the process of dying (e.g., saying I love you, I forgive you, and thank you), rather than on life's trivialities, such as the details of Medicare law. Consequently, there should be no Medicare denials for care related to the terminal illness during a hospice election period. If such denials occur, they may stem from a billing error made by the hospice or another health care provider. Thus any Medicare denial for care related to the terminal illness during an election period should be brought to the attention of the hospice, with an eye on the appeal clock, just in case the denial needs to be formally appealed.

§5.12   THE MEDICARE PRESCRIPTION DRUG, IMPROVEMENT, AND MODERNIZATION ACT OF 2003

[A]   Prescription Drug Coverage[114]

The Medicare Prescription Drug, Improvement, and Modernization Act of 2003[115] added prescription drug coverage as a potential Medicare benefit. If a hospice patient has signed-up for a Part D plan,[116] then whether the hospice, Medicare Part B, the beneficiary's Part D plan, or the beneficiary is responsible for paying for the hospice patient's medications will depend in large part on the medication's purpose.

Palliative medications related to the hospice patient's terminal illness should be paid for by the beneficiary's hospice provider.[117] Curative medications related to the patient's terminal illness will not be paid for by the hospice provider, Medicare Part B or the beneficiary's Medicare Part D plan.[118] Medications prescribed for the treatment of illness not related to the patient's terminal illness should be billed to Part B,[119] when they are coverable by Part B, and when they are not coverable by Part B, they should be billed to the patient's Part D plan.[120] If the patient receives Medicare-covered inpatient care for a condition not related to his or her terminal illness, then the medications that he or she receives in the inpatient facility that are not related to the terminal illness will be covered under the Medicare Part A benefit for hospital[121] or skilled nursing facility care.[122] The medications that are related to the terminal illness, should continue to be paid for by the hospice provider.

---

[114] See **Chapter 11**.

[115] Medicare Prescription Drug, Improvement, and Modernization Act of 2003, Pub. L. No. 108-173, 117 Stat. 2066.

[116] See **§11.01**.

[117] See **§5.09**.

[118] See **§5.01**.

[119] See **§6.03**.

[120] See **§11.04**.

[121] See **§2.05[C]**.

[122] See **Chapter 3**.

[B] §512 of the Act, Coverage of Hospice Consultation Services

If a Medicare beneficiary is terminally ill and has not yet elected the hospice benefit, Medicare will pay for a consultation visit with the hospice medical director or physicians who are employees of a hospice program. During this visit, the physician may: evaluate the individual's need for pain and symptom management; counsel the individual with respect to end-of-life issues and care options; and advise the individual regarding advanced care planning. Hospices receive payment for this service that is equal to the amount established for an office or other out-patient visit for evaluation and management associated with presenting problems of moderate severity under the established Medicare physician fee schedule other than the portion of the amount attributable to the practice expense component. The physician, if not a volunteer, will be paid by the hospice.

[C] §408 of the Act, Nurse Practitioners Services

In addition to coverage for the physician who certifies that a beneficiary is terminally ill, Medicare payments are made for the services of a nurse practitioner chosen by the beneficiary instead of a physician as having the most significant role in the determination and delivery of the beneficiary's medical care. The nurse will not be authorized to certify the beneficiary as terminally ill, but will be able to review hospice plans of care.

[D] §946 of the Act, Provision of Core Hospice Services

A hospice may, under extraordinary circumstances, enter into arrangements with another hospice to provide core hospice services to Medicare beneficiaries. These extraordinary circumstances include: unanticipated high patient loads, staffing shortages due to illness or other events, or temporary travel of a patient outside a hospice program's service area. The hospice program making these arrangements bills Medicare and is paid for the hospice care.

[E] §409 of the Act, Rural Hospice Demonstration Project

Three hospice programs will be selected to take part in a demonstration project, which will last no longer than five years. The chosen hospices will provide hospice care to Medicare beneficiaries who live in rural areas and who do not have able caregivers. The hospice care will be provided in facilities that have 20 or fewer beds and offer the full range of services usually provided by hospice programs. Payments to the demonstration hospice programs will be the same as payments made to non-demonstration hospice programs.

APPENDIX 5-1

CMS PROGRAM MEMORANDUM, TRANSMITTAL AB-01-09
(JAN. 24, 2001)

Program Memorandum **Intermediaries/Carriers**	Department of Health and Human Services (DHHS) HEALTH CARE FINANCING ADMINISTRATION (HCFA)

Transmittal AB-01-09	Date: JANUARY 24, 2001

CHANGE REQUEST 1502

SUBJECT: Clarification of Physician Certification Requirements for Medicare Hospice

Section 1814(a)(7) of the Social Security Act (the Act) contains the requirements for Medicare hospice that a physician certify in writing, at the beginning of a benefit period, that a beneficiary is terminally ill. Section 1861(dd)(3)(A) explains that an individual is considered to be "terminally ill" if the individual has a medical prognosis that the individual's life expectancy is 6 months or less. Federal Regulations at 42 CFR 418.3 further clarify that an individual is considered to be terminally ill if they have a medical prognosis of a life expectancy of 6 months or less *if the illness runs its normal course.*

Subtitle C, §322, of the Benefits Protection and Improvement Act (BIPA) of 2000 amends §1814(a)(7) of the Act by clarifying that the certification of terminal illness of an individual who elects hospice "shall be based on the physician's or medical director's clinical judgment regarding the normal course of the individual's illness." This clarification is effective for certifications made on or after the date of BIPA enactment, which was December 21, 2000.

The amendment to §1814(a)(7) of the Act clarifies current policy, that the certification is based on clinical judgment regarding the normal course of illness, and further emphasizes the understanding that making medical prognostication of life expectancy is not always exact.

Intermediaries should inform hospice providers of this statutory clarification of current Medicare policy within 30 days of the implementation date.

Carriers should publish this instruction in their next regularly scheduled bulletin following the implementation date.

The *effective date* for this Program Memorandum (PM) is December 21, 2000.

The *implementation date* for this PM is February 1, 2001.

These instructions should be implemented within your current operating budget.

This PM may be discarded after February 1, 2002.

If you have any questions contact Lynn Riley at (410) 786-1286.

HCFA-Pub. 60AB

CHAPTER 6

MEDICARE PART B: SUPPLEMENTAL MEDICAL INSURANCE

§6.01 INTRODUCTION

[A] Services

Part B of the Medicare program, Supplemental Medical Insurance, provides coverage for a host of services for beneficiaries, including:

- Physician services;

- Services and supplies incident to a physician's professional services, including drugs and biologicals that cannot be self-administered, including chemotherapy;[1]

- Outpatient hospital services;

- Physical and occupational therapy services;

- Speech therapy services;

- X-ray, laboratory, and other diagnostic tests;

- Surgical dressings and devices for reduction of fractures;

- Durable medical equipment; and

- Prosthetic devices.[2]

[B] Administration

Part B is financed by premiums paid by individuals enrolled in the program and by general revenues from the federal government. Since 1993, individuals receiving Social Security retirement benefits, individuals receiving Social Security disability benefits for 24 months, and individuals otherwise entitled to Medicare Part A are automatically enrolled in Part B unless they decline coverage.

Section 911 of the Medicare Prescription Drug Improvement and Modernization Act of 2003 (MMA), as part of the government's regulatory reform initiative, creates a new Section 1874A of the Social Security Act, that modifies and consolidates the administration of the Medicare Program. In particular, the Secretary of Health and Human Services (HHS) now has the authority to contract with an eligible entity known as a "Medicare Administrative Contractor."

---

[1] 42 U.S.C. §§1395k, 1395x.

[2] *Id.* Definitions of Medicare-covered services, along with critical Medicare terms, are found at 42 U.S.C. §1395x. Definitions include §1395x(a) (spell of illness); §1395x(b) (inpatient hospital services); §1395x(c) (inpatient psychiatric hospital services); §1395x(e) (definition of hospital); §1395x(f) (psychiatric hospital); §1395x(g) (outpatient occupational therapy services); §1395x(h) (extended care services); §1395x(i) (post hospital extended care services); §1395x(j) (skilled nursing facility); §1395x(m) (home health services); §1395x(o) (home health agency); §1395x(p) (outpatient physical therapy services); §1395x(q) (physician services); §1395x(r) (physician); §1395x(s) (medical and other services, including durable medical equipment (DME), prosthetic devices, and ambulance services).

This entity will perform certain functions previously performed by contractors (Part B) and Intermediaries (Part A). Functions include determining payment amounts, local medical coverage decisions, beneficiary education, technical assistance, and other functions.[3]

The MMA also calls for the appointment of a Medicare Beneficiary Ombudsman, located in HHS. The Ombudsman is to assist beneficiaries with appeals and related matters in fee-for-service and Medicare Advantage (formerly called Medicare + Choice) settings.[4]

§6.02   ENROLLMENT AND PAYMENT REQUIREMENTS

[A]   Eligibility

Medicare Part B, the Supplemental Insurance Program, is a voluntary program for eligible enrollees who enroll and pay a monthly premium.[5] An eligible enrollee is a person who is either entitled to Part A[6] or anyone age 65 or older who is a citizen or who has been a lawful permanent resident for five years preceding the month of application.[7] Persons not entitled to Part A benefits may request enrollment in Part B.[8] Persons convicted of crimes against national security (subversive activity) may not enroll.[9]

[B]   Enrollment

[1]   Enrollment Periods

Persons enrolled in Part A are presumed to want Part B; however, one can opt out of Part B before coverage begins or within a specified period (not

---

[3] Section 911 of the MMA, Pub. L. No. 108-173, December 8, 2003. Section 911 also makes conforming modifications to 42 U.S.C. §1395h, 1395u to remove references to fiscal intermediaries and carriers. The flexibility in Medicare Administration provisions is effective October 1, 2005. Provider education and technical assistance and information security provisions are effective upon enactment of the Act.

[4] Provision is effective one year from date of enactment of MMA. *See* Section 923, amending 1808 of the Social Security Act.

[5] *See* 42 U.S.C. §§1395j–1395w. The Part B monthly premium in 2006 is $88.50 and in 2007 _____. Premiums for a subsequent year are announced in the Federal Register prior to October of the preceding year. The Part B deductible in 2006 is $110 and in 2007 _____. In subsequent years, it will be increased by the same percentage as the Part B premium (monthly actuarial value of benefits payable under Part B), rounded up to the nearest dollar. Section 629 of the Medicare Modernization Act (MMA), amending §1833(b) of the Social Security Act, 42 U.S.C. §1395l(b).

[6] 42 U.S.C. §1395o; 42 C.F.R. §407.10.

[7] 42 U.S.C. §1395i-2; 42 C.F.R. §407.10(a)(2)(i)–(iii).

[8] 42 C.F.R. §407.22(a)(1).

[9] 42 C.F.R. §407.10(b).

less than two months) beginning after notice that Part B coverage has started.[10]

Enrollment in Part B, and Medicare generally, is automatic for most persons who qualify for Medicare Part A. For others, it is usually handled through the local office of the Social Security Administration (SSA). An application for benefits can be submitted by mail or in person. If one wishes to decline Part B, a signed statement to that effect should be sent to the local SSA office.[11]

Most beneficiaries enroll during their initial enrollment period, which includes the seven-month period beginning on the first day of the third month before the month when all eligibility requirements are met and extends for seven months from that date.[12] Generally, early application is recommended so as to avoid gaps in coverage.[13] For example, if an individual enrolls in the first three months of the initial enrollment period, entitlement begins with the first month of eligibility.[14] If the individual enrolls during the fourth month of the initial enroll- ment period, entitlement begins with the following month.[15] If the individual enrolls in the fifth month of the initial enrollment period, entitlement begins the second month after the month of enrollment.[16] If the individual waits until the last two months of the initial enrollment period to enroll, entitlement begins the third month after the month of enrollment.[17]

Beneficiaries who continue to be covered by an employer group health plan which covers 20 or more employees through their own active employment or the active employment of their spouse[18] may delay their enrollment in Medicare Part B without incurring a penalty. Such beneficiaries will be entitled to a special enroll- ment period when the earlier of two things occurs: the employment through which they have the insurance ends or the insurance terminates. The special enrollment period runs for a period of eight months.[19]

Persons enrolling late, because they missed their initial enrollment period and were not eligible for a special enrollment period, must wait for a general

---

[10] 42 C.F.R. §407.17(b).

[11] *Id.*

[12] 42 U.S.C. §1395p(d); 42 C.F.R. §407.14(a)(1). Under the Medicare Advantage (formerly called Medicare+Choice) program, enrollees must make an election whether to be in the original fee-for-service Medicare program or to participate in a Medicare Advantage managed care option. *See* 42 C.F.R §§422.62 *et seq.*

[13] *See* 42 U.S.C. §1395q; 42 C.F.R. §407.25.

[14] 42 C.F.R. §407.25(a)(1).

[15] 42 C.F.R. §407.25(a)(2).

[16] 42 C.F.R. §407.25(a)(3).

[17] 42 C.F.R. §407.25 (a)(4).

[18] Individuals entitled to Medicare on the basis of disability (except ESRD) may qualify for a SEP if they are covered by a large group health plan ($\geq$ 100 employees) through their own employment or the employment of a family member. 42 C.F.R. §407.20(d)(2).

[19] 42 U.S.C. §1395p(i).

enrollment period to apply.[20] There is a general enrollment period each year from January 1st through March 31st.[21] There may be penalties attached to enrollment during a general enrollment period, however, as explained in detail below.

[2] Penalty for Late Enrollment

As a general matter, persons eligible for Part B should consider filing an application for benefits at the earliest possible time.[22] There is a ten percent penalty added to the premium for each full year of late enrollment.[23] The penalty has no durational limit.[24] There is no increase in premium if the late enrollment gap is less than 12 months.[25] Late enrollment is allowed only during the first three months of each calendar year (coverage becomes effective July 1 of that calendar year).[26]

There is no late enrollment period if the delay is the result of error, fault, or delay by a federal government official or agent of the government.[27] The enrollee must establish that he or she with good cause relied on erroneous information provided by such an official, for example, an SSA or Medicare official.[28]

[C] Premiums

[1] Standard Monthly Premium

Persons enrolled in Medicare Part B are required to pay a monthly premium, the amount of which is established annually by the Department of Health and Human Services (HHS).[29] Payments are either deducted from government benefits or by direct payment or remittance as provided in the law.[30]

---

[20] 42 C.F.R. §§406.24, 407.25.

[21] 42 U.S.C. §1395p(e).

[22] In addition, advocates should advise their low-income clients of Medicaid provisions that require states to pay the premiums for Medicare beneficiaries with incomes at or below the federal poverty level and resources at or below twice the Supplemental Security Income (SSI) limit. *See* 42 U.S.C. §§1396a, 1396d(p) of the Medicaid statute. Medicaid buy-in for low-income Medicare beneficiaries is discussed elsewhere in this book.

[23] 42 U.S.C. §1395(r); 42 C.F.R. §408.22.

[24] For disabled beneficiaries, under age 65, the penalty will end when they turn 65.

[25] 42 C.F.R. §408.22.

[26] 42 C.F.R. §§407.15(a), 407.25.

[27] 42 C.F.R. §407.32. For disabled beneficiaries, Social Security's Program Operation Manual provides for equitable relief when the delay in enrollment was caused by incorrect information provided by their employer or group health plan. (SSA POMS, HI 00805.320).

[28] *Id.*

[29] 42 U.S.C. §1395r; *see also* 42 C.F.R. §§408.4(a), 407.17(b) (automatic enrollment). (*See* discussion of special provisions for payment of Medicare premiums, copayments, and deductibles for persons with low income and resources found elsewhere in this book).

[30] 42 U.S.C. §1395r; 42 C.F.R. §408.20 (monthly premiums); 42 C.F.R. §408.40 (deduction from monthly benefits).

Premiums are deducted from Social Security, Railroad Retirement, or federal civil service retirement benefits.[31] Part B premiums are generally billed quarterly but can be billed monthly where the beneficiary is unwilling or unable to pay quarterly.[32]

If the beneficiary receives only a civil service annuity and has a spouse who is eligible for Medicare Supplemental Insurance, the beneficiary may authorize the deduction of the spouse's premium from the beneficiary's check.[33]

If benefits are suspended for excess earnings, and are to be resumed before the close of the taxable year, the individual is not billed for Part B premiums, but can continue to pay such premiums to keep his or her coverage.[34] If payment of premiums is not to be resumed before the end of the taxable year, the individual is billed directly for premiums.[35]

The grace period for failing to pay the initial premium or subsequent monthly premium ends with the last day of the third month after the billing month; termination of coverage for nonpayment is effective with the first month following the end of the grace period.[36] Overdue payments remain an obligation and can be deducted from future Social Security or Railroad Retirement or offset against any Part B payments otherwise due, or can be collected directly from the enrollee or the enrollee's estate.[37]

In general, Medicare beneficiaries pay approximately 25 percent of Medicare Part B program costs, with some beneficiaries paying slightly more if they have incurred an increased enrollment premium for late enrollment or re-enrollment.[38] Approximately 75 percent of the Medicare Part B premium is subsidized by the Federal Government through contributions to the Federal Supplemental Insurance Trust Fund.[39]

[2] Part B Income-Related Premium

While representing savings to the Medicare Supplemental Trust Fund, the Part B income-related premium implements a public policy shift whereby, based on income, Medicare beneficiaries will pay more in premiums depending on

---

[31] 42 C.F.R. §§408.42, 408.43, 408.44.

[32] 42 C.F.R. §408.60(b).

[33] 42 C.F.R. §408.44.

[34] 42 C.F.R. §408.46(a).

[35] 42 C.F.R. §408.46(b).

[36] 42 C.F.R. §408.8.

[37] 42 C.F.R. §408.4(b).

[38] 42 C.F.R. §408.20(c)(1). Note, too, Medicare Advantage (MA) plans can provide a reduction in Medicare Part B premium as an additional benefit. *See*, 42 C.F.R. §408.21.

[39] 42 U.S.C. §1395r. Note, since January 2003, Medicare Advantage (MA) plans may elect to receive a reduction in its payments if 80 percent of the reduction is applied to reduce the standard Medicare Part B premiums of its Medicare enrollees, and the Medicare Part B premium is reduced monthly and is offered to all Medicare enrollees in a specific plan benefit package. 42 C.F.R. §408.21(a). In addition, the reduction can not be greater than the standard premium amount determined for the year, however, it can be less. 42 C.F.R. §408.21(b).

income. Under the provisions, the responsibility for determining the income-related portion of the Part B premium will reside with SSA, using individual federal income tax data from the IRS. In resolving administrative disputes about the amount of an income-related Part B premium, SSA will use its administrative review process for determinations of rights regarding non-medical issues.

Starting in January 2007, Medicare beneficiaries with higher incomes will be required to pay a greater portion of the Part B premium costs.[40] This higher premium is called the Part B income-related premium and is added to the Medicare Part B standard monthly premium, plus any applicable premium increase for late enrollment or re-enrollment.[41]

The higher premium amount will apply to beneficiaries with federal modified adjusted gross taxable income (as defined by the Internal Revenue Service) over the threshold income amount of $80,000 per individual or $160,000 for a couple.[42] It will be phased in from calendar year 2007 through calendar year 2009.[43] At or above this amount, the beneficiary will have to pay an income-related monthly adjustment amount.[44]

The purpose of the income-related monthly adjustment amount is to reduce the Federal subsidy of the Medicare Part B program for beneficiaries with modified adjusted gross income above an established threshold.[45] The Centers for Medicare & Medicaid Services (CMS) will publish the threshold amounts annually in September in the Federal Register. Published threshold amounts will be effective January 1 of the next calendar year for the full calendar year.[46]

---

[40] The income-related premium is a requirement of the Medicare Modernization Act (MMA) of 2003, §811, Pub. L. 108-173, enacted December 8, 2003. The Office of Management and Budget (OMB) has determined that implementing the Part B income-related premium will result in an overall savings to the Medicare Supplementary Medical Insurance Trust Fund of roughly $7.7 billion over the period of fiscal years 2007-2011. The Social Security Administration (SSA) will administer the income-related premium. SSA's administrative expenses in connection with Part B income-related premium is stated as amounting to $200 million over that same 5-year period. *See* proposed regulations, 71 Fed. Reg. 10926, at 10931 (Mar. 3, 2006).

[41] *Id.* The income-related premium provision amends §1839 of the Social Security Act, 42 U.S.C. §1395r. The Deficit Reduction Act (DRA) of 2005, §5111, Pub. L. 109-171, further amended §1839(i) of the Social Security Act to provide that the payment of the full amount of the income-related monthly adjustment amount will be phased in starting in 2007 and will be completed in 2009, with a 33 percent phase-in in 2007, 67 percent in 2008, and 100 percent in 2009. Before DRA, there was a five-year phase-in period. 42 U.S.C §1395r(i)(3)(B).

[42] *See* proposed 20 C.F.R. §418.1105(b)

[43] *See* proposed 20 C.F.R. §418.1001(b); §418.1130 (how SSA will phase in the income-related monthly adjustment amount).

[44] *Id.*

[45] *See* proposed 20 C.F.R. §418.1005, found at 71 Fed. Reg. 10926 *et seq.*

[46] *See*, proposed regulations of the Social Security Administration (SSA), the agency that will administer the Part B Income-related premium process in conjunction with the Internal Revenue Service (IRS) of the U.S. Department of the Treasury, and the Centers for Medicare & Medicaid Services (CMS) of the Department of Health and Human Services (DHHS). 71 Fed. Reg. 10926.

[a] Higher Income Medicare Beneficiary Payment Amount Elements

A beneficiary with income above the threshold amount will pay:[47]

1. The Medicare Part B standard monthly premium; plus

2. Any applicable increase in the standard monthly premium for late enrollment or re-enrollment; plus

3. An income-related monthly adjustment amount.

The federal premium subsidy is the portion of the full cost of providing Medicare Part B coverage that is paid by the federal government through transfers into the Federal Supplementary Medical Insurance Trust Fund, and the income-related monthly adjustment amount is an additional amount of premium that beneficiaries will pay for Medicare Part B coverage if one has income above the threshold. The amount of one's income-related monthly adjustment amount is based on his or her modified adjusted gross income.[48]

Medicare beneficiaries required to pay an income-related monthly adjustment amount will not be eligible for the limitation on Medicare Part B standard monthly premium increase beyond the amount of one's Social Security (or tier 1 railroad retirement) cost-of-living adjustments.[49] Those who are Medicare beneficiaries prior to January 1, 2007, and required to pay an income-related monthly adjustment amount in 2007, will receive notification at the end of 2006 about the additional amount of premium owed and about any related changes in the amount of Social Security monthly benefits or other payments to be withheld.[50]

Those who enroll in Medicare after January 1, 2007, and who are determined to be responsible for an income-related Part B premium, will be notified shortly after enrolling in Medicare Part B.[51] For a person who becomes a Medicare beneficiary during 2007 or after, the Social Security Administration (SSA) will notify the person prior to the start of each year if required to pay an income-related Part B premium.[52]

The Centers for Medicare & Medicaid Services (CMS), in the Department of Health and Human Services (DHHS) publishes the Medicare part B standard monthly premium each year.[53] CMS also establishes rules for entitlement to a nonstandard premium as well as premium penalties for late enrollment or reenrollment.[54]

---

[47] See proposed 20 C.F.R. §418.1005.

[48] See proposed 20 C.F.R. §418.1001.

[49] See 71 Fed. Reg. 10,927 (Mar. 3, 2006).

[50] Id.

[51] Id.

[52] Id.

[53] 42 C.F.R. §408.20.

[54] 42 C.F.R. §408.20(e).

A nonstandard premium may be established in individual cases only if the individual is entitled to old age or disability benefits for the months of November and December, and actually receives the corresponding benefit checks in December and January.[55] For calendar years after 1988, beginning with calendar year 1989, a premium increase greater than the cost-of-living increase is still a perquisite for a nonstandard premium.[56] A nonstandard premium, however, is not precluded solely because the cash benefit is further reduced as a result of government pension offset or workers' compensation payment.[57] The nonstandard premium is the greater of the following: the premium paid for December; the standard premium promulgated for January, reduced as necessary to compensate for (A) the fact that the cost-of-living increase was less than the increase in the standard premium; or (B) the further reduction in benefit because of government pension offset of workers' compensation payments.[58]

[b] Determining the Amount to be Paid

SSA will use information that it gets from the IRS to determine if beneficiaries who are enrolled in Medicare Part B are required to pay an income-related monthly adjustment amount. SSA also changes income-related monthly adjustment amount determinations using information provided by a beneficiary under circumstances. SSA also notifies beneficiaries when the Social Security benefit amounts they receive will change based on its income-related monthly adjustment amount determination.

SSA will determine one's income-related monthly adjustment amount using the beneficiary's tax filing status and modified adjusted gross income. A beneficiary's income-related premium amount will be determined using a set of tables reflecting modified adjusted gross income ranges. For each range, an unsubsidized Medicare Part B premium percentage is assigned. The remainder is subsidized from the Federal Supplementary Medical Insurance Trust Fund. For example, in 2007, a beneficiary with a modified adjusted gross income in the range of $80,000 but less than or equal to $100,000 will pay 35 percent of the Part B premium cost, with a Federal premium subsidy of 65 percent.[59]

[c] New Subpart B (Proposed Rule)

SSA proposes to add a new subpart B, Medicare Part B Income-Related Monthly Adjustment Amount. It would be codified in the Code of Federal

---

[55] 42 C.F.R. §408.20(e)(1) (basic rule).

[56] 42 C.F.R. §408.20(e)(3)(i).

[57] 42 C.F.R. §408.20(e)(3)(ii).

[58] 42 C.F.R. §408.20(e)(4).

[59] *See* Table, at 71 Fed. Reg. 10,934 (Mar. 3, 2005).

Regulations at 20 C.F.R., Part 418, which will contain the rules that SSA will use to determine when one will be required to pay an income-related monthly adjustment amount in addition to one's Medicare Part B standard monthly premium plus any applicable premium increase for late enrollment or reenrollment.[60]

Section 811 of the MMA amended the Social Security Act to provide that the limitation on increases in the Medicare Part B standard monthly premium for some beneficiaries will not apply to beneficiaries who are responsible for an income-related premium.[61] The standard Part B Medicare premium is set by to cover approximately 25 percent of the Medicare Part B program costs. The other 75 percent is subsidized in large part by the federal government by contributions to the Federal Supplementary Medical Insurance Trust Fund.[62]

In determining whether one is required to pay an income-related premium, SSA will request information about a beneficiary's modified adjusted gross income from IRS. SSA will specify the tax year involved in its request for information, including Federal income tax return information and the beneficiary's modified adjusted gross income for the tax year which is two years before the effective year of SSA' determination.[63] If the beneficiary must pay an income-related monthly adjustment amount, the beneficiary will not be eligible for the limitation on Medicare Part B standard monthly premium increase beyond the amount of his or her Social Security (or tier 1 railroad retirement) cost-of-living adjustments.[64]

Modified adjusted gross income is defined at 26 U.S.C. §62 and in related regulations, and includes certain other forms of income that may be excluded from adjusted gross income for purposes of determining the amount of Federal income tax that one must pay.[65] The definition includes the beneficiary's adjusted gross income as defined by the IRS, plus the following forms of tax-exempt income:[66]

1. Tax-exempt interest income;

2. Income from United States savings bonds used to pay higher education tuition and fees;

3. Foreign earned income;

4. Income derived from sources within Guam, American Samoa, or the Northern Mariana islands; and

5. Income from sources within Puerto Rico.

---

[60] *See* 71 Fed. Reg. 10,929 (Mar. 3, 2006).

[61] *See* 71 Fed. Reg. 10,926 (Mar. 3, 2006).

[62] *See* 71 Fed. Reg. 10,926 (Mar. 3, 2006).

[63] *See* proposed 20 C.F.R. §§418.1130–418.1250.

[64] *See* 71 Fed. Reg. 10,927 (Mar. 3, 2006).

[65] *See* 71 Fed. Reg. 10,927 (Mar. 3, 2006).

[66] *See* proposed 20 C.F.R. §418.1010(6).

If modified adjusted gross income information is not available from IRS for the tax year two years before the effective year of SSA's determination, IRS will send the beneficiary's modified adjusted gross income information for the tax years three years before that year if it exceeds the threshold, but SSA will use three years of tax information only until information for two years prior becomes available.[67]

If three years of IRS information is used, the beneficiary may request that SSA use information provided by the beneficiary for the tax year two years before that year. SSA will use this information if it will result in a lower income-related monthly adjustment amount. In order to make an initial determination based on beneficiary-supplied information, the beneficiary must provide a copy of his or her federal income tax return for that year, a copy that the beneficiary has requested for that year from IRS, or a an IRS transcript of the beneficiary's return; and if the beneficiary supplies a copy of his or her retained IRS return, SSA will also very this information with IRS.[68]

In some cases, IRS will not have data to provide SSA regarding an individual's modified adjusted gross income because the amount of the individual's income is below the level for which an income tax return must be filed. SSA will not be making income-related monthly adjustment amount determinations in such situations because this individual's income would also be below the modified adjusted gross income threshold; but, if, however, SSA receives information which indicates that an individual who has not filed a tax return has income which exceeds the established threshold for an income-related monthly adjustment amount, SSA will make such a determination.[69] The statute requires that the Secretary of Health and Human Services (HHS), in conjunction with the Secretary of the Treasury, issue regulations that "provide for the treatment of the premium adjustment with respect to such individuals.[70]

[d]   The Sliding Scale Formula and How It Applies

Section 1839(i) of the Social Security Act, 42 U.S.C §1395r, prescribes a sliding scale formula that SSA will use to establish annually four income-related monthly adjustment amounts beginning in 2007.[71] The calculation of the income-related monthly adjustment amount reduces a beneficiary's Medicare Part B premium subsidy using specified percentages; and the amount of this premium subsidy reduction is the income-related monthly adjustment amount.[72]

---

[67] See proposed 20 C.F.R. §§418.1135–418.1150.

[68] See proposed 20 C.F.R. §418.1240.

[69] See 71 Fed. Reg. 10,927 (Mar. 3, 2006).

[70] Id.

[71] Id. at 10,928.

[72] Id.

To determine each income-related monthly adjustment amount, CMS will use the unsubsidized Medicare Part B premium (approximately four times the Medicare Part B standard monthly premium) and multiply it by a specified percentage.[73] The percentage used in the calculation increases as the amount of modified adjusted gross income increases.[74] The premium subsidy is the amount of the Part of the Part B premium paid by the Supplemental Medical Insurance Trust Fund.[75] Currently, beneficiaries pay 25 percent of monthly premium costs.[76]

[e] Applicable Modified Adjusted Gross Income Ranges

The range amounts for individuals who are married filing jointly are double the range amounts for single income tax filers, with IRS recognizing three additional filing statuses: head of household, qualifying widow(er), and married filing separately.[77]

The 2007 modified adjusted gross income ranges for individuals with a federal tax filing status of single, head of household, qualifying widow(er) with dependent child, and married filing separately when the individual has lived apart from his/her spouse for the entire tax year for the year SSA used to make its income-related monthly adjustment amount:[78]

1. Greater than $80,000 and less than or equal to $100,000;

2. Greater than $100,000 and less than or equal to $150,000;

3. Greater than $150,000 and less than or equal to $200,000; and

4. Greater than $200,000.

In 2007, the modified adjusted gross income ranges for individuals who are married and file a joint tax return for the tax year used by SSA to make its income-related monthly adjustment amount determinations are as follows:[79]

1. Greater than $160,000 and less than or equal to $200,000;

2. Greater than $200,000 and less than or equal to $300,000;

3. Greater than $300,000 and less than or equal to $400,000; and

4. Greater than $400,000.

---

[73] See 71 Fed. Reg. 10,928 (Mar. 3, 2006).

[74] Id.

[75] Id.

[76] Id. at 10927.

[77] See proposed 20 C.F.R. §418.1110(a).

[78] Id. at §418.1110(b).

[79] Id. at §418.1110(c).

In 2007, the modified adjusted gross income ranges for married individuals who file a separate return and have lived with their spouse at any time during the tax year used by SSA to make the income-related monthly adjustment amount determinations are as follows:[80]

1. Greater than $80,000 and less than or equal to $120,000; and

2. Greater than $120.000.

Section 1839(i)(3)(C)(iii), (42 U.S.C. §1395r), provides for the modified adjusted gross income ranges for individuals who file their federal income tax return with a filing status of married filing separately and who also have lived with their spouse at any time during the year to be reduced by the threshold amount established for that calendar year which may resulting a higher income-related monthly adjustment amount for these individuals.[81] Section 1839(i)(1), however, provides a threshold amount which is $80,000 in 2007 but will change in subsequent years due to indexing that is applicable to all income-related monthly adjustment amount demonstration. Thus, the lowest range amount can not be lower than the threshold; for 2007, this results in the following two ranges for married filing separately: (1) $80,000 to less than or equal to $120,000, and (2) more than 120,000.[82]

Starting in 2007 for calendar year 2008, and annually thereafter for each following year, SSA will publish the annual modified adjusted gross income ranges and income-related monthly adjustment amounts that are associated with each range.[83] SSA will use this published information to determine which amount applies to a beneficiary based on the beneficiary's tax filing status in the tax year SSA is using to determine the beneficiary's income-related monthly adjustment amount.[84]

If a beneficiary files an amended tax return for the tax year SSA used to make a determination of his or her income-related monthly adjustment amount, the beneficiary may request that SSA use the beneficiary's amended tax return for that year; the beneficiary must provide to SSA proof that he or she filed an amended tax return with IRS, including the beneficiary's retained copy of the amended tax return, and a letter from IRS verifying receipt of the return, or an IRS transcript of his or her amended tax return; if the beneficiary believes that IRS provided incorrect modified adjusted gross income information and SSA used that information to determine the beneficiary's income related monthly adjustment amount, the beneficiary may request that SSA make a new income-related monthly adjustment amount determination.[85]

---

[80] *Id.* at §418.1110(d).

[81] *See* 71 Fed. Reg. 10,928 (Mar. 3, 2006).

[82] *Id.*

[83] *See* proposed 20 C.F.R. §418.1110(e).

[84] *Id.*

[85] *See* 71 Fed. Reg. 10,928 (Mar. 3, 2006).

[f] Applicable Modified Adjusted Gross Income Adjustment Amount

Section 1839(i)(3)(B) requires the amount of the full income-related monthly adjustment to be phased in over a three-year period beginning in 2007; the effect is that from 2007 through 2009 the amount of the income-related monthly adjustment amount will increase because the subsidy will decrease, and the percentage will change each year so that the income-related monthly adjustment amount will gradually increase, until the full amount is phased in starting in 2009.[86]

Beginning in 2008, §1839(i)(5) of the Act requires an annual inflation adjustment for the threshold amount and the amounts used in the modified adjusted gross income ranges, to be based on the percentage increase in the Consumer Price Index for all urban consumers rounded to the nearest $1,000.[87] SSA will publish these amounts annually.[88]

[g] When SSA Will Use a More Recent Tax Year (Major Life Changing Events)

The Secretary of HHS is to establish procedures in conjunction with the Secretary of the Treasury for determining one's modified adjusted gross income for a tax year more recent than the information ordinarily provided by IRS when:[89]

- The beneficiary experiences a major life-changing event.

- The major life-changing event in question results in a significant reduction in your modified adjusted gross income;

- The beneficiary requests that SSA use a more recent tax year's modified adjusted gross income; and

- The beneficiary provides evidence of the event and evidence of the reduction in modified adjusted gross income.

Such events include marriage, divorce, death of a spouse; partial or full work stoppage, loss of income from income-producing property (when the loss is not at the beneficiary's direction, for example, loss of income from real property due to a natural disaster in a Presidentially or Gubernatorially declared disaster area, or due to arson, or destruction of livestock or crops).[90]

Life-changing events also include a reduction or loss of certain forms of pension income due to termination or reorganization of the pension plan, or a

---

[86] Id.

[87] See 71 Fed. Reg. 10,928 (Mar. 3, 2006).

[88] Id.

[89] See proposed 20 C.F.R. §418.1201.

[90] See proposed 20 C.F.R. §418.1205; §418.1225.

scheduled cessation of one's pension benefits.[91] For reductions made in income-related monthly adjustment amount determination based on one's request due to a qualifying major life-changing event, the determination will generally be effective on January 1 of the calendar year for which SSA makes the determination; and if the beneficiary enrolled in Medicare part B after January 1 of the year for which SSA makes an income-related monthly adjustment amount determination based on the beneficiary's request due to a major life-changing event, the determination will be effective the month of the beneficiary's Medicare part B enrollment.[92]

A life-changing event does not include events that affect expenses but not your income; in addition, a life-changing event does not include events that result in the loss of dividend income.[93]

When a beneficiary asks SSA to use a more recent tax year on account of a life-changing event, SSA will ask the beneficiary to provide evidence of the major life-changing event and evidence as to how the event significantly reduced the beneficiary's modified adjusted gross income.[94] Unless SSA has information in its records that raises a doubt about the evidence presented, additional evidence documenting the life-changing event will not be necessary.[95]

The effective date of a income-related monthly adjustment amount initial determination based on a more recent tax year is as follows: when the beneficiary makes the request prior to January 1, 2007, SSA' initial determination is effective on January 1, 2007.[96] For requests made during or after 2007 and the beneficiary's modified adjusted gross income for the more recent tax year is significantly reduced as a result of a major life-changing event, SSA' initial determination is generally effective on January 1 of the year in which the beneficiary makes his or her request.[97] If the beneficiary's first month of enrollment or re-enrollment in Medicare part B is after January of the year for which he or she makes a request for use of a more recent tax year, SSA' initial determination is effective on the first day of the beneficiary's entitlement to Medicare Part B enrollment or re-enrollment.[98]

If a beneficiary knows of changes in the information provided to SSA that will result in the use a more recent tax year, the beneficiary is to inform SSA, allowing SSA to ascertain whether the beneficiary's income-related monthly adjustment amount should be eliminated or adjusted.[99] SSA will accept new

---

[91] *See* proposed 20 C.F.R. §418.1205(e).

[92] *See* proposed 20 C.F.R. §418.1230.

[93] *See* proposed 20 C.F.R. §418.1210.

[94] *See* proposed 20 C.F.R. §418.1230.

[95] *See* proposed 20 C.F.R. §418.1220.

[96] *See* proposed §418.1235.

[97] *See* proposed §418.1235(b).

[98] *See* proposed §418.1235(c).

[99] *See* proposed §§418.1245, 418.1250.

modified adjusted gross income information at any time after the beneficiary's request until the end of the calendar year following the more recent tax year(s) SSA used.[100]

[h] Appealing an Income-Related Monthly Adjustment

[i] General Provisions

When SSA decides that a beneficiary must pay an income-related monthly adjustment, and the amount of any adjustment, based on information SSA receives from IRS or the beneficiary, IRS will send the beneficiary a notice of its initial determination, explaining that, if the beneficiary disagrees, he or she may request that SSA reconsider the determination within 60 days after the date the beneficiary receive notice of SSA' initial determination.[101] The notice will explain that the beneficiary may request a new initial determination, rather than reconsideration, if he or she believes the information SSA used in its initial determination was correct, but the beneficiary wants SSA to use different information about his or her modified adjusted gross income.[102]

In making initial determinations and reconsiderations, SSA will use the rules for the administrative review process that it uses for determinations of beneficiary rights regarding non-medical issues under title II of the Act. These are the same rules that are uses when making initial determinations and reconsiderations regarding application for and entitlement to Medicare benefits under 42 C.F.R. §405.904(a)(1).

If dissatisfied with SSA's reconsideration, the beneficiary may request further review, including a hearing before an administrative law judge from the Office of Medicare Hearings and Appeals (OMHA) at HHS, review by the Medicare Appeals Council (MAC) and judicial review, consistent with 42 C.F.R. Part 405, Subpart I.[103] As part of the request, the beneficiary will be required to provide consent to HHS for the agency to release relevant tax return information to OMHA or the MAC for the purposes of adjudicating any appeal of the amount of an income-related adjustment to the Part B premium subsidy and for any judicial review of that appeal.[104]

An initial determination is the determination SSA will make about a beneficiary's income-related monthly adjustment amount that is subject to administrative review.[105] For the purposes of administering the income-related

---

[100] *See* proposed §418.1245.

[101] *See* 71 Fed. Reg. 10,929 (Mar. 3, 2006); proposed §418.1305.

[102] *See* proposed §§418.1315, 418.1320.

[103] *See* proposed 20 C.F.R. §418.1330; *see also* 71 Fed. Reg. 10,929 (Mar. 3, 2006).

[104] *See* proposed 20 C.F.R. §418.1340.

[105] *See* proposed 20 C.F.R. §§418.1303–418.1310.

monthly adjustment amount, initial determinations include but are not limited to determinations about: (a) the amount of the beneficiary's income-related monthly adjustment amount based on information provided by IRS; and (b) any change in one's income-related monthly adjustment amount based on a request for a new determination.[106]

[ii] New Initial Determination

SSA proposes to establish a new procedure a request for a "new initial determination"—that a beneficiary may use when he or she does not dispute the accuracy of the IRS modified adjusted gross income information SSA used, or the determination SSA made based on that information, but the beneficiary wants SSA to use different information.[107] The beneficiary may provide evidence of his or her modified adjusted gross income for a more recent tax year than the information provided by IRS when the beneficiary has experienced a major life-changing event that significantly reduces his or her income or when IRS has provided modified adjusted gross income information from three years prior to the premium effective year and the beneficiary supplies a retained copy of his or her federal income tax return for the tax year two years prior.[108]

SSA proposes to establish this alternative procedure in view of the nature of the information that it is required by the MMA to use in making determinations regarding the income-related monthly adjustment amount.[109] SSA anticipates that the use of this new procedure will allow it to make timely adjustments when beneficiaries update information about their modified adjusted gross income, or when they prove the IRS information SSA used is incorrect.[110] This process does not affect the beneficiary's right to appeal any initial determination that SSA makes about a beneficiary's income-related monthly adjustment amount, but allows the beneficiary to choose an alternative of requesting that SSA use other information to make a new initial determination.[111]

[D] Copayments and Deductibles

Under Part B, a beneficiary is responsible for an annual deductible and co-payment (or coinsurance amount) for covered items and services,[112] which is based

---

[106] *See* proposed 20 C.F.R. §418.1305.

[107] *See* proposed 20 C.F.R. §418.1320.

[108] *Id.*

[109] *See* 71 Fed. Reg. 10,929 (Mar. 3, 2006).

[110] *Id.*

[111] *Id.*

[112] 42 U.S.C. §1395l.

on the Medicare-approved amount (not the actual charge) for incurred expenses.[113] The annual deductible is offset against first incurred expenses in a given calendar year.[114]

Generally, Medicare requires beneficiaries to pay a 20 percent copayment amount based on the Medicare-approved amount for most Part B services.[115] Medicare then reimburses the Part B provider or supplier 80 percent of the Medicare-approved amount.[116]

§6.03 COVERED MEDICAL AND OTHER HEALTH CARE SERVICES

[A] Covered Service

[1] Medically Reasonable and Necessary Medical and Other Health Services

Medicare Part B provides coverage for expenses incurred by beneficiaries for medically reasonable and necessary medical and other health services.[117] Advocates should consult the Medicare Coverage Issues Manual for updates

---

[113] 42 U.S.C. §1395l(b); 42 C.F.R. §410.160. *See* 42 U.S.C. §1395u(b)(3). The Medicare-approved charge is sometimes referred to as the Medicare reasonable charge amount. The reasonable charge amount is a complicated calculation. It is generally the (1) lowest of the physician's actual charge; (2) the physician's customary charge to other Medicare beneficiaries for similar services as determined by the carrier according to its profile of that physician's charges; and (3) the local or geographic prevailing charge recognized by the carrier for similar services provided by physicians to Medicare patients. *See also* 42 C.F.R. §405.501.

[114] *See* note 42.

[115] 42 U.S.C. §1395l(a); 42 C.F.R. §410.152(b). (Exceptions include clinical diagnostic laboratory tests provided by laboratories and physicians who participate in the Medicare assignment program; home health care; used durable medical equipment that is purchased at a price that is at least 25 percent less than the reasonable charge for comparable new equipment; outpatient and ambulatory surgical services; pneumococcal vaccine; donation of a kidney for transplant surgery.) *See also* list of covered services found below. Note, too, that with respect to outpatient hospital services reimbursed under Part B, the beneficiary copayment amount was being based on actual charges rather than the Medicare-approved amount. *See* Stephenson v. Shalala, 87 F.3d 350 (9th Cir. 1996). Also, BBA '97 required the establishment of a Prospective Payment System for Hospital Outpatient Department Services, including fee schedules and coinsurance amounts, effective for services on or after January 1, 1999. (Pub. L. No. 105-33, §4523(a), amending 1833(t) of the Social Security Act, 42 U.S.C. §1395l(t).) This payment system has resulted in beneficiaries' sometimes paying substantially more than 20 percent for some outpatient services.

[116] 42 U.S.C. §1395l(a); 42 C.F.R. §410.152(b).

[117] 42 U.S.C. §1395y(a)(1)(A).

and modifications to Medicare coverage policy.[118] Medicare provides coverage for categories of services as follows:[119]

- Physician services, including surgery, consultation, and office and institutional calls (visits), and services and supplies, including drugs and biologicals that cannot be self-administered, furnished incident to a physician's professional service;[120]

- Outpatient rehabilitation services;[121]

- Outpatient hospital services furnished incident to physician services;

- Outpatient physical therapy; outpatient speech pathology services; and diagnostic X-ray tests, laboratory tests, and other diagnostic tests;[122]

- X-ray, radium, and radioactive isotope therapy;

- Surgical dressings, and splints, casts, and other devices used for reduction of fractures and dislocations;

- Rental or purchase of durable medical equipment for use in the patient's home;[123]

- Ambulance service;[124]

- Prosthetic devices that replace all or part of an internal body organ;

- Leg, arm, back, and neck braces and artificial legs, arms, and eyes;

- Certain medical supplies used in connection with home dialysis delivery systems;[125]

---

[118] Medicare Coverage Issues Manual; *see* Center for Medicare and Medicaid Services (CMS) Coverage Issues Manual, CMS Pub. 6, Section 30 (Clinical Trials); Section 35 (Medical Procedures); Section 45 (Supplies-Drugs); Section 50 (Diagnostic Services/Dialysis Equipment); Section 60 (DME/Prosthetic Devices); Section 70 (Braces-Trusses-Artificial Limbs and Eyes); Section 80 (Patient Education Programs); Section 90 (Nursing Services). Note, too, CMS is moving to an online system for its various manuals. Please check <www.cms.hhs.gov/manuals>. They are in the process of "cross-walking" sections and have descriptions of their cross-walking approach. The process is uneven, thus the caution to check the CMS Web site described above for the best information and location of provisions. In addition, the CMS website has undergone a recent re-design which has in some instances further complicated finding items.

[119] 42 U.S.C. §§1395k(a), 1395x; Medicare Carriers Manual, MCM, 100-2, 15, 10 (Oct. 31, 2003). Note old "Coverage and Limitations" materials are being reissued in CMS's "Medicare Benefit Policy Manual."

[120] *See also* 42 C.F.R. §§410.20(b), 410.22–410.25.

[121] *See also* 42 C.F.R. §§410.61, 410.100.

[122] *See also* 42 C.F.R. §§410.61, 410.100.

[123] Rules for customized items of durable medical equipment are located at 42 C.F.R. §414.224.

[124] *See* 42 C.F.R. §410.40.

[125] Special rules governing payment for suppliers of home dialysis supplies and equipment are found at 42 C.F.R. §414.330.

- Rural health clinic (RHC) services;[126]

- Ambulatory surgical center (ASC) services;

- Antigens and blood-clotting factors;

- Influenza, pneumococcal, and hepatitis B vaccines;

- Some health maintenance organization services;

- Some Pap smear screenings;

- Some mammography screenings;[127]

- Qualified psychologist services; and

- Therapeutic shoes for patients with severe diabetic foot disease.

Medicare Part B also covers home health visits not covered under Part A, and outpatient hospital services not reimbursed by an Intermediary (an entity under contract with the Health Care Financing Administration for the administration of Part A services).

It should also be noted that some medical services may be considered for coverage under more than one of the categories of services mentioned above; for example, EKG services. In those instances, if the requirements for one category of service are met, payment is available.[128]

The Balanced Budget Act of 1997 (BBA '97) added a set of preventive services to the Medicare program. They include:

- An annual mammogram for women age 40 and over, effective for mammograms performed on or after January 1, 1998 (deductible does not apply).[129]

- Annual pap smears and pelvic exams for beneficiaries considered at high risk or following an abnormal Pap smear; for women not in these groups, coverage is for Pap smears and pelvic exams once every two years (deductible does not apply).[130]

- [Text with footnote reserved][131]

- Prostate cancer screening for men over age 50 (effective January 1, 2000).[132]

- Colorectal cancer screening tests for beneficiaries age 50 and older. Frequency and payment limits are to be determined by the Secretary. A formula for

---

[126] *See also* 42 C.F.R. §§405.2401–405.2417.

[127] Medicare will pay for annual mammograms for female beneficiaries age 40 and over. The Part B annual deductible is waived for these services.

[128] Medicare Carrier's Manual, MCM, 100-2, 15, 10 (Oct. 31, 2003).

[129] 42 U.S.C. §§1395l(b), 1395m(c)(2)(A).

[130] 42 U.S.C. §§1395l(b), 1395x(nn).

[131] [Reserved.]

[132] 42 U.S.C. §§1395l(h)(1)(A), 1395x(oo).

deductibles and copayments is included in the legislation (effective January 1, 1998).[133] The Part B related deductible for colorectal screenings was eliminated by the DRA, effective January 1, 2007.[134]

- Outpatient diabetes self-management training services, blood testing strips and monitors (effective dates for training services and monitors are July 1, 1998, for testing strips, January 1, 1998).[135]

- Medical nutrition therapy services for beneficiaries who have diabetes or renal disease who have not received diabetes outpatient self-management training services within a time period determined by the Secretary, are not receiving maintenance dialysis for which Medicare payment is being made, and who meet such other criteria determined by the Secretary, effective January 2002.

- Bone mass measurements made on or after July 1, 1998, for qualified high-risk individuals (frequency standards to be established by the Secretary).[136]

- Glaucoma screening for individuals determined to be at high risk for glaucoma, individuals with a family history of glaucoma, and individuals with diabetes, effective January 1, 2002.[137]

- Telehealth services when a beneficiary resides in a rural county designated as a health professional shortage area and where other criteria are met (effective January 1, 1999).[138]

Advocates should also be aware that in making coverage decisions, Medicare uses screens and norms of treatment. These norms and screens generally go to the issue of frequency of use of certain services and procedures. They are not to be used to deny services outright but can be used as a tool for identifying certain usage patterns and trends. When used, beneficiaries are to be provided an opportunity to rebut any unfavorable coverage assumptions made on the basis of such screens and norms.[139]

---

[133] 42 U.S.C. §§1395m, 1395x.

[134] §5113 of the DRA, amending 42 U.S.C. §§1395l and 1395m.

[135] 42 U.S.C. §1395x.

[136] 42 U.S.C. §1395x. High-risk persons include an estrogen-deficient woman at clinical risk for osteoporosis; an individual with vertebral abnormalities; an individual receiving long-term gluco-corticoid steroid therapy; an individual with primary hyperparathyroidism; or an individual being monitored to assess the response to or efficacy of an approved osteoporosis drug therapy.

[137] 42 U.S.C. §1395x(s)(2).

[138] 42 U.S.C. §1395m(m); 42 C.F.R. §410.78.

[139] See Vorster v. Bowen, 709 F. Supp. 934 (C.D. Cal. 1989) (Part B—frequency of service screens); Fox v. Bowen, 656 F. Supp. 1236 (D. Conn. 1987) (Part A—access to physical therapy services in a skilled nursing facility).

The Medicare Prescription Drug, Improvement, and Modernization Act of 2003 (MMA) added more preventive services. These new services include:

- *Preventive Physical Exams.* The exam is for an initial physical exam performed no later than six months after the individual's initial date of coverage under Part B.[140] The term "initial preventive physical examination" means physicians' services consisting of a physical examination (including measurement of height, weight, and blood pressure, and an electrocardiograph) with the goal of health promotion and disease detection and includes education, counseling, and referral with respect to screening and other preventive services described in the (b)(2) section of the provision,[141] but does not include clinical laboratory tests.[142]

- *Cardiovascular Screening Tests.* This is a blood test for the early detection of cardiovascular disease. The tests can only be performed once every two years. The provision is effective on January 1, 2005.[143]

- *Diabetes Laboratory Diagnostic Tests.* The tests include fasting plasma glucose tests as well as other tests and modifications. It applies to individuals at risk of diabetes or who have any combination of the following: hypertension; dyslipidemia; obesity (body mass index greater than or equal to 30kg/m2; previous identification of an elevated impaired glucose tolerance; a risk factor consisting of at least two of the following characteristics: overweight, defined as body mass index greater than 25, but less than 30, kg/m2; a family history of diabetes; a history of gestational diabetes mellitus or delivery of a baby weighing greater than 9 pounds; 65 years of age or older.[144]

- *Abdominal aortic aneurysm screening.* The DRA adds coverage for this screening test for certain Medicare beneficiaries as of January 1, 2007, and eliminates the Medicare Part B Premium for this screening test.[145]

[2] Medicare Caps for Physical Therapy / Speech Pathology Services and Occupational Therapy

[a] *Background*

The BBA '97 placed limitations on the amount of financial coverage in Medicare for beneficiaries receiving outpatient therapy services, including

---

[140] Section 611 of the MMA, adding §1861(ww) and amending §§1861(s)(2), 1833(a)(1), and 1848(j)(3) of the Social Security Act. Effective Jan. 1, 2005, 42 U.S.C. §§1395x(s)(2), 1395l(a)(1), and 1395w-4(j).

[141] *Id. See* §611(b)(1) and (2).

[142] *Id. See* §611(b)(1).

[143] *Id. See* §612 of the MMA, amending §§1861(s)(2) and 1862(a)(1) and adding §1861(xx)(1) to the Social Security Act, 42 U.S.C. §§1395x(s)(2), 1395l(a)(1) and 1395w-4(j).

[144] *Id. See* §613 of the MMA.

[145] DRA §5112, amending 42 U.S.C. §1395x.

physical therapy, speech-language pathology services, and occupational therapy. Two categories were defined, one covering physical therapy services and speech-language pathology services combined, and the other covering occupational therapy services. These so-called "therapy caps" are indexed each year by the Medicare Economic Index (MEI), per the BBA. The caps were intended to become effective in 1999.

In 1999, Congress passed a Balanced Budget Refinement Act that placed a moratorium on the "therapy caps." Except for a short time in 2003, Congress had continued this moratorium through December 2005. The moratorium was not renewed for 2006 though, and the caps were set at $1,740 for each of the two categories.

To compensate for the re-introduction of such a limitation, Congress passed an "exceptions process" in the Deficit Reduction Act of 2005 (signed in February 2006). The exceptions process allows for specific diagnoses and procedures to receive continued Medicare financial coverage even once the beneficiary has met their "therapy cap" for the year. Alternatively, a provider can request an exception if the particular problem to be treated is not automatically covered under the given exceptions. This exceptions process though, as it currently stands, will end January 1, 2007.

[b] Therapy Caps

Two distinct caps were placed on therapy services: one for physical therapy and speech therapy (now labeled speech-language pathology) combined, and the other for occupational therapy services.[146] Each category of services received can receive up to $1740 in Medicare covered expenses. A beneficiary must first cover the deductible, which has been set at $124 for 2006. The beneficiary is also responsible for 20 percent (the co-pay) of the total for the services rendered. Medicare covers 80 percent following the co-pay, up to the $1740 financial limitation for 2006.

[c] Exceptions Process

Either a provider or the beneficiary can submit a request for an exception. Exception requests fall into two categories: (1) those that will be automatically approved ("automatic exceptions") and (2) those that require a "manual" approval by the Medicare contractor ("manual exceptions").[147]

---

[146] DRA, Title V, Subtitle B, Ch. 1, §5107–Revisions to Payments for Therapy Services; *see also* 42 U.S.C. §1395l(g).

[147] CMS Medicare Claims Processing Manual (CMS Pub. 100-04) Ch. 5, §10.2—The Financial Limitation (also released by CMS as a revision notice at: <http://www.cms.hhs.gov/transmittals/downloads/R855CP.pdf>).

In either category, the most important aspect for approval of an exception is the "medical necessity" of the requested therapy. Any request for an exception to a therapy cap requires that the therapy be "medically necessary" for the treatment of the condition.[148]

[i] Automatic Exceptions

Automatic exceptions can cover diagnoses and procedures that are either directly related to the *condition*, any associated *complexities* that may negatively impact recovery from that condition, and/or particular *evaluation* services.

A list of *condition* codes that fall into the "automatically" excepted category can be found at *http://www.cms.hhs.gov/transmittals/downloads/R855CP.pdf*. Diagnoses and procedures that qualify as automatic exceptions do not require specific documentation for submission to the Medicare contractor. Documentation must be maintained in case of a claim review though. Any documentation demonstrating the "medical necessity" of the automatically excepted diagnosis is all that needs to be submitted.

For *evaluation* services to be excepted from the therapy cap, they must be contained in the following list of Outpatient Rehabilitation HCPCS Codes, and will only be excepted from the cap once the cap is reached (a retroactive exception): 92506 (evaluation of speech), 92597 (oral speech device evaluation), 92607 (evaluation for prescription for speech-generating AAC device), 92608 (each additional 30 minutes required for evaluation), 92610-92611-92612-92614-92616 (swallow evaluations), 96105 (assessment of aphasia), 97001 (physical therapy evaluation), 97002 (physical therapy re-evaluation), 97003 (occupational therapy evaluation), 97004 (occupational therapy re-evaluation). These codes are also "automatically" excepted procedures, but again, they are only excepted from the cap once the cap is reached.

Though not specifically stated by CMS, *complexities* appear to be of two varieties: (1) physical ailments that lead to complexities in treating the targeted condition of the body, and (2) complications of management flow leading to a potential delay in treatment.

Depending on the nature of the complexity, an exception should be approved for any complexity affecting the beneficiary's ability to recover from the condition. Complexities due to physical ailments must also be connected to a condition, especially if they are to qualify as an automatic exception. Some complexities though will qualify as an automatic exception even if they are connected to a

---

[148] CMS Medicare Benefit Policy Manual (CMS Pub. 100-02) Ch. 15, §220.3.5—Documentation Requirements for Therapy Services (also released by CMS as a revision notice at: <http://www.cms.hhs.gov/transmittals/downloads/R47BP.pdf>). *See also*, CMS Medicare Program Integrity Manual (CMS Pub. 100-08) Ch. 3, §3.4.1.2.1—Exception From the Uniform Dollar Limitation (also released by CMS as a revision notice at: <http://www.cms.hhs.gov/transmittals/downloads/R140PI.pdf>).

condition that is not specifically listed in the ICD-9 list of automatically excepted diagnoses. This can happen for an unrelated condition that causes a complexity affecting the rate of recovery for the originally diagnosed condition that is the purpose of the therapy. For example, if the beneficiary is experiencing a musculoskeletal problem that is not associated with the condition receiving therapy (example given by CMS: a wrist injury that prevents the use of a cane), but it does impact the ability for the patient to recover, then this complexity can qualify as an automatic exception for any additional treatment required because of the complexity.

"Complexities" due to management flow issues can be excepted for a variety of CMS provided reasons, such as if a beneficiary requires treatment within 30 treatment days of being discharged from a hospital or SNF, or if a beneficiary needs to return to a pre-morbid living situation, or if a beneficiary is unable to reach an outpatient hospital therapy service due to lack of access (thus resulting in approval for treatment at a non-hospital based facility). Additionally, if a beneficiary requires both physical therapy and speech therapy simultaneously, then this particular type of complexity will be excepted once this double treatment reaches the cap.

[ii] Manual Exceptions

If the beneficiary does not qualify for one of the automatic exceptions, either the provider or the beneficiary may request an exception from the Medicare contractor to exceed the cap for a medically necessary procedure. For a so-called "manual" exception, specific documentation must be submitted. Required documentation includes: the initial evaluation or reevaluation, current plan of care, treatment notes, and any progress reports that will provide the contractor with the beneficiary's current state of recovery as well as the reason that therapy needs to be continued.

[iii] Limitations

Only 15 additional days of treatment may be requested at any one time. However, a plan justifying any additional treatment days, including any days beyond the initial 15, must be submitted with the exceptions request.

[d] Contractor's Decision Process

In requesting an exception from the Medicare contractor, if the contractor does not make a decision within ten days, the services are automatically considered "medically necessary" and the requested therapy treatment is automatically approved. The CMS information on this ten day window for contractors to make a decision though infers that the contractor does not need to notify the beneficiary of a decision within those ten days, so the beneficiary or his/her provider may need to inquire after the window has closed to ascertain the determination.

[e] Permanent Exception

One exception, and possibly the loophole in the cap process altogether (at least for beneficiaries), is that the financial limitation, or cap, does not apply to therapy services rendered in an outpatient hospital facility or in emergency rooms. Therefore, beneficiaries that have reached their limit of Medicare coverage for therapy can be referred to an outpatient hospital setting where the therapy cap does not apply. This exception does not include therapy services at SNFs however.

[f] Appeals

CMS's notices on the therapy cap exceptions process notes that because the caps are statutorily based they are difficult to appeal. However, an appeal is obviously not precluded. Advocates should approach these appeals as any other Part B appeal.

[B] Excluded Services

Medicare Part B, as described above, is fairly comprehensive, but not complete. Certain categories of services and procedures are excluded from its purview.[149]

Services are also denied on the basis of local medical review policies (LMRPs). These policies are often hidden and not explicitly discussed in denial motions. Of late, CMS has developed a Web site where LMRPs can be found.[150] There are more than 8,000 LMRPs. Advocates should ask carriers and hearing officers whether an LMRP is the basis of a denial of coverage and ask that the LMRP be made available.

Among the categories of services and procedures that are excluded are the following:

- Services that are not medically reasonable or necessary;

- Custodial care;

- Personal comfort items and services;

- Care that does not meaningfully contribute to the treatment of illness, injury, or a malformed body member;

---

[149] See generally 42 U.S.C. §1395y(a).

[150] See <http://www.LMRP.net>. See also Medicare Coverage Database at <www.cms.hhs.gov/med/search.asp>.

- Prescription drugs that do not require administration by a physician;

- Routine physical checkups;

- Eyeglasses or contact lenses in most cases;

- Eye examinations for purpose of prescribing, fitting, or changing eyeglasses or contact lenses;

- Hearing aids and examinations for hearing aids;

- Immunizations except for pneumococcal and hepatitis B vaccine;

- Orthopedic shoes and other supportive devices for the foot unless intended as an instrumental part of a leg brace;

- Cosmetic surgery;

- Most dental services; and

- Routine foot care.

[C] Waiver of Liability Payment for Certain Excluded Items and Services

As described above, Medicare pays for covered services that are deemed reasonable and necessary, and not otherwise excluded. There are circumstances, however, in which Medicare will pay for excluded services. The general rule is that neither the beneficiary nor the provider knew or should have known that the service at issue was excluded.[151] Further, if Medicare determines that the beneficiary was unaware of an exclusion, but the provider knew or should have known, Medicare will indemnify the beneficiary or release the beneficiary from liability for payment.[152]

Under these circumstances, the provider is not entitled to payment for the excluded service either from the beneficiary or from Medicare.[153] Providers with persistent problems in this regard, or with poor track records, lose the presumption of lack of knowledge of whether an item or service is covered, and their requests for payment for excluded items and services will be denied.[154]

---

[151] 42 U.S.C. §1395pp; 42 C.F.R. §411.400. Provider knowledge of Medicare rules is presumed through written notices of noncoverage from Medicare carriers and intermediaries to providers, utilization review committees, and other communications; beneficiary knowledge is imputed through having received denials of coverage under comparable circumstances. *See* 42 C.F.R. §§411.404, 411.406.

[152] 42 U.S.C. §1395pp; 42 C.F.R. §§411.400 *et seq.*

[153] *Id.*

[154] 42 C.F.R. §411.406.

[D] Special Problem Coverage Areas

[1] Ambulance Service

Ambulance service is covered under Part B of the Medicare Program if certain conditions are met.[155] Generally, the ambulance supplier must meet the ambulance vehicle, staff, billing, and reporting standards established by CMS in regulations,[156] and no payment is made directly or indirectly for ambulance services under Part A.[157] A national fee schedule for ambulance services, starting April 1, 2002, is being phased in over a five-year period.[158]

Ambulance regulations clarify rules defining medical necessity for ambulance transport, amending 42 C.F.R. §410.40 to state that for non-emergency transport, bed confinement is not the sole criterion in determining medical necessity of ambulance transport.[159]

In addition, in April 1, 2002, CMS established a fee schedule for the payment of ambulance services, including requiring ambulance service providers to accept assignment, thus limiting patient liability.[160]

In addition, medical necessity and origin and destination requirements must be met. Payment for ambulance services under Part B is available for ambulance trips within the United States for basic life support (BLS) services and advanced life support (ALS) services, and for paramedic ALS intercept services.[161] CMS, in its recently proposed regulations, is planning to amend its definition of an emergency response entity to mean an ambulance entity that maintains readiness to

---

[155] 42 C.F.R. §410.40. CMS provides for two separate reasonable charge rates for ambulance reimbursement, one for basic life support (BLS) ambulance service and one for advanced life support (ALS) ambulance service. *See* Medicare Claims Processing Manual, 100-4, §15-20.22–20.6. *See also* 415 of the MMA, amending 42 U.S.C. §1395m(l), with respect to rural air ambulance.

[156] 42 C.F.R. §§410.40, 410.41.

[157] 42 C.F.R. §410.10(a)(2).

[158] *See* 42 C.F.R. §414.615.

[159] Amending 42 C.F.R. §410.40(d).

[160] 42 C.F.R. §414.610(a)-(g). New §414.610(b) addresses payment, including mandatory assignment for claims filed on or after April 1, 2002. *See also* 69 Fed. Reg. 40288–40292 (July 1, 2004), adding interim final rules on payment increases for rural and urban ambulance services. This notice implements 414 of the MMA.

[161] 42 C.F.R. §410.40(a)(2)(b)(1)-(3). Paramedic ALS intercept services must be furnished in a rural area as defined in 42 C.F.R. §412.62(f) and must be furnished under contract with one or more volunteer ambulance services that are certified to furnish ambulance service; that furnish services only at the BLS level; and that are prohibited by State law from billing for any service. They can also be furnished by a paramedic ALS intercept supplier certified to furnish ALS services as provided in 42 C.F.R. §410.41(b)(2) and that bills all the recipients who receive ALS intercept services for the entity, regardless of whether those recipients are Medicare beneficiaries. *Id.* For purposes of payment for paramedic intercept ambulance services, a rural area is an area designated as a rural area by any law or regulation of the state or if it is located in a rural census tract of a metropolitan statistical area (as determined under the most recent Goldsmith Modification).

respond to urgent callas at the BLS or ALSI level of service; and responds immediately at BLS or ALSI level of service to 911 calls, the equivalent in areas without a 911 call system or radio calls within a hospital system when the ambulance entity is owned and operated by the hospital.[162]

With respect to medical necessity, ambulance service is available under Medicare only if the services are furnished to a beneficiary with a medical condition such that other modes of transportation are contraindicated.[163] If the ambulance trip is necessary for non-emergency services, the beneficiary must be unable to get up from bed without assistance; the beneficiary must be unable to ambulate; and the beneficiary must be unable to sit in a chair or wheelchair.[164]

Medicare covers scheduled non-emergency ambulance services if the ambulance supplier, in advance of the service, obtains a written order from the treating physician certifying that the medical necessity requirements of the coverage regulations are met. The order must be dated no earlier than 60 days before the ambulance service is provided.[165]

For ambulance service for a resident of a facility who is under the care of a physician, the physician must certify that the trip meets the above described medical necessity requirements within 48 hours after the trip.[166] If the trip is for a

---

With respect to rural areas, CMS in recently proposed regulations, 71 Fed. Reg. 30,359 (May 26, 2006) proposed to amend the definition of rural area to mean "an area located outside an urban area, or a rural census tract within a Metropolitan Statistical Area (MSA) as determined under the most recent version of the Goldsmith modification as determined by the Office of Rural Health Policy of the Health Resources and Services Administration." Definitions applicable to ambulance services, both land and water (referred to as "ground") are found at 42 C.F.R. §414.605.

With respect to specialty care transport (SCT), CMS proposes to amend its definitions to provide that: SCT means the hospital-to-hospital transportation of a critically injured or ill beneficiary by a ground ambulance vehicle, including medically necessary supplies and services, at a level of service beyond the scope of the EMT-Paramedic. SCT is necessary when a beneficiary's condition requires ongoing care that must be furnished by one or more health professionals in an appropriate specialty area, for example, nursing, emergency medicine, respiratory care, cardiovascular care, or a paramedic with additional training." *Id.*

Urban area means a MSA, as defined by the Executive Office of Management and Budget. *Id.*

[162] *See,* proposed 42 C.F.R. §414.605(1), (2), 71 Fed. Reg. 30,364 (May 26, 2006).

[163] 42 U.S.C. §1395x(s)(7); 42 C.F.R. §410.40(d).

[164] 42 C.F.R. §410.40(d)(1)(i)-(iii).

[165] 42 C.F.R. §410.40(d)(2).

[166] 42 C.F.R. §410.40(d)(3)(i). CMS is interpreting its rules such that physician certification can be signed by a physician's assistant, a nurse practitioner, or a clinical nurse specialist, acting under the supervision of the physician, as recognized under state law. Further, for purposes of certification with respect to unscheduled, nonemergency ambulance transports, a registered nurse who is employed by the attending physician or who is an employee of the hospital or facility where the patient is being treated may sign a physician certification statement on oral orders from the physician or other qualified practitioner. Also consult the Web sites of the durable medical equipment regional carriers (DMERCs). Often coverage criteria for DME items are available on the Web.

beneficiary residing at home or in a facility and is not under the direct care of a physician, no certification is required.[167]

Origin and destination requirements for ambulance service coverage are as follows:[168]

- From any point of origin to the nearest hospital, critical access hospital (CAH), or skilled nursing facility that is capable of furnishing the required level and type of care for the beneficiary's illness or injury, including the necessary physician specialists needed to treat the beneficiary's condition;

- From a hospital, CAH, or skilled nursing facility to the beneficiary's home;

- From a skilled nursing facility to the nearest supplier of medically necessary services not available at the skilled nursing facility where the beneficiary is a resident, including the return trip;

- For a beneficiary who is receiving renal dialysis for treatment of end-stage renal disease (ESRD), from the beneficiary's home to the nearest facility that furnishes renal dialysis, including the return trip.

[2] Durable Medical Equipment

[a] General

Coverage is available under Part B for the rental, purchase, or lease of durable medical equipment (DME) for use in the home.[169] Generally, items of DME include such things as iron lungs, wheelchairs, hospital beds, walkers, canes, oxygen systems, and dialysis systems. A physician's order is generally necessary to obtain DME.[170] Under the DME rules, the Medicare program pays 80 percent of the payment basis and schedules established by the Secretary's exclusive authority to set payment amounts under the program.[171]

The issue of whether to rent, purchase, or lease DME is often a problem. The best approach is to work closely with the carrier and physician to determine the appropriate DME for the individual and the coverage rationale for its use. It is also important to understand that Medicare, under guidelines established by the

---

[167] 42 C.F.R. §410.40(d)(3)(ii).

[168] 42 C.F.R. §410.40(e)(1)–(4).

[169] 42 U.S.C. §1395m(a); 42 C.F.R. §410.38. Advocates should consult the Medicare Coverage Issues Manual (CMS Pub. 6) 60, Durable Medical Equipment, for the most up-to-date DME coverage listings. This listing is generally given great weight in the administrative review process and in federal court review. It is particularly helpful in understanding the specific coverage criteria, including medical factors, that are necessary for coverage.

[170] 42 U.S.C. §1395m(a)(11)(B).

[171] 42 U.S.C. §1395m(a)(1)(A), (B), (C).

Secretary, makes the determination of whether DME should be rented, purchased, or leased, and how much Medicare will pay for such equipment.[172]
[Text with footnote reserved][173]

Where customized items of DME are involved, it is important to show how the item is uniquely designed to meet the needs of the particular beneficiary, consistent with Medicare's requirements of medical necessity, and not merely an item of convenience.[174]

[b] Medicare Coverage of Power Mobility Devices

On May 5, 2005, CMS issued its National Coverage Determination (NCD) defining access to Medicare covered mobility assistive equipment (MAEs) such as power wheelchairs, and scooters (three-wheel devices). These devices are under the broad umbrella of power mobility devices (PMDs).[175] In making its coverage determination with the appropriateness of such equipment for a particular beneficiary, CMS has moved away from a chair or bed confined standard, and is now basing coverage decisions on an evaluation of a beneficiary's ability to engage in certain mobility-related activities of daily living such as toileting, feeding, and bathing in customary locations in the home. Where such criteria are met, and properly documented, CMS will consider the item of DME at issue reasonable and necessary as defined in the Medicare law.[176]

In April 2006, CMS issued, through its "Medicare Learning Network," a detailed treatment of access to PMDs, including power wheelchairs and power operated vehicles (POVs).[177] It provides the following useful definitions:[178]

> **Power Mobility Devices:** PMDs are defines as covered items of Durable Medical Equipment (DME) that are in a class of wheelchairs that includes

---

[172] 42 U.S.C. §1395m(a)(1)(C), 1395m(a)(1)(A)–(C); 42 C.F.R. §410.210. Also, note that the Health Care Financing Administration (HCFA) has established a system of DMERCs. *See* 42 U.S.C. §1395m(a)(12). These carriers have established protocols and coverage criteria that they employ in making DME coverage decisions. In many instances, the protocols reflect Medicare national coverage determinations and thus a uniform coverage policy. In other instances, from region to region, DMERCs may employ differing approaches to coverage of the same item or category of DME. *See* Durable Medical Equipment, Prosthesis, Orthotics, and Supplies (DMEPOS), Information Resource for Medicare, <http://www.cms.hhs.gov/suppliers/dmepos>. This resource includes HIPAA information and a Medicare Participating Suppliers Directory by state.

[173] [Reserved.]

[174] *See* 42 C.F.R. §414.224.

[175] *See* Decision Memo for Mobility Assistive Equipment (CAG-00274N), found at: <http://www.cms.hhs.gov/mcd/viewdecisionmemo.asp?id = 143>. Other important citations on access to Power Mobility Devices under Medicare include: the Mobility Assistive Equipment Web Page: <www.cms.hhs.gov/CoverageGenInfo/06_wheelchair.asp>; and Medicare Coverage Data Base: <www.cms.hhs.gov/mcd/search.asp>; Medicare Claims Processing Manual: <www.cms.hhs.gov/Manuals/IOM/list.asp>.

[176] *See* §1862(a)(1)(A) of the Social Security Act, 42 U.S.C. §1395y(a)(1)(A).

[177] *See* <http://www.cms.hhs.gov/MLNProducts/downloads/webWCFS_4-20-06.pdf>.

[178] *Id.*

power wheelchairs (four-wheeled motorized vehicles whose steering is oper-ated by an electronic device or joystick to control direction and turning) or POVs (three- or four-wheeled motorized scooters that are operated by a tiller) that a beneficiary uses in the home.

Power (Motorized) Wheelchairs: Most beneficiaries who require power wheelchairs are non-ambulatory and have severe weakness of the upper extremities due to a neurological or muscular condition. Under the new MAE national coverage policy, power wheelchairs may be medically necessary for beneficiaries who cannot effectively perform Mobility-Related Activities of Daily Living (MRADLs) in the home using a cane, walker, manual operated wheelchair, or a POV/scooter. In addition, the beneficiary must demonstrate the ability to safely and effectively operate the power wheel-chair in the hoe environment.

Power Operated Vehicles (POVs or scooters): These vehicles have been appropriately used in the home environment to improve the ability of chronically disabled persons to cope with normal domestic, vocational, and social activities. Under the new MAE national coverage policy, POVs may be medically necessary for beneficiaries who cannot effectively perform MRADLS in the home using a cane, walker, or manually operated wheelchair. In addition, the beneficiary must demonstrate sufficient strength and postural stability to safely and effectively operate the POV in the home environment.

In its NCD issuance, CMS sets forth new function-based criteria for PMD, setting out an algorithmic process called the "Clinical Criteria for MAE Cover-age." It replaces the older "bed or chair-confined" standard.[179] It is felt that this new approach gives greater consideration to the beneficiary's abilities to engage mobility activities within the home. Moreover, the issuance does not preclude use of the PMD outside the home. The chief concern is to establish that the beneficiary has a mobility limitation such that a PMD is medically necessary and that the beneficiary has the physical and mental ability to use the equipment in the home and is willing to do so. When these factors are appropriately documented by physicians and treating practitioners, the beneficiary is free to use the MOE both in the home, and out in the community (but not primarily for the pursuit of leisure or recreational activities).

In making an assessment whether an item of PMD is appropriate the physi-cian or treating practitioner must conduct a face-to-face evaluation of the beneficiary before writing a prescription. The decision memorandum provides the additional clarification that Medicare no longer restricts the type of physician able to prescribe a PMD. Also, a physician assistant, nurse practitioner, or clinical nurse specialist may prescribe a PMD. In addition the prescription for the PMD must be writing and signed and dated by the physician or treating practitioner who performed the face-to-face examination, and must be received by the PMD sup-plier within 30 days of the face-to-face examination (45 days after the face-to-face examination beginning June 5, 2006). Note, however, a separate face-to-face

---

[179] *See* note 171; <http://www.cms.hhs.gov/MLNProducts/downloads/ webWCFS_4-20-06.pdf>.

examination is not required when (a) the beneficiary is discharged from a hospital if the treating physician or treating practitioner that performed the face-to-face evaluation during the hospital stay issues the PMD prescription and supporting documentation to the supplier with 30 days after the date of discharge (45 days after the date of discharge beginning June 5, 2006); (b) when only accessories for PMDs are being ordered.[180]

Other supporting information that the physician or treating practitioner must provide the supplier of the PMD that includes:[181]

• The medical necessity for the use of the PMD in the home,

• Relevant information from the beneficiary's medical record, and

• Information establishing that the beneficiary or caregiver is capable of operating the PMD.

With respect to prior documentation, CMS clarifies that the information in the record at the face-to-face evaluation will be sufficient to support medical necessity. It notes, however, that prior documentation may be necessary when the information from the face-to-face examination refers to previous notes in the medical record.[182]

[3] National Coverage Determinations

The Medicare statute gives the Secretary the obligation and authority to make determinations about what specific items and services are covered under the Medicare program.[183] CMS uses its national coverage determination process to discharge this responsibility.[184] National coverage decisions are binding on all

---

[180] *See* <http://www.cms.hhs.gov/MLNProducts/downloads/webWCFS_4-20-06.pdf>.

[181] *Id.*

[182] *See* <http://www.cms.hhs.gov/MLNProducts/downloads/webWCFS_4-20-06.pdf>.

[183] 42 U.S.C. §§1395y(a)(1)(A), 1395ff(b)(3), 1395hh. *See also* 42 C.F.R. §§405.732, 405.860, 405.205. *See also* Medicare National Coverage Determinations Manual, <http://www.cms.hhs.gov/manuals/103_cov_determ/ndc103c01oct03.pdf>.

[184] *See* 64 Fed. Reg. 22,619 (Apr. 27, 1999), 54 Fed. Reg. 4,302 (Jan. 30, 1989), and 52 Fed. Reg. 15,560 (Apr. 29, 1987) for a discussion of HCFA's understanding of its authority and background information about the national coverage process; *see also* Linoz v. Heckler, 899 F.2d 871 (9th Cir. 1986); Jameson v. Heckler, [1987-1 Transfer Binder] Medicare & Medicaid Guide (CCH) 36,073 (E.D. Cal. 1987) (regarding Social Security Act §1862(a)(1)(A), 42 U.S.C. §1395y(a), and failure to use the Administrative Procedures Act process for public input into the coverage determinations process). Note current Medicare authority to make national coverage determinations without the requirement of notice-and-comment rule-making procedures, §§1871(a)(2), 1869(b)(3)(B) of the Social Security Act, 42 U.S.C. §§1395hh(a)(2), 1395ff(b)(3)(B). *See also* 68 Fed. Reg. 74,607 (Dec. 24, 2003) (procedures for maintaining code lists in the Negotiated NCDs for Clinical Diagnostic Services).

Medicare carriers, fiscal intermediaries, peer review organizations (also known as quality improvement organizations (QIOs)), health maintenance organizations, competitive medical plans, and health care prepayment plans when published in the *Federal Register*.[185] They may not be set aside by administrative law judges,[186] and the federal courts may only set aside a national coverage determination after it has received and considered the Secretary's rationale for the coverage determination.[187]

Advocates encounter problems with the national coverage determinations process when they seek coverage for new procedures. Problem areas usually revolve around getting access to the national coverage process itself; the lack of the ability to participate in the process in a meaningful way such that information in support of coverage is fairly and fully heard and utilized in making national coverage decisions; and the extremely slow nature of the process itself.

CMS is embarking on new initiatives designed to make more public and open its national coverage process, including the time lines that it uses in making national coverage decisions. The current process, and relevant definitions, effective December 8, 2003, are set out in the new final regulations:[188]

A National Coverage Determination (NCD) is a decision that CMS makes whether to cover a particular service nationally under the Medicare program. It does not include a determination of what code, if any, is assigned to a service or a determination with respect to the amount of payment to be made for the service.[189] NCDs are determined on the basis of the reasonable and necessary criteria of the Social Security Act; are binding on all Medicare carriers, fiscal intermediaries, QIOs, HMOs, CMPs, HCPPs, the Medicare Appeals Council, and administrative law judges (ALJs); an ALJ may not disregard, set aside, or otherwise review an NDC; an ALJ may review the facts of a particular case to determine whether the NCD has been applied correctly to the claim; for initial determinations and NCD challenges arising before October 1, 2002, a court's review of an NCD is limited to whether the record is incomplete or otherwise lacks adequate information to support the validity of the decision, unless the case has been remanded to the Secretary to supplement the record regarding the NCDs, and the court may not invalidate an NCD except upon review of the supplemental record.[190]

---

[185] 42 C.F.R. §405.860(a).

[186] 42 U.S.C §1395ff(b)(3); 42 C.F.R. §§405.732, 405.860. Section 522 of the Medicare, Medicaid, and SCHIP Benefits Improvement and Protection Act of 2000 provides for Departmental Appeals Board (DAB) review of national coverage determinations. A DAB decision would constitute final HHS action and would be subject to judicial review.

[187] 42 U.S.C. §1395ff(b)(3).

[188] *See* 68 Fed. Reg. 63,692 (preamble), pp. 63,715ff (regulatory text). For background discussion, *see* 64 Fed. Reg. 22,619–22,625 (Apr. 27, 1999).

[189] 42 C.F.R. §§400.202 (Definitions specific to Medicare); 405.732 (Review of an NCD).

[190] 42 C.F.R. §§405.732(a)-(c), 405.860(a)-(c), 426.100–426.587 (review of local and national coverage determinations, including the process and timelines for review) (Nov. 7, 2003).

A Local Coverage Determination (LCD) is a decision by a fiscal intermediary or a carrier under Medicare Part A or Part B, whether to cover a particular service on an intermediary-wide or carrier-wide basis in accordance with Medicare's reasonable and necessary criteria; it may provide that a service is not reasonable and necessary for certain diagnoses and/or for certain diagnosis codes; but it does not include a determination of which procedure code, if any, is assigned to a service or a determination with respect to the amount of payment to be made for the service.[191]

With respect to LCD and NCD reviews and individual claim appeals, an aggrieved party (a Medicare beneficiary or the estate of a Medicare beneficiary)[192] must notify the ALJ or the Departmental Appeals Board, as appropriate, regarding the submission and disposition of any pending claim or appeal relating to the subject of the aggrieved party's LCD and NCD complaint; this reporting obligation continues through the entire LCD and NCD review process.[193] Only an aggrieved party may initiate a review of an LCD and NCD and must do so through filing an acceptable complaint.[194] Only currently effective (no drafts or other predecisional material) LCDs or NCDs (or deemed NCDs) may be challenged.[195] During the review of an NCD or LCD, the aggrieved party bears the burden of proof and the burden of persuasion for the issue(s) raised in a complaint; the burden of proof is judged by a preponderance of the evidence.[196]

§6.04   MEDICARE ASSIGNMENT PROGRAM

[A]   Overview

The Medicare assignment program was established in 1984 and initially focused on physicians.[197] The program now includes both physicians and suppliers.[198] Under this program, physicians and suppliers agree to accept the Medicare reasonable charge amount (the Medicare approved amount) as payment in full (no balance billing) with the beneficiary being responsible for a 20 percent copayment.[199]

---

[191] 42 C.F.R. §400.202 (definitions specific to Medicare).

[192] 42 C.F.R. §426.110.

[193] 42 C.F.R. §426.310.

[194] 42 C.F.R. §426.320.

[195] 42 C.F.R. §426.325.

[196] 42 C.F.R. §426.330.

[197] 42 U.S.C. §1395u(b)(4). *See also* Medicare Carriers Manual, Part 3, Chapter XVII, 17000-17002 (Participating Program and Billing Limitations).

[198] *See* 42 C.F.R. §§424.55 (payment to supplier), 414.48 (limits on actual charges of nonparticipating suppliers), 400.202 (definition specific to Medicare, including payment on an assignment-related basis).

[199] 42 U.S.C. §1395u(b)(3)(B)(ii); 42 C.F.R. §410.152. *See also* 42 U.S.C §1395n; 42 C.F.R. §424.55(b).

In order to participate, physicians and suppliers must make an annual election whether to participate and sign a participation agreement. Physicians and suppliers who do not elect to participate may participate on a case-by-case basis.[200] Physicians and suppliers who participate are designated as participating physicians and suppliers, are listed in directories of Medicare participating physicians and suppliers, and receive certain insignia they can use in their offices to identify themselves as participants in the Medicare assignment program. Participating physicians and suppliers also receive a five percent higher Medicare fee schedule amount.[201]

[B] Fee Schedules and Limiting Charge Amounts

Beginning in November 1989, Congress enacted additional physician payment reforms that limited what physicians who do not participate in the Medicare assignment program can charge their Medicare patients, effective January 1, 1991.[202] The current limiting charge amount that nonparticipating physicians can charge their Medicare patients is no more than 115 percent above the Medicare fee schedule amount, which is the recognized payment amount or limiting charge.[203] For example, if Medicare sets the recognized payment amount for a service at $100, even though the nonparticipating physician might bill non-Medicare patients at $175, the physician can bill his or her Medicare patient for the service no more than $115.

Physicians who treat patients eligible for Medicaid, including qualified Medicare beneficiaries (QMBs), must bill on an assignment-only basis.[204] Moreover, if the services of a nonparticipating physician to Medicare beneficiaries are determined not to be medically necessary, the physician must return the billed amount to the beneficiary.[205] With respect to elective surgery costing $500 or

---

[200] 42 U.S.C. §1395u(h)(2)–(6).

[201] 42 U.S.C. §§1395w-4(g), 1395u(b)(4)(A)(iv). *See also* Whitney v. Heckler, 780 F.2d 963, 970-972 (11th Cir. 1986) (upholding the 5 percent cost differential).

[202] *See* Omnibus Budget Reconciliation Act of 1989 (OBRA '89), Pub. L. No. 101-239, 6102 (adding 1848(g) to the Social Security Act, 42 U.S.C. §1395w-4(g) (limitation on beneficiary liability)); 42 C.F.R. §415.48.

[203] 42 U.S.C. §1395w-4(g)(2)(B), (C). It should be noted that states can establish more stringent balance billing limits, given that Congress has not totally preempted the field. See Pennsylvania Med. Soc'y v. Marconis, 942 F.2d 842 (3d Cir 1991); Massachusetts Med. Soc'y v. Dukakis, 815 F.2d 790 (1st Cir. 1987); Medical Soc'y of N.Y. State v. Cuomo, 777 F. Supp. 1157 (S.D.N.Y. 1991); Downhour v. Somani, 85 F.3d 261 (6th Cir.), *cert. denied*, 519 U.S. 965 (1996). In addition, New York Medicare beneficiaries have been found to have a private right of action against hospitals to seek repayment against a hospital for physician overcharges under Medicare and state law that limits charge laws. *See* Medicare Beneficiaries Def. Fund v. Memorial Sloan-Kettering Cancer Ctr., 603 N.Y.S.2d 1016 (Sup. Ct. 1993).

[204] 42 U.S.C. §1395w-4(g)(3) (applies to services furnished on or after April 1, 1990).

[205] 42 C.F.R. §411.408.

more, nonparticipating physicians must provide the beneficiary with written information that sets out the difference in the Medicare reimbursement and the physician's full charge.[206] In addition, physicians must submit all claims, both assigned and unassigned, for their Medicare beneficiaries; they cannot charge extra for this service, and claims have to be submitted within one year of the date of providing services(s) for which reimbursement is sought.[207] Note, too, effective April 1, 2002, all payments for ambulance services are made on an assignment-only basis. Providers can collect from beneficiaries only the unmet Part B deductible and Part B coinsurance amounts.[208]

Congress amended its formula for setting physician fee rates, correcting a formula flaw. The change, effective March 1, 2003, allowed physicians in 2003 through April 14, 2003 to make participation elections.[209]

[C] New Limited Prior Determination Process

Section 938 amends of the MMA, 42 U.S.C. §1395ff(b),[210] to create a, limited prior determination process regarding physician services determined by the Secretary to be subject to the process. Under the process, a participating physician who has permission from the patient or an individual who has received an advance beneficiary notice (ABN) may ask the appropriate Medicare contractor for a determination of whether Medicare will pay for a service before actually receiving the service.

The Secretary may require that the request be accompanied by a description of the physicians' service, supporting medical necessity documentation, the ABN if the requester is the individual, and other appropriate documents. The contractor must then provide a written notice, within 45 days of receipt of the request, as to whether the service is covered, is not covered, or the contractor lacks sufficient information to make a coverage determination. The contractor must inform the beneficiary of the decision if the request was made by the physician.

A determination that a service is covered is binding on the contractor in the absence of fraud or misrepresentation of the facts. If the determination is not favorable, the individual has no appeal rights. However, the individual may still receive the service and have a claim submitted to the contractor. If the claim for services received is denied, the individual may then pursue an appeal through the regular appeals process. Similarly, an individual who decides not to go through the prior determination process, but who chooses instead to receive the service and seek reimbursement, retains current appeals rights.

---

[206] 42 U.S.C. §1395w-4(g).

[207] 42 U.S.C. §1395w-4(g)(4).

[208] 67 Fed. Reg. 9099, at 9134, amending 22 C.F.R. §414.610(a)–(g) by adding new §414.610(b).

[209] *See* 68 Fed. Reg. 9567 (Feb. 28, 2003). *See also* Consolidated Appropriations Resolution of 2003 (CAR), Pub. L. No. 108-7, §402(a), amending §1848(i)(1)(G) of the Social Security Act.

[210] 938 of the MMA, Pub. L. No. 108-173.

The Secretary is to implement the prior determination process no later than June 2005. The process ends or "sunsets" five years later. During this time period, the Secretary also must establish a process for collecting information about instances in which beneficiaries who receive an ABN decide not to receive the service, and must establish an outreach and education program for beneficiaries and providers about the appropriate use of ABNs. The General Accounting Office (GAO) must report on the use of ABNs and the response by beneficiaries within 18 months of enactment, and report on the use of the prior determination process within 36 months of enactment.

[D]   Private Physician Contracts

BBA '97 established an option allowing Medicare beneficiaries to enter into private contracts with their physicians (either a provider group, a network of providers, or an individual provider) to pay privately for services otherwise covered by the Medicare program.[211] Medicare limitations on actual charges and the physician requirement to submit claims do not apply.[212] For purposes of this provision, a Medicare beneficiary is an individual who is entitled to benefits under Part A or enrolled under Part B.[213]

Contracts under this provision are outside the Medicare program and physicians must agree not to bill any Medicare beneficiary for Medicare-covered service for a period of two years and submit a written affidavit to the Secretary of Health and Human Services to that effect.[214] A copy of the affidavit of the physician showing that the physician has advised the beneficiary of his or her rights under this provision must be filed with the Secretary of Health and Human Services within ten days after the first such contract has been signed.[215]

Moreover, the provider of service must warn the beneficiary that Medicare balance billing limits do not apply, and that Medicare Supplemental Insurance (Medigap) may not provide coverage under these circumstances.[216] In addition, the provision stipulates that a Medicare beneficiary who has entered such a contract is free to use his or her Medicare card with other physicians who have not signed such a contract.[217] The new law also provides that such contracts cannot be entered when the beneficiary is facing the need for emergency or urgently needed care.[218]

---

[211] 42 U.S.C. §1395a(b)(1)-(4).

[212] 42 U.S.C. §1395a(b)(4).

[213] *Id.*

[214] 42 U.S.C. §1395a(b)(3).

[215] *Id.*

[216] 42 U.S.C. §1395a(b)(2).

[217] *Id.*

[218] *Id.*

Contracts must clearly indicate that the beneficiary:[219]

- Agrees not to submit a claim (or request that a physician or practitioner submit a claim) to Medicare for covered services;

- Agrees to be responsible, whether through insurance or otherwise, for payment for services provided and that no reimbursement will be provided from Medicare;

- Acknowledges that no fee schedule or balance billing limits will apply to physician or provider charges;

- Acknowledges that Medigap plans do not, and that other supplemental insurance plans may not, elect to make payments for such services because payment is not made under Medicare; and

- Acknowledges that the Medicare beneficiary has the right to use other physicians who have not entered into such contracts.

§6.05   FILING MEDICARE PART B CLAIMS

Claims for Part B services, including physician services and other services reimbursable on a charge basis or fee schedule basis, must be filed no later than the end of the calendar year following the year in which the services were furnished. The time limit on filing claims for services furnished in the last three months of the year is the same as if the services had been furnished in the subsequent year (i.e., December 31 of the following year).[220]

For services furnished on or after September 1, 1990, physicians and suppliers are required to complete and submit both assigned and nonassigned Part B claims for their Medicare patients within 12 months of the date of the services received.[221] Physicians and suppliers who submit claims beyond this time period will have their claims reduced by 10 percent of the amount that would otherwise be paid; physicians who submit nonassigned claims late are subject to monetary penalties.[222]

With respect to the submission of claims, a claim is any writing submitted by or on behalf of the claimant, indicating a request or claim for payment from

---

[219] 42 U.S.C. §1395a(b)(2)(B).

[220] 42 C.F.R §424.44; Medicare Carriers Manual, CMS Pub. 14-3, 100-4, 1-70, 70.1.

[221] 42 U.S.C. §1395w-4(g)(3); Medicare Carriers Manual, CMS Pub. 14-3, 100-1, 1-70, 70.1 *et seq.* Claims submitted for Part B services received from a nonparticipating hospital or for services received out of the United States must be submitted in accordance with the rules described above. *See* 42 C.F.R. §§424.100 *et seq.* See Medicare Claims Processing Manual, CMS, 10.2.1 (revised Oct. 1, 2003); <www.cms.hhs.gov/manuals/104_claims/clm104c01.pdf>. *See also* 42 U.S.C. §1395u(b)(6) (who can receive payment).

[222] 42 U.S.C. §§1395w-4(g)(4).

Medicare in connection with the receipt of medical services. No particular claim form is required, although a variety of Medicare billing forms are prepared and recognized by CMS. Claims should identify the beneficiary and the services received, although the identification of services does not have to be complete. Claims are considered filed when mailed or delivered to CMS, any carrier (entity under contract with CMS to administer Part B claims), or any intermediary (entity under contract with CMS to administer Part A claims).[223]

Carrier jurisdiction for the submission and processing of claims is generally the geographic area in which the physician's or supplier's office is located. If the physician or supplier maintains offices in more than one carrier service area, each office is serviced for that area. If the physician does not maintain an office but uses his or her home address, that address determines the carrier jurisdiction. If the office where the service is rendered is in another carrier's jurisdiction, the claim must be transferred to that carrier.[224]

§6.06 INFORMATION ABOUT COVERAGE

[A] Annual Notice to Beneficiaries

The BBA '97 required the Secretary to provide Medicare beneficiaries with an Annual Notice to Beneficiaries, instructing beneficiaries to check carefully their explanations of benefits or itemized statements for accuracy, along with a toll-free telephone number for reporting errors and questionable charges, including fraud and abuse reporting.[225] The annual notice to beneficiaries also must tell them that they have a right to request of their physician, provider, supplier, or other entity providing services, an itemized statement of Medicare-covered items and services provided.

The requested itemization is to be provided no later than 30 days from the date of the request.[226] Failure to provide the requested itemization can result in civil money penalties of $100 for each such failure.[227] The beneficiary has 90 days from the date of receipt of the itemization to submit a written request to the Secretary for review of the itemization.[228]

---

[223] Medicare Carriers Manual, CMS Pub. 14-3, 100-4, 1-70.7.1.

[224] MCM, CMS Pub. 14-3, 100-4, 1-10.1.1; Medicare Claims Processing Manual, Chapter 21, Medicare Summary Notices, 10.1.1 *et seq.*, <http://www.cms.hhs.gov/manuals/104_claims/clm104c21.pdf>.

[225] 42 U.S.C. §1395b-2. The annual notice requirement became effective on the date of the enactment of BBA '97, Aug. 5, 1997.

[226] 42 U.S.C. §1395b-7.

[227] *Id.* Effective date of the itemization requirement is January 1999.

[228] *Id.*

[B] Explanation of Medicare Benefits

An Explanation of Medicare Benefits (EOMB) must be obtained before a beneficiary has a right to appeal. The EOMB, or initial determination, is the written notice that briefly explains what Medicare will pay on a Part B claim.[229] It is prepared by the carrier.

The EOMB is important to initiating a review of a denial of a service. Following the receipt of an EOMB, the beneficiary is entitled to have the carrier review its unfavorable decision.[230]

Beneficiaries should pay close attention to the EOMB. Many claims are denied in whole or in part due to insufficient information and mistakes. Similarly, it is important to monitor the way in which information about initial determinations is presented on the EOMB. This is an ongoing quality of notice concern.[231] Moreover, the EOMB is likely to be the first document that the beneficiary will get that will have specific, although summary, information about the denial, in whole or in part, of a specific item or service.

Reviews of initial determinations must be filed within six months of the date of the initial determination.[232] Claims can be filed at the local SSA or CMS office or the office of the carrier.[233]

[C] Medicare Summary Notices

Medicare is using its Medicare Summary Notices (MSNs) to inform beneficiaries of action taken on intermediary-processed claims. This applies generally to Medicare Part A services and to Medicare Part B outpatient claims, replacing the EOMB for outpatient claims.[234] The MSN is a summary notice form, containing a title section, claims information section, message section, and appeals information section. It looks much like the EOMB and provides a similar range of information.

---

[229] *See* 42 C.F.R. §405.803(b), providing a list of decisions that are initial determinations. *See generally* 42 C.F.R. §§405.803–405.806.

[230] 42 C.F.R. §405.810.

[231] While CMS is making strides in improving the quality of its notice information throughout the Medicare program, serious quality of notice concerns have been raised over the years. *See* David v. Heckler, 591 F. Supp. 1033 (E.D.N.Y. 1984).

[232] 42 C.F.R. §405.807.

[233] *Id.*

[234] Effective July 1, 2002, the MSN is used by all carriers and intermediaries. Medicare Claims Processing Manual, Chapter 21, MSN, 10.3.2 (basic concepts and approaches) and 10.3.6 (claim information section).

§6.07 APPEALS

[A] Appeals Arising Under Parts A and B of Medicare

New rules regarding Medicare appeals were published in the Federal Register on March 8, 2005, and are codified at Subpart G, of Part 405.[235] For Part B claims, the rules were phased-in over the course of 2005 and fully in place by January 1, 2006. The rules establish a combined Part A and Part B appeals process.

The background to these new rules is that in 2000, Congress enacted legislation designed to streamline and make uniform the appeals systems for claims arising under Parts A and B of Medicare. Although the new provisions were supposed to go into effect in 2002, the Centers for Medicare & Medicaid Services (CMS) only effectuated changes concerning the time for filing appeals from initial decisions and the reduced amount in controversy for hearings on Part B claims. Congress made additional changes to the appeals process in 2003, including authorizing the transfer of administrative law judges (ALJs) from the Social Security Administration (SSA) to the Department of Health and Human Services (HHS), and negating some of the earlier time savings by extending the time in which contractors must complete their decisions.

CMS' regulations, referred to above, implement the changes to the appeals process for Medicare Part A and Part B claims, and to implement changes to ALJ hearing process for all Medicare claims, including managed care claims and future prescription drug claims.[236] For Part B claims that are currently decided by Medicare fiscal intermediaries (for example, outpatient hospital claims), these new appeal rules will apply for all redeterminations issued on or after May 1, 2005. For Part B claims that are currently decided by a Medicare carrier, these new appeal procedures will be effective for redeterminations (the substitute for the current Part B review determination) issued on of after January 1, 2006.[237]

[B] Initial Determinations and Redeterminations

As in the past, the claims process begins when the Medicare contractor issues an initial determination of a claim submitted by a provider. The regulations make clear that the initial determination goes only to the beneficiary, even when the contractor is aware that the beneficiary has an appointed representative. Someone who wants to appeal from the initial determination must submit a written, signed request for a redetermination within 120 days of the initial determination; the regulations assume the notice is received 5 days after the date of the notice. Requests for redeterminations must be filed with the contractor; beneficiaries can no longer file requests with Social Security offices.

---

[235] *See* 42 C.F.R. §§405.701 *et seq.*

[236] 70 Fed. Reg. 11,420 (Mar. 8, 2005).

[237] *Id.* at 11,425.

The regulations also, for the first time, allow providers and suppliers to request appeal of a denial of an initial determination, raising the possibility that both the beneficiary and the provider or supplier will initiate the appeals process. In such a case the Medicare carrier (called "Medicare contractor" in the interim final regulations) must consolidate the appeals. The contractor has 60 days from receipt of the redetermination request to issue a decision. If more than one party files a request, the time period runs from the date the last request is received. For example, if a beneficiary files a redetermination request on day 1, but the provider files on day 50, the 60-day time period for the contractor to act starts on day 50.

Unlike the MSN, the notice of the redetermination will be sent to a beneficiary's appointed representative. The notice will explain the facts, policies, and law relied upon in making the redetermination decision; the right to request a reconsideration and the process for doing so; and a statement of specific missing documents that must be submitted. The notice will state that providers, but not beneficiaries (unless they are represented by a provider), must submit all of their evidence at the next level of review in order for the evidence to be considered at any further stage of the appeals process. It is unclear whether CMS will require contractors to send different notices to beneficiaries and providers, or whether CMS will include in the redetermination notice a statement that evidentiary limitations do not apply to beneficiaries. In addition, contractors will not be required to send redetermination notices to multiple beneficiaries in overpayment cases brought by providers if the beneficiary allegedly has no liability for the claim. It is unclear how the contractor will determine in such cases whether the beneficiary has already paid for the service in question.

The regulations create a new reopening process to be used instead of the redetermination process to correct minor errors or omissions in initial determinations. This process responds to a new section of the Medicare law that allows providers to correct minor mistakes without going through the appeals process. Reopenings can also be used at subsequent levels of review. Questions remain concerning the relationship of the new reopening process and the process for deciding remanded cases, as well as the ability of a contractor to reopen a decision in favor of the beneficiary.

[C] The QICs—Reconsideration Determinations

The 2000 law created a third level of review, the reconsideration. Reconsiderations are conducted by a new group of Medicare contractors called Qualified Independent Contractors (QICs).[238] The use of the QICs became effective for

---

[238] 42 C.F.R. §405.960. The QIC's jurisdiction over reconsideration determinations commenced on May 1, 2005, for all Part A determinations and those Part B determinations made by a QIO or fiscal intermediary. The QIC's jurisdiction over Part B reconsideration determinations for all determination currently made by a Medicare Part B carrier commenced January 1, 2006. See 70 Fed. Reg. 11,424–11,426 (Mar. 8, 2005).

part B claims currently handled by Medicare carriers, with respect to redeterminations issued on or after January 1, 2006. Beneficiaries and other parties to the redetermination have 180 days to request a reconsideration by filing a request at the location indicated on the redetermination notice.[239] Reconsiderations filed by both a beneficiary and a provider or supplier will be consolidated, and the time for the QIC to issue a decision runs from receipt of the last-filed appeal.[240]

The reconsideration level of review is a paper review; CMS states clearly in the preamble to the final regulations that QICs will not be conducting hearings. However, the QIC may solicit the view of the beneficiary.[241] As noted above, if providers or suppliers appeal from the QIO to the QIC, they are required to submit all of the evidence they want considered in the claim to the QIC. Evidence not submitted by providers or suppliers to the QIC may be excluded at subsequent levels of review.[242] However, beneficiaries who appeal (except those who are represented by a provider) may present evidence at further levels of appeal.[243]

The QIC is supposed to complete its reconsideration within 60 days of the reconsideration request.[244] Again, the time frame runs from the last request filed if more than one party seeks reconsideration; the QIC must so notify a party who filed an earlier request.[245] The regulations do not indicate how QICs are supposed to document receipt or how beneficiaries are to know when the 60-day period ends. Although the statute allows a party to the reconsideration to ask for an extension of not more than 14 days for the QIC to conclude the reconsideration, the regulations add 14 days to the reconsideration time frame each time that additional evidence is submitted.[246]

In making its reconsideration determination, the QIC is bound by national coverage determinations (NCDs) promulgated by Medicare and CMS Rulings, as well as statute and regulations.[247] It is not bound by local coverage determinations made by Medicare contractors, nor by Medicare policy issued by CMS itself; however, the QIC must give "substantial deference" to these determinations and policy in making its decision.[248] If the QIC declines to apply them, the QIC's decision must state the reason why they were not followed.[249]

---

[239] 42 C.F.R. §405.962.

[240] 42 C.F.R. §405.964(c).

[241] 70 Fed. Reg. 11,447–11,478 (Mar. 8, 2005).

[242] 42 C.F.R. §405.966(a) and (c).

[243] 42 C.F.R. §405.966(c).

[244] 42 C.F.R. §405.970(a).

[245] 42 C.F.R. §405.970(b)(2).

[246] 42 C.F.R. §405.970(b)(3).

[247] 42 C.F.R. §405.1050(a)(4).

[248] 42 C.F.R. §405.968(b)(1) and (2).

[249] 42 C.F.R. §405.968(b)(3).

[D]   Escalation

The MMA introduced the concept of "escalation" into the Medicare appeals process. Commencing at the reconsideration level of appeal, if a decision is not rendered within a set time frame,[250] a party to the appeal may "escalate" the appeal to the next level. For Part B claims currently processed by a Medicare carrier, the escalation process will not be in effect, with respect to reconsiderations after January 1, 2006. The interim final regulations set out many possible situations in which extensions of the time frame for the adjudicator to render its decision may occur.[251] Among these situations is the submission of additional evidence to the adjudicator by a party.

Generally, however, if a QIC does not issue a timely reconsideration decision (60 days from the date of its receipt of the request for reconsideration), the statute and regulations allow a party to request that the appeal be escalated to the next level of review, the ALJ level. The regulations give the QIC five days to either issue a decision or acknowledge the escalation request and send it to the ALJ level of review. The regulations indicate that an appeal escalated to the ALJ level must be completed within 180 days of receipt, rather than the statutorily mandated 90 days for ALJ decisions. Even at the ALJ level, however, additional extensions of the time frame for issuing a decision can occur.[252]

[E]   Part B Administrative Law Judge Hearings

Under the regulations, beneficiaries and other parties will have 60 days from receipt of the reconsideration determination to file a request for an administrative law judge hearing.[253] The request for hearing must be filed at the address indicated on the reconsideration determination.[254] In addition, a party may escalate to the ALJ hearing from the QIC, when the QIC fails to issue a timely decision.[255] However, if an appeal is escalated to the ALJ, the 90-day time frame for deciding an ALJ appeal is automatically extended to 180 days, with the possibility for additional extensions beyond the 180 days.[256]

---

[250] The time frames are: 60 days for the QIC to render a reconsideration determination; 90 days for an ALJ to issue a hearing decision; 180 days for the Medicare Appeals Council (MAC) to issue its decision.

[251] 42 C.F.R. §§405.970(b) and 42 405.1002(a) [reconsideration level]; 42 C.F.R. §§405.1016(a)–(d) and 405.1104 [administrative law judge level]; 42 C.F.R. §§405.1106(b) and 405.1132 [Medicare Appeals Council level].

[252] Id.

[253] Extension of this 60-day time frame may be granted upon a showing of good cause. 42 C.F.R. §405.1014(c).

[254] 42 C.F.R. §405.1014(b).

[255] 42 C.F.R. §405.1002(b)(1)–(3).

[256] 42 C.F.R. §405.1016(c). Among the bases for an extension are: CMS is a party and a party requests discovery against another party [42 C.F.R. §405.1016(d)]; submission of additional evidence

Many significant changes to the administrative law judge appeal level have been made, and are set forth in the regulations.[257] Not the least of these significant changes is the transfer of jurisdiction for administrative law judge hearing from the Social Security Administration to the U.S. Department of Health and Human Services, a change which was mandated by the MMA. According to CMS, ALJs will operate out of four locations: Miami; Cleveland; Irvine, California; and Falls Church, Virginia. These are the only hearing offices in which Medicare administrative law judges are housed, effective on or after July 1, 2005.[258]

Currently, in-person hearings are all but a thing of the past, except in "special or extraordinary circumstances."[259] Instead, beneficiaries are being offered a video teleconference (VTC) hearing, or if no VTC technology exists in a location near the beneficiary, a telephone hearing.[260]

The regulations do not spell out what constitutes a "special circumstance" that would justify an in-person hearing.[261] Even if such special circumstances are established, the in-person hearing will be for the requestor's own testimony, but not to the entire hearing.[262] In addition, when an in-person hearing is requested and granted, the limited time frame for an ALJ to render his or her decision is deemed waived.[263]

Another important change is that CMS or its contractors may participate in or be made a party to the Administrative Law Judge hearings, with rights to submit "position papers" and present witnesses (if they are "participants") and the right to cross-examine the other party's witnesses (if they are "parties").[264] An administrative law judge may seek to have CMS or its contractors participate or be joined as parties, and CMS itself can request that it be a participant or party.[265] Under the regulations, an ALJ must permit CMS or its contractors to participate or be joined as parties, if they so request.

---

by a party later than ten days after receiving a notice of hearing [42 C.F.R. §405.1018(b)]; a party's request for a copy of all or part of the administrative record [42 C.F.R. §405.1042(b)(2)]; and a granted request for postponement of the hearing [42 C.F.R. §405.1020(h)].

[257] 42 C.F.R. §§405.1004 *et seq.*

[258] *See* <www.cms.hhs.gov>; *see also* 70 Fed. Reg. 11,425 (Mar. 8, 2005).

[259] 42 C.F.R. §405.1020(b)(2).

[260] 42 C.F.R. §405.1020(b).

[261] The preamble to the interim final regulations discusses some circumstances which might warrant an in-person hearing. Among these is when the case "presents complex challenging or novel presentation issues" or based upon "the appellant's proximity to and ability to go to the local hearing office." 70 Fed. Reg. 11,457 (Mar. 8, 2005).

[262] 42 C.F.R. §405.1020(c). These provisions in 42 C.F.R. §405.1020 apply to Part B hearings requested on or after July 1, 2005. Other ALJ provisions discussed herein are not effective for Part B cases that are currently handled by a Medicare carrier until January 1, 2006. 70 Fed. Reg. 11,457 (Mar. 8, 2005).

[263] 42 C.F.R. §405.1020(i)(4).

[264] 42 C.F.R. §§405.1010 (participants) and 405.1012 (parties).

[265] *Id.* and 42 C.F.R. §405.1010(a).

A notice of the hearing must be given to all parties, the Medicare contractor, and the QIC, advising them of the time and date for the hearing at least 20 days prior to the date of its scheduled date.[266] All of those receiving a notice of hearing are required to acknowledge whether they plan to attend the hearing or object to the proposed time and/or place of the hearing.[267] An objection to the time and/or place must be in writing and state the reasons for the objection.[268] If a party objects to the issues as stated in the notice of hearing, that party must notify the ALJ in writing no later than five days prior to the hearing of the objections, and send a copy of the objections to all other parties to the appeal.[269] The ALJ will make a decision with respect to the objections either in writing or at the hearing.[270]

Any new written evidence which a beneficiary wishes to submit must be submitted with the request for hearing or within ten days prior to the scheduled date of the hearing.[271] Evidence may be submitted later than ten days prior to the hearing, but the time frame for the ALJ's issuance of his or her decision is tolled for the period between when the evidence was required to be submitted and when it was actually received.[272] Although providers are generally required to submit all relevant evidence at the QIC level of appeal, they may submit additional evidence if they establish "good cause" for failing to do so earlier.[273] The ALJ must review the new evidence submitted by the provider and notify all parties whether it is excluded.[274]

Although generally the issues at the hearing will include all issues brought out at any prior level of appeal which were not decided in a party's favor, the ALJ may also include as an issue any portion of any prior determination that was decided favorably.[275] The parties must be notified of all issues before the hearing.[276] New issues may be raised at any time prior to the start of the hearing, if those new issues could have a material impact on the claims that are the subject of the request for hearing.[277]

Discovery at the ALJ level of appeal is permissible only when CMS elects to be made a party to the hearing.[278] Discovery is permissible with respect to any

---

[266] 42 C.F.R. §§405.1020(c) and 405.1022(a).

[267] 42 C.F.R. §405.1200(c)(2).

[268] 42 C.F.R. §405.1020(e).

[269] 42 C.F.R. §405.1024(a) and (b).

[270] 42 C.F.R. §405.1024(c).

[271] 42 C.F.R. §405.1018(a). This provision does not apply to unrepresented beneficiaries. 42 C.F.R. §405.1018(d).

[272] 42 C.F.R. §405.1018(b).

[273] 42 C.F.R. §405.1018(c).

[274] 42 C.F.R. §405.1028(a)-(d).

[275] 42 C.F.R. §405.1032(a).

[276] 42 C.F.R. §405.1032.

[277] 42 C.F.R. §405.1032(b). Certain limitations apply. *See* 42 C.F.R. §405.980.

[278] 42 C.F.R. §405.1037(a).

matter that is relevant to the subject matter of the hearing, although the party from whom discovery is sought may raise objections based on the assertion that the material sought is privileged or otherwise protected.[279] Additionally, an ALJ may deny a request for discovery if s/he concludes that the discovery request is unreasonable, unduly burdensome or expensive, or otherwise inappropriate.[280] Discovery is limited. A party may request reasonable production of documents for inspection and copying, but depositions may not be taken unless the deponent agrees or the ALJ finds the proposed deposition is appropriate and necessary.[281] Similarly, requests for admissions and interrogatories are generally not permitted.[282]

The ALJ may hold a prehearing or a posthearing conference, either at his or her own initiative or at the request of a party.[283] The ALJ must inform the parties of the time, place, and purpose of the conference at least seven calendar days prior to the conference date.[284] The ALJ may consider matters in addition to those stated on the notice of hearing, if the parties consent in writing.[285] A record of the hearing will be made, and the ALJ must issue an order stating all agreements and actions resulting from the conference.[286]

An administrative record, including marked exhibits, will be made.[287] Under the interim final regulations, a party may review the record at the hearing or, if a hearing is not held, at any time prior to the issuance of an ALJ decision.[288] However, given that hearings will most often not be held in person, the regulations offer no explanation as to how such a review can be accomplished. A party may request and receive a copy of all or part of the record; however, the party can be asked to pay the costs of providing the requested items.[289]

Once a hearing has been held,[290] the ALJ must issue a written decision that sets out findings of fact, conclusions of law, and the reasons for the decision.[291] The decision must be mailed to each party, the Medicare contractors, and the QIC.[292]

---

[279] 42 C.F.R. §405.1037(a)(2).

[280] Id.

[281] 42 C.F.R. §405.1037(b)(1) and (2).

[282] 42 C.F.R. §405.1037(b)(3).

[283] 42 C.F.R. §405.1040.

[284] 42 C.F.R. §405.1040(b).

[285] 42 C.F.R. §405.1040(c).

[286] Id. and §405.1404(d).

[287] 42 C.F.R. §405.1042.

[288] 42 C.F.R. §405.1042(a)(3).

[289] 42 C.F.R. §405.1042(b)(1).

[290] Parties are free to waive the right to a hearing, and have a decision issued solely on the administrative record. 42 C.F.R. §§405.1020(d) and 405.1038(b). In addition, an ALJ may, without holding a hearing, issue a decision that is fully favorable to the appellant(s) if the hearing record supports such a finding. 42 C.F.R. §405.1038(a).

[291] 42 C.F.R. §405.1046(a).

[292] Id.

If an ALJ decision is not rendered within the appropriate time frame for the circumstances of the case, a party may escalate the appeal to the Medicare Appeals Council.[293] The request for escalation must be filed with the ALJ.[294] Once the request is received, the ALJ has five days to either issue a decision, remand the case to the QIC,[295] or notify the parties that a timely decision cannot be issued.[296] At that point, the QIC decision becomes the decision which the MAC will review.[297] In addition, the Medicare Appeals Council may, on its own initiative, remove a case from the ALJ and assume responsibility for holding a hearing and adjudicating the case itself.[298]

[F] Medicare Appeals Council Review[299]

A party who is dissatisfied with an ALJ decision may request review by the Medicare Appeals Council (MAC).[300] A written request for MAC review must be filed with the MAC or the appropriate ALJ office.[301] The request must identify those parts of the ALJ decision (or other determination being appealed, if the case is before the MAC due to escalation) to which the party objects, and state the reasons for those objections.[302] Unless the appellant is an unrepresented beneficiary, the MAC will limit its review to those parts of the decision below specifically identified as objectionable in the request for review.

If a party has requested review because s/he is dissatisfied with an ALJ decision, or has escalated an appeal from the ALJ to the MAC, the MAC will review *de novo* the decision below.[303] A party seeking MAC review does not have

---

[293] 42 C.F.R. §405.1104.

[294] 42 C.F.R. §405.1104(a)(1).

[295] 42 C.F.R. §§405.1104(a)(2) and 405.1034.

[296] 42 C.F.R. §405.1104(b)(2) and (3).

[297] 42 C.F.R. §405.1104(b)(3).

[298] 42 C.F.R. §405.1050.

[299] As with other provisions of the regulations, the provisions described in the section will not be effective in Part B cases currently handled by a Medicare carrier until a QIC reconsideration determination has been issued on or after January 1, 2006, in the case, and an appeal taken from that reconsideration determination.

[300] The MAC may also exercise its "own motion" review. 42 C.F.R. §405.1110. This review can occur upon the initiative of the MAC or when a CMS (or any of its contractors) refers a case to the MAC that they think has been erroneously decided or the decision presents a broad policy or procedural issue that may affect the public interest. This, of course, gives CMS the ability to tightly control the decision-making process and its outcomes, even though the MMA requires the independence of administrative law judges.

[301] 42 C.F.R. §405.1112(a).

[302] 42 C.F.R. §405.1112(b).

[303] 42 C.F.R. §405.1108.

a right to a new hearing; however, the MAC, in its discretion, may conduct any additional proceedings, including holding a hearing.[304]

Generally, absent good cause,[305] no additional evidence may be introduced at the MAC level of appeal, unless the ALJ decision being reviewed decides a new issue about which the parties were not afforded an opportunity to address before the ALJ.[306] However, a party to the MAC review which is before the MAC because of escalation may file a request for a subpoena of specified documents within 10 days of the request for escalation.[307]

The parties have the right to file briefs or other written statements with the MAC.[308] In addition, the MAC may request (but cannot require) CMS or its contractors to file a brief or position paper, if the MAC determines that it is necessary to resolve the issues in the case.[309] In some instances, the MAC may permit, or seek, oral argument on the appeal.[310]

The MAC may dispose of the case in a number of ways: it may remand the case to the ALJ;[311] it may dismiss the request for MAC review;[312] or it may issue a decision.[313] If the MAC fails to issue its decision within the required 90-day time frame from its receipt of the request for MAC review,[314] the appellant may request escalation to federal court.[315] If, upon filing of the escalation request and the lapse of the permissible time plus five additional days, the MAC is unable to issue a decision, remand, or dismissal, it must notify the appellant informing him or her that it is not able to do so.[316] A party may file an action in federal district court within 60 days after the date it receives this notification from the MAC.[317]

---

[304] 42 C.F.R. §405.1108(a) and (d)(3).

[305] 42 C.F.R. §405.1122(c).

[306] 42 C.F.R. §405.1122(a).

[307] 42 C.F.R. §405.1122(d)(1)–(4).

[308] 42 C.F.R. §405.1120.

[309] *Id.*

[310] 42 C.F.R. §405.1124.

[311] 42 C.F.R. §405.1108(d)(3).

[312] 42 C.F.R. §405.1108(c) and (d)(4) and (5).

[313] 42 C.F.R. §405.1108(a) and (d)(1).

[314] 42 C.F.R. §405.1132. As with the other levels of appeal, the time frame for issuing a determination is subject to various extensions. *See*, for example, 42 C.F.R. §405.1114 [extension when party seeks evidence from the MAC]; 42 C.F.R. §405.1120 [extension when briefs are filed]; 42 C.F.R. §405.1122(e)(2)(ii) [stay upon issuance of subpoena].

[315] 42 C.F.R. §405.1132.

[316] 42 C.F.R. §405.1132(a)(2).

[317] 42 C.F.R. §405.1132(b).

[G] Judicial Review[318]

A party to a MAC decision, who is dissatisfied with that decision, may obtain judicial review if the amount in controversy requirements are met.[319] The civil action must be filed within 60 days after receipt of notice of the MAC decision.[320] Provisions exist in the regulations for applying to the MAC for extension of the filing time.[321] The civil action must be filed in the district court for the judicial district in which the beneficiary resides or, if filed by a provider, in the judicial district where it has its principal place of business.[322] The Secretary of the Department of Health and Human Services (DHHS) in his or her official capacity is the proper defendant.[323] The standard of review for the court is whether the Secretary's decision is supported by substantial evidence.[324]

In addition, Section 932 of the MMA modified 42 U.S.C. §1395ff(b) to create expedited access to the judicial review process whereby beneficiaries, providers, and suppliers can have expedited access to judicial review in certain appeals of Medicare Part A or Part B claims.[325] The new expedited appeals process also applies to provider contract disputes—primarily nursing home enforcement cases.[326] Expedited review is available when it is determined both that the Medicare Appeals Council (MAC) lacks authority to decide a question of law or regulation relevant to the case and that there is no material issue of fact in dispute.[327]

A beneficiary may file a request for expedited access to judicial review at the same time as, or after, filing a request for an ALJ hearing.[328] A review entity made up of three reviewers who are ALJs or members of the DAB has 60 days after receipt of the request to issue a written decision.[329] The review entity may request appropriate documents and materials from the beneficiary to support his or her contention that (1) no material issues of fact exist and (2) the MAC lacks authority to decide the relevant question of law or regulations.[330] If the review entity agrees

---

[318] As with other provisions of the interim final regulations, the provisions described in the section will not be effective in Part B cases currently handled by a Medicare carrier until a QIC reconsideration determination has been issued on or after January 1, 2006, in the case, and an appeal taken from that reconsideration determination.

[319] 42 C.F.R. §405.1136.
[320] 42 C.F.R. §405.1130.
[321] 42 C.F.R. §405.1134.
[322] 42 C.F.R. §405.1136(b).
[323] 42 C.F.R. §405.1136(d).
[324] 42 C.F.R. §405.1136(f).
[325] 42 C.F.R. §405.990.
[326] 42 C.F.R. §405.906(a)–(c); §405.990(e).
[327] 42 C.F.R. §405.990(a)(2).
[328] 42 C.F.R. §405.990(d)(2).
[329] 42 C.F.R. §405.990(a)(1).
[330] 42 C.F.R. §405.990(c).

with the beneficiary's request for expedited review, or if the review entity fails to act within 60 days of receipt of the request, the beneficiary skips ALJ and DAB review and may go directly to district court.[331] If the review entity finds against the beneficiary, she has no further recourse, and may not make another request for expedited review regarding the matter in dispute.[332]

§6.08 APPOINTMENTS OF REPRESENTATIVES AND ATTORNEYS' FEES

The regulations also specify the elements of a proper appointment of representative, its duration, and rules about collection of fees for representing Medicare beneficiaries in an appeal of a Medicare denial.[333] These rules are applicable to all Medicare appeals, including Part B appeals currently being handled by a Medicare carrier, effective May 1, 2005.[334]

A valid appointment of representation form must:

- Be in writing and signed and dated by both the beneficiary and the representative.

- Authorize the representative to act on behalf of the beneficiary and authorize the adjudicator to release identifiable health information to the representative.

- Include an explanation of the purpose and scope of the representation.

- Include the name, phone number, and address for the beneficiary and the representative.

- Include the beneficiary's Medicare health insurance claim number.

- Include the representative's professional status or relationship to the beneficiary.

- Be filed with the entity processing the party's initial determination or appeal.[335]

If a form is defective, the representative will be given an opportunity to correct the defect. Otherwise, the representative will not have the authority to act on behalf of the beneficiary or to receive health information.[336]

The regulations limit the duration of the appointment of representation form to one year. A duly appointed representative may file multiple appeals on behalf of an individual beneficiary during the course of that year, but must submit a copy of the original appointment form with each additional appeal filed. Once an

---

[331] 42 C.F.R. §405.990(f)(4).

[332] 42 C.F.R. §405.990(h)(3)(i).

[333] 42 C.F.R. §§405.910 and 405.912.

[334] 70 Fed. Reg. 11,425 (Mar. 8, 2005).

[335] 42 C.F.R. §405.910(c).

[336] 42 C.F.R. §405.910(d).

appointment of representation form has been filed in a case, the appointment lasts for the duration of the appeal unless it is revoked.[337]

The regulations prohibit an appointed representative from delegating the appointment to another person without the beneficiary's consent. Thus, a family member who already serves as an appointed representative cannot delegate that appointment to an advocate for purposes of pursing an appeal unless the beneficiary signs a written notice. A signed statement is not required where both the appointed and new representatives are attorneys (but not paralegals) in the same law firm or organization. When a beneficiary lacks the capacity to sign an appointment of representation form or form acknowledging delegation of the appointment, state law determines who has authority to authorize representation on his or her behalf.[338]

Under the regulations, a beneficiary's appointed representative (but not a provider or supplier's representative) who wishes to charge a fee for services at the administrative law judge (ALJ) and Medicare Appeals Council (MAC) levels of review must obtain approval of the fee from the Secretary. The regulations also say that no award of fees or costs may be made against the Medicare trust fund, and that limitations on the amount of fees that apply in Social Security and SSI disability cases do not apply to Medicare appeals.[339]

The regulations do not contain a standard by which fee requests will be judged. However, the preamble indicates that guidelines for the application of Equal Access to Justice Act (EAJA) claims before the Secretary may be applicable to Medicare appeals.[340] The preamble further states that HHS will review the guidelines to determine whether they need to be changed in light of the new provision.[341]

The preamble justifies the policy change by saying that a change in the Medicare Act makes provisions concerning approval of fee arrangements from back awards of Social Security disability benefits applicable to Medicare appeals.[342] The preamble goes on to acknowledge, however, that, unlike Social Security cases, there is no back award of benefits from which attorneys can be paid, and that the limitation on Social Security attorneys' fees does not apply.[343]

In appeals brought to federal district court, attorneys' fees are generally available for cases under the Social Security Act, either through the Social Security Act Title II provisions[344] or under the Equal Access to Justice Act (EAJA).[345]

---

[337] 42 C.F.R. §§405.910(e) and 405.912(e).

[338] 42 C.F.R. §405.911(l).

[339] 42 C.F.R. §405.910(f).

[340] 70 Fed. Reg. 11,430 (Mar. 8, 2005).

[341] *Id.*

[342] 70 Fed. Reg. 11,429 (Mar. 8, 2005).

[343] *Id.*

[344] *See* 42 U.S.C. §406(b).

[345] *See* 28 U.S.C. §2412.

Under EAJA, fees are available to prevailing parties against the government in civil cases where the government's position is deemed not "substantially justified" or where there are special circumstances that would make an award unjust.[346] Proving entitlement to benefits is generally regarded as meeting the prevailing party status.[347] Having established prevailing party status, the burden shifts to the government to prove that its position was substantially justified.[348] The government must meet a strong burden of showing that its position was substantially justified.[349] Fees are awarded in accordance with the statute's fee provisions.[350]

---

[346] 28 U.S.C. §2412(d)(1)(A).

[347] *See* McGill v. Secretary of HHS, 712 F.2d 28, 32 (2d Cir. 1983), *cert. denied*, 465 U.S. 1068 (1984).

[348] 28 U.S.C. §2412(d)(1)(A).

[349] Pierce v. Underwood, 487 U.S. 552 (1988).

[350] *See* 28 U.S.C. §2412(d)(2). *See* **Appendix 6-7.**

APPENDIX 6-1

TITLE 42—PUBLIC HEALTH
(CODE OF FEDERAL REGULATIONS):

PART 405—FEDERAL HEALTH INSURANCE
FOR THE AGED AND DISABLED

Subpart H—Appeals Under The Medicare Part B Program
[Revised as of October 1, 2005]

See the chart following §6.07[G].

Sec. 405.801   Part B appeals—general description.

Authority: Secs. 1102, 1842(b)(3)(C), 1869(b), and 1871 of the Social Security Act (42 U.S.C. 1302, 1395u(b)(3)(C), 1395ff(b), and 1395hh).

Source: 32 FR 18028, Dec. 16, 1967, unless otherwise noted. Redesignated at 42 FR 52826, Sept. 30, 1977.

(a) The Medicare carrier makes an initial determination when a request for payment for Part B benefits is submitted. If an individual beneficiary is dissatisfied with the initial determination, he or she may request, and the carrier will perform, a review of the claim. Following the carrier's review determination, the beneficiary may obtain a carrier hearing if the amount remaining in controversy is at least $100. The beneficiary is also entitled to a carrier hearing without the benefit of a review determination when the initial request for payment is not being acted upon with reasonable promptness (as defined in Sec. 405.802). Following the carrier hearing, the beneficiary may obtain a hearing before an ALJ if the amount remaining in controversy is at least $500. If the beneficiary is dissatisfied with the decision of the ALJ, he or she may request the Departmental Appeals Board (DAB) to review the case. Following the action of the DAB, the beneficiary may file suit in Federal district court if the amount remaining in controversy is at least $1,000.

(b) The rights of a beneficiary under paragraph (a) of this section to appeal the carrier's initial determination are granted also to—

(1) A physician or supplier that furnishes services to a beneficiary and that accepts an assignment from the beneficiary, or

(2) A physician who meets the conditions of section 1842(l)(1)(A) of the Act pertaining to refund requirements for nonparticipating physicians who have not taken assignment on the claim(s) at issue.

(c) Procedures governing the determinations by SSA as to whether an individual has met basic Part B entitlement requirements are covered in subpart G of this part and 20 CFR part 404, subpart J. Subparts J and R of 20 CFR part 404 are also applicable to ALJ, DAB, and judicial review conducted under subpart H, except to the extent that specific provisions are contained in this subpart.

[62 FR 25853, May 12, 1997]
***

Sec. 405.807   Request for review of initial determination.

(a) General. A party to an initial determination by a carrier, that is dissatisfied with the initial determination and wants to appeal the matter, may request that the carrier review the determination. The request for review by the party to an initial determination must clearly indicate that he or she is dissatisfied with the initial determination and wants to appeal the matter. The request for review does not constitute a waiver of the party's right to a hearing (under Sec. 405.815) after the review.

(b) Place and method of filing a request. A request by a party for a carrier to review the initial determination may be made in one of the following ways:

(1) In writing and filed at an office of the carrier, SSA, or CMS.

(2) By telephone to the telephone number designated by the carrier as the appropriate number for the receipt of requests for review.

(c) Time of filing request. (1) The carrier must provide a period of 6 months after the date of the notice of the initial determination within which the party to the initial determination may request a review.

(2) The carrier may, upon request by the party, extend the period for requesting the review of the initial determination.

[64 FR 52670, Sept. 30, 1999]
***

Sec. 405.815   Amount in controversy for carrier hearing, ALJ hearing and judicial review.

Any party designated in Sec. 405.822 is entitled to a carrier hearing after a review determination has been made by the carrier if the amount remaining in controversy is $100 or more and the party meets the requirements of Sec. 405.821 of this subpart. To be entitled to a hearing before an ALJ following the carrier hearing, the amount remaining in controversy must be $500 or more, and for judicial review following the ALJ hearing and Departmental Appeals Board Review, the amount remaining in controversy must be $1000 or more.

[59 FR 12182, Mar. 16, 1994, as amended at 61 FR 32348, June 24, 1996]
***

Sec. 405.821   Request for carrier hearing.

(a) A request for a carrier hearing is any clear expression in writing by a claimant asking for a hearing to adjudicate a claim when not acted upon with reasonable promptness or by a party to a review determination who states, in effect, that he or she is dissatisfied with the carrier's review determination and wants further opportunity to appeal the matter to the carrier.

(b) The hearing request must be filed at an office of the carrier or at an office of SSA or CMS.

(c) Except when a carrier hearing is held because the carrier did not act upon a claim with reasonable promptness, a party to the review determination may request a carrier hearing within six months after the date of the notice of the review determination. The carrier may, upon request by the party affected, extend the period for filing the request for hearing.

[59 FR 12183, Mar. 16, 1994, as amended at 62 FR 25855, May 12, 1997]
***

Sec. 405.855   ALJ hearing.

(a) **Right to hearing.** A party to the carrier hearing has a right to a hearing before an ALJ if—

(1) The party files a written request for an ALJ hearing within 60 days after receipt of the notice of the carrier hearing decision; and

(2) The amount remaining in controversy is $500 or more.

(b) **Place of filing hearing request.** The request for an ALJ hearing must be made in writing and filed with the carrier that issued the decision, a Social Security office, or, in the case of a qualified railroad retirement beneficiary, an office of the Railroad Retirement Board.

(c) **Effect of ALJ hearing decision.** (1) An ALJ's decision is binding on all parties to the hearing unless—

(i) The DAB reviews the ALJ decision;

(ii) The DAB does not review the ALJ decision, and the party requests judicial review;

(iii) The decision is revised by the DAB or an ALJ in accordance with the provisions of Sec. 405.750 of this chapter; or

(iv) The expedited appeals process is used.

[62 FR 25854, May 12, 1997]

APPENDIX 6-2

TITLE 42—PUBLIC HEALTH
(CODE OF FEDERAL REGULATIONS):

PART 406—HOSPITAL INSURANCE ELIGIBILITY AND ENTITLEMENT

Subpart C—Premium Hospital Insurance
[Revised as of October 1, 2003]

[Note: These regulations have been compiled and annotated by the editors.]

Sec. 406.24   Special enrollment period.[1]

(a) **Terminology.** As used in this subpart, the following terms have the indicated meanings.

(1) Current employment status has the meaning given this term in Sec. 411.104 of this chapter.

(2) Family member has the meaning given this term in Sec. 411.201 of this chapter.

(3) Group health plan (GHP) and large group health plan (LGHP) have the meanings given those terms in Sec. 411.101 of this chapter, except that the "former employee" language of those definitions does not apply with respect to SEPs because—

(i) Section 1837(i)(1)(A) of the Act explicitly requires that GHP coverage of an individual age 65 or older be by reason of the individual's (or the individual's spouse's) current employment status; and

(ii) The sentence following section 1837(i)(1)(B) of the Act refers to "large group health plan." Under section 1862(b)(1)(B)(i), as amended by OBRA '93, LGHP coverage of a disabled individual must be "by virtue of the individual's or a family member's current employment status with an employer."

(4) Special enrollment period (SEP) is a period provided by statute to enable certain individuals to enroll in Medicare without having to wait for the general enrollment period.

(b) **Duration of SEP.**[2] (1) The SEP includes any month during any part of which—

(i) An individual over age 65 is enrolled in a GHP by reason of the current employment status of the individual or the individual's spouse; or

(ii) An individual under age 65 and disabled—

---

[1] Before August 1986, SEPs were available only for enrollment in supplementary medical insurance, not for enrollment in premium hospital insurance.

[2] Before March 1995, SEPs began on the first day of the first month the individual was no longer covered under a GHP or LGHP by reason of current employment status.

(A) Is enrolled in a GHP by reason of the current employment status of the individual or the individual's spouse; or

(B) Is enrolled in an LGHP by reason of the current employment status of the individual or a member of the individual's family.

(2) The SEP ends on the last day of the eighth consecutive month during which the individual is at no time enrolled in a GHP or an LGHP by reason of current employment status.

(c) Conditions for use of a SEP.[3] In order to use a SEP, the individual must meet the following conditions:

(1) When first eligible to enroll for premium hospital insurance under Sec. 406.20(b) or (c), the individual was—

(i) Age 65 or over and covered under a GHP by reason of the current employment status of the individual or the individual's spouse;

(ii) Under age 65 and covered under an LGHP by reason of the current employment status of the individual or a member of the individual's family; or

(iii) Under age 65 and covered under a GHP by reason of the current employment status of the individual or the individual's spouse.

(2) For all the months thereafter, the individual has maintained coverage either under hospital insurance or a GHP or LGHP.

(d) Special rule: Additional SEPs. (1) Generally, if an individual fails to enroll during any available SEP, he or she is not entitled to any additional SEPs.

(2) However, if an individual fails to enroll during a SEP, because coverage under the same or a different GHP or LGHP was restored before the end of that particular SEP, that failure to enroll does not preclude additional SEPs.

(e) Effective date of coverage. (1) If the individual enrolls in a month during any part of which he or she is covered under a GHP or LGHP on the basis of current employment status, or in the first full month when no longer so covered, coverage begins on the first day of the month of enrollment or, at the individual's option, on the first day of any of the three following months.

(2) If the individual enrolls in any month of the SEP other than the months specified in paragraph (e)(1) of this section, coverage begins on the first day of the month following the month of enrollment.

[61 FR 40346, Aug. 2, 1996]

---

[3] Before August 10, 1993, an individual under age 65 could qualify for a SEP only if he or she had LGHP coverage as an "active individual," which the statute defined as "an employee, employer, self-employed individual (such as the employer), individual associated with the employer in a business relationship, or as a member of the family of any of those persons."

APPENDIX 6-3

TITLE 42—PUBLIC HEALTH
(CODE OF FEDERAL REGULATIONS):

PART 407—SUPPLEMENTARY MEDICAL INSURANCE (SMI) ENROLLMENT AND ENTITLEMENT

Subpart B—Individual Enrollment and Entitlement For SMI
[Revised as of October 1, 2003]

Sec. 407.10   Eligibility to enroll.

(a) Basic rule. Except as specified in paragraph (b) of this section, an individual is eligible to enroll for SMI if he or she—

(1) Is entitled to hospital insurance under any of the rules set forth in Secs. 406.10 through 406.15 of this chapter; or

(2) Meets the following requirements:

(i) Has attained age 65. (An individual is considered to have attained age 65 on the day before the 65th anniversary of his or her birth.)

(ii) Is a resident of the United States.

(iii) Is a citizen of the United States, or an alien lawfully admitted for permanent residence who has resided continuously in the United States during the 5 years preceding the month in which he or she applies for enrollment.

(b) Exception. An individual is not eligible to enroll for SMI if he or she has been convicted of—

(1) Spying, sabotage, treason, or subversive activities under chapter 37, 105, or 115 of title 18 of the United States Code; or

(2) Conspiracy to establish dictatorship under section 4 of the Internal Security Act of 1950.
***

Sec. 407.12   General enrollment provisions.

(a) Opportunity to enroll. (1) An individual who is eligible to enroll for SMI may do so during an initial enrollment period or a general enrollment period as specified in Secs. 407.14 and 407.15. An individual who meets the conditions specified in Sec. 407.20 may enroll during a special enrollment period, as provided in that section.

(2) An individual who fails to enroll during his or her initial enrollment period or whose enrollment has been terminated may enroll or reenroll during a general enrollment period, or, if he or she meets the specified conditions, during a special enrollment period.

(b) Enrollment periods ending on a nonworkday. (1) If an enrollment period ends on a Federal nonworkday, that period is automatically extended to the next succeeding workday.

(2) A Federal nonworkday is any Saturday, Sunday, or Federal legal holiday or a day that is declared by statute or executive order to be a day on which Federal employees are not required to work.
***

Sec. 407.14 Initial enrollment period.

(a) Duration. (1) The initial enrollment period is the 7-month period that begins 3 months before the month an individual first meets the eligibility requirements of Sec. 407.10 and ends 3 months after that first month of eligibility.

(2) In determining the initial enrollment period of an individual who is age 65 or over and eligible for enrollment solely because of entitlement to hospital insurance, the individual is considered as first meeting the eligibility requirements for SMI on the first day he or she becomes entitled to hospital insurance or would have been entitled if he or she filed an application for that program.

(b) Deemed initial enrollment period. (1) SSA or CMS will establish a deemed initial enrollment period for an individual who fails to enroll during the initial enrollment period because of a belief, based on erroneous documentary evidence, that he or she had not yet attained age 65. The period will be established as though the individual had attained age 65 on the date indicated by the incorrect information.

(2) A deemed initial enrollment period established under paragraph (b)(1) of this section is used to determine the individual's premium and right to enroll in a general enrollment period if that is advantageous to the individual.
***

Sec. 407.15 Eligibility to enroll.

(a) Except as specified in paragraph (b) of this section, the general enrollment period is January through March of each calendar year.

(b) An unlimited general enrollment period existed between April 1 and September 30, 1981. Any eligible individual whose initial enrollment period had ended, or whose previous period of entitlement had terminated, could have enrolled or reenrolled during any month of that 6-month period.
***

Sec. 407.17 Automatic enrollment.

(a) Who is automatically enrolled. An individual is automatically enrolled for SMI if he or she:

(1) Resides in the United States, except in Puerto Rico;

(2) Becomes entitled to hospital insurance under any of the provisions set forth in Secs. 406.10 through 406.15 of this chapter; and

(3) Does not decline SMI enrollment.

(b) Opportunity to decline automatic enrollment. (1) SSA will notify an individual that he or she is automatically enrolled under paragraph (a) of this section and grant the individual a specified period (at least 2 months after the month the notice is mailed) to decline enrollment.

(2) The individual may decline enrollment by submitting to SSA or CMS a signed statement that he or she does not wish SMI.

(3) The statement must be submitted before entitlement begins, or if later, within the time limits set in the notice of enrollment.

***

Sec. 407.20 Special enrollment period related to coverage under group health plans.

(a) Terminology—(1) Group health plan (GHP) and large group health plan (LGHP). These terms have the meanings given them in Sec. 411.101 of this chapter except that the "former employee" language of those definitions does not apply with respect to SEPs for the reasons specified in Sec. 406.24(a)(3) of this chapter.

(2) Special enrollment period (SEP). This term has the meaning set forth in Sec. 406.24(a)(4) of this chapter. In order to use a SEP, an individual must meet the conditions of paragraph (b) and of paragraph (c) or (d) of this section, as appropriate.

(b) General rule. All individuals must meet the following conditions:

(1) They are eligible to enroll for SMI on the basis of age or disability, but not on the basis of end-stage renal disease.

(2) When first eligible for SMI coverage (4th month of their initial enrollment period), they were covered under a GHP or LGHP on the basis of current employment status or, if not so covered, they enrolled in SMI during their initial enrollment period; and

(3) For all months thereafter, they maintained coverage under either SMI or a GHP or LGHP. (Generally, if an individual fails to enroll in SMI during any available SEP, he or she is not entitled to any additional SEPs. However, if an individual fails to enroll during a SEP because coverage under the same or a different GHP or LGHP was restored before the end of that particular SEP, that failure to enroll does not preclude additional SEPs.)

(c) Special rule: Individual age 65 or over. For an individual who is or was covered under a GHP, coverage must be by reason of the current employment status of the individual or the individual's spouse.

(d) Special rules: Disabled individual.[1] Individuals entitled on the basis of disability (but not on the basis of end-stage renal disease) must meet conditions that vary depending on whether they were covered under a GHP or an LGHP.

(1) For a disabled individual who is or was covered under a GHP, coverage must be on the basis of the current employment status of the individual or the individual's spouse.

(2) For a disabled individual who is or was covered under an LGHP, coverage must be as follows:

(i) Before August 10, 1993, as an "active individual," that is, as an employee, employer, self-employed individual (such as the employer), individual associated with the employer in a business relationship, or as a member of the family of any of those persons.

(ii) On or after August 10, 1993, by reason of current employment status of the individual or a member of the individual's family.

(e) Effective date of coverage. The rule set forth in Sec. 406.24(d) for Medicare Part A applies equally to Medicare Part B.

[61 FR 40346, Aug. 2, 1996]
***

Sec. 407.25   Beginning of entitlement: Individual enrollment.

The following apply whether an individual is self-enrolled or automatically enrolled in SMI:

(a) Enrollment during initial enrollment period. (1) If an individual enrolls during the first three months of the initial enrollment period, entitlement begins with the first month of eligibility.

(2) If an individual enrolls during the fourth month of the initial enrollment period, entitlement begins with the following month.

(3) If an individual enrolls during the fifth month of the initial enrollment period, entitlement begins with the second month after the month of enrollment.

(4) If an individual enrolls in either of the last two months of the initial enrollment period, entitlement begins with the third month after the month of enrollment.

(5) **Example.** An individual first meets the eligibility requirements for enrollment in April. The initial enrollment period is January through July. The month in

---

[1] Under the current statute, the SEP provision applicable to disabled individuals covered under an LGHP expires in September 1998. Unless Congress changes that date, the last SEP available under those provisions will begin with June 1998.

which the individual enrolls determines the month that begins the period of entitlement, as follows:

Enrolls in initial enrollment period	Entitlement begins on—
January	April 1 (month eligibility requirements first met)
February	April 1
March	April 1
April	May 1 (month following month of enrollment)
May	July 1 (second month after month of enrollment)
June	September 1 (third month after month of enrollment)
July	October 1 (third month after month of enrollment)

(b) Enrollment or reenrollment during general enrollment period. (1) If an individual enrolls or reenrolls during a general enrollment period before April 1, 1981, or after September 30, 1981, entitlement begins on July 1 of that calendar year.

(2) If an individual enrolled or reenrolled during the general enrollment period between April 1, 1981, and September 20, 1981, entitlement began with the third month after the month in which the enrollment request was filed.

(c) Enrollment or reenrollment during a SEP. The rules set forth in Sec. 406.24(d) of this chapter apply.

[53 FR 47204, Nov. 22, 1988, as amended at 61 FR 40347, Aug. 2, 1996]
***

Sec. 407.32 Prejudice to enrollment rights because of Federal Government misrepresentation, inaction, or error.

If an individual's enrollment or nonenrollment in SMI is unintentional, inadvertent, or erroneous because of the error, misrepresentation, or inaction of a Federal employee or any person authorized by the Federal Government to act in its behalf, the Social Security Administration or CMS may take whatever action it determines is necessary to provide appropriate relief. The action may include:

(a) Designation of a special initial or general enrollment period;

(b) Designation of an entitlement period based on that enrollment period;

(c) Adjustment of premiums;

(d) Any combination of actions under paragraphs (a) through (c) of this section; or

(e) Any other remedial action that may be necessary to correct or eliminate the effects of the error, misrepresentation, or inaction.

APPENDIX 6-4

TITLE 42—PUBLIC HEALTH
(CODE OF FEDERAL REGULATIONS):

PART 408—PREMIUMS FOR SUPPLEMENTARY
MEDICAL INSURANCE

Subpart B—Amount of Monthly Premiums
[Revised as of October 1, 2003]

Sec. 408.22 Increased premiums for late enrollment and for reenrollment.

For an individual who enrolls after expiration of his or her initial enrollment period or reenrolls after termination of a coverage period, the standard monthly premium determined under Sec. 408.20 is increased by ten percent for each full twelve months in the periods specified in Secs. 408.24 and 408.25.

APPENDIX 6-5

TITLE 42—PUBLIC HEALTH
(CODE OF FEDERAL REGULATIONS):

PART 410—SUPPLEMENTARY MEDICAL INSURANCE
(SMI) BENEFITS

Subpart B—Medical and Other Health Services
[Revised as of October 1, 2003]

Sec. 410.10   Medical and other health services: Included services.

Subject to the conditions and limitations specified in this subpart, "medical and other health services" includes the following services:

(a) Physicians' services.

(b) Services and supplies furnished incident to a physician's professional services, of kinds that are commonly furnished in physicians' offices and are commonly either furnished without charge or included in the physicians' bills.

(c) Services and supplies, including partial hospitalization services, that are incident to physician services and are furnished to outpatients by or under arrangements made by a hospital or a CAH.

(d) Diagnostic services furnished to outpatients by or under arrangements made by a hospital or a CAH if the services are services that the hospital or CAH ordinarily furnishes to its outpatients for diagnostic study.

(e) Diagnostic laboratory and X-ray tests (including diagnostic mammography that meets the conditions for coverage specified in Sec. 410.34(b) of this subpart) and other diagnostic tests.

(f) X-ray therapy and other radiation therapy services.

(g) Medical supplies, appliances, and devices.

(h) Durable medical equipment.

(i) Ambulance services.

(j) Rural health clinic services.

(k) Home dialysis supplies and equipment; on or after July 1, 1991, epoetin (EPO) for home dialysis patients, and, on or after January 1, 1994, for dialysis patients, competent to use the drug; self-care home dialysis support services; and institutional dialysis services and supplies.

(l) Pneumococcal vaccinations.

(m) Outpatient physical therapy and speech pathology services.

(n) Cardiac pacemakers and pacemaker leads.

(o) Additional services furnished to enrollees of HMOs or CMPs, as described in Sec. 410.58.

(p) Hepatitis B vaccine.

(q) Blood clotting factors for hemophilia patients competent to use these factors without medical or other supervision.

(r) Screening mammography services.

(s) Federally qualified health center services.

(t) Services of a certified registered nurse anesthetist or an anesthesiologist's assistant.

(u) Prescription drugs used in immunosuppressive therapy.

(v) Clinical psychologist services and services and supplies furnished as an incident to the services of a clinical psychologist, as provided in Sec. 410.71.

(w) Clinical social worker services, as provided in Sec. 410.73.

(x) Services of physicians and other practitioners furnished in or at the direction of an HIS or Indian tribe hospital or clinic.

[51 FR 41339, Nov. 14, 1986, as amended at 52 FR 27765, July 23, 1987; 55 FR 22790, June 4, 1990; 55 FR 53522, Dec. 31, 1990; 56 FR 8841, Mar. 1, 1991; 56 FR 43709, Sept. 4, 1991; 57 FR 24981, June 12, 1992; 57 FR 33896, July 31, 1992; 58 FR 30668, May 26, 1993; 59 FR 26959, May 25, 1994; 59 FR 49833, Sept. 30, 1994; 60 FR 8955, Feb. 16, 1995; 63 FR 20128, Apr. 23, 1998; 66 FR 55328, Nov. 1, 2001]
***

Sec. 410.12　Medical and other health services: Basic conditions and limitations.

(a) **Basic conditions.** The medical and other health services specified in Sec. 410.10 are covered by Medicare Part B only if they are not excluded under subpart A of part 411 of this chapter, and if they meet the following conditions:

(1) When the services must be furnished. The services must be furnished while the individual is in a period of entitlement. (The rules on entitlement are set forth in part 406 of this chapter.)

(2) By whom the services must be furnished. The services must be furnished by a facility or other entity as specified in Secs. 410.14 through 410.69.

(3) Physician certification and recertification requirements. If the services are subject to physician certification requirements, they must be certified as being medically necessary, and as meeting other applicable requirements, in accordance with subpart B of part 424 of this chapter.

(b) **Limitations on payment.** Payment for medical and other health services is subject to limitations on the amounts of payment as specified in Secs. 410.152 and 410.155 and to the annual and blood deductibles as set forth in Secs. 410.160 and 410.161.

[51 FR 41339, Nov. 14, 1986, as amended at 53 FR 6648, Mar. 2, 1988; 57 FR 33896, July 31, 1992]
***

Sec. 410.14 Special requirements for services furnished outside the United States.

Medicare Part B pays for physicians' services and ambulance services furnished outside the United States if the services meet the applicable conditions of Sec. 410.12 and are furnished in connection with covered inpatient hospital services that meet the specific requirements and conditions set forth in subpart H of part 424 of this chapter.

[51 FR 41339, Nov. 14, 1986, as amended at 53 FR 6648, Mar. 2, 1988]
***

Sec. 410.20 Physicians' services.

(a) **Included services.** Medicare Part B pays for physicians' services, including diagnosis, therapy, surgery, consultations, and home, office, and institutional calls.

(b) **By whom services must be furnished.** Medicare Part B pays for the services specified in paragraph (a) of this section if they are furnished by one of the following professionals who is legally authorized to practice by the State in which he or she performs the functions or actions, and who is acting within the scope of his or her license.

(1) A doctor of medicine or osteopathy, including an osteopathic practitioner recognized in section 1101(a)(7) of the Act.

(2) A doctor of dental surgery or dental medicine.

(3) A doctor of podiatric medicine.

(4) A doctor of optometry.

(5) A chiropractor who meets the qualifications specified in Sec. 410.22.

(c) **Limitations on services.** The Services specified in paragraph (a) of this section may be covered under Medicare Part B if they are furnished within the limitations specified in Secs. 410.22 through 410.25.
***

Sec. 410.22 Limitations on services of an optometrist.

Medicare Part B pays for the services of a doctor of optometry, which he or she is legally authorized to perform in the State in which he or she performs them, if the services are among those described in section 1861(s) of the Act and Sec. 410.10 of this part.

[64 FR 59439, Nov. 2, 1999. Redesignated at 66 FR 55328, Nov. 1, 2001]
***

Sec. 410.23   Screening for glaucoma: Conditions for and limitations on coverage.

(a) Definitions. As used in this section, the following definitions apply:

(1) Direct supervision in the office setting means the optometrist or the ophthalmologist must be present in the office suite and be immediately available to furnish assistance and direction throughout the performance of the procedure. It does not mean the physician must be present in the room when the procedure is performed.

(2) Eligible beneficiary means individuals in the following high risk categories:

(i) Individual with diabetes mellitus;

(ii) Individual with a family history of glaucoma; or

(iii) African-Americans age 50 and over.

(3) Screening for glaucoma means the following procedures furnished to an individual for the early detection of glaucoma:

(i) A dilated eye examination with an intraocular pressure measurement.

(ii) A direct ophthalmoscopy examination, or a slit-lamp biomicroscopic examination.

(b) Condition for coverage of screening for glaucoma. Medicare Part B pays for glaucoma screening examinations provided to eligible beneficiaries as described in paragraph (a)(2) of this section if they are furnished by or under the direct supervision in the office setting of an optometrist or ophthalmologist who is legally authorized to perform these services under State law (or the State regulatory mechanism provided by State law) of the State in which the services are furnished, as would otherwise be covered if furnished by a physician or incident to a physician's professional service.

(c) Limitations on coverage of glaucoma screening examinations.

(1) Payment may not be made for a glaucoma screening examination that is performed for an individual who is not an eligible beneficiary as described in paragraph (a)(2) of this section.

(2) Payment may be made for a glaucoma screening examination that is performed on an individual who is an eligible beneficiary as described in paragraph (a)(2) of this section, after at least 11 months have passed following the month in which the last glaucoma screening examination was performed.

[66 FR 55328, Nov. 1, 2001]
***

Sec. 410.24   Limitations on services of a doctor of dental surgery or dental medicine.

Medicare Part B pays for services furnished by a doctor of dental surgery or dental medicine within the scope of his or her license, if the services would be covered as physicians' services when performed by a doctor of medicine or osteopathy.[1]

[51 FR 41339, Nov. 14, 1986, as amended at 56 FR 8852, Mar. 1, 1991]
***

Sec. 410.25 Limitations on services of a podiatrist.

Medicare Part B pays for the services of a doctor of podiatric medicine, acting within the scope of his or her license, if the services would be covered as physicians' services when performed by a doctor of medicine or osteopathy.
***

Sec. 410.26 Services and supplies incident to a physician's professional services: Conditions.

(a) Definitions. For purposes of this section, the following definitions apply:

(1) Auxiliary personnel means any individual who is acting under the supervision of a physician (or other practitioner), regardless of whether the individual is an employee, leased employee, or independent contractor of the physician (or other practitioner) or of the same entity that employs or contracts with the physician (or other practitioner).

(2) Direct supervision means the level of supervision by the physician (or other practitioner) of auxiliary personnel as defined in Sec. 410.32(b)(3)(ii).

(3) Independent contractor means an individual (or an entity that has hired such an individual) who performs part-time or full-time work for which the individual (or the entity that has hired such an individual) receives an IRS-1099 form.

(4) Leased employment means an employment relationship that is recognized by applicable State law and that is established by two employers by a contract such that one employer hires the services of an employee of the other employer.

(5) Noninstitutional setting means all settings other than a hospital or skilled nursing facility.

(6) Practitioner means a non-physician practitioner who is authorized by the Act to receive payment for services incident to his or her own services.

(7) Services and supplies means any services or supplies (including drugs or biologicals that are not usually self-administered) that are included in section 1861(s)(2)(A) of the Act and are not specifically listed in the Act as a separate benefit included in the Medicare program.

---

[1] For services furnished before July 1, 1981, Medicare Part B paid only for the following services of a doctor of dental surgery or dental medicine:

Surgery on the jaw or any adjoining structure, and
Reduction of a fracture of the jaw or other facial bone.

(b) **Medicare Part B pays for services and supplies incident to the service of a physician (or other practitioner).**

(1) Services and supplies must be furnished in a noninstitutional setting to noninstitutional patients.

(2) Services and supplies must be an integral, though incidental, part of the service of a physician (or other practitioner) in the course of diagnosis or treatment of an injury or illness.

(3) Services and supplies must be commonly furnished without charge or included in the bill of a physician (or other practitioner).

(4) Services and supplies must be of a type that are commonly furnished in the office or clinic of a physician (or other practitioner).

(5) Services and supplies must be furnished under the direct supervision of the physician (or other practitioner). The physician (or other practitioner) directly supervising the auxiliary personnel need not be the same physician (or other practitioner) upon whose professional service the incident to service is based.

(6) Services and supplies must be furnished by the physician, practitioner with an incident to benefit, or auxiliary personnel.

(7) A physician (or other practitioner) may be an employee or an independent contractor.

(c) Limitation. Drugs and biologicals are also subject to the limitations specified in Sec. 410.29.

[51 FR 41339, Nov. 14, 1986, as amended at 66 FR 55328, Nov. 1, 2001; 67 FR 20684, Apr. 26, 2002]
***

Sec. 410.27 Outpatient hospital services and supplies incident to physician services: Conditions.

(a) Medicare Part B pays for hospital services and supplies furnished incident to physicians' services to outpatients, including drugs and biologicals that cannot be self-administered, if—

(1) They are furnished—

(i) By or under arrangements made by a participating hospital, except in the case of an SNF resident as provided in Sec. 411.15(p) of this chapter;

(ii) As an integral though incidental part of a physician's services; and

(iii) In the hospital or at a location (other than an RHC or FQHC) that CMS designates as a department of a provider under Sec. 413.65 of this chapter.

(2) In the case of partial hospitalization services, also meet the conditions of paragraph (d) of this section.

(b) Drugs and biologicals are also subject to the limitations specified in Sec. 410.168.

(c) Rules on emergency services furnished to outpatients by nonparticipating hospitals are specified in Sec. 410.168.

(d) Medicare Part B pays for partial hospitalization services if they are—

(1) Prescribed by a physician who certifies and recertifies the need for the services in accordance with subpart B of part 424 of this chapter; and

(2) Furnished under a plan of treatment as required under subpart B of part 424 of this chapter.

(e) Services furnished by an entity other than the hospital are subject to the limitations specified in Sec. 410.42(a).

(f) Services furnished at a location (other than an RHC or an FQHC) that CMS designates as a department of a provider under Sec. 413.65 of this chapter must be under the direct supervision of a physician. "Direct supervision" means the physician must be present and on the premises of the location and immediately available to furnish assistance and direction throughout the performance of the procedure. It does not mean that the physician must be present in the room when the procedure is performed.

[56 FR 8841, Mar. 1, 1991, as amended at 63 FR 26307, May 12, 1998; 65 FR 18536, Apr. 7, 2000]
***

Sec. 410.28   Hospital or CAH diagnostic services furnished to outpatients: Conditions.

(a) Medicare Part B pays for hospital or CAH diagnostic services furnished to outpatients, including drugs and biologicals required in the performance of the services (even if those drugs or biologicals are self-administered), if those services meet the following conditions:

(1) They are furnished by or under arrangements made by a participating hospital or participating CAH, except in the case of an SNF resident as provided in Sec. 411.15(p) of this chapter.

(2) They are ordinarily furnished by, or under arrangements made by, the hospital or CAH to its outpatients for the purpose of diagnostic study.

(3) They would be covered as inpatient hospital services if furnished to an inpatient.

(b) Drugs and biologicals are also subject to the limitations specified in Sec. 410.29(b) and (c).

(c) Diagnostic services furnished by an entity other than the hospital or CAH are subject to the limitations specified in Sec. 410.42(a).

(d) Rules on emergency services furnished to outpatients by nonparticipating hospitals are set forth in subpart G of part 424 of this chapter.

(e) Medicare Part B makes payment under section 1833(t) of the Act for diagnostic services furnished at a facility (other than an RHC or an FQHC) that CMS designates as having provider-based status only when the diagnostic services are furnished under the appropriate level of physician supervision specified by CMS in accordance with the definitions in Sec. 410.32(b)(3)(i), (b)(3)(ii), and (b)(3)(iii). Under general supervision at a facility accorded provider-based status, the training of the nonphysician personnel who actually perform the diagnostic procedure and the maintenance of the necessary equipment and supplies are the continuing responsibility of the facility.

(f) The rules for clinical diagnostic laboratory tests set forth in Secs. 410.32(a) and (d)(2) through (d)(4) of this subpart are applicable to those tests when furnished in hospitals and CAHs.

[51 FR 41339, Nov. 14, 1986, as amended at 58 FR 30668, May 26, 1993; 63 FR 26307, May 12, 1998; 65 FR 18536, Apr. 7, 2000; 66 FR 58809, Nov. 23, 2001]
***

Sec. 410.29   Limitations on drugs and biologicals.

Medicare Part B does not pay for the following:

(a) Except as provided in Sec. 410.28(a) for outpatient diagnostic services and Sec. 410.63(b) for blood clotting factors, and except for EPO, any drug or biological that can be self-administered.

(b) Any drug product that meets all of the following conditions:

(1) The drug product was approved by the Food and Drug Administration (FDA) before October 10, 1962.

(2) The drug product is available only through prescription.

(3) The drug product is the subject of a notice of opportunity for hearing issued under section 505(e) of the Federal Food, Drug, and Cosmetic Act and published in the Federal Register on a proposed order of FDA to withdraw its approval for the drug product because it has determined that the product is less than effective for all its labeled indications.

(4) The drug product is presently not subject to a determination by FDA, made under its efficacy review program, that there is a compelling justification of the drug product's medical need. (21 CFR 310.6 contains an explanation of the efficacy review program.)

(c) Any drug product that is identical, related, or similar, as defined in 21 CFR 310.6, to a drug product that meets the conditions of paragraph (b) of this section.

[51 FR 41339, Nov. 14, 1986, as amended at 55 FR 22790, June 4, 1990; 56 FR 43709, Sept. 4, 1991]
***

Sec. 410.32   Diagnostic x-ray tests, diagnostic laboratory tests, and other diagnostic tests: Conditions.

(a) Ordering diagnostic tests. All diagnostic x-ray tests, diagnostic laboratory tests, and other diagnostic tests must be ordered by the physician who is treating the beneficiary, that is, the physician who furnishes a consultation or treats a beneficiary for a specific medical problem and who uses the results in the management of the beneficiary's specific medical problem. Tests not ordered by the physician who is treating the beneficiary are not reasonable and necessary (*see* Sec. 411.15(k)(1) of this chapter).

(1) **Chiropractic exception.** A physician may order an x-ray to be used by a chiropractor to demonstrate the subluxation of the spine that is the basis for a beneficiary to receive manual manipulation treatments even though the physician does not treat the beneficiary.

(2) **Mammography exception.** A physician who meets the qualification requirements for an interpreting physician under section 354 of the Public Health Service Act as provided in Sec. 410.34(a)(7) may order a diagnostic mammogram based on the findings of a screening mammogram even though the physician does not treat the beneficiary.

(3) **Application to nonphysician practitioners.** Nonphysician practitioners (that is, clinical nurse specialists, clinical psychologists, clinical social workers, nurse-midwives, nurse practitioners, and physician assistants) who furnish services that would be physician services if furnished by a physician, and who are operating within the scope of their authority under State law and within the scope of their Medicare statutory benefit, may be treated the same as physicians treating beneficiaries for the purpose of this paragraph.

(b) **Diagnostic x-ray and other diagnostic tests—(1) Basic rule.** Except as indicated in paragraph (b)(2) of this section, all diagnostic x-ray and other diagnostic tests covered under section 1861(s)(3) of the Act and payable under the physician fee schedule must be furnished under the appropriate level of supervision by a physician as defined in section 1861(r) of the Act. Services furnished without the required level of supervision are not reasonable and necessary (*see* Sec. 411.15(k)(1) of this chapter).

(2) **Exceptions.** The following diagnostic tests payable under the physician fee schedule are excluded from the basic rule set forth in paragraph (b)(1) of this section:

(i) Diagnostic mammography procedures, which are regulated by the Food and Drug Administration.

(ii) Diagnostic tests personally furnished by a qualified audiologist as defined in section 1861(ll)(3) of the Act.

(iii) Diagnostic psychological testing services personally furnished by a clinical psychologist or a qualified independent psychologist as defined in program instructions.

(iv) Diagnostic tests (as established through program instructions) personally performed by a physical therapist who is certified by the American Board of Physical Therapy Specialties as a qualified electrophysiologic clinical specialist and permitted to provide the service under State law.

(3) **Levels of supervision.** Except where otherwise indicated, all diagnostic x-ray and other diagnostic tests subject to this provision and payable under the physician fee schedule must be furnished under at least a general level of physician

supervision as defined in paragraph (b)(3)(i) of this section. In addition, some of these tests also require either direct or personal supervision as defined in paragraphs (b)(3)(ii) or (b)(3)(iii) of this section, respectively. (However, diagnostic tests performed by a physician assistant (PA) that the PA is legally authorized to perform under State law require only a general level of physician supervision.) When direct or personal supervision is required, physician supervision at the specified level is required throughout the performance of the test.

(i) General supervision means the procedure is furnished under the physician's overall direction and control, but the physician's presence is not required during the performance of the procedure. Under general supervision, the training of the nonphysician personnel who actually perform the diagnostic procedure and the maintenance of the necessary equipment and supplies are the continuing responsibility of the physician.

(ii) Direct supervision in the office setting means the physician must be present in the office suite and immediately available to furnish assistance and direction throughout the performance of the procedure. It does not mean that the physician must be present in the room when the procedure is performed.

(iii) Personal supervision means a physician must be in attendance in the room during the performance of the procedure.

(c) Portable x-ray services. Portable x-ray services furnished in a place of residence used as the patient's home are covered if the following conditions are met:

(1) These services are furnished under the general supervision of a physician, as defined in paragraph (b)(3)(i) of this section.

(2) The supplier of these services meets the requirements set forth in part 486, subpart C of this chapter, concerning conditions for coverage for portable x-ray services.

(3) The procedures are limited to—

(i) Skeletal films involving the extremities, pelvis, vertebral column, or skull;

(ii) Chest or abdominal films that do not involve the use of contrast media; and

(iii) Diagnostic mammograms if the approved portable x-ray supplier, as defined in subpart C of part 486 of this chapter, meets the certification requirements of section 354 of the Public Health Service Act, as implemented by 21 CFR part 900, subpart B.

(d) Diagnostic laboratory tests. (1) Who may furnish services. Medicare Part B pays for covered diagnostic laboratory tests that are furnished by any of the following:

(i) A participating hospital or participating RPCH.

(ii) A nonparticipating hospital that meets the requirements for emergency outpatient services specified in subpart G of part 424 of this chapter and the laboratory requirements specified in part 493 of this chapter.

(iii) The office of the patient's attending or consulting physician if that physician is a doctor of medicine, osteopathy, podiatric medicine, dental surgery, or dental medicine.

(iv) An RHC.

(v) A laboratory, if it meets the applicable requirements for laboratories of part 493 of this chapter, including the laboratory of a nonparticipating hospital that does not meet the requirements for emergency outpatient services in subpart G of part 424 of this chapter.

(vi) An FQHC.

(vii) An SNF to its resident under Sec. 411.15(p) of this chapter, either directly (in accordance with Sec. 483.75(k)(1)(i) of this chapter) or under an arrangement (as defined in Sec. 409.3 of this chapter) with another entity described in this paragraph.

(2) Documentation and recordkeeping requirements.

(i) Ordering the service. The physician or (qualified nonphysican practitioner, as defined in paragraph (a)(3) of this section), who orders the service must maintain documentation of medical necessity in the beneficiary's medical record.

(ii) Submitting the claim. The entity submitting the claim must maintain the following documentation:

(A) The documentation that it receives from the ordering physician or nonphysician practitioner.

(B) The documentation that the information that it submitted with the claim accurately reflects the information it received from the ordering physician or nonphysician practitioner.

(iii) Requesting additional information. The entity submitting the claim may request additional diagnostic and other medical information to document that the services it bills are reasonable and necessary. If the entity requests additional documentation, it must request material relevant to the medical necessity of the specific test(s), taking into consideration current rules and regulations on patient confidentiality.

(3) Claims review. (i) Documentation requirements. Upon request by CMS, the entity submitting the claim must provide the following information:

(A) Documentation of the order for the service billed (including information sufficient to enable CMS to identify and contact the ordering physician or nonphysician practitioner).

(B) Documentation showing accurate processing of the order and submission of the claim.

(C) Diagnostic or other medical information supplied to the laboratory by the ordering physician or nonphysician practitioner, including any ICD-9-CM code or narrative description supplied.

(ii) Services that are not reasonable and necessary. If the documentation provided under paragraph (d)(3)(i) of this section does not demonstrate that the service is reasonable and necessary, CMS takes the following actions:

(A) Provides the ordering physician or nonphysician practitioner information sufficient to identify the claim being reviewed.

(B) Requests from the ordering physician or nonphysician practitioner those parts of a beneficiary's medical record that are relevant to the specific claim(s) being reviewed.

(C) If the ordering physician or nonphysician practitioner does not supply the documentation requested, informs the entity submitting the claim(s) that the documentation has not been supplied and denies the claim.

(iii) **Medical necessity.** The entity submitting the claim may request additional diagnostic and other medical information from the ordering physician or nonphysician practitioner to document that the services it bills are reasonable and necessary. If the entity requests additional documentation, it must request material relevant to the medical necessity of the specific test(s), taking into consideration current rules and regulations on patient confidentiality.

(4) **Automatic denial and manual review. (i) General rule.** Except as provided in paragraph (d)(4)(ii) of this section, CMS does not deny a claim for services that exceed utilization parameters without reviewing all relevant documentation that is submitted with the claim (for example, justifications prepared by providers, primary and secondary diagnoses, and copies of medical records).

(ii) **Exceptions.** CMS may automatically deny a claim without manual review if a national coverage decision or LMRP specifies the circumstances under which the service is denied, or the service is specifically excluded from Medicare coverage by law.

(e) **Diagnostic laboratory tests furnished in hospitals and CAHs.** The provisions of paragraphs (a) and (d)(2) through (d)(4), inclusive, of this section apply to all diagnostic laboratory test furnished by hospitals and CAHs to outpatients.

[62 FR 59098, Oct. 31, 1997, as amended at 63 FR 26308, May 12, 1998; 63 FR 53307, Oct. 5, 1998; 63 FR 58906, Nov. 2, 1998; 64 FR 59440, Nov. 2, 1999; 66 FR 58809, Nov. 23, 2001]
***

Sec. 410.34   Mammography services: Conditions for and limitations on coverage.

(a) **Definitions.** As used in this section, the following definitions apply:

(1) Diagnostic mammography means a radiologic procedure furnished to a man or woman with signs or symptoms of breast disease, or a personal history of breast cancer, or a personal history of biopsy-proven benign breast disease, and includes a physician's interpretation of the results of the procedure.

(2) Screening mammography means a radiologic procedure furnished to a woman without signs or symptoms of breast disease, for the purpose of early detection of breast cancer, and includes a physician's interpretation of the results of the procedure.

(3) Supplier of diagnostic mammography means a facility that is certified and responsible for ensuring that all diagnostic mammography services furnished to Medicare beneficiaries meet the conditions for coverage of diagnostic mammography services as specified in paragraph (b) of this section.

(4) Supplier of screening mammography means a facility that is certified and responsible for ensuring that all screening mammography services furnished to Medicare beneficiaries meet the conditions and limitations for coverage of screening mammography services as specified in paragraphs (c) and (d) of this section.

(5) Certificate means the certificate described in 21 CFR 900.2(b) that may be issued to, or renewed for, a facility that meets the requirements for conducting an examination or procedure involving mammography.

(6) Provisional certificate means the provisional certificate described in 21 CFR 900.2(m) that may be issued to a facility to enable the facility to qualify to meet the requirements for conducting an examination or procedure involving mammography.

(7) The term meets the certification requirements of section 354 of the Public Health Service (PHS) Act means that in order to qualify for coverage of its services under the Medicare program, a supplier of diagnostic or screening mammography services must meet the following requirements:

(i) Must have a valid provisional certificate, or a valid certificate, that has been issued by FDA indicating that the supplier meets the certification requirements of section 354 of the PHS Act, as implemented by 21 CFR part 900, subpart B.

(ii) Has not been issued a written notification by FDA that states that the supplier must cease conducting mammography examinations because the supplier is not in compliance with certain critical certification requirements of section 354 of the PHS Act, implemented by 21 CFR part 900, subpart B.

(iii) Must not employ for provision of the professional component of mammography services a physician or physicians for whom the facility has received written notification by FDA that the physician (or physicians) is (or are) in violation of the certification requirements set forth in section 354 of the PHS Act, as implemented by 21 CFR 900.12(a)(1)(i).

(b) Conditions for coverage of diagnostic mammography services. Medicare Part B pays for diagnostic mammography services if they meet the following conditions:

(1) They are ordered by a doctor of medicine or osteopathy (as defined in section 1861(r)(1) of the Act).

(2) They are furnished by a supplier of diagnostic mammography services that meets the certification requirements of section 354 of the PHS Act, as implemented by 21 CFR part 900, subpart B.

(c) Conditions for coverage of screening mammography services. Medicare Part B pays for screening mammography services if they are furnished by a supplier of screening mammography services that meets the certification requirements of section 354 of the PHS Act, as implemented by 21 CFR part 900, subpart B.

(d) Limitations on coverage of screening mammography services. The following limitations apply to coverage of screening mammography services as described in paragraphs (c) and (d) of this section:

(1) The service must be, at a minimum a two-view exposure (that is, a craniocaudal and a medial lateral oblique view) of each breast.

(2) Payment may not be made for screening mammography performed on a woman under age 35.

(3) Payment may be made for only 1 screening mammography performed on a woman over age 34, but under age 40.

(4) For an asymptomatic woman over 39 years of age, payment may be made for a screening mammography performed after at least 11 months have passed following the month in which the last screening mammography was performed.

[59 FR 49833, Sept. 30, 1994, as amended at 60 FR 14224, Mar. 16, 1995; 60 FR 63176, Dec. 8, 1995; 62 FR 59100, Oct. 31, 1997; 63 FR 4596, Jan. 30, 1998]
***

Sec. 410.36   Medical supplies, appliances, and devices: Scope.

(a) Medicare Part B pays for the following medical supplies, appliances and devices:

(1) Surgical dressings, and splints, casts, and other devices used for reduction of fractures and dislocations.

(2) Prosthetic devices, other than dental, that replace all or part of an internal body organ, including colostomy bags and supplies directly related to colostomy care, including—

(i) Replacement of prosthetic devices; and

(ii) One pair of conventional eyeglasses or conventional contact lenses furnished after each cataract surgery during which an intraocular lens is inserted.

(3) Leg, arm, back, and neck braces and artificial legs, arms, and eyes, including replacements if required because of a change in the individual's physical condition.

(b) As a requirement for payment, CMS may determine through carrier instructions, or carriers may determine, that an item listed in paragraph (a) of this section requires a written physician order before delivery of the item.

[51 FR 41339, Nov. 14, 1986, as amended at 57 FR 36014, Aug. 12, 1992; 57 FR 57688, Dec. 7, 1992]
***

Sec. 410.38   Durable medical equipment: Scope and conditions.

(a) Medicare Part B pays for the rental or purchase of durable medical equipment, including iron lungs, oxygen tents, hospital beds, and wheelchairs, if the equipment is used in the patient's home or in an institution that is used as a home.

(b) An institution that is used as a home may not be a hospital or a CAH or a SNF as defined in sections 1861(e)(1), 1861(mm)(1) and 1819(a)(1) of the Act, respectively.

(c) Wheelchairs may include a power-operated vehicle that may be appropriately used as a wheelchair, but only if the vehicle—

(1) Is determined to be necessary on the basis of the individual's medical and physical condition;

(2) Meets any safety requirements specified by CMS; and

(3) Except as provided in paragraph (c)(2) of this section, is ordered in writing by a specialist in physical medicine, orthopedic surgery, neurology, or rheumatology, the written order is furnished to the supplier before the delivery of the vehicle to the beneficiary, and the beneficiary requires the vehicle and is capable of using it.

(4) A written prescription from the beneficiary's physician is acceptable for ordering a power-operated vehicle if a specialist in physical medicine, orthopedic surgery, neurology, or rheumatology is not reasonably accessible. For example, if travel to the specialist would be more than one day's trip from the beneficiary's home or if the beneficiary's medical condition precluded travel to the nearest available specialist, these circumstances would satisfy the "not reasonably accessible" requirement.

(d) Medicare Part B pays for medically necessary equipment that is used for treatment of decubitus ulcers if—

(1) The equipment is ordered in writing by the beneficiary's attending physician, or by a specialty physician on referral from the beneficiary's attending physician, and the written order is furnished to the supplier before the delivery of the equipment; and

(2) The prescribing physician has specified in the prescription that he or she will be supervising the use of the equipment in connection with the course of treatment.

(e) Medicare Part B pays for a medically necessary seat-lift if it—

(1) Is ordered in writing by the beneficiary's attending physician, or by a specialty physician on referral from the beneficiary's attending physician, and the written order is furnished to the supplier before the delivery of the seat-lift;

(2) Is for a beneficiary who has a diagnosis designated by CMS as requiring a seat-lift; and

(3) Meets safety requirements specified by CMS.

(f) Medicare Part B pays for transcutaneous electrical nerve stimulator units that are—

(1) Determined to be medically necessary; and

(2) Ordered in writing by the beneficiary's attending physician, or by a specialty physician on referral from the beneficiary's attending physician, and the written order is furnished to the supplier before the delivery of the unit to the beneficiary.

(g) As a requirement for payment, CMS may determine through carrier instructions, or carriers may determine that an item of durable medical equipment requires a written physician order before delivery of the item.

[51 FR 41339, Nov. 14, 1986, as amended at 57 FR 57688, Dec. 7, 1992; 58 FR 30668, May 26, 1993]
***

Sec. 410.40   Coverage of ambulance services.

(a) Basic rules. Medicare Part B covers ambulance services if the following conditions are met:

(1) The supplier meets the applicable vehicle, staff, and billing and reporting requirements of Sec. 410.41 and the service meets the medical necessity and origin and destination requirements of paragraphs (d) and (e) of this section.

(2) Medicare Part A payment is not made directly or indirectly for the services.

(b) Levels of services. Medicare covers the following levels of ambulance service, which are defined in Sec. 414.605 of this chapter:

(1) Basic life support (BLS) (emergency and nonemergency).

(2) Advanced life support, level 1 (ALS1) (emergency and nonemergency).

(3) Advanced life support, level 2 (ALS2).

(4) Paramedic ALS intercept (PI).

(5) Specialty care transport (SCT).

(6) Fixed wing transport (FW).

(7) Rotary wing transport (RW).

(c) Paramedic ALS intercept services. Paramedic ALS intercept services must meet the following requirements:

(1) Be furnished in an area that is designated as a rural area by any law or regulation of the State or that is located in a rural census tract of a metropolitan statistical area (as determined under the most recent Goldsmith Modification). (The Goldsmith Modification is a methodology to identify small towns and rural areas within large metropolitan counties that are isolated from central areas by distance or other features.)

(2) Be furnished under contract with one or more volunteer ambulance services that meet the following conditions:

(i) Are certified to furnish ambulance services as required under Sec. 410.41.

(ii) Furnish services only at the BLS level.

(iii) Be prohibited by State law from billing for any service.

(3) Be furnished by a paramedic ALS intercept supplier that meets the following conditions:

(i) Is certified to furnish ALS services as required in Sec. 410.41(b)(2).

(ii) Bills all the recipients who receive ALS intercept services from the entity, regardless of whether or not those recipients are Medicare beneficiaries.

(d) Medical necessity requirements—(1) General rule. Medicare covers ambulance services, including fixed wing and rotary wing ambulance services, only if they are furnished to a beneficiary whose medical condition is such that other means of transportation are contraindicated. The beneficiary's condition must require both the ambulance transportation itself and the level of service provided in order for the billed service to be considered medically necessary. Nonemergency transportation by ambulance is appropriate if either: the beneficiary is bed-confined, and it is documented that the beneficiary's condition is such that other methods of transportation are contraindicated; or, if his or her medical condition, regardless of bed confinement, is such that transportation by ambulance is medically required. Thus, bed confinement is not the sole criterion in determining the medical necessity of ambulance transportation. It is one factor that is considered in medical necessity determinations. For a beneficiary to be considered bed-confined, the following criteria must be met:

(i) The beneficiary is unable to get up from bed without assistance.

(ii) The beneficiary is unable to ambulate.

(iii) The beneficiary is unable to sit in a chair or wheelchair.

(2) Special rule for nonemergency, scheduled, repetitive ambulance services. Medicare covers medically necessary nonemergency, scheduled, repetitive ambulance services if the ambulance provider or supplier, before furnishing the service to the beneficiary, obtains a written order from the beneficiary's attending physician certifying that the medical necessity requirements of paragraph (d)(1) of this section are met. The physician's order must be dated no earlier than 60 days before the date the service is furnished.

(3) Special rule for nonemergency ambulance services that are either unscheduled or that are scheduled on a nonrepetitive basis. Medicare covers medically necessary nonemergency ambulance services that are either unscheduled or that are scheduled on a nonrepetitive basis under one of the following circumstances:

(i) For a resident of a facility who is under the care of a physician if the ambulance provider or supplier obtains a written order from the beneficiary's attending physician, within 48 hours after the transport, certifying that the medical necessity requirements of paragraph (d)(1) of this section are met.

(ii) For a beneficiary residing at home or in a facility who is not under the direct care of a physician. A physician certification is not required.

(iii) If the ambulance provider or supplier is unable to obtain a signed physician certification statement from the beneficiary's attending physician, a signed certification statement must be obtained from either the physician assistant (PA), nurse practitioner (NP), clinical nurse specialist (CNS), registered nurse (RN), or discharge planner, who has personal knowledge of the beneficiary's condition at the time the ambulance transport is ordered or the service is furnished. This individual must be employed by the beneficiary's attending physician or by the hospital or facility where the beneficiary is being treated and from which the beneficiary is transported. Medicare regulations for PAs, NPs, and CNSs apply and all applicable State licensure laws apply; or,

(iv) If the ambulance provider or supplier is unable to obtain the required certification within 21 calendar days following the date of the service, the ambulance supplier must document its attempts to obtain the requested certification and may then submit the claim. Acceptable documentation includes a signed return receipt from the U.S. Postal Service or other similar service that evidences that the ambulance supplier attempted to obtain the required signature from the beneficiary's attending physician or other individual named in paragraph (d)(3)(iii) of this section.

(v) In all cases, the provider or supplier must keep appropriate documentation on file and, upon request, present it to the contractor. The presence of the signed certification statement or signed return receipt does not alone demonstrate that the ambulance transport was medically necessary. All other program criteria must be met in order for payment to be made.

(e) **Origin and destination requirements.** Medicare covers the following ambulance transportation:

(1) From any point of origin to the nearest hospital, CAH, or SNF that is capable of furnishing the required level and type of care for the beneficiary's illness or injury. The hospital or CAH must have available the type of physician or physician specialist needed to treat the beneficiary's condition.

(2) From a hospital, CAH, or SNF to the beneficiary's home.

(3) From a SNF to the nearest supplier of medically necessary services not available at the SNF where the beneficiary is a resident, including the return trip.

(4) For a beneficiary who is receiving renal dialysis for treatment of ESRD, from the beneficiary's home to the nearest facility that furnishes renal dialysis, including the return trip.

(f) **Specific limits on coverage of ambulance services outside the United States.** If services are furnished outside the United States, Medicare Part B covers ambulance transportation to a foreign hospital only in conjunction with the beneficiary's admission for medically necessary inpatient services as specified in subpart H of part 424 of this chapter.

[64 FR 3648, Jan. 25, 1999, as amended at 65 FR 13914, Mar. 15, 2000; 67 FR 9132, Feb. 27, 2002]
***

Sec. 410.45   Rural health clinic services: Scope and conditions.

(a) Medicare Part B pays for the following rural health clinic services, if they are furnished in accordance with the requirements and conditions specified in part 405, subpart X, and part 491 of this chapter:

(1) Physicians' services.

(2) Services and supplies furnished as an incident to physicians' professional services.

(3) Nurse practitioner and physician assistant services.

(4) Services and supplies furnished as an incident to nurse practitioners' or physician assistants' services.

(5) Visiting nurse services.

(b) Medicare pays for rural health clinic services when they are furnished at the clinic, at a hospital or other medical facility, or at the beneficiary's place of residence.
***

Sec. 410.50   Institutional dialysis services and supplies: Scope and conditions.

Medicare Part B pays for the following institutional dialysis services and supplies if they are furnished in approved ESRD facilities:

(a) All services, items, supplies, and equipment necessary to perform dialysis and drugs medically necessary in the treatment of the patient for ESRD.

(b) Routine dialysis monitoring tests (i.e., hematocrit and clotting time) used by the facility to monitor the patients' fluids incident to each dialysis treatment, when performed by qualified staff of the facility under the direction of a physician, as provided in Sec. 405.2163(b) of this chapter, even if the facility does not meet the conditions for coverage of services of independent laboratories in subpart M of part 405 of this chapter.

(c) Routine diagnostic tests.

(d) Epoetin (EPO) and its administration.

[51 FR 41339, Nov. 14, 1986, as amended at 56 FR 43709, Sept. 4, 1991; 59 FR 1285, Jan. 10, 1994]
***

Sec. 410.52   Home dialysis services, supplies, and equipment: Scope and conditions.

(a) Medicare Part B pays for the following services, supplies, and equipment furnished to an ESRD patient in his or her home:

(1) Purchase or rental, installation, and maintenance of all dialysis equipment necessary for home dialysis, and reconditioning of this equipment. Dialysis equipment includes, but is not limited to, artificial kidney and automated peritoneal dialysis machines, and support equipment such as blood pumps, bubble detectors, and other alarm systems.

(2) Items and supplies required for dialysis, including (but not limited to) dialyzers, syringes and needles, forceps, scissors, scales, sphygmomanometer with cuff and stethoscope, alcohol wipes, sterile drapes, and rubber gloves.

(3) Home dialysis support services furnished by an approved ESRD facility, including periodic monitoring of the patient's home adaptation, emergency visits by qualified provider or facility personnel, any of the tests specified in paragraphs (b) through (d) of Sec. 410.50, personnel costs associated with the installation and maintenance of dialysis equipment, testing and appropriate treatment of water, and ordering of supplies on an ongoing basis.

(4) On or after July 1, 1991, epoetin (EPO) for use at home by a home dialysis patient and, on or after January 1, 1994, by a dialysis patient, if it has been determined, in accordance with Sec. 405.2163 of this chapter, that the patient is competent to use the drug safely and effectively.

(b) Home dialysis support services specified in paragraph (a)(3) of this section must be furnished in accordance with a written treatment plan that is prepared and reviewed by a team consisting of the individual's physician and other qualified professionals. (Section 405.2137 of this chapter contains specific details.)

[51 FR 41339, Nov. 14, 1986, as amended at 56 FR 43709, Sept. 4, 1991; 59 FR 26959, May 25, 1994]
***

Sec. 410.55   Services related to kidney donations: Conditions.

Medicare Part B pays for medical and other health services covered under this subpart that are furnished in connection with a kidney donation—
(a) If the kidney is intended for an individual who has end-stage renal disease and is entitled to Medicare benefits; and
(b) Regardless of whether the donor is entitled to Medicare.
***

Sec. 410.57   Pneumococcal vaccine and flu vaccine.

(a) Medicare Part B pays for pneumococcal vaccine and its administration when reasonable and necessary for the prevention of disease, if the vaccine is ordered by a doctor of medicine or osteopathy.
(b) Medicare Part B pays for the influenza virus vaccine and its administration.

[63 FR 35066, June 26, 1998]
***

Sec. 410.58   Additional services to HMO and CMP enrollees.

Services not usually covered under Medicare Part B may be covered as medical and other health services if they are furnished to an enrollee of an HMO or a CMP and the following conditions are met:
(a) The services are—
(1) Furnished by a physician assistant or nurse practitioner as defined in Sec. 491.2 of this chapter, or are incident to services furnished by such a practitioner; or
(2) Furnished by a clinical psychologist as defined in Sec. 417.416 of this chapter to an enrollee of an HMO or CMP that participates in Medicare under a risk-sharing contract, or are incident to those services.

(b) The services are services that would be covered under Medicare Part B if they were furnished by a physician or as incident to a physician's professional services.

***

Sec. 410.60   Outpatient physical therapy services: Conditions.

(a) Basic rule. Medicare Part B pays for outpatient physical therapy services if they meet the following conditions:

(1) They are furnished to a beneficiary while he or she is under the care of a physician who is a doctor of medicine, osteopathy, or podiatric medicine.

(2) They are furnished under a written plan of treatment that meets the requirements of Sec. 410.61.

(3) They are furnished—

(i) By a provider as defined in Sec. 489.2 of this chapter, or by others under arrangements with, and under the supervision of, a provider; or

(ii) By or under the personal supervision of a physical therapist in private practice as described in paragraph (c) of this section.

(b) Outpatient physical therapy services furnished to certain inpatients of a hospital or a CAH or SNF. Medicare Part B pays for outpatient physical therapy services furnished to an inpatient of a hospital, CAH, or SNF who requires them but who has exhausted or is otherwise ineligible for benefit days under Medicare Part A.

(c) Special provisions for services furnished by physical therapists in private practice. (1) Basic qualifications. In order to qualify under Medicare as a supplier of outpatient physical therapy services, each individual physical therapist in private practice must meet the following requirements:

(i) Be legally authorized (if applicable, licensed, certified, or registered) to engage in the private practice of physical therapy by the State in which he or she practices, and practice only within the scope of his or her license, certification, or registration.

(ii) Engage in the private practice of physical therapy on a regular basis as an individual, in one of the following practice types:

(A) An unincorporated solo practice.

(B) An unincorporated partnership or unincorporated group practice.

(C) An unincorporated solo practice, partnership, or group practice, or a professional corporation or other incorporated physical therapy practice.

(D) An employee of a physician group.

(E) An employee of a group that is not a professional corporation.

(iii) Bill Medicare only for services furnished in his or her private practice office space, or in the patient's home. A therapist's private practice office space refers to the location(s) where the practice is operated, in the State(s) where the therapist (and practice, if applicable) is legally authorized to furnish services, during the hours that the therapist engages in practice at that location. When services are furnished in private practice office space, that space must be owned, leased, or rented by the practice and used for the exclusive purpose of operating the practice. A patient's home does not include any institution that is a hospital, a CAH, or a SNF.

(iv) Treat individuals who are patients of the practice and for whom the practice collects fees for the services furnished.

(2) Supervision of physical therapy services. Physical therapy services are performed by, or under the personal supervision of, the physical therapist in private practice. All services not performed personally by the therapist must be performed by employees of the practice, personally supervised by the therapist, and included in the fee for the therapist's services.

(d) Excluded services. No service is included as an outpatient physical therapy service if it would not be included as an inpatient hospital service if furnished to a hospital or CAH inpatient.

(e) Annual limitation on incurred expenses. (1) Amount of limitation. (i) In 1999, 2000, and 2001, no more than $1,500 of allowable charges incurred in a calendar year for outpatient physical therapy services are recognized incurred expenses.

(ii) In 2002 and thereafter, the limitation shall be determined by increasing the limitation in effect in the previous calendar year by the increase in the Medicare Economic Index for the current year.

(2) For purposes of applying the limitation, outpatient physical therapy includes:

(i) Except as provided in paragraph (e)(3) of this section, outpatient physical therapy services furnished under this section;

(ii) Except as provided in paragraph (e)(3) of this section outpatient speech-language pathology services furnished under Sec. 410.62;

(iii) Outpatient physical therapy and speech-language pathology services furnished by a comprehensive outpatient rehabilitation facility;

(iv) Outpatient physical therapy and speech-language pathology services furnished by a physician or incident to a physician's service;

(v) Outpatient physical therapy and speech-language pathology services furnished by a nurse practitioner, clinical nurse specialist, or physician assistant or incident to their services.

(3) For purposes of applying the limitation, outpatient physical therapy excludes services furnished by a hospital or CAH directly or under arrangements.

[63 FR 58906, Nov. 2, 1998, as amended at 67 FR 80041, Dec. 31, 2002]
***

Sec. 410.62   Outpatient speech-language pathology services: Conditions and exclusions.

(a) **Basic rule.** Medicare Part B pays for outpatient speech pathology services if they meet the following conditions:

(1) They are furnished to a beneficiary while he or she is under the care of a physician who is a doctor of medicine or osteopathy. (2) They are furnished under a written plan of treatment that—

(i) Is established by a physician or, effective January 1, 1982, by either a physician or the speech pathologist who will provide the services to the particular individual;

(ii) Is periodically reviewed by a physician; and

(iii) Meets the requirements of Sec. 410.63.

(3) They are furnished by a provider as defined in Sec. 489.2 of this chapter or by others under arrangements with, or under the supervision of, a provider.

(b) **Outpatient speech pathology services to certain inpatients of a hospital, CAH, or SNF.** Medicare Part B pays for outpatient speech pathology services furnished to an inpatient of a hospital, CAH, or SNF who requires them but has exhausted or is otherwise ineligible for benefit days under Medicare Part A.

(c) **Excluded services.** No service is included as an outpatient speech pathology service if it would not be included as an inpatient hospital service if furnished to a hospital or CAH inpatient.

(d) **Limitation.** After 1998, outpatient speech-language pathology services are subject to the limitation in Sec. 410.60(e).

[51 FR 41339, Nov. 14, 1986, as amended at 53 FR 6648, Mar. 2, 1988; 56 FR 8852, Mar. 1, 1991; 56 FR 23022, May 20, 1991; 58 FR 30668, May 26, 1993; 63 FR 58907, Nov. 2, 1998]
***

Sec. 411.400   Payment for custodial care and services not reasonable and necessary.

(a) **Conditions for payment.** Notwithstanding the exclusions set forth in Sec. 411.15(g) and (k), Medicare pays for "custodial care" and "services not reasonable and necessary" if the following conditions are met:

(1) The services were furnished by a provider or by a practitioner or supplier that had accepted assignment of benefits for those services.

(2) Neither the beneficiary nor the provider, practitioner, or supplier knew, or could reasonably have been expected to know, that the services were excluded from coverage under Sec. 411.15(g) or (k).

(b) **Time limits on payment. (1) Basic rule.** Except as provided in paragraph (b)(2) of this section, payment may not be made for inpatient hospital care, posthospital SNF care, or home health services furnished after the earlier of the following:

(i) The day on which the beneficiary has been determined, under Sec. 411.404, to have knowledge, actual or imputed, that the services were excluded from coverage by reason of Sec. 411.15(g) or Sec. 411.15(k).

(ii) The day on which the provider has been determined, under Sec. 411.406, to have knowledge, actual or imputed, that the services are excluded from coverage by reason of Sec. 411.15(g) or Sec. 411.15(k).

(2) Exception. Payment may be made for services furnished during the first day after the limit established in paragraph (b)(1) of this section, if the QIO or the intermediary determines that the additional period of one day is necessary for planning post-discharge care. If the QIO or the intermediary determines that yet another day is necessary for planning post-discharge care, payment may be made for services furnished during the second day after the limit established in paragraph (b)(1) of this section.

***

Sec. 411.404 Criteria for determining that a beneficiary knew that services were excluded from coverage as custodial care or as not reasonable and necessary.

(a) Basic rule. A beneficiary who receives services that constitute custodial care under Sec. 411.15(g) or that are not reasonable and necessary under Sec. 411.15(k), is considered to have known that the services were not covered if the criteria of paragraphs (b) and (c) of this section are met.

(b) Written notice. Written notice has been given to the beneficiary, or to someone acting on his or her behalf, that the services were not covered because they did not meet Medicare coverage guidelines. A notice concerning similar or reasonably comparable services furnished on a previous occasion also meets this criterion. For example, program payment may not be made for the treatment of obesity, no matter what form the treatment may take. After the beneficiary who is treated for obesity with dietary control is informed in writing that Medicare will not pay for treatment of obesity, he or she will be presumed to know that there will be no Medicare payment for any form of subsequent treatment of this condition, including use of a combination of exercise, machine treatment, diet, and medication.

(c) Source of notice. The notice was given by one of the following:

(1) The QIO, intermediary, or carrier.

(2) The group or committee responsible for utilization review for the provider that furnished the services.

(3) The provider, practitioner, or supplier that furnished the service.

APPENDIX 6-6

TITLE 42—PUBLIC HEALTH
(CODE OF FEDERAL REGULATIONS):

PART 411—EXCLUSIONS FROM MEDICARE
AND LIMITATIONS ON MEDICARE PAYMENT

Subpart K—Payment For Certain Excluded Services
[Revised as of October 1, 2003]

Sec. 411.406   Criteria for determining that a provider, practitioner, or supplier knew that services were excluded from coverage as custodial care or as not reasonable and necessary.

(a) **Basic rule.** A provider, practitioner, or supplier that furnished services which constitute custodial care under Sec. 411.15(g) or that are not reasonable and necessary under Sec. 411.15(k) is considered to have known that the services were not covered if any one of the conditions specified in paragraphs (b) through (e) of this section is met.

(b) **Notice from the QIO, intermediary or carrier.** The QIO, intermediary, or carrier had informed the provider, practitioner, or supplier that the services furnished were not covered, or that similar or reasonably comparable services were not covered.

(c) **Notice from the utilization review committee or the beneficiary's attending physician.** The utilization review group or committee for the provider or the beneficiary's attending physician had informed the provider that these services were not covered.

(d) **Notice from the provider, practitioner, or supplier to the beneficiary.** Before the services were furnished, the provider, practitioner or supplier informed the beneficiary that—

(1) The services were not covered; or

(2) The beneficiary no longer needed covered services.

(e) **Knowledge based on experience, actual notice, or constructive notice.** It is clear that the provider, practitioner, or supplier could have been expected to have known that the services were excluded from coverage on the basis of the following:

(1) Its receipt of CMS notices, including manual issuances, bulletins, or other written guides or directives from intermediaries, carriers, or QIOs, including notification of QIO screening criteria specific to the condition of the beneficiary for whom the furnished services are at issue and of medical procedures subject to preadmission review by a QIO.

(2) Federal Register publications containing notice of national coverage decisions or of other specifications regarding noncoverage of an item or service.

(3) Its knowledge of what are considered acceptable standards of practice by the local medical community.

[54 FR 41734, Oct. 11, 1989, as amended at 60 FR 48425, Sept. 19, 1995]

APPENDIX 6-7

MEDICARE SUMMARY NOTICE

CMS/ Medicare Summary Notice

CUSTOMER SERVICE INFORMATION

BENEFICIARY NAME
STREET ADDRESS
CITY, STATE ZIP CODE

Your Medicare Number: 111-11-1111A

If you have questions, write or call:
Medicare
555 Medicare Blvd., Suite 200
Medicare Building
Medicare, US XXXXX-XXXX

BE INFORMED: Beware of "free" medical services or products. If it sounds too good to be true, it probably is.

Local: (XXX) XXX-XXXX
Toll-free: 1-800-XXX-XXXX
TTY for Hearing Impaired: 1-800-XXX-XXXX

This is a summary of claims processed from 05/15/2004 through 06/10/2004.

PART A HOSPITAL INSURANCE – INPATIENT CLAIMS

Dates of Service	Benefit Days Used	Non-Covered Charges	Deductible and Coinsurance	You May Be Billed	See Notes Section
Claim Number: 12435-84956-84556-45621					a
Cure Hospital, 213 Sick Lane, Dallas, TX 75555					
Referred by: Paul Jones, M.D.					
04/25/04 – 05/09/04	14 days	$0.00	$876.00	$776.00	b, c
Claim Number: 12435-84956-845556-45622					
Continued Care Hospital, 124 Sick Lane, Dallas, TX 75555					
Referred by: Paul Jones, M.D.					
05/09/04 – 06/20/04	11 days	$0.00	$0.00	$0.00	

PART B MEDICAL INSURANCE – OUTPATIENT FACILITY CLAIMS

Dates of Service	Services Provided	Amount Charged	Non-Covered Charges	Deductible and Coinsurance	You May Be Billed	See Notes Section
Claim Number: 12435-8956-8458						d
Medicare Hospital, 123 Medicare Lane, Dallas, TX 75209						
Referred by: Paul Jones, M.D.						
04/02/04	L.V. Therapy (Q0081)	$33.00	$0.00	$6.60	$6.60	
	Lab (3810)	1,140.50	0.00	228.10	228.10	
	Operating Room (31628)	786.50	0.00	157.30	157.30	
	Observation Room (99201)	293.00	0.00	58.60	58.60	
	Claim Total	**$2,253.00**	**$0.00**	**$450.60**	**$450.60**	(continued)

THIS IS NOT A BILL – Keep this notice for your records.

Your Medicare Number: 111-11-1111A

Notes Section:

a The amount Medicare paid the provider for this claim is $XXXX.XX.

b $776.00 was applied to your inpatient deductible.

c $30.00 was applied to your blood deductible.

d The amount Medicare paid the provider for this claim is $XXXX.XX.

Deductible Information:

You have met the Part A deductible for this benefit period.

You have met the Part B deductible for 2004.

You have met the blood deductible for 2004.

General Information:

You have the right to make a request in writing for an itemized statement which details each Medicare item or service which you have received from your physician, hospital, or any other health supplier or health professional. Please contact them directly, in writing, if you would like an itemized statement.

Compare the services you receive with those that appear on your Medicare Summary Notice. If you have questions, call your doctor or provider. If you feel further investigation is needed due to possible fraud and abuse, call the phone number in the Customer Service Information Box.

Appeals Information – Part A (Inpatient) and Part B (Outpatient)

If you disagree with any claims decision on either Part A or Part B of this notice, you can request an appeal by **November 1, 2004**. Follow the instructions below:

1) Circle the item(s) you disagree with and explain why you disagree.

2) Send this notice, or a copy, to the address in the "Customer Service Information" box on Page 1. (You may also send any additional information you may have about your appeal.)

3) Sign here _____ Phone number _____

Revised 02/04

IMPORTANT INFORMATION YOU SHOULD KNOW ABOUT YOUR MEDICARE BENEFITS

For more information about services covered by Medicare, please see your Medicare Handbook.

PART A HOSPITAL INSURANCE (INPATIENT) helps pay for inpatient hospital care, inpatient care in a skilled nursing facility following a hospital stay, home health care and hospice care. Inpatient services are measured in benefit periods. A benefit period begins the first time you receive Medicare covered inpatient hospital care and ends when you have been out of the hospital or skilled nursing facility for 60 consecutive days. There is no limit to the number of benefit periods you may have.

THE AMOUNT YOU MAY BE BILLED for **Part A** services includes:

- **an inpatient hospital deductible** once during each benefit period,

- **a coinsurance amount for the 61st through the 90th days** of a hospital stay during each benefit period,

- **a coinsurance amount for each Lifetime Reserve Day**, which can be used if you have to stay in the hospital more than 90 days in one benefit period. Lifetime Reserve Days may be used only once,

- **a blood deductible** for the first three pints of unreplaced blood furnished to you in a calendar year in some states,

- **an inpatient coinsurance for the 21st through the 100th days** of a Medicare covered stay in a **skilled nursing facility,**

- charges for services or supplies that are **not covered** by Medicare. You may not have to pay for certain denied services. If so, a NOTE on the front will tell you.

PART B MEDICAL INSURANCE (OUTPATIENT FACILITIES) helps pay for care provided by certified medical facilities, such as hospital outpatient departments, renal dialysis facilities, and community health centers.

THE AMOUNT YOU MAY BE BILLED for **Part B** services includes:

- **an annual deductible,** the first $100 of Medicare Part B charges each year,

- after the deductible has been met for the year, depending on services received, a **coinsurance amount** (20% of the amount charged), or a fixed **copayment** for each service,

- charges for services or supplies that are **not covered** by Medicare. You may not have to pay for certain denied services. If so, a NOTE on the front will tell you.

If you have supplemental insurance, it may help to pay the amounts you may be billed. If you use this notice to claim supplemental benefits from another insurance company, make a copy for your records.

WHEN OTHER INSURANCE PAYS FIRST: All Medicare payments are made on the condition that you will pay Medicare back if benefits could be paid by insurance that is primary to Medicare. Types of insurance that should pay before Medicare include employer group health plans, no-fault insurance, automobile medical insurance, liability insurance and workers' compensation. Notify us right away if you have filed or could file a claim with insurance that is primary to Medicare.

YOUR RIGHT TO APPEAL: If you disagree with any decision on this notice, you have a right to appeal. For **PART A** and **PART B** decisions, you must file an appeal within **120 days of the date of this notice.** Follow the appeal instructions for Part A or Part B on the front of the last page of the notice. If you want **help with your appeal,** you can have a friend or someone else help you. There are also groups, such as legal aid services, that will provide free advisory services if you qualify. To contact us for the names and telephone numbers of groups in your area, please see our Customer Service Information box on the front of this Summary Notice.

HELP STOP MEDICARE FRAUD: Fraud is a false representation by a person or business to get Medicare payments. Some examples of fraud include:

- offers of goods or money in exchange for your Medicare Number,

- telephone or door-to-door offers for free medical services or items, and

- claims for Medicare services/items you did not receive.

If you think a person or business is involved in fraud, you should call Medicare at the Customer Service telephone number on the front of this notice.

INSURANCE COUNSELING AND ASSISTANCE: Insurance Counseling and Assistance programs are located in every State. These programs have volunteer counselors who can give you free assistance with Medicare questions, including enrollment, entitlement, Medigap, and premium issues. If you would like to know how to get in touch with your local Insurance Counseling and Assistance Program Counselor, please call us at the number shown in the Customer Service Information box on the front of this notice.

Centers for Medicare & Medicaid Services

50 - Categories and Identification Numbers for Approved MSN Messages

(Rev. 1, 10-01-03)

A3-3726.14A, B3-7014, PMs A-99-48, AB-02-106, B-02-047, AB-02-155, B-02-029

MSN messages are separated into the following categories. Within each category, messages are numbered beginning with 1 (e.g., ambulance messages are from 1.1 through 1.11; blood messages are from 2.1 through 2.2). Each MSN has a unique number when the category number is included. Numbers are the same for carriers and intermediaries, including DMERCs and RHHIs. However, the message number is not printed on the MSN, and contractors are free to use any internal numbering system appropriate for their systems.

Contractors are instructed to use the most appropriate message for each situation regardless of message category. The categories are to facilitate reference.

    1 - Ambulance

    2 - Blood

    3 - Chiropractic

    4 - End-Stage Renal Disease (ESRD)

    5 - Number/Name/Enrollment

    6 - Drugs

    7 - Duplicate Bills

    8 - Durable Medical Equipment (DME)

    9 - Failure to Furnish Information

    10 - Foot Care

    11 - Transfer of Claims or Parts of Claims

    12 - Hearing Aids

    13 - Skilled Nursing Facility

    14 - Laboratory

    15 - Medical Necessity

    16 - Miscellaneous

MEDICARE ADVANTAGE: COORDINATED CARE PLANS, PRIVATE FEE-FOR-SERVICE, AND OTHER DELIVERY OF SERVICES OPTIONS

§7.01 INTRODUCTION

Medicare provides for a variety of delivery of care options for the receipt of Medicare covered services, including managed care.[1] These services are found in Part C of the Medicare Statute, formerly known as the Medicare+Choice (M+C) Program,[2] and now known as Medicare Advantage (MA). This change was required by the Medicare Prescription Drug, Improvement and Modernization Act of 2003 (MMA), and the Centers for Medicare & Medicaid Services (CMS) has largely completed its transition from using the term, "Medicare+ Choice," to "Medicare Advantage" (MA) as descriptive of the Medicare Program's (1) coordinated care plan options, (including managed care arrangements such as Health Maintenance Organizations (HMOs), Provider Sponsored Organizations (PSOs), regional or local Preferred Provider organizations (PPOs), and other network plans (except Medicare Savings Accounts (MSAs) and Private Fee-for-Service Plans); (2) Medicare Medical Savings Accounts (MMSA), Health Savings Accounts (HSAs); and (3) Private Fee-for-Service Plans (PFFS) and Religious Fraternal Benefit Society Plans.[3] The transition to the complete use of the term "Medicare Advantage" as descriptive of this group of options was completed as of January 1, 2006.[4]

The delivery of Medicare Advantage services remains in a state of flux as plans leave some markets and enter others. Between 1999 and 2003, almost half of all Medicare managed care plans had stopped offering services completely or cut back on the counties served, affecting about 2.4 million beneficiaries.[5] To address this instability, the MMA made substantial increases to the payment rates applicable to Medicare Advantage (MA) plans.[6] Plan participation increased through 2006 as a result of increased payments and is likely so stay relatively stable in 2007. There is general concern, however, that the new rates are inflated and represent significant overpayments to plans and yet may not provide sufficient incentives to retain plan participation over time.[7]

---

[1] 42 U.S.C. §1395w-21, Pub. L. No. 105-33, Title IV, 4001 (Aug. 5, 1997); *see also* Pub. L. No. 108-173, 201(c). Managed care is used generally in this chapter to refer to all Medicare Part C plans. Manual provisions concerning Medicare Managed care are found in the CMS online manuals which are available on the CMS website: <http://www.cms.hhs.gov/manuals>. *See*, Medicare Managed Care Manual, CMS Pub. 100-16.

[2] 42 U.S.C. §1395w-21.

[3] Pub. L. No. 108-173, 201(c); 42 C.F.R. §422.4 (types of MA plans).

[4] Pub. L. No. 108-173, 201(c).

[5] Public Citizen Congress Watch, "Private Insurance Plans and Medicare, the Disappointing History" (June 2003).

[6] *See* §211 of the MMA, Pub. L. No. 108-173, amending 42 U.S.C. §1395w-23 (Payment to Medicare+Choice Organizations). 42 C.F.R. §§422.304–422.311. Rates and related data are posted on the CMS website at <http://www.cms.hhs.gov/healthplans/reportfilesdata/default.asp?>.

[7] *See*, King, Kathleen M., and Mark Schlesigner, (eds.), Final Report of the Study Panel on Medicare and Markets—*The Role of Private Health Plans in Medicare: Lessons from the Past,*

Early trend data analysis by Mathematica Policy Research, Inc., indicates that there are more MA plan options available in 2006 generally, except for in Alaska and parts of New England. With favorable rate treatment and plan expansion in rural areas, there is likely to be more plan stability.[8] Rural area growth is concentrated among Private Fee for Service Plans (PFFCs) and regional PPOs.

Advocates should watch closely the growth and use of MA options, paying particular attention to plan structure and benefits, scope of coverage, and beneficiary appeal rights, in an environment of increased copayments for services, and the push toward vouchers and other defined contribution approaches.[9]

§7.02   ADVANTAGES AND DISADVANTAGES OF MEDICARE ADVANTAGE OPTIONS

As a general matter, MA options focus on at least some level of utilization management and cost containment in which savings are often passed on to beneficiaries in the form of reduced costs or additional services.

[A] Advantages

There are several advantages in choosing a Medicare Advantage Option:

- *No claims.* Generally, a beneficiary need not submit unless emergency or urgent care is received while outside the service area.

Looking to the Future (Washington, D.C: National Academy of Social Insurance, September 2003). In addition, persons following the issue of plan participation may wish to visit the Medicare Health Plan Tracker, Monthly Tracking Report, prepared by Mathematica Policy Research, Inc., found on the Kaiser Family Foundation webpage at: <http://www.kff.org/medicare/loader.cfm?url=/common-spot/security/getfile.cfm&PageID=52248>.

[8] Marsha Gold, Sc.D., Mathematica Policy Research, Inc., presentation for the Alliance for Health Reform, May 19, 2006; see also Mathematica Policy Research, Inc., Publication #82 (May 15, 2006). "Tracking Medicare Health and Prescription Drug Plans, Monthy Report for Apr. 2006), <http://www.mathematica-mpr.com/>.

[9] *See* Marilyn Moon, *Restructuring Medicare: Impacts on Beneficiaries* (Urban Inst., Jan. 1999); Brian Biles, Susan Raetzman, Susan Joseph and Karen Davis, *Issue Brief: The Future of Medicare* (Commonwealth Fund, Nov. 1998). Benefit package issues for 2006 and beyond remain key factors in plan utilization and plan satisfaction. Plan flexibility in benefit design, plus favorable reimbursement rates, will continue to be a driver with respect to beneficiary utilization. Brian Biles, Lauren Hersch Nicholas, and Stuart Guterman, have released an Issue Brief (May 2006), for the Commonwealth Fund, Commonwealth Fund pub. #927, entitled "Medicare Beneficiary Out-of-Pocket Costs: Are Medicare Advantage Plans a Better Deal?" In his paper, he posits that broad generalizations about the advantages of MA plans for seniors may be misleading. His caution is that seniors' out-of-pocket costs vary widely. Thus, the caution to look at one's overall health status, drug needs, and other factors before making a decision whether to elect an MA plan. *See also*, Marilyn Moon, Medicare A Policy Primer (The Urban Institute Press 2006) Washington, D.C.

- *Emphasis on preventive care.* Preventive health care, including annual physical exams, as well as health care screening services not covered under the Medicare "fee-for-service" program, are often provided and encouraged.

- *Comprehensive services.* These services, which are not covered under the Medicare "fee-for-service" program, often include vision care, prescription drugs, dental care, and hearing exams.

- *No need for Medigap insurance.* Managed care plans should provide beneficiaries with all or most of the benefits offered by a Medigap policy.

- *Easier to budget health care expenses.* Beneficiaries should know the amount of any premiums and copayments for doctor services in advance.

- *Avoid unnecessary surgeries.* Plans are interested in avoiding unnecessary risks and have no financial incentive to perform unnecessary procedures. Consequently, if a plan recommends surgery a beneficiary can be relatively certain that it is necessary.

[B] Disadvantages

Some disadvantages include:

- *Plan terminations.* Plans may decide to terminate services and make elections whether to participate in a given market annually.

- *Limitations on receiving specialized care.* Many plans require a beneficiary to have the prior approval of his or her primary care physician to see a specialist. Because of financial incentives, some primary care physicians resist making referrals.

- *Financial incentives to limit service.* Plans receive the same payment from Medicare whether a beneficiary receives services or not. Some physicians may treat managed care patients differently from fee-for-service patients. Waiting time may be longer, fewer tests may be performed, or services may be limited. Limiting services based on financial considerations may result in questionable quality of care.

- *Requirement to use plan providers.* In most plans, a beneficiary is not free to go to any physician or hospital he or she may choose. Beneficiaries are often "locked in" and must use the plan's providers and facilities. In other plans, a beneficiary must pay more to see "non-network" providers.

- *Out-of-area care limitations.* If a beneficiary lives outside the plan service area for more than a specified period of time, the plan may not sell a beneficiary a plan or may disenroll a beneficiary. Plans cover emergency and urgent care if a beneficiary is out of the service area for a brief time, but a beneficiary must return to the area for routine care. The plan may offer a separate option that covers out-of-area care, but the beneficiary will have to pay an additional premium.

- *Service locations.* There are limited locations where a beneficiary can receive care.

- *Higher copayments and deductibles.* Some plans are beginning to charge higher copayments and deductibles than traditional Medicare for services needed by beneficiaries with greater health care needs. Larger copayments may be charged for hospital, skilled nursing facility (SNF), and home health services and for durable medical equipment (DME), including oxygen. This has been criticized as a way of cherry picking, for example, forcing heavy care patients out of the managed care plan.

- *Disenrollment.* It can take up to 30 days to disenroll, and a beneficiary must continue to use the health plan during this time. Even after the disenrollment becomes effective, Medicare's computers may not be updated, and some Medicare "fee-for-service" claims will be erroneously rejected.

§7.03 GUIDELINES FOR CONSIDERING MEDICARE ADVANTAGE OPTIONS

Beneficiaries should make informed decisions before enrolling. Following some simple rules before enrolling in a plan can avoid problems and disappointment later. These guidelines will help to ensure that beneficiaries make wise decisions about MA options. After careful evaluation, some Medicare beneficiaries will choose managed care, while others may determine that the original Medicare "fee-for-service" program better suits their needs. Beneficiaries should consider the following:

1. Review coverage provided by the original Medicare program and by Medigap insurance policies. Beneficiaries should understand the coverage and costs available through the original fee-for-service system combined with an appropriate Medigap policy.

2. Read each plan's literature to see what kind of plan it is, what it pays for, and what copayments are required for different kinds of services.

3. Determine what plan services are provided at additional cost and how much the cost. All preventive services should be identified, as well as any limitations associated with visits or services. The beneficiary should fully understand where to go for emergency, urgently needed, and routine care.

4. Review for any coverage for prescription drugs carefully. Consider whether the plan covers brand names or only generics, imposes different copayments based on the type of drug, or provides coverage on a monthly, quarterly, or yearly basis. In addition, one should compare

drug coverage with prescription drug plans available, starting in 2006, under Medicare Part D.

5. If plan materials do not provide answers to all questions, contact the plan for additional information. Beneficiaries should make a note of how plan staff responds to such inquiries and use that information in evaluating the plan.

6. Ask about plan physicians, determine if their physicians are in the plan, and find out how to change physicians if a satisfactory relationship with a plan physician cannot be established. In addition, beneficiaries should ask which hospitals, SNFs, and home care agencies the plan contracts with to ensure that there are satisfactory choices available.

7. Know how to use the plan's complaint system and how appeals and grievances are handled.

8. Inquire among friends and relatives to determine if any are currently enrolled in managed care plans or have been enrolled in the past. Beneficiaries should ask them about their experience with the plan.

9. Ask the plan representative if member satisfaction surveys are conducted and if the results are available for review.

10. Contact the CMS Regional Office of Beneficiary Services to determine if a plan has failed to comply with CMS regulations.

§7.04 MEDICARE ADVANTAGE

[A] Overview

The Secretary of Health and Human Services (HHS) is required to establish standards, regulations, and rules for Medicare Part C that are consistent with existing standards and regulations governing the Medicare program.[10] Regulations implementing MA changes have been published[11] and are discussed in this chapter.

---

[10] 42 U.S.C. §1395w-24(f).

[11] *See* 70 Fed. Reg. 4588–4741 (Jan. 28, 2005), effective March 22, 2005, except for the following changes effective January 1, 2006: amendment of §417.600(b) (applying the beneficiary appeals and grievance provisions to Medicare contracts with HMOs and CMPs under §1876 of the Social Security Act), removal of §§417.602 through 417.638 (Subpart Q-HMO/CMP Beneficiary Appeals, starting with the definitions section, through reopening and determinations and decisions), and amendments to §417.832(d) (administrative law judge hearings, Medicare Appeals Council review, and judicial review), and §417.840 (Health Care Prepayment Plans (HCPPs) must apply the time frames and other rules of §§422.568 through 422.619).

[B]   Requirements

Each Medicare Advantage organization (MA organization)[12] must provide the services currently available under Medicare Parts A and B.[13] The MA organization, through its MA plan[14] or plans, however, may impose different copayments and deductibles than under Parts A and B, as long as the monthly premium and cost sharing are actuarially equivalent to cost sharing under traditional Medicare.[15] The plans must also pass on to beneficiaries any cost savings achieved through efficient plan administration in the form of additional benefits.[16] Plans may offer supplemental benefits for which a separate premium may be charged, but the separate premium may not vary among individuals within the plan and must not exceed certain actuarial and community rating requirements.[17]

With respect to Medicare Part D drug coverage, MA sponsors must offer drug coverage unless the sponsor offers plans with and without drug coverage. PFFPs do not have to offer drug coverage. This becomes important when choosing health plans.

In addition, MA plans are allowed to offer reduced Medicare Part B premiums as an additional benefit to its enrollees. Information about Part B premium reductions would be included with the information beneficiaries receive about plans during the annual open enrollment period.[18]

MA plans must tell an enrollee about hospice care, if a hospice program is located within the MA organization's service area, or, if not located within the

---

[12] An MA organization means a public or private entity organized and licensed by a state as a risk-bearing entity (with the exception of provider-sponsor organizations receiving waivers), that is, certified by CMS as meeting MA contract requirements. 42 C.F.R. §422.2 (definitions).

[13] 42 U.S.C. §1395w-22(a); 42 C.F.R. §422.101. Note, 42 C.F.R. §422.2 (Medicare Advantage definitions) and 42 C.F.R. §423.4 (Voluntary Prescription Drug Benefit, Medicare Part D, definitions) contain an important explanatory list of terms of importance in discussing and understanding the MA program. An MA-Prescription drug (PD) plan, for example, is one that provides qualified prescription, drug coverage (*see also* 42 C.F.R. §423.4), and MA regional plans are coordinated care plans structured as a preferred provider organization (PPO) that serve one or more entire regions and, in keeping with CMS requirements, have a network of contracting providers that have agreed to a specific reimbursement for the plan's covered services and must pay for all covered services whether provided in or out of the network. *Id.*

[14] An MA Plan means health benefits coverage offered through a policy or contract with an MA Organization that includes a specific set of health benefits offered at a uniform premium and uniform level of cost sharing to all Medicare beneficiaries residing in the service area of the MA plan (or individual segments of a service area). 42 C.F.R. §422.2 (definitions). Though different in meaning, "MA Organization" and "MA Plan" are often used interchangeably. In general, an MA Organization is the overarching structure that may comprise one or more MA Plans.

[15] 42 U.S.C. §1395w-24(e).

[16] 42 C.F.R. §422.312.

[17] 42 U.S.C. §1395w-22; 42 C.F.R. §422.102.

[18] Section 606 of the Medicare, Medicaid, and SCHIP Benefits Improvement and Protection Act of 2000 (BIPA), Pub. L. No. 106-554 (Dec. 21, 2000).

service area, if it is common to refer patients to hospice programs outside the service area.[19] If the patient elects hospice care, CMS makes payments directly to the hospice program, and makes monthly payments to the MA organization for additional benefits not provided by hospice care.[20]

Medicare Advantage plans must accept eligible beneficiaries who elect that organization's plan during an open enrollment period, without restrictions.[21] The statute provides a process and priorities for limiting enrollment in the case of potential over-enrollment, unless the result would be unrepresentative of the area's Medicare population.[22]

[C] Medicare Advantage Options[23]

[1] Coordinated Care Plans

In order to offer an MA coordinated care plan in an area, the MA organization offering the plan must offer qualified Part D coverage that includes the requirements related to qualified prescription drug coverage.[24] These plans include the following:[25]

- *Health Maintenance Organizations (HMOs).* A type of managed care plan that can take a variety of forms such as a staff-based facility of service providers and/or a group of independent practice associations that acts as both insurer and provider of services to its members; services and benefits usually financed through a capitated payment; copayments may apply;

- *Provider Sponsored Organizations (PSOs).* An organization created by health care providers to act as insurer for a defined group of enrollees, including physician-based models, hospital-based models, or a combination of service delivery models; and

- *Preferred Provider Organizations (PPOs).* Managed care entities that contract with networks or panels of providers for serving the PPOs' enrolled population(s) and are paid on the basis of a contractually specified reimbursement for covered benefits with the organization offering the plan and provide

---

[19] 42 U.S.C. §1395w-23(h); 42 C.F.R. §422.266(a).

[20] 42 U.S.C. §1395w-23(h); 42 C.F.R. §422.266(c).

[21] 42 U.S.C. §1395w-21(g); 42 C.F.R. §422.60(a)(1), (2).

[22] 42 U.S.C. §1395w-21(g); 42 C.F.R. §422.60(b)(2).

[23] 42 U.S.C. §1395w-21; 42 C.F.R. §422.4.

[24] 42 C.F.R. §422.4(c)(1); 42 C.F.R. §422.104. See **Chapter 11** for details.

[25] 42 C.F.R. §422.4(a)(1).

[26] 42 C.F.R. §422.4(a)(1)(v).

reimbursement for all covered benefits regardless of whether the benefits are provided within the network of providers.[26]

Health services provided by HMOs, PPOs, and PSOs can be with or without a point-of-service option, or the ability to use plan or out-of-plan health care providers.

[2]   Medicare Medical Savings Account (MSA)

MA organizations offering MSA plans are not permitted to offer prescription drug coverage, other than that required under part A and B of the Medicare statute.[27] The MMA makes the previously and never used Medicare Saving Account (MSA) demonstration a permanent Medicare option, starting with contract years beginning January 1, 2006; removes the capacity limits and the deadline for enrollment; and eliminates the requirement for a quality assurance program because MSAs are bank accounts and not plans.[28]

As with the old MSA demonstration, the new option combines the use of a health care savings account with a high deductible catastrophic health plan. To participate in an MA MSA, the beneficiary has to enroll in an MA MSA health plan.[29]

Under rules established by the Secretary, an individual is not eligible to enroll (or continue enrollment) in an MSA plan for a year unless the individual provides assurances satisfactory to the Secretary that the individual will reside in the United States for at least 183 days during the year.[30] Individuals must enroll during an initial enrollment period or an annual coordinated election period.[31]

[3]   Health Savings Accounts

This option, outside the Medicare program, and under the Internal Revenue Code, is added to the law by the MMA.[32] Under this provision, an individual opens a Health Savings Account (HSA) in connection with the purchase of high deductible private health insurance. The HSA offers significant advantages over the MSAs in considerable income tax savings. The individual can also carry over unspent balances from year to year. Funds deposited in the HSA trust account are to

---

[27] 42 C.F.R. §422.4(c)(2).

[28] 233, of the MMA, amending 1851(b)(4), 1851(e)(5)(A), 1852, 1852(e)(1), and 1852(k) of the Social Security Act., 42 U.S.C. §§1395w-21(b)(4), 1395w-21(e)(5)(A), 1395w-22, 1395w-22(e)(1), and 1395w-22(k). There is not much use of this option to date.

[29] 42 C.F.R. §422.4(a)(2).

[30] Id.

[31] Id.

[32] §1201 of the MMA, Internal Revenue Code (IRS), 223.

be used for the sole purpose of paying qualified medical expenses of beneficiaries. An individual will be able to withdraw sums from his or her HSA trust account to cover deductibles and other health care expenses, in connection with a related high deductible health insurance policy. Deposits into the trust account each year will be excluded from taxable income, earnings on the accounts are not taxed, nor are amounts withdrawn from the trust account to pay health expenses.[33]

[4] Private Fee-for-Service Plans

MA organizations offering private fee-for-service (PFFS) plans may choose to offer qualified Part D coverage that meets the requirement for that coverage.[34] A private fee-for-service plan is a Medicare Advantage plan that:

- Reimburses hospitals, physicians, and other providers at a rate determined by the plan on a fee-for-service basis without placing the provider at financial risk;

- Does not vary such rates for such a provider based on utilization relating to such provider; and

- Does not restrict the selection of providers among those who are lawfully authorized to provide the covered services and who agree to accept the terms and conditions of payment established by the plan.[35]

The Medicare program will make a capitated payment to the private pay fee-for-service plan just as it would to an HMO or PSO.[36] A physician, provider of service, or other entity that has a contract for Medicare services furnished to Medicare enrollees must accept as payment in full for covered services an amount not to exceed (including any permitted deductibles, coinsurance, copayments, or balance billing) 115 percent of its contracted rate.[37] The plan must establish procedures to enforce its billing limits. If the plan fails to adhere to its billing limits, the plan may be subject to sanctions. Beneficiaries must be provided with an appropriate explanation of benefits, consistent with current beneficiary information requirements for Medicare Parts A and B, and for applicable Medicare Supplemental policies.[38] The explanation must include a clear statement of the amount of the enrollee's liability, including any allowable balance billing.

---

[33] *Id.*

[34] 42 C.F.R. §422.4(c)(3). See the discussion of Part D drug plan requirements in **Chapter 11.**

[35] 42 U.S.C. §1395w-28(b)(2); 42 C.F.R. §422.4(a)(3).

[36] 42 U.S.C. §1395w-23. PPOs are likely to be more common in 2006 than PSOs.

[37] 42 U.S.C. §§1395w-22(k), 1395w-24.

[38] 42 U.S.C. §1395w-22(k); 42 C.F.R. §422.111 (disclosure requirements), §422.112 (access to services), §422.113 (special rules for ambulance services, emergency and urgently needed services, and maintenance and post-stabilization care services), §422.114 (access to services under an MA private fee-for-service plan), §422.133 (return to home skill nursing facility).

The private fee-for-service plan must provide the Medicare beneficiary with advance balance billing information before incurring inpatient hospital services (and certain other services to be identified by the Secretary) for which balance billing amounts could be substantial.[39]

[5] Religious Fraternal Benefit Society Plans

Medicare Advantage allows a religious fraternal benefit (RFB) society to establish a plan that limits enrollment to members of the church, convention, or group with which it is affiliated.[40] Such plans must be exempt from taxation as provided under the Internal Revenue Code of 1986,[41] and be affiliated with, carry out the tenets of, and share a religious bond with a church or convention or association of churches or an affiliated group of churches.[42] In addition, the society must meet certain requirements and the Secretary can adjust the payment amounts.[43]

[6] Local and Regional Medicare Advantage Plans

Earlier, CMS sponsored a demonstration program to offer PPO coverage to Medicare beneficiaries. The demonstration project closed in 2006 and no new local PPOs can be offered.[44]

An MA local PPO is defined as an MA plan that is not an MA regional plan.[45] Local and regional MA plans are structured as Preferred Provider Organizations (PPOs).[46] An MA Regional PPO is an MA Plan that has a network of providers that has a contractual agreement with CMS for a specified reimbursement to provide covered benefits regardless of whether such benefits are provided within the network of providers, and the regional PPO service area covers one or more entire MA regions.[47]

---

[39] Check the Web sites of specific plans and of CMS for plan details and locations.

[40] 42 U.S.C. §1395w-28(c); 42 C.F.R. §422.57.

[41] 42 C.F.R. §422.2.

[42] 42 U.S.C. §1395w-28(e).

[43] *Id.*

[44] *See* 42 U.S.C. §1395w-21(a)(2)(A).

[45] 42 U.S.C. §1395w-28(b)(5).

[46] *See* <http://www.cms.hhs.gov/medicarereform/mmaregions/>, for a description of the Regional PPO program; and *see* <http://www.cms.hhs.gov/medicarereform/mmaregions/PPORegionEst2005. pdf>, for a chart of the Medicare Advantage PPO regions including number of beneficiaries in each region and related information. There are 26 MA regions. *Id.*

[47] 42 C.F.R. §422.4(a)(1)(v).

There are special cost-sharing rules for MA regional plans. To the extent such plans apply a deductible, they are only permitted to have a single deductible related to combined Medicare Part A and Part B services.[48] The applicability of the single deductible may be differential for specific in-network services and may also be waived for preventative services or other items and services.[49]

MA regional plans are required to provide for a catastrophic limit on beneficiary out-of-pocket expenditures for in-network and out-of-network benefits under original fee-for-service Medicare program.[50] The total out-of-pocket catastrophic limit may be higher than the in-network catastrophic limit, but may not increase the total catastrophic limit.[51] MA regional plans are required to track the deductibles and catastrophic limits and are to notify members and health care providers when the limits have been reached.[52]

MA regional plans are required to provide reimbursement for all covered benefits, regardless of whether those benefits are provided within or outside of the network of contracted providers.[53] In applying the actuarially equivalent level of cost sharing on MA bids related to benefits under the original Medicare program option, only the catastrophic limit on out-of-pocket expenses for in-network benefits will be taken into account.[54]

[7] Specialized MA Plans (SNP) for Special Needs Individuals

The MMA adds specialized MA plans for people with special needs. These plans are defined as an MA plan that exclusively serves people who are institutionalized; are entitled to medical assistance under a State plan under Title 19 (Medicaid) of the Social Security Act; or meet such requirements as the Secretary may determine would benefit from enrollment in a specialized MA plan for individuals with severe or disabling chronic conditions.[55] Special rules for SNP enrollment and eligibility have been established by the Secretary.[56]

---

[48] 42 C.F.R. §422.101(d)(1).

[49] *Id.*

[50] 42 C.F.R. §422.101(d)(2).

[51] 42 C.F.R. §422.101(d)(3).

[52] 42 C.F.R. §422.101(d)(4).

[53] 42 C.F.R. §422.101(e)(1).

[54] 42 C.F.R. §422.101(e)(2); *see also* §422.256(b)(3).

[55] 42 U.S.C. §1395w-28(b)(6).

[56] 42 C.F.R. §422.52. *See* discussion of SNP in Part D of **Chapter 11**. Note, the Secretary may designate certain MA plans that disproportionally serve special needs individuals as SNPs. *See*, 42 C.F.R. §422.52(f).

[D] Medicare Advantage Eligibility

[1] Eligible Persons

To be eligible for an MA plan, an individual must be entitled to benefits under Part A and enrolled in Medicare Part B.[57] To enroll in an MA plan, an individual must complete and sign an election form or complete a CMS-approved election method offered by the MA organization.[58]

Persons with end-stage renal disease (ESRD) are excluded, except that an individual who develops ESRD while enrolled in an MA Plan may continue to be enrolled in that plan.[59] Such an individual may also enroll in another MA Plan if the ESRD beneficiary loses MA Plan coverage when his or her plan terminates its contract with CMS or reduces its service area. Note, however, an individual with end-stage renal disease may elect an MA special needs plan as long as that plan has opted to enroll ESRD individuals.[60]

An individual is eligible to enroll in a particular MA Plan if the plan serves the geographic area in which the individual resides.[61] If, after enrolling in a plan, the individual leaves the geographic area, the plan can offer the individual the option of staying in the plan if the plan provides the individual with reasonable geographic access to all basic plan benefits.

[2] Persons Ineligible to Enroll

An individual who is a Qualified Medicare Beneficiary (QMB), a Qualified Disabled and Working individual, a Specified Low-Income Medicare Beneficiary, or otherwise eligible for Medicaid, and entitled to Medicare cost-sharing under a state Medicaid program, may not enroll in an MA MSA plan.[62]

Federal Employee Health Benefit Plan (FEHBP) members will need to make sure that plan choices under consideration are those that have been certified by the Director of the Office of Management and Budget (OMB) to the Secretary that the Office of Personnel Management (OPM) has adopted policies that ensure that the enrollment of FEHBP individuals in such plans will not result in increased expenditures for health benefits under FEHBP.[63] Similar rules may be applied to individuals eligible for health care from either the Veterans Administration (VA) or the Department of Defense (DOD).[64]

---

[57] 42 U.S.C. §1395w-21; 42 C.F.R. §422.50(a)(1).

[58] 42 C.F.R. §422.50(a)(5).

[59] 42 C.F.R. §422.50(a)(2).

[60] *See* §422.50(a)(2)(iii). An MA special needs plan is defined in §422.2.

[61] 42 C.F.R. §422.50(a)(3).

[62] 42 U.S.C. §1395w-21(b)(3).

[63] 42 U.S.C. §1395w-21(b)(2)(A).

[64] 42 U.S.C. §1395w-21(b)(1)(2)(B).

[E] Process for Exercising Choice

The Secretary of HHS must establish a process through which Medicare beneficiaries can elect how they wish to obtain their Medicare covered services. Elections are made or changed only during coverage election periods.[65]

At the time of enrollment and every year thereafter, MA plans must disclose to enrollees their service area emergency service options and procedures for obtaining emergency services; out-of-state service coverage; optional supplemental coverage and costs; prior authorization rules; grievance and appeals procedures; quality assurance mechanisms; the number of grievances and appeals and their disposition; and a summary of the method of compensating doctors.[66]

[1] Initial Coverage Election Period

If there are one or more Medicare Advantage plans offered in an individual's service area at the time the individual first becomes entitled to benefits under Part A and enrolled under Part B, the individual must make the election during a defined election period beginning three months before the individual is entitled to both Parts A and B and ending the last month preceding the month of entitlement.[67] An election is considered to have been made on the date the election form is received by the MA Plan.[68]

Beneficiaries who do not make an election will remain in the original fee-for-service Medicare program. If an individual does not make an election and is in an HMO, that individual will remain in the HMO if the HMO offers an MA Plan.[69]

[2] Annual Coordinated Election Period

Each November, the Secretary of HHS must conduct an annual coordinated election period during which time a beneficiary may choose to enroll in an MA Plan, change to a different MA Plan, or return to fee-for-service Medicare.[70] An election made during this time period becomes effective on January 1 of the following year. A beneficiary who makes no election will remain in fee-for-service Medicare or in the MA Plan in which she or he is enrolled. The Secretary of HHS must mail written comparative information about plan choices to all beneficiaries

---

[65] 42 U.S.C. §1395w-21(c); 42 C.F.R. §422.60 (election process), §422.62 (election of coverage under an MA plan), §422.66 (coordination of enrollment and disenrollment through MA organizations), §422.74 (disenrollment by the MA organization).

[66] 42 U.S.C. §1395w-22(c); 42 C.F.R. §422.111.

[67] 42 U.S.C. §1395w-22(c); 42 C.F.R. §422.622.

[68] 42 C.F.R. §422.60 (election process).

[69] 42 U.S.C. §1395w-21(c)(3) (default); 42 C.F.R. §422.66(d).

[70] 42 U.S.C. §1395w-21(c)(1)–(3).

who live in an area in which at least one MA Plan is offered at least 15 days before the annual coordinated enrollment period.[71]

During the annual coordinated election period, an individual eligible to enroll in an MA plan may change his or her election from an MA plan to original Medicare or to a different MA plan, or from original Medicare to an MA plan; and if an individual changes his or her election from an MA plan that offers prescription drug coverage to original Medicare, he or she may also elect a Prescription Drug Plan (PDP).[72]

[3] Open Enrollment Periods

The rules concerning open enrollment and disenrollment are referred to as the "lock-in" rules.

[a] *Open Enrollment and Disenrollment Beginning in 2007*

For 2007 and subsequent years, except (1) as provided for newly eligible MA individuals,[73] (2) for elections made or changed during the annual coordinated election period,[74] (3) or for an individual eligible to elect an MA plan who is institutionalized as defined by CMS,[75] an individual who is not enrolled in an MA plan but is eligible to elect an MA plan may make an election into an MA plan once during the first three (3) months of the year.[76]

[i] *MA-PD Plans*

An individual who is enrolled in an MA-PD plan may elect another MA-PD plan or original Medicare and coverage under a PDP; an individual who is in original Medicare and has coverage under a PDP may elect an MA-PD plan.[77] Such an individual may not elect an MA plan that does not provide qualified prescription drug coverage.[78]

---

[71] 42 U.S.C. §1395w-21(d)(1)–(7); Note for 2006, an exception to the general rule, allowing for a longer annual coordinated election period, on November 15, 2005 through May 15, 2006. This period coincided with the first enrollment period for the new prescription drug benefit.

[72] *See* 42 C.F.R. §422.62(a)(2).

[73] *See* 42 C.F.R. §422.62(a)(5)(ii).

[74] *See* 42 C.F.R. §422.62(a)(5)(iii).

[75] *See* 42 C.F.R. §422.62(a)(6).

[76] 42 C.F.R. §422.62(a)(5).

[77] 42 C.F.R. §422.62(a)(5)(A).

[78] *Id.*

[ii]   MA Plan Without Prescription Drugs

An individual who is enrolled in an MA plan that does not provide qualified prescription drug coverage may elect another MA plan that does not provide that coverage or original Medicare; an individual who is in original Medicare and does not have coverage under a PDP may elect an MA plan that does not provide qualified prescription drug coverage.[79] Such an individual may not elect an MA-PD plan or coverage under a PDP.[80]

[b]   Newly Eligible MA Individual During 2007

An individual who becomes MA eligible during 2007 or later may elect an MA plan, including a plan with prescription drug coverage, or change his or her election once during the period that begins the month the individual is entitled to both Part A and Part B and ends on the last day of the third month of the entitlement, or on December 31, whichever is earlier.[81] This individual cannot elect an MA plan that does not provide qualified prescription drug coverage,[82] although if in original Medicare and without coverage under a PDP, he or she may elect an MA plan that does not provide prescription drug coverage.[83] In the latter circumstance, the individual may not elect an MA-PD plan or coverage under a PDP.[84]

The limitations to one election or change during the first part of each calendar year do not apply to elections made or changes made during the annual coordinated election period specified in paragraph (a)(2) (annual coordinated election period) of this section or during a special election period specified in paragraph (b) (special election periods) which begins in November of each year.[85]

[c]   Open Enrollment Period for Institutionalized Individuals

After 2005, an individual who is eligible to elect an MA plan and who is institutionalized is not limited, except as provided for in special rules for MA MSA plans, in the number of elections or changes he or she may make.[86] Subject to the MA plan being open to enrollees, an MA eligible institutionalized individual may

---

[79] 42 C.F.R. §422.62(a)(5)(B).

[80] *Id.*

[81] 42 C.F.R. §422.62(a)(5)(B)(ii).

[82] 42 C.F.R. §422.62(a)(5)(A).

[83] 42 C.F.R. §422.62(a)(5)(B).

[84] *Id.*

[85] *See* 42 C.F.R. §422.62(a)(5)(B)(iii).

[86] 42 C.F.R. §422.62(a)(6).

at any time elect an MA plan or change his or her election from an MA plan, or from original Medicare to an MA plan.[87]

A beneficiary who is an inpatient in an institution such as a skilled nursing facility or a rehabilitation hospital may elect to enroll in a MA Plan or to change MA plans at any time.

[4] Special Election Periods

An individual may at any time change his or her election in the form and manner specified by CMS, from an MA plan to original Medicare or to a different MA plan under any of the following special circumstances:[88]

(a) CMS or the organization has terminated the organization's contract for the plan, discontinued the plan, discontinued the plan in the area in which the individual resides, or the organization has notified the individual of the impending termination of the plan, or the impending discontinuation of the plan in the area in which the individual resides;

(b) The individual is not eligible to remain enrolled in the plan because of a change in his or her place of residence to a location out of the service area or continuation area or other change in circumstances as determined by CMS but not including terminations resulting from a failure to make timely payment of an MA plan monthly or supplemental beneficiary premium, or from disruptive behavior;

(c) The individual demonstrates to CMS, that—

(i) the organization offering the plan substantially violated a material provision of its contract in relation to the individual, such as (a) failing to provide the beneficiary on a timely basis medically necessary services for which benefits are available under the plan; (b) failing to provide medical services in accordance with applicable quality standards; or the organization (or its agent, representative, or plan provider) materially misrepresented the plan's provisions in marketing the plan to the individual.

(ii) the organization (or its agent, representative, or plan provider) materially misrepresents the plan's provisions in marketing the plan to an individual.

(d) The individual meets such other exceptional conditions as CMS may provide.

---

[87] *See* 42 C.F.R. §422.62(a)(6).
[88] 42 C.F.R. §422.62(b).

[5] Coordination of Enrollment and Disenrollment through MA Organizations

The enrollment and disenrollment of an individual in an MA plan of an MA organization is governed by the election of coverage under MA plans.[89] An individual may elect a different MA plan by filing the appropriate election with the MA;[90] or submit a request for disenrollment to the MA in the form and manner prescribed by CMS, or file the appropriate disenrollment form through other mechanisms as determined by CMS.[91] A disenrollment request is considered to have been made on the date the disenrollment request is received by the MA organization.[92]

The MA organization or plan must submit a disenrollment notice to CMS within time frames specified by CMS,[93] and provide the enrollee with notice of disenrollment, and include in the notice a statement explaining that the enrollee remains enrolled until the effective date of disenrollment; and that until that date, neither the MA organization nor CMS pays for services not provided or arranged for by the MA plan in which the enrollee is enrolled; and file and retain disenrollment request for the period specified in CMS instructions.[94]

[a] Failure to Submit Disenrollment Notice to CMS Promptly

If the MA organization fails to submit the correct and complete required notice, the MA organization must reimburse CMS for any capitation payments received after the month in which payment would have ceased if the requirement had been met timely.[95]

Retroactive active disenrollment may be granted by CMS in the following cases: there never was a legally valid enrollment; or a valid request for disenrollment was properly made but not processed or acted upon.[96] Note, an individual who fails to make an election during the initial coverage election period is deemed to have elected original Medicare.[97]

---

[89] 42 C.F.R. §422.66(a), (b).

[90] 42 C.F.R. §422.66(b)(i).

[91] 42 C.F.R. §422.66(b)(ii).

[92] 42 C.F.R. §422.66(b)(2).

[93] 42 C.F.R. §422.66((b)(3)(i).

[94] 42 C.F.R. §422.66(b)(3)(i)–(iv).

[95] 42 C.F.R. §422.66(b)(4).

[96] 42 C.F.R. §422.66(b)(5).

[97] 42 C.F.R. §422.66(c). The Medicare Managed Care Manual defines "passive" election as when the beneficiary has been informed by the MA plan that he or she may make an election of a different plan but takes no action. *See* Medicare Managed Care Manual, CMS Pub. 100-16, Ch. 2, §20.4.2.

[6] Conversion of Enrollment (Seamless Continuation of Coverage)

An MA plan offered by an MA organization must accept any individual (regardless of whether the individual has end-stage renal disease) who is enrolled in a health plan offered by the MA organization during the month immediately preceding the month in which he or she is entitled to both Part A and Part B, and who meets the MA plan eligibility requirements.[98]

Subject to CMS's approval, an MA organization may set aside a reasonable number of vacancies in order to accommodate enrollment of conversions. Any set aside vacancies that are not filled within a reasonable time must be made available to other MA eligible individuals.[99]

If an individual chooses to remain enrolled with the MA organization as an MA enrollee, the individual's conversion to an MA enrollee is effective the month in which he or she is entitled to both Part A and Part B.[100] With respect to conversions, the MA organization may only disenroll an individual in accordance with applicable disenrollment provisions.[101] Moreover, the individual who is converting must complete an election as prescribed in the MA election process.[102] The MA organization must transmit the information necessary for CMS to add the individual to its records as specified in the election requirements.[103]

[7] Maintenance of Enrollment

An individual who has made an election is considered to have continued that election until either: (i) the individual changes the election; (ii) the elected MA plan is discontinued or no longer serves the area in which the individual resides; or (iii) the organization does not offer or the individual does not elect the option of continuing enrollment.[104]

An individual enrolled in an MA plan that becomes an MA-PD plan on January 1, 2006, will be deemed to have elected to enroll in that MA-PD plan.[105] An individual who has elected an MA plan that does not provide prescription drug coverage will not be deemed to have elected an MA-PD plan and will

---

[98] 42 C.F.R. §422.66(d)(1). Note, eligibility requirements to elect an MA plan are at 42 C.F.R. §422.50.

[99] 42 C.F.R. §422.66(d)(2).

[100] 42 C.F.R. §422.66(d)(3).

[101] 42 C.F.R. §422.66(d)(4), *see* §422.74 (disenrollment by the MA organization).

[102] 42 C.F.R. §422.66(d)(5), *see* §422.60 (election process requirements).

[103] 42 C.F.R. §422.66(d)(6).

[104] 42 C.F.R. §422.66(e)(1)(i)–(ii).

[105] 42 C.F.R. §422.66(e)(2).

remain enrolled in the MA plan.[106] An individual enrolled in an MA-PD plan as of December 31 of a year is deemed to have elected to remain enrolled in that plan on January 1 of the following year.[107]

[8] Exception for Employer Group Health Plans

In cases when an MA organization has both a Medicare contract and a contract with an employer group health plan, and in which the MA organization arranges for the employer to process election forms for Medicare-entitled group members who wish to disenroll from the Medicare contract, the effective date of the election may be retroactive; a retroactive effective date may be made for up to a 90-day period.[108] Upon receipt of the election from the employer, the MA organization must submit a disenrollment notice to CMS.[109]

[9] Effective Dates of Coverage and Change of Coverage

[a] Initial Coverage Election Period

An election made during an initial coverage election period is effective as of the first day of the month of entitlement to both Part A and Part B.[110]

[b] Annual Coordinated Election

For an election or change of election made during the annual coordinated election period, coverage is effective as of the first day of the following calendar year.[111]

[c] Open Enrollment Periods

For an election, or change in election, made during an open enrollment period, coverage is effective as of the first day of the first calendar month following the month in which the election is made.[112]

---

[106] 42 C.F.R. §422.66(e)(4).
[107] 42 C.F.R. §422.66(e)(5).
[108] 42 C.F.R. §422.66(f)(1).
[109] 42 C.F.R. §422.66(f)(2).
[110] 42 C.F.R. §422.68(a).
[111] 42 C.F.R. §422.68(b).
[112] 42 C.F.R. §422.68(c).

[d] Special Election Periods

CMS determines the effective date of an election or change of election made during a special election period.[113] To the extent practicable, it is to make such changes in a manner consistent with protecting the continuity of health benefits coverage.[114]

[e] Special Election Period for Individual Age 65

For an election of coverage under original Medicare made during a special election period for an individual age 65, coverage is effective as of the first day of the calendar month following the month in which the election is made.[115]

[10] Disenrollment by the MA Organization

[a] Basis for Disenrollment

An MA organization may not disenroll an individual from any MA plan it offers, nor by any action or inaction, request or encourage an individual to disenroll,[116] except as follows:

[i] Optional Disenrollment

An MA organization may disenroll an individual from an MA plan it offers in any of the following circumstances: (i) any monthly basic and supplementary beneficiary premiums are not paid on a timely basis, subject to the grace period for late; (ii) the individual has engaged in disruptive behavior; and (iii) the individual provides fraudulent information on his or her election form or permits abuse of his or her enrollment card.[117]

[ii] Required Disenrollment

An MA organization must disenroll an individual from any MA plan it offers in any of the following circumstances: (1) the individual no longer resides in the MA plan's service area as specified in the plan; (2) is no longer eligible under the plan, and optional continued enrollment has not been offered or elected under the continuation of enrollment rules of this section; (3) the individual loses

---

[113] 42 C.F.R. §422.68(d).

[114] *Id.*

[115] 42 C.F.R. §422.66(e).

[116] 42 C.F.R. §422.74(a)(1)–(2).

[117] 42 C.F.R. §422.74(b)(i)–(iii).

entitlement under Part A or Part B benefits; (4) the individual has engaged in disruptive behavior as specified herein.[118]

[b] Plan Termination or Reduction of Area Where Plan Is Available

General rule: An MA organization that has its MA plan terminated, or terminates an MA plan, or that discontinues offering the plan in any portion of the area where the plan had previously been available, must disenroll affected enrollees.[119]

Exception: When an MA organization discontinues offering an MA plan in a portion of its service area, the MA organization may elect to offer enrollees residing in all or portions of the affected area the option to continue enrollment in plan offered by the organization, provided that there is no other MA plan offered in the affected area at the time of the discontinuation.[120] The organization may require an enrollee who chooses to continue enrollment to agree to receive the full range of basic benefits (excluding emergency and urgently needed care) exclusively through facilities designated by the organization within the plan service area.[121]

[c] Notice Requirement

If the disenrollment is for reasons such as failure to pay premiums, disruptive behavior, or provision of fraudulent information with respect to plan election (other than death or loss of entitlement to Part A or Part B), the MA organization must give the individual a written notice of the disenrollment, with an explanation of the reasons for disenrollment provided to the individual before submission of the disenrollment to CMS. Moreover, the notice must include an explanation of the individual's right to a hearing under MA organization's grievance procedures.[122]

[d] Process for Disenrollment

[i] Monthly Basic and Supplementary Premiums Are Not Paid Timely

An MA organization may disenroll an individual from the MA plan for failure to pay basic and supplemental premiums if:

(1) the MA organization can demonstrate to CMS that it made reasonable efforts to collect the unpaid premium amount. Such efforts include alerting

---

[118] 42 C.F.R. §422.74(b)(2).

[119] 42 C.F.R. §422.74(b)(3).

[120] *Id.*

[121] 42 C.F.R. §422.74(b)(3).

[122] 42 C.F.R. §422.74(c).

the individual that the premiums are due and providing the individual with a grace period, that is, an opportunity to pay past due premiums in full; (2) the length of the grace period will be, at minimum, one month and will begin on the first day of the month for which the premium is unpaid; and the MA plan demonstrates to CMS that it has advised the individual that failure to pay the premiums by the end of the grace period will result in termination of MA coverage.[123]

Further, the MA organization must demonstrate to CMS that it has provided the enrollee with notice of disenrollment.[124] If the enrollee fails to pay the premiums for optional services, but pays the premium for basic and mandatory supplemental services, the MA organization has the option to discontinue the optional supplemental benefits and retain the individual as an MA enrollee.[125]

[ii] Disruptive Behavior[126]

An MA plan enrollee is disruptive if his or her behavior substantially impairs the plan's ability to arrange for or provide services to the individual or other plan members. An individual cannot be considered disruptive if such behavior is related to the use of medical service or compliance (or noncompliance) with medical advice or treatment. Plans must make efforts to resolve the problems, and document the enrollee's behavior and its efforts to resolve the problem. In addition, CMS will review the information on the matter as submitted by the plan and the enrollee and make a decision whether to approve or deny the disenrollment. If CMS permits the disenrollment of a disruptive individual, disenrollment is the first day of the calendar month after the month in which the MA organization gives the individual notice of its plan to disenroll the individual for disruptive behavior.[127]

[F] Appeal and Grievance in Medicare Advantage Plans

Medicare Advantage appeal procedures include an internal grievance process and a formal appeal process with external review. The grievance and appeal processes are intended for different kinds of complaints. MA Organizations must ensure that all enrollees receive written information about the grievance and appeal procedures that are available to them.[128]

---

[123] 42 C.F.R. §422.74(d)(1).

[124] Id.

[125] 42 C.F.R. §422.74(d)((1)(C) (iii).

[126] 42 C.F.R. §422.74(d)(2)(i)–(vi).

[127] 42 C.F.R. §422.564(a)(1).

[128] 42 C.F.R. §422.564(a)(1).

[1] Grivances

[a] Generally

Each MA organization must provide meaningful procedures for timely hearing and resolving grievances between enrollees and the organization or any other entity or individual through which the organization provides health care services under any MA plan it offers.[129] Grievance procedures are separate and distinct from appeals.[130] Appeals address concerns and disagreements with organizational determinations (whether an item, service, or procedure is covered). Grievances go to issues about the quality of services received, time and location of services, and related matters.[131] In addition, the MA plan's grievance process is separate from the quality of care complaint filed with a Quality Improvement Organization (QIO), which address beneficiaries' written complaints about the quality of services received under the Medicare program. For quality of care issues, the beneficiary may file a written complaint with the MA organization or the QIO, or both.[132]

In addition, the MA organization must have an established recordkeeping process for tracking records on all grievances received, both orally and in writing. The record is to contain, at a minimum, the date of receipt of the grievance, and the final disposition of the grievance, and the date that the MA organization notified the enrollee of the disposition.[133]

[b] Expedited Grievances

Expedited grievances must be responded to within 24 hours. This process is available if the complaint involves an MA organization's decision to invoke an extension relating to an organization determination or reconsideration, or the MA organization's refusal to grant an enrollee's request for an expedited organization determination.[134]

---

[129] 42 C.F.R. §422.564(a).

[130] 42 C.F.R. §422.564(b); *see also*, 42 C.F.R. §422.566(a)–(b) for definition of an organization determination.

[131] 42 C.F.R. §422.564(b).

[132] 42 C.F.R. §422.564(c); for the functions of the QIO, see U.S.C. 1320c-3(a)(14).

[133] 42 C.F.R. §422.564(e).

[134] 42 C.F.R. §422.564((d)(1)–(2).

[c]   *Grievance Process*

CMS defines a grievance as an issue that does *not* involve organization determinations,[135] and that is:

> any complaint or dispute, other than one that constitutes an organization determination, expressing dissatisfaction with any aspect of an MA Organization's or provider's operations, activities, or behavior regardless of whether remedial action is requested.[136]

The grievance process is designed to provide a remedy for Medicare Advantage beneficiaries who have concerns about things other than coverage of benefits. For example, a grievance might be brought concerning rudeness of staff members, inconvenience of facilities, location and hours of service, or receipt of membership materials. Every MA Organization is required to provide "meaningful procedures for timely resolution of grievances between enrollees and the organization."[137] Grievances also include disputes with "any other entity or individual through which the organization provides health care services."[138]

An enrollee may file a grievance with an MA plan, either orally or in writing. The grievance must be filed no later than 60 days after the event or incident that precipitates the grievance.[139] The MA plan must notify the enrollee of its decision as expeditiously as possible, based on health status, but no later than 30 days of receipt of grievance.[140] The MA organization may extend the 30-day time frame by up to 14 days if the enrollee requests the extension, or if the MA organization justifies a need for additional information and documents how the delay is in the interest of the enrollee. If the MA organization extends the deadline, it must notify the enrollee in writing of the reasons for the delay.[141]

Grievances submitted in writing must be responded to in writing; grievances submitted orally may be responded to either orally or in writing, unless the enrollee requests a written response.[142] Grievances related to quality of care, regardless of how filed, must be responded to in writing and must include a description of the enrollee's right to file a written complaint with the QIO. In addition, the MA organization must cooperate with the QIO in resolving the complaint.[143]

---

[135] 42 C.F.R. §422.564(b).

[136] *See* 42 C.F.R. §422.564. The procedures distinguish grievances from appeals; from Quality Improvement Organization (QIO) complaints, and includes an expedited grievance.

[137] 42 C.F.R. §422.564(a)(1).

[138] *Id.*

[139] 42 C.F.R. §422.564(e)(1).

[140] 42 C.F.R. §422.564(e)(1).

[141] 42 C.F.R. §422.564(e)(2).

[142] 42 C.F.R. §422.564(e)(3)(i)–(iii).

[143] 42 C.F.R. §422.564(e)(3)(iii).

Upon receiving a complaint, an MA organization must promptly determine and inform the enrollee whether the complaint is subject to its grievance procedures or its appeal procedures.[144]

[2] Organization Determinations

[a] *Generally*

Each MA organization must have a procedure for making timely organization determinations regarding the benefits to which the enrollee is entitled under the MA plan, including such things as basic benefits, mandatory and optional supplemental benefits, and the amount, if any, the beneficiary is to pay.[145]

An organization determination is any determination made by a MA organization with respect to: (1) payment for temporary out of the area renal dialysis services, emergency services, post-stabilization care or urgent care; (2) payment for any other health services furnished by a provider other than the MA organization that the enrollee believes are covered under Medicare or if not covered under Medicare, should be furnished, arranged for, or reimbursed by the MA organization; (3) the MA organization's refusal to provide or pay for services, in whole or in part, including the type or level of services, that the enrollee believes should be furnished or arranged for by the MA organization; and (4) discontinuation of a service if the enrollee believes that continuation of the service is medically necessary; the failure of the MA organization to approve, furnish, arrange for, or provide payment for health care services in a timely manner; or (5) the provision of timely notice to an enrollee with respect to an adverse determination, such that the delay would adversely affect the health of the enrollee.[146]

An expedited organization determination, as explained below, can be requested by an enrollee (including his or her authorized representative) or a physician (regardless of whether the physician is affiliated with the MA organization.[147]

[b] *Who Can Request an Organization Determination?*

Individuals or entities who can request an organization determination are the enrollee (including his or her authorized representative); any provider that furnishes, or intends to furnish, services to the enrollee; or the legal representative of a deceased enrollee's estate.[148]

---

[144] 42 C.F.R. §422.564(b).

[145] 42 C.F.R. §422.566(a).

[146] 42 C.F.R. §422.566(b).

[147] 42 C.F.R. §422.566(c)(2)(i)–(ii).

[148] 42 C.F.R. §422.566(c)(1)(i)–(iii).

[c] Standard Time Frames and Notice—Organization Determinations

[i] Time Frame for Requests for Service

When a party has made a request for a service, the MA organization must notify the enrollee of its determination as expeditiously as the enrollee's health condition requires, but no later than 14 calendar days after the day the organization receives a request for a standard review.[149] The MA organization may extend the time frame by up to 14 calendar days upon request of the enrollee or of the MA organization if it justifies the need for the extension and shows how the delay is in the interest of the enrollee.[150] The enrollees must be informed in writing of the MA organization's decision to extend the time frame, and its reasons, and the MA organization must inform the beneficiary of his or her right to file an expedited grievance if he or she disagrees with the MA organization's decision.[151]

[ii] Time Frame for Request of Payment

The MA organization must process requests for payment according to the Secretary's "prompt payment" provisions which call for paying 95 percent of clean claims (no obvious errors on the face of the claim) within 30 days, with all other claims to be paid, or denied, within 60 days from the date of the request.[152]

[iii] Written Notification of Organization Denials

If the MA organization decides to deny service or payment in whole or in part, or if an enrollee disagrees with an MA organization's decision to discontinue or reduce the level of care for an ongoing course of treatment, the organization must give the enrollee written notice of the determination.[153]

[iv] Parties to the Organization Determination

Parties to an organization determination include the enrollee (including his or her representative), or an assignee of the enrollee (a physician or other service

---

[149] 42 C.F.R. §422.568(a).

[150] 42 C.F.R. §422.566(a); prompt payment rules are set forth in 42 C.F.R. §422.520.

[151] 42 C.F.R. §422.566(a).

[152] 42 C.F.R. §422.568(b).

[153] 42 C.F.R. §422.568(c).

provider who waives any right to payment from the enrollee for that service), the legal representative of a deceased enrollee's estate, as well as any provider or entity (other than the MA organization) determined to have an appealable interest.[154] The effect of an organization determination is binding on all parties unless it is reconsidered or reopened.[155]

[v] Expediting Certain Organization Determinations

An enrollee or physician must submit an oral or written request directly to the MA organization or, if applicable, to the entity responsible for making the determination as directed by the MA organization. A physician may provide oral or written support for a request for an expedited determination.[156]

To ask for an expedited determination, an enrollee or a physician must submit an oral or written request directly to the MA organization; if applicable, to the entity responsible for making the determination, as directed by the MA organization.[157] A physician may provide oral or written support for a request for an expedited determination.[158]

An MA plan that processes expedited requests must establish an efficient and convenient means for individuals to submit oral or written requests, and document in case files requests made by enrollees. In addition, the MA organization must determine that using the standard time frame could seriously jeopardize the life or health of the enrollee or the enrollee's ability to regain maximum function.[159]

The MA organization must provide an expedited determination if the physician indicates that applying the standard time frame for making a determination could seriously jeopardize the life or health of the enrollee or the enrollee's ability to regain maximum function.[160]

[vi] Actions Following a Denial

The MA plan is to transfer automatically a request to the standard time frame and make the determination within 14 days (from the date the MA organization received the request), give the enrollee prompt oral notice of the denial, and within 3 days, a written letter explaining that the request will be processed using the 14-day

---

[154] 42 C.F.R. §422.574.

[155] 42 C.F.R. §422.576. *See*, 42 C.F.R. §§422.578–422.596 (reconsideration), 42 C.F.R. §422.616 (reopening).

[156] 42 C.F.R. §422.570(a).

[157] 42 C.F.R. §422.570(b)(1).

[158] 42 C.F.R. §422.570(b)(2).

[159] 42 C.F.R. §422.570(c).

[160] 42 C.F.R. §422.570(c)(ii).

standard time frame, as well as explain that the enrollee has the right to submit an expedited grievance, and a right to re-submit the request with physician support.[161]

[vii]   Timeline for Expedited Organization Determinations

MA plans must make adverse or favorable determination as expeditiously as the enrollee's health condition requires, but not later than 72 hours. A 14-day extension can be granted if the enrollee requests it, or if the organization justifies the need for additional information, and must notify enrollee in writing of reasons for the delay; and inform the enrollee that he or she can file an expedited griev-ance.[162] Moreover, if notice is oral, the MA must confirm it in writing within three days of oral notice.[163]

[d]   Right to Reconsideration

Any party to an organization determination may request that the determina-tion be reconsidered under the procedures described in §422.582 (requests for a standard reconsideration).[164] An enrollee or a physician (acting on behalf of an enrollee) can request an expedited reconsideration.[165]

[i]   Reconsideration Defined

A reconsideration is defined as consisting of a review of an adverse organization determination, the evidence and findings upon which it was based, and any other evidence the parties submit or the MA organization or CMS obtains.[166] A party to an organization determination must ask for a reconsideration of the determination by making a written request to the MA organization that made the organization determination. The MA organization may adopt a policy for accepting oral requests.[167]

[ii]   Filing a Request for Reconsideration

A party must file a request for reconsideration within 60 calendar days from the date of the notice of the organization determination.[168] If a party shows good

---

[161] 42 C.F.R. §422.570(d).

[162] 42 C.F.R. §422.572.

[163] *Id.*

[164] 42 C.F.R. §422.578.

[165] 42 C.F.R. §422.584.

[166] 42 C.F.R. §422.580.

[167] 42 C.F.R. §422.582(a).

[168] 42 C.F.R. §422.582(b).

cause, the MA organization may extend the time frame for filing a request for reconsideration.[169]

If the 60-day period in which to file a request for reconsideration has expired, a party to the org. determination may file a request for a reconsideration with the MA organization. The request for reconsideration and to extend time must be in writing; and must state why the request for reconsideration was not filed timely.[170]

[iii]   Parties to Reconsideration

The parties to the reconsideration are the parties to the organization determination, and any other provider or entity (other than the MA organization) whose rights with respect to the organization determination may be affected by the reconsideration, as determined by the entity that conducts the reconsideration.[171] The party who files a request for reconsideration may withdraw it by filing a written request for withdrawal to the MA organization.[172]

[iv]   Time Frames and Responsibilities for Reconsiderations

Standard reconsideration: Requests for services—determinations completely favorable to the enrollee must be issued as expeditiously as the beneficiary's health condition requires, but not later than 30 calendar days from the date the MA org. received the request for a standard review.[173]

The MA organization may extend the time frame by up to 14 calendar days if the enrollee requests or if the MA organization justifies a need for additional information and how the delay is in the interest of the enrollee; the MA organization must notify the enrollee in writing of the reasons for the delay, and inform the enrollee of his or her right to file an expedited grievance; for extensions, decisions must be made as expeditiously as the patient's condition requires but within the time period of the extension.[174]

If the MA organization fails to provide a reconsideration determination within the specified time frames, the failure constitutes an affirmation of its adverse organization determination, and the organization must submit the file to the Independent Review Entity (IRE).[175]

---

[169] 42 C.F.R. §422.582(c).

[170] 42 C.F.R. §422.582(c)(2).

[171] 42 C.F.R. §422.582(d).

[172] 42 C.F.R. §422.582(e).

[173] 42 C.F.R. §422.590(a).

[174] 42 C.F.R. §422.590(b).

[175] 42 C.F.R. §422.590; 42 C.F.R. §422.590(c)(b).

The MA organization that approves a request for expedited reconsideration must complete its reconsideration and give the enrollee (and physician if involved) notice of its decision as expeditiously as the enrollee's health condition requires but no later than 72 hours after receiving the request.[176]

The MA organization may extend the 72-hour deadline by up to 14 calendar days if the enrollee requests the extension or if the organization justifies a need for additional information. In addition, the MA organization must notify the enrollee in writing with reasons for the delay, and an explanation of the enrollee's right to file an expedited grievance; and must make its decision no later than upon the expiration of the extension.[177] If the MA organization first notified an enrollee of a completely favorable expedited reconsideration, it must mail written confirmation to the enrollee within three calendar days.[178]

[v]   Expediting Certain Reconsiderations

Excluding requests for payment for services already furnished, an enrollee or a physician (regardless of whether he or she is affiliated with the MA organization) may request an expedited reconsideration.[179] An enrollee, or a physician acting on behalf of an enrollee, must submit an oral or written request directly to the MA organization or, if applicable, to the entity responsible for making the reconsideration, as directed by the MA organization.[180] A physician may provide oral or written support for the request.[181]

The MA organization must establish and maintain efficient and convenient means to submit oral and written requests and documents and maintain the documentation in the case file, and make prompt decisions whether to expedite the reconsideration or follow the standard time frame.[182] When requested by an enrollee, the MA organization must decide whether to expedite its decision, or where the request is made or supported by a physician, make its reconsideration on an expedited basis.[183]

If the request for expedited reconsideration is denied, the MA organization must transfer a request to a standard time frame and make determination within the 30 days that begins the day the MA organization received the request for expedited reconsideration and must give the enrollee prompt oral notice, followed within 3

[176] 42 C.F.R. §422.590(d)(1).
[177] 42 C.F.R. §422.590(d)(2).
[178] 42 C.F.R. §422.590(d)(3).
[179] 42 C.F.R. §422.584(a).
[180] 42 C.F.R. §422.584(b).
[181] 42 C.F.R. §422,584(b)(2).
[182] 42 C.F.R. §422.584(c).
[183] Id.

calendar days by written letter, explaining that the request will be processed using the 30-day standard time frame for reconsiderations.[184]

If an MA organization grants a request for expedited reconsideration, it must conduct the reconsideration and give notice as required by the regulations.[185] Moreover, if the MA organization must receive medical information from non-contract providers, the organization must request the necessary information within 24 hours of the initial request for an expedited reconsideration.[186] Non-contractors are to make a diligent effort to supply the information, and the MA organization is still responsible for meeting the time frame and notice requirements.[187]

If the MA organization affirms in whole or in part, it must submit a written explanation and the case file to the Independent Review Entity (IRE) contracted by CMS as expeditiously as the enrollee's health condition requires, but not later than within 24 hours of its affirmation. In addition, the organization must make a reasonable and diligent effort to gather and forward the information to the IRE.[188] If the MA organization refers the matter to the Independent Review Entity (IRE), it must concurrently notify the enrollee of that action.[189]

If the MA organization fails to provide the enrollee with timely results of its reconsideration within the time frame set out above, the failure constitutes an adverse reconsideration predetermination, and the MA organization must submit the file to the IRE within 24 hours of expiration of the above described time frame.[190]

[vi]   Who Can Hear an Adverse MA Organization Determination

Persons not involved in the organization determination may hear an adverse MA organization determination; medical necessity determinations must be made by a physician with expertise in the field of medicine that is appropriate for the service at issue,[191] although the physician need not in all cases be of the same specialty or subspecialty as the treating physician.[192]

---

[184] 42 C.F.R. §422.584(d).

[185] 42 C.F.R. §422.584(d); *see also* §422.590.

[186] *Id.*

[187] *Id.*

[188] 42 C.F.R. §422.590(d)(5).

[189] 42 C.F.R. §422.590(e).

[190] 42 C.F.R. §422.590(f).

[191] 42 C.F.R. §422.590(f).

[192] *Id.*

[e] Reconsideration by an Independent Entity

When the MA organization affirms, in whole or part, its adverse organization determinations, the issues that remain in dispute must be reviewed and resolved by an independent, outside entity that contracts with CMS; the entity must meet contract deadlines for its decisions; the parties to a reconsideration are the same as those before the MA organization's reconsideration, with the addition of the MA organization.[193] The independent entity is responsible for mailing a notice of its reconsideration determination to the parties and for sending a copy to CMS; the notice must state the specific reasons for the entity's decision in understandable language; and if the decision is adverse, it must inform the parties of their right to ALJ review if the amount in controversy is $100 or more; and describe the procedures for obtaining ALJ review.[194]

A reconsidered determination is final and binding on all parties unless a party other than the MA organization files a request for a hearing under the provisions for request for an Administrative Law Judge (ALJ) review, or unless the reconsidered determination is revised.[195] If the amount remaining in controversy after reconsideration meets the threshold requirement established annually by the Secretary, any party to the reconsideration (except the MA organization) who is dissatisfied with the reconsideration determination has a right to a hearing before an ALJ.[196]

[f] Right to ALJ Hearing and Amount in Controversy

The amount remaining in controversy, which can include any combination of Part A and Part B services, is computed by the Secretary.[197] The parties to a hearing are the parties to the reconsideration, the MA organization, and any other person or entity whose rights with the respect to the reconsideration may be affected by the hearing, as determined by the ALJ.[198]

A party must file a written request for a hearing with the entity specified in the IRE's reconsideration notice, and except when an ALJ extends the time frame, a party must file a request within 60 days of the notice of a reconsideration determination.[199] The parties to a hearing are the parties to the reconsideration, the MA

---

[193] 42 C.F.R. §422.592.

[194] 42 C.F.R. §422.594.

[195] 42 C.F.R. §422.596; *see* §422.616 (reopening and revising determinations and decisions).

[196] 42 C.F.R. §422.600(a).

[197] 42 C.F.R. §422.600(b). The jurisdictional amounts for 2007 were unavailable at the time of publication.

[198] 42 C.F.R. §422.600(c).

[199] 42 C.F.R. §§422.602(a), (b).

organization, and any other party or entity whose rights with respect to the reconsideration may be affected by the hearing, as determined by the ALJ.[200]

If a request for a hearing clearly shows that the amount in controversy is less than that required jurisdictional amount, the ALJ dismisses the request; if the hearing is initiated, and the ALJ finds the amount in controversy is less than required jurisdictional amount, the ALJ discontinues the hearing and does not rule on the substantive issues raised in the appeal.[201]

[g] Medicare Appeals Council Review

Any party to the hearing, including the MA organization, who is dissatisfied with the ALJ hearing decision, may request the Medicare Appeals Council (MAC) review the ALJ's decision or dismissal. The regulations under part 405 apply to matters addressed by this subpart to the extent they are appropriate.[202]

[h] Judicial Review

Any party, including the MA organization may request judicial review (upon notifying the other parties) of an ALJ's decision if the MAC denied the party's request for review; and the amount in controversy meets the threshold requirement established annually by the Secretary.[203]

With respect to a review of a MAC decision, any party, including the MA organization, may request judicial review (upon notifying the other parties) of the MAC decision if it is the final decision of CMS and the amount in controversy meets the threshold established by the Secretary.[204]

In order to request judicial review, a party must file a civil action in a district court of the United States in accordance with Section 205(g) of the Social Security Act.[205]

---

[200] 42 C.F.R. §422.602(c).

[201] 42 C.F.R. §422.602(d). This provision implements §1869(b)(1)(E)(iii) (Amount in Controversy) (MMA) of the Social Security Act, 42 U.S.C. §1395w-22(g)(5). The preamble to the interim final regulations, at 70 Fed. Reg. 11,423 (Mar. 8, 2005), provides "revisions to the appeals time frames and amount in Controversy." The amount in controversy (AIC) requirement for ALJ hearing requests and judicial review is amended so that it will be adjusted annually by the Secretary, beginning January 1, 2005, by the percentage increase in the medical care component of the consumer price index (CPI) for all urban consumers and rounded to the nearest multiple of $10. See 42 C.F.R. §§405.950(a), 405.970(a), and 405.1006.

[202] 42 C.F.R. §422.608.

[203] 42 C.F.R. §422.612.

[204] 42 C.F.R. §422.612.

[205] 42 C.F.R. §422.612(c). (See part 405 of 42 C.F.R. for a description of the procedures to follow in requesting judicial review.)

[i] Reopening and Revising Determinations and Decisions

An organization or reconsidered determination made by an MA organization, a reconsidered determination made by the Independent Entity, or the decision of an ALJ, or of the MAC, may be reopened and revised by the entity that made the determination or decision.[206]

[j] Effectuating Standard Reconsidered Determinations and Decisions

[i] For a request for service, if on reconsideration, the MA organization completely reverses its organization determination, the MA organization must authorize or provide the service under dispute as expeditiously as the enrollee's condition requires, but no later than 30 calendar days after the date MA organization receives the request for reconsideration (or no later than the end of an extension).[207]

[ii] For a request for payment, if on reconsideration, the MA organization completely reverses its organization determination, the organization must pay for the service no later than 60 days after the date the MA organization receives the request for reconsideration.[208]

[k] Effectuating Reversals by the Independent, Outside Review Entity

For a request for service, the independent, outside review entity (IRE) must authorize the service within 72 hours from the date it receives notice reversing the determination, and with respect to request for payment, the IRE must authorize payment within 30 calendar days from the date it receives notice reversing the organization determination.[209]

[i] Effectuating Standard Reconsideration

For reversals other than by the MA organization or the Independent review entity, decisions by an ALJ or higher level of appeal must be effectuated as expeditiously as the enrollee's health requires, but no later than 60 calendar days from the date it receives notice reversing the decision.[210] When, however, the MA

---

[206] 42 C.F.R. §422.616.

[207] 42 C.F.R. §422.618(a)(1).

[208] 42 C.F.R. §422.618(a)(2).

[209] 42 C.F.R. §422.618(b)(1)-(2).

[210] 42 C.F.R. §422.618(c)(1).

organization files an appeal with the MAC, the MA organization may await the outcome of the review before it pays for, authorizes, or provides the service under dispute. The MA organization must concurrently send a copy of its appeal request and any accompanying documents to the enrollee and must notify the outside entity that it has requested an appeal.[211]

[ii]   Effectuating Expedited Reconsidered Determinations

If the MA organization completely reverses its determination, the service must be authorized as expeditiously as the enrollee's health condition requires, but no later than 72 hours after receipt of the request for reconsideration (or no later than upon expiration of any extension).[212]

[iii]   Effectuating Reversals by the Independent Review Entity, Expedited Reconsideration

If the MA organization's decision is reversed in whole or in part, the decision must be effectuated as expeditiously as the enrollee's condition requires, but no later than 72 hours from the date it receives the notice reversing the determination.[213]

[iv]   Effectuating Expedited Reversals by Other Than the MA Organization or the IRE

If reversed in whole or in part by the ALJ or higher level of appeal, the MA organization must authorize payment as expeditiously as the enrollee's condition requires, but no later than 60 days from the date it receives the notice reversing the determination.[214] The MA organization may await the outcome of the review before it authorizes or provides the service under dispute, and if the MA organization files an appeal with the MAC, it must concurrently notify the enrollee and notify the Independent Review Entity.[215]

---

[211] 42 C.F.R. §422.618(c)(2).

[212] 42 C.F.R. §422.619(a).

[213] 42 C.F.R. §422.619(b).

[214] 42 C.F.R. §422.619(c)(1).

[215] 42 C.F.R. §422.619(c)(2).

[l] MA Organization Enrollee Notice of Non-Covered Inpatient Hospital Care

[i] Written Notice of Non-Coverage

The MA organization must provide written notice to the enrollee when the beneficiary disagrees with the discharge decision, or if the MA organization or its designate is not discharging the individual, but no longer intends to continue coverage of the inpatient stay.[216] Under these circumstances, an enrollee is entitled to coverage until at least noon of the day after such notice is provided (coverage is extended under QIO review rules if QIO review is requested).[217]

[ii] Physician Concurrence Required

Before discharging an individual or changing the level of care in an inpatient hospital setting, the MA organization must obtain the concurrence of the physician who is responsible for the enrollee's inpatient care.[218]

[iii] Timing and Content of Notice of Noncoverage

When applicable, the written notice of non-coverage must be issued no later than the day before hospital coverage ends. It must include the reason why inpatient care is no longer covered; the effective date and time of the enrollee's liability for continued inpatient care; the enrollee's appeal rights; the new lower level of care, if applicable; and any other information required by CMS.[219]

---

[216] 42 C.F.R. §422.620(a); The notice protections for hospitalized MA enrollees are likely to be expanded as the result of a settlement agreement in Weichardt v. Thompson, C.A. No. 03 5490 VRW (N.D.Cal. Settlement Agreement, October 28, 2005). Proposed regulations implementing this settlement have been published by CMS. *See* Medicare Program; Notification Procedures for Hospital Discharges, 71 Fed. Reg. 17052 - 17062 (April 5, 2006) (to be codified at 42 C.F.R. §§405.1205, 405.1206, 422.620, and 422.622, *inter alia*.) If adopted, the new system will include both a generic and a specific notice of discharge. The hospital will be required to deliver a generic notice of a discharge decision to the patient on the day before a planned discharge. This notice describes the process for immediate appeal of the discharge, and the financial consequences of the appeal options. 42 C.F.R. §422.620 (proposed). If a patient decides to request expedited appeal, the MA organization must deliver a second, detailed notice by the end of the day when appeal is requested. This notice sets out the factual and legal reasons why the MA believes hospital services are no longer covered. 42 C.F.R. §422.622(c) (proposed).

[217] *Id.*

[218] 42 C.F.R. §422.620(b).

[219] 42 C.F.R. §422.620(c).

[iv] Requesting Immediate QIO Review of Noncoverage of Inpatient Hospital Care

Person requesting immediate QIO review may remain in the hospital with no additional financial liability; persons who fail to request immediate QIO review may request expedited reconsideration, but the financial liability rules apply.[220]

The financial liability rules provide that when the MA organization determines that hospital services are not, or are no longer, covered, the organization continues to be financially responsible for the costs of the hospital stay, when a timely appeal is filed, until noon of the calendar day following the day the QIO notifies the enrollee of its review determination.[221] If coverage of the hospital admission was never approved by the MA organization (or the admission does not constitute emergency or urgently needed care), the MA organization is liable for the hospital costs only if it is determined on appeal that the hospital stay should have been covered under the MA plan.[222] The hospital may not charge the MA organization (or the enrollee) if it was the hospital (acting on behalf of the enrollee) that filed the request for immediate QIO review; and the QIO upholds the noncoverage determination made by the MA organization.[223]

If the hospital determines that inpatient hospital services are no longer necessary, and the enrollee could not reasonably be expected to know that the services would not be covered, the hospital may not charge the enrollee for inpatient services received before noon of the calendar day following the day the QIO notifies the enrollee of its review determination.[224]

[v] Procedures for Immediate QIO Review

An enrollee must submit the request to the QIO that has an agreement with CMS, in writing, by noon of the first working day after receipt of written notice that the MA organization or hospital believes that the hospital stay is no longer necessary.[225] On receipt, the QIO must notify the MA organization that the enrollee has filed a request for immediate review, and the MA organization must supply any information (by phone or in writing) requested by the QIO for its review by the close of business of the first full working day immediately following the day the enrollee submits the request for review.[226]

---

[220] 42 C.F.R. §422.622 (a)(1)–(2); §422.622(c)(financial liability).

[221] 42 C.F.R. §422.622(c).

[222] *Id.*

[223] 42 C.F.R. §422.622(c)((1)(A)–(B).

[224] 42 C.F.R. §422.622(c)(2).

[225] 42 C.F.R. §422.622(b).

[226] *Id.*

In response to request from the MA organization, the hospital must submit medical records and other information to the QIO by close of business of the first full working day immediately following the day the organization makes its request; and the QIO must solicit the views of the enrollee who requested the review.[227] In addition, the QIO must make a determination and notify the enrollee, the hospital, and the MA organization by the close of business of the first working day after it receives all necessary information from the hospital, or the organization, or both.[228]

[m] Notifying Enrollees of MA Organization Provider Termination of Services

[i] Timing of Notice

Before terminating covered services authorized by an MA organization, an advance written notice must be provided to an enrollee by providers of service, including Home Health Agencies (HHAs), Skilled Nursing Facilities (SNFs), and Comprehensive Outpatient Rehabilitation Facilities (CORFs).[229] This includes the cessation of coverage at the end of a course of treatment, regardless of whether the enrollee agrees with the termination.[230] Prior to any termination of service, the provider must deliver advance written notice to the enrollee of the MA's decision to terminate services; provider must use a standardized notice, required by the Secretary.[231] The notice is to be provided no later than two days before the proposed end of services.[232] If services are expected to be fewer than two days in duration, notify the enrollee at the time of admission to the provider; for noninstitutional settings if the span of time between services exceeds two days, the notice should be given no later than the next to last time services are furnished.[233]

[ii] Content of Notice

Standardized notice to include: date that coverage ends; date of enrollee's liability; a description of the enrollee's right to a fast-track appeal, described below, to the IRE; an enrollee's right to submit evidence that services should continue; availability of other MA appeal procedures; the right to receive detailed information about the IRE process; and other information required by the Secretary.[234]

---

[227] 42 C.F.R. §422.622(b).

[228] Id.

[229] 42 C.F.R. §422.624(a).

[230] Id.

[231] 42 C.F.R. §422.624(b).

[232] 42 C.F.R. §422.624(b)(1).

[233] Id.

[234] 42 C.F.R. §422.624(b)(2).

[iii]   When Delivery of Notice is Valid

Delivery not valid unless: (1) the enrollee (or authorized rep) has signed and dated the notice to indicate receipt and comprehension of content; (2) notice is delivered as described above and has the notice content described above (*see* **§7.04[F][2][m][i], [ii]**).[235]

[iv]   Financial Liability for Failure to Deliver Valid Notice

An MA organization is financially liable for continued services until two days after the enrollee receives valid notice; an enrollee may waive continuation of service if he or she agrees with being discharged sooner than two days after receiving the notice.[236]

[n]   Fast-Track Appeals to Independent Review Entities

[i]   Right to Fast-Track Appeal

An enrollee of an MA organization has a right to a fast-track appeal of an MA organization decision to terminate provider services, which can be requested of the Independent Review Entities (IRE) in writing or by telephone by noon of the first day after the day of delivery of the termination notice (or by noon of the next day that the IRE is open for business).[237] If the enrollee fails to make a timely request to the IRE, he or she may request an expedited reconsideration by the MA organization.[238] If, after delivery of the termination notice, the enrollee chooses to leave a provider or discontinue receipt of services on or before the proposed termination, the enrollee cannot later assert a right to IRE appeal for the services at issue.[239]

[ii]   Continuation of Coverage

Coverage of provider services continues until the date and time designated on the termination notice, unless the enrollee appeals and the IRE reverses the MA organization decision.[240] If the decision is delayed because the provider did not

---

[235] 42 C.F.R. §422.624(b).

[236] 42 C.F.R. §422.624(d).

[237] 42 C.F.R. §422.626(a); CMS Manual Provisions on Fast Track can be found in the Medicare Managed Care Manual, CMS Pub. 100-16, Ch. 13, §90.8 (revised 12-03-04) (online publication, <www.cms.hhs.gov>).

[238] 42 C.F.R. §422.626(a)(2)–(3).

[239] *Id.*

[240] 42 C.F.R. §422.626(b).

submit requested information timely, the MA organization is liable for any additional coverage required by the delayed IRE decision; if the IRE finds that enrollee did not receive valid notice, coverage continues until at least two days after valid notice is received, unless the continued coverage poses a threat to the enrollee's health and safety.[241]

[iii] Burden of Proof

The burden of proof rests with the MA organization to demonstrate that termination of coverage is the correct decision, either based on medical necessity, or based on other Medicare coverage policies.[242]

[iv] Procedures IRE Must Follow

On the date of receipt of enrollee's request for an appeal, the IRE must immediately notify the MA organization and the provider of the appeal request, and of its responsibility to submit documentation as requested by the IRE.[243] The IRE must make a decision and notify the enrollee, the MA organization, and the provider, by close of business of the day after it receives the necessary information for decision.[244] It can defer the decision until it receives necessary information from the MA, and until it does, coverage continues until the IRE makes its decision.[245]

[v] Responsibilities of the MA Organization

The MA organization is to provide detailed notice to the enrollee about why services are either no longer reasonable and necessary or no longer covered, and is to include in the notice a description of any applicable Medicare coverage rule, instruction, policy, including citation, or any applicable MA rationale or contract provision, or facts specific to the enrollee, and other information required by CMS, including cost for copying documents, as well as any information required by the IRE.[246]

---

[241] *Id.*

[242] 42 C.F.R. §422.626(c).

[243] 42 C.F.R. §422.626(d).

[244] *Id.*

[245] *Id.*

[246] 42 C.F.R. §422.626(e).

[vi]   Reconsiderations of IRE Decisions

An enrollee may request reconsideration no later than 60 days after notification that the IRE has upheld the decision.[247] The reconsideration must be rendered expeditiously, but no later than within 14 days of receipt of the enrollee's request.[248] If affirmed in whole or part, the enrollee may appeal to the ALJ, the DAB, or a federal court as provided in these rules.[249]

§7.05   MEDICARE ADVANTAGE QUALITY IMPROVEMENT PROGRAM

[A]   Overview

MA plans are to establish a series of quality of care protections through a quality improvement program for the health services they provide.[250] The primary goal of this program is to ensure ongoing quality improvement for health care services provided to individuals enrolled in MA Plans.[251] Advocates should study this ambitious and multifaceted approach to quality improvement and monitoring mechanisms carefully to ascertain how quality improvement mechanisms might facilitate coverage and access to services. Similarly, advocates should assess the impact of quality improvement programs on grievance and appeal processes where services are denied, reduced, or terminated.

In the past, advocates encountered these mechanisms most frequently in the hospital Prospective Payment System (PPS) and HMO environments where capitated payments may well militate against more costly care even where such care may provide a more advantageous patient outcome. Unfortunately, advocates have had limited success in using quality assessment and monitoring mechanisms, including utilization review (UR), to advocate for certain procedures.

Advocates have found it difficult to challenge utilization determinations where issues under consideration did not lend themselves to defined standards, for example, where a standard of medical practice is evolving. In addition, much of the quality review process continues to be based on medical peer review, an approach that appears, overall, less favorable to beneficiaries than does a neutral

---

[247] 42 C.F.R. §422.626(e).

[248] *Id.*

[249] *Id.*

[250] *See* 42 U.S.C. §§1395w-22(e) *et seq.*; 42 C.F.R. §422.152 (Quality Improvement Program). It should be noted that there is a different quality assurance program for MA private fee-for-service plans and non-network MSA plans, *see* 42 U.S.C. §1395w-22(e)(2)(B) requiring MA Plans to include a separate focus on racial and ethnic minorities.

[251] 42 U.S.C. §1395w-22(e)(1).

fact finder trained in the weighing of evidence, such as an ALJ.[252] The HHS policy allowed the investigation reports of independent QIOs to be released to complainants only with the consent of the persons against whom a complaint has been made. A court decision has held that this policy, which discouraged beneficiaries from filing complaints, violated the Medicare statute.[253]

Information on quality assurance and its interplay with access to services in the managed care context is very important. For beneficiary advocates, this has been a relatively obscure aspect of obtaining necessary services for our clients. Given the increased federal and state focus on delivering services through managed care entities, quality concerns necessarily become more central to discussions about coverage and access to services. As such, a focus on monitoring and enforcing certain quality of care standards becomes an additional resource for promoting access to services.

[B] The Quality Improvement Program

[1] In General

Each MA organization (other than MA private fee-for-service and MSA plans) that offers one or more MA plans must have, for each of those plans, an ongoing quality improvement program that meets the applicable requirements of the Quality Improvement Program for the services it furnishes to MA enrollees.[254] As part of its ongoing quality improvement program, a plan must (1) have a chronic care improvement program that meets the requirements of subparagraph (c) of these regulations (described below), concerning elements of a chronic care program; (2) conduct quality improvement projects that can be expected to have a favorable effect on health outcomes and enrollee satisfaction, and meet the requirements of paragraph (d) (described below) of this section; and (3) encourage its providers to participate in CMS and HHS quality improvement initiatives.[255]

[2] Requirements for MA Coordinated Care Plans

An MA coordinated care plan's quality improvement plan (except for regional PPO plans and local PPO plans as defined in paragraph (e) of these regulations), described below, must (1) in processing requests for initial or continued authorization of services, follow written policies and procedures that reflect current standards of medical practice; (2) have in effect mechanisms to

---

[252] This is an area for empirical study. Anecdotal experience suggests that beneficiaries receive more favorable results when using the neutral fact-finder approach.

[253] Public Citizen Inc. v. DHHS, 332 F.3d 654 (D.C. Cir. 2003).

[254] 42 C.F.R. §422.152(a).

[255] 42 C.F.R. §422.152(a)(1)–(3).

detect both underutilization and overutilization of services; (3) measure and report performance.[256]

The organization offering the plan must do the following: (1) measure performance under the plan, using the measurement tools required by CMS, and report its performance to CMS; and (2) make available to CMS information on quality and outcomes measures that will enable beneficiaries to compare health coverage options and select among them as provided in these regulations.[257]

[3]　Chronic Care Improvement Program Requirements

These programs must develop criteria for a chronic care improvement program. The criteria must include (1) methods for identifying MA enrollees with multiple or sufficiently severe chronic conditions that would benefit from participating in a chronic care improvement program; and (2) have mechanisms for monitoring MA enrollees that are participating in the chronic care improvement program.[258]

[4]　Quality Improvement Projects

Quality improvement projects are an organization's initiatives that focus on specified clinical and non-clinical areas and that involve the following: (1) measurement of performance; (2) systematic and periodic follow-up on the effect of the interventions, and for each project, the organization must assess performance under the plan using quality indicators that are (a) objective, clearly and unambiguously defined, and based on current clinical knowledge or health services research; and (b) capable of measuring outcomes such as changes in health status, functional status and enrollee satisfaction, or valid proxies of those outcomes.[259]

Performance assessment on the selected indicators must be based on systematic ongoing collection and analysis of valid and reliable data.[260] Interventions must achieve demonstrable improvement,[261] the organization must report the status and results of each project to CMS as requested.[262]

---

[256] 42 C.F.R. §422.152(b)(1) and (2).

[257] 42 C.F.R. §422.152(b)(3)(i) and (ii), including a reference to §422.64(c)(10) (information about the MA plan). Note the January 28, 2005, rules revisions, effective March 22, 2005, do not revise §422.64. There is no §422.64(c)(10) in the previous §422.64. Note too that MA local PPO-type plans that are offered by an organization that is licensed or organized under State law as a health maintenance organization must meet the requirements specified in paragraphs (b)(1) through (b)(3).

[258] 42 C.F.R. §422.152(c)(1) and (2).

[259] 42 C.F.R. §422.152(d)(1) and (2).

[260] 42 C.F.R. §422.152(d)(3).

[261] 42 C.F.R. §422.152(d)(4).

[262] 42 C.F.R. §422.152.(d)(5).

[5] Requirements for MA Regional Plans

A local preferred provider organization plan means an MA plan that (i) has a network of providers that have agreed to a contractually specified reimbursement for covered benefits with the organization offering the plan; (ii) provides for reimbursement for all covered benefits regardless of whether the benefits are provided within the network of providers; and (iii) is offered by an organization that is not licensed or organized under State law as a health maintenance organization.[263]

MA organizations offering an MA regional plan or local PPO plan must (i) measure performance under the plan using standard measures required by CMS and report its performance to CMS; the standard measures may be specified in uniform data collection and reporting instruments required by CMS; (ii) evaluate the continuity and coordination of care furnished to enrollees; (iii) if the organization uses written protocols for utilization review, the organization must (a) base those protocols on current standards of medical practice; and (b) have mechanisms to evaluate utilization of services and to inform enrollees and providers of services of the results of the evaluation.[264]

[6] Requirements for All Types of Plans

For all types of plans offered, an MA organization must maintain a health information system that collects, analyzes, and integrates the data necessary to implement its quality improvement program; ensure that the information it receives from providers of services is reliable and complete; and make all collected information available to CMS.[265]

For each plan, there must be in effect a process for formal evaluation, at least annually, of the impact and effectiveness of its quality improvement program.[266] For each plan, the MA organization must correct all problems that come to its attention through internal surveillance, complaints, or other mechanisms.[267]

[C] Compliance Deemed on the Basis of Accreditation

If the Secretary finds that a plan has consistently maintained an excellent record of quality improvement and compliance, in accordance with the MA program, he may waive the requirement of an agreement with an independent

---

[263] 42 C.F.R. §422.152(e)(1)(i)-(iii).

[264] 42 C.F.R. §422.152(e)(2)(i)–(iii).

[265] 42 C.F.R. §422.152(f)(1)(i)–(ii).

[266] 42 C.F.R. §422.152(f)(2).

[267] 42 C.F.R. §422.152(f)(3).

quality review and improvement organization.[268] Moreover, the Secretary shall provide that an MA Organization is deemed to meet the requirement of this section, including confidentiality and accuracy of patients' records,[269] if the plan is accredited (and periodically reaccredited) by a private organization that meets accreditation standards at least as stringent as those of the Secretary.[270]

A Medicare Advantage Organization is deemed to meet Medicare requirements if it submits to surveys by CMS to validate its accreditation process and authorizes its accreditation organization to release to CMS a copy of its most recent accreditation survey, together with any survey-related information that CMS may require, including corrective action plans and summaries of unmet CMS requirements.[271]

In order for an organization to have "deemed status," it must be fully accredited (and periodically reaccredited) by a private, national accreditation organization approved by the CMS,[272] and the accreditation organization must use CMS standards.[273] The quality improvement and performance improvement requirements and the confidentiality and accuracy of enrollee records requirements are "deemable."[274] Deemed status becomes effective on either the date on which the organization is approved by CMS or the date it is accredited by the accrediting organization.[275]

Deemed status is removed when CMS removes part or all of such status for any of the following reasons:[276]

- On the basis of CMS's own survey or the results of the accreditation survey, it finds that the organization does not meet Medicare requirements for deemed status already granted; or

- CMS withdraws approval of the accreditation organization that made the accreditation finding; or the Medicare Advantage Organization fails to meet the survey requirements described above. Moreover, CMS retains the right to bring

---

[268] 42 U.S.C. §1395w-22(e)(3)(C).

[269] 42 U.S.C. §1395w-25(h)(1)–(2); 42 C.F.R. §422.156.

[270] Pub. L. No. 105-33 4001(e)(4); 42 C.F.R. §422.157.

[271] 42 C.F.R. §422.156(d)(1)–(2).

[272] Deeming should be viewed cautiously, particularly as a statutory requirement. A recent HCFA report rejected deeming of accreditation for nursing homes. *See* Study of Private Accreditation (Deeming) of Nursing Homes, Regulatory Incentives and Non-regulatory Incentives and Effectiveness of the Survey and Certification System (July 1998) (summary available at <http://www.hcfa.gov>).

[273] 42 C.F.R. §422.156(a)(1)–(2).

[274] 42 C.F.R. §422.156(b)(1)–(2) ("deemable"—a term of the regulations).

[275] 42 C.F.R. §422.156(c)(1)–(2).

[276] 42 C.F.R. §422.156(e)(1)–(3).

enforcement action against any Medicare Advantage Plan with respect to deemed accreditation.[277]

It is particularly important that CMS is explicitly retaining its enforcement authority. Whether and to what extent CMS uses this authority will likely determine the strength and success of quality improvement programs.

Moreover, the failure to have an accredited quality assurance program would jeopardize a plan's ability to participate in the MA Plan as the quality assurance program is mandatory to the extent described above.

---

[277] 42 C.F.R. §422.156(f).

APPENDIX 7-1

TITLE 42—PUBLIC HEALTH
(CODE OF FEDERAL REGULATIONS)

PART 422—MEDICARE ADVANTAGE PROGRAM

Subpart B—Eligibility, Election, and Enrollment

Sec. 422.50   Eligibility to elect an MA plan.

Source: 63 FR 35071, June 26, 1998, unless otherwise noted.

For this subpart, all references to an MA plan include MA-PD and both MA local and MA regional plans, as defined in Sec. 422.2 unless specifically noted otherwise.

(a) An individual is eligible to elect an MA plan if he or she—

(1) Is entitled to Medicare under Part A and enrolled in Part B (except that an individual entitled only to Part B and who was enrolled in an HMO or CMP with a risk contract under part 417 of this chapter on December 31, 1998 may continue to be nrolled in the MA organization as an MA plan enrollee);

(2) Has not been medically determined to have end-stage renal disease, except that—

(i) An individual who develops end-stage renal disease while enrolled in an MA plan or in a health plan offered by the MA organization is eligible to elect an MA plan offered by that organization;

(ii) An individual with end-stage renal disease whose enrollment in an MA plan was terminated or discontinued after December 31, 1998, because CMS or the MA organization terminated the MA organization's contract for the plan or discontinued the plan in the area in which the individual resides, is eligible to elect another MA plan. If the plan so elected is later terminated or discontinued in the area in which the individual resides, he or she may elect another MA plan; and

(iii) An individual with end-stage renal disease may elect an MA special needs plan as defined in Sec. 422.2, as long as that plan has opted to enroll ESRD individuals.

(3) Meets either of the following residency requirements:

(i) Resides in the service area of the MA plan.

(ii) Resides outside of the service area of the MA plan and is enrolled in a health plan offered by the MA organization during the month immediately preceding the month in which the individual is entitled to both Medicare Part A and Part B, provided that an MA organization chooses to offer this option and that CMS determines that all applicable MA access requirements of Sec. 422.112 are met for that individual through the MA plan's established provider network. The MA organization must furnish the same benefits to these enrollees as to enrollees who reside in the service area;

(4) Has been a member of an Employer Group Health Plan (EGHP) that includes the elected MA plan, even if the individual lives outside of the MA plan service area, provided that an MA organization chooses to offer this option and that CMS determines that all applicable MA access requirements at Sec. 422.112 are met for that individual through the MA plan's established provider network. The MA organization must furnish the same benefits to all enrollees, regardless of whether they reside in the service area;

(5) Completes and signs an election form or completes another CMS-approved election method offered by the MA organization and provides information required for enrollment; and

(6) Agrees to abide by the rules of the MA organization after they are disclosed to him or her in connection with the election process.

(b) An MA eligible individual may not be enrolled in more than one MA plan at any given time.

[63 FR 35071, June 26, 1998; 63 FR 52611, Oct. 1, 1998, as amended at 65 FR 40316, June 29, 2000; 68 FR 50855, Aug. 22, 2003; 70 FR 4715, Jan. 28, 2005; 70 FR 52026, Sept. 1, 2005]
***

Sec. 422.62   Election of coverage under an MA plan.

(a) **General: Coverage election periods—(1) Initial coverage election period for MA.** The initial coverage election period is the period during which a newly MA-eligible individual may make an initial election. This period begins 3 months before the month the individual is first entitled to both Part A and Part B and ends on the later of—

(i) The last day of the month preceding the month of entitlement; or

(ii) If after May 15, 2006, the last day of the individual's Part B initial enrollment period.

(2) **Annual coordinated election period.** (i) Beginning with 2002, the annual coordinated election period for the following calendar year is November 15th through December 31st, except for 2006.

(ii) For 2006, the annual coordinated election period begins on November 15, 2005 and ends on May 15, 2006.

(iii) During the annual coordinated election period, an individual eligible to enroll in an MA plan may change his or her election from an MA plan to original Medicare or to a different MA plan, or from original Medicare to an MA plan. If an individual changes his or her election to original Medicare, he or she may also elect a PDP.

(3) **Open enrollment and disenrollment opportunities through 2005.** Through 2005, the number of elections or changes that an MA eligible individual may make is not limited (except as provided for in paragraph (d) of this section for MA MSA plans). Subject to the MA plan being open to enrollees as provided under

Sec. 422.60(a)(2), an individual eligible to elect an MA plan may change his or her election from an MA plan to original Medicare or to a different MA plan, or from original Medicare to an MA plan.

(4) Open enrollment and disenrollment during 2006. (i) Except as provided in paragraphs (a)(4)(ii), (a)(4)(iii), and (a)(6) of this section, an individual who is not enrolled in an MA plan, but who is eligible to elect an MA plan in 2006, may elect an MA plan only once during the first 6 months of the year.

(A) An individual who is enrolled in an MA-PD plan may elect another MA-PD plan or original Medicare and coverage under a PDP. Such an individual may not elect an MA plan that does not provide qualified prescription drug coverage.

(B) An individual who is enrolled in an MA plan that does not provide qualified prescription drug coverage may elect another MA plan that does not provide that coverage or original Medicare. Such an individual may not elect an MA-PD plan or coverage under a PDP.

(ii) Newly eligible MA individual. An individual who becomes MA eligible during 2006 may elect an MA plan or change his or her election once during the period that begins the month the individual is entitled to both Part A and Part B and ends on the last day of the 6th month of the entitlement, or on December 31, whichever is earlier, subject to the limitations in paragraphs (a)(4)(i)(A) and (a)(4)(i)(B) of this section.

(iii) The limitation to one election or change in paragraphs (a)(4)(i) and (a)(4)(ii) of this section does not apply to elections or changes made during the annual coordinated election period specified in paragraph (a)(2) of this section or during a special election period specified in paragraph (b) of this section.

(5) Open enrollment and disenrollment beginning in 2007. (i) For 2007 and subsequent years, except as provided in paragraphs (a)(5)(ii), (a)(5)(iii), and (a)(6) of this section, an individual who is not enrolled in an MA plan but is eligible to elect an MA plan may make an election into an MA plan once during the first 3 months of the year.

(A) An individual who is enrolled in an MA-PD plan may elect another MA-PD plan or original Medicare and coverage under a PDP. An individual who is in original Medicare and has coverage under a PDP may elect a MA-PD plan. Such an individual may not elect an MA plan that does not provide qualified prescription drug coverage.

(B) An individual who is enrolled in an MA plan that does not provide qualified prescription drug coverage may elect another MA plan that does not provide that coverage or original Medicare. An individual who is in original Medicare and does not have coverage under a PDP may elect an MA plan that does not provide qualified prescription drug coverage. Such an individual may not elect an MA-PD plan or coverage under a PDP.

(ii) Newly eligible MA individual. An individual who becomes MA eligible during 2007 or later may elect an MA plan or change his or her election once during the period that begins the month the individual is entitled to both Part A and Part B and ends on the last day of the 3rd month of the entitlement, or on December 31, whichever is earlier subject to the limitations in paragraphs (a)(5)(i)(A) and (a)(5)(i)(B) of this section.

(iii) The limitation to one election or change in paragraph (a)(5)(i) and (a)(5)(ii) of this section does not apply to elections made or changes made during the annual coordinated election period specified in paragraph (a)(2) of this section or during a special election period specified in paragraph (b) of this section.

(6) Open enrollment period for institutionalized individuals. After 2005, an individual who is eligible to elect an MA plan and who is institutionalized, as defined by CMS, is not limited (except as provided for in paragraph (d) of this section for MA MSA plans) in the number of elections or changes he or she may make. Subject to the MA plan being open to enrollees as provided under Sec. 422.60(a)(2), an MA eligible institutionalized individual may at any time elect an MA plan or change his or her election from an MA plan to original Medicare, to a different MA plan, or from original Medicare to an MA plan.

(b) Special election periods. An individual may at any time (that is, not limited to the annual coordinated election period) discontinue the election of an MA plan offered by an MA organization and change his or her election, in the form and manner specified by CMS, from an MA plan to original Medicare or to a different MA plan under any of the following circumstances:

(1) CMS or the organization has terminated the organization's contract for the plan, discontinued the plan in the area in which the individual resides, or the organization has notified the individual of the impending termination of the plan, or the impending discontinuation of the plan in the area in which the individual resides.

(2) The individual is not eligible to remain enrolled in the plan because of a change in his or her place of residence to a location out of the service area or continuation area or other change in circumstances as determined by CMS but not including terminations resulting from a failure to make timely payment of an MA monthly or supplemental beneficiary premium, or from disruptive behavior.

(3) The individual demonstrates to CMS, in accordance with guidelines issued by CMS, that—

(i) The organization offering the plan substantially violated a material provision of its contract under this part in relation to the individual, including, but not limited to the following:

(A) Failure to provide the beneficiary on a timely basis medically necessary services for which benefits are available under the plan.

(B) Failure to provide medical services in accordance with applicable quality standards; or

(ii) The organization (or its agent, representative, or plan provider) materially misrepresented the plan's provisions in marketing the plan to the individual.

(4) The individual meets such other exceptional conditions as CMS may provide.

(c) Special election period for individual age 65. Effective January 1, 2002, an MA eligible individual who elects an MA plan during the initial enrollment period, as defined under section 1837(d) of the Act, that surrounds his or her 65th birthday (this period begins 3 months before and ends 3 months after the month of the individual's 65th birthday) may discontinue the election of that plan and elect coverage under original Medicare at any time during the 12-month period that begins on the effective date of enrollment in the MA plan.

(d) Special rules for MA MSA plans—(1) Enrollment. An individual may enroll in an MA MSA plan only during an initial coverage election period or annual coordinated election period described in paragraphs (a)(1) and (a)(2) of this section.

(2) Disenrollment. (i) Except as provided in paragraph (d)(2)(ii) of this section, an individual may disenroll from an MA MSA plan only during—

(A) An annual election period; or

(B) The special election period described in paragraph (b) of this section.

(ii) Exception. An individual who elects an MA MSA plan during an annual election period and has never before elected an MA MSA plan may revoke that election, no later than December 15 of that same year, by submitting to the organization that offers the MA MSA plan a signed and dated request in the form and manner prescribed by CMS or by filing the appropriate disenrollment form through other mechanisms as determined by CMS.

[63 FR 35071, June 26, 1998; 63 FR 52612, Oct. 1, 1998, as amended at 65 FR 40317, June 29, 2000; 70 FR 4717, Jan. 28, 2005]
***

Sec. 422.562   General provisions.

(a) Responsibilities of the MA organization. (1) An MA organization, with respect to each MA plan that it offers, must establish and maintain—

(i) A grievance procedure as described in Sec. 422.564 for addressing issues that do not involve organization determinations;

(ii) Aprocedure for making timely organization determinations;

(iii) Appeal procedures that meet the requirements of this subpart for issues that involve organization determinations; and

(2) An MA organization must ensure that all enrollees receive written information about the—

(i) Grievance and appeal procedures that are available to them through the MA organization; and

(ii) Complaint process available to the enrollee under the QIO process as set forth under section 1154(a)(14) of the Act.

(3) In accordance with subpart K of this part, if the MA organization delegates any of its responsibilities under this subpart to another entity or individual through which the organization provides health care services, the MA organization is ultimately responsible for ensuring that the entity or individual satisfies the relevant requirements of this subpart.

(b) Rights of MA enrollees. In accordance with the provisions of this subpart, enrollees have the following rights:

(1) The right to have grievances between the enrollee and the MA organization heard and resolved, as described in Sec. 422.564.

(2) The right to a timely organization determination, as provided under Sec. 422.566.

(3) The right to request an expedited organization determination, as provided under Sec. 422.570.

(4) If dissatisfied with any part of an organization determination, the following appeal rights:

(i) The right to a reconsideration of the adverse organization determination by the MA organization, as provided under Sec. 422.578.

(ii) The right to request an expedited reconsideration, as provided under Sec. 422.584.

(iii) If, as a result of a reconsideration, an MA organization affirms, in whole or in part, its adverse organization determination, the right to an automatic reconsidered determination made by an independent, outside entity contracted by CMS, as provided in Sec. 422.592.

(iv) The right to an ALJ hearing if the amount in controversy is met, as provided in Sec. 422.600.

(v) The right to request MAC review of the ALJ hearing decision, as provided in Sec. 422.608.

(vi) The right to judicial review of the hearing decision if the amount in controversy is met, as provided in Sec. 422.612.

(c) Limits on when this subpart applies. (1) If an enrollee receives immediate QIO review (as provided in Sec. 422.622) of a determination of noncoverage of inpatient hospital care—

(i) The enrollee is not entitled to review of that issue by the MA organization; and

(ii) The QIO review decision is subject only to the appeal procedures set forth in parts 476 and 478 of this chapter.

(2) If an enrollee has no further liability to pay for services that were furnished by an MA organization, a determination regarding these services is not subject to appeal.

(d) When other regulations apply. Unless this subpart provides otherwise, the regulations in part 405 of this chapter (concerning the administrative review and hearing processes and representation of parties under titles II and XVIII of the Act), apply under this subpart to the extent they are appropriate.

[63 FR 35067, June 26, 1998, as amended at 65 FR 40329, June 29, 2000; 70 FR 4738, Jan. 28, 2005; 70 FR 52027, Sept. 1, 2005]
***

Sec. 422.568   Standard timeframes and notice requirements for organization determinations.

(a) **Timeframe for requests for service.** When a party has made a request for a service, the MA organization must notify the enrollee of its determination as expeditiously as the enrollee's health condition requires, but no later than 14 calendar days after the date the organization receives the request for a standard organization determination. The MA organization may extend the timeframe by up to 14 calendar days if the enrollee requests the extension or if the organization justifies a need for additional information and how the delay is in the interest of the enrollee (for example, the receipt of additional medical evidence from noncontract providers may change an MA organization's decision to deny). When the MA organization extends the timeframe, it must notify the enrollee in writing of the reasons for the delay, and inform the enrollee of the right to file an expedited grievance if he or she disagrees with the MA organization's decision to grant an extension.

(b) **Timeframe for requests for payment.** The MA organization must process requests for payment according to the "prompt payment" provisions set forth in Sec. 422.520.

(c) **Written notice for MA organization denials.** If an MA organization decides to deny service or payment in whole or in part, or if an enrollee disagrees with an MA organization's decision to discontinue or reduce the level of care for an ongoing course of treatment, the organization must give the enrollee written notice of the determination.

(d) **Written notice for MA Organization denials.** If an enrollee requests an MA organization to provide an explanation of a practitioner's denial of an item or service, in whole or in part, the MA organization must give the enrollee a written notice.

(e) **Form and content of the MA organization notice.** The notice of any denial under paragraph (d) of this section must—

(1) Use approved notice language in a readable and understandable form;

(2) State the specific reasons for the denial;

(3) Inform the enrollee of his or her right to a reconsideration;

(4)(i) For service denials, describe both the standard and expedited reconsideration processes, including the enrollee's right to, and conditions for, obtaining an expedited reconsideration and the rest of the appeal process; and

(ii) For payment denials, describe the standard reconsideration process and the rest of the appeal process; and

(5) Comply with any other notice requirements specified by CMS.

(f) Effect of failure to provide timely notice. If the MA organization fails to provide the enrollee with timely notice of an organization determination as specified in this section, this failure itself constitutes an adverse organization determination and may be appealed.

[65 FR 40329, June 29, 2000, as amended at 70 FR 4739, Jan. 28, 2005; 70 FR 52027, Sept. 1, 2005]
***

Sec. 422.570   Expediting certain organization determinations.

(a) **Request for expedited determination.** An enrollee or a physician (regardless of whether the physician is affiliated with the M+C organization) may request that an M+C organization expedite an organization determination involving the issues described in Sec. 422.566(b)(3) and (b)(4). (This does not include requests for payment of services already furnished.)

(b) **How to make a request.** (1) To ask for an expedited determination, an enrollee or a physician must submit an oral or written request directly to the M+C organization or, if applicable, to the entity responsible for making the determination, as directed by the M+C organization.

(2) A physician may provide oral or written support for a request for an expedited determination.

(c) **How the M+C organization must process requests.** The M+C organization must establish and maintain the following procedures for processing requests for expedited determinations:

(1) Establish an efficient and convenient means for individuals to submit oral or written requests. The M+C organization must document all oral requests in writing and maintain the documentation in the case file.

(2) Promptly decide whether to expedite a determination, based on the following requirements:

(i) For a request made by an enrollee the M+C organization must provide an expedited determination if it determines that applying the standard timeframe for making a determination could seriously jeopardize the life or health of the enrollee or the enrollee's ability to regain maximum function.

(ii) For a request made or supported by a physician, the M+C organization must provide an expedited determination if the physician indicates that applying the standard timeframe for making a determination could seriously jeopardize the life or health of the enrollee or the enrollee's ability to regain maximum function.

(d) **Actions following denial.** If an M+C organization denies a request for expedited determination, it must take the following actions:

(1) Automatically transfer a request to the standard timeframe and make the determination within the 14-day timeframe established in Sec. 422.568 for a standard determination. The 14-day period begins with the day the M+C organization receives the request for expedited determination.

(2) Give the enrollee prompt oral notice of the denial and subsequently deliver, within 3 calendar days, a written letter that—

(i) Explains that the M+C organization will process the request using the 14-day timeframe for standard determinations;

(ii) Informs the enrollee of the right to file a grievance if he or she disagrees with the M+C organization's decision not to expedite; and

(iii) Informs the enrollee of the right to resubmit a request for an expedited determination with any physician's support; and

(iv) Provides instructions about the grievance process and its timeframes.

(e) Action on accepted request for expedited determination. If an M+C organization grants a request for expedited determination, it must make the determination and give notice in accordance with Sec. 422.572.

(f) Prohibition of punitive action. An M+C organization may not take or threaten to take any punitive action against a physician acting on behalf or in support of an enrollee in requesting an expedited determination.

[63 FR 35107, June 26, 1998, as amended at 65 FR 40329, June 29, 2000]
***

Sec. 422.576   Effect of an organization determination.

The organization determination is binding on all parties unless it is reconsidered under Secs. 422.578 through 422.596 or is reopened and revised under Sec. 422.616.
***

Sec. 422.578   Right to a reconsideration.

Any party to an organization determination (including one that has been reopened and revised as described in Sec. 422.616) may request that the determination be reconsidered under the procedures described in Sec. 422.582, which address requests for a standard reconsideration. An enrollee or physician (acting on behalf of an enrollee) may request an expedited reconsideration as described in Sec. 422.584.
***

Sec. 422.592   Reconsideration by an independent entity.

(a) When the M+C organization affirms, in whole or in part, its adverse organization determination, the issues that remain in dispute must be reviewed and resolved by an independent, outside entity that contracts with CMS.

(b) The independent outside entity must conduct the review as expeditiously as the enrollee's health condition requires but must not exceed the deadlines specified in the contract.

(c) When the independent entity conducts a reconsideration, the parties to the reconsideration are the same parties listed in Sec. 422.582(d) who qualified during the M+C organization's reconsideration, with the addition of the M+C organization.
***

Sec. 422.594   Notice of reconsidered determination by the independent entity.

(a) **Responsibility for the notice.** When the independent entity makes the reconsidered determination, it is responsible for mailing a notice of its reconsidered determination to the parties and for sending a copy to CMS.

(b) **Content of the notice.** The notice must—

(1) State the specific reasons for the entity's decisions in understandable language;

(2) If the reconsidered determination is adverse (that is, does not completely reverse the MA organization's adverse organization determination), inform the parties of their right to an ALJ hearing if the amount in controversy is $100 or more;

(3) Describe the procedures that a party must follow to obtain an ALJ hearing; and

(4) Comply with any other requirements specified by CMS.

[63 FR 35107, June 26, 1998, as amended at 65 FR 40330, June 29, 2000]
***

Sec. 422.600   Right to a hearing.

(a) If the amount remaining in controversy is $100 or more, any party to the reconsideration (except the M+C organization) who is dissatisfied with the reconsidered determination has a right to a hearing before an ALJ. The M+C organization does not have the right to request a hearing before an ALJ.

(b) The amount remaining in controversy, which can include any combination of Part A and Part B services, is computed in accordance with Sec. 405.740 of this chapter for Part A services and Sec. 405.817 of this chapter for Part B services.

(c) If the basis for the appeal is the M+C organization's refusal to provide services, CMS uses the projected value of those services to compute the amount remaining in controversy.
***

Sec. 422.612   Judicial review.

(a) **Review of ALJ's decision.** Any party, including the MA organization, may request judicial review (upon notifying the other parties) of an ALJ's decision if—

(1) The Board denied the party's request for review; and

(2) The amount in controversy meets the threshold requirement established annually by the Secretary.

(b) **Review of MAC decision.** Any party, including the MA organization, may request judicial review (upon notifying the other parties) of the MAC decision if it is the final decision of CMS and the amount in controversy meets the threshold established in paragraph (a)(2) of this section.

(c) **How to request judicial review.** In order to request judicial review, a party must file a civil action in a district court of the United States in accordance with section 205(g) of the Act. See part 405 of this chapter for a description of the procedures to follow in requesting judicial review.

[63 FR 35107, June 26, 1998; 63 FR 52614, Oct. 1, 1998, as amended at 65 FR 40331, June 29, 2000; 70 FR 4740, Jan. 28, 2005]
***

Sec. 422.616 Reopening and revising determinations and decisions.

(a) An organization or reconsidered determination made by an MA organization, a reconsidered determination made by the independent entity described in Sec. 422.592, or the decision of an ALJ or the MAC that is otherwise final and binding may be reopened and revised by the entity that made the determination or decision, under the rules in part 405 of this chapter.

(b) Reopening may be at the instigation of any party.

(c) The filing of a request for reopening does not relieve the MA organization of its obligation to make payment or provide services as specified in Sec. 422.618.

(d) Once an entity issues a revised determination or decision, any party may file an appeal.

[63 FR 35107, June 26, 1998; 63 FR 52614, Oct. 1, 1998, as amended at 70 FR 4740, Jan. 28, 2005]
***

Sec. 422.618 How an MA organization must effectuate standard reconsidered determinations or decisions.

(a) **Reversals by the MA organization—(1) Requests for service.** If, on reconsideration of a request for service, the MA organization completely reverses its organization determination, the organization must authorize or provide the service under dispute as expeditiously as the enrollee's health condition requires, but no later than 30 calendar days after the date the MA organization receives the request for reconsideration (or no later than upon expiration of an extension described in Sec. 422.590(a)(1)).

(2) **Requests for payment.** If, on reconsideration of a request for payment, the MA organization completely reverses its organization determination, the organization must pay for the service no later than 60 calendar days after the date the MA organization receives the request for reconsideration.

(b) **Reversals by the independent outside entity. (1) Requests for service.** If, on reconsideration of a request for service, the MA organization's determination is reversed in whole or in part by the independent outside entity, the MA organization must authorize the service under dispute within 72 hours from the date it receives notice reversing the determination, or provide the service under dispute as expeditiously as the enrollee's health condition requires, but no later than 14 calendar days from that date. The MA organization must inform the independent outside entity that the organization has effectuated the decision.

(2) **Requests for payment.** If, on reconsideration of a request for payment, the MA organization's determination is reversed in whole or in part by the independent outside entity, the MA organization must pay for the service no later than 30 calendar days from the date it receives notice reversing the organization determination. The MA organization must inform the independent outside entity that the organization has effectuated the decision.

(c) **Reversals other than by the MA organization or the independent outside entity.**—(1) **General rule.** If the independent outside entity's determination is reversed in whole or in part by the ALJ, or at a higher level of appeal, the MA organization must pay for, authorize, or provide the service under dispute as expeditiously as the enrollee's health condition requires, but no later than 60 calendar days from the date it receives notice reversing the determination. The MA organization must inform the independent outside entity that the organization has effectuated the decision or that it has appealed the decision.

(2) **Effectuation exception when the MA organization files an appeal with the Medicare Appeals Council.** If the MA organization requests Medicare Appeals Council (the Board) review consistent with Sec. 422.608, the MA organization may await the outcome of the review before it pays for, authorizes, or provides the service under dispute. A MA organization that files an appeal with the Board must concurrently send a copy of its appeal request and any accompanying documents to the enrollee and must notify the independent outside entity that it has requested an appeal.

[63 FR 35107, June 26, 1998, as amended at 65 FR 40331, June 29, 2000; 68 FR 50858, Aug. 22, 2003]
***

Sec. 422.619   How an MA organization must effectuate expedited reconsidered determinations.

(a) Reversals by the MA organization. If on reconsideration of an expedited request for service, the MA organization completely reverses its organization determination, the MA organization must authorize or provide the service under dispute as expeditiously as the enrollee's health condition requires, but no later than 72 hours after the date the MA organization receives the request for reconsideration (or no later than upon expiration of an extension described in Sec. 422.590(d)(2)).

(b) Reversals by the independent outside entity. If the MA organization's determination is reversed in whole or in part by the independent outside entity, the MA organization must authorize or provide the service under dispute as expeditiously as the enrollee's health condition requires but no later than 72 hours from the date it receives notice reversing the determination. The MA organization must inform the independent outside entity that the organization has effectuated the decision.

(c) Reversals other than by the MA organization or the independent outside entity—(1) General rule. If the independent outside entity's expedited determination is reversed in whole or in part by the ALJ, or at a higher level of appeal, the MA organization must authorize or provide the service under dispute as expeditiously as the enrollee's health condition requires, but no later than 60 days from the date it receives notice reversing the determination. The MA organization must inform the independent outside entity that the organization has effectuated the decision.

(2) Effectuation exception when the MA organization files an appeal with the Medicare Appeals Council. If the MA organization requests Medicare Appeals Council (the Board) review consistent with Sec. 422.608, the MA organization may await the outcome of the review before it authorizes or provides the service under dispute. A MA organization that files an appeal with the Board must concurrently send a copy of its appeal request and any accompanying documents to the enrollee and must notify the independent outside entity that it has requested an appeal.

[65 FR 40331, June 29, 2000, as amended at 68 FR 50859, Aug. 22, 2003]
***

Sec. 422.620   How enrollees of MA organizations must be notified of noncovered inpatient hospital care.

(a) **Enrollee's entitlement.** (1) Where an MA organization has authorized coverage of the inpatient admission of an enrollee, either directly or by delegation (or the admission constitutes emergency or urgently needed care, as described in Sec. Sec. 422.2 and 422.113), the MA organization (or hospital that has been delegated the authority to make the discharge decision) must provide a written notice of noncoverage when—

(i) The beneficiary disagrees with the discharge decision; or

(ii) The MA organization (or the hospital that has been delegated the authority to make the discharge decision) is not discharging the individual but no longer intends to continue coverage of the inpatient stay.

(2) An enrollee is entitled to coverage until at least noon of the day after such notice is provided. If QIO review is requested under Sec. 422.622, coverage is extended as provided in that section.

(b) **Physician concurrence required.** Before discharging an individual or changing the level of care in an inpatient hospital setting, the MA organization must obtain the concurrence of the physician who is responsible for the enrollee's inpatient care.

(c) Notice to the enrollee. When applicable, the written notice of non-coverage must be issued no later than the day before hospital coverage ends. The written notice must include the following elements:

(1) The reason why inpatient hospital care is no longer needed or covered;

(2) The effective date and time of the enrollee's liability for continued inpatient care;

(3) The enrollee's appeal rights;

(4) If applicable, the new lower level of care being covered in the hospital setting; and

(5) Any additional information specified by CMS.

[68 FR 16667, Apr. 4, 2003, as amended at 70 FR 4740, Jan. 28, 2005]

Effective Date Note: At 68 FR 20349, Apr. 4, 2003, **Sec. 422.620** was revised. This section contains information collection and recordkeeping requirements and will not become effective until approval has been given by the Office of Management and Budget.
***

Sec. 422.626   Fast-track appeals of service terminations to independent review entities (IREs).

(a) Enrollee's right to a fast-track appeal of an MA organization's termination decision. An enrollee of an MA organization has a right to a fast-track appeal of an MA organization's decision to terminate provider services.

(1) An enrollee who desires a fast-track appeal must submit a request for an appeal to an IRE under contract with CMS, in writing or by telephone, by noon of the first day after the day of delivery of the termination notice. If, due to an emergency, the IRE is closed and unable to accept the enrollee's request for a fast-track appeal, the enrollee must file a request by noon of the next day that the IRE is open for business.

(2) When an enrollee fails to make a timely request to an IRE, he or she may request an expedited reconsideration by the MA organization as described in Sec. 422.584.

(3) If, after delivery of the termination notice, an enrollee chooses to leave a provider or discontinue receipt of covered services on or before the proposed termination date, the enrollee may not later assert fast-track IRE appeal rights under this section relative to the services or expect the services to resume, even if the enrollee requests an appeal before the discontinuation date in the termination notice.

(b) Coverage of provider services. Coverage of provider services continues until the date and time designated on the termination notice, unless the enrollee appeals and the IRE reverses the MA organization's decision. If the IRE's decision is delayed because the MA organization did not timely supply necessary information or records, the MA organization is liable for the costs of any additional coverage required by the delayed IRE decision. If the IRE finds that the enrollee did not receive valid notice, coverage of provider services by the MA organization continues until at least two days after valid notice has been received. Continuation of coverage is not required if the IRE determines that coverage could pose a threat to the enrollee's health or safety.

(c) **Burden of proof.** When an enrollee appeals an MA organization's decision to terminate services to an IRE, the burden of proof rests with the MA organization to demonstrate that termination of coverage is the correct decision, either on the basis of medical necessity, or based on other Medicare coverage policies.

(1) To meet this burden, the MA organization must supply any and all information that an IRE requires to sustain the MA organization's termination decision, consistent with paragraph (e) of this section.

(2) The enrollee may submit evidence to be considered by an IRE in making its decision.

(3) The MA organization or an IRE may require an enrollee to authorize release to the IRE of his or her medical records, to the extent that the records are necessary for the MA organization to demonstrate the correctness of its decision or for an IRE to determine the appeal.

(d) **Procedures an IRE must follow.** (1) On the date an IRE receives the enrollee's request for an appeal, the IRE must immediately notify the MA organization and the provider that the enrollee has filed a request for a fast-track appeal, and of the MA organization's responsibility to submit documentation consistent with paragraph (e)(3) of this section.

(2) When an enrollee requests a fast-track appeal, the IRE must determine whether the provider delivered a valid notice of the termination decision, and whether a detailed notice has been provided, consistent with paragraph (e)(1) of this section.

(3) The IRE must notify CMS about each case in which it determines that improper notification occurs.

(4) Before making its decision, the IRE must solicit the enrollee's views regarding the reason(s) for termination of services as specified in the detailed written notice provided by the MA organization, or regarding any other reason that the IRE uses as the basis of its review determination.

(5) An IRE must make a decision on an appeal and notify the enrollee, the MA organization, and the provider of services, by close of business of the day after it receives the information necessary to make the decision. If the IRE does not receive the information needed to sustain an MA organization's decision to terminate services, it may make a decision on the case based on the information at hand, or it may defer its decision until it receives the necessary information. If the IRE defers its decision, coverage of the services by the MA organization would continue until the decision is made, consistent with paragraph (b) of this section, but no additional termination notice would be required.

(e) Responsibilities of the MA organization. (1) When an IRE notifies an MA organization that an enrollee has requested a fast-track appeal, the MA organization must send a detailed notice to the enrollee by close of business of the day of the IRE's notification. The detailed termination notice must include the following information:

(i) A specific and detailed explanation why services are either no longer reasonable and necessary or are no longer covered.

(ii) A description of any applicable Medicare coverage rule, instruction or other Medicare policy including citations, to the applicable Medicare policy rules, or the information about how the enrollee may obtain a copy of the Medicare policy from the MA organization.

(iii) Any applicable MA organization policy, contract provision, or rationale upon which the termination decision was based.

(iv) Facts specific to the enrollee and relevant to the coverage determination that are sufficient to advise the enrollee of the applicability of the coverage rule or policy to the enrollee's case.

(v) Any other information required by CMS.

(2) Upon an enrollee's request, the MA organization must provide the enrollee a copy of, or access to, any documentation sent to the IRE by the MA organization, including records of any information provided by telephone. The MA organization may charge the enrollee a reasonable amount to cover the costs of duplicating the information for the enrollee and/or delivering the documentation to the enrollee. The MA organization must accommodate such a request by no later than close of business of the first day after the day the material is requested.

(3) Upon notification by the IRE of a fast-track appeal, the MA organization must supply any and all information, including a copy of the notice sent to the enrollee, that the IRE needs to decide on the appeal. The MA organization must supply this information as soon as possible, but no later than by close of business of the day that the IRE notifies the MA organization that an appeal has been received from the enrollee. The MA organization must make the information available by phone (with a written record made of what is transmitted in this manner) and/or in writing, as determined by the IRE.

(4) An MA organization is financially responsible for coverage of services as provided in paragraph (b) of this section, regardless of whether it has delegated responsibility for authorizing coverage or termination decisions to its providers.

(5) If an IRE reverses an MA organization's termination decision, the MA organization must provide the enrollee with a new notice consistent with Sec. 422.624(b).

(f) Reconsiderations of IRE decisions. (1) If the IRE upholds an MA organization's termination decision in whole or in part, the enrollee may request, no later than 60 days after notification that the IRE has upheld the decision that the IRE reconsider its original decision.

(2) The IRE must issue its reconsidered determination as expeditiously as the enrollee's health condition requires but no later than within 14 days of receipt of the enrollee's request for a reconsideration.

(3) If the IRE reaffirms its decision, in whole or in part, the enrollee may to appeal the IRE's reconsidered determination to an ALJ, the MAC, or a federal court, as provided for under this subpart.

(4) If on reconsideration the IRE determines that coverage of provider services should terminate on a given date, the enrollee is liable for the costs of continued services after that date unless the IRE's decision is reversed on appeal. If the IRE's decision is reversed on appeal, the MA organization must reimburse the enrollee, consistent with the appealed decision, for the costs of any covered services for which the enrollee has already paid the MA organization or provider.

Effective Date Note: At 68 FR 20349, Apr. 4, 2003, **Sec. 422.626** was added. This section contains information collection and recordkeeping requirements and will not become effective until approval has been given by the Office of Management and Budget.

APPENDIX 7-2

FORMS

FORM 7A

NOTICE OF DENIAL OF PAYMENT

NOTICE OF DENIAL OF PAYMENT

Date: Member ID Number:

Beneficiary's name:

We,_____,
recently received a claim for: _____
_____
_____
provided to you by _____on _____
We will not pay for _____
_____
_____
_____
because:_____
_____
_____
_____
_____
_____

OMB Approval No. 0938-0829   Form No. CMS-10003-NDP (June 2001)

IMPORTANT INFORMATION ABOUT YOUR APPEAL RIGHTS
For more information about your appeal rights, call us or see your Evidence of Coverage.

What If I Don't Agree With This Decision?

You have the right to appeal. To exercise it, file your appeal in writing within 60 calendar days after the date of this notice. We can give you more time if you have a good reason for missing the deadline.

Who May File An Appeal?
You or someone you name to act for you (your **authorized representative**) may file an appeal. You can name a relative, friend, advocate, attorney, doctor, or someone else to act for you. Others also already may be authorized under State law to act for you.

You can call us at: (___)_____ to learn how to name your authorized representative. [If you have a hearing or speech impairment, please call us at TTY/TTD (___)_____].

If you want someone to act for you, you and your authorized representative must sign, date and send us a statement naming that person to act for you.

How Do I File An Appeal?
You or your authorized representative should mail or deliver your written appeal to the address(es) below:

We must give you a decision no later than 60 calendar days after we receive your appeal.

What Do I Include With My Appeal?
You should include: your name, address, Member ID number, reasons for appealing, and any evidence you wish to attach. You may send in supporting medical records, doctors' letters, or other information that explains why we should pay for the service. Call your doctor if you need this information to help you with your appeal. You may send in this information or present this information in person if you wish.

What Happens Next?
If you appeal, we will review our decision. After we review our decision, if payment for any of your claims is still denied, Medicare will provide you with a new and impartial review of your case by a reviewer outside of your Medicare+Choice Organization. If you disagree with that decision, you will have further appeal rights. You will be notified of those appeal rights if this happens.

Contact Information:
If you need information or help, call us at:

Toll Free:
TTY/TTD:

Other Resources To Help You:
Medicare Rights Center
Toll Free: 1-888-HMO-9050

Elder Care Locator
Toll Free: 1-800-677-1116

1-800-MEDICARE (1-800-633-4227)
TTY/TDD: 1-877-486-2048

OMB Approval No. 0938-0829   Form No. CMS-10003-NDP (June 2001)

FORM 7B

NOTICE OF DENIAL OF MEDICAL COVERAGE

NOTICE OF DENIAL OF MEDICAL COVERAGE

Date:

Beneficiary's name: Member ID Number:

We have denied coverage of the following medical services or items that you or your physician requested:_____

_____

_____

_____

We denied this request because:_____

_____

_____

_____

What If I Don't Agree With This Decision?

You have the right to appeal. To exercise it, file your appeal in writing within 60 calendar days after the date of this notice. We can give you more time if you have a good reason for missing the deadline.

Who May File An Appeal?

You or someone you name to act for you (your **authorized representative**) may file an appeal. You can name a relative, friend, advocate, attorney, doctor, or someone else to act for you. Others also already may be authorized under State law to act for you.

You can call us at: (___) _____ to learn how to name your authorized representative. If you have a hearing or speech impairment, please call us at TTY/ TDD (___) _____ .

If you want someone to act for you, you and your authorized representative must sign, date, and send us a statement naming that person to act for you.

OMB Approval No. 0938-0829   Form No. CMS-10003-NDMC (June 2001)

IMPORTANT INFORMATION ABOUT YOUR APPEAL RIGHTS

For more information about your appeal rights, call us or see your Evidence of Coverage.

There Are Two Kinds of Appeals You Can File

Standard (30 days)- You can ask for a standard appeal. We must give you a decision no later than 30 days after we get your appeal. (We may extend this time by up to 14 days if you request an extension, or if we need additional information and the extension benefits you.)

Fast (72 hour review)- You can ask for a fast appeal if you or your doctor believe that your health could be seriously harmed by waiting too long for a decision. We must decide on a fast appeal no later than 72 hours after we get your appeal. (We may extend this time by up to 14 days if you request an extension, or if we need additional information and the extension benefits you.)

- **If any doctor** asks for a fast appeal for you, or supports you in asking for one, and the doctor indicates that waiting for 30 days could seriously harm your health, **we will automatically give you a fast appeal.**
- If you ask for a fast appeal without support from a doctor, we will decide if your health requires a fast appeal. If we do not give you a fast appeal, we will decide your appeal within 30 days.

What Do I Include With My Appeal?

You should include: your name, address, Member ID number, reasons for appealing, and any evidence you wish to attach. You may send in supporting medical records, doctors' letters, or other information that explains why we should provide the service. Call your doctor if you need this information to help you with your appeal. You may send in this information or present this information in person if you wish.

How Do I File An Appeal?

For a Standard Appeal: You or your authorized representative should mail or deliver your written appeal to the address(es) below:

For a Fast Appeal: You or your authorized representative should contact us by telephone or fax:

What Happens Next? If you appeal, we will review our decision. After we review our decision, if any of the services you requested are still denied, Medicare will provide you with a new and impartial review of your case by a reviewer outside of your Medicare+Choice Organization. If you disagree with that decision, you will have further appeal rights. You will be notified of those appeal rights if this happens.

Contact Information:
If you need information or help, call us at:

Toll Free:
TTY/TTD:

Other Resources To Help You:
Medicare Rights Center:
Toll Free: 1-888-HMO-9050
TTY/TTD:

Elder Care Locator
Toll Free: 1-800-677-1116

1-800-MEDICARE (1-800-633-4227)
TTY/TTD: 1-877-486-2048

OMB Approval No. 0938-0829   Form No. CMS-10003-NDMC   (June 2001)

FORM 7C

NOTICE OF DISCHARGE AND MEDICARE APPEAL RIGHTS

(Rev. 22, 05-09-03)

NOTICE OF DISCHARGE & MEDICARE APPEAL RIGHTS

Enrollee's Name:	Date of Notice:
Health Insurance Claim (HIC) Number:	Admission Date:
Attending Physician:	Discharge Date:
Hospital:	Health Plan:

YOUR IMMEDIATE ATTENTION IS REQUIRED

Your doctor has reviewed your medical condition and has determined that you can be discharged from the Hospital because: [check one]

_____You no longer require inpatient hospital care.

_____You can safely get any medical care you need in another setting.

_____Other_____ _____.

[Fill in details.]

This also means that, if you stay in the hospital, it is likely that your hospital charges for [**specify date of first noncovered day**], and thereafter will not be covered by your Health Plan.

The Hospital has developed a discharge plan which explains any follow-up care or medications you need. If you have questions about this follow-up care, you should discuss them with your doctor. If you have not received a discharge plan and wish to do so, please contact your nurse, social worker or doctor.

If you agree with your doctor's discharge decision, you can either read further to learn more about your appeal rights, or you can skip to the end of this notice and sign to show that you have received this notice.

However, if you disagree with your Doctor's discharge decision, Medicare gives you the right to appeal. In that case, please continue reading to learn how to appeal a discharge decision, what happens when you appeal, and how much money you may owe.

IF YOU THINK YOU'RE BEING ASKED TO LEAVE THE HOSPITAL TOO SOON, REQUEST AN IMMEDIATE REVIEW

HOW DO YOU GET AN IMMEDIATE REVIEW?

1. The [Name of QIO] is the name of the Quality Improvement Organization - sometimes called a QIO - authorized by Medicare to review the Hospital care provided to Medicare patients. You or your authorized representative, attorney, or court appointed guardian must contact the QIO by telephone or in writing: [**Name, address, telephone and fax number of the QIO**]. If you file a written request, please write, "I want an immediate review".

2. Your request must be made no later than noon of the first working day after you receive this notice.

3. The QIO will make a decision within one full working day after it receives your request, your medical records, and any other information it needs to make a decision.

4. While you remain in the Hospital, your Health Plan will continue to be responsible for paying the costs of your stay until noon of the calendar day following the day the QIO notifies you of its official Medicare coverage decision.

WHAT IF THE QIO AGREES WITH YOUR DOCTOR'S DISCHARGE DECISION?

If the QIO agrees, you will be responsible for paying the cost of your Hospital stay beginning at noon of the calendar day following the day the QIO notifies you of its Medicare coverage decision.

WHAT IF THE QIO DISAGREES WITH YOUR DOCTOR'S DISCHARGE DECISION?

You will not be responsible for paying the cost of your additional Hospital days, except for certain convenience services or items not covered by your Health Plan.

WHAT IF YOU DON'T REQUEST AN IMMEDIATE REVIEW?

If you remain in the Hospital and do not request an immediate review by the QIO, you may be financially responsible for the cost of many of the services you receive beginning [specify date of first noncovered day].

If you leave before [specify date of first noncovered day], you will not be responsible for the cost of care. As with all hospitalizations, you may have to pay for certain convenience services or items not covered by your Health Plan.

WHAT IF YOU ARE LATE OR MISS THE DEADLINE TO FILE FOR AN IMMEDIATE REVIEW?

If you are late or miss the noon deadline to file for an immediate review by your QIO, you may still request an expedited (fast) appeal from your Health Plan. A "fast" appeal means your Health Plan will have to review your request within 72 hours. However, you will not have automatic financial protection during the course of your appeal. This means you could be responsible for paying the costs of your Hospital stay beginning [specify date of first noncovered day].

HOW DO YOU REQUEST A FAST APPEAL?

You may call or fax your request to your Health Plan:

> Stamp or Print Here
> Name of Health Plan
> Address
> Phone # and Fax #

If you filed a request for immediate QIO review but were late in filing the request, the QIO will forward your request to your Health Plan as a request for a fast appeal.

If you're filing a written request, please write, "I want a fast appeal."

If you or any doctor asks your Health Plan to give you a fast appeal, your Health Plan must process your appeal within 72 hours of your request.

Your Health Plan may take up to 14 extra calendar days to make a decision if you request an extension or if your Health Plan can justify how the extra days will benefit you. For example, you should request an extension if you believe that you or your Health Plan need more time to gather additional medical information. Keep in mind that you may end up paying for this extended hospital stay.

Please sign to let us know you have received this notice of discharge and appeal rights. By signing this notice, you do not give up your right to appeal this discharge.

_____

Signature of Medicare Enrollee or Authorized Representative   Date

cc: [Health Plan]

FORM 7D

WAIVER OF LIABILITY STATEMENT

(Rev. 22, 05-09-03)

WAIVER OF LIABILITY STATEMENT

_____
Medicare/HIC Number

_____
Enrollee's Name

_____   _____
Provider   Dates of Service

_____
Health Plan

I hereby waive any right to collect payment from the above-mentioned enrollee for the aforementioned services for which payment has been denied by the above-referenced health plan. I understand that the signing of this waiver does not negate my right to request further appeal under 42 CFR 422.600.

_____   _____
Signature   Date

FORM 7E

NOTICE OF MEDICARE NON-COVERAGE
[Insert Logo Here]

NOTICE OF MEDICARE NON-COVERAGE

THE EFFECTIVE DATE YOUR *{INSERT TYPE}* SERVICES WILL END:
{insert effective date}

- Your Medicare+Choice (M+C) plan believes that you will no longer have Medicare coverage of these services after the effective date of this notice. You may have to pay for any *{insert type}* services you receive after that date.

YOUR RIGHT TO APPEAL THIS DECISION

- You have the right to an immediate, independent medical review (appeal) of the decision to end coverage of these services while your services continue.

- If you choose to appeal, the independent reviewer will ask for your opinion. The reviewer will also look at your medical records or other relevant information. You do not have to prepare anything in writing, but you have the right to do so if you wish.

- If you choose to appeal, you and the independent reviewer will each receive a copy of the detailed explanation about why your coverage for services should not continue. You will receive this form only after you request an appeal.

- If you choose to appeal, and the independent reviewer agrees that services should no longer be covered after the effective date, neither Medicare nor your M+C plan will pay for these services after that date.

- If you stop services no later than the effective date indicated on this form, you will avoid financial liability.

HOW TO ASK FOR AN IMMEDIATE APPEAL

- You must make your request to your Quality Improvement Organization (also known as a QIO). A QIO is the independent reviewer authorized by Medicare to review the decision to end these services.

- Your request for an immediate appeal should be made as soon as possible, but no later than noon of the day before the effective date of this notice.

- The QIO will notify you of its decision as soon as possible, generally by no later than the effective date of this notice.

- Call your QIO at: *{insert name and number of QIO}* to appeal, or if you have questions.

See the back of this form for more information.

Page 1 of 2. Form No. CMS-10095-A (December 2003)

OTHER APPEAL RIGHTS:

- If you miss the deadline for requesting an immediate appeal with the QIO, you still may request an expedited appeal from your M+C plan.

- Contact your M+C plan or 1-800-MEDICARE (1-800-633-4227), or TTY/TDD: 1-877-486-2048 for more information about the M+C appeals process.

Please sign below to indicate that you have received this notice.

I have been notified that Medicare coverage of my services will end on the effective date of this notice and that I may appeal this decision by contacting my QIO.

_____   _____
Signature of Patient or Authorized Representative   **Date**

FORM 7F

DETAILED EXPLANATION OF NON-COVERAGE
[Insert Logo Here]

DETAILED EXPLANATION OF NON-COVERAGE

Date:

Patient Name: Member ID Number:

Because you requested an appeal, you are receiving this detailed explanation of why your M+C plan believes your Medicare coverage for *{insert type}* services should end. **This notice is not the decision on your appeal.** The decision on your appeal will come from your Quality Improvement Organization (QIO).

- **We have reviewed your case and decided that Medicare coverage of your *{insert type}* services should end.**

  {Insert relevant text about who made the decision}

- **The facts used to make this decision:**

  {Insert relevant text}

- **Detailed explanation of why your services are no longer covered under your M+C plan, and the specific Medicare coverage rules and policy used to make this decision:**

  {Insert relevant text}

- **_{Insert M+C plan}_ policy, provision, or rationale used in making the decision:**

  {Insert relevant text}

  If you would like a copy of the policy or coverage guidelines used to make this decision, or a copy of the documents sent to the QIO, please call us at *{insert M+C plan or provider telephone number}*:

Form No. CMS-10095-B   (December 2003)

Please see CMS's "Notice Initiative" on its webpage, (http:/www.cms.hhs.gov/medicare/bni/default.asp). This site is updated regularly with new notices as they become available for review and comment, and for use in Medicare claims and appeals activities.

CHAPTER **8**

MEDIGAP SERVICES

§8.01 INTRODUCTION

Despite the protections offered by Medicare, there are gaps in the Medicare benefit package in the form of deductibles, copayments, and other limitations. Medigap insurance is provided by private insurance companies to supplement Medicare coverage and, sometimes, to cover services not included in Medicare's benefit package. Since Medicare generally only pays a portion of a beneficiary's medical expenses, Medigap insurance is intended to "bridge the gap" between what Medicare pays and the balance of a beneficiary's medical bills.

Medigap insurance is meant to work in tandem with the fee-for-service Medicare program. Medigap insurance will generally only cover services that Medicare has already approved for payment. Generally, if Medicare denies coverage for an item or service, the Medigap policy will also refuse to pay its portion of the bill, unless coverage is specified in the policy.

Medigap coverage is a key component of health insurance protection for individuals who rely upon the original Medicare program to finance their health care. Consumers need to be clear about the benefits they need and what the various plans cover in order to ensure that they pay only for what they need and get the coverage to which they are entitled. Elder law attorneys should help guide this process. Attorneys should also be aware of the important consumer protections and responsibilities which may affect their clients' Medigap coverage—and hence the ability of their clients to pay for necessary health care.

§8.02 MEDICARE CERTIFICATION OF POLICIES

Beginning in 1990, the Health Care Financing Administration (HCFA), now the Centers for Medicare and Medicaid Services (CMS), began a program of mandatory certification of Medigap policies and created ten standard plans.[1] Under this authority, the Secretary is required to establish a procedure whereby Medigap policies are certified as meeting minimum standards and requirements.[2] The Medicare statute deems certification by the Secretary to Medigap policies that

---

[1] *See* §4353(a) of the Omnibus Budget Reconciliation Act of 1990 (OBRA '90) (effective Nov. 5, 1990) (codified at 42 U.S.C. §1395ss(a)), applicable to policies sold after July 1992; such policies must conform to one of the 10 standardized model policies developed by the National Association of Insurance Commissioners (NAIC). (*See* standardized table of Medigap policies at **§8.03**.) Previously, certification was voluntary as provided in 507(a) of the Social Security Disability Amendments of 1980, Pub. L. No. 96-265. (*See* 42 U.S.C. §1395ss(b)–(f) for a full discussion of the state and federal certification processes and §1395ss(i)–(n) for a full discussion and history of the effective dates for adopting and meeting the NAIC Model Regulation or federal model standards.)

[2] 42 U.S.C. §1395ss(a)(1). The Secretary's authority to promulgate rules for the administration of its certification program for Medigap policies is found at 42 U.S.C. §1395ss(h). The requirements for certification by the Secretary are found at 42 U.S.C. §1395ss(c). Procedures for certification are found in the regulations at 42 C.F.R. §403.232.

meet regulatory requirements established under state law if the state regulatory programs provide for the application and enforcement of standards that are equal to or are more stringent than the National Association of Insurance Commissioners (NAIC) Model standards.[3] The Secretary is to review periodically the compliance of states with these requirements[4] and is also to submit a report to Congress at least once every two years that evaluates the effectiveness of the certification process.[5]

The Medicare Prescription Drug, Improvement and Modernization Act of 2003 (the Medicare Act)[6] added two new standardized plans and changed the benefits under three existing plans, starting in 2006. In addition, the Medicare Act authorized NAIC to review and revise the model standards to incorporate the new plans and reflect the changes in the existing plans.

§8.03   STANDARDIZED PLANS

In all states except Minnesota, Massachusetts and Wisconsin,[7] federal law requires insurers to sell Medigap policies that are one of the 12 standard supplemental plans.[8] These 12 plans are labeled with the letters A through L to make it easier for consumers to compare plans.[9] Medigap policies pay most, if not all, of the original Medicare plan's coinsurance amounts and may provide coverage for deductibles as well. Some of the 12 standardized plans pay for services not covered by Medicare such as outpatient prescription drugs,[10] preventive screening services, and emergency medical care while traveling outside the United States. When describing the benefits of each of the Medigap policies, insurance companies must use the same format, language, and definitions to make it easier for consumers to compare policies.[11]

---

[3] *See* 42 U.S.C. §1395ss(g)(2)(A). NAIC Model Standards are found at 42 C.F.R. §403.210.

[4] 42 U.S.C. §1395ss(b).

[5] 42 U.S.C. §1395ss(f)(2).

[6] Medicare Prescription Drug, Improvement and Modernization Act of 2003, Pub. L. No. 108–173 (Dec. 8, 2003), amending 42 U.S.C. §1395ss.

[7] Information on these three states' Medigap plans as well as the ten standardized plans can be found on the CMS Web site at <http://www.medicare.gov/medigap.>

[8] 42 U.S.C. §1395ss(a).

[9] Policies sold before July 31, 1992, were not standardized and, although these policies are no longer offered for sale, many beneficiaries continue to renew their existing pre-standardization policies.

[10] Effective January 1, 2006, no new standardized Medigap policies that provide outpatient prescription drug benefits will be sold. Consumers who are enrolled in those plans as of December 1, 2005, will be able to retain and renew those policies. 42 U.S.C. §1395ss(v), as added by Public L. No. 108–173.

[11] 42 U.S.C. §1395ss(e).

MEDIGAP

STANDARD MEDICARE SUPPLEMENT PLANS

Core Benefits	A	B	C	D	E	F	G	H	I	J
Hospital Coinsurance: Days 61 to 91	•	•	•	•	•	•	•	•	•	•
Hospital Coinsurance: Days 91 to 150	•	•	•	•	•	•	•	•	•	•
Hospital Payment in full: 365 additional days	•	•	•	•	•	•	•	•	•	•
Part A and Part B Blood Deductible: First three pints of blood	•	•	•	•	•	•	•	•	•	•
Part B 20% Coinsurance: Physician and other services	•	•	•	•	•	•	•	•	•	•

Additional Benefits	A	B	C	D	E	F	G	H	I	J
Skilled Nursing Facility Coinsurance: Days 21 to 100—$124 per day in 2007			•	•	•	•	•	•	•	•
Part A Hospital Deductible: $992 in 2007		•	•	•	•	•	•	•	•	•
Part B Annual Deductible: $131 in 2007			•			•				•
Part B Excess Charges: Coverage for up to 115% percent of Medicare's approved charge (Medigap policy will either pay 80% or 100% of excess charge)						100%	80%		100%	100%
Foreign Travel Emergency: $250 deductible,, 80% of the cost of emergency care during the first two months of the trip, $50,000 lifetime limit			•	•	•	•	•	•	•	•
At-Home Recovery: Maximum benefit of $1,600 annually				•			•		•	•

Prescription Drugs—   • •
  Basic Benefit: $250
  annual deductible;
  50% of prescription
  drug costs; Maximum
  benefit of $1,250
  annually

Prescription Drugs—   •
  Extended Benefit:
  $250 annual
  deductible; 50% of
  prescription drug
  costs; Maximum
  benefit of $3,000
  annually[12]

Preventive Medical   •   •
  Care: $120 maximum
  annually for
  preventive services
  ordered by doctor

Plan A contains the basic or "core" benefits. The other 11 policies contain the core benefits plus one or more additional benefits. The following is a list of the benefits that are contained in the core policy and that must be contained in all new Medigap policies sold since July 31, 1992:[13]

1. Part A hospital coinsurance for days 61 to 90 ($248 per day in the year 2007;

2. Part A lifetime reserve coinsurance for days 91 to 150 ($496 in 2007));

3. 365 lifetime hospital days beyond Medicare coverage;

4. Parts A and B Three Pint Blood Deductible;

5. Part B 20 percent coinsurance.

Additional benefits are offered in Policies B through L. Each plan offers a different combination of these benefits in addition to the core benefits. The Medigap Chart shows which plans contain which benefits.[14] Additional benefits are:

1. Part A Skilled Nursing Facility (SNF) coinsurance for days 21 to 100 ($124 per day in 2007));

2. Part A hospital deductible ($992 in 2007);

---

[12] No new policies offering prescription drug coverage may be sold on or after January 1, 2006. 42 U.S.C. §1395ss(v).

[13] 42 U.S.C. §1395ss(o).

[14] This information can also be found at the CMS Web site at <http://www.medicare.gov>.

3. Part B deductible ($131 in 2007);

4. Part B charges above the Medicare approved amount (if the provider does not accept assignment);

5. Foreign travel emergency coverage;

6. At-home recovery (home health aide services);

7. Prescription drug coverage (basic or extended);[15]

8. Preventive medical care.

§8.04 HIGH DEDUCTIBLE PLANS

Medigap policies F and J also have a high deductible option. These high deductible plans offer the same basic benefits as plans F and J but the beneficiary enrolled in the high deductible option must pay a deductible ($1,790 in 2006)[16] each year before the policy pays anything. Additional deductibles must be met, including a separate prescription drug deductible of $250 per year for Plan J and a separate foreign travel emergency deductible of $250 per year for Plans F and J.[17] Because of these additional deductibles, the premiums for these plans may be significantly lower than for plans without the high deductible.

§8.05 MEDICARE SELECT

Sections 4358(a) and (b) of OBRA '90 authorize approval of certain Medigap policies as Medicare SELECT policies if the policies meet the NAIC model standards and otherwise comply with the statute. Medicare SELECT is the same as standard Medigap insurance in nearly all ways. The only difference is that Medicare SELECT policies limit full benefits to items and services furnished by a network of providers, except in emergency situations. Reduced benefits may be provided for items and services furnished by non-network providers. Medicare SELECT policies generally have lower premiums because of this limitation.[18]

Medicare SELECT policies meet the NAIC or federal regulations if:

• Full benefits are provided for items and services furnished through a network of entities which have entered into contracts or agreements with the issuer of the policy;

---

[15] *See* note 12.

[16] For subsequent years the deductible is increased by the percentage increase in the Consumer Price Index for all urban consumers for the 12-month period ending with August of the preceding year. *See* 42 U.S.C. §1395ss(p)(11)(C)(ii).

[17] 42 U.S.C. §1395ss(p)(11).

[18] 42 U.S.C. §1395ss(t)(1).

- Full benefits are provided for medically necessary and immediately required services because of an unforeseen illness, injury, or condition and it is not reasonable given the circumstances to obtain the services through the network;

- The network offers sufficient access;

- The issuer of the policy has arrangements for an ongoing quality assurance program for items and services furnished through the network;

- The insurer provides each enrollee at the time of enrollment (and the enrollee acknowledges receipt of) an explanation of the restrictions on obtaining services through the network, out-of-network services, coverage of emergency services, and urgently needed care; and

- The insurer provides each enrollee an explanation regarding the availability and cost of other Medigap policies offered by the insurer that do not include the network restrictions.[19]

The Secretary is authorized to impose civil money penalties against the issuer of a policy up to $25,000 for each of the following violations:

- Substantial failure to provide medically necessary items and services to enrollees through the network, if the failure has adversely affected or has a substantial likelihood of adversely affecting the enrollee;

- Imposition of premiums on enrollees in excess of premiums approved by the state;

- Actions to expel an enrollee for reasons other than nonpayment of premiums;

- Failure to provide the enrollee with a written explanation of the policy's restrictions on payment outside the network, out-of-area coverage, coverage of emergency and urgently needed care, and availability and cost of a policy without a network restriction; and

- Failure to obtain an acknowledgment from the enrollee that he or she received the above-described explanation at the time of enrollment.[20]

§8.06   CHANGES TO POLICIES EFFECTIVE IN 2006

Congress, in the Medicare Act of 2003, made changes to existing standard plans H, I, and J, and created two new Medigap plans. The changes to the existing plans and the sale of the new plans became effective on January 1, 2006, the day that the new Medicare drug provisions (Part D) went into effect.

---

[19] 42 U.S.C. §1395ss(t)(1)(A)–(F).
[20] 42 U.S.C. §1395ss(t)(2).

On or after that date, Medigap Plans H, I, and J cannot be sold, issued, or renewed to anyone with Medicare who is enrolled in or eligible for Medicare Part D. The Act created an exception for people with a plan H, I, or J policy that was issued before January 1, 2006.[21] Those policies may be renewed for such individuals as long as the individuals are not enrolled in a Medicare Part D prescription drug plan. If someone decides to keep a Mcdigap prescription drug plan, upon enrollment in a Medicare Part D drug plan, the Medigap plan's coverage will be modified to eliminate prescription drug coverage for expenses of prescription drugs incurred after the effective date of coverage under Part D. Premiums will also be adjusted to reflect the elimination of this coverage. Certain consumer protections, discussed below, will be provided to individuals who have Medigap prescription drug plans and want to change to a different plan.

Two new Medigap policies can also be offered. The first benefit package, Plan K, will cover 50 percent of cost sharing applicable under Medicare parts A and B, except for the Part B deductible. It will cover 100 percent cost sharing for preventive benefits, all inpatient hospital coinsurance, and 365 extra lifetime days of coverage of inpatient hospital services. There will also be a limitation on annual out-of-pocket expenses under Parts A and B of $4,000 in 2006, adjusted for inflation in subsequent years. The second benefit package, Plan L, will be the same as the first except that it will cover seventy-five percent (75 percent) of cost sharing applicable under Parts A and B, and the limit on annual out-of-pocket expenses will be $2,000 in 2006.[22]

The Medicare Act authorizes the NAIC to review and revise the standard benefit packages, taking into account the changes to Plans H, I, and J and the addition of the two new benefit packages. The revisions are to be consistent with existing NAIC model regulations. The Act requires, to the extent practicable, that the revised standards be implemented as of January 1, 2006.[23]

Note that the Medicare Act does not modify the standard plans to require that any or all of them pay the cost sharing under the new Medicare Part D prescription drug benefit. Thus, neither the existing nor new Medigap policies will cover any of the out-of-pocket costs associated with prescription drug benefits provided under Part D.

§8.07 CONSUMER PROTECTIONS

Pursuant to federal law, all Medicare beneficiaries have an "open enroll-ment" period during the first six months they are both at least 65 years of age and enrolled in Medicare Part B. During this time period, a Medicare beneficiary can purchase any of the standard Medigap policies. This is a "guaranteed issue

---

[21] 42 U.S.C. §1395ss(v).

[22] 42 U.S.C. §1395ss(w)(2).

[23] 42 U.S.C. §1395ss(w)(1).

period," which means that insurance companies are prohibited from denying a policy to any Medicare beneficiary who meets the open enrollment requirements.

Medicare beneficiaries who are at least 65 years old are also guaranteed issuance of certain Medigap policies if they apply within 63 days of the following events:

- A Medicare beneficiary who enrolled in a Medicare Advantage (MA) (formerly Medicare + Choice) Plan upon first becoming eligible for Medicare who subsequently disenrolled within 12 months is guaranteed issuance of any Medigap policy offered for sale in the beneficiary's state. That period is extended for another 12 months if the MA Plan terminated its contract with CMS or the beneficiary was otherwise involuntarily disenrolled within the first 12 months of enrollment and enrolled in another MA Plan.[24]

- A Medicare beneficiary who dropped a Medigap policy upon enrolling for the first time in an MA Plan but who subsequently disenrolled within 12 months is guaranteed issuance of the same Medigap policy from the same insurance company *if that policy* is still being offered for sale. Otherwise, such an individual is entitled to guaranteed issuance of Medigap plans A, B, C, or F. That period is extended for an additional 12 months if the MA Plan terminated its contract with CMS or the beneficiary was otherwise involuntarily disenrolled within the first 12 months of enrollment and enrolled in another MA Plan.[25]

- A Medicare beneficiary who moved out of the area or whose plan terminated service to her area became bankrupt or violated or misrepresented a provision of the plan or engaged in marketing violations is guaranteed issuance of Medigap plans A, B, C, or F. These same rights apply to Medicare beneficiaries whose employer stops providing employee or retiree health insurance coverage, or when COBRA health care continuation insurance ends.[26]

Once a beneficiary purchases a Medigap policy he is also guaranteed renewal of that policy unless the beneficiary does not pay the policy premiums or for material misrepresentation. The health status of the individual is not a valid reason to cancel or to refuse to renew a policy.[27]

Each Medigap policy shall provide that benefits and premiums can be suspended at the request of the policy holder for a period up to 24 months when the policy holder has applied for and is determined to be eligible for medical assistance under the Medicaid program, provided the policy holder notifies the issuer of the policy within 90 days after the entitlement to such assistance. If the beneficiary's Medicaid entitlement is suspended or terminated, the Medigap policy can be

---

[24] 42 U.S.C. §1395ss(s).

[25] *Id.*

[26] *Id.*

[27] 42 U.S.C. §1395ss(q)(1)(A)–(B).

automatically reinstated effective the day of the suspension or termination.[28] There are penalties for insurers who fail to abide by these provisions.[29] The Ticket to Work Incentives Improvement Act of 1999 provides for suspension of Medigap coverage and premiums for disabled workers entitled to Medicare Part A who are covered under certain group health plans. It also requires reinstatement of a Medigap policy if group coverage is lost provided that the policyholder gives notice of the loss of such coverage within 90 days.[30]

§8.08 PROHIBITION AGAINST SALE OF DUPLICATE POLICIES

Another important consumer protection found in federal law is the prohibition against the sale of a second Medigap policy to a beneficiary.[31] It is also unlawful for a person to knowingly sell or issue a Medigap policy that duplicates health benefits to which the individual is entitled under Title 19 (Medicaid) or other benefit programs under a state or federal law.[32] An insurance agent is required to disclose this provision of the law to Medicare beneficiaries and must obtain a written acknowledgment of their receipt of this information. A new policy may be sold to replace an existing policy, but this fact must also be acknowledged in writing. However, a beneficiary may keep or purchase another medical insurance policy that is not a Medigap policy. Such policies include hospital indemnification coverage, which only provides benefits for hospitalization and nothing else, and long-term care insurance.[33] When an insurance company or independent insurance agent sells such a policy, the specific coverage must be disclosed and it must be certified that the policy is not a Medigap policy.[34]

In addition, since January 2006, issuers of Medigap policies are required to eliminate coverage that duplicates prescription drug benefits for individuals who have a Medigap prescription drug policy[35] and who enroll in a Medicare Part D prescription drug plan. Affected individuals can either enroll in a Medicare

---

[28] 42 U.S.C. §1395ss(q)(5)(A).

[29] 42 U.S.C. §1395ss(q)(5)(C).

[30] 42 U.S.C. §1395ss(q)(6).

[31] It is also not illegal for a beneficiary to renew existing policies. For that reason, there are a few beneficiaries who do have more than one Medigap policy because the policies were purchased before this provision of the law took effect.

[32] 42 U.S.C. §1395ss(d)(3).

[33] Id.

[34] State law can and does, in many instances, offer additional consumer protections to beneficiaries purchasing Medigap policies. Medicare beneficiaries should check with their state's insurance commissioner for additional information.

[35] A Medigap prescription drug policy is defined as Plans H, I, and J, including a high deductible Plan J, or a policy to which the standards do not apply but which provides prescription drug benefits. 42 U.S.C. §1395ss(v)(6)(A).

supplemental policy without prescription drug coverage, or they can remain in their current plan, which will be modified to eliminate the drug benefit.[36]

§8.09 REQUIRED RATIO OF AGGREGATE BENEFITS TO AGGREGATE PREMIUMS

Medigap policies may not be issued or renewed in any state unless the policy can be expected to provide a return to policyholders in the form of aggregate benefits provided under the policy of at least 75 percent of the aggregate amount of premiums collected in the case of group policies, and at least 65 percent in the case of individual policies.[37] Issuers of policies must provide for a proportional refund or credit against future premiums in order to ensure this required ratio of aggregate benefits provided as compared to the aggregate premiums collected, also known as loss ratios.[38] Refunds or credits must include interest from the end of the calendar year involved until the date of the refund or credit at a rate specified by the Secretary.[39]

In addition, since 1993 the Secretary has been required to submit an annual report each October on loss ratios under Medigap policies to the Committees on Energy and Commerce and Ways and Means of the House of Representatives and the Committee on Finance of the Senate.[40] The Comptroller General is required to perform audits to ascertain compliance with the loss ratio requirements at least once every three years and to report the results of the audits to the state involved and to the Secretary.[41] The Secretary also has independent audit authority.[42] An insurer who fails to provide the required premium refunds or credits is subject to fines of up to $25,000 for each policy issued for which such failure occurred.[43]

§8.10 COVERAGE OF PREEXISTING CONDITIONS

In general, insurance companies can sell Medigap policies with exclusions for coverage of preexisting conditions for a period of up to six months. A preexisting condition is a medical condition present prior to obtaining the health insurance coverage. Under the Health Insurance Portability and Accountability

---

[36] 42 U.S.C. §1395ss(v)(2)(A).

[37] 42 U.S.C. §1395ss(r)(1)(A). For purposes of this provision, only policies issued as a result of solicitations of individuals through the mail or by mass media advertising shall be deemed to be individual policies.

[38] 42 U.S.C. §1395ss(r)(1)(B).

[39] 42 U.S.C. §1395ss(r)(2)(A)–(D).

[40] 42 U.S.C. §1395ss(r)(4)–(5).

[41] 42 U.S.C. §1395ss(r)(5)(A).

[42] 42 U.S.C. §1395ss(r)(5)(B).

[43] 42 U.S.C. §1395ss(r)(6)(A).

Act (HIPAA)[44] such exclusions *cannot* be imposed on an individual who applies for a Medigap policy during his or her initial open enrollment period who has at least six months of creditable coverage, and who has not had a break in creditable coverage of more than 63 days of applying for the Medigap policy.[45]

A beneficiary's initial open enrollment period occurs during the first six months the beneficiary is both age 65 or older and enrolled in Medicare Part B. Creditable coverage is defined as coverage under:

- A group health plan;
- Health insurance coverage;
- Part A or Part B of Medicare;
- Medicaid;
- A medical program on the Indian Health Service or tribal organization;
- A state health benefits risk pool;
- CHAMPUS (Civilian Health and Medical Program of the Uniformed Services);
- The Federal Employees Health Benefit Plan;
- A public health plan; or
- A health plan under the Peace Corps Act.[46]

For beneficiaries who are switching from one Medigap policy to another, the issuer of the replacement Medigap policy must waive any time periods applicable to preexisting conditions, waiting periods, elimination periods, and probation periods in the new Medigap policy for similar benefits to the extent of time spent under the original policy.[47]

In addition, since 1997, pursuant to the Balanced Budget Act of 1997, Medicare beneficiaries who are at least 65 years old are also guaranteed issuance of certain Medigap policies with no wait for coverage of preexisting conditions if they apply within 63 days under certain circumstances.[48] The circumstances under which these rights exist are as follows:

- A Medicare beneficiary whose employer stopped providing employee retirement health benefits or whose COBRA health care continuation insurance coverage ends is guaranteed issuance of Medigap policies A, B, C, or F.

---

[44] 42 U.S.C. §300gg.

[45] 42 U.S.C. §1395ss(s)(2)(D).

[46] 42 U.S.C. §300gg(c)(1).

[47] 42 U.S.C. §1395ss(s)(1).

[48] 42 U.S.C. §1395ss(s)(3).

- A Medicare beneficiary who enrolled in a Medicare managed care plan upon first becoming eligible for Medicare who subsequently disenrolled within 12 months is guaranteed issuance of any Medigap policy sold in his or her state.

- A Medicare beneficiary who dropped a Medigap policy upon enrolling for the first time in a Medicare managed care plan but who subsequently disenrolled within 12 months is guaranteed issuance of the same Medigap policy from the same insurance company if that policy is still being offered for sale. Otherwise, such an individual is entitled to guaranteed issuance of Medigap policies A, B, C, or F from any insurance company selling Medigap policies in his or her state.

- A Medicare beneficiary who moved out of the area served by his or her Medicare managed care plan or whose Medicare managed care plan terminated service to his or her area, became bankrupt, or violated or misrepresented a provision of the plan is guaranteed issuance of Medigap policies A, B, C, or F.

§8.11   DISSEMINATION OF INFORMATION ABOUT MEDIGAP POLICY BENEFITS

The Secretary is required to provide Medicare beneficiaries with information that will assist them in evaluating whether a Medigap policy will be of value to them and with information that will be helpful in comparing Medigap policies.[49] Pursuant to this requirement, beneficiaries are to be provided information about the actions and practices that are subject to sanctions under Medicare, the manner in which such actions and practices may be reported, and a toll-free telephone number for individuals to report suspected violations.[50] In addition, beneficiaries are to be provided a listing, including addresses and telephone numbers, of state and federal agencies and offices that provide information and assistance to individuals on selecting Medigap policies.[51] The Secretary is also to provide a toll-free telephone number for information about Medigap policies, including the relationship of state Medicaid programs to Medigap policies.[52] Much of this required information is found on CMS's Web site at *http://www.medicare.gov*.

The MMA requires issuers of Medicare prescription drug policies[53] to provide written notice, during the 60 days immediately before the initial Medicare Part D prescription drug enrollment period,[54] to everyone who holds a Medigap prescription drug policy. The notice must meet standards devised by the Secretary

---

[49] 42 U.S.C. §1395ss(e)(1).

[50] 42 U.S.C. §1395ss(e)(2)(A).

[51] 42 U.S.C. §1395ss(e)(3).

[52] 42 U.S.C. §1395ss(f)(3).

[53] *See* note 36.

[54] The initial enrollment period for Part D begins November 15, 2005. Medicare Act 101(a) adding §1860D-1(b)(2)(A) of the Social Security Act.

and by NAIC. It must advise the policy holders that if they enroll in a Part D plan, they can (1) continue in their prescription drug plan but the plan will be modified to eliminate the drug benefit, or (2) they can enroll in a Plan A, B, C, or F. The notice must further advise the policy holders that if they do not enroll in a Part D plan, they may continue in their Medigap prescription drug policy, with prescription drug benefits, but that (1) they may not be guaranteed enrollment in another Medigap policy if they subsequently decide to change policies and (2) the coverage under the Medigap drug policy may not count as creditable coverage, raising that possibility of limited enrollment periods should they subsequently decide to enroll in a Part D plan. The Secretary, along with NAIC, may require issuers to include additional information in the notice, including that people who retain Medigap prescription drug plans may have to pay increased premiums for a Part D plan should they choose to enroll after the initial enrollment period.[55]

---

[55] 42 U.S.C. §1395ss(v)(2)(B).

APPENDIX 8-1

TITLE 42—PUBLIC HEALTH
(CODE OF FEDERAL REGULATIONS):

PART 403—SPECIAL PROGRAMS AND PROJECTS

Subpart B—Medicare Supplemental Policies
[Revised as of October 1, 2003]

Sec. 403.215   Loss ratio standards.

(a) The policy must be expected to return to the policyholders, in the form of aggregate benefits provided under the policy—

(1) At least 75 percent of the aggregate amount of premiums in the case of group policies; and

(2) At least 60 percent of the aggregate amount of premiums in the case of individual policies.

(b) For purposes of loss ratio requirements, policies issued as a result of solicitation of individuals through the mail or by mass media advertising are considered individual policies.

* * *

Sec. 403.232   Requirements and procedures for obtaining certification.

(a) To be certified by CMS, a policy must meet—

(1) The NAIC model standards specified in Sec. 403.210;

(2) The loss ratio standards specified in Sec. 403.215; and

(3) Any State requirements applicable to a policy—

(i) Issued in that State; or

(ii) Marketed in that State.

(b) An insuring organization requesting certification of a policy must submit the following to CMS for review—

(1) A copy of the policy form (including all the documents that would constitute the contract of insurance that is proposed to be marketed as a certified policy).

(2) A copy of the application form including all attachments.

(3) A copy of the uniform certificate issued under a group policy.

(4) A copy of the outline of coverage, in the form prescribed by the NAIC model standards.

(5) A copy of the Medicare supplement buyers' guide to be provided to all applicants if the buyers' guide is not the CMS/NAIC buyers' guide.

(6) A statement of when and how the outline of coverage and the buyers' guide will be delivered and copies of applicable receipt forms.

(7) A copy of the notice of replacement and statement as to when and how that notice will be delivered.

(8) A list of States in which the policy is authorized for sale. If the policy was approved under a deemer provision in any State, the conditions involved must be specified.

(9) A copy of the loss ratio calculations, as specified in Sec. 403.250.

(10) Loss ratio supporting data, as specified in Sec. 403.256.

(11) A statement of actuarial opinion, as specified in Sec. 403.258.

(12) A statement that the insuring organization will notify the policyholders in writing, within the period of time specified in Sec. 403.245(c), if the policy is identified as a certified policy at the time of sale and later loses certification.

(13) A signed statement in which the president of the insuring organization, or a designee, attests that—

(i) The policy meets the requirements specified in paragraph (a) of this section; and

(ii) The information submitted to CMS for review is accurate and complete and does not misrepresent any material fact.

APPENDIX 8-2

TITLE 42—THE PUBLIC HEALTH AND WELFARE
(UNITED STATES CODE):

CHAPTER 7—SOCIAL SECURITY:

SUBCHAPTER XVIII—HEALTH INSURANCE FOR AGED AND DISABLED

(SUBPART D—MISCELLANEOUS PROVISIONS)

Sec. 1395gg   Overpayment on behalf of individuals and settlement of claims for benefits on behalf of deceased individuals.

(c) Exception to subsection (b) payment adjustment. There shall be no adjustment as provided in subsection (b) of this section (nor shall there be recovery) in any case where the incorrect payment has been made (including payments under section 1395f(e) of this title) with respect to an individual who is without fault or where the adjustment (or recovery) would be made by decreasing payments to which another person who is without fault is entitled as provided in subsection (b)(4) of this section, if such adjustment (or recovery) would defeat the purposes of subchapter II or subchapter XVIII of this chapter or would be against equity and good conscience. Adjustment or recovery of an incorrect payment (or only such part of an incorrect payment as the Secretary determines to be inconsistent with the purposes of this subchapter) against an individual who is without fault shall be deemed to be against equity and good conscience if (A) the incorrect payment was made for expenses incurred for items or services for which payment may not be made under this subchapter by reason of the provisions of paragraph (1) or (9) of section 1395y(a) of this title and (B) if the Secretary's determination that such payment was incorrect was made subsequent to the third year following the year in which notice of such payment was sent to such individual; except that the Secretary may reduce such three-year period to not less than one year if he finds such reduction is consistent with the objectives of this subchapter.
* * *

Sec. 1395ss   Certification of medicare supplemental health insurance policies.

(a) Submission of policy by insurer.
(1) The Secretary shall establish a procedure whereby Medicare supplemental policies (as defined in subsection (g)(1) of this section) may be certified by the Secretary as meeting minimum standards and requirements set forth in subsection (c) of this section. Such procedure shall provide an opportunity for any insurer to submit any such policy, and such additional data as the Secretary

finds necessary, to the Secretary for his examination and for his certification thereof as meeting the standards and requirements set forth in subsection (c) of this section. Subject to subsections (k)(3), (m), and (n) of this section, such certification shall remain in effect if the insurer files a notarized statement with the Secretary no later than June 30 of each year stating that the policy continues to meet such standards and requirements and if the insurer submits such additional data as the Secretary finds necessary to independently verify the accuracy of such notarized statement. Where the Secretary determines such a policy meets (or continues to meet) such standards and requirements, he shall authorize the insurer to have printed on such policy (but only in accordance with such requirements and conditions as the Secretary may prescribe) an emblem which the Secretary shall cause to be designed for use as an indication that a policy has received the Secretary's certification. The Secretary shall provide each State commissioner or superintendent of insurance with a list of all the policies which have received his certification.

(2) No Medicare supplemental policy may be issued in a State on or after the date specified in subsection (p)(1)(C) of this section unless—

(A) the State's regulatory program under subsection (b)(1) of this section provides for the application and enforcement of the standards and requirements set forth in such subsection (including the 1991 NAIC Model Regulation or 1991 Federal Regulation (as the case may be)) by the date specified in subsection (p)(1)(C) of this section; or

(B) if the State's program does not provide for the application and enforcement of such standards and requirements, the policy has been certified by the Secretary under paragraph (1) as meeting the standards and requirements set forth in subsection (c) of this section (including such applicable standards) by such date.

Any person who issues a Medicare supplemental policy, on and after the effective date specified in subsection (p)(1)(C) of this section, in violation of this paragraph is subject to a civil money penalty of not to exceed $25,000 for each such violation. The provisions of section 1320a-7a of this title (other than the first sentence of subsection (a) and other than subsection (b)) shall apply to a civil money penalty under the previous sentence in the same manner as such provisions apply to a penalty or proceeding under section 1320a-7a(a) of this title.

CHAPTER 9

MEDICARE'S RELATIONSHIP WITH PRIVATE INSURANCE

§9.01 INTRODUCTION

In 1980 Congress prohibited Medicare from paying for health services that are also covered by other insurers through its creation of the Medicare Secondary Payer (MSP) program.[1] The MSP program has been modified and expanded by subsequent legislation in order to shift more health care costs from the federal government to private insurers.

The MSP law makes Medicare payment secondary to payment by two kinds of private insurers: first, those providing group health insurance for currently working employees;[2] and second, those providing coverage under automobile, liability, and workers' compensation policies.[3]

§9.02 EMPLOYER GROUP HEALTH PLANS (EGHPS)

[A] Medicare Secondary to EGHPs

The Medicare statute makes Medicare secondary to employer group health insurance in a number of situations. Employer group health insurance plans of specified sizes are prohibited from discriminating in health insurance benefits available to workers and their spouses who are eligible for Medicare because they are disabled or age 65 or older.[4]

Medicare provides only limited, secondary coverage for EGHP-eligible beneficiaries. It will take steps to recover payments previously made when it discovers that an EGHP should have paid as primary insurer.[5]

[B] Which Medicare Beneficiaries Are Covered Under an EGHP?

A Medicare beneficiary may be able to obtain coverage under an EGHP offered to currently working employees, their spouses, and their dependents; under a retiree health plan offered to retirees, their spouses, and their dependents; or under the Consolidated Omnibus Budget Reconciliation Act (COBRA)[6] health care continuation coverage. In all three situations, if the plan is offered by a private employer or union, the plan must meet the requirements of another federal law known as the Employee Retirement Income Security Act, or ERISA,[7] which sets certain standards for employment-related health insurance.

---

[1] Omnibus Budget Reconciliation Act (OBRA) of 1980, Pub. L. No. 96-499, §953.

[2] 42 U.S.C. §1395y(b)(2)(A)(i)

[3] 42 U.S.C. §1395y(b)(2)(A)(ii).

[4] 42 U.S.C. §1395y(b)(1)(A)(i).

[5] 42 U.S.C. §1395y(b)(2)(B)(iii).

[6] 29 U.S.C. §1161; 42 U.S.C. §§300bb-1 *et seq. See* discussion at **§9.05.**

[7] 29 U.S.C. §1001.

ERISA does not require employers to offer group health insurance to their employees. Employers that offer health insurance do so voluntarily.[8] If a health insurance plan is offered, ERISA generally allows the plan sponsor, i.e., the employer or union, to set the eligibility criteria for participation in the health plan offered to active employees. Someone who does not meet the criteria established by the plan sponsor is not eligible to join in the health plan, and Medicare is the primary insurer.

Similarly, employers who offer group health insurance to currently working employees are not required to offer retiree health insurance to retired workers. An employer may choose to offer retiree health insurance to some classes of retirees and not others.

Unlike Medicare, which specifies some benefits and services to be covered, an EGHP generally is not required to provide a specific level of services or coverage. Congress originally intended ERISA to protect pension benefits.[9] Only ERISA's fiduciary duty provisions, the disclosure provisions, and the cause-of-action provisions were made applicable to health plans.[10] This has left employers free, with some exceptions, to decide what benefits to offer, to change health insurance, to reduce the level of benefits, and even to eliminate coverage entirely without any protection for employees or retirees.[11] Most pertinent to Medicare beneficiaries, the addition of a Medicare prescription drug benefit has caused some employers and unions to reconsider the prescription drug coverage they provide through their retiree health plans. Because the drug coverage they offer is not separate from other retiree health benefits, many employers and unions informed their retirees that enrollment in a Medicare Part D drug plan would result in the loss of all of their retiree health coverage. As a result some individuals with retiree health coverage who are dually eligible for Medicare and Medicaid, and who were automatically enrolled in a Part D plan, lost all of their retiree health coverage for themselves and their dependents. The loss of such coverage was particularly problematic for spouses and other dependents who lacked any other health insurance.[12]

Some states require that health plans offered in their state cover certain benefits. However, ERISA preempts such state law requirements for self-insured plans, i.e., plans that set aside their own funds and assume the risk of meeting the health claims of employees and dependents.[13] As a result, even if state law

---

[8] Hawaii is the only state permitted to require employers to offer health insurance. General Accounting Office, *Employment-Based Health Insurance: Medium and Large Employers Can Purchase Coverage, But Some Workers Are Not Eligible*, GAO/HEHS-98-184 (July 1998).

[9] 29 U.S.C. §1001(c).

[10] 29 U.S.C. §§1003, 1051, 1081, 1101.

[11] *See, e.g.,* Sprague v. General Motors Corp., 133 F.3d 388 (6th Cir. 1998); McGann v. H H Music, 946 F.2d 401 (5th Cir. 1991).

[12] *See* discussion in **Chapter 11** Medicare Part D.

[13] 29 U.S.C. §1144.

mandates that certain services such as mental health benefits be included in the benefit package, a self-insured health plan subject to ERISA does not have to offer the mandated benefit.

[C] Definitions of MSP Employer Group Health Plans

[1] Health Plans That Are Affected by MSP Rules[14]

An EGHP, regardless of whether it is subject to ERISA, is included within the scope of the basic MSP program when the sponsoring employer employs 20 or more full- or part-time employees, one of whom is age 65 or older, or is married to a spouse who is age 65 or older.[15] In addition, a large group health plan with 100 or more full- or part-time employees is subject to the MSP statute when an employee is disabled or has a family member who is disabled.[16] EGHPs, regardless of size, are primary under MSP rules for Medicare beneficiaries with end-stage renal disease only for 30 months.[17]

[2] Health Insurance That Is Not Affected by MSP Rules

Certain kinds of health insurance are not made primary to Medicare under the MSP statute and regulations. These unaffected types of insurance include retiree health insurance benefits and insurance that is purchased voluntarily by a former employee or spouse. Insurance purchased under COBRA by a beneficiary eligible for Medicare when he initially purchased the private policy would not be affected. Private health insurance unrelated to employment, including Medicare supplemental health insurance (MediGap) that is privately purchased, is also not affected by the EGHP law.

Persons insured under health insurance that is not subject to MSP requirements are entitled to receive Medicare benefits as their primary source of health insurance, and their private health insurer can be secondary to Medicare.

§9.03 CALCULATION OF MEDICARE SECONDARY PAYMENT AMOUNT IN EGHP CASES

The Medicare statute and regulations set out a complex set of formulas for determining how much Medicare will pay when it is secondary to an EGHP.[18]

---

[14] CMS established a Web site to provide information about coordination of benefits with Medicare at <http://www.cms.hhs.gov/COBGeneralInformation>.

[15] 42 U.S.C. §1395y(b)(1)(A).

[16] 42 U.S.C. §1395y(b)(1)(B).

[17] 42 U.S.C. §1395y(b)(1)(C).

[18] 42 U.S.C. §1395y(b)(4); 42 C.F.R. §411.33.

Under these rules, Medicare will pay when the provider's charge for the service is not fully paid by the primary plan. The amount that Medicare will pay is the lowest of the following amounts, calculated without reduction by the usual coinsurance or deductibles:

1. The Medicare payment amount if there were no EGHP;

2. For payments calculated by Medicare on a cost-related basis (mostly Part A), the Medicare payment amount minus the EGHP payment;

3. For payments calculated by Medicare on a basis other than cost (mostly reasonable charge basis payments under Part B), the higher of the EGHP allowed amount or the Medicare allowed amount, minus the payment actually paid by the EGHP.

When the EGHP is a managed care organization (MCO), Medicare will not pay for services for which the MCO denied coverage, unless the beneficiary was unaware that Medicare would not pay.[19] This has caused problems for beneficiaries who have gone out of plan for services or counted on Medicare's less restrictive application of coverage rules to fill gaps in services available from the employer's managed care plan.

§9.04   ENFORCEMENT OF EGHP CLAIMS

[A]   EGHP Enforcement and Recovery Powers

When Medicare believes that an EGHP is liable as primary insurer for a Medicare beneficiary, it will refuse to make payment. If the EGHP refuses to pay for health services, Medicare has the statutory authority to seek double damages from the plan.[20]

CMS also has the authority to seek a recovery of payments for health services it made by mistake ("overpayments") when an EGHP should have been primary payer. It can recover overpayments from the EGHP, or from a beneficiary in situations where the beneficiary is deemed not to be cooperating with HCFA in a recovery action.

[B]   Individual Enforcement of EGHP Claims

An individual who believes that the EGHP is responsible for a health claim may file an appeal through the EGHP's appeals process. When a worker or beneficiary first becomes covered under a health plan, and periodically thereafter,

---

[19] Medicare Secondary Payer Manual, CMS Pub. 100-5, Ch. 5, §§40.1.2, 40.1.2.1.

[20] 42 U.S.C. §1395y(b)(2)(B)(iii).

he or she is given a "summary plan description" (SPD), or plan brochure.[21] The SPD describes in plain terms the coverage under the plan, how to apply for benefits, and how to file an appeal if a claim is denied.[22] Individuals should consult their SPD to determine the proper procedure for filing an appeal.

An EGHP that is subject to ERISA must comply with the claims procedure established under that statute and implementing regulations issued by the Department of Labor.[23] The worker or beneficiary must complete any internal administrative appeal rights he or she has under the plan before going to court.[24] The worker or beneficiary may not need to exhaust or complete the health plan's appeal process if serious procedural violations are shown or where exhaustion would be futile.[25]

When health care has been denied, the individual or his or her advocate should request a review of the adverse decision pursuant to the claims procedures described in the SPD. Department of Labor regulations require that decisions on review be within a "reasonable amount of time," which they define as no more than 60 days.[26] Plans may extend the time period for response to 120 days after receipt of the request for review if there are special circumstances, such as the need to hold a hearing or wait for a meeting of the board of trustees.[27] Expedited consideration is available for claims involving urgent care.[28]

If the plan denies the appeal, the individual may file a court action. Civil actions that may be brought under ERISA include suits to recover benefits due under the plan, to enforce rights under the plan, or to clarify rights to future benefits. Affected individuals may also seek to enjoin violations of ERISA as well as to obtain any other equitable relief to redress violations or to enforce provisions of the statute.[29]

§9.05 COORDINATION OF COBRA RIGHTS AND MEDICARE

Medicare beneficiaries who want to exercise their option to purchase health care under the COBRA continuation of care provisions[30] need to understand how COBRA coordinates with Medicare.

---

[21] 29 U.S.C. §§1021, 1024(b).

[22] 29 U.S.C. §1022.

[23] 29 U.S.C. §§1132, 1133; 29 C.F.R. §2560.503-1.

[24] 29 U.S.C. §1132.

[25] *See, e.g.,* Curry v. Contract Fabricants Profit Sharing Plan, 891 F.2d 842 (11th Cir. 1990).

[26] 29 C.F.R. §2560.503-1(i)(1)(i).

[27] *Id.*

[28] 29 C.F.R. §2560.503-1(i)(2)(i), (m)(1).

[29] 29 U.S.C. §1132(a)(2), (3).

[30] Consolidated Omnibus Budget Reconciliation Act of 1985 (COBRA), Pub. L. No. 99-272, 100 Stat. 222 (Apr. 7, 1986), codified at 26 U.S.C. §4980(b), 29 U.S.C. §§1161 *et seq.*, 42 U.S.C. §§300bb-1 *et seq.*

[A] What Is COBRA?

Private employers who offer an EGHP and who normally employed 20 or more workers on a typical business day during the preceding calendar year must offer COBRA to employees and their dependents who lose their health insurance because of certain specified events, discussed below.[31] State and local governments employing more than 20 employees also must offer COBRA continuation coverage.[32]

[B] Eligibility and Coverage

An individual eligible to purchase COBRA is referred to as a "qualified beneficiary."[33] In order to be a qualified beneficiary, the individual must have been covered under a group health plan on the day before a "qualifying event."[34] Qualified beneficiaries include:

• Covered employees;

• Spouses;

• Dependent children; and

• Retirees, their dependents, or their surviving spouses if the retiree's former employer files a petition for bankruptcy.[35]

Covered employees, or workers, are only eligible for COBRA based on termination of their employment or reduction in their hours.[36]

Eligibility to elect COBRA continuation coverage arises upon the occurrence of one of six "qualifying events" that result in the loss of health coverage:

1. The death of the covered employee;

2. The termination, other than for gross misconduct, or reduction in hours of the covered employee's employment;

3. The divorce or legal separation of the covered employee from the employee's spouse;

4. The covered employee's entitlement to Medicare;

---

[31] 29 U.S.C. §1161(b).

[32] 42 U.S.C. §300bb-1(a), (b)(1). Federal employees have their own health care continuation coverage. 5 U.S.C. §8905a.

[33] 29 U.S.C. §1161(a). The COBRA premium may not exceed 102 percent of the applicable premium for the continuation period. 29 U.S.C. §1162(3).

[34] 29 U.S.C. §1167(3). *See infra*, discussion of qualifying events.

[35] 29 U.S.C. §1167(2), (3).

[36] 29 U.S.C. §1163(2), 1167(2).

5. A dependent child's losing dependent status;

6. The filing for bankruptcy by a retiree's former employer.[37]

Covered employees and their dependents must be given notice of their COBRA rights when first eligible to participate under the plan.[38] Often the notice is included in the SPD that describes plan benefits and plan rights. They receive a second notice of COBRA rights generally within 45 days after they experience a qualifying event.[39] The qualified beneficiaries then have 60 days in which to elect COBRA coverage.[40]

The coverage offered to qualified beneficiaries must be identical to the coverage provided to employees in the same kind of job who have not experienced a qualifying event.[41] Thus, an employer cannot offer Medicare wrap-around coverage as a COBRA benefit when similarly situated active employees are entitled to full health insurance coverage. If, however, coverage is expanded or reduced for current workers, it must be modified in the same manner for qualified beneficiaries.[42]

A plan may not condition COBRA coverage upon or discriminate because of lack of evidence of insurability.[43] Thus, a plan may not deny COBRA coverage or limit the scope of coverage available to qualified beneficiaries because of their health status or medical conditions.

COBRA coverage lasts 18 or 36 months, depending on the qualifying event.[44] For events that have an 18-month period, coverage may be extended beyond that period, for a total of 36 months, if the qualified beneficiary experiences another qualifying event during that time frame.[45]

However, an Internal Revenue Service Ruling clarifies that where the second qualifying event is the covered employee's becoming entitled to Medicare, and where Medicare entitlement would not result in a loss of coverage, the qualified beneficiary is not entitled to an extension of COBRA coverage.[46]

COBRA coverage will end early if:

1. The employer stops offering group health coverage;

2. The qualified beneficiary fails to pay premiums;

---

[37] 29 U.S.C. §1163.

[38] 29 U.S.C. §1166(a), 26 C.F.R. §2590.606-1, §2590.606-4, and appendices.

[39] *Id.*

[40] 29 U.S.C. §1166(a)(2), (4)(b).

[41] 29 U.S.C. §1162(1).

[42] *Id.*

[43] 29 U.S.C. §1162(4).

[44] 29 U.S.C. §1162(2)(A). Coverage for retirees whose employer filed for bankruptcy extends for the lifetime of the retiree.

[45] 29 U.S.C. §1162(2)(A)(ii).

[46] IRS Rev. Rul. 2004-22, Internal Revenue Bulletin 2004-10 (Mar. 8, 2004).

3. The qualified beneficiary becomes entitled to Medicare;

4. The qualified beneficiary becomes covered under another group health plan that contains no limitation for preexisting conditions.[47]

[C] Coordination of COBRA and Medicare

As explained earlier, Medicare is the primary payer for a Medicare beneficiary who is also covered under COBRA health care continuation insurance. The more confusing relationship involves the role Medicare entitlement plays in determining whether an individual may elect COBRA and the duration of COBRA coverage.

[1] What Is "Medicare Entitlement"?

Both the statutory sections on COBRA qualifying events and COBRA maximum coverage periods use the term "Medicare entitlement" rather than Medicare eligibility.[48] COBRA regulations clarify that being eligible to enroll in Medicare does not constitute being entitled to Medicare for purposes of electing COBRA.[49] A qualified beneficiary becomes entitled to Medicare upon the effective date of enrollment in either Part A or Part B, whichever occurs first.[50] Thus, an individual who continues working at age 65 and does not elect to receive social security benefits and Medicare at that time is not entitled to Medicare for purposes of COBRA eligibility.

[2] Coverage Period If the Qualifying Event Is
Medicare Entitlement

The maximum coverage period for a qualified beneficiary who loses health insurance as a result of a covered employee's becoming entitled to Medicare is 36 months.[51] The 36-month period begins to run at the time of Medicare entitlement, even if the qualified beneficiary does not lose health coverage until he or she experiences a subsequent qualifying event that occurs less than 18 months after the Medicare entitlement.[52] As a result of this complicated provision, the qualified beneficiary often will not be covered for the full 36-month period.

---

[47] 29 U.S.C. §1162(2)(B), (C), (D).

[48] 29 U.S.C. §§1162(2)(A), §1163.

[49] 26 C.F.R. §§54.4980B-7, Q & A-3.

[50] Id.

[51] 29 U.S.C. §1162(2)(A)(iv).

[52] 29 U.S.C. §1162(2)(A)(v).

Consider the following examples involving Medicare entitlement as a qualifying event:

Example 1: An employee becomes entitled to Medicare on May 1, 2006, causing his dependents to lose health insurance as of that date. In this situation the dependents are entitled to 36 months of COBRA, starting on May 1, 2006.

Example 2: Again, the employee becomes entitled to Medicare on May 1, but the dependents do not lose their health coverage until the employee retires on October 1, 2006. They are technically entitled to 36 months of COBRA starting on May 1, 2006, the date of Medicare entitlement. Because of the way the coverage period is calculated, and because they do not lose insurance until October 1, they only have COBRA coverage for the 31-month period starting in October.

Example 3: If the dependents do not lose health insurance until the employee retires on May 1, 2008, they are not entitled to the coverage period for a qualifying event based on Medicare entitlement. The subsequent qualifying event that caused the loss of health coverage occurred more than 18 months after the employee became entitled to Medicare. The dependents are entitled to the coverage period for a qualifying event of termination of employment, which is 18 months from the date of retirement, May 1, 2008.[53]

[3] Extended COBRA Coverage Until Medicare Entitlement

To avoid a gap in health coverage before Medicare entitlement begins,[54] workers or their dependents determined to be disabled under Title II or Title XVI of the Social Security Act may receive 29 months of extended COBRA coverage if certain conditions are met.[55] The disability onset date, i.e., the date the individual is found disabled, must occur sometime during the first 60 days of continuation coverage.[56] The individual must also notify the health plan administrator within 60 days of the determination. Individuals who do not meet these requirements, e.g., their disability onset date is later than the first 60 days of COBRA, or they fail to notify the plan administrator in a timely manner, are not eligible for extended coverage. Health plans may increase the COBRA premium for the 19th through the 29th month of extended coverage,[57] making it difficult for some individuals to continue purchasing coverage.

---

[53] 29 U.S.C. §1162(2)(A)(i).

[54] Individuals under age 65 become entitled to Medicare if they have been entitled to Social Security disability benefits for 25 months. 42 C.F.R. §406.12.

[55] 29 U.S.C. §1162(2)(A). *See also* Meadows v. Cagle's, 954 F.2d 686 (11th Cir. 1992).

[56] 29 U.S.C. §1162(2)(A).

[57] 29 U.S.C. §1162(3)(B).

[4]   COBRA Eligibility for Beneficiaries Already on Medicare

Individuals who were already receiving Medicare or who were covered under a second group health plan at the time of their qualifying event are eligible to elect COBRA.[58] If the health plan requires participants to enroll in all other health benefits for which they are eligible, the plan may require them to enroll in Medicare Part B.

[5]   COBRA and Special Enrollment Periods

COBRA qualified beneficiaries who have delayed enrollment in Medicare Part B do not qualify for a special enrollment period (SEP) to enroll in Part B after their COBRA coverage ends.[59] Only individuals who delayed enrolling in Part B because they were covered under an EGHP by reason of current employment may take advantage of the SEP rules.[60] Individuals on COBRA do not meet the definition of having current employment status.[61] Thus, they have to wait to enroll in Part B until the general enrollment period, and they have to pay the applicable premium for delayed enrollment.

Some COBRA qualified beneficiaries may have delayed enrollment in a Part D drug plan because the drug coverage they had under COBRA constitutes creditable coverage, i.e., was determined to be as good as Medicare drug coverage. Because these individuals will lose their creditable drug coverage when their COBRA coverage ends, they may have a special enrollment period (SEP) that would allow them to choose and enroll in a Part D plan before the next annual coordinated enrollment period. The SEP begins with the month they are advised of the loss of creditable drug coverage and ends 60 days from the loss of coverage or from the date of the notice, whichever is later.[62]

§9.06   MSP RULES APPLICABLE TO MEDICARE ADVANTAGE PLANS

Medicare Advantage (MA) plans (formerly Medicare+Choice (M+C) Organizations) are also subject to MSP rules.[63] The statute and regulations require MA Plans to identify other payers that should be primary and coordinate benefits to Medicare enrollees with them.[64]

---

[58] Geissal v. Moore Med., 118 S. Ct. 186 (1998); 26 C.F.R. §54.4980B-7 Q 3(a).

[59] 42 C.F.R. §§407.20, 406.24(a)(3).

[60] 42 C.F.R. §407.20(b), (c).

[61] 42 C.F.R. §411.104.

[62] PDP Eligibility, Enrollment, and Disenrollment Guidance §20.3.5 <http://www.cms.hhs.gov/PrescriptionDrugCovContra/Downloads/CurrentPDPEnrollmentGuidance.pdf>.

[63] 42 U.S.C. §1395w-22(a)(4).

[64] 42 C.F.R. §422.108.

The MA Plan is authorized to charge or allow its providers to charge any other insurer that should be primary—liability insurers, workers' compensation insurers, and EGHPs—for Medicare-covered services. The MA and its providers are also authorized to collect for services rendered by them from either the primary insurer or from the beneficiary, if he or she has received payment from the primary insurer.[65] However, one court held that there is no cause of action for an MA Plan to bring suit in federal court to recover the cost of care it provided to a beneficiary.[66]

Surprisingly, the statute and regulation do not limit the MSP amount that the MAs and their providers can charge or recover to the rates that they receive under the Medicare program. Beneficiary advocates should keep in mind that they have the opportunity to appeal and/or request waiver of MSP recovery claims. Beneficiaries must be informed of this right at the time repayment is requested; however, MA collection notices may not advise them of this right. They should be prepared to cite the criteria for waiver and the appeal rights set out in the Medicare Secondary Payer Manual.[67]

§9.07 CONDITIONAL PAYMENT AND THIRD-PARTY RECOVERY

If an injured Medicare beneficiary's medical expenses are covered by liability insurance, including no-fault and med-pay, Medicare will pay for medical services only when the third-party insurance payment will not be "prompt." Such Medicare payments are described as "conditional" and the program expects to recover them when the private insurance payment "has been or could be made."[68] When there has been a conditional Medicare payment, the hospital must accept payment at the Medicare rate and cannot seek additional payment from the liability insurance recovery.[69]

The Medicare program through the Centers for Medicare and Medicaid Services (CMS) is given specific collection powers with respect to its conditional payment recovery claims by statute. CMS has both subrogation rights and the right to bring an independent action to recover its conditional payments. It is authorized to bring such actions against "any or all entities that are or were required or responsible (directly, as an insurer or self-insurer, as a third-party administrator . . . or otherwise) to make payment with respect to the same item or

---

[65] Id.

[66] Care Choices HMO v. Engstrom, 330 F.3d 786 (6th Cir. 2003).

[67] Medicare Secondary Payer Manual, CMS Pub. 100-5, Ch. 7, §§50.5.4.4–50.6.5.4.

[68] 42 U.S.C. §1395y(b)(2)(A)(ii), (b)(2)(B); 42 C.F.R. §411.20, 411.50(c).

[69] Rybicki v. Hartley, 792 F.2d 260 (1st Cir. 1986); Holle v. Moline Pub. Hosp., 598 F. Supp. 1017 (C.D. Ill. 1984). However, a provider can choose not to bill Medicare but to instead bill a liability insurer or assert a lien on the beneficiary's insurance settlement. Medicare Program: Third Party Liability Insurance Regulations, 68 Fed. Reg. 43940 (2003), modifying 42 C.F.R. §§411.54 and 489.20.

service . . . under a primary plan" and to collect double damages against that [primary plan] entity.[70] It is further authorized to bring actions against "any other entity [including any physician or provider] that has received payment from that [primary plan] entity."[71]

Several court decisions restricted MSP recovery by interpreting the statute to prevent Medicare from recovering conditional payments from settlement funds established in class action litigation.[72] Congress responded in 2003 by amending the Medicare statute to expand the definitions of self-insured entities and responsible primary plans from which MSP recovery could be required.[73]

[A]   Amount of Medicare Recovery

In general, "CMS may recover an amount equal to the Medicare payment or the amount payable by the third party, whichever is less."[74] The amount of the Medicare recovery stops accruing as of the time of settlement. There is no MSP recovery for services covered by Medicare after that time unless the settlement included a specific allocation for future medical services.[75] In cases involving liability insurers, "Medicare reduces its recovery to take account of the cost of procuring the judgment or settlement. . . ."[76] Under this provision, a proportionate share of attorney's fees and costs should be subtracted from the amount recovered by Medicare. If the primary insurer's payment is less than the MSP claim, Medicare will take it all, minus the costs of procurement.

> **Example:** Following her auto accident, for which liability was disputed, Vicki Victim received a settlement of $50,000. Her medical expenses were $40,000, of which Medicare paid $25,000; her pain and suffering were valued at $10,000; lost wages were $20,000; and her permanent loss of limb was valued at $30,000.

Despite the fact that Vicki's settlement was only 50 percent of her $100,000 damages, Medicare would demand recovery of its entire $25,000 outlay, reduced only by its proportionate share of the procurement costs. Assuming a 30 percent

---

[70] 42 U.S.C. §1395y(b)(2)(B)(ii).

[71] 42 U.S.C. §1395y(b)(2)(B), (3).

[72] Thompson v. Goetzman, 334 F.3d 489 (5th Cir. 2003); Mason v. American Tobacco Co., 2003 WL 22255601 (2d Cir. 2003); United States v. Phillip Morris, 116 F. Supp. 2d 131, 145 (D.D.C. 2000).

[73] 42 U.S.C. §1395y(b)(2)(A) and (B), Medicare Prescription Drug, Improvement, and Modernization Act of 2003, Section 301(b)(1) and (2). These changes are retroactive to 1980.

[74] 42 C.F.R. §411.24(c).

[75] Letter of July 3, 2002, from Thomas Bosserman, CMS Region IX Health Insurance Specialist, to Sally Hart.

[76] 42 C.F.R. §411.37.

contingency fee arrangement, Medicare would actually take $17,500, Victim's personal injury attorney would receive a fee of $15,000, and Vicki would receive only $17,500, leaving $82,500 in uncompensated losses.

This basic formula is limited to Medicare outlays for health services resulting from the accident or other incident that gave rise to liability. Thus, Medicare should not recover for health services to the extent that they were aggravated by, for example, a preexisting heart condition. Advocates should examine the list of conditional payments presented by Medicare and object to the inclusion of any that were not caused entirely by the incident that triggered third-party insurer liability.[77]

[B] MSP Collection Duties of Personal Injury Attorneys

CMS asserts that personal injury attorneys have statutory obligations to affirmatively assist Medicare in its MSP recovery efforts,[78] but beneficiary advocates dispute this assertion. Advocates believe the CMS position is based on a misreading of the Medicare statute that (1) incorrectly gives MSP recovery claims the status of liens, and (2) inaccurately extends certain punitive powers over insurance companies to the attorneys for beneficiaries.

In *Zinman v. Shalala,* a nationwide class action, a federal district court held that Medicare has no lien rights with respect to its MSP recovery claims, and ordered Medicare to stop using the term "lien" in its collection efforts.[79] Several consequences flow from the fact that the MSP recovery claim does not have lien status.

First, an attorney does not owe Medicare the duty to protect its recovery claim against his or her client. The Medicare regulations do impose (1) on the beneficiary, a duty of cooperation[80] and (2) on the other insurance company, a duty to notify Medicare.[81] In 1998 CMS proposed regulations that would require the beneficiary *or the beneficiary's representative* to give Medicare notice of an insurance claim within 60 days and notice of settlement within 30 days, but these proposed regulations have never been finalized.[82] Consequently, the regulations

---

[77] One court held that a beneficiary could dispute whether the health services for which MSP recovery is sought actually resulted from the accident producing the award even if the original liability claim alleged that they had. United States v. Weinberg, No. 01-CV-0679, Medicare & Medicaid Guide (CCH) 301,136, 2002 U.S. Dist. LEXIS 12289 (E.D. Pa. 2002).

[78] *Compare* Thomas J. Nyzio, *Medicare Recovery in Liability Cases*, S.C. Law. 20-24 (May/June 1996); Glenn E. Bradford & Melinda M. Ward, *The Medicare "Super Lien" Revisited*, J. Mo. B. 44-49 (Jan./Feb. 2000).

[79] 835 F. Supp. 1163, 1171 (N.D. Cal. 1993), *aff'd*, 67 F.3d 841 (9th Cir. 1995).

[80] 42 C.F.R. §411.23.

[81] 42 C.F.R. §411.24(a).

[82] 63 Fed. Reg. 14,506 (Mar. 25, 1998).

currently require only that the beneficiary reimburse Medicare within 60 days of receipt of third-party payment.[83]

Second, if the client chooses to receive his or her portion of the insurance proceeds from his or her attorney and deal with Medicare directly, the MSP statute and regulations impose no penalty on the attorney. Under ethical rules of practice, the attorney should advise the client of the MSP recovery program, but the client should then be allowed to decide whether he or she wants the attorney to pay Medicare directly or disburse the proceeds so that the client can handle the MSP claim him- or herself. The client should be advised of the possibility of collection action or termination of future benefits if the MSP recovery claim is not paid. The client should also be advised of the possibility of qualifying for a waiver of MSP recovery pursuant to the provisions described above if he or she received the proceeds from the attorney and used them for necessary items.

The Medicare statute does give CMS a right of action to recover from an attorney who has liability proceeds in his or her possession. In contrast, it gives CMS a broader right of action to recover from an insurance company (a "primary payer") that has transferred proceeds, e.g., to its insured, without paying Medicare.[84] The key to understanding this statutory language is the cross-reference to §1395y(b)(3)(A), which imposes double damages only on primary plans, together with the broad definition of entities responsible under a "primary plan" in the preceding section.[85] Carefully read, the statute clearly distinguishes between actions against insurers, which can be for double damages, and actions against other entities, such as attorneys who have received a payment from the insurer, which can only be for the payment itself.[86]

The language of the regulations makes the same distinction between Medicare's double collection rights against third-party payers and its rights against others such as attorneys.[87] Like the statute, the regulations define "third-party payer" as "an insurance policy, plan, or program that is primary to Medicare."[88] Thus, they provide no authority for Medicare to recover double damages from attorneys who have received liability insurance proceeds but then passed them on to their clients.

---

[83] 42 C.F.R. §411.24(h).

[84] 42 U.S.C. §1395y(b)(2)(B)(iii); Manning v. Utilities Mut. Ins. & Niagara Mohawk Dist. Power Co., 254 F.3d 387 (2d Cir. 2001).

[85] 42 U.S.C. §1395y(b)(2)(A) and (b)(2)(B)(iii).

[86] *See also* Health Ins. Ass'n of Am. & Blue Cross & Blue Shield Ass'n of Am. v. Shalala, 23 F.3d 412 (D.C. Cir. 1994). In that case the D.C. Circuit struck down several MSP regulations as going too far in imposing collection liability on insurance companies, including one extending MSP recovery provisions against insurance companies to such companies when they act as administrators for self-insured employer plans, and another authorizing recovery against insurance companies even when policy filing deadlines had passed.

[87] *Compare* closely the provisions of 42 C.F.R. §411.24(g), which confers collection rights against attorneys, *with* 42 C.F.R. §411.24(i), which confers broader collection rights against third-party payers.

[88] 42 C.F.R. §411.21. For MSP enforcement, use the analogous state statute of limitations.

§9.08 MSP WORKERS' COMPENSATION RECOVERY

The Medicare Secondary Payer program also makes workers' compensation programs primary payers of medical expenses for persons receiving workers' compensation benefits.[89]

Sometimes workers' compensation claims are settled by agreement for a lump sum payout rather than continuing payments for the lifetime of the disabled worker. In such cases, unlike its policy with respect to liability insurance settlements, Medicare will recognize an apportionment set out in the settlement agreement of the lump sum between future medical expenses and other damages (lost wages), so long as the amount allocated to future medical expenses appears to be reasonable and not an attempt to shift the burden of payment for work-related medical services to Medicare.[90]

Medicare will pay for all the beneficiary's covered health care after the portion of the settlement allocated to medical expenses for work-related conditions has been spent for such services. Beneficiaries should keep records of their expenditures for medical services from this portion of the settlement so they can establish when it has been exhausted and Medicare should become primary payer. This record keeping could be done under a "set-aside arrangement" established to administer the medical expense portion of the settlement in cases where the settlement is a commutation of future benefits rather than a compromise, but there is no requirement for doing so.[91]

§9.09 MEDICARE SECONDARY PAYER COLLECTION PROCEDURES

The Medicare Secondary Payer Manual (MSP) is an online program guide for the administration of the Medicare secondary payer law posted on the CMS Web site. It is used by providers, insurers, and advocates in working through the day-to-day administration of the Medicare program. The manual includes a form letter for use by entities under contract with CMS in making initial MSP recovery demands to beneficiaries.[92] Typically, although not always, Medicare initiates collection procedures when a beneficiary's personal injury attorney notifies it that a settlement is expected. Medicare also may learn about the existence of third-party liability claims through questionnaires to beneficiaries, intermediary[93] and carrier[94] screening of claims for injury-related services, and information-sharing with the Internal Revenue Service.

---

[89] 42 U.S.C. §1395y(b)(2)(B); MSP Manual, Ch. 7, §40.3.

[90] MSP Manual, Ch. 7, §§40.3.4 through 40.3.5.

[91] Procedures for obtaining CMS approval of a set-aside arrangement from the Regional Office are described in the MSP Manual, at Ch. 7, §§40.3.5 through 40.3.5.1.

[92] MSP Manual, Ch. 7, §50.5.1.1, Exhibit 2.

[93] An intermediary is an entity under contract for the administration of Part A claims.

[94] A carrier is an entity under contract for the administration of Part B claims.

The CMS collection letter advises beneficiaries of the amount claimed as an overpayment by Medicare, sets out the repayment process, and describes the beneficiary waiver and appeal procedures.[95] It encourages beneficiaries to pay Medicare immediately by asserting a right to interest accruing on unpaid claims even during the pendency of unsuccessful beneficiary requests for waiver and/or appeals. The collection letter further states that Medicare may arrange for the amount of an overdue MSP claim to be deducted from the beneficiary's Social Security check. Advocates have criticized this letter as unduly threatening and an exaggeration of Medicare's actual MSP recovery practices.

§9.10   BENEFICIARY RIGHTS TO SEEK WAIVER OR APPEAL THE MSP RECOVERY CLAIM

Under the Medicare statute, beneficiaries have the right to appeal the amount of MSP recovery claims if they believe the amount of a claim is not correct.[96] They also have the right to ask Medicare to waive or compromise recovery under several different provisions of the law.[97]

[A]   Appeals of MSP Recovery Claims

If it appears that Medicare is demanding more of a beneficiary's award than it is entitled to under these rules, there is an administrative appeals process that can be pursued.[98] This is the usual Medicare Part A appeals process, consisting of a paper reconsideration by the intermediary, followed by a hearing before an Office of Medicare Hearings and Appeals administrative law judge if the amount in controversy is $110 (2006 amount) or more, paper review by the Departmental Appeals Board, and finally judicial review in federal district court if the amount in controversy is $1,090 (2006 amount) or more. The jurisdictional amounts may increase yearly.

[B]   Compromise of MSP Recovery Claims

The second opportunity for a beneficiary to reduce the amount Medicare takes is to request waiver or compromise of the MSP recovery claim.[99]

---

[95] The data compilation function of the MSP recording program is performed by a coordination of benefits (COB) contractor.

[96] 42 U.S.C. §1395ff.

[97] 42 U.S.C. §1395y(b)(2)(B)(v) (waiver provisions in the MSP statute), 1395gg(c) (general provisions for waiver of Medicare overpayments); 31 U.S.C. §3711 (Federal Claims Collection Act).

[98] 42 U.S.C. §1395ff; 42 C.F.R. §§404.900 *et seq.*

[99] 42 U.S.C. §1395y(b)(2)(B)(iv).

The Medicare statute and regulations set out three grounds for waiver or compromise:[100]

1. When the probability of recovery or the amount involved does not warrant pursuit of the claim;[101]

2. When waiver is in the best interests of the Medicare program;[102]

3. When the beneficiary is without fault (presumed for MSP waivers) and recovery would either defeat the purpose of the Social Security and Medicare programs or would be against equity and good conscience.[103]

The CMS staff in the regional offices handle all requests for waiver pursuant to the first two grounds.[104] An attorney who wishes to obtain a reduction of MSP recovery as part of an overall settlement package prior to resolution of personal injury claims or litigation should contact his or her CMS Regional Office. It can be very useful to bring CMS into negotiations before a judicial settlement officer who urges all parties, including Medicare, to accept compromise in the interests of justice.

[C] Waiver of MSP Recovery Claims

The third ground for waiver is handled by the Medicare contractors, and it is the one commonly used to produce a reduction in MSP recovery claims after a beneficiary has received a personal injury award that is inadequate to compensate him or her fully or where recovery will otherwise cause the beneficiary to suffer financial hardship.

The MSP Manual sets out factors to be considered in granting waiver:

• Out-of-pocket expenses incurred by the beneficiary;

• The age of the beneficiary;

• The beneficiary's assets, monthly income, and expenses; and

• Any physical or mental impairments the beneficiary may have.[105]

The MSP Manual broadly defines out-of-pocket medical expenses not covered by Medicare to include such health-related costs as housing renovation to accommodate a disabled beneficiary, adult diapers, and coinsurance payments.[106]

---

[100] 42 C.F.R. §411.28.

[101] Federal Claims Collection Act, 31 U.S.C. §3711.

[102] *See* MSP section of the Medicare statute, 42 U.S.C. §1395y(b)(2)(B)(iv).

[103] *See* overpayment recovery provision of the Medicare statute, 42 U.S.C. §1395gg(c).

[104] MSP Manual, Ch. 7, §50.4.2.

[105] MSP Manual, Ch. 7, §§50.6.2 *et seq.*

[106] MSP Manual, Ch. 7, §50.6.2.1.B.

However, the MIM states that out-of-pocket expenses are not automatically allowed and may be denied where the beneficiary can afford to pay them from other funds.

In order to obtain a waiver the beneficiary must supply a list of specific expenses, even when the expenses are for future medical services or other needs. Documentation in the form of sworn statements, actual bills, or canceled checks is required for out-of-pocket medical expenses. Unfortunately, Medicare often denies waiver without comment in cases where it could be justified under the MIM provisions if a particular kind of evidence were supplied. The advocate should ask Medicare MSP collection staff what specific evidence they require to justify granting waiver.

The "defeat the purposes of the Social Security or Medicare laws" criterion under 1395gg(c) is met when a beneficiary does not have an income or resources sufficient to meet his or her ordinary and necessary expenses.[107] Such expenses include food, shelter, utilities, insurance, medical, and other health expenses not covered by other insurance, as well as support payments and other expenses necessary to maintain the beneficiary's standard of living. Examples of financial hardship include a case where the beneficiary has already spent the insurance proceeds and would have inadequate living expenses if the beneficiary repaid Medicare; a case where the beneficiary is living at the poverty level (although preexisting poverty is not in itself enough to justify waiver); and a case where some unforeseen financial circumstance occurs, such as grandchildren becoming the financial responsibility of the beneficiary.[108]

The second §1395gg(c) waiver ground, "against equity and good conscience," looks to the following factors:

- The degree to which the beneficiary did not contribute to causing the overpayment;

- The degree to which Medicare did contribute to causing the overpayment;

- The degree to which repayment would cause undue hardship to the beneficiary; and

- Whether the beneficiary would be unjustly enriched by waiver, or was harmed by relying on erroneous Medicare information.[109]

---

[107] MSP Manual, Ch.7, §§50.6.5, *et seq.*

[108] *Id.*

[109] MSP Manual, Ch.7, §550.6.5.1.

APPENDIX 9-1

29 C.F.R. §2560.503-1

Sec. 2560.503-1 Claims procedure.

(a) Scope and purpose. In accordance with the authority of sections 503 and 505 of the Employee Retirement Income Security Act of 1974 (ERISA or the Act), 29 U.S.C. 1133, 1135, this section sets forth minimum requirements for employee benefit plan procedures pertaining to claims for benefits by participants and beneficiaries (hereinafter referred to as claimants). Except as otherwise specifically provided in this section, these requirements apply to every employee benefit plan described in section 4(a) and not exempted under section 4(b) of the Act.

(b) Obligation to establish and maintain reasonable claims procedures. Every employee benefit plan shall establish and maintain reasonable procedures governing the filing of benefit claims, notification of benefit determinations, and appeal of adverse benefit determinations (hereinafter collectively referred to as claims procedures). The claims procedures for a plan will be deemed to be reasonable only if—

(1) The claims procedures comply with the requirements of paragraphs (c), (d), (e), (f), (g), (h), (i), and (j) of this section, as appropriate, except to the extent that the claims procedures are deemed to comply with some or all of such provisions pursuant to paragraph (b)(6) of this section;

(2) A description of all claims procedures (including, in the case of a group health plan within the meaning of paragraph (m)(6) of this section, any procedures for obtaining prior approval as a prerequisite for obtaining a benefit, such as preauthorization procedures or utilization review procedures) and the applicable time frames is included as part of a summary plan description meeting the requirements of 29 C.F.R 2520.102-3;

(3) The claims procedures do not contain any provision, and are not administered in a way, that unduly inhibits or hampers the initiation or processing of claims for benefits. For example, a provision or practice that requires payment of a fee or costs as a condition to making a claim or to appealing an adverse benefit determination would be considered to unduly inhibit the initiation and processing of claims for benefits. Also, the denial of a claim for failure to obtain a prior approval under circumstances that would make obtaining such prior approval impossible or where application of the prior approval process could seriously jeopardize the life or health of the claimant (e.g., in the case of a group health plan, the claimant is unconscious and in need of immediate care at the time medical treatment is required) would constitute a practice that unduly inhibits the initiation and processing of a claim;

(4) The claims procedures do not preclude an authorized representative of a claimant from acting on behalf of such claimant in pursuing a benefit claim or

appeal of an adverse benefit determination. Nevertheless, a plan may establish reasonable procedures for determining whether an individual has been authorized to act on behalf of a claimant, provided that, in the case of a claim involving urgent care, within the meaning of paragraph (m)(1) of this section, a health care professional, within the meaning of paragraph (m)(7) of this section, with knowledge of a claimant's medical condition shall be permitted to act as the authorized representative of the claimant; and

(5) The claims procedures contain administrative processes and safeguards designed to ensure and to verify that benefit claim determinations are made in accordance with governing plan documents and that, where appropriate, the plan provisions have been applied consistently with respect to similarly situated claimants.

(6) In the case of a plan established and maintained pursuant to a collective bargaining agreement (other than a plan subject to the provisions of section 302(c)(5) of the Labor Management Relations Act, 1947 concerning joint representation on the board of trustees)—

(i) Such plan will be deemed to comply with the provisions of paragraphs (c) through (j) of this section if the collective bargaining agreement pursuant to which the plan is established or maintained sets forth or incorporates by specific reference—

(A) Provisions concerning the filing of benefit claims and the initial disposition of benefit claims, and

(B) A grievance and arbitration procedure to which adverse benefit determinations are subject.

(ii) Such plan will be deemed to comply with the provisions of paragraphs (h), (i), and (j) of this section (but will not be deemed to comply with paragraphs (c) through (g) of this section) if the collective bargaining agreement pursuant to which the plan is established or maintained sets forth or incorporates by specific reference a grievance and arbitration procedure to which adverse benefit determinations are subject (but not provisions concerning the filing and initial disposition of benefit claims).

(c) Group health plans. The claims procedures of a group health plan will be deemed to be reasonable only if, in addition to complying with the requirements of paragraph (b) of this section—

(i) The claims procedures provide that, in the case of a failure by a claimant or an authorized representative of a claimant to follow the plan's procedures for filing a pre-service claim, within the meaning of paragraph (m)(2) of this section, the claimant or representative shall be notified of the failure and the proper procedures to be followed in filing a claim for benefits. This notification shall be provided to the claimant or authorized representative, as appropriate, as soon as possible, but not later than 5 days (24 hours in the case of a failure to file a claim involving urgent care) following the failure. Notification may be oral, unless written notification is requested by the claimant or authorized representative.

(ii) Paragraph (c)(1)(i) of this section shall apply only in the case of a failure that—

(A) Is a communication by a claimant or an authorized representative of a claimant that is received by a person or organizational unit customarily responsible for handling benefit matters; and

(B) Is a communication that names a specific claimant; a specific medical condition or symptom; and a specific treatment, service, or product for which approval is requested.

(3) The claims procedures do not contain any provision, and are not administered in a way, that requires a claimant to file more than two appeals of an adverse benefit determination prior to bringing a civil action under section 502(a) of the Act;

(3) To the extent that a plan offers voluntary levels of appeal (except to the extent that the plan is required to do so by State law), including voluntary arbitration or any other form of dispute resolution, in addition to those permitted by paragraph (c)(2) of this section, the claims procedures provide that:

(i) The plan waives any right to assert that a claimant has failed to exhaust administrative remedies because the claimant did not elect to submit a benefit dispute to any such voluntary level of appeal provided by the plan;

(ii) The plan agrees that any statute of limitations or other defense based on timeliness is tolled during the time that any such voluntary appeal is pending;

(iii) The claims procedures provide that a claimant may elect to submit a benefit dispute to such voluntary level of appeal only after exhaustion of the appeals permitted by paragraph (c)(2) of this section;

(iv) The plan provides to any claimant, upon request, sufficient information relating to the voluntary level of appeal to enable the claimant to make an informed judgment about whether to submit a benefit dispute to the voluntary level of appeal, including a statement that the decision of a claimant as to whether or not to submit a benefit dispute to the voluntary level of appeal will have no effect on the claimant's rights to any other benefits under the plan and information about the applicable rules, the claimant's right to representation, the process for selecting the decisionmaker, and the circumstances, if any, that may affect the impartiality of the decisionmaker, such as any financial or personal interests in the result or any past or present relationship with any party to the review process; and

(v) No fees or costs are imposed on the claimant as part of the voluntary level of appeal.

(4) The claims procedures do not contain any provision for the mandatory arbitration of adverse benefit determinations, except to the extent that the plan or procedures provide that:

(i) The arbitration is conducted as one of the two appeals described in paragraph (c)(2) of this section and in accordance with the requirements applicable to such appeals; and

(ii) The claimant is not precluded from challenging the decision under section 502(a) of the Act or other applicable law.

(d) Plans providing disability benefits. The claims procedures of a plan that provides disability benefits will be deemed to be reasonable only if the claims procedures comply, with respect to claims for disability benefits, with the requirements of paragraphs (b), (c)(2), (c)(3), and (c)(4) of this section.

(e) Claim for benefits. For purposes of this section, a claim for benefits is a request for a plan benefit or benefits made by a claimant in accordance with a plan's reasonable procedure for filing benefit claims. In the case of a group health plan, a claim for benefits includes any pre-service claims within the meaning of paragraph (m)(2) of this section and any post-service claims within the meaning of paragraph (m)(3) of this section.

(f) Timing of notification of benefit determination. (1) In general. Except as provided in paragraphs (f)(2) and (f)(3) of this section, if a claim is wholly or partially denied, the plan administrator shall notify the claimant, in accordance with paragraph (g) of this section, of the plan's adverse benefit determination within a reasonable period of time, but not later than 90 days after receipt of the claim by the plan, unless the plan administrator determines that special circumstances require an extension of time for processing the claim. If the plan administrator determines that an extension of time for processing is required, written notice of the extension shall be furnished to the claimant prior to the termination of the initial 90-day period. In no event shall such extension exceed a period of 90 days from the end of such initial period. The extension notice shall indicate the special circumstances requiring an extension of time and the date by which the plan expects to render the benefit determination.

(2) Group health plans. In the case of a group health plan, the plan administrator shall notify a claimant of the plan's benefit determination in accordance with paragraph (f)(2)(i), (f)(2)(ii), or (f)(2)(iii) of this section, as appropriate.

(i) Urgent care claims. In the case of a claim involving urgent care, the plan administrator shall notify the claimant of the plan's benefit determination (whether adverse or not) as soon as possible, taking into account the medical exigencies, but not later than 72 hours after receipt of the claim by the plan, unless the claimant fails to provide sufficient information to determine whether, or to what extent, benefits are covered or payable under the plan. In the case of such a failure, the plan administrator shall notify the claimant as soon as possible, but not later than 24 hours after receipt of the claim by the plan, of the specific information necessary to complete the claim. The claimant shall be afforded a reasonable amount of time, taking into account the circumstances, but not less than 48 hours, to provide the specified information. Notification of any adverse benefit determination pursuant to this paragraph (f)(2)(i) shall be made in accordance with paragraph (g) of this section. The plan administrator shall notify the claimant of the plan's benefit determination as soon as possible, but in no case later than 48 hours after the earlier of—

(A) The plan's receipt of the specified information, or

(B) The end of the period afforded the claimant to provide the specified additional information.

(ii) Concurrent care decisions. If a group health plan has approved an ongoing course of treatment to be provided over a period of time or number of treatments—

(A) Any reduction or termination by the plan of such course of treatment (other than by plan amendment or termination) before the end of such period of time or number of treatments shall constitute an adverse benefit determination. The plan administrator shall notify the claimant, in accordance with paragraph (g) of this section, of the adverse benefit determination at a time sufficiently in advance of the reduction or termination to allow the claimant to appeal and obtain a determination on review of that adverse benefit determination before the benefit is reduced or terminated.

(B) Any request by a claimant to extend the course of treatment beyond the period of time or number of treatments that is a claim involving urgent care shall be decided as soon as possible, taking into account the medical exigencies, and the plan administrator shall notify the claimant of the benefit determination, whether adverse or not, within 24 hours after receipt of the claim by the plan, provided that any such claim is made to the plan at least 24 hours prior to the expiration of the prescribed period of time or number of treatments. Notification of any adverse benefit determination concerning a request to extend the course of treatment, whether involving urgent care or not, shall be made in accordance with paragraph (g) of this section, and appeal shall be governed by paragraph (i)(2)(i), (i)(2)(ii), or (i)(2)(iii), as appropriate.

(iii) Other claims. In the case of a claim not described in paragraphs (f)(2)(i) or (f)(2)(ii) of this section, the plan administrator shall notify the claimant of the plan's benefit determination in accordance with either paragraph (f)(2)(iii)(A) or (f)(2)(iii)(B) of this section, as appropriate.

(A) Pre-service claims. In the case of a pre-service claim, the plan administrator shall notify the claimant of the plan's benefit determination (whether adverse or not) within a reasonable period of time appropriate to the medical circumstances, but not later than 15 days after receipt of the claim by the plan. This period may be extended one time by the plan for up to 15 days, provided that the plan administrator both determines that such an extension is necessary due to matters beyond the control of the plan and notifies the claimant, prior to the expiration of the initial 15-day period, of the circumstances requiring the extension of time and the date by which the plan expects to render a decision. If such an extension is necessary due to a failure of the claimant to submit the information necessary to decide the claim, the notice of extension shall specifically describe the required information, and the claimant shall be afforded at least 45 days from receipt of the notice within which to provide the specified information. Notification of any adverse benefit determination pursuant to this paragraph (f)(2)(iii)(A) shall be made in accordance with paragraph (g) of this section.

(B) Post-service claims. In the case of a post-service claim, the plan administrator shall notify the claimant, in accordance with paragraph (g) of this section, of the plan's adverse benefit determination within a reasonable period of time, but not later than 30 days after receipt of the claim. This period may be extended one time by the plan for up to 15 days, provided that the plan administrator both determines that such an extension is necessary due to matters beyond the control of the plan and notifies the claimant, prior to the expiration of the initial 30-day period, of the circumstances requiring the extension of time and the date by which the plan expects to render a decision. If such an extension is necessary due to a failure of the claimant to submit the information necessary to decide the claim, the notice of extension shall specifically describe the required information, and the claimant shall be afforded at least 45 days from receipt of the notice within which to provide the specified information.

(3) Disability claims. In the case of a claim for disability benefits, the plan administrator shall notify the claimant, in accordance with paragraph (g) of this section, of the plan's adverse benefit determination within a reasonable period of time, but not later than 45 days after receipt of the claim by the plan. This period may be extended by the plan for up to 30 days, provided that the plan administrator both determines that such an extension is necessary due to matters beyond the control of the plan and notifies the claimant, prior to the expiration of the initial 45-day period, of the circumstances requiring the extension of time and the date by which the plan expects to render a decision. If, prior to the end of the first 30-day extension period, the administrator determines that, due to matters beyond the control of the plan, a decision cannot be rendered within that extension period, the period for making the determination may be extended for up to an additional 30 days, provided that the plan administrator notifies the claimant, prior to the expiration of the first 30-day extension period, of the circumstances requiring the extension and the date as of which the plan expects to render a decision. In the case of any extension under this paragraph (f)(3), the notice of extension shall specifically explain the standards on which entitlement to a benefit is based, the unresolved issues that prevent a decision on the claim, and the additional information needed to resolve those issues, and the claimant shall be afforded at least 45 days within which to provide the specified information.

(4) Calculating time periods. For purposes of paragraph (f) of this section, the period of time within which a benefit determination is required to be made shall begin at the time a claim is filed in accordance with the reasonable procedures of a plan, without regard to whether all the information necessary to make a benefit determination accompanies the filing. In the event that a period of time is extended as permitted pursuant to paragraph (f)(2)(iii) or (f)(3) of this section due to a claimant's failure to submit information necessary to decide a claim, the period for making the benefit determination shall be tolled from the date on which the notification of the extension is sent to the claimant until the date on which the claimant responds to the request for additional information.

(g) Manner and content of notification of benefit determination. (1) Except as provided in paragraph (g)(2) of this section, the plan administrator shall provide a claimant with written or electronic notification of any adverse benefit determination. Any electronic notification shall comply with the standards imposed by 29 C.F.R 2520.104b-1(c)(1)(i), (iii), and (iv). The notification shall set forth, in a manner calculated to be understood by the claimant—

(i) The specific reason or reasons for the adverse determination;

(ii) Reference to the specific plan provisions on which the determination is based;

(iii) A description of any additional material or information necessary for the claimant to perfect the claim and an explanation of why such material or information is necessary;

(iv) A description of the plan's review procedures and the time limits applicable to such procedures, including a statement of the claimant's right to bring a civil action under section 502(a) of the Act following an adverse benefit determination on review;

(v) In the case of an adverse benefit determination by a group health plan or a plan providing disability benefits,

(A) If an internal rule, guideline, protocol, or other similar criterion was relied upon in making the adverse determination, either the specific rule, guideline, protocol, or other similar criterion; or a statement that such a rule, guideline, protocol, or other similar criterion was relied upon in making the adverse determination and that a copy of such rule, guideline, protocol, or other criterion will be provided free of charge to the claimant upon request; or

(B) If the adverse benefit determination is based on a medical necessity or experimental treatment or similar exclusion or limit, either an explanation of the scientific or clinical judgment for the determination, applying the terms of the plan to the claimant's medical circumstances, or a statement that such explanation will be provided free of charge upon request.

(vi) (vi) In the case of an adverse benefit determination by a group health plan concerning a claim involving urgent care, a description of the expedited review process applicable to such claims.

(2) In the case of an adverse benefit determination by a group health plan concerning a claim insvolving urgent care, the information described in paragraph (g)(1) of this section may be provided to the claimant orally within the time frame prescribed in paragraph (f)(2)(i) of this section, provided that a written or electronic notification in accordance with paragraph (g)(1) of this section is furnished to the claimant not later than 3 days after the oral notification.

(h) Appeal of adverse benefit determinations. (1) In general. Every employee benefit plan shall establish and maintain a procedure by which a claimant shall have a reasonable opportunity to appeal an adverse benefit determination to an appropriate named fiduciary of the plan, and under which there will be a full and fair review of the claim and the adverse benefit determination.

(2) Full and fair review. Except as provided in paragraphs (h)(3) and (h)(4) of this section, the claims procedures of a plan will not be deemed to provide a claimant with a reasonable opportunity for a full and fair review of a claim and adverse benefit determination unless the claims procedures—

(i) Provide claimants at least 60 days following receipt of a notification of an adverse benefit determination within which to appeal the determination;

(ii) (ii) Provide claimants the opportunity to submit written comments, documents, records, and other information relating to the claim for benefits;

(iii) (iii) Provide that a claimant shall be provided, upon request and free of charge, reasonable access to, and copies of, all documents, records, and other information relevant to the claimant's claim for benefits. Whether a document, record, or other information is relevant to a claim for benefits shall be determined by reference to paragraph (m)(8) of this section;

(iv) (iv) Provide for a review that takes into account all comments, documents, records, and other information submitted by the claimant relating to the claim, without regard to whether such information was submitted or considered in the initial benefit determination.

(3) Group health plans. The claims procedures of a group health plan will not be deemed to provide a claimant with a reasonable opportunity for a full and fair review of a claim and adverse benefit determination unless, in addition to complying with the requirements of paragraphs (h)(2)(ii) through (iv) of this section, the claims procedures—

(i) Provide claimants at least 180 days following receipt of a notification of an adverse benefit determination within which to appeal the determination;

(ii) Provide for a review that does not afford deference to the initial adverse benefit determination and that is conducted by an appropriate named fiduciary of the plan who is neither the individual who made the adverse benefit determination that is the subject of the appeal, nor the subordinate of such individual;

(iii) Provide that, in deciding an appeal of any adverse benefit determination that is based in whole or in part on a medical judgment, including determinations with regard to whether a particular treatment, drug, or other item is experimental, investigational, or not medically necessary or appropriate, the appropriate named fiduciary shall consult with a health care professional who has appropriate training and experience in the field of medicine involved in the medical judgment;

(iv) Provide for the identification of medical or vocational experts whose advice was obtained on behalf of the plan in connection with a claimant's adverse benefit determination, without regard to whether the advice was relied upon in making the benefit determination;

(v) Provide that the health care professional engaged for purposes of a consultation under paragraph (h)(3)(iii) of this section shall be an individual who is neither an individual who was consulted in connection with the adverse benefit determination that is the subject of the appeal, nor the subordinate of any such individual; and

(vi) Provide, in the case of a claim involving urgent care, for an expedited review process pursuant to which—

(A) A request for an expedited appeal of an adverse benefit determination may be submitted orally or in writing by the claimant; and

(B) All necessary information, including the plan's benefit determination on review, shall be transmitted between the plan and the claimant by telephone, facsimile, or other available similarly expeditious method.

(4) Plans providing disability benefits. The claims procedures of a plan providing disability benefits will not, with respect to claims for such benefits, be deemed to provide a claimant with a reasonable opportunity for a full and fair review of a claim and adverse benefit determination unless the claims procedures comply with the requirements of paragraphs (h)(2)(ii) through (iv) and (h)(3)(i) through (v) of this section.

(i) **Timing of notification of benefit determination on review. (1) In general.** (i) Except as provided in paragraphs (i)(1)(ii), (i)(2), and (i)(3) of this section, the plan administrator shall notify a claimant in accordance with paragraph (j) of this section of the plan's benefit determination on review within a reasonable period of time, but not later than 60 days after receipt of the claimant's request for review by the plan, unless the plan administrator determines that special circumstances (such as the need to hold a hearing, if the plan's procedures provide for a hearing) require an extension of time for processing the claim. If the plan administrator determines that an extension of time for processing is required, written notice of the extension shall be furnished to the claimant prior to the termination of the initial 60-day period. In no event shall such extension exceed a period of 60 days from the end of the initial period. The extension notice shall indicate the special circumstances requiring an extension of time and the date by which the plan expects to render the determination on review.

(ii) In the case of a plan with a committee or board of trustees designated as the appropriate named fiduciary that holds regularly scheduled meetings at least quarterly, paragraph (i)(1)(i) of this section shall not apply, and, except as provided in paragraphs (i)(2) and (i)(3) of this section, the appropriate named fiduciary shall instead make a benefit determination no later than the date of the meeting of the committee or board that immediately follows the plan's receipt of a request for review, unless the request for review is filed within 30 days preceding the date of such meeting. In such case, a benefit determination may be made by no later than the date of the second meeting following the plan's receipt of the request for review. If special circumstances (such as the need to hold a hearing, if the plan's procedures provide for a hearing) require a further extension of time for processing, a benefit determination shall be rendered not later than the third meeting of the committee or board following the plan's receipt of the request for review. If such an extension of time for review is required because of special circumstances, the plan administrator shall provide the claimant with written notice of the extension, describing the special circumstances and the date as of which the benefit determination will be made, prior to the commencement of the extension. The plan administrator shall notify the claimant, in accordance with paragraph (j) of this section, of the benefit determination as soon as possible, but not later than 5 days after the benefit determination is made.

(2) **Group health plans.** In the case of a group health plan, the plan administrator shall notify a claimant of the plan's benefit determination on review in accordance with paragraphs (i)(2)(i) through (iii), as appropriate.

(ii) **Urgent care claims.** In the case of a claim involving urgent care, the plan administrator shall notify the claimant, in accordance with paragraph (j) of this section, of the plan's benefit determination on review as soon as possible, taking into account the medical exigencies, but not later than 72 hours after receipt of the claimant's request for review of an adverse benefit determination by the plan.

(ii) Pre-service claims. In the case of a pre-service claim, the plan administrator shall notify the claimant, in accordance with paragraph (j) of this section, of the plan's benefit determination on review within a reasonable period of time appropriate to the medical circumstances. In the case of a group health plan that provides for one appeal of an adverse benefit determination, such notification shall be provided not later than 30 days after receipt by the plan of the claimant's request for review of an adverse benefit determination. In the case of a group health plan that provides for two appeals of an adverse determination, such notification shall be provided, with respect to any one of such two appeals, not later than 15 days after receipt by the plan of the claimant's request for review of the adverse determination.

(ii) Post-service claims. (A) In the case of a post-service claim, except as provided in paragraph (i)(2)(iii)(B) of this section, the plan administrator shall notify the claimant, in accordance with paragraph (j) of this section, of the plan's benefit determination on review within a reasonable period of time. In the case of a group health plan that provides for one appeal of an adverse benefit determination, such notification shall be provided not later than 60 days after receipt by the plan of the claimant's request for review of an adverse benefit determination. In the case of a group health plan that provides for two appeals of an adverse determination, such notification shall be provided, with respect to any one of such two appeals, not later than 30 days after receipt by the plan of the claimant's request for review of the adverse determination.

(B) In the case of a multiemployer plan with a committee or board of trustees designated as the appropriate named fiduciary that holds regularly scheduled meetings at least quarterly, paragraph (i)(2)(iii)(A) of this section shall not apply, and the appropriate named fiduciary shall instead make a benefit determination no later than the date of the meeting of the committee or board that immediately follows the plan's receipt of a request for review, unless the request for review is filed within 30 days preceding the date of such meeting. In such case, a benefit determination may be made by no later than the date of the second meeting following the plan's receipt of the request for review. If special circumstances (such as the need to hold a hearing, if the plan's procedures provide for a hearing) require a further extension of time for processing, a benefit determination shall be rendered not later than the third meeting of the committee or board following the plan's receipt of the request for review. If such an extension of time for review is required because of special circumstances, the plan administrator shall notify the claimant in writing of the extension, describing the special circumstances and the date as of which the benefit determination will be made, prior to the commencement of the extension. The plan administrator shall notify the claimant, in accordance with paragraph (j) of this section, of the benefit determination as soon as possible, but not later than 5 days after the benefit determination is made.

(3) Disability claims. (i) Except as provided in paragraph (i)(3)(ii) of this section, claims involving disability benefits (whether the plan provides for one or two appeals) shall be governed by paragraph (i)(1) of this section, except that a period of 45 days shall apply instead of 60 days for purposes of that paragraph.

(ii). In the case of a multiemployer plan with a committee or board of trustees designated as the appropriate named fiduciary that holds regularly scheduled meetings at least quarterly, paragraph (i)(3)(i) of this section shall not apply, and the appropriate named fiduciary shall instead make a benefit determination no later than the date of the meeting of the committee or board that immediately follows the plan's receipt of a request for review, unless the request for review is filed within 30 days preceding the date of such meeting. In such case, a benefit determination may be made by no later than the date of the second meeting following the plan's receipt of the request for review. If special circumstances (such as the need to hold a hearing, if the plan's procedures provide for a hearing) require a further extension of time for processing, a benefit determination shall be rendered not later than the third meeting of the committee or board following the plan's receipt of the request for review. If such an extension of time for review is required because of special circumstances, the plan administrator shall notify the claimant in writing of the extension, describing the special circumstances and the date as of which the benefit determination will be made, prior to the commencement of the extension. The plan administrator shall notify the claimant, in accordance with paragraph (j) of this section, of the benefit determination as soon as possible, but not later than 5 days after the benefit determination is made.

(4) Calculating time periods. For purposes of paragraph (i) of this section, the period of time within which a benefit determination on review is required to be made shall begin at the time an appeal is filed in accordance with the reasonable procedures of a plan, without regard to whether all the information necessary to make a benefit determination on review accompanies the filing. In the event that a period of time is extended as permitted pursuant to paragraph (i)(1), (i)(2)(iii)(B), or (i)(3) of this section due to a claimant's failure to submit information necessary to decide a claim, the period for making the benefit determination on review shall be tolled from the date on which the notification of the extension is sent to the claimant until the date on which the claimant responds to the request for additional information.

(5) Furnishing documents. In the case of an adverse benefit determination on review, the plan administrator shall provide such access to, and copies of, documents, records, and other information described in paragraphs (j)(3), (j)(4), and (j)(5) of this section as is appropriate.

(j) Manner and content of notification of benefit determination on review. The plan administrator shall provide a claimant with written or electronic notification of a plan's benefit determination on review. Any electronic notification shall comply with the standards imposed by 29 C.F.R 2520.104b-1(c)(1)(i), (iii), and (iv). In the case of an adverse benefit determination, the notification shall set forth, in a manner calculated to be understood by the claimant—

(1) The specific reason or reasons for the adverse determination;

(2) Reference to the specific plan provisions on which the benefit determination is based;

(3) A statement that the claimant is entitled to receive, upon request and free of charge, reasonable access to, and copies of, all documents, records, and other information relevant to the claimant's claim for benefits. Whether a document, record, or other information is relevant to a claim for benefits shall be determined by reference to paragraph (m)(8) of this section;

(4) A statement describing any voluntary appeal procedures offered by the plan and the claimant's right to obtain the information about such procedures described in paragraph (c)(3)(iv) of this section, and a statement of the claimant's right to bring an action under section 502(a) of the Act; and

(5) In the case of a group health plan or a plan providing disability benefits—

(i) If an internal rule, guideline, protocol, or other similar criterion was relied upon in making the adverse determination, either the specific rule, guideline, protocol, or other similar criterion; or a statement that such rule, guideline, protocol, or other similar criterion was relied upon in making the adverse determination and that a copy of the rule, guideline, protocol, or other similar criterion will be provided free of charge to the claimant upon request;

(ii) If the adverse benefit determination is based on a medical necessity or experimental treatment or similar exclusion or limit, either an explanation of the scientific or clinical judgment for the determination, applying the terms of the plan to the claimant's medical circumstances, or a statement that such explanation will be provided free of charge upon request; and

(iii) The following statement: "You and your plan may have other voluntary alternative dispute resolution options, such as mediation. One way to find out what may be available is to contact your local U.S. Department of Labor Office and your State insurance regulatory agency."

(k) Preemption of State law. (1) Nothing in this section shall be construed to supersede any provision of State law that regulates insurance, except to the extent that such law prevents the application of a requirement of this section.

(2)(i) For purposes of paragraph (k)(1) of this section, a State law regulating insurance shall not be considered to prevent the application of a requirement of this section merely because such State law establishes a review procedure to evaluate and resolve disputes involving adverse benefit determinations under group health plans so long as the review procedure is conducted by a person or entity other than the insurer, the plan, plan fiduciaries, the employer, or any employee or agent of any of the foregoing.

(ii) The State law procedures described in paragraph (k)(2)(i) of this section are not part of the full and fair review required by section 503 of the Act. Claimants therefore need not exhaust such State law procedures prior to bringing suit under section 502(a) of the Act.

(l) Failure to establish and follow reasonable claims procedures. In the case of the failure of a plan to establish or follow claims procedures consistent with the requirements of this section, a claimant shall be deemed to have exhausted the administrative remedies available under the plan and shall be entitled to pursue any available remedies under section 502(a) of the Act on the basis that the plan has failed to provide a reasonable claims procedure that would yield a decision on the merits of the claim.

(m) Definitions. The following terms shall have the meaning ascribed to such terms in this paragraph (m) whenever such term is used in this section:

1.(i) A "claim involving urgent care" is any claim for medical care or treatment with respect to which the application of the time periods for making non-urgent care determinations—

(A) Could seriously jeopardize the life or health of the claimant or the ability of the claimant to regain maximum function, or,

(B) In the opinion of a physician with knowledge of the claimant's medical condition, would subject the claimant to severe pain that cannot be adequately managed without the care or treatment that is the subject of the claim.

(ii) Except as provided in paragraph (m)(1)(iii) of this section, whether a claim is a "claim involving urgent care" within the meaning of paragraph (m)(1)(i)(A) of this section is to be determined by an individual acting on behalf of the plan applying the judgment of a prudent layperson who possesses an average knowledge of health and medicine.

(iii) Any claim that a physician with knowledge of the claimant's medical condition determines is a "claim involving urgent care" within the meaning of paragraph (m)(1)(i) of this section shall be treated as a "claim involving urgent care" for purposes of this section.

(2) The term "pre-service claim" means any claim for a benefit under a group health plan with respect to which the terms of the plan condition receipt of the benefit, in whole or in part, on approval of the benefit in advance of obtaining medical care.

(3) The term "post-service claim" means any claim for a benefit under a group health plan that is not a pre-service claim within the meaning of paragraph (m)(2) of this section.

(4) The term "adverse benefit determination" means any of the following: a denial, reduction, or termination of, or a failure to provide or make payment (in whole or in part) for, a benefit, including any such denial, reduction, termination, or failure to provide or make payment that is based on a determination of a participant's or beneficiary's eligibility to participate in a plan, and including, with respect to group health plans, a denial, reduction, or termination of, or a failure to provide or make payment (in whole or in part) for, a benefit resulting from the application of any utilization review, as well as a failure to cover an item or service for which benefits are otherwise provided because it is determined to be experimental or investigational or not medically necessary or appropriate.

(5) The term "notice" or "notification" means the delivery or furnishing of information to an individual in a manner that satisfies the standards of 29 C.F.R 2520.104b-1(b) as appropriate with respect to material required to be furnished or made available to an individual.

(6) The term "group health plan" means an employee welfare benefit plan within the meaning of section 3(1) of the Act to the extent that such plan provides "medical care" within the meaning of section 733(a) of the Act.

(7) The term "health care professional" means a physician or other health care professional licensed, accredited, or certified to perform specified health services consistent with State law.

(8) A document, record, or other information shall be considered "relevant" to a claimant's claim if such document, record, or other information

(i) Was relied upon in making the benefit determination;

(ii) Was submitted, considered, or generated in the course of making the benefit determination, without regard to whether such document, record, or other information was relied upon in making the benefit determination;

(iii) Demonstrates compliance with the administrative processes and safeguards required pursuant to paragraph (b)(5) of this section in making the benefit determination; or

(iv) In the case of a group health plan or a plan providing disability benefits, constitutes a statement of policy or guidance with respect to the plan concerning the denied treatment option or benefit for the claimant's diagnosis, without regard to whether such advice or statement was relied upon in making the benefit determination.

(n) Apprenticeship plans. This section does not apply to employee benefit plans that solely provide apprenticeship training benefits.

(o) Applicability dates. (1) Except as provided in paragraph (o)(2) of this section, this section shall apply to claims filed under a plan on or after January 1, 2002.

(2) This section shall apply to claims filed under a group health plan on or after the first day of the first plan year beginning on or after July 1, 2002, but in no event later than January 1, 2003.

[65 FR 70265, Nov. 21, 2000, as amended at 66 FR 35887, July 9, 2001]

APPENDIX 9-2

MEDICARE SECONDARY PAYER MANUAL

Chapter 7—Contractor MSP Recovery Rules

50.5.4.4.3—Timely Processing of Waiver Determinations
(Rev. 1, 10-01-03)
A3-3418.18

Waiver determinations should be completed within 120 days from the date a waiver request is received (and date stamped) in the contractor mailroom.

50.6—Contractor Criteria for Waiver Determinations
(Rev. 1, 10-01-03)
A3-3418.11

There are three statutory authorities under which Medicare may accept less than the full amount of its claim:

- §1870(c) of the Social Security Act;

- §1862(b) of the Social Security Act; and

- The Federal Claims Collection Act (FCCA).

Each statute contains different criteria upon which decisions to compromise, waive, suspend, or terminate Medicare's claim may be made. Likewise, the exercise of each authority is limited to specific entities.

Medicare contractors have authority to consider beneficiary requests for waivers under §1870(c) of the Act. Authority to waive Medicare claims under §1862(b) and to compromise claims, or to suspend or terminate recovery action under FCCA, is reserved exclusively to CMS CO and/or RO staffs.

However, FCCA and §1862(b) provisions are described at §50.7.2 and §50.7.1, to assist the contractor in identifying the types of inquiries/circumstances in which the RO must be involved, and to assist the contractor in understanding the terms which apply to each authority. Distinctions between waiver, partial waiver and compromise are important and are found at Chapter 1, §20, where each term is defined.

50.6.1—Waiver Determination Under §1870(c): Step 1 Collect All Pertinent Data
(Rev. 1, 10-01-03)
A3-3418.12

The contractor sends the beneficiary a Form SSA-632-BK, (obtained from the following Social Security Administration (SSA) internet address: *http:// www.ssa.gov/online/ssa-632.pdf*), with appropriate supporting documentation. Enclose this form with Exhibit 11. The beneficiary does **not** need to complete Section 1 "Without Fault"—of the SSA-632-BK, since at this time, beneficiaries are deemed to be without fault. At the time the Form SSA-632-BK—Request for

Waiver of Overpayment is submitted, the beneficiary must also provide supporting documentation for:

- Procurement costs;

- Accident-related out-of-pocket medical expenses incurred; and

- Expenses and income information that demonstrate financial hardship (if the beneficiary is alleging financial hardship).

50.6.2—Waiver Determination Under 1870(c): Step 2—Apply Waiver Criteria (Rev. 1, 10-01-03)
A3-3418.13
The contractor determines whether the beneficiary meets the criteria for waiver determinations under §1870(c) of the Act (42 C.F.R 405.355 and 20 C.F.R. 404.506-512). Section 1870(c) of the Act provides that CMS may waive all or part of its recovery in any case where an overpayment under title XVIII has been made with respect to a beneficiary:

a.   Who is without fault, and

b.   When adjustment or recovery would either:

   1.   Defeat the purpose of title II or title XVIII of the Act, **or**

   2.   Be against equity and good conscience.

50.6.3—Factors to Consider in Determining if a Full or Partial Waiver is Warranted: Step 3
(Rev. 1, 10-01-03)
A3-3418.14

50.6.3.1—Allowing Out-of-Pocket Expenses in Waiver Determinations
(Rev. 1, 10-01-03)
Out-of-pocket expenses should be considered in determining if a full or partial waiver is warranted. Out-of-pocket expenses are defined as those medical expenses for which a beneficiary has paid or is responsible to pay incurred for injuries directly related to the accident and that are **not** covered by insurance (including Medicare), settlement proceeds, or court-awarded damages.

A waiver of all or part of the out-of-pocket expenses may be granted only if the following criteria have been met. In determining the amount of out-of-pocket expenses to be waived, each case must be considered on its own merits.

A—Beneficiary Documents Out-Of-Pocket Expenses.
The following documentation should be considered proper proof of the expenses paid:

- Notarized/sworn statement which attests to the validity of the expenses;

- Canceled checks (which correlate to bills received);

- Receipts for services furnished; and

- Copies of bills demonstrating services furnished.

B—Beneficiary's Assets Insufficient To Repay Medicare

The contractor must not automatically assume that out-of-pockets should be waived. Using assets reported on the Form SSA-632-BK—Request for Waiver of Overpayment, it determines whether the beneficiary was actually able to afford the out-of-pocket expenses.

The following are types of out-of-pocket expenses that may support granting a waiver:

- Housing renovation—beneficiary's residence had to be modified to accommodate beneficiary because of an accident-related injury e.g., addition of a ramp to accommodate a wheel chair;

- Adult diapers—where the accident caused loss of bladder use;

- Prescriptions for medication needed as a result of an accident-related injury;

- Private duty nursing or custodial care not covered by Medicare;

- Coinsurance and deductibles not covered by supplemental insurance; and

- Expenses for dental work caused by the accident.

- Contractors should not consider:

- Funeral expenses; or

- Travel for relatives (even if accident-related).

50.6.3.2—Other factual data in Determining if a Full or Partial Waiver is Warranted
(Rev. 1, 10-01-03)
A3-3418.14.B

Other factual data contractors should use in determining if a full or partial waiver is warranted are:

- Age of beneficiary;

- Beneficiary's assets;

- Beneficiary's monthly income and expenses; and

- Physical or mental impairments.

50.6.4—Determining Beneficiary Fault
(Rev. 1, 10-01-03)
A3-3418.13.A

Based on the CMS application of the SSA definition of fault, found at 20 C.F.R. 404.507, CMS deems that beneficiaries are without fault.

50.6.5—When Recovery Would Defeat the Purpose of Title II or Title XVIII
   (Rev. 1, 10-01-03)
   A3-3418.13.B

This means recovery would defeat the purpose of benefits under these titles, i.e., would cause financial hardship by depriving a beneficiary of income required for ordinary and necessary living expenses. This depends upon whether the beneficiary has an income or financial resources sufficient for more than ordinary and necessary expenses, or is dependent upon all of their current benefits for such needs. A beneficiary's ordinary and necessary expenses include:

- Fixed living expenses, such as food and clothing, rent, mortgage payments, utilities, maintenance, insurance (e.g., life, accident, and health insurance, including premiums for supplementary medical insurance benefits under title XVIII), taxes, installment payments, etc.;

- Medical, hospitalization, and other similar expenses not covered by Medicare or any other insurer;

- Expenses for the support of others for whom the beneficiary is legally responsible; and

- Other miscellaneous expenses which may reasonably be considered necessary to maintain the beneficiary's current standard of living.

50.6.5.1—Examples of Financial Hardship
   (Rev. 1, 10-01-03)
   A3-3418.13.B

Following are examples of determining financial hardship on a Medicare beneficiary:

- The beneficiary has spent the settlement proceeds and the only remaining income from which the beneficiary could attempt to satisfy Medicare's claim would be from the money that is needed for the beneficiary's monthly living expenses. Waiver may be appropriate under this aspect of the waiver criteria. If documented and appropriate monthly expenses consume the entire amount of money available, a full waiver may be warranted. A partial waiver may be appropriate if the beneficiary retains at least some (for example $25.00) discretionary income each month;

- The demonstrated beneficiary income and resources are at a poverty level standard, such as being in an SSI pay status. A beneficiary may demonstrate proof of SSI pay status by requesting the Form SSA-2458, Benefit Verification, from a SSA office. If Medicare's claim would have to be satisfied from income and resources that meet an established level of poverty, waiver **may** be appropriate. However, **preexisting financial hardship alone may be an insufficient basis for granting a waiver.** All factors, not just the existence of poverty, must be weighed before a waiver decision can be made; or

- An unforeseen severe financial circumstance existing at the time Medicare's claim comes into existence can also constitute financial hardship. If a beneficiary has become legally financially responsible for an unforeseen obligation, has acted in good faith at all times with respect to Medicare's claim, **and** has no other financial resources to meet this legal obligation, waiver may be warranted. For example, waiver would be appropriate if a beneficiary's grandchildren became the legal responsibility under a will or trust that came into existence upon the sudden death of the beneficiary's child (the parent of the grandchildren).

NOTE: The contractor should assume in **all** waiver examples that the attorney has already taken attorney fees from the settlement proceeds, and the beneficiary does not have to pay the attorney from the settlement figure shown. Also, it should assume that the settlement proceeds are being retained in an escrow account by the attorney and have not been spent. In cases where the funds have already been spent by the beneficiary, the beneficiary's monthly financial situation and the likelihood of recouping the monies will be significant factors.

In the following situations, Medicare's full recovery would create the kind of financial hardship in which granting waiver would be appropriate.

A—Example 1

Facts: The beneficiary was injured in a slip and fall accident. A liability suit awarded a settlement of $4,500 to the beneficiary. The attorney's fees were $1,500. The beneficiary incurred $1,700 in allowable, properly documented out-of-pocket medical expenses. The beneficiary is left with $1,300, but there will be future medical expenses that are not likely to be covered by Medicare. The beneficiary submitted documentation indicating Social Security benefits are received and there is still a monthly shortfall of $200. Medicare's recovery after reducing for Medicare's share of procurement costs is $537.

Analysis: While Medicare's claim is very small, so is the settlement. The money the beneficiary would use to repay Medicare could be used to pay the additional medical expenses and pay the beneficiary for out-of-pocket expenses. The beneficiary is already experiencing financial hardship. Medicare's recovery would produce additional financial hardship.

Action: Grant full waiver.

B—Example 2

Facts: The beneficiary sustained serious injuries from a fall on a bus. The beneficiary sued the bus company and received a settlement of $5,000. Medicare made conditional payments of $6,369. Attorney's fees total $1,667. After reducing its claim to share in the procurement costs, Medicare's net conditional payments total $3,333. (When Medicare's payments exceed the amount of the settlement, Medicare's recovery becomes the amount of the settlement, less total procurement costs.) The beneficiary's monthly income and expenses are equal. The beneficiary incurred noncovered out-of-pocket medical expenses of $3,000, of which $1,500 is properly documented.

Analysis: After reducing for procurement costs, Medicare is entitled to recover $3,333.33, the remainder of the settlement funds. If the beneficiary repaid Medicare the total amount owed after reduction for procurement costs, there would be no funds left with which to pay out-of-pocket medical expenses. Repayment to Medicare would create a financial hardship with respect to the out-of-pocket costs. Therefore, Medicare may further reduce its claim to avoid causing a financial hardship for the beneficiary.

Action: Grant a partial waiver of the amount owed.

50.6.5.2—Recovery Would Be Against Equity and Good Conscience
(Rev. 1, 10-01-03)
A3-3418.13.C

"Equity and good conscience" is applied to Medicare overpayment recoveries when required, based on the totality of the circumstances in a particular case. In applying the standard of "equity and good conscience," factors to consider include, but are not limited to, the following:

- The degree to which the beneficiary contributed to causing the overpayment;

- The degree to which Medicare and/or its contractors contributed to causing the overpayment;

- The degree to which recovery or adjustment would cause undue hardship for the beneficiary;

- Whether the beneficiary would be unjustly enriched by a waiver or adjustment of recovery; and

- Whether the beneficiary changed their position to their material detriment as a result of receiving the overpayment or as a result of relying on erroneous information supplied to the beneficiary by Medicare.

Below are several Medicare overpayment situations when application of "equity and good conscience" is likely to result in a waiver of adjustment and recovery. These situations are:

- The beneficiary made a personal financial decision, based on written information from an official CMS source, that the overpayment was correct, and recovery would change the beneficiary's position for the worse; or

- Recovery of the full overpayment amount is contraindicated by especially compelling mitigating facts and circumstances of the beneficiary's case.

Below are examples where it would be against equity and good conscience for Medicare to recover its total payments.

A—Example 1

Facts: The beneficiary sustained injuries in an automobile accident. Medicare made conditional payments in the amount of $7,500 on the beneficiary's behalf. The beneficiary later filed suit for the injuries and damages suffered as a result of the accident and received a $5,000 settlement. There were no attorneys fees, thus Medicare's claim is $5,000. The beneficiary requested a waiver of the overpayment. The beneficiary submitted documentation demonstrating that the money received was used to replace the automobile that was totaled in the accident.

Analysis: If Medicare seeks full recovery, the beneficiary will likely have to sell the replacement vehicle to repay Medicare. The beneficiary's vehicle was the only means of transportation used for a part-time job to supplement income as well as transportation to doctors, etc. Selling the vehicle to repay Medicare would cause the beneficiary to be placed in a worse position than before the accident, which would be against equity and good conscience.

Action: Either full or partial waiver may be granted. Obviously, Medicare may seek its entire recovery. However, since the beneficiary's documentation indicates that the entire $5,000 was needed to replace the car, full waiver would be more appropriate.

NOTE: Using the settlement money to replace the totaled car was considered appropriate only because loss of the beneficiary's car was complete. It would be inappropriate to grant waiver simply because the beneficiary chose to purchase a car from the proceeds.

B—Example 2

Facts: The beneficiary sustained multiple injuries in an automobile accident, including a permanent injury that will preclude employment ever again. Monthly income equals monthly expenses. Medicare's conditional payments were $8,500. The beneficiary received a liability insurance payment of $5,000 (which was the limit of the policy). No attorney was retained. Therefore, Medicare's recovery becomes $5,000. The beneficiary incurred allowable, properly documented out-of-pocket medical expenses of $4,500.

Analysis: Since the beneficiary is now unable to work, the ability to absorb the out-of-pocket medical expenses has greatly diminished. Since a valuable right, i.e., the right to be gainfully employed, is a change in one's position, it would be against equity and good conscience for Medicare to recoup its entire recovery. In accordance with §50.7.1, since Medicare stands to recover 100 percent of the settlement amount, it may waive 100 percent of the out-of-pocket costs. It would not be feasible to pursue recovery of the remaining $500.

Action: Grant full waiver.

50.6.5.3—When the Beneficiary Fails to Meet Either Waiver Criterion Under 1870(c)
(Rev. 1, 10-01-03)
A3-3418.13.D

When the beneficiary requests a waiver, but does not meet either of the two criteria, the request for waiver should be denied. The following examples illustrate such circumstances.

A—Example 1

Facts: The beneficiary broke a leg and is now unable to work. Medicare's conditional payments total $7,000. The beneficiary received a settlement of $20,000. After reducing Medicare's claim to allow for procurement costs, Medicare should recover $4,667. The total beneficiary monthly income is $1,004 (interest income and social security benefits), with monthly expenses of $585. Out-of-pocket incurred expenses total $870 and the beneficiary has requested a full waiver.

Analysis: Wavier criteria is not met because the beneficiary has not shown that daily living expenses could not be met, nor that repayment would be unfair. This determination is based upon the information provided, which documents that the beneficiary is able to meet daily living expenses, and has excess funds ($285 excess per month), even without the settlement received. Moreover, the beneficiary received a large enough settlement to pay the noncovered out-of-pocket expenses and to repay Medicare without incurring a financial hardship. Repayment under these circumstances is equitable.

Action: Waiver request is denied.

B—Example 2

Facts: The beneficiary was unemployed before injury that triggered Medicare conditional payments. However, the accident has reduced the probability that the beneficiary will ever be able to work again. Medicare's recovery is $11,000. No attorney was used in procuring the settlement, nor were there other procurement costs. Therefore, no procurement costs were subtracted from the amount of Medicare's recovery. The beneficiary received a $55,000 settlement. Documented out-of-pocket medical expenses equal $10,000. Monthly expenses are $2,068 and monthly income is $1,150 ($771 social security benefits, $344 unemployment, $35 interest income).

Analysis: The beneficiary has a monthly shortfall of $918, which appears to constitute a financial hardship. However, this financial hardship existed before the accident. **RepayingMedicare** must be the circumstance that causes financial hardship. Preexisting financial hardship **alone** is not a sufficient reason to grant waiver. Additionally, after repaying Medicare and paying for out-of-pocket expenses, the beneficiary retains $33,221 of the settlement proceeds. Repayment of Medicare's claim will not deprive the beneficiary of any valuable right or put the beneficiary in a worse position than before the accident. For this reason, repaying Medicare is not against equity and good conscience.

Action: Waiver request is denied.

50.6.5.4—Waiver Indicators
(Rev. 1, 10-01-03)
A3-3418.13.E

Waiver decisions are rarely, if ever, straightforward and uncomplicated. However, there are a few indicators to consider. The following are just examples and are in no way conclusive determinations of whether waiver should or should not be granted. Every waiver decision must be made on the merits of the facts in the case in question.

A—Indicators that support granting full or partial waiver include:

- Medicare's recovery exceeds settlement amount (this is often true with small settlements);

- Beneficiary sustained the type of permanent injuries, or has documented lost wages, or became unemployed;

- There are noncovered out-of-pocket accident related expenses; and

- Beneficiary's living expenses are equal to or higher than income.

B—Indicators that support denying waiver (where financial hardship is alleged) include:

- Medicare asserted its right to recover before the settlement proceeds were disbursed (and there is correspondence in the case file which provides documentation of Medicare's timely assertion);

- Beneficiary receives a large settlement;

- Beneficiary's income exceeds ordinary living expenses;

- After repaying Medicare and allowing for out-of-pocket medical costs (if such allowances are necessary), the beneficiary will be left with a substantial amount of the settlement proceeds; and

- Beneficiary has substantial assets.

In order to make proper use of these indicators it is imperative to carefully collect information from the beneficiary. Consistent use of the Form SSA-632-BK form is essential.

50.6.5.4.1—Letter for Granting a Full Waiver (Exhibit 4)
   (Rev. 1, 10-01-03)
   A3-3418.12.D

Exhibit 4—Letter for Granting a Full Waiver

If granting a full waiver, the contractor sends the Standard Letter Granting Full Waiver shown below. Use of this letter is mandatory. Substitutes may **not** be used. The contractor retains copies for the file.

STANDARD LETTER GRANTING FULL WAIVER

Re: Name of Beneficiary HIC #

Dear Beneficiary/Attorney:

We have reviewed your/your client's request to waive the amount owed to Medicare and have determined that you qualify for a full waiver.

This qualification is based upon the requirements of §1870(c) of the Act (42 U.S.C. 1395gg(c)), and the regulations found at 42 C.F.R 405.355-405.356, and 20 C.F.R 404.506 et seq. These regulations provide that a beneficiary's overpayment may be waived if the beneficiary is without fault in causing the overpayment, **and** if recovery would either defeat the purpose of the Social Security Act or Medicare program, **or** if recovery would be against equity and good conscience. Because you/your client meet(s) these qualifications, we are granting a full waiver.

You have shown [include explanation of the reasons the qualifications for waiver have been met].

The Medicare conditional payment in this case was $ _____. You (Your client) received a settlement of $ _____. The procurement costs in this case, including attorney fees were _____. After allowing $ _____ as Medicare's share of procurement costs, the amount which would have been due to Medicare is $ _____.

However, for the reasons stated above, Medicare is waiving recovery of this amount.

Please sign the enclosed release agreement form within 10 days and return it to this office. Should you/your client have any questions concerning this letter, please contact _____ on _____.

Medicare Contractor
Enclosure(s): Release Agreement

50.6.5.4.2—Letter for Granting A Partial Waiver (Exhibit 5)
   (Rev. 1, 10-01-03)
   A3-3418.12.D

Exhibit 5—Letter for Granting a Partial Waiver

If granting a partial waiver, the contractor sends the Standard Letter Granting Partial Waiver shown below. Use of this letter is mandatory. Substitutes may **not** be used. The contractor retains copies for the file.

STANDARD LETTER GRANTING PARTIAL WAIVER

Re: Name of Beneficiary HIC #

Dear Beneficiary/Attorney:

We have completed our review of your/your client's request to waive monies owed to Medicare. It is our decision to partially waive Medicare's claim.

The authority to waive recovery of a Medicare overpayment is found in 1870(c) of the Social Security Act (42 U.S.C. 1395gg(c)). Under this provision, and the regulations found at 42 C.F.R. 405.355-405.356, if a beneficiary is without fault in causing the overpayment **and** recovery would either defeat the purpose of the Social Security Act or Medicare program, **or** would be against equity and good conscience, recovery may be waived. In making these decisions, Medicare applies the rules found in Social Security regulations at 20 C.F.R. 404.506-404.509, 404.510a, and 404.512.

In applying these rules, we found the following:

The contractor enters reasons for partial deductions:

Example

This partial waiver is granted because it would be against equity and good conscience to recover the full amount of the claim. The settlement proceeds in this particular case were very small considering the injuries suffered; therefore, it would be against equity and good conscience for Medicare to take the entire settlement.

OR

Example

You have documented financial hardship and we have determined that it would defeat the purpose of the Social Security Act to request repayment of the entire claim. Therefore, we are granting a partial waiver in the amount of $ _____, and $ _____ must be repaid to Medicare.

Medicare's conditional payment in this case was $ _____. You (your client) received a settlement of $ _____. The procurement costs in this case, including attorney fees were $ _____. After allowing _____ as Medicare's share of procurement costs per 42 C.F.R. 411.37, Medicare's net conditional claim was $ _____.

However, in accordance with this determination, we are granting a partial waiver in the amount of $ _____. The total amount now due to Medicare is $(principle and interest).

In accordance with this determination, a check in the amount of _____, made payable to Medicare, should be sent to:

Medicare contractor
Address

Your/the beneficiary's name and health insurance claim number should be included on the check made payable to Medicare.

On (date that exhibit 2 was sent) _____, we notified you that interest would be assessed on any debt not repaid in full within 60 days of that date, regardless of whether you chose to appeal or to seek waiver of the debt. We advised you that repaying the debt would not affect your right to dispute, appeal, or request waiver of the debt. Because you did not repay the debt within 60 days of (the date that exhibit 2 was sent), you owe Medicare $ _____, in interest charges.

Please sign the enclosed release agreement form within 10 days and return it to this office.

If you disagree with the decision not to grant a full waiver of recovery of this overpayment, you have 60 days from the date you receive this letter to request a reconsideration. The request can be submitted directly to the address above.

If you decide to exercise your appeal rights, and if you want help with your appeal, you can have a friend, lawyer, or someone else help you. There are groups, such as lawyer referral services and public interest advocacy groups that can help you find a lawyer.

There are also groups, such as legal aide services, who provide free legal services if you meet eligibility requirements. Should you/your client have any questions concerning this letter, please contact _____ on _____.

Medicare Contractor
Enclosure(s): Release Agreement Form
Pre-addressed envelope

50.6.5.4.3—Letter if Waiver Criteria Are Not Met (Exhibit 6) (Rev. 1, 10-01-03) A3-3418.12.E

Exhibit 6—Letter if Waiver Criteria Are Not Met

The contractor sends the Standard Letter Denying Waiver Request shown below, providing a full explanation of the reasons for the denial. Use of this letter is mandatory. Substitutes may **not** be used. The contractor retains copies for the file.

STANDARD LETTER DENYING WAIVER REQUEST

Medicare Beneficiary
HIC # XXX-XX-XXXX

We have completed our review of your request for waiver of the outstanding Medicare claim against the settlement or recovery proceeds you have received with respect to your accident. It is our determination that your circumstances do not fall within the criteria used to grant waiver, as set forth in our letter to you dated. These circumstances are:

[Insert substantive and fact-driven reasoning, applying the waiver criteria and explaining how particular expenses were or were not accident-related. Be sure to address or rebut the beneficiary's reasons for requesting a waiver, including if no reason was given.] For these reasons, we are denying your request that Medicare waive its recovery.

Medicare's conditional payment in this case was $ _____. The liability settlement received was $ _____. The procurement costs totaled $ _____. After allowing $ _____ as Medicare's share of procurement costs under 42 C.F.R 411.37(c), Medicare has a claim in the amount of $ _____ against your settlement or recovery proceeds. Also, on (date that exhibit 2 was sent) _____, we notified you that interest would be assessed on any debt not repaid in full within 60 days of that date, regardless of whether you chose to appeal or to seek waiver of the debt. We advised you that repaying the debt would not have affect your right to dispute, appeal, or request waiver of the debt.

Because you did not repay the debt within 60 days of (date that exhibit 2 was sent), you owe Medicare $ _____ in interest charges.

Therefore, in accordance with this determination, the amount which must be repaid to Medicare is $ _____. A check in the amount of $ _____, made payable to Medicare, should be sent within 30 days of your receipt of this determination in the enclosed envelope to:

Medicare contractor
Address

Your/the beneficiary's name and health insurance claim number should be included on the check made payable to Medicare.

If you disagree with the decision not to grant waiver of recovery of this overpayment, you have 60 days from the date you receive this letter to request a reconsideration. The request can be submitted directly to the address above.

If you decide to exercise your appeal rights, and if you want help with your appeal, you can have a friend, lawyer, or someone else help you. There are groups, such as lawyer referral services and public interest advocacy groups, that can help you find a lawyer.

There are also groups, such as legal aide services, who provide free legal services if you meet eligibility requirements. Should you/your client have any questions concerning this letter, please contact _____ on _____.

Medicare Contractor
Enclosure(s)

50.7—Waiver and/or Compromise Exercised Only by CMS
   (Rev. 1, 10-01-03)

50.7.1—Waiver Under 1862(b) of the Social Security Act
   (Rev. 1, 10-01-03)
   A3-3418.15
   This section of the Act grants the Secretary the right to waive MSP liability recoveries if doing so would be "in the best interests of the program." Authority to grant waivers under this section of the Act may be exercised only by CMS CO or RO staff. Waivers granted under this authority may not be appealed because they are granted at CMS' discretion. (See 42 C.F.R. 405.705(d).)

50.7.2—Compromise of Claim, or Suspension or Termination of Collection, Under the Federal Claims Collection Act (31 U.S.C. 3711)
   (Rev. 1, 10-01-03)
   A3-3418.16
   This statutory provision gives Federal agencies the authority to compromise where:

- The cost of collection does not justify the enforced collection of the full amount of the claim;

- There is an inability to pay within a reasonable time on the part of the individual against whom the claim is made; or

- The chances of successful litigation are questionable, making it advisable to seek a compromise settlement.

   These criteria are provided here for contractor information, since only RO or CO staff, not Medicare contractors, are permitted to compromise Medicare claims. If a beneficiary, attorney, or beneficiary's representative offers to pay Medicare less than the full amount of its claim, the contractor informs the inquiring party of their rights to request waiver, appeal, or compromise of the claim. It advises them that while contractors may assist them in securing a waiver or appeal, contractors are not permitted to compromise claims on behalf of the United States Government. Then, it follows the instructions at §50.4.2, which provide that a resolution through the FCCA is available **through the RO** at any time after the contractor is aware that Medicare has made conditional payments in a liability situation.
   When a beneficiary agrees to a compromise settlement under the FCCA, the beneficiary also agrees not to appeal the matter further.

CHAPTER **10**

DUAL ELIGIBILITY: ISSUES FOR MEDICARE BENEFICIARIES ALSO ELIGIBLE FOR MEDICAID

§10.01   INTRODUCTION

About 7.5 million older people and people with disabilities are eligible for both Medicare and some form of Medicaid. These beneficiaries are rather inartfully referred to as "dual eligibles," because of their simultaneous entitlement to Medicare and Medicaid.[1] Their demographic and health utilization characteristics distinguish them from other Medicare beneficiaries. Generally speaking, they are poorer and sicker than the rest of the Medicare population. They use the emergency room more often and fewer have a particular doctor. They are 16 percent of the Medicare population but account for 24 percent of Medicare expenditures.[2] They are 14 percent of the Medicaid population but account for 40 percent of Medicaid expenditures.[3]

For those eligible for Medicare Parts A and B and for full Medicaid benefits, Medicaid provides wrap-around coverage, operating as a Medigap policy—both by paying some or all of the Medicare cost-sharing requirements and by extending coverage, since Medicaid fills the gaping hole that exists in the Medicare program coverage due to the lack of comprehensive long-term care coverage. (Prior to January 1, 2006, Medicaid also provided prescription drug coverage for dual eligibles since, prior to that date, Medicare provided only very limited drug coverage.

Ironically, entitlement to the benefits of both Medicare and Medicaid can result in less rather than more health care. This is due at least in part to confusion that arises from statutory and regulatory differences between the two programs. Medicare and Medicaid are programs with different medical necessity definitions, coverage definitions, provider participation requirements, and reimbursement structures.

For those dually eligible who are entitled to full Medicaid benefits, Medicaid is the payer of last resort. Generally, in fee for service Medicare, this means that Medicare determines the allowable amount, pays its portion, then sends the remainder of the bill to Medicaid to pay the balance. However, when the Medicare allowable amount is either more or less than the Medicaid reimbursement for the same service, when the definition of what the covered service is differs, or when the Medicare beneficiary is enrolled in a managed care program, administrative and other complications can result in the beneficiary's being denied access to care or having his or her care delayed.

Starting January 1, 2006, dually eligible beneficiaries were no longer eligible for prescription drug coverage under Medicaid.[4] They are entitled to Medicare

---

[1] *Dual Eligibles: Medicaid's Role for Low-Income Medicare Beneficiaries,* The Kaiser Commission on Medicaid and the Uninsured: Medicaid Facts (Feb. 2006).

[2] Medicare Payment Advisory Commission (MedPac), "A Data Book- Health Care Spending and the Medicare Program (June 2006).

[3] *Dual Eligibles: Medicaid's Role for Low-Income Medicare Beneficiaries,* The Kaiser Commission on Medicaid and the Uninsured: Medicaid Facts (Feb. 2006).

[4] 42 U.S.C. §1396u-5(d)(1).

Part D prescription drug coverage and were automatically enrolled in a Part D plan if they had not chosen a plan on their own by December 31, 2005.[5] This change is discussed in detail in **Chapter 11** on Prescription Drug Coverage. As beneficiaries become newly dually eligible, they will also be enrolled in plans if they have not chosen one themselves.

This chapter discusses and analyzes issues that affect dually eligible individuals. It includes descriptions of Medicaid eligibility and services as they pertain to Medicare beneficiaries.

§10.02   PROFILE OF THE DUALLY ELIGIBLE[6]

[A]   Demographic Data

Compared with other Medicare beneficiaries, those who are dually eligible are both older and younger, poorer, more often minorities, disproportionately women, more likely to never have been married, and much more likely to be in an institution. They are considerably less well educated.

- *Older.* 15 percent are over age 85, compared with 11 percent of non-dually eligible beneficiaries.

- *Younger.* 37 percent are under 65, compared with 10 percent of non-dually eligible beneficiaries.

- *Poorer.* They are more than six times as likely to have incomes below $10,000.

- *Disproportionately minority.* They are about three times as likely to belong to a racial or ethnic minority.

- *Disproportionately women.* 62 percent are women, compared with 55 percent of non-dually eligible beneficiaries.

- *More likely to be in an institution.* They are seven times more likely to be in an institution than non-dually eligible Medicare beneficiaries.[7]

- *Less well educated.* They are more than twice as likely to have no high school diploma and considerably less than half as likely to have attended some college.

---

[5] 42 U.S.C. §1396u-5(c)(6).

[6] Profile compiled from several sources. MedPac, "A Data Book—Health Care Spending and the Medicare Program" (June 2006); *Dual Eligibles: Medicaid's Role for Low-Income Medicare Beneficiaries,* The Kaiser Commission on Medicaid and the Uninsured: Medicaid Facts (Feb. 2006); CMS "The Characteristics and Perceptions of the Medicare Population (2002) Section 8 How do Dual Eligible Medicare Beneficiaries compare to Non Dual Eligible Beneficiaries." <http://www.cms.hhs.gov/apps/mcbs/CMSsrc/2002/sec8.pdf> (site visited July 14, 2006).

[7] Institutionalization, in fact, is likely to *create* dual eligibility, since it is the most common path to Medicaid eligibility for older people. That is to say, people become eligible for Medicaid because the cost of nursing home care far exceeds their income, so, in the parlance of the Medicaid program, they become "medically needy."

[B] Health and Functional Status of the Dually Eligible

Compared with other Medicare beneficiaries, dually eligible beneficiaries are more likely to need help with activities of daily living (ADLs), have significantly worse self-reported health status, are more likely to have chronic or serious medical conditions, and are more likely to have cognitive impairments.

- *ADLs.* They are nearly twice as likely to have limitations with one or more ADLs (walking, toileting, eating, dressing, bathing, and transferring).

- *Self-reported health status.* They are more than twice as likely to self-report poor health.

- *Chronic or serious medical conditions.* They are more likely to have stroke, diabetes, and other chronic conditions.

- *Cognitive impairments.* They are four times more likely to have Alzheimer's disease.

§10.03   SUMMARY OF MEDICAID ELIGIBILITY AND MEDICAID BENEFITS

Unlike Medicare, Medicaid is a needs-based program, which means that all those who receive benefits do so by virtue of having very low incomes and resources and/or very high medical bills. In addition to being poor or near poor, an individual must fit into a category that is covered by a state's Medicaid program. States must cover some categories of individuals and are given the option to cover others. Among those to whom they must provide full Medicaid coverage are very poor—incomes at or below 75 percent of the federal income poverty guidelines—aged, blind, and disabled individuals; in addition, they must provide Medicare cost-sharing coverage for poor Medicare beneficiaries called Qualified Medicare Beneficiaries (QMBs), and premium payments for near poor Medicare beneficiaries called Specified Low-income Medicare Beneficiaries (SLMBs),[8] Qualified Disabled and Working Individuals (QDWIs),[9] and Qualified Individuals (QIs).[10] Collectively, these programs are known as the Medicare Savings Programs (MSPs).

Generally speaking, states use the same methodology for determining eligibility for Medicaid, QMB, SLMB, QDWI, and QI eligibility that is used for determining eligibility for the Supplemental Security Income (SSI) program. This methodology allows a disregard of $20 of unearned income per month, as well

---

[8] See **§10.04[B].**

[9] See **§10.04[D][2].**

[10] *See id.* For this group, coverage need only be provided up to the limit of the state's block grant. Coverage for QI-1s has been extended through the end of fiscal year 2007.

as a disregard of the first $65 per month of earned income, plus one-half the remainder.[11] Other disregards are available for individuals with specific circumstances, such as amounts set aside in a plan for achieving self-support.[12] Certain resources are excluded from consideration, including the homestead, personal possessions, a car, a burial plot, a separate burial fund, and a very limited amount of life insurance.[13] States may use methodologies for determining Medicaid and MSP eligibility that are more generous than SSI's, but not less generous.[14] In 2005, about 40 states use some methodology that is more generous than SSI's, at least for their MSP programs.[15]

Individuals who qualify for full Medicaid benefits do so by fitting into one of many categories or groups:

1. Individuals who receive SSI or a mandatory state supplement to SSI;[16]

2. Individuals who formerly received SSI and are qualified severely impaired individuals, as defined by law, who qualify for SSI if their earnings are not counted;[17]

3. Individuals who formerly received SSI and are in one of several categories of people deemed to receive SSI in order to ensure continued Medicaid coverage.[18]

---

[11] 42 U.S.C. §1382a(b)(2)(A), (b)(4); 20 C.F.R. §§416.1112, 416.1124.

[12] 20 C.F.R. §416.1112(c).

[13] 42 U.S.C. §1382b; 20 C.F.R. §416.1210.

[14] 42 U.S.C. §1396a(r)(2).

[15] This estimate is based on data gathered in a soon-to-be published survey of state Medicaid programs, but is not 100 percent reliable as not all states have verified the accuracy of the data collected from various Internet sources. Survey results will be published in a report to be issued in 2005, prepared by the Center for Medicare Advocacy, Inc. for the Kaiser Family Foundation. *See, generally*, Patricia B. Nemore, Jacqueline A. Bender, and Wey-Wey Kwok, "Toward Making Medicare Work for Low-Income Beneficiaries: A Baseline Comparison of the Part D Low-Income Subsidy and Medicare Savings Programs Eligibility and Enrollment Rules," Kaiser Family Foundation (May 2006).

[16] 42 U.S.C. §1396a(a)(10)(A)(i)(II); 42 U.S.C. §1396a note, referring to 13(c) of Pub. L. No. 93-233. Individuals are entitled to a mandatory state supplement if they were receiving supplemental assistance from their state prior to the start of the federal SSI program. The provision was intended to ensure that such individuals did not receive less assistance under SSI than they had previously received through their state program.

[17] 42 U.S.C. §1396d(q).

[18] These are "Pickle people," who have received SSI in the past and who would continue to be eligible for SSI but for cost-of-living increases in Title II in 1977 and thereafter, 42 U.S.C. §1396a note; "Kennelly Widows," who are widows and widowers between age 60 and age 65 who lose SSI due to eligibility for early widows' benefits under the Social Security survivors program and are considered to be receiving SSI for Medicaid eligibility purposes until they are entitled to Medicare at age 65, 42 U.S.C. §1383c(d); disabled adult children (DACs) who are individuals age 18 and over who had received SSI based on a disability that began before age 22 and who subsequently became eligible for children's benefits under Title II. They are deemed eligible for SSI for Medicaid purposes.

Generally speaking, each of these three paths to Medicaid eligibility must be included in a state's Medicaid program; individuals in these categories are referred to as mandatory categorically eligible.[19] In addition, states have the option of choosing to cover other groups:

1. Individuals who are eligible for but not receiving SSI or an optional state supplement.[20]

2. Individuals who have been in an institution for 30 days and who meet an income standard set by the state equal to or less than 300 percent of the SSI federal benefit rate.[21]

3. Individuals who receive home and community-based services under a waiver of certain Medicaid requirements,[22] or under a State Plan Amendment as authorized by the Deficit Reduction Act of 2005.[23]

4. Individuals who would be eligible if they were in an institution, who are terminally ill, and who receive only hospice care.[24]

5. Individuals who receive an optional state supplement to SSI.[25]

6. Individuals who are aged or disabled with income under 100 percent of the federal poverty level.[26]

---

42 U.S.C. §1383c(c). A fourth category of "deemed SSI recipients" are children who lost SSI due to a change in eligibility rules in the 1996 welfare law. These children are unlikely to be Medicare beneficiaries and therefore are unlikely to be dually eligible.

[19] The exception to coverage of these otherwise mandatory categories is for states that have chosen the so-called 209(b) option. This option, named for the section of the public law in which it was enacted, is set out at 42 U.S.C. §1396a(f). It permits states to use more restrictive eligibility rules, if they expressly choose to do so. When Congress enacted the all-federal SSI program, replacing federal-state programs of aid to the aged, blind, and disabled, it provided states with an option to otherwise mandatory Medicaid coverage: they may establish eligibility standards in their Medicaid program that are more restrictive than SSI, but no more restrictive than the eligibility rules that were in effect in the state in January 1972. Congress provided this option to encourage states that would have had dramatic increases in their Medicaid populations due to the higher SSI standards not to drop out of Medicaid altogether. Eleven states currently use this option: Connecticut, Hawaii, Illinois, Indiana, Minnesota, Missouri, New Hampshire, North Dakota, Ohio, Oklahoma, and Virginia.

[20] 42 U.S.C. §1396a(a)(10)(A)(ii)(I).

[21] 42 U.S.C. §1396a(a)(10)(A)(ii)(V). Identifying states that have chosen this option is more difficult than one would think. For reasons unfathomable to the authors, every reliable source of information on this subject lists the states somewhat differently. As best as can be determined, through a recently undertaken survey relying on various sources, current "income cap" states are Alabama, Alaska, Arizona, Colorado, Delaware, Georgia, Idaho, Mississippi, Nevada, New Mexico, Oregon, South Carolina, South Dakota, Texas, and Wyoming.

[22] 42 U.S.C. §1396a(a)(10)(A)(ii)(VI).

[23] Pub. L. No. 109-171, §6086 amending 42 U.S.C. §1396n by adding subsection (i).

[24] 42 U.S.C. §1396a(a)(10)(A)(ii)(VII).

[25] 42 U.S.C. §1396a(a)(10)(A)(ii)(XI).

[26] 42 U.S.C. §1396a(a)(10)(A)(ii)(X), referring to §1396a(m)(1).

7. Individuals who are aged, blind, or disabled and are "medically needy" due to high medical bills.[27] Individuals in this group must show incurred or paid medical expenses that, when deducted from their income, reduce their income to an amount called the Medically Needy Income Level (MNIL), which is often substantially below the SSI benefit rate.[28] The amount of incurred or paid medical expense they must document is referred to as their "spenddown."

Individuals in groups 1 through 6 are referred to as the Optional Categorically Needy; individuals in group 7 are referred to as the Medically Needy.

States are required to provide certain services to the Mandatory and Optional Categorically Needy, and have the option of including other services. Required Medicaid services are:

- Inpatient hospital services;

- Outpatient hospital services;

- Laboratory and x-ray services;

- Nursing facility services for people age 21 or over;

- Early and periodic screening, diagnosis, and treatment for people under 21;

- Family planning services and supplies for individuals of child-bearing age;

- Physicians' services and some dental services;

- Midwife services;

- Services furnished by certain certified nurse practitioners; and

- Home health services for people entitled to nursing facility services.[29]

---

[27] 42 U.S.C. §1396a(a)(10)(C), referring to 42 U.S.C. §1396d(a).

[28] The MNIL has been limited for years by statutory language that prohibits federal Medicaid payments for people with incomes in excess of 133-1/3 percent of the state's standard for a family receiving Aid to Families with Dependent Children (AFDC). 42 U.S.C. §1396b(f). This standard, in most states, was substantially below federal poverty levels and even below the SSI level, which is 75 percent of the poverty level. Although AFDC was repealed in 1996 and replaced with a block grant called Temporary Assistance for Needy Families, the old AFDC standard, indexed for inflation, is still used. A separate statutory provision, at 42 U.S.C. §1396a(r)(2), permits states to use methodologies for determining eligibility for Medicaid that are less restrictive than the income program they relate to, but not more restrictive. The Health Care Financing Administration (HCFA), then the name of the federal agency that administers Medicare and Medicaid (now called the Centers for Medicare and Medicaid Services (CMS)), interpreted that provision as being circumscribed by the payment limit provision. An amendment to the regulation at 42 C.F.R. §435.1007 that became effective August 4, 2001, changes that interpretation to allow states to apply their less restrictive methodologies to income *before* measuring it against the payment limit. 66 Fed. Reg. 33,810 (June 25, 2001).

[29] 42 U.S.C. §1396a(a)(10)(D), referring to 42 U.S.C. §1396d(a).

Optional services include:

- Prescription drugs (but not after December 31, 2005 for the dually eligible);
- Physical therapy;
- Occupational therapy;
- Dentures;
- Prosthetic devices;
- Eyeglasses;
- Personal care;
- Podiatry;
- Optometry; and
- Transportation.

Generally speaking, when a state offers an optional service to one group of categorically needy individuals, it must offer the same service to all groups.[30] It does not have to offer all services to the Medically Needy.

Because Medicare is the primary payer for those who are dually eligible, some Medicaid services are more important to these beneficiaries than others. Prescription drug coverage, for example, was a Medicaid service that filled a gap in Medicare coverage (until January 1, 2006); older people and people with disabilities tend to have high prescription drug usage.[31] Another significant Medicaid service for this population is long-term care, both in an institution and in the community. It is, therefore, extremely useful to low-income Medicare beneficiaries to qualify for full Medicaid benefits in addition to assistance with Medicare cost-sharing.

---

[30] 42 U.S.C. §1396a(a)(10)(B)(i) (services shall be not less in amount, duration, and scope than those available to other categorically needy groups); 42 C.F.R. §440.240(b). *But see*, Deficit Reduction Act of 2005, Pub. L. No. 109-171, §6044 that allows states to establish specific benefit packages for specific groups of people. Dual eligibles are exempt from coverage under this new option.

[31] *See, e.g.*, Harriet L. Komisar, Judith Feder, Judity Kasper, *Unmet Long-Term Care Needs: An Analysis of Medicare-Medicaid Dual Eligibles* (The Commonwealth Fund Oct. 2005 Vol. 14) <http://www.cmwf.org/publications/publications_show.htm?doc_id=307206> (site visited July 18, 2006); *Dual Eligibles: Medicaid's Role for Low-Income Medicare Beneficiaries,* The Kaiser Commission on Medicaid and the Uninsured: Medicaid Facts (Feb. 2006); Becky Briesacher, Bruce Stuart, Jalpa Doshi, Sachin Kamal-Bahl, & Dennis Shea, *Medicare's Disabled Beneficiaries: The Forgotten Population in the Debate over Drug Benefits* (The Commonwealth Fund Sept. 2002); Issue Brief: "Dual Eligibles: Medicaid's Role in Filling Medicare's Gaps," Kaiser Commission on Medicaid and the Uninsured (Mar. 2004). As noted elsewhere, in January 2006, dual eligibles began to get prescription drug coverage only through Medicare's new Part D benefit. Federal Medicaid dollars will not be available to provide wrap-around coverage even for drugs not included in an individual's Part D plan.

§10.04   UNIVERSE OF DUAL ELIGIBILITY

[A]   Categories of Dually Eligible Individuals

The term "dually eligible" is used differently in different settings or situations. It is helpful to understand the categories that may be included in references to dual eligibility so as to begin an analysis with a common understanding of the terminology. The federal Centers for Medicare and Medicaid Services (CMS), which administers the Medicare program and, in partnership with the states, the Medicaid program, describes a broad universe in its definition of dual eligibility.[32] CMS's universe comprises three primary subgroups of low-income Medicare beneficiaries:

1. QMBs or SLMBs either with full Medicaid benefits and Medicare cost-sharing (QMB or SLMB-plus) or with Medicare cost-sharing assistance, but without any additional Medicaid coverage (QMB or SLMB-only);

2. Individuals with full Medicaid benefits but not Medicare cost-sharing as QMBs or SLMBs;

3. Individuals entitled to Medicaid benefits only to pay for Medicare premiums, with no additional Medicaid coverage for other Medicare out-of-pocket costs, and without full Medicaid benefits. This category comprises, in addition to the SLMB-only named above, two different groups:
    (a) QI-1s[33]
    (b) QDWIs

Most data sources, including the GAO, do not reflect a separate count of QDWI enrollment; a 1999 survey of all state Medicaid programs yielded the number 41 for nationwide QDWI enrollment.[34]

It is useful to understand that the Medicare Prescription Drug, Improvement, and Modernization Act of 2003 (MMA)[35] uses a different definition of dual eligible. It refers to "full benefit dual eligibles" and defines those people as Medicare beneficiaries entitled to full Medicaid benefits.[36] This definition excludes those in group 3 above, as well as those in group 1 who receive assistance only with Medicare cost sharing.

---

[32] "List and Definition of Medicare/Medicaid Dual Eligibles," found at <http://www.cms.hhs.gov/DualEligible/02_DualEligibleCategories.asp#TopOfPage> (site visited June 16, 2006).

[33] QI-1s are authorized through fiscal year 2007, which ends September 30, 2007. Another group, QI-2, was authorized from 1998 through 2002. The authorization for that group was not renewed.

[34] Patricia B. Nemore, *Variations in State Medicaid Buy-in Practices for Low-Income Medicare Beneficiaries: A 1999 Update*, prepared for the Henry J. Kaiser Family Foundation (Dec. 1999).

[35] Pub. L. No. 108-173 (Dec. 8, 2003), adding 42 U.S.C. §§1395w-101 *et seq.* (2005 supplement).

[36] 42 U.S.C. §1396u-5(c)(6); 42 C.F.R. §423.902.

[B] QMB or SLMB with Full Medicaid Benefits and Medicare Cost Sharing (QMB/SLMB-Plus) or with Only Medicare Cost-Sharing Assistance (QMB/SLMB-Only)

A QMB is an aged or disabled individual with Medicare Part A whose countable income is at or below the federal poverty level and whose countable resources are less than $4,000 ($6,000 for a couple).[37] The QMB benefit is payment by Medicaid of the cost sharing that is imposed on a Medicare beneficiary, that is, the Medicare Part B premium, which would otherwise generally be deducted automatically from the Social Security or Railroad Retirement check each month, the Part A premium for voluntary enrollees (i.e., those who do not receive premium-free Part A), as well as all deductibles and coinsurance imposed under Medicare Part A and Medicare Part B and copayments charged by Medicare Advantage Plans.[38] States have the option of paying premiums or enrollment fees charged by MA Plans.[39] In essence, the QMB benefit operates like a basic Medicare supplemental health insurance policy (often called a "Medigap" policy). QMB coverage can save a recipient hundreds or even thousands of dollars each year.[40] Unlike virtually all other Medicaid benefits, QMB coverage cannot be granted for months prior to the application.[41] The benefit is available in the first month after the month eligibility is determined.[42] An individual can be eligible for both the QMB benefit and full Medicaid coverage, or for only the QMB benefit.

A SLMB is an individual who would be a QMB but for his or her countable income, which must be between 100 and 120 percent of the federal

---

[37] The eligibility level for 2006, beginning in March, is $ 837 per month for an individual in the 48 states, slightly higher for those in Alaska and Hawaii. The amount includes a $20-per-month federally mandated income disregard that is available to all applicants. In addition to the $20, states must disregard a portion of earned income and may disregard other income, effectively expanding coverage. Likewise, they may offer more generous resource exclusions than federal law requires. About 40 states have some provision for MSP populations that is more generous than the federal rules. Income Poverty Guidelines are published each year in February or March by the Department of Health and Human Services. The new poverty rates are effective for the MSP programs in the month following publication.

[38] 42 U.S.C. §§1396d(p)(3), 1396a(n)(2); Medicaid Manual (SMM) Part 3, Eligibility (HCFA Pub. 45) 3490.12. See **Appendix 10-1**. *See also* Memorandum of November 22, 1991, from Director, Office of Medicaid Management, MB, Subject: State Requirement to Pay Premiums for Qualified Medicare Beneficiaries (QMB)—ACTION to Deputy Chief Counsel, Office of General Counsel. See **Appendix 10-2.**

[39] 42 U.S.C. §§1396d(p)(3), 1396a(n)(2); Medicaid Manual (SMM) Part 3, Eligibility (HCFA Pub. 45).

[40] The Congressional Budget Office estimates Medicare cost-sharing at $3,000 for 2006. Congressional Budget Office (CBO) "A Detailed Description of CBS's Cost Estimate for Medicare Prescription Drug Benefit" (July 2004). <http://www.cbo.gov/showdoc.cfm?index=5668&sequence=0> (site visited July 14, 2006).

[41] 42 U.S.C. §1396d(a).

[42] *Id.*

poverty level.[43] The SLMB benefit is payment by Medicaid of the Medicare Part B premium. Thus, a SLMB does not have the Medicare Part B premium deducted from his or her Social Security or Railroad Retirement check each month. However, unlike the QMB benefit, no additional Medicare cost-sharing is included in the SLMB benefit. A SLMB without full Medicaid coverage should consider the need for a Medicare supplemental (Medigap) policy to cover the costs of other Medicare out-of-pocket expenses, such as copayments and deductibles. SLMB coverage can be granted for up to three months prior to the date of application if the individual was eligible during those months.[44] An individual could be eligible for both SLMB benefits and full Medicaid benefits or for only SLMB benefits.

[C]   Recipients of Full Medicaid Benefits But Not Full Medicare Cost Sharing as a QMB

These individuals are receiving Medicare Part A and/or Medicare Part B and receive full Medicaid benefits. The group comprises two slightly different populations. First, there are those whose incomes are under 100 percent of poverty, but who do not have Part A premium free and whose state does not pay their Part A premium for them. The lack of Part A prevents them from being QMBs and thus entitled to full Medicare benefits, which may include better hospitalization, home health, or rehabilitation therapy coverage than they have under their state Medicaid program. CMS has told states they must purchase Part A for their Medicaid recipients whose income is under 100 percent of poverty to ensure their enrollment as QMBs.[45] CMS has not, however, enforced this requirement.

The second group comprises those whose income is above 100 percent of poverty who are precluded from QMB coverage for that reason, even if they have Medicare Part A. Generally, these would be individuals entitled to Medicaid under a special income cap or as medically needy because they are receiving costly long-term care services or, prior to January 1, 2006, had high prescription drug costs. If they are not entitled to payment of their Medicare Part B premium as SLMBs, the state nonetheless has the option of paying their Part B premium.[46] If the state

---

[43] 42 U.S.C. §1396a(a)(10)(E)(iii). The eligibility limit for SLMB for 2006 is $1,000 monthly for an individual in the 48 states, slightly higher for Alaska and Hawaii. This amount includes the $20 income disregard.

[44] 42 U.S.C. §1396d(a).

[45] State Medicaid Manual (SMM), Part 3, Eligibility (HCFA Pub. 45) 3490.13, *Payment of Monthly Premiums for Medicare Part B and for Premium Hospital Insurance Under Medicare Part A. See* **Appendix 10-1**. *See also* Memorandum of Nov. 22, 1991, from Director, Office of Medicaid Management, MB, Subject: State Requirement to Pay Medicare Premiums for Qualified Medicare Beneficiaries (QMB)—ACTION to Deputy Chief Counsel, Office of the General Counsel. *See* **Appendix 10-2**.

[46] 42 U.S.C. §1395v authorizes states to enter into "buy-in" agreements with the federal Centers for Medicare and Medicaid Services through which states purchase Medicare Part B coverage for

chooses not to pay the Part B premium, it cannot receive its federal share of the Medicaid payment for a Medicaid service that is also covered by Medicare Part B if the individual could have been enrolled in Part B but was not.[47]

[D] Recipients of Medicaid Payments for Medicare Premiums Only

In addition to individuals with SLMB-only eligibility who are entitled to payment only of the Medicare Part B premium, two other groups are entitled to Medicaid payments only for Medicare premiums. To be eligible for either of these benefits, an individual cannot otherwise be eligible for Medicaid, i.e., cannot be eligible for full Medicaid benefits.

[1] Qualified Individual-1 (QI-1)

This group comprises individuals with Medicare Part A whose countable income is between 120 percent and 135 percent of poverty and whose countable resources are twice those allowed for SSI, $4,000 for an individual and $6,000 for a couple.[48] The benefit for a QI-1 is payment of the Part B premium, from a block grant to the state that was authorized to be available from January 1998 through December 2002.[49] The benefit has been extended through September 2007 the end of fiscal year 2007.[50]

Although the QI-1 benefit is the same amount as the SLMB benefit, the difference between the two programs, in addition to the higher eligibility threshold for QI-1, is that SLMB is an entitlement for the individual and QI-1 is not. Thus, all individuals who are found eligible for SLMB will receive the benefit; individuals found eligible for QI-1 will receive the benefit only as long as the state still has

---

Medicaid recipients; 42 U.S.C. §1395i-2(g) authorizes modifications of such agreements to permit the states also to purchase Part A. *See* 42 C.F.R. §407.42 for the eligibility groups that states can include in their buy-in agreements, and 42 C.F.R. §431.625 for authorization for states to receive federal matching dollars, known as federal financial participation (FFP) for their buy-in costs. 42 U.S.C. §1395v can be found at **Appendix 10-5**.

[47] 42 U.S.C. §1396b(b)(1), 42 C.F.R. §431.625(d)(3). *See also* Medicaid Source Book: Background Data and Analysis 366 (1993 Update), A Report prepared by the Congressional Research Service for the Subcommittee on Health and the Environment of the Committee on Energy and Commerce, U.S. House of Representatives (Jan. 1993). According to a report from the Kaiser Commission on Medicaid and the Uninsured, 19 states do not pay Medicare premiums for their medically needy beneficiaries. Stephanie E. Anthony, Christy Schroer, Sharon Silow-Carroll, & Jack A. Meyer, *Medicaid Managed Care for Dual Eligibles: State Profiles 101* (The Henry J. Kaiser Family Foundation, Oct. 2000).

[48] 42 U.S.C. §1396a(a)(10)(E)(iv)(I). The monthly income eligibility limit for QI-1 for 2006 is $1,122.50 for an individual in the 48 states, slightly higher for Alaska and Hawaii.

[49] 42 U.S.C. §1396u-3(d).

[50] Pub. L. No. 109-91 (Oct. 20, 2005).

funds in its block grant. States must pay the benefit on a first-come, first-served basis, and while individuals must reapply each year, priority is given to those who received the benefit in the previous year.[51] Recipients are entitled to three months retroactive coverage if they were eligible in the three months prior to their application.[52]

[2] Qualified Disabled and Working Individual

A Qualified Disabled and Working Individual (QDWI) is an individual who is disabled and working under a work incentive plan, who has exhausted premium-free Part A coverage (available for a period of eight and one-half years, including a trial work period) under such plan, whose countable income is not more than 200 percent of poverty and whose countable resources are not more than twice those allowed for SSI.[53] The benefit for a QDWI is payment for the Medicare Part A premium, not the Part B premium. (A QDWI wanting Part B would have to pay for it himself or herself.) Like the QMB and SLMB benefit, the QDWI benefit is an entitlement so that anyone found eligible should get it. Like SLMB and QI-1, QDWI is available up to three months prior to application, if the individual was eligible during those months.

§10.05   ENROLLMENT ISSUES FOR MEDICARE SAVINGS PROGRAMS POPULATION

[A] Overview

Medicare Savings Programs (MSP)[54]—QMB, SLMB, QI-1, and QDWI—that pay all or some of the Medicare out-of-pocket costs provide critical links to the health care system for low-income Medicare beneficiaries. Without help paying for Medicare cost-sharing, beneficiaries may either forgo health care for which they must pay or forgo other necessities of life such as food, clothing, or utility payments, in order to be able to pay their out-of-pocket medical costs. Yet an estimated 67 percent of those eligible for QMB-only benefits, and about 87 percent of those

---

[51] 42 U.S.C. §1396u-3(b).

[52] 42 U.S.C. §1396d.

[53] 42 U.S.C. §§1396a(a)(10)(E)(ii), 1396d(s). For 2006, the monthly income limit for an individual in the 48 states is $1,653, slightly higher for Alaska and Hawaii.

[54] Past editions of this Handbook have referred to these programs as "buy-in programs," following the common terminology used among advocates until recent years. A few years ago, CMS formally named the programs collectively the Medicare Savings Programs; that is now the name most commonly used.

eligible for SLMB benefits, are not participating in the programs.[55] Barriers to program participation have been identified in numerous reports:

- Very restrictive asset ceilings used in determining eligibility;

- Lack of effective outreach to program beneficiaries;

- Lack of knowledge of the programs on the part of welfare workers, Social Security employees, and community-based organizations;

- Cumbersome and obstacle-laden enrollment processes that require long waits in welfare offices, face-to-face interviews, and extensive documentation of income and assets;

- Difficulties with language and transportation; and

- Medicaid rules, such as required estate recovery.[56]

Some of these problems arise because MSP benefits are disconnected from the Medicare program: instead of applying for Medicare and MSP at the same time and place, an individual must go through the Social Security Administration for Medicare and through the state Medicaid or welfare system for MSP benefits.[57]

---

[55] The Congressional Budget Office estimates Medicare cost-sharing at $3,000 for 2006. Congressional Budget Office (CBO) "A Detailed Description of CBS's Cost Estimate for Medicare Prescription Drug Benefit" (July 2004). <www.cbo.gov/showdoc.cfm?index=5668&sequence=0> (site visited July 14, 2006).

[56] Jack Ebeler, Paul N. Van de Water, and Cyanne Demchak (ed.) 2006 "Improving the Medicare Savings Programs." (Washington: National Academy of Social Insurance 2006); Dalia K. Remler and Sherry A. Glied "What Other Programs Can Teach Us: Increasing Participation in Health Insurance Programs." *American Journal of Public Health,* January 2003, Kim Glaun, *Medicaid Programs to Assist Low-Income Medicare Beneficiaries: Medicare Savings Programs Case Study Findings,* prepared for the Kaiser Commission for Medicaid and the Uninsured (2003); Patricia B. Nemore, *Variations in State Medicaid Buy-in Practices for Low-Income Medicare Beneficiaries: A 1999 Update,* prepared for the Henry J. Kaiser Family Foundation (Dec. 1999); General Accounting Office, *Low-Income Medicare Beneficiaries: Further Outreach and Administrative Simplification Could Increase Enrollment,* GAO/HEHS-99-61 (Apr. 1999); AARP Pub. Pol'y Inst. *Bridging the Gaps Between Medicare and Medicaid: The Case of QMBs and SLMBs* (Washington, D.C., AARP Jan. 1999); Families USA, *Shortchanged: Billions Withheld from Medicare Beneficiaries* (Washington, D.C., Families USA 1998); Patricia B. Nemore, *Variations in State Medicaid Buy-in Practices for Low-Income Medicare Beneficiaries* (Washington, D.C., The Henry J. Kaiser Family Foundation, Nov. 1997); Peter J. Neumann, Mimi D. Bernardin, Ellen J. Bayer, and William N. Evans, *Identifying Barriers to Elderly Participation in the Qualified Medicare Beneficiary Program,* Final Report submitted to HCFA (1994); General Accounting Office, *Medicare and Medicaid— Many Eligible People Not Enrolled in Qualified Medicare Beneficiary Program,* GAO/HEHS-94-52 (Jan. 1994); Families USA, *The Medicare Buy-In: A Promise Unfulfilled* (Washington, D.C., Families USA Mar. 1993); Families USA, *The Medicare Buy-In: Still a Government Secret* (Washington, D.C., Families USA Mar. 1992); Families USA, *The Secret Benefit—The Failure to Provide the Medicare Buy-In to Poor Seniors* (Washington, D.C., Families USA 1991).

[57] The Medicare, Medicaid, and SCHIP Benefits Improvement and Protection Act of 2000, Pub. L. No. 106-554 (Dec. 21, 2000) (BIPA), included two provisions attempting to address enrollment

Other issues arise because MSP benefits are needs based, requiring people to both disclose information about their income and assets and provide documentation to support their disclosures. Several of the more complex issues are discussed below.

[B] Failure of State Medicaid Systems and Workers to Identify Buy-In Eligibility When Processing Medicaid Applications

State Medicaid agencies are required to operate their programs in a manner consistent with simplicity of administration and in the best interests of recipients.[58] The agency, moreover, must consider the applicant's eligibility for any program for which she qualifies.[59] Yet eligibility workers are often unfamiliar with the MSP programs and state Medicaid agencies fail to have computer prompts available for the workers to enhance the probability that Medicaid applicants will be properly screened. Because each state's Medicaid program has many paths to eligibility, it is difficult, if not impossible, for an applicant herself to identify with precision the particular coverage group for which she is applying. The applicant is unlikely to ask explicitly to be considered for full Medicaid, for QMB, for SLMB, and for QI, although in some states, the applicant must check off on the application all Medicaid categories for which she wishes to be considered.

Being screened for all possible categories of eligibility will matter if, for example, the applicant is found to have too much income to be eligible for the full package of Medicaid benefits, but little enough to qualify for an MSP program,[60] and the applicant should be considered for each one. However, if eligibility determination systems are not fully coordinated to ensure such a result, the applicant may be erroneously denied benefits.

A different MSP eligibility issue may arise every January when Social Security cost-of-living adjustments (COLAs) become effective. Because income poverty guidelines, which are also adjusted for inflation each year, are not published until February or March each year, effective the following month, there is a

---

difficulties experienced by those eligible for Medicare Savings Programs. One provision requires the Secretary of the Department of Health and Human Services to create a single simplified application form for MSP benefits that states may adopt if they choose. BIPA 709. This application form is available at <http://www.cms.hhs.gov/DualEligible/03_ModelApplicationforMedicareSavingsPrograms. asp#TopOfPage>; site visited on June 16, 2006. The second provision requires the Commissioner of the Social Security Administration to conduct outreach to identify individuals who might be eligible for MSP benefits, to notify them of their potential eligibility, and to notify each state of the names and addresses of those whom the Commissioner had identified who are residents of that state. BIPA 911.

[58] 42 U.S.C. §1396a(a)(19); 42 C.F.R. §435.902.

[59] 42 U.S.C. §1396a(a)(10); 42 C.F.R. §435.902; State Medicaid Manual 3490.3.

[60] Because MSP program eligibility is at or above 100 percent of poverty, and because the most available path to full Medicaid benefits for older people and people with disabilities is SSI eligibility, which is at about 75 percent of poverty, many people not eligible for full Medicaid could be eligible for one of the Medicare Savings Programs.

period of several months when an individual's income may exceed the poverty level standard for the MSP in which the individual is enrolled. Congress recognized the harm caused by this disconnect in operation of two different annual adjusters and amended the statute to require that Social Security cost-of-living increases must be disregarded in determining eligibility until the second month after the month in which new poverty guidelines are published.[61] Advocates may need to remind workers of the income disregard in the early months of each year.

These systems and worker failures to screen for MSP eligibility often result in dually eligible applicants being found eligible for categories of Medicaid that may not be as useful to them as MSP benefits would be. For example, an individual may be found eligible for a medically needy coverage group, with an income spend-down requirement, rather than for QMB benefits. Medically needy individuals must spend precious income on medical bills before their Medicaid entitlement is effective while remaining liable for all Medicare cost sharing or perhaps paying for a Medigap supplemental policy to cover some of the Medicare cost-sharing obligation. Conversely, it may be in an applicant's interest to forgo MSP benefits and use Medicare cost sharing, especially the monthly Part B premium payment, to meet a spenddown that would then grant access to full Medicaid benefits. In past years, this was most likely to be true if the individual's spenddown is small and her prescription drug costs, not then covered by Medicare but covered by Medicaid, were high. This particular situation is no longer relevant since dually eligible beneficiaries lost Medicaid prescription drug coverage in January 2006.

Similarly, institutionalized individuals may be found eligible for a long-term care coverage group with a share of cost obligation, with MSP entitlement never assessed. When this happens, they may incur two potential sources of liability to the nursing facility where none should be occurring: share of cost under Medicaid and a Medicare copayment charge for the 21st through the 100th day of a Medicare Part A covered stay. This issue is addressed in more detail at **§10.06.**

In these kinds of situations, advocates can assist their clients in evaluating trade-offs between Medicare Savings Program eligibility and full Medicaid eligibility through meeting a spenddown.

[C] Complexities of Enrolling in Medicare Part A for Eligibility for Qualified Medicare Beneficiary Benefits

To be eligible as a Qualified Medicare Beneficiary for state Medicaid payment of Medicare cost-sharing obligations, applicants must have Medicare Part A.[62] Most Medicare beneficiaries receive Part A without payment of a premium, due to receipt of Social Security income or related benefits, such as Civil Service or Railroad Retirement. Some people, however, are not entitled to

---

[61] 42 U.S.C. §1396d(p)(2)(D).

[62] 42 U.S.C. §1396d(p).

premium-free Medicare Part A. For example, individuals who do not have a long enough work history under the Social Security system may not have sufficient quarters of coverage to obtain Social Security benefits. Such individuals can purchase Part A for a premium of $393 per month in 2006 ($[] per month in 2007).[63] Purchase of Part A is called "voluntary enrollment."

The cost of the Medicare Part A premium represents a significant financial burden for lower income persons: it is nearly 50 percent of monthly income for a person in poverty. Although states are required to pay the Part A premium for QMBs who must voluntarily enroll,[64] an individual must have Part A to be eligible as a QMB. To circumvent this apparent Catch-22, in about 1989 the Health Care Financing Administration (HCFA), now CMS, created a "conditional" enrollment process, through which a potential QMB enrolls in Part A conditioned upon his or her being found eligible for QMB benefits.[65]

The conditional enrollment process is complex. The individual must contact a Social Security Administration office to enroll in Part A. She should attach a statement to her enrollment to the following effect:

> I wish to enroll for Hospital Insurance under Medicare on a monthly premium basis. I understand that the state will pay my premium based on my eligibility for Medicaid (Medical Assistance) as a Qualified Medicare Beneficiary. If my application for the Qualified Medicare Beneficiary Program is denied, this conditional application for Hospital Insurance will be dropped. I also understand that if I am terminated under Medicaid as a Qualified Medicare Beneficiary, I will have to pay my premium if I wish to keep my Medicare Hospital Insurance.

She then takes proof of her enrollment to the state Medicaid office, where she applies for QMB benefits, appending a copy of her Part A enrollment application to her Medicaid application.

Generally, persons who fail to voluntarily enroll in Medicare Parts A and B during their initial eligibility period (the seven months surrounding their 65th birthday) must wait for a general enrollment period to enroll. They are penalized financially for late enrollment and their Medicare coverage is not effective until July 1 of that year. A general enrollment period occurs only once each year from January through March.

For potential QMBs, states can avoid the enrollment limitations, the penalty, and even the complex conditional enrollment process by having buy-in agreements

---

[63] Those with at least 30 quarters of Social Security coverage pay a lower premium ($216 in 2006 and $[ ] in 2007).

[64] *See, e.g.*, Notice of Hearing: Reconsideration of Disapproval of Michigan State Plan Amendment, 57 Fed. Reg. 57,469 (Dec. 4, 1992).

[65] Advocates advising clients about conditional enrollment should first check with both their state Medicaid office and their local Social Security office. Despite the legal requirement for states to pay the Part A premium, where necessary, it is not clear that all states honor conditional enrollment, nor that all Social Security offices even know about it in those states that do honor it.

with the federal government that permit them to enroll individuals in Part A at any time of the year.[66] Not all states have such buy-in agreements, however; states without them effectively deny potential beneficiaries access to the QMB benefit during those nine months of the year when Medicare enrollment is closed and subject their applicants to the multi-step and complicated conditional enrollment process during the brief three-month general enrollment period.[67]

Even in the 36 jurisdictions (35 states and the District of Columbia) that do have Medicare Part A buy-in agreements authorizing enrollment in Medicare Part A at any time, significant barriers are sometimes placed in the way of applicants. In some such states, individuals are still directed to the Social Security Administration to enroll conditionally in Medicare.

Even individuals entitled to full *Medicaid* benefits may be put through the conditional enrollment hoops to get Medicare Part A if they are not already enrolled in Medicare Part A. This could be avoided because states have income and resource information on such individuals. States can already identify whether they are potential QMBs (i.e., under 100 percent of poverty), and, if they do not already have it, states can get Medicare information about such persons from CMS. Yet many states make little effort to identify these individuals so they can enroll them for Medicare Part A automatically, giving such persons access to the full range of Medicare Part A benefits. Part A benefits can be useful even to a recipient of full Medicaid benefits because they entitle the individual to hospital, skilled nursing facility (SNF), home health, and hospice benefits that are often more extensive than those offered by the state Medicaid program, and because they enable the individual to reduce her Medicaid estate recovery liability.

[D] Medicare Savings Programs and the Medicare Part D Low-Income Subsidy

The subsidy available to low-income Medicare beneficiaries to help with Part D covered drugs[68] is closely related to the Medicare Savings Programs in both design and administration. Eligibility rules for the two programs are similar though not identical and states are required by law to make LIS eligibility determinations through their Medicaid programs. Moreover, the law requires states, when they are assisting beneficiaries with low-income subsidy (LIS) applications, to screen them for eligibility for Medicare Savings Programs and, if eligible, offer

---

[66] 42 U.S.C. §1395v, 42 C.F.R. §406.26. "Buy-in," used in connection with agreements between state Medicaid programs and the federal government to describe a process for paying Medicare premiums, is a term of art, used in statute and regulation.

[67] The states that do not have Part A buy-in agreements are Alabama, Arizona, California, Colorado, Illinois, Kansas, Kentucky, Missouri, Nebraska, New Jersey, New Mexico, Oregon, South Carolina, Utah, and Virginia.

[68] *See* discussion of Low-Income Subsidy in **Chapter 11**.

them an opportunity to enroll.[69] Finally, individuals enrolled in QMB, SLMB, or QI programs are deemed eligible for the LIS without having to apply or separately qualify by meeting the LIS income and asset eligibility rules.

The screen and enroll requirement, which does not apply to LIS applications taken through the Social Security Administration, is significant for two reasons. First, because it is piggybacked on an application for assistance with paying for prescription drugs (the LIS), it may promote a higher enrollment rate in the Medicare Savings Programs themselves, since drug coverage may be a more attractive and necessary benefit than premium assistance. And, because Medicare Savings Program eligibility rules are more liberal in at least some respect in 40 states than the nationally uniform LIS rules, enrollment in an MSP provides a back-door route to eligibility for the LIS for some who would not otherwise qualify.[70]

Advocates assisting clients with enrolling in Medicare Savings Programs can enhance their assistance by helping them to understand the complexities of enrollment choices for the low-income subsidy. It may be more expeditious for a client to make one trip to Medicaid rather than two separate trips, one to Medicaid for MSP and one to Social Security for LIS, but clients will need to be clear about what they are seeking when they go to their Medicaid office.

§10.06   ACCESS ISSUES FOR THE DUALLY ELIGIBLE POPULATION

[A]   Prescription Drug Coverage and Medicare Part D

Prior to January 1, 2006, dually eligible beneficiaries received their prescription drug coverage exclusively from Medicaid, with the exception of drugs covered under Medicare Parts A and B, delivered in institutions or in physicians' offices.

However, beginning January 1, 2006, any individual eligible to enroll in a Medicare Part D plan who is receiving full Medicaid services cannot receive prescription drug coverage through Medicaid.[71] This is true regardless of whether the individual has actually enrolled in a Part D plan and regardless of whether the plan covers the specific drug needed. Concomitantly, the state cannot receive federal matching payments for such services.

[1]   Definition of Dual Eligibles

For purposes of Part D, dual eligibles are defined as individuals who have coverage under a Part D plan and who are eligible for full Medicaid benefits

---

[69] 42 U.S.C. §1396u-5(a)(3).

[70] For a detailed discussion of the interrelationships between MSPs and LIS, *see* Toward Making Medicare Work, *supra* note 15.

[71] 42 U.S.C. §1396u-5(d)(1). For a more detailed discussion of the entire Medicare drug benefit, *see* **Chapter 11**.

under any category of a state Medicaid plan. Those with full coverage under a so-called §1115 research and demonstration waiver fall within the definition; individuals receiving prescription drug coverage under a §1115 Pharmacy Plus waiver do not.[72] This definition differs from and is narrower than that offered in **§10.04**.

[2] Assignment of Dual Eligibles to Drug Plans

Presumably because of the loss of Medicaid drug coverage and because of the high prescription usage of the dually eligible population, Congress required the automatic enrollment in a drug plan of any dual eligible who does not voluntarily enroll.[73] Auto enrollment must be into Part D plans with premiums at or below the average (or "benchmark") plan premium for the region. In the fall of 2005, CMS began to notify duals of the plan to which they had been assigned, telling them that if they did not choose a plan on their own by December 31, 2005, they would be enrolled in the designated plan. After January 1, 2006, difficulties developed when dual eligibles could not identify the plan in which they were enrolled, or received cards from more than one plan, or had premiums incorrectly deducted from their Social Security checks or were unable to use their low income subsidy and had to pay large co-payments. Beneficiaries filed litigation challenging the Department of Health and Human Services' failure to implement Part D to assure drug coverage for dual eligibles.[74]

Enrollment for Medicaid-eligible individuals who become eligible for Medicare after January 1, 2006, is effective on the first day of the month the individual becomes eligible for Part D. Regulations state that enrollment for Part D eligibles who become newly eligible for Medicaid becomes effective as soon as practicable after being identified as dual eligible by CMS.[75] However, more recently, CMS has issued subregulatory guidance that makes the effective date for such individuals the first day of the month in which the individual becomes Medicaid eligible.[76]

Unlike other Medicare beneficiaries dual eligibles retain the right to switch plans at any time.[77] Thus, individuals assigned to plans whose formularies do not include the prescriptions they use may switch to a more appropriate plan.

---

[72] 42 C.F.R. §423.772.

[73] 42 U.S.C. §1396u-5(c)(6).

[74] Situ, et al. v. Leavitt, C06-02841 TEH (NDCA, Complaint filed April 26, 2006)

[75] 42 C.F.R. §423.34(f).

[76] Letter of March 17, 2006 to Medicare Prescription Drug Plans (PDPs) from Anthony J. Culotta, Acting Director, Medicare Enrollment and Appeals Group, Re: Update Guidance—Changes to Effective Date and PDP Notice Requirements for Auto-Enrollment and Facilitated Enrollment. **Appendix 10-6**.

[77] 42 C.F.R. §423.38(c).

[3] Medicaid Wrap-Around

The elimination of coverage for an otherwise covered Medicaid service represents a substantial departure from the historic Medicare-Medicaid relationship for dual eligibles, under which Medicaid has paid Medicare's cost-sharing and provided "wrap-around coverage" for services where, as with home health, Medicare coverage is more limited than Medicaid's or where, as with prescription drugs before January 1, 2006 and long-term care, Medicare coverage was or is nearly non-existent. The significance of this situation cannot be overstated. Because of the design of the Medicare drug benefit, many dual eligibles find themselves with less prescription drug coverage than they had under Medicaid and potentially less protection during appeals processes to challenge denials or other barriers to coverage. Further, all but those who are institutionalized will have to pay copayments for their prescriptions, with the copayment amounts increasing yearly. Copayments are not required under federal Medicaid law and a number of states do not use them or use them only for certain drugs. Moreover, in the past, their use was not enforceable.[78]

Medicaid can continue to cover for dual eligibles, using both federal and state funding, those drugs that it is permitted but not required by law to cover for any Medicaid beneficiary and that are not, by definition, Part D covered drugs. Such drugs include benzodiazepines (used for anxiety, panic attacks, seizure disorders, and muscle spasms), barbiturates (used for seizures), weight gain and weight loss drugs (used in connection with HIV treatments), prescription vitamins, cough and cold relief drugs, and non-prescription drugs, among others. States also have the option of paying co-payments for dual eligibles and/or for drugs that are not on a plan's formulary. However, they will receive no federal matching payments and must use only state funds if they assist dual eligibles with this cost sharing.

The January 2006 transition from Medicaid to Medicare coverage for prescription drugs was so chaotic for dual eligibles that 44 states initiated some sort of emergency coverage programs, some declaring a health care emergency in the state. A handful of these programs continued to operate at mid-year; it is unclear if any states will keep such programs in place indefinitely.[79]

[4] Nursing Facility Residents and Other Beneficiaries Receiving Long-Term Care Services

In addition to the problems experienced by other dually eligible individuals, those who reside in nursing homes and other institutions will experience problems that arise because of the setting in which they live. For example, there is no assurance that a dually eligible resident who does not choose a plan for herself will be automatically

---

[78] *See* 42 C.F.R. §447.53(e); The non-enforceability of co-pays was changed by the Deficit Reduction Act of 2006, Pub. L. No. 109-171, §6041 (signed Feb. 8, 2006).

[79] *See* <www.ncsl.org/programs/health/PartDPatch.htm> (site visited June 27, 2006).

assigned to a plan that includes the pharmacy used by her nursing facility, although plans are required to include long-term care pharmacies in their networks.

Dually eligible individuals who reside in a nursing facility pay no co-payment for their medications. This benefit is not extended to residents of assisted living facilities and others who are receiving home and community-based services pursuant to a Section 1915 waiver, even though these individuals must meet the medical eligibility requirements for a nursing facility to get community-based services. Those individuals must pay co-payments of between $1 and $5 (between $1 and $5.35 for 2007), depending on their income and on the particular drug.[80]

[5] Transitioning into a Part D Plan

When Medicare beneficiaries transition from another source of payment for their prescriptions to a Part D plan, they may encounter difficulties caused by changes in formularies and other utilization management tools used by Part D plans to contain costs. The transition may be particularly difficult for those dual eligibles who are transitioning from more generous Medicaid programs.

All Part D plans are required to establish a transition process for new enrollees who are already taking Medicare-covered drugs that are not on the plan's formulary.[81] Each plan has the flexibility to design its own process as long as the process is consistent with sub-regulatory guidance issued by CMS. CMS' guidance for 2007 directs plans to provide a temporary 30-day one-time supply of non-formulary medication for new enrollees at any time during the first 90 days after enrollment. Residents of long-term care facilities, both dual eligibles and others, should be able to get multiple 31-day supplies during the 90 day period.[82] Although the guidance recognizes that other transitions may occur, for example, when someone goes from the hospital or from home to a long-term care facility, the guidance suggests no transitional time periods. Instead, CMS indicates that beneficiaries may use the exceptions and appeals process to seek coverage for their non-formulary medications in those situations.[83]

[B] Payment of Medicare Cost Sharing at Medicaid Rates

Prior to passage of the Balanced Budget Act of 1997 (BBA '97),[84] at least four federal Circuit Courts of Appeal had found that states must reimburse

---

[80] 42 C.F.R. §§423.772, 423.782(a)(2)(ii).

[81] 42 C.F.R. §423.120(b)(3).

[82] "Transition Process Requirements for Part D Sponsors" (April 2006), Centers for Medicare and Medicaid Services, *see* **Appendix 10-7**. CMS uses 31 instead of 30 days for long-term care facilities in recognition that long-term care pharmacies usually dispense medications in 31 day supplies.

[83] *Id.*

[84] Balanced Budget Act of 1997, Pub. L. No. 105-33 [hereinafter BBA '97].

Medicare cost-sharing to providers of services to QMBs at the full Medicare rate,[85] which is usually higher than a state's Medicaid rate for the same service. A provision in BBA '97 gave states the option to reimburse providers for services provided to dually eligible beneficiaries at their lower Medicaid rate.[86] (However, federal law also authorizes states to pay at the higher of the two reimbursement rates.[87]) Under the BBA '97 provision, if the Medicare share (80 percent of the Medicare allowable amount for most Part B services) is more than the states' Medicaid rate for the same service, the state need pay nothing.

> **Example:** If the Medicare approved rate is $100, the Medicare payment would be $80 and the beneficiary coinsurance would be $20. However, if the Medicaid rate for the service is only $75, the state would make no payment for the beneficiary's share, since Medicare has already paid above the state reimbursement rate. Thus, the provider would get $20 less than she would from a privately insured beneficiary. The QMB is not liable for the unreimbursed state portion.

Since the enactment of BBA '97, courts have held, even in cases that predated BBA '97, that states *may* reimburse at the lower of the two reimbursement rates.[88] Thus, dually eligible beneficiaries are treated as Medicaid rather than Medicare beneficiaries, with respect to provider reimbursement. Advocates fear that this change has a serious potential for increasing barriers to health care, which the QMB program was originally intended to overcome. Since passage of BBA '97, at least 15 states have reduced their reimbursement to the lower Medicaid rate; as of 1999, 35 states were paying at the lower rate.[89] A 2003 study of the effects of this provision on access to services concluded that payment reductions reduced utilization. It did not, however, evaluate the effect of reduced utilization on health outcomes.[90] The report recommended no changes.

The BBA '97 provision authorizing lower payments to providers also expressly prohibits providers from billing dually eligible patients; that is, providers

---

[85] Rehabilitation Ass'n of Va. v. Kozlowski, 42 F.3d 1444 (4th Cir. 1994); Haynes Ambulance Service, Inc. v. State of Alabama, 36 F.3d 1074 (11th Cir. 1994); Pennsylvania Med. Soc'y v. Snider, 29 F.3d 886 (3d Cir. 1994); New York City Health & Hosp. Corp. v. Perales, 954 F.2d 854 (2d Cir. 1992), *cert. denied*, 506 U.S. 972 (1999).

[86] BBA '97, 4714, amending 42 U.S.C.A. §1396a(n) (Supp. 2005) by adding subparagraphs (2) and (3).

[87] 42 U.S.C. §1396a(n)(1).

[88] Beverly Cmty. Hosp. Ass'n v. Belshe, 132 F.3d 1259 (9th Cir. 1997); Stohler v. Menke, 998 F. Supp. 836 (E.D. Tenn. 1997).

[89] Patricia B. Nemore, *Variations in State Medicaid Buy-in Practices for Low-Income Medicare Beneficiaries: A 1999 Update*, prepared for The Henry J. Kaiser Family Foundation (Dec. 1999).

[90] Report to Congress, State Payment Limitations for Medicare Cost-Sharing, Tommy G. Thompson, Secretary of Health and Human Services 2003, transmitted by letter of May 20, 2003 to Speaker of the House of Representatives, J. Dennis Hastert.

must accept the Medicare payment and the Medicaid payment, if any, as payment in full.[91]

CMS interprets these requirements to permit providers to choose whether to accept a patient as private pay, QMB-only, or, if applicable, full Medicaid.[92] This interpretation eviscerates the statutory protection, since the provider can avoid its reach by telling the beneficiary he will serve her only as private pay. Unfortunately, this interpretation has not been challenged. Advocates may find better protection in state law.

[C] Skilled Nursing Facilities/Nursing Facilities: Inappropriate Transfers and Obstruction of Medicaid Services

Medicare pays for *skilled* nursing or rehabilitative care, following a three- (or more) day hospitalization, for a condition related to the hospitalization. The care must be provided in a certified skilled nursing facitlity (SNF) and coverage is available for up to 100 days. After the 20th day, the beneficiary must pay a copayment ($119 in 2006 and $xxx in 2007). *Medicaid* pays for nursing or rehabilitative care that can only be provided in a nursing facility on an inpatient basis. A "nursing facility" in Medicaid is a place that provides both skilled care and "health related care and services."[93] The care must be provided in a certified nursing facility; there is no limit on the number of days of coverage as long as the services are medically necessary. Medicaid requires the individual to pay a "share of cost" that comprises the individual's whole monthly income less certain required and permitted deductions. Medicaid then pays the facility the difference between the individual's share of cost and the Medicaid rate.

Difficulties can arise for dually eligible beneficiaries because facilities may not be certified for both Medicare and Medicaid or may have separate wings certified for each program.[94] If such a beneficiary enters the facility with Medicaid paying for her stay, and is subsequently hospitalized for three days, she will then

---

[91] BBA '97, 4714(a)(1)(B). Contrary to this explicit prohibition in the law, a home care trade journal reported a state trade association spokesperson as saying that providers can refuse to accept assignment and ask for full payment up front from clients. "Once indigent patients understand that they must pay $100 up-front and only collect $80 at a later date, 'they'll decline to do business with you,' [the spokesperson] counsels." *Some States Crack Down on Copays for Dual Eligibles*, 6 Eli's Home Care Wk. 196 (Apr. 26, 1999).

[92] State Medicaid Manual 3490.14B.

[93] 42 U.S.C.A. §1396r(a) (Supp. 2005).

[94] Although national data for 2005 report that about 83 percent of all nursing home beds in the country that are certified for either program are certified for both programs and that more than 88 percent of all facilities are certified for both programs (CMS Online Survey, Certification and Reporting (OSCAR) Data—Current Surveys—Dec. 2005), nursing home advocates report that movement between wings separately certified continues to be an issue for dually eligible beneficiaries.

be eligible for a period of skilled nursing coverage under Medicare. She may be told—either by the facility or by the state Medicaid program—that she cannot return to her Medicaid bed but must be placed in a bed in a Medicare-only certified portion of the facility. The facility might tell her this if it will receive a higher reimbursement rate under Medicare than Medicaid; the state might try to force her to get Medicare coverage because of its obligation under federal law to seek reimbursement from all liable third parties.

Under the law, however, if her old bed is available, or, if not, if another one is, the facility must readmit her to it, regardless of whether it can get higher reimbursement if she is in a bed in a Medicare-certified portion of the facility.[95] Moreover, with respect to the state's concern about third-party liability, the Centers for Medicare and Medicaid Services has said on at least one occasion that states are required to seek third-party coverage only where such coverage exists; if a resident is in a bed in a portion of a facility not certified for Medicare, there would be no Medicare coverage for that bed, and so there would be no third-party liability.[96]

Conversely, a dually eligible beneficiary might enter the facility for the first time needing skilled care after a three-day hospitalization, and so be entitled to Medicare coverage right away. When that coverage ends, she may be told by the facility that she must move because it needs the bed for another Medicare resident. While the law gives the beneficiary an absolute right to refuse this transfer,[97] she will not be able to get Medicaid to pay for her continued stay unless her bed is also certified for Medicaid.

As a general matter, when a facility asks a resident to move from one part of the facility to another, an advocate or family member will want to find out what the certification is for both parts of the facility. If they are certified differently—e.g., one is only Medicare-certified and the other is only Medicaid-certified—the resident is entitled to a notice of the reasons for the transfer and an opportunity for a fair hearing to challenge the transfer.[98] If the move is merely from one room to

---

[95] *See* 42 U.S.C. §1396r(c)(2)(D) concerning a Medicaid resident's right to notice of state bed hold policies when she is being transferred to a hospital. Although states are not required to pay nursing facilities to hold beds while residents are absent, they may do so, and the resident must be informed of the state's policy and her right to return to the bed the state paid for, if any, or to the first available bed in the facility. In addition to this right of the nursing home resident, Medicaid provides a generic right of free choice of provider to all beneficiaries. 42 U.S.C. §1396a(a)(23).

[96] Letter of March 31, 1999 from Associate Regional Administrator, Region I, Health Care Financing Administration (precursor to the Centers for Medicare and Medicaid Services) to Center for Medicare Advocacy, Inc. [Preston letter] *See* **Appendix 10-4**. Advocates are cautioned that while the principles enunciated in this letter are embodied in the law, actual state policy and practice is likely to be less favorable and the state may refuse to pay for a resident who has declined Medicare coverage. Advocates are encouraged, nonetheless, to make these arguments for clients who wish to return to a non-Medicare-certified bed.

[97] 42 U.S.C. §1395i-3(c)(1)(A)(x) [Medicare], §1396r(c)(1)(A)(x) [Medicaid].

[98] Federal law limits the permissible reasons for transfers. The reasons, which apply to all nursing home residents, not just to those dually eligible, are: (1) the resident's welfare cannot be met by the

another within a certified portion of the facility, the resident is entitled only to notification, not to a hearing, but may nonetheless be able to prevent the relocation by invoking federal standards that promote self-determination, participation and accommodation of the resident's need.[99]

From the resident's perspective, the best way to resolve these problems is for the state to require that all beds in facilities be certified for both Medicare and Medicaid.

[D] Medicaid Individual Share of Cost Issues During a Skilled Nursing Facility Benefit Period

If a dually eligible individual's nursing home stay is paid for by Medicaid, she will pay all of her income, less deductions allowed for personal needs, for the support of family members and for a few other purposes,[100] to the facility as her share of cost (also called Net Available Monthly Income (NAMI), patient pay amount, or applied income). Medicaid then pays the difference between the share of cost and the established Medicaid rate for the facility.

However, when a portion of her stay is paid for by Medicare, different rules apply. If the individual is a QMB (income does not exceed 100 percent of federal income poverty guidelines, about $837/month in 2006 for one person, slightly higher in Alaska and Hawaii), she should have no share of cost for any portion of her nursing home stay that is covered by Medicare. This is because Medicare will cover fully the first 20 days of her Medicare-covered stay and the copayment ($119 for 2006) for days 21 to 100 is Medicaid's responsibility. The nursing home can neither charge her for the copayment, nor receive her Medicaid share of cost for that period of time.

Sometimes, nursing facilities and Medicaid agencies are not as clear as they could be in informing residents about their rights and obligations with respect to

---

facility, (2) the resident no longer needs the facility's services because of improved health, (3) safety of individuals in the facility is endangered, (4) health of individuals in the facility would be endangered, (5) resident has failed to pay, and (6) facility ceases to operate. 42 U.S.C. §§1396r(c)(2)(A)(i)–(vi), 1351-3(c)(2)(A)(i)–(vi). In addition, a resident can refuse a transfer to or from a Medicare-certified portion of the facility when the purpose is to relocate her from or to a non-Medicare certified portion of the facility. *See* note 99.

[99] *See, e.g.,* 42 C.F.R. §483.15(b), (e) (2005).

[100] 42 U.S.C. §§1396a(r)(1), 1396r-5(d)(1); 42 C.F.R. §§435.725, 435.733, 435.832. The deductions from gross income include incurred medical expenses, a personal needs allowance of at least $30 a month, monies diverted to create a minimum monthly needs allowance for a community spouse, and/or a family allowance for other dependents, if any, and certain reparation payments. Although the above-cited regulations do, indeed, describe permissible deductions from income before determining share of cost, advocates should not rely on them as they do not reflect changes that have been made in the law since 1987.

share of cost; advocates can help their clients by making sure they are not paying a share of cost when they should not be.[101]

[E] Wheelchairs, Supplies, and Other Durable Medical Equipment

Generally, Medicare pays for wheelchairs only if, without the chair, the individuals would be confined to bed or to a stationary chair. Other items that might be thought of as durable medical equipment, such as bathroom grab bars, are explicitly excluded from Medicare coverage. Conditions of coverage for durable medical equipment are contained in the Medicare Coverage Issues Manual.[102] Durable medical equipment is covered when needed for use in the home. Medicaid coverage rules may be more expansive, and must include a process for a beneficiary to request coverage for a non-covered item.[103]

When a physician believes that a patient requires Medicare-covered DME, she refers the patient to a medical equipment supplier who then obtains a Certificate of Medical Necessity from the physician. The supplier provides the equipment to the patient and then submits a claim to the regional DME carrier for a determination as to Medicare coverage. As with most Medicare coverage decisions, determinations as to whether DME will be covered are generally made after the equipment has been provided to the patient. If Medicare coverage is denied, the patient, or a third-party payer such as Medicaid, may be liable.

A Program Memorandum (PM) authorizes suppliers of DME, regardless of whether they take assignment, to bill beneficiaries for "upgrades" by issuing them an advance beneficiary notice (ABN) informing the beneficiary that the upgrade is not likely to be paid for by Medicare.[104] The definition of upgrade in the PM is "an item with features that go beyond what the physician ordered."[105] If the supplier has labeled some portion of the equipment an "upgrade," it may be difficult to

---

[101] *See, e.g.*, Conrad v. Perales, 92 F. Supp. 2d 175 (W.D.N.Y. 2000) for discussion of a variation on this theme.

[102] Available at <http://www.cms.hhs.gov/manuals/downloads/Pub06_PART_60.pdf> (site visited July 7, 2006). With respect to power operated vehicles (POVs) which, together with power wheelchairs, Medicare now refers to as power mobility devices, this transmittal has not been updated to reflect new regulations published April 5, 2006 at 71 Fed. Reg. 17,021. The new regulations liberalize the former requirement concerning who could prescribe a POV. They amend regulations for durable medical equipment at 42 C.F.R. §410.38.

[103] *See, e.g.,* Lankford v. Sherman, 2006 WL 1699600 (8th Cir. 2006); DeSario v. Thomas, 139 F.3d 80 (2d Cir. 1998).

[104] Program Memorandum No. B-01-64 (Oct. 22, 2001) (Subject: DMERCs-Advance Beneficiary Notices (ABNs) for "Upgrades"), <http://www.cms.hhs.gov/Transmittals> (site visited July 7, 2006) At this site, click on CMS program memoranda, then scroll down the long list to the B section.

[105] *Id.*

argue that Medicaid should pay for it, but advocates should seek an independent Medicaid determination of medical necessity because the Medicaid statute has a more expansive definition of medical necessity than does the Medicare statute and includes a greater focus on independence.[106]

In addition to limiting coverage for wheelchairs, Medicare reimburses at a rate lower than that of many state Medicaid programs, whose fee structures for wheelchairs are often more generous.[107] Medical supplies are also treated differently by the two programs: for example, a month's supply of catheters under Medicare is 30; a state Medicaid program may pay for 31 in a 31-day month. These disparities result in claims for dually eligible individuals being denied or reduced by Medicare, then the balance paid by Medicaid only at the lower rate or not at all.

In the past, states told providers serving dually eligible individuals that they were required to serve them on an assignment-related basis, even though this was not required by law. "Assignment-related basis" means they cannot receive more than the Medicare approved amount for the supply or service. Because this amount is often less than they would receive from Medicaid for a Medicaid-only client, and because they are prohibited from billing a dually eligible person the way they would a non-dually eligible Medicare beneficiary, providers are reluctant to serve dually eligible individuals. These state practices can be challenged as violations of comparability requirements in the Medicaid program and possibly as violations of state medical necessity law.[108]

The BBA '97 prohibits providers from billing dually eligible clients more than the provider receives from Medicare and Medicaid together, regardless of what that amount is.[109] It does not require, however, that the payment be limited to the Medicare rate.[110]

---

[106] Concerning the definition of medical necessity, Medicare pays for services that are "reasonable and necessary for the diagnosis or treatment of illness or injury or to improve the functioning of a malformed body member." 42 U.S.C. §1395y(a)(1)(A). Medicaid pays for "necessary medical services and . . . rehabilitation and other services to help . . . individuals attain or retain capability for independence or self-care." 42 U.S.C. §1396.

[107] As a general matter, in most states, Medicaid pays less for similar services than does Medicare. Customized wheelchairs and certain medical supplies are anomalous in this regard.

[108] *See, e.g.*, Charpentier v. Belshe, Civ. No. 90-758 EJG/PAN, Medicare & Medicaid Guide (CCH) 43,123 (N.D. Cal. 1994), holding that policies resulting in no access to certain Medicaid services for categorically needy individuals who were also eligible for Medicare, where such access was not so limited for individuals not "dually eligible," violated comparability requirements. *But see* Ralabate v. Wing, 1996 WL 377204, Medicare & Medicaid Guide (CCH) 44,550 (W.D.N.Y. 1996).

[109] BBA '97, 4714(a)(1)(B), amending 42 U.S.C.A. §1396a(n) by adding subparagraphs (2) and (3). (2005 Supp.)

[110] 42 U.S.C. §1396a(n)(1) (2005 Supp.).

[F] Differing Home Care Coverage Standards in Medicare and Medicaid Programs

Medicare covers a defined package of home health services when specified coverage criteria are met.[111] Medicare covers a finite amount (no more than 35 hours per week) of skilled nursing care and home health aide services to assist with personal care. In addition, the Medicare home health benefit covers skilled physical therapy, occupational therapy, speech and language therapy, medical social work services, and some medical equipment and supplies.

Several Medicare requirements restrict the availability of the Medicare home health benefit. To qualify for home health services, a Medicare beneficiary must be homebound[112] and must require a skilled service.[113] While the requirement that an individual be homebound is included in the statute,[114] interpretations by both home health providers and Medicare Contractors (formerly called Fiscal Intermediaries) are often more narrow than necessary and operate to limit the availability of the Medicare home health benefit.

For example, any absence from the home setting may lead to a decision by the home health agency that the patient is not homebound and therefore does not qualify for Medicare coverage. As a result of such a determination, the agency will no longer bill Medicare. If the beneficiary can pay to continue the services, she can ask the agency to submit a "demand bill," to Medicare to get an official coverage determination by Medicare. A demand bill is submitted when the agency itself does not believe there is Medicare coverage but the beneficiary wishes an official determination which is a condition precedent to a Medicare appeal. There is no right under Medicare, as there is in Medicaid,[115] to continued coverage pending the outcome of an appeal. Accordingly, unless another payment source exists, as a practical matter, the home health agency makes final decisions regarding Medicare coverage.

Individuals who are dually eligible may need to look to Medicaid home care benefits to meet some or all of their needs as well as to sustain their Medicare appeals. Medicaid mandatory home health care coverage rules are similar to Medicare rules, with two significant exceptions: they require neither homebound

---

[111] 42 U.S.C. §§1395f(a)(28)(C), 1395x(m) (2005 Supp.).

[112] 42 U.S.C. §§1395f(a)(8), 1395n(a)(2)(F).

[113] 42 U.S.C. §1395f(a)(2)(C).

[114] 42 U.S.C. §§1395f(a)(8), 1395n(a)(2)(F). The statutory language is "confined to the home." Under an amendment to this section passed in 2000, beneficiaries receiving therapeutic, psychosocial, or medical treatment in an adult day care program may still be considered "homebound." Moreover, absences from home for the purpose of attending a religious service are deemed to be of infrequent or short duration, in keeping with the statutory standard.

[115] 42 U.S.C. §1396a(a)(3); 42 C.F.R. §431.220; Goldberg v. Kelly, 397 U.S. 254 (1970). This concept is often referred to as aid paid pending. It is a hallmark of the Medicaid program that advocates seek to have expanded to all health care recipients.

status nor that a skilled service be needed.[116] In addition to mandatory home health, all states include in their Medicaid programs home and community-based services provided to limited populations through waiver of certain federal Medicaid requirements or modifications of State Plan Amendments.[117] These programs vary widely in their eligibility and services. They usually offer "nonmedical" services, such as companion services, chore services, or adult day care, in addition to the more traditional home health care services offered by Medicare and the Medicaid mandatory home health benefit.

While some dual eligibles may need the services of one or the other program, many could benefit from enhanced coordination of the services offered by Medicare and Medicaid. This is particularly true with respect to coordination between Medicare and the Medicaid waiver home care programs. The Balanced Budget Act imposed a statutory limit on the amount of certain key home health services for which Medicare will pay. BBA '97 explicitly defined the "part-time or intermittent" quantitative standard for Medicare home health services to mean less than 35 hours a week of a combination of skilled nursing and home health aide services. That is the maximum amount of those services that Medicare will cover. (Although Medicaid home health regulations adopt the "part-time or intermittent" language from Medicare, the Medicaid statute contains no such limitation. The regulations, therefore, may be subject to challenge.) Most waiver programs also limit coverage through a cap on the amount of money or hours of care available to a beneficiary. Coordination of Medicare and Medicaid benefits can, thus, enhance the total quantity of care that may be offered to an individual and, in doing so, can also enhance the quality of care and quality of life for the beneficiary. Indeed, it can make the difference between being able to remain in a home setting and being forced to accept a residential long-term care placement.

§10.07 MANAGED CARE ISSUES FOR DUALLY ELIGIBLE INDIVIDUALS

[A] Overview

Dual eligibility presents a particularly wide spectrum of complexity when enrollment in managed care is introduced into the mix of possibilities. While both

---

[116] 42 U.S.C. §§1396a(a)(10)(D), 1396d. Although neither the Medicaid statute nor the Medicaid regulations use the "homebound" standard, states have, in the past, incorporated it into their Medicaid home health programs. CMS has informed states that such a requirement is impermissible under Medicaid regulations at 42 C.F.R. §§440.230(c) and 440.240(b). State Medicaid Director Letter of July 25, 2000, Olmstead Update No. 3, Attachment 3-g, found at <www.cms.hhs.gov/smdl/downloads/smd072500b.pdf> (site visited July 18, 2006).

[117] 42 U.S.C. §1396a(a)(10)(D). These programs are referred to as waiver programs because certain Medicaid statutory requirements are waived by the federal government for limited purposes. The Deficit Reduction Act of 2005 authorizes states to provide such services as part of their regular Medicaid program, without having to seek a waiver. Pub. L. No. 109-171, §6086 amending 42 U.S.C.A. §1396n by adding subsection (i).

Medicare and Medicaid offer managed care options, with limited exceptions, neither program requires those who are dually eligible to enroll. In fact, less than seven percent of Medicare beneficiaries who are dually eligible are enrolled in Medicare managed care, now called Medicare Advantage (formerly known as Medicare+Choice).[118] In the past, programmatic differences between Medicare and Medicaid in requirements for participating managed care organizations and in requirements for beneficiaries have made coordination between the two programs difficult and thus resulted in few states promoting enrollment of dually eligible individuals into Medicaid managed care; fewer states require them to enroll.[119]

Some policymakers favor a so-called integrated approach to care for the dually eligible that blends Medicare and Medicaid dollars and covers both acute care (now primarily paid for by Medicare) and long-term care (now primarily paid for by Medicaid). Programs of All-Inclusive Care for the Elderly (PACE) which have operated for about 20 years are one such model, but PACE programs are limited in their scope, currently serving less than 1% of the dually eligible population.[120]

A provision in the MMA may change the landscape relating to dual eligibles and managed care. The provision authorized the creation of special Medicare Advantage plans called Special Needs Plans (SNPs) for certain populations; the dually eligible are one such population.[121] According to an issue brief published in November 2005

> In 2006, 276 SNPs will serve Medicare beneficiaries, and the majority of approved plans will serve dual eligible beneficiaries. Some are Medicaid managed care plans seeking to enter the Medicare market. In many respects these plans, with their state contracts and experience serving special needs individuals such as dual eligibles, represent the "ideal" SNP. However, many approved SNPs do not have contracts with state Medicaid agencies and are new to serving special needs individuals. Although it is clear that the new SNP option will generate different models for treating special needs individuals, it is not known whether fully integrated care will result.[122]

---

[118] Edith Walsh, Angela Greene, Sonja Hoover, and Christine Layton, Case Studies of Managed Care Arrangements for Dually Eligible Beneficiaries, Research Triangle Institute for the Centers for Medicare and Medicaid, September 26, 2003. Also found at <www.cms.hhs.gov/Reports/downloads/walsh_2003_2.pdf> (site visited July 18, 2006) [Case studies]. The range of participation among the states is remarkable: Oregon has 36.5 percent of its dual eligibles in Medicare Advantage plans while Mississippi has .1 percent (one-tenth of one percent).

[119] At least 21 states have some dual eligibles enrolled in Medicaid managed care. *Id.* citing to The National Academy for State Health Policy (NASHP) (Kaye et al., 1999).

[120] *See* "Quality Initiatives—General Information: Programs of All Inclusive Care for the Elderly," Centers for Medicare and Medicaid Services Web site at <http://www.cms.hhs.gov/QualityInitiativesGenInfo/10_PACE.asp> (site visited July 11, 2006) [Quality Initiatives]

[121] Pub. L. No. 108-173, §231 amending 42 U.S.C.A. §1395w-21(a)(2)(A) and 1395w-28.

[122] Christie Provost Peters, "Medicare Advantage SNPs: A New Opportunity for Integrated Care?" National Health Policy Forum, Issue Brief # 808 (Nov. 11, 2005), available at <http://www.nhpf.org/pdfs_ib/IB808_SNP_11-11-05.pdf> (site visited July 11, 2006)

[B] Managed Care/Fee-for-Service Matrix

At least four combinations of health care coverage for dually eligible individuals are possible when managed care is offered into the mix. A dually eligible individual can be in

- Medicaid fee-for-service/Medicare fee-for-service
- Medicaid fee-for-service/Medicare Advantage
- Medicaid managed care/Medicare fee-for-service
- Medicaid managed care/Medicare Advantage

In the last case, the individual could be enrolled in two different managed care plans and become very confused as to which plan she should look to for which coverage. Managed care issues arise concerning state obligations to pay managed care cost-sharing for QMBs, as well as concerning Medicare Advantage organizations' efforts to limit their liability for providing care by trying to shift coverage to the Medicaid program. Additional issues arise with respect to a dually eligible individual's right to choose a nursing facility if she is in a Medicare Advantage HMO that has a network of nursing facilities. These issues are discussed below.

[C] State Medicaid Payment of Cost Sharing for Medicare Managed Care Enrollees

Although dually eligible individuals are enrolled in Medicare HMOs at a very low rate, those who are enrolled and who are QMBs are entitled to have their states pay HMO copayments.[123] Despite this requirement, many states do not pay Medicare cost sharing (for QMBs) outside of the fee-for-service setting.[124] Among those states that do, many do not have systems to identify their QMBs who are so enrolled; they rely on the beneficiary or a provider to alert them. Information is

---

[123] 42 U.S.C. §1396d(p)(3); State Medicaid Manual (HCFA Pub. 45) 3490.12; Policy Memorandum of June 30, 2000, from Director, Disabled and Elderly Health Program Group to Associate Regional Administrators, Subject: Policy Memorandum on Medicaid Obligations to Pay Medicare Cost-Sharing Expenses for Qualified Medicare Beneficiaries in Medicare Health Maintenance Organizations or Competitive Medical Plans or Medicare Plus Choice Organizations—INFORMATION. *See* **Appendix 10-3.**

[124] *See* Patricia B. Nemore, *Variations in State Medicaid Buy-in Practices for Low-Income Medicare Beneficiaries: A 1999 Update*, prepared for The Henry J. Kaiser Family Foundation (Dec. 1999). Only 19 states responded affirmatively to a survey question asking whether the state pays copays in Medicare managed care. Eighteen states reported that they did not; the remaining states either did not answer or do not have Medicare managed care in their state. The author is not aware of more recent data on this subject.

available from CMS to identify Medicare Advantage HMO enrollees;[125] advocates can press their states to get this information and use it. Until a state has such a system in place, advocates should advise clients to inform their state of their HMO enrollment, and have the HMO bill the state for any copayments for which the individual is responsible.

[D] Managed Long-Term Care

Several problematic scenarios can arise if an individual enrolled in a Medicare HMO needs or is receiving nursing home care.

> **Scenario One:** A dually eligible beneficiary living at home and enrolled in a Medicare HMO needs skilled nursing home care. The HMO waives the Medicare three-day prior hospitalization requirement. The beneficiary wants to move to an out-of-network nursing home; the HMO says it will not cover such care. The state Medicaid agency refuses to pay for Medicaid coverage since the individual could have received Medicare coverage through the HMO in which she chose to enroll.

Until July 1, 2006, a solution to this problem was to disenroll from the Medicare HMO. Disenrollment is effective the month following the individual's notice to disenroll; the beneficiary is then free to choose a nursing facility and have Medicaid pay, since she would not have met the three-day prior hospitalization requirement for Medicare coverage. Beginning in 2006, however, beneficiaries are able to make only one change relative to their Medicare Advantage plan in the first six months of that year, and one change during the first three months of subsequent years.

> **Scenario Two:** The same beneficiary needs a nursing home placement, but does not need skilled care. There is no possibility of Medicare coverage for the nursing home stay.

Even though she chooses an out-of-network nursing facility, Medicaid will pay because the Medicare HMO has no liability for non-Medicare-covered nursing facility care.[126]

---

[125] *See* SMDL No. 02-001, Jan. 9, 2002, informing states how to request a customized extract from the Medicare Enrollment Database (EDB) at <http://www.cms.hhs.gov/PrivProtectedData/downloads/EDBCustomizedStateFile.pdf> (site visited July 18, 2006). CMS had earlier discussed the EDB as "the authoritative source for all Medicare entitlement information . . . comprehensive and updated daily. . . ." Letter of June 21, 2000, from Timothy M. Westmoreland, Director, Center for Medicaid and State Operations, and Gary G. Christoph, Ph.D., Chief Information Officer to State Medicaid Directors at <http://www.cms.hhs.gov/smdl/downloads/smd062100.pdf> (site visited July 18, 2006) and Letter of Sept. 6, 2000, from Mary Hogan, Director, Data and Systems Group, to State Medicaid Directors. The latter letter is available at <http://www.cms.hhs.gov/smdl/downloads/smd090600.pdf> (site visited July 18, 2006).

[126] *See, e.g.,* Preston letter, *supra* note 98. A copy of the letter can be found in **Appendix 10-4.**

> **Scenario Three:** A dually eligible individual enrolled in a Medicare HMO resides in a non-Medicare-certified bed in a nursing facility. She becomes eligible for the Medicare SNF benefit after a three-day hospitalization. Would she be required to move to an in-network Medicare certified bed or would she be allowed to waive her right to Medicare coverage and remain in the non-Medicare-certified bed, with Medicaid as the payer?

The Medicaid law requires states to allow beneficiaries to receive services from any certified provider who chooses to serve them.[127] While there is legal support for the view that if the individual chooses to remain in a bed in which she could not receive Medicare services, there is no Medicare liability and Medicaid must pay, it is unlikely that many states interpret their obligations that way.[128]

Legislation enacted in December 2000 addressed a fourth variation of the nursing home musical bed game for dually eligible beneficiaries enrolled in a Medicare HMO: the situation where an HMO enrollee in a non-network SNF is transferred to a hospital and seeks to return to her former skilled nursing facility instead of going to an in-network facility.[129] The legislation permits the enrollee to choose to return to the former (out-of-network) facility, if the facility agrees to accept the HMO payment for services. This provision appears to actually undermine existing rights of dually eligible individuals, although the situation it addresses seems unlikely to arise very often.

As noted earlier, enrollment of dually eligible beneficiaries in Medicare and Medicaid managed care has been considerably more limited than such enrollment of non-dual populations in both programs. This situation appears to be shifting, bolstered by the MMA provision for Medicare Advantage plans for special populations and by state Medicaid programs' increased interest in using managed care for this population. Advocates should be attentive to such developments in their states and seek to ensure that programs seeking to provide "integrated" Medicare and Medicaid services cover all services required by each separate program and provide beneficiaries with all protections allowed by each program.

§10.08 PROGRAMS OF ALL-INCLUSIVE CARE FOR THE ELDERLY

As noted briefly earlier, Programs of All-Inclusive Care for the Elderly (PACE) are operated under both the Medicare and Medicaid programs[130] to

---

[127] 42 U.S.C. §1396a(a)(23).

[128] *But see* Preston letter, *supra*, note 98.

[129] BIPA, 621.

[130] The principal statutory provisions governing PACE, 42 U.S.C. §1395eee (Medicare) and 42 U.S.C. §1396u-4 (Medicaid), are substantially the same. Interim final regulations are at 42 C.F.R. Pt. 460, 64 Fed. Reg. 66,233 (Nov. 24, 1999). While most enrollees in PACE programs will be dually eligible, such dual enrollment is not a requirement for the program. However, for those who are

replicate the comprehensive services delivery and financing model for acute and long-term care created by On Lok Senior Health Services in San Francisco in the late 1970s. Until the BBA '97, PACE programs were operated under waivers of both Medicare and Medicaid requirements. The BBA '97 amended both Medicare and Medicaid to establish PACE as a nonwaiver program, with states having the option to include PACE in their Medicaid program. PACE is the embodiment of the "integrated" approach to serving dually eligible older people, putting Medicare and Medicaid dollars and acute and long-term care services together and thus avoiding many of the confusions and complexities described elsewhere in this chapter. A goal of PACE is to provide a full array of long-term care services to frail older people in a community-based setting.

To be eligible for PACE services, enrollees must need the level of health care required from a nursing facility under Medicaid.[131] But PACE programs are not merely long-term care programs: generally speaking, they must provide the full array of both acute and long-term care services required under Medicare and Medicaid as well as any services determined necessary for the individual enrollee by her interdisciplinary team.[132]

An individual can disenroll from a PACE program at any time.[133] In addition, she can be disenrolled involuntarily for one of six reasons:

1. Failure to pay a premium due;

2. Engaging in disruptive behavior;

3. Moving out of the service area;

4. No longer needing nursing facility level of care;

5. Termination of PACE agreement with CMS;

6. Inability of PACE program to offer services due to loss of licensing or contracts with outside providers.[134]

The second reason, engaging in disruptive or threatening behavior, is not grounds for involuntary disenrollment if the behavior is related to the participant's mental or physical condition, unless the behavior is a threat to safety.[135]

PACE grievance and appeals procedures raise serious concerns about protection of beneficiary rights that reflect the complexity of dual eligibility.

---

enrolled in either Medicare or Medicaid or both, regulations for those programs will govern beneficiaries' rights and entitlements, in addition to the provisions of the PACE regulations. A second set of interim final regulations was published at 67 Fed. Reg. 61,496 (Oct. 1, 2002).

[131] 42 C.F.R. §460.150(b)(2).

[132] *See generally* 42 C.F.R. §460.92.

[133] 42 C.F.R. §460.162.

[134] 42 C.F.R. §460.164(a).

[135] *Id.* at §460.164(d)(1).

The regulation creates a PACE organization appeal process[136] separate from and in addition to appeals available under Medicare and Medicaid. However, the regulation does not define the relationship of this process to the other two processes, nor does it describe the next appropriate step after completing the PACE appeal process. The regulation requires PACE organizations to inform individuals of their rights under Medicare and Medicaid but does not clarify how individuals would coordinate rights under both programs, nor where they would enter the Medicare or Medicaid processes if they so chose. In the past, Medicaid agencies have denied dually eligible beneficiaries access to Medicaid appeals if they have not exhausted their Medicare appeals, even if the Medicare appeals were not available because no formal claim had been made.[137]

PACE is, at least conceptually, a paradigm of integrated care for dual eligibles. It has, however, for whatever reasons, been very slow to develop. A document dated March 2006 on the Web site of the National PACE Association lists 43 sites in the country; CMS's Web site, updated in February 2006, states that 17,000 individuals are served by the programs.[138] In contrast, after their authorization in the 2003 MMA, 276 Medicare Advantage Special Needs Plans existed in 2006, most of them for dual eligibles. SNPs are a little known entity; while they may have great potential for serving this population, advocates should be attentive to whether their dually eligible clients are actually getting services to which they are entitled under both Medicare and Medicaid.

---

[136] *Id.* at §460.122.

[137] *See, e.g.*, Charpentier v. Belshe, Civ. No. 90-758 EJG/PAN, Medicare & Medicaid Guide (CCH) 43,123 (N.D. Cal. 1994).

[138] National PACE Association "PACE and Pre-PACE Providers at <http://www.npaonline.org/website/download.asp?id=745> (site visited July 11, 2006); Quality Initiatives, *supra* note 125.

APPENDIX 10-1

CMS PUB. 45: STATE MEDICAID MANUAL, PART 3 ELIGIBILITY

§3490.12 *Medicare Cost Sharing Expenses and Federal Financial Participation and*

§3490.13 *Payment of Monthly Premiums for Medicare Part B and for Premium Hospital Insurance Under Medicare Part A*

3490.12 Medicare Cost Sharing Expenses and Federal Financial Participation.— FFP is available for medical assistance for Medicare cost sharing expenses. These expenses are defined as:

- Monthly premiums for Medicare Part B and, where applicable, for Premium Hospital Insurance under Medicare Part A;

- Medicare Part A and Part B deductibles and coinsurance, including deductibles and coinsurance that HMOs and CMPs charge their Medicare enrollees in lieu of the Medicare deductibles and coinsurance that the beneficiaries would pay if they were not enrolled in an HMO or CMP; and

- At your option, premiums for enrollment with a Health Maintenance Organization (HMO) or a Competitive Medical Plan (CMP) under §§1876 of the Act.

Note that FFP is available for Medicare cost sharing expenses at the beginning of the month after the month in which you determine an individual is eligible for Medicaid as a QMB.

3490.13 Payment of Monthly Premiums for Medicare Part B and for Premium Hospital Insurance Under Medicare Part A.—You are required to pay the full amount of monthly premiums for Medicare Part B and, where applicable, for Premium Hospital Insurance under Medicare Part A. You may enroll QMBs and pay the Medicare Part B premiums under the State buy-in process under §§1843 of the Act. Effective January 1, 1990, a State may request and obtain a buy-in agreement modification to include payment of Part A premiums on behalf of QMBs. Payment of premiums through buy-in is advantageous because premiums paid through this method are not subject to the increases otherwise applicable in the case of late enrollment or re-enrollment. States without a buy-in agreement for Part B and/or Part A, are billed for the premiums (which may include any penalty applicable to the QMB for late enrollment) when the State seeks to enroll the QMB in Part A or Part B.

APPENDIX 10-2

November 22, 1991, Memorandum from Director of Office of Medicaid Management, MB, to Deputy Chief Counsel, Office of the General Counsel, Re: State Requirement to Pay Medicare Premiums for Qualified Medicare Beneficiaries (QMB)—Action

DEPARTMENT OF HEALTH & HUMAN SERVICES

Health Care
Financing Administration

Memorandum

Date: NOV 2 2 1991   Refer to: FMC-13

From: Director
Office of Medicaid Management, MB

Subject: State Requirement to Pay Medicare Premiums for Qualified
Medicare Beneficiaries (QMB)—ACTION

To: Deputy Chief Counsel
Office of the General Counsel

ISSUE

It has come to our attention that as many as 3 million Medicare beneficiaries may not be receiving the benefits to which they are entitled under section 1902(a)(10)(E) of the Social Security Act (the QMB provision).

We seek to confirm that the Federal Government has the authority necessary to compel States to: (a) enroll these individuals as QMBs, and (b) provide such individuals with all the benefits to which they are entitled under the QMB provision. Can the Health Care Financing Administration (HCFA) unilaterally accrete likely QMBs in Part A buy-in States and all other States without any State approval up front?

BACKGROUND

The Medicare Catastrophic Coverage Act of 1988 amended the Social Security Act to make coverage of certain Medicare beneficiaries for Medicare cost-sharing expenses a mandatory Medicaid coverage group.

The State Medicaid Manual (SMM), Part 3, Eligibility, was revised to instruct the States as to their obligations under this section. A QMB is defined as an individual who:

o   is entitled to Medicare hospital insurance benefits under Part A, with or without payment of premiums;

o   has income (as determined for Supplemental Security Income (SSI) purposes) that does not exceed 100 percent of the Federal poverty level; and

o   has resources (as determined for SSI purposes) that do not exceed twice the maximum amount established for SSI eligibility.

Page 2 - Deputy Chief Counsel, OGC

Potential QMBs Currently Without Part A

Part A Buy-in States

As a result of the Omnibus Budget Reconciliation Act of 1989, States are permitted, at their option, to modify their Part B buy-in agreement (copy attached) to include paying Part A premiums for QMBs. On February 7, 1990, we sent a letter to all State Medicaid Directors informing States of this option.

Thirty-Four States currently participate in Part A buy-in. The buy-in process allows States to accrete individuals as QMBs and to automatically enroll them in Part A. States are required (SMM section 3490.5) to conduct a review of all recipients currently eligible under the State plan and who also are entitled under Part A of Medicare to determine whether they meet the eligibility requirements for QMB status.

At the time the buy-in process became effective, there were 270,000 individuals in the 34 buy-in States for whom the States were purchasing Part B coverage on their behalf but who lacked Part A coverage and should have been accreted as QMBs through the Part A buy-in process. Of these, only 124,458 individuals have been accreted as QMBs. These States have had more than 15 months to perform the required review of their records, and accrete the remaining 145,000 individuals as QMBs, but have failed to do so.

We have sent a letter to the 18 most egregious States asking that they review the records of the remaining individuals in order to make the QMB determination and accrete them as QMBs. We have asked that they let us know what they plan to do in this regard.

It is our intention that after a period of 6 weeks from the date of our letter (October 10) HCFA will accrete the remaining individuals as QMBs and bill the State for the Part A premium. The State will then have an opportunity to delete any individuals they have determined do not meet the QMB eligibility criteria.

Page 3   Deputy Chief Counsel, OGC

Non-Part A Buy-in States

In the 16 States which did not modify their buy-in agreement, there were 250,000 individuals who could have been QMBs except for their lack of enrollment in Part A. In these States the individual must enroll in Part A. In 1989 we made available an easy method for the States to have these individuals enroll in Part A. An SSA-795 contact form was modified permitting the individual to sign a preprinted statement asking to be enrolled in Part A with the understanding that the State would be billed for the premium. To date, only 34,962 individuals have enrolled using this process. This is due, we believe, to State failure to inform the individual of this process.

It is our intention to mail the form directly to the remaining individuals, explaining the benefit to them, and instructing them to sign and return the form to us. Having thus established their enrollment in Part A, we intend to accrete these individuals as QMBs in a manner similar to that described earlier for the Part A buy-in States.

Potential QMBs Already Entitled to Part A

Finally, approximately 3.2 million Medicaid recipients are currently covered under Part A and have their Part B coverage purchased by States on their behalf. The vast majority of these individuals are SSI recipients. Of these, only 845,000 have been identified as QMBs.

Although States are paying the $358.80 annual Part B premium, the beneficiary is not guaranteed the financial protection afforded under the statute for other costs, e.g., the $100 annual Part B deductible and 20-percent copayment for physician charges in excess of the deductible.

It is our intention to insert the required QMB identifier in the records of these 3.2 million individuals, and to inform the State of the QMB status of these individuals.

We are writing seeking your concurrence with these intended actions. Your prompt reply is appreciated. Should you have any questions please contact Mike Sparacino on extension 6-5918.

David McNally

Attachment

FMC-33:MSparacino:SGullick:MPSMISC DISK:A:OGCNOTE:11-12-91

APPENDIX 10-3

June 30, 2000, Memorandum from Director, Disabled and Elderly Health Programs Group, to Associate Regional Administrators, Re: Policy

DEPARTMENT OF HEALTH & HUMAN SERVICES
Health Care Financing Administration
Center for Medicaid and State Operations

MEMORANDUM

RECEIVED

JUL 0 5 2000

HCFA-DMSO

DATE: JUN 30 2000

FROM: Director
        Disabled and Elderly Health Programs Group

SUBJECT: Policy Memorandum on Medicaid Obligations to Pay Medicare
           Cost-sharing Expenses for Qualified Medicare Beneficiaries in Medicare
           Health Maintenance Organizations or Competitive Medical Plans or
           Medicare Plus Choice Organizations—INFORMATION

TO: Associate Regional Administrators
      Division of Medicaid and State Operations
      Regions I - X

This policy memorandum provides clarification about State Medicaid agency obligations to pay Medicare cost-sharing expenses for Qualified Medicare Beneficiaries (QMBs) enrolled in Medicare Health Maintenance Organizations (HMOs) or Competitive Medical Plans (CMPs) or in Medicare Plus Choice (M-C) plans through M+C organizations.

Qualified Medicare Beneficiaries (QMBs)

QMBs are individuals who meet the definition in §1905(p)(1) of the Social Security Act (the Act) (further described at §3490.2 of the State Medicaid Manual (SMM)). All QMBs are Medicare beneficiaries, entitled to the full range of Medicare covered services and Medicare provider options, without regard to whether those services are covered under the Medicaid State Plan, and eligible for Medicaid payment of their Medicare cost-sharing expenses. QMBs include both:

- **QMB** - Medicare beneficiaries who are eligible for Medicaid under the QMB definition and only receive Medicare services. Medicaid pays for their Medicare cost-sharing expenses.

- **QMB Plus** - Medicare beneficiaries who are eligible for Medicaid under the QMB definition and also are eligible under another Medicaid eligibility group and, in addition to the above, receive Medicaid services. Medicaid pays for their Medicare cost-sharing and for Medicaid services.

Medicare Cost-sharing

Section 3490.12 of the SMM defines the Medicare cost-sharing expenses that Medicaid must pay for a QMB as including:

- Medicare Part A and Part B deductibles and coinsurance, including deductibles and coinsurance that HMOs and Competitive Medical Plans (CMPs) charge their Medicare enrollees in lieu of the Medicare deductibles and coinsurance that the beneficiaries would pay if they were not enrolled in an HMO or CMP; and

- At the State's option, premiums for enrollment with an HMO or CMP under §1876 of the Social Security Act (the Act).

This language interprets §1905(p)(3) of the Act, which clearly states that Medicare cost-sharing expenses include, subject to §1902(n)(2) of the Act, Medicare deductibles and coinsurance, and may include, at the option of the State, premiums for enrollment of QMBs with an eligible organization under §1876 of the Act. §1902(n)(2) of the Act provides that a State is not required to provide any payment for deductibles, coinsurance, or copayments for Medicare cost-sharing to the extent that payment under Medicare for the service would exceed the payment amount that otherwise would be made under the Medicaid State plan for such service if provided to an eligible recipient other than a Medicare beneficiary. Clearly, the Medicaid State plan (Supplement 1 to Attachment 4.19-B) is controlling as to the amount (the Medicare rate, the State plan rate, or somewhere in between) Medicaid must pay for Medicare cost-sharing.

Medicare Plus Choice (M+C) Options

The Balanced Budget Act of 1997 (BBA) introduced a new Part C to title XVIII of the Act, the M+C program. M+C provides Medicare beneficiaries with some new options for receiving Medicare benefits through private health plans, including provision for provider-sponsored organizations (PSO), preferred provider organization (PPO) plans, private fee-for-service plans, and a medical savings account (MSA) option that currently is not available because no private insurer has chosen to participate.

Most organizations that previously contracted on a risk basis under §1876 as HMOs and CMPs now contract with Medicare as M+C organizations under Part C. Only a limited number of grandfathered cost-reimbursed HMOs or CMPs still contract under §1876. Although Medicare cost-sharing under §1905(p)(3) of the Act does not expressly provide for States to include premiums for M+C organizations, we believe that Congress intended to permit States to include premiums under Medicare contracts with private health plans, and that §1905(p)(3) should thus be read to permit M+C premiums for M+C plans to be included, at State option, in cost-sharing under the same terms as §1876 contracts. For ease of reference, references to M+C organizations will include any remaining cost-contracting HMOs or CMPs under §1876 of the Act.

Monthly Premiums in M+C Organizations

Monthly premiums are fixed monthly amounts that an M+C organization can charge its enrollees. If the M+C organization charges monthly premiums, the premiums generally cover the basic package of Medicare covered benefits, but may include additional premium amounts for supplemental benefits, which are not otherwise covered under Medicare. Medicaid is liable for payment of monthly premium amounts for QMBs and QMB Plus categories for the basic package of Medicare covered benefits only, if so elected in the Medicaid State plan (page 29-3.2(a)(1)(i)). In addition, since QMB Plus is also eligible for full Medicaid benefits, Medicaid may also pay premiums for supplemental benefits not covered by Medicare, but which are covered by Medicaid, if so elected in the Medicaid State plan (page 29b-3.2(a)(2)).

Medicare Cost-sharing

Deductibles are fixed dollar amounts that an individual must pay out-of-pocket before the costs of services are covered by the M+C organization. Coinsurance charges are a percentage of costs for services. Copayments are fixed dollar amounts that a beneficiary must pay when he or she uses a particular service. For purposes of the provisions discussed in this memorandum, coinsurance includes the copayments that M+C organizations charge when beneficiaries use services. Medicaid is liable for these Medicare cost-sharing expenses for Medicare covered services to the payment amount specified in the Medicaid State plan (Supplement 1 to Attachment 4.19-B). If the payment amount is not specified, or the payment amount is the State plan payment rate and Medicaid does not cover the service, so there is no State plan payment rate, Medicaid will be liable for the full Medicare cost-sharing.

State Options and Responsibilities

It is optional for State Medicaid agencies to include as "cost-sharing" under §1905(p)(3) of the Act, premium charges imposed by M+C organizations for enrollment. When the State Medicaid agency has opted to include the premium charges as cost-sharing and is paying the premium as described above, the QMB is relieved of liability for such premiums. In this case, when the State is paying for the charges in the basic benefit package attributable to Medicare covered services, the QMB would be entitled to the full range of Medicare covered services. When the State has opted to pay M+C organization premiums, it must treat all M+C organizations the same.

For individuals eligible as **QMB Plus**, the Medicaid agency must pay for any services in their Medicaid State plan provided by a Medicaid provider, whether within the M+C organization or outside the M+C organization. If some of these services are included in the group of supplemental benefits that are part of the M+C organization's benefits package, the State may find it cost-effective to choose to pay for the portion of the premium attributable to the supplemental benefits. However, since these supplemental benefits are non-Medicare covered services when they are offered on an optional basis, they may never be included in Medicare cost-sharing under §1905(p)(3).

When a Medicare M+C organization has chosen to impose deductibles, coinsurance or copayment charges for Medicare covered services on their enrollees (not as a premium, but as amounts charged when services are furnished) the Medicaid agency is **required** to include those costs as Medicare cost-sharing for QMBs without regard to whether it has elected to include premiums in cost-sharing. These costs must be paid by the State in full or to a lesser extent as indicated in the Medicaid State plan.

If an individual eligible as a **QMB Plus** is enrolled in an M+C organization, and uses out-of-plan Medicaid providers for M+C covered Medicaid services under non-emergency conditions, Medicaid can deny payment for the services that should have been provided through the M+C organization, if the service is available at no cost to the individual. If the State has opted to pay premiums for enrollment of a such an individual in an M+C organization, and is paying deductibles and coinsurance copayments, that M+C organization coverage is available to the recipient at no cost. In this case, the M+C organization can be considered a third party resource which the State must take into account in determining the extent of medical assistance payment. The State can deny payment for the individual's Medicaid coverage in an amount corresponding to the value of this available resource. Where both the M+C organization and the State Medicaid agency appropriately deny payment, a provider may seek payment from the QMB Plus as a Medicaid recipient.

Please forward the information in this memorandum to the State agencies in your region. Questions on Medicaid policy in this area can be directed to Robert Nakielny at (410) 786-4466 or by E-mail at Rnakielny@hcfa.gov.

Thomas E. Hamilton

Attachment

Attachment

State Liability for QMB Payments

Summary	QMB	QMB Plus
Part B Premiums	Required	Required
Part A Premiums, when necessary	Required	Required
Deductibles	Required	Required
Coinsurance	Required	Required
Copayments	Required	Required
Enrollment Premiums	Optional	Optional
Other M+C Premiums (non basic Medicare)	None	Optional

APPENDIX 10-4

Letter of March 31, 1999, from the Associate Regional Administrator, Region 1, Health Care Financing Administration, to Hilary S. Dalin, Staff Attorney, Center for Medicare Advocacy, Inc., Concerning Dually Eligible Individuals in Nursing Facilities

Region I
J.F.K. Federal Building
Government Center
Boston, MA 02203

March 31, 1999

Hilary S. Dalin
Staff Attorney
Center for Medicare Advocacy, Inc.
P.O. Box 350
Willimantic, Connecticut 06226

Dear Ms. Dalin:

This letter is the response to the questions you asked us by letter, dated February 10, 1999. Your questions and our responses follow below.

1. If a dually eligible individual who is enrolled in a Medicare HMO sought nursing home admission due solely to a need for custodial care and the Medicare HMO denied Medicare coverage on the grounds that the nursing facility was out-of-network, would Medicaid reimbursement also be precluded?

Neither Medicaid nor Medicare cover custodial care. However, if the individual met the nursing facility (NF) level of care requirements for Medicaid, then coverage by Medicaid would not be precluded. Medicare only covers skilled nursing facility (SNF) services, so Medicare or the Medicare HMO would not be a liable third party in this situation.

2. If a dually eligible individual who was enrolled in a Medicare HMO and resided in a non-Medicare-certified bed in a NF became eligible for the Medicare SNF benefit, would the resident be compelled to move to an in-network Medicare-certified bed or would such an individual be allowed to waive her right to Medicare coverage and remain in the non-Medicare-certified bed, with Medicaid as the payor?

Our answer is that the individual would not have to move, and thus Medicare would not be an available third party resource. A State may not, as a condition of eligibility, require an individual entitled to Medicare to obtain a "Medicare bed" in order to utilize her Medicare benefits. A liable third party resource exists for Medicaid purposes only to the extent that the services the individual receives from the provider of her choice are covered by the third party entity. According to section 1902(a)(23) of the Social Security Act (the Act), a Medicaid eligible individual may obtain Medicaid covered services from any qualified provider who undertakes to provide her the services.

In general, if the individual is in a "Medicaid bed" that is not also a "Medicare bed," then Medicare is not a liable third party and the Medicaid agency must pay the full amount allowed under the Medicaid payment schedule (42 CFR 433.139(c)). However, if a Medicaid/Medicare bed is available *at no cost* to the individual, *at the time of placement in a facility*, then the State may deny or reduce payment for a Medicaid only bed in an amount corresponding to the value of the available resource (section 1902(a)(17)(B) of the Act). In other words, Medicaid would only be liable for that amount of the Medicaid rate which exceeded the amount the third party would have paid, if any, had the individual been placed in an available Medicare covered bed.

I trust I have answered your questions fully. Should you have further questions, do not hesitate to contact me.

Sincerely

Ronald Preston
Associate Regional Administrator

APPENDIX 10-5

TITLE 42—THE PUBLIC HEALTH AND WELFARE
(UNITED STATES CODE),

CHAPTER 7—SOCIAL SECURITY

SUBCHAPTER XVIII—HEALTH INSURANCE FOR AGED AND DISABLED,

PART B—Supplementary Medical Insurance Benefits for
Aged and Disabled

Sec. 1395v. Agreements with States

(a) Duty of Secretary; enrollment of eligible individuals

The Secretary shall, at the request of a State made before January 1, 1970, or during 1981 or after 1988, enter into an agreement with such State pursuant to which all eligible individuals in either of the coverage groups described in subsection (b) of this section (as specified in the agreement) will be enrolled under the program established by this part.

(b) Coverage of groups to which applicable

An agreement entered into with any State pursuant to subsection (a) of this section may be applicable to either of the following coverage groups:

(1) individuals receiving money payments under the plan of such State approved under subchapter I of this chapter or subchapter XVI of this chapter; or

(2) individuals receiving money payments under all of the plans of such State approved under subchapters I, X, XIV, and XVI of this chapter, and part A of subchapter IV of this chapter.

Except as provided in subsection (g) of this section, there shall be excluded from any coverage group any individual who is entitled to monthly insurance benefits under subchapter II of this chapter or who is entitled to receive an annuity under the Railroad Retirement Act of 1974 (45 U.S.C. 231 et seq.). Effective January 1, 1974, and subject to section 1396a(f) of this title, the Secretary shall, at the request of any State not eligible to participate in the State plan program established under subchapter XVI of this chapter, continue in effect the agreement entered into under this section with such State subject to such modifications as the Secretary may by regulations provide to take account of the termination of any plans of such State approved under subchapters I, X, XIV, and XVI of this chapter and the establishment of the supplemental security income program under subchapter XVI of this chapter.

(c) Eligible individuals

For purposes of this section, an individual shall be treated as an eligible individual only if he is an eligible individual (within the meaning of section 1395o of this title) on the date an agreement covering him is entered into under subsection (a) of this section or he becomes an eligible individual (within the meaning of such section) at any time after such date; and he shall be treated as receiving money payments described in subsection (b) of this section if he receives such payments for the month in which the agreement is entered into or any month thereafter.

(d) Monthly premiums; coverage periods

In the case of any individual enrolled pursuant to this section—

(1) the monthly premium to be paid by the State shall be determined under section 1395r of this title (without any increase under subsection (b) thereof);

(2) his coverage period shall begin on whichever of the following is the latest:

(A) July 1, 1966;

(B) the first day of the third month following the month in which the State agreement is entered into;

(C) the first day of the first month in which he is both an eligible individual and a member of a coverage group specified in the agreement under this section; or

(D) such date as may be specified in the agreement; and

(3) his coverage period attributable to the agreement with the State under this section shall end on the last day of whichever of the following first occurs:

(A) the month in which he is determined by the State agency to have become ineligible both for money payments of a kind specified in the agreement and (if there is in effect a modification entered into under subsection (h) of this section) for medical assistance, or

(B) the month preceding the first month for which he becomes entitled to monthly benefits under subchapter II of this chapter or to an annuity or pension under the Railroad Retirement Act of 1974 (45 U.S.C. 231 et seq.).

(e) Subsection (d)(3) terminations deemed resulting in section 1395p enrollment

Any individual whose coverage period attributable to the State agreement is terminated pursuant to subsection (d)(3) of this section shall be deemed for purposes of this part (including the continuation of his coverage period under this part) to have enrolled under section 1395p of this title in the initial general enrollment period provided by section 1395p(c) of this title. The coverage period under this part of any such individual who (in the last month of his coverage period attributable to the State agreement or in any of the following six months) files notice that he no longer wishes to participate in the insurance program established by this part, shall terminate at the close of the month in which the notice is filed.

(f) "Carrier" as including State agency; provisions facilitating deductions, coinsurance, etc., and leading to economy and efficiency of operation

With respect to eligible individuals receiving money payments under the plan of a State approved under subchapter I, X, XIV, or XVI of this chapter, or part A of subchapter IV of this chapter, or eligible to receive medical assistance under the plan of such State approved under subchapter XIX of this chapter, if the agreement entered into under this section so provides, the term "carrier" as defined in section 1395u(f) of this title also includes the State agency, specified in such agreement, which administers or supervises the administration of the plan of such State approved under subchapter I, XVI, or XIX of this chapter. The agreement shall also contain such provisions as will facilitate the financial transactions of the State and the carrier with respect to deductions, coinsurance, and otherwise, and as will lead to economy and efficiency of operation, with respect to individuals receiving money payments under plans of the State approved under subchapters I, X, XIV, and XVI of this chapter, and part A of subchapter IV of this chapter, and individuals eligible to receive medical assistance under the plan of the State approved under subchapter XIX of this chapter.

(g) Subsection (b) exclusions from coverage groups

(1) The Secretary shall, at the request of a State made before January 1, 1970, or during 1981 or after 1988, enter into a modification of an agreement entered into with such State pursuant to subsection (a) of this section under which the second sentence of subsection (b) of this section shall not apply with respect to such agreement.

(2) In the case of any individual who would (but for this subsection) be excluded from the applicable coverage group described in subsection (b) of this section by the second sentence of such subsection—

(A) subsections (c) and (d)(2) of this section shall be applied as if such subsections referred to the modification under this subsection (in lieu of the agreement under subsection (a) of this section), and

(B) subsection (d)(3)(B) of this section shall not apply so long as there is in effect a modification entered into by the State under this subsection.

(h) Modifications respecting subsection (b) coverage groups

(1) The Secretary shall, at the request of a State made before January 1, 1970, or during 1981 or after 1988, enter into a modification of an agreement entered into with such State pursuant to subsection (a) of this section under which the coverage group described in subsection (b) of this section and specified in such agreement is broadened to include (A) individuals who are eligible to receive medical assistance under the plan of such State approved under subchapter XIX of this chapter, or (B) qualified medicare beneficiaries (as defined in section 1396d(p)(1) of this title).

(2) For purposes of this section, an individual shall be treated as eligible to receive medical assistance under the plan of the State approved under subchapter XIX of this chapter if, for the month in which the modification is entered into under this subsection or for any month thereafter, he has been determined to be eligible to receive medical assistance under such plan. In the case of any individual who would (but for this subsection) be excluded from the agreement, subsections (c) and (d)(2) of this section shall be applied as if they referred to the modification under this subsection (in lieu of the agreement under subsection (a) of this section), and subsection (d)(2)(C) of this section shall be applied (except in the case of qualified medicare beneficiaries, as defined in section 1396d(p)(1) of this title) by substituting "second month following the first month" for "first month."

(3) In this subsection, the term "qualified medicare beneficiary" also includes an individual described in section 1396a(a)(10)(E)(iii) of this title.

(i) Enrollment of qualified medicare beneficiaries

For provisions relating to enrollment of qualified medicare beneficiaries under part A of this subchapter, see section 1395i-2(g) of this title.

(Aug. 14, 1935, ch. 531, title XVIII, Sec. 1843, as added July 30, 1965, Pub. L. 89-97, title I, Sec. 102(a), 79 Stat. 312; amended Apr. 8, 1966, Pub. L. 89-384, Sec. 4(a), (b), 80 Stat. 105; Jan. 2, 1968, Pub. L. 90-248, title II, Sec. 222(a), (b), (e), 241(e), 81 Stat. 900, 901, 917; Dec. 31, 1973, Pub. L. 93-233, Sec. 18(l), 87 Stat. 970; Oct. 16, 1974, Pub. L. 93-445, title III, Sec. 308, 88 Stat. 1358; Dec. 5, 1980, Pub. L. 96-499, title IX, Sec. 945(e), 947(a), (c), 94 Stat. 2642, 2643; Apr. 20, 1983, Pub. L. 98-21, title VI, Sec. 606(a)(3)(E), 97 Stat. 171; July 18, 1984, Pub. L. 98-369, div. B, title III, Sec. 2354(b)(15), 98 Stat. 1101; July 1, 1988, Pub. L. 100-360, title III, Sec. 301(e)(1), 102 Stat. 749; Oct. 13, 1988, Pub. L. 100-485, title VI, Sec. 608(d)(14)(H), 102 Stat. 2416; Dec. 19, 1989, Pub. L. 101-239, title VI, Sec. 6013(b), 103 Stat. 2164; Nov. 5, 1990, Pub. L. 101-508, title IV, Sec. 4501(d), 104 Stat. 1388-165.)

References in Text

Part A of subchapter IV of this chapter, referred to in subsecs. (b)(2) and (f), is classified to section 601 et seq. of this title. The Railroad Retirement Act of 1974, referred to in subsec. (d)(3)(B), is act Aug. 29, 1935, ch. 812, as amended generally by Pub. L. 93-445, title I, Sec. 101, Oct. 16, 1974, 88 Stat. 1305, which is classified generally to subchapter IV (Sec. 231 et seq.) of chapter 9 of Title 45, Railroads. For further details and complete classification of this Act to the Code, see Codification note set out preceding section 231 of Title 45, section 231 of Title 45, and Tables.

Part A of this subchapter, referred to in subsec. (i), is classified to section 1395c et seq. of this title.

Amendments

1990—Subsec. (h)(3). Pub. L. 101-508 added par. (3).

1989—Subsec. (i). Pub. L. 101-239 added subsec. (i).

1988—Subsecs. (a), (g)(1). Pub. L. 100-360, Sec. 301(e)(1)(A), formerly Sec. 301(e)(1), as redesignated by Pub. L. 100-485, Sec. 608(d)(14)(H)(i), inserted "or after 1988" after "during 1981."

Subsec. (h)(1). Pub. L. 100-360, Sec. 301(e)(1)(A), formerly Sec. 301(e)(1), as redesignated by Pub. L. 100-485, Sec. 608(d)(14)(H)(i), inserted "or after 1988" after "during 1981."

Pub. L. 100-360, Sec. 301(e)(1)(B), as added by Pub. L. 100-485, Sec. 608(d)(14)(H)(ii), inserted cl. (A) designation after "include" and added cl. (B).

Subsec. (h)(2). Pub. L. 100-360, Sec. 301(e)(1)(C), as added by Pub. L. 100-485, Sec. 608(d)(14)(H)(ii), inserted "(except in the case of qualified medicare beneficiaries, as defined in section 1396d(p)(1) of this title)" after "shall be applied."

1984—Subsec. (d)(3)(B). Pub. L. 98-369 substituted "1974" for "1937."

1983—Subsec. (d)(1). Pub. L. 98-21 substituted "without any increase under subsection (b) thereof" for "without any increase under subsection (c) thereof."

1980—Subsec. (a). Pub. L. 96-499, Sec. 945(e), inserted "or during 1981," after "January 1, 1970."

Subsec. (e). Pub. L. 96-499, Sec. 947(a), inserted provision that the coverage period under this part of any individual who filed notice that he no longer wished to participate in the insurance program established by this part was to terminate at the close of the month in which the notice was filed.

Subsec. (g)(1). Pub. L. 96-499, Sec. 945(e), inserted "or during 1981," after "January 1, 1970."

Subsec. (g)(2)(C). Pub. L. 96-499, Sec. 947(c)(3), struck out cl. (C) which authorized individuals facing exclusion from the applicable coverage group to terminate their enrollment under this part by the filing of a notice indicating he no longer wished to participate in the insurance program established by this part.

Subsec. (h)(1). Pub. L. 96-499, Sec. 945(e), inserted "or during 1981," after "January 1, 1970."

1974—Subsec. (b). Pub. L. 93-445 substituted "under the Railroad Retirement Act of 1974" for "or pension under the Railroad Retirement Act of 1937."

1973—Subsec. (b). Pub. L. 93-233 provided for continuation of State agreements for coverage of certain individuals in connection with establishment of supplemental security income program.

1968—Pub. L. 90-248, Sec. 222(b)(4), inserted "(or are eligible for medical assistance)" in section catchline.

Subsec. (a). Pub. L. 90-248, Sec. 222(e)(1), substituted "1970" for "1968."

Subsec. (b)(2). Pub. L. 90-248, Sec. 241(e)(1), struck out "IV," after "I," and inserted ", and part A of subchapter IV of this chapter" after "XVI of this chapter."

Subsec. (c). Pub. L. 90-248, Sec. 222(e)(2), struck out "and before January 1, 1968" after "such date" and "before January 1968" after "thereafter" just before the period.

Subsec. (d)(2)(D). Pub. L. 90-248, Sec. 222(e)(3), struck out "(not later than January 1, 1968)" after "such date."

Subsec. (d)(3)(A). Pub. L. 90-248, Sec. 222(b)(1), substituted "ineligible both for money payments of a kind specified in the agreement and (if there is in effect a modification entered into under subsection (h) of this section) for medical assistance" for "ineligible for money payments of a kind specified in the agreement."

Subsec. (f). Pub. L. 90-248, Sec. 222(b)(2), inserted "or eligible to receive medical assistance under the plan of such State approved under subchapter XIX of this chapter" and ", and individuals eligible to receive medical assistance under the plan of the State approved under subchapter XIX of this chapter" after "or part A of subchapter IV of this chapter" and ", and part A of subchapter IV of this chapter," respectively.

Pub. L. 90-248, Sec. 241(e)(2), struck out "IV," before "X," in two places, and inserted "or part A of subchapter IV of this chapter," after "XVI of this chapter," first place it appears in first sentence and, "and part A of subchapter IV of this chapter" after "XVI of this chapter" in second sentence.

Subsec. (g)(1). Pub. L. 90-248, Sec. 222(b)(3), substituted "1970" for "1968."

Subsec. (h). Pub. L. 90-248, Sec. 222(a), added subsec. (h).

1966—Subsec. (b). Pub. L. 89-384, Sec. 4(a), inserted reference to subsec. (g) in exclusionary provision.

Subsec. (g). Pub. L. 89-384, Sec. 4(b), added subsec. (g).

Effective Date of 1990 Amendment

Amendment by Pub. L. 101-508 applicable to calendar quarters beginning on or after Jan. 1, 1991, without regard to whether or not regulations to implement such amendment are promulgated by such date, see section 4501(f) of Pub. L. 101-508, set out as a note under section 1396a of this title.

Effective Date of 1989 Amendment

Amendment by Pub. L. 101-239 effective Jan. 1, 1990, see section 6013(c) of Pub. L. 101-239, set out as a note under section 1395i-2 of this title.

Effective Date of 1988 Amendments

Amendment by Pub. L. 100-485 effective as if included in the enactment of the Medicare Catastrophic Coverage Act of 1988, Pub. L. 100-360, see section 608(g)(1) of Pub. L. 100-485, set out as a note under section 704 of this title.

Section 301(e)(3) of Pub. L. 100-360 provided that: "The amendment made by paragraph (1) (amending this section) shall take effect on January 1, 1989, and the amendments made by paragraph (2) (amending section 1396a of this title) shall take effect on July 1, 1989."

Effective Date of 1984 Amendment

Amendment by Pub. L. 98-369 effective July 18, 1984, but not to be construed as changing or affecting any right, liability, status, or interpretation which existed (under the provisions of law involved) before that date, see section 2354(e)(1) of Pub. L. 98-369, set out as a note under section 1320a-1 of this title.

Effective Date of 1983 Amendment; Transitional Rule

Amendment by Pub. L. 98-21 applicable to premiums for months beginning with January 1984, but for months after June 1983 and before January 1984, the monthly premium for June 1983 shall apply to individuals enrolled under parts A and B of this subchapter, see section 606(c) of Pub. L. 98-21, set out as a note under section 1395r of this title.

Effective Date of 1980 Amendment

Section 947(d) of Pub. L. 96-499 provided that: "The amendments made by this section (amending this section and section 1395q of this title) apply to notices filed after the third calendar month beginning after the date of the enactment of this Act (Dec. 5, 1980)."

Effective Date of 1974 Amendment

Amendment by Pub. L. 93-445 effective Jan. 1, 1975, see section 603 of Pub. L. 93-445, set out as a note under section 402 of this title.

Effective Date of 1973 Amendment

Amendment by Pub. L. 93-233 effective Jan. 1, 1974, see section 18(z-3)(1) of Pub. L. 93-233.

Termination Period for Certain Individuals Covered Pursuant to State Agreements

Section 947(e) of Pub. L. 96-499 provided that: "The coverage period under part B of title XVIII of the Social Security Act (this part) of an individual whose coverage period attributable to a State agreement under section 1843 of such Act (this section) is terminated and who has filed notice before the end of the third calendar month beginning after the date of the enactment of this Act (Dec. 5, 1980) that he no longer wishes to participate in the insurance program established by part B of title XVIII shall terminate on the earlier of (1) the day specified in section 1838 (section 1395q of this title) without the amendments made by this section, or (2) (unless the individual files notice before the day specified in this clause that he wishes his coverage period to terminate as provided in clause (1)) the day on which his coverage period would terminate if the individual filed notice in the fourth calendar month beginning after the date of the enactment of this Act."

District of Columbia; Agreement of Commissioner with Secretary for Supplementary Medical Insurance

Pub. L. 90-227, Sec. 2, Dec. 27, 1967, 81 Stat. 745, provided that: "The Commissioner (now Mayor of District of Columbia) may enter into an agreement (and any modifications of such agreement) with the Secretary under section 1843 of the Social Security Act (this section) pursuant to which (1) eligible individuals (as defined in section 1836 of the Social Security Act) (section 1395o of this title) who are eligible to receive medical assistance under the District of Columbia's plan for medical assistance approved under title XIX of the Social Security Act (subchapter XIX of this chapter) will be enrolled in the supplementary medical insurance program established under part B of title XVIII of the Social Security Act (this part), and (2) provisions will be made for payment of the monthly premiums of such individuals for such program."

Section Referred to in Other Sections

This section is referred to in sections 1395i-2, 1395q, 1395s, 1396a of this title.

APPENDIX 10-6

Updated Guidance—Changes to Effective Date and PDP Notice Requirements for Auto-Enrollment and Facilitated Enrollment (March 17, 2006)

DEPARTMENT OF HEALTH & HUMAN SERVICES
Centers for Medicare & Medicaid Services
7500 Security Boulevard
Baltimore, Maryland 21244-1850

CENTER FOR BENEFICIARY CHOICES

To: Medicare Prescription Drug Plans (PDPs)

From: Anthony J. Culotta, Acting Director /s/
                Medicare Enrollment and Appeals Group

Subject: Updated Guidance – Changes to Effective Date and PDP Notice
                Requirements for Auto-Enrollment and Facilitated Enrollment

Date: March 17, 2006

The purpose of this memo is to provide information and guidance about the following:

- The first round of facilitated enrollment, effective May 1, 2006
- Effective dates for future auto-enrollment actions
- Retroactive enrollments for full-dual beneficiaries who have voluntarily enrolled in a PDP

Earlier this week, CMS released two transaction files to PDPs that contain information about beneficiaries to be facilitated or auto-enrolled into Part D. This memo outlines requirements associated with both the facilitated enrollment and auto-enrollment processes, and provides updated guidance. The first file, released on March 13, includes those beneficiaries who have been auto-enrolled or facilitated enrolled. The second, released on March 15, was a special Transaction Reply Report that includes only the facilitated enrollment population.

CMS is changing the effective date of auto-enrollment for certain subsets of full-benefit dual eligibles. In addition, CMS is modifying previous guidance provided on November 10, 2005 as to when PDPs must provide a confirmation notice to new auto-enrollees, and is extending this requirement to facilitated enrollees. CMS is also changing the effective date of the initial round of facilitated enrollment for non-full benefit dual eligibles who are eligible for the low-income subsidy from June 1, 2006 to May 1, 2006.

<u>Facilitated Enrollment Effective May 1, 2006</u>

The effective date of facilitated enrollment for beneficiaries included in the special March 15 Transaction Reply Report will be May 1, 2006. Facilitated enrollments can be distinguished by looking for the following: Field 21 – Enrollment Source = C (facilitated enrollment); and Transaction Reply Code = 118 (facilitated enrollment).

Thus, the effective date of facilitated enrollment of non-full benefit dual eligibles who are eligible for the low-income subsidy remains prospective, i.e. the first day of the second month after the beneficiary is included in a monthly facilitated enrollment run, as outlined in section 30.1.5.B of CMS' PDP Eligibility, Enrollment and Disenrollment Guidance).

New Guidance on Auto-Enrollment Effective Date

Under our existing PDP Eligibility, Enrollment and Disenrollment Guidance (Section 30.1.4.B.), the auto-enrollment effective date for full-benefit dual eligibles who are first Medicare eligible and subsequently become Medicaid eligible, is the first day of the second month after the person is identified by CMS (i.e., included in our monthly auto-enrollment process. However, this policy may result in a gap in prescription drug coverage for these individuals. Likewise, full-benefit dual eligibles who voluntarily enroll in a Part D may experience a gap in prescription drug coverage, since that enrollment is effective prospectively.

Therefore, effective immediately, the effective date of auto-enrollment for full-benefit dual eligibles who are Medicare eligible and subsequently become Medicaid eligible will be the first day of the month of Medicaid eligibility or January 1, 2006, whichever is later. This includes those individuals who become eligible for both Medicare and Medicaid in the same month. This updated guidance supersedes instructions in Section 30.1.4.B of CMS' PDP Eligibility, Enrollment and Disenrollment Guidance as applicable to this subset of auto-enrollees. CMS will continue to calculate the effective date of auto-enrollments and provide this information on the Transaction Reply Report (TRR) and the PDP notification file.

Revised Guidance on Auto-Enrollment Effective Date for Full-Benefit Dual Eligibles With Previous Enrollment in a Part D Plan

Also, effective immediately, the auto-enrollment effective date for full-benefit dual eligibles who had previously been enrolled in a Part D plan, but disenrolled and failed to enroll in a new Part D plan, is the first day of the month after the disenrollment effective date from the previous Part D plan. This updated guidance supersedes Section 30.1.4.B of CMS' PDP Eligibility, Enrollment and Disenrollment Guidance as applicable to this subset of auto-enrollees.

Thus, all auto-enrollments will now have a retroactive effective date, as follows:

- New full-benefit dual eligibles who are Medicare eligible first will be auto-enrolled retroactive to the start of Medicaid eligibility;
- New full-benefit dual eligibles who are Medicaid eligible first will be auto-enrolled retroactive to the start of Medicare Part D eligibility as outlined in Section 30.1.4.D. (which remains unchanged for the population who is Medicaid first and then becomes Medicare eligible);
- Full-benefit dual eligibles with previous Part D plan enrollment will be auto-enrolled retroactive to the day after the end of that previous coverage.

<u>Revised Guidance on Effective Date of Voluntary Enrollment by Full-Benefit Dual Eligibles
with Out-of-Pocket Costs in Previous Uncovered Months</u>

In limited instances, a full-benefit dual eligible voluntarily enrolls in a Part D plan in the
month(s) before the individual would otherwise have been auto-enrolled. Individuals with
active elections are not included in our auto-enrollment process. However, since an individual's
elected enrollment normally would not be effective until the first day of the following month,
this would mean that the individual would have a coverage gap before the effective date of the
election and thus would likely incur out-of-pocket prescription drug costs.

To remedy this situation, we are establishing a Special Enrollment Period (SEP) that will permit
such individuals to have their voluntary enrollment be retroactive to the first day of the previous
un-covered month(s). The effective date is retroactive only to the beginning of the month in
which there were out-of-pocket costs, not necessarily all months in which there was no Part D
plan enrollment. Please note that the beneficiary must have been a full-benefit dual eligible
during each of the uncovered month(s), and incurred out-of-pocket costs during this time.
Where these cases originate with CMS, caseworkers in CMS' Regional Offices will take the
appropriate action and notify the PDP. If a full-benefit dual eligible member requests this
retroactive coverage directly from the PDP, the PDP must develop the retroactive request and
submit it to CMS Division of Payment Operations.

<u>Revised Guidance on Deadline for PDP Confirmation Notice to New Auto- and Facilitated
Enrollees</u>

Beginning in June 2006, PDPs must provide the confirmation notice to new auto- and facilitated
enrollees within seven (7) business days of receiving the weekly TRR with confirmation of
auto- or facilitated enrollment, or the PDP notification file (monthly file listing assignments,
that also includes address data), whichever is later. This requirement must be met for new auto-
and facilitated enrollees beginning in June 2006, and replaces guidance issued on November 10,
2005 (see Q&A #5) for auto-enrollees, and section 30.1.5.D of the PDP Guidance.

<u>Further Information</u>

We appreciate PDPs' continued cooperation in ensuring full-benefit dual eligibles do not
experience coverage gaps, and that all auto- and facilitated enrollees are notified in a timely
manner that their enrollment is confirmed. If you have any questions, please contact Sharon
Donovan at (410) 786-2561, or sharon.donovan@cms.hhs.gov

APPENDIX 10-7

Transition Process Requirements for Part D Sponsors (April 2006)

Overview

CMS's review of plan formularies will ensure that plans offer a comprehensive array of drugs that reflects best practices in the pharmacy industry, as well as current treatment standards. We expect plan formularies and benefit designs to include the full range of treatment options and, at the same time, reflect drug benefit management tools that are proven and in widespread use in prescription drug plans today. As described in detail in our Formulary Guidance for 2007, our goal is to ensure beneficiaries receive clinically appropriate medications at the lowest possible cost. In reaching this goal, we also need to account for the specific needs of individuals who are already stabilized on certain drug regimens. In addition, it is important to recognize the needs of new full-benefit dual eligibles who may be auto-enrolled in a prescription drug plan and who, despite education and outreach efforts on the changing nature of their drug coverage under the Medicare drug benefit, may be unaware of the impact of the prescription drug plan's formulary or utilization management practices on their existing drug regimens.

An effective transition process for new enrollees must assure timely access to needed drugs while allowing for the flexibility necessary for Part D plans to develop a benefit design that promotes beneficiary choice and affordable access to medically necessary drugs. We will review each plan sponsor's transition process as part of our plan benefit design review.

While each drug plan must cover multiple drugs that have been shown to be similarly safe and effective for the vast majority of beneficiaries, the specific drugs used by an individual beneficiary may initially differ from those covered by the plan's formulary. To address the needs of individuals who are stabilized on certain drug regimens when they join a plan, Part D plans are required to establish an appropriate transition process for new enrollees who are transitioning to a Part D plan from other prescription drug coverage – including other Part D plans – and whose current drug therapies may not be included in their new Part D plan's formulary. Plan transition processes must address situations in which enrollees are stabilized on formulary drugs that require prior authorization or step therapy under a plan's utilization management rules. Transition processes must also address cases in which a beneficiary changes their setting of care, for example from a hospital to a home or institutional setting, to provide uninterrupted access to needed drugs.

Based on our experience with implementing the Part D benefit in 2006 – and in order to ensure the smoothest possible transition for new plan enrollees in 2007 – this document establishes a minimum set of standards for a Part D sponsor transition process. These minimum standards specify the components of a transition process beyond simply the assurance of a temporary supply of non-formulary drugs or a transition period constituting a particular length of time. These standards are based on policy clarifications provided to Part D plans in early 2006, but we emphasize that these standards are minimums and that plans are encouraged to go beyond these minimum requirements – particularly for enrollees with extenuating circumstances. We also note that since plans have attested to meeting the requirements of this transition guidance, violation of any of these requirements is subject to corrective action by CMS per our established compliance processes.

Plans must submit their transition processes for 2007 to PartDformularies@cms.hhs.gov by Monday, May 1, 2006 at 5 p.m. EST. We will provide further instructions on how plans must submit this information.

I. General Transition Process Requirements

In creating standards for a transition process, we have attempted to balance safeguards for a smooth transition process for plan enrollees with maximum flexibility for plan sponsors in managing their prescription drug benefit offerings. A transition process is necessary with respect to: (1) the transition of new enrollees into prescription drug plans on January 1, 2007 following the 2006 annual coordinated election period; (2) the transition of newly eligible Medicare beneficiaries from other coverage in 2007; (3) the transition of individuals who switch from one plan to another after January 1, 2007; and (4) enrollees residing in long-term care (LTC) facilities Plans should also consider how to expedite transitions to formulary drugs for enrollees who change treatment settings due to changes in level of care.

In addition, transition process requirements will be applicable to non-formulary drugs, meaning both: (1) Part D drugs that are not on a plan's formulary, and (2) Part D drugs that are on a plan's formulary but require prior authorization or step therapy under a plan's utilization management rules, since a formulary drug whose access is restricted via utilization management requirements is essentially equivalent to a non-formulary Part D drug to the extent that the relevant utilization management requirements are not met for a particular enrollee.

P&T Committee Role

At a minimum, a transition process will address procedures for medical review of non-formulary drug requests and, when appropriate, a process for switching new Part D plan enrollees to therapeutically appropriate formulary alternatives failing an affirmative medical necessity determination. We will look to transition process submissions for assurances that a plan's pharmacy and therapeutics (P&T) committee will review and provide recommendations regarding the procedures for medical review of non-formulary drug requests. P&T committee involvement will help ensure that transition decisions appropriately address situations involving enrollees stabilized on drugs that are not on the plan's formulary (or that are on the formulary but require prior authorization or step therapy under a plan's utilization management requirements) and which are known to have risks associated with any changes in the prescribed regimen.

Temporary One-Time Fills

A plan's transition process must address situations in which an individual first presents at a participating pharmacy with a prescription for a drug that is not on the formulary, unaware of what is covered by the plan or of the plan's exception process to provide access to Part D drugs that are not covered. This may be particularly true for full-benefit dual eligible beneficiaries who are auto-enrolled in a plan and who do not make an affirmative choice based on review of a plan's benefit relative to their existing medication needs. Plans must have systems capabilities that allow them to provide a one-time, temporary supply of non-formulary Part D drugs (including Part D drugs that are on a plan's formulary but require prior authorization or step therapy under a plan's utilization management rules) in order to accommodate the immediate needs of an enrollee, as well as to allow the plan and/or the enrollee sufficient time to work out with the prescriber an appropriate switch to a therapeutically equivalent medication or the completion of an exception request to maintain coverage of an existing drug based on medical necessity reasons.

A plan may charge cost-sharing for a temporary supply of drugs provided under its transition process. Cost-sharing for transition supplies for low-income subsidy (LIS) eligibles can never exceed the statutory maximum copayment amounts ($3 or $5 copays, or 15% coinsurance, depending on the level of LIS for which a particular enrollee qualifies). For non-LIS enrollees, a plan must charge cost-sharing based on one of its approved drug cost-sharing tiers (if the plan has a tiered benefit design), and this cost-sharing must be consistent with cost-sharing that the plan would charge for non-formulary drugs approved under a coverage exception.

Transition Timeframes

In order to balance the need for a smooth transition with plans' ability to effectively manage their benefits, we believe it makes sense to both limit and define the amount of time during which a transition process is applicable to new enrollees. To that end, plans will be required to provide a temporary supply fill anytime during the first 90 days of a beneficiary's enrollment in a plan. Because it is possible that beneficiaries transitioning from other prescription drug coverage will have obtained extended (e.g., 90-day) supplies of maintenance drugs prior to the last effective date of their previous coverage, plans must provide a temporary 30-day fill (unless the enrollee presents with a prescription written for less than 30 days) when a beneficiary presents at a pharmacy to request a refill of a non-formulary drug (including Part D drugs that are on a plan's formulary but require prior authorization or step therapy under a plan's utilization management rules) within the first 90 days of their coverage under the new plan. Since certain enrollees may join a plan at any time during the year, this requirement will apply beginning on an enrollee's first effective date of coverage, and not only to the first 90 days of the contract year.

Edits for Transition Supplies

One of our most important goals for a transition process is to ensure that a new enrollee is able to leave a pharmacy with a temporary supply of non-formulary Part D drugs without unnecessary delays. To this end, plans should used sound business and clinical decision-making with regard to the establishment of certain edits associated with temporary supplies of non-formulary Part D drugs at the point of sale. While Part D plans may implement additional step therapy or prior authorization edits during transition, they may do so only if such edits are resolved at the point of sale. For example, if a prescriber writes a prescription for 5mg tablets at 2 tablets daily, Part D plans might have dose optimization edits in place to require the prescription to be changed to 10mg tablets, one tablet daily. However, during transition, Part D plans would need to allow pharmacies to override this edit if the prescriber will not authorize the change at point of sale. In other words, the beneficiary should leave the pharmacy with sufficient quantity of medication (either 5mg or 10mg tablets) to last the plan allowable days supply, unless the prescriber originally wrote for a lesser days supply. If the dose optimization edit (or any other step therapy/prior authorization edit) is overridden at point of sale for transition purposes only, but not permanently, the beneficiary must be so notified so that he or she can begin the exception process if necessary. As part of their transition process submissions to CMS, plans should describe any edits on transition drugs and their process for resolving those edits at the point of sale.

We note that although Part D plans may implement quantity limits for safety purposes or drug utilization edits that are based upon approved product labeling during a beneficiary's transition period, to the extent that the prescription is dispensed for less than the written amount due to a plan edit, plans must provide refills for that transition supply (up to a 30-day supply in a retail setting and a 90-day supply in a long-term care setting). For example, if a beneficiary presents at a retail pharmacy with a prescription for one tablet per day for 30 days and a plan has a quantity limit edit in place that limits the days supply to 14 per prescription for safety purposes, the beneficiary would receive a 14-day supply (consistent with the safety edit). At the conclusion of the 14-day supply, the beneficiary should be entitled to another 14-day supply while he/she continues to pursue an exception with the Part D plan, or a switch to a therapeutic alternative that is on the plan's formulary.

Irrespective of transition, all of these edits are subject to exceptions and appeals. For example, if a quantity limit edit (based upon maximum recommended daily dose) results in the dispensing of a quantity that is less than indicated on the prescription and is less than the plan allowable days supply (as determined by the prescribed daily dose), Part D sponsors must ensure that beneficiaries are made aware of this quantity limit and that an exception is required to obtain a greater quantity. Part D plans must expeditiously process such exception requests so that beneficiaries will not experience unintended interruptions in medically necessary Part D drug therapies and/or will not inappropriately pay additional cost-sharing associated with multiple fills of lesser quantities when the originally prescribed doses of Part D drugs are medically necessary.

New Prescriptions versus Ongoing Medication Therapy

We are aware that it may be difficult for plans to distinguish between new prescriptions for non-formulary Part D drugs and refills for ongoing medication therapy involving non-formulary Part D drugs. For example, some new enrollees may need to switch pharmacies when they enroll in a new Part D plan (or when they enroll in Part D for the first time) and, depending on state law, their prescriptions may not transfer from pharmacy to pharmacy. In other words, some enrollees may need to present at their new network pharmacy with a new prescription for use at that pharmacy, even if that prescription is for ongoing medication therapy. We recognize that it may be difficult for plans to distinguish between ongoing medication therapy and a brand-new prescription for a non-formulary Part D drug. Although plans may attempt to follow up with prescribing physicians and pharmacies to ascertain the status of a prescription presented during the transition period, we clarify that if a plan is unable to make this distinction at the point of sale, it will be required to apply all transition process standards specified by CMS in this document to a new prescription for a non-formulary Part D drug. In other words, a brand-new prescription for a non-formulary drug will not be treated any differently than an ongoing prescription for a non-formulary drug when a distinction cannot be made at the point of sale.

Transition Notices

A successful transition process is contingent upon informing enrollees and their caretakers about their options for ensuring that enrollees' medical needs are safely accommodated within a Part D plan's formulary. An enrollee who receives a temporary supply of a non-formulary Part D drug at a network pharmacy might simply assume that, by virtue of filling his or her prescription, that the plan will cover that drug for the remainder of a the plan year. For this reason, plans must provide enrollees with appropriate notice regarding their transition process within a reasonable amount of time after providing a temporary supply of non-formulary Part D drugs (including Part D drugs that are on a plan's formulary but require prior authorization or step therapy under a plan's utilization management rules).

Plans will be required to send a written notice, via U.S. mail, to each enrollee who receives a transition fill. This standard is consistent with our requirement that other beneficiary communications, including formulary change notices and explanations of benefits, be sent via U.S. mail. In addition, this notice must be sent to each affected enrollee within three business days of the temporary fill. We believe this turnaround is necessary in order to provide an affected enrollee with sufficient time -- especially in light of our 30-day transition fill policy in the retail setting -- to work with his or her prescriber to switch to a therapeutically equivalent drug that is on the plan's formulary or to process an exceptions request.

The notice must include the following elements: (1) an explanation of the temporary nature of the transition supply an enrollee has received; (2) instructions for working with the plan sponsor and the enrollee's prescriber to identify appropriate therapeutic alternatives that are on the plan's formulary; (3) an explanation of the enrollee's right to request a formulary exception; and (4) a description of the procedures for requesting a formulary exception. As we did in 2006, we will provide plans with a model letter that they may submit to CMS under the file and use certification process. Given that a notice that conforms with our model letter will be generic, we expect that plans will make prior authorization or exception request forms available upon request to both enrollees and prescribing physicians and via a variety of mechanisms -- including by mail, fax, email, and on plan websites. While plans must, at a minimum, send affected enrollees a generic notice, we encourage plans to provide more detailed transition notices -- including the reason for a transition fill, alternative formulary drugs, and any prior authorization or exception request forms a beneficiary will need to effectuate a transition -- to the extent they have that capacity.

In addition, we strongly encourage point-of-sale notification of enrollees about transition supplies by pharmacists. We are working with the pharmacy and drug benefit industry, including the National Council for Prescription Drug Programs (NCPDP), to incorporate a work-around process for using structured payment coding in the message field of billing transaction responses indicating that a particular fill is a transition supply. This process will be consistent with the current NCPDP 5.1 standard. We will require plans to adopt this coding, as well as require their trading partners (including pharmacies) to use and implement it for 2007 and until such time as such messaging is superceded by a new HIPAA-approved standard with appropriate coding.

Public Notice of Transition Process

As a general matter, we believe plan sponsors must make general information about their transition processes available to beneficiaries in a manner similar to information provided on formularies and benefit design. It is likely that individuals will base their decision on which prescription drug best meets their needs on a variety of factors. Matching their current medication list with a Part D plan's formulary may be only one factor in the decision making process. Other factors, such as cost issues and inclusion of the retail pharmacy that they are most familiar with in the plan's network, may bear more weight in the final decision-making process. Having information about a plan's transition process in plan enrollment materials and websites, as well as on the Medicare Prescription Drug Plan Finder, may reassure beneficiaries that there will be procedures in place to assist them in switching to therapeutic alternatives or in obtaining a formulary exception where appropriate. It will also serve to educate advocates and other interested third parties – for example, state Medicaid agencies – about plan transition processes.

To this end, we will make available plan transition process information via a required link from the Medicare Prescription Drug Plan Finder to individual plan websites. This is consistent with the manner in which current enrollees, prospective enrollees, and other stakeholders will be able to access information about plan exception and appeals processes in 2007. We will provide plans with model submission forms so that plan transition process information is presented consistently from plan to plan. We will provide these model submission forms to plans very shortly. Via our marketing guidelines, we will also require that plans include transition process information in their pre- and post-enrollment materials as appropriate.

II. Transition Process in the Retail Setting

The minimum transition process standards described in Section I will apply to beneficiaries obtaining their drugs in a retail setting (or via home infusion, safety-net, or I/T/U pharmacies). However, we clarify that, in the retail setting, the one-time, temporary supply of non-formulary Part D drugs – including Part D drugs that are on a plan's formulary but require prior authorization or step therapy under a plan's utilization management rules – must be for at least 30 days of medication, unless the prescription is written by a prescriber for less than 30 days. Plans should note that, outside the long-term care setting, such a temporary fill may be a one-time fill only.

III. Transition Process in the LTC Setting

It is important that the transition process take into account the unique needs of residents of LTC facilities who enroll in a new Part D plan. Residents of LTC facilities are more likely to be receiving multiple medications for which simultaneous changes could significantly impact the condition of the enrollee. In addition, given that a large proportion of LTC facility residents may be dually eligible for both Medicare and full Medicaid benefits, and could be auto-enrolled into the plan without making an affirmative selection based on the individual's existing treatment needs, it is critical that the transition process address access to medications at the filling of the first prescription. When possible, we encourage plan sponsors to ensure that LTC pharmacies in the plan's network that have relationships with LTC facilities work with those facilities prior to the effective date of enrollment to ensure a seamless transition of the facility's residents.

Transition Period Immediately After Enrollment for LTC Facility Residents

The minimum transition process standards described in Section I will apply to beneficiaries obtaining their drugs in a long-term care setting. The temporary supply of non-formulary Part D drugs – including Part D drugs that are on a plan's formulary but require prior authorization or step therapy under a plan's utilization management rules – for a new enrollee in a LTC facility must be for at least 31 days (unless the prescription is written for less than 31 days). We are requiring a 31-day transition supply given that many LTC pharmacies and facilities dispense medications in 31-day increments. However, unlike in the retail setting, plans must honor multiple fills of non-formulary Part D drugs, including Part D drugs that are on a plan's formulary but require prior authorization or step therapy under a plan's utilization management rules, as necessary during the entire length of the 90-day transition period.

Emergency Supply for Current Enrollees

Since, as a matter of general practice, LTC facility residents must receive their medications as ordered without delay, Part D plans must cover an emergency supply of non-formulary Part D drugs for LTC facility residents as part of their transition process. During the first 90 days after a beneficiary's enrollment, he or she will receive a transition supply via the process described above. However, to the extent that an enrollee in a LTC setting is outside his or her 90-day transition period, the plan must still provide an emergency supply of non-formulary Part D drugs – including Part D drugs that are on a plan's formulary but require prior authorization or step therapy under a plan's utilization management rules – while an exception is being processed. These emergency supplies of non-formulary Part D drugs – including Part D drugs that are on a plan's formulary but require prior authorization or step therapy under a plan's utilization management rules – must be for at least 31 days of medication, unless the prescription is written by a prescriber for less than 31 days. We are requiring a 31-day emergency supply given that many LTC pharmacies and facilities dispense medications in 31-day increments.

III. Current Enrollee Transitions

In addition to circumstances impacting new enrollees who may enter a plan with a medication list that contains non-formulary Part D drugs, other circumstances exist in which unplanned transitions for current enrollees could arise and in which prescribed drug regimens may not be on plan formularies. These circumstances usually involve level of care changes in which a beneficiary is changing from one treatment setting to another. For example, beneficiaries who enter LTC facilities from hospitals are sometimes accompanied by a discharge list of medications from the hospital formulary, with very short term planning taken into account (often under 8 hours). Similar situations may exist, for example, for beneficiaries who are discharged from a hospital to a home; for beneficiaries who end their skilled nursing facility Medicare Part A stay (where payments include all pharmacy charges) and who need to revert to their Part D plan formulary; for beneficiaries who give up hospice status to revert to standard Medicare Part A and B benefits; for beneficiaries who end a long-term care facility stay and return to the community; and for beneficiaries who are discharged from psychiatric hospitals with medication regimens that are highly individualized.

For these unplanned transitions, beneficiaries and providers must clearly avail themselves of plan exceptions and appeals processes. We have streamlined the grievance, coverage determination, and appeals process requirements in order to ensure that beneficiaries receive quick determinations regarding the medications they need. In all cases, we make it clear that a Part D plan sponsor is required to make coverage determinations and redeterminations as expeditiously as the enrollee's health condition requires. In addition, and as described above, current enrollees entering LTC settings from other care settings will be provided emergency supplies of non-formulary drugs – including Part D drugs that are on a plan's formulary but require prior authorization or step therapy under a plan's utilization management rules.

However, even with these protections, there may exist some period of time in which beneficiaries with level of care changes have a temporary gap in coverage while an exception is processed. For this reason, we strongly encourage plans to incorporate processes in their transition plans that allow for transition supplies to be provided to current enrollees with level of care changes.

In addition, we learned in 2006 that many plans were rejecting claims based on early refill edits in cases in which an enrollee was admitted to or discharged from a LTC facility. An early refill edit is a utilization management tool used to promote compliance and to prevent waste. An early refill edit cannot be used to limit appropriate and necessary access to an enrollee's Part D benefit. For example, if a patient gets a prescription for 30 tablets for a 30 days supply (i.e. 1 tablet daily), but the prescriber changes the dose to 2 tablets daily after only 10 days, it would be inappropriate for a plan to deny as "too soon" a claim for a new prescription with the new dosage because the enrollee will not have enough medication to last until the originally scheduled refill date. Similarly, when an enrollee is admitted to or discharged from a LTC facility, he or she will not have access to the remainder of the previously dispensed prescription (through no fault of his or her own) and, therefore, plans must allow the enrollee to access a refill upon admission or discharge.

CHAPTER 11

PRESCRIPTION DRUG COVERAGE

§11.01   INTRODUCTION

Effective January 2006, Medicare beneficiaries have limited assistance paying for prescription drugs through a new Medicare Part D. The drug benefit, added by the Medicare Prescription Drug, Improvement, and Modernization Act of 2003 (MMA),[1] is not part of the traditional Medicare program, but rather is offered through private insurance plans.

The Part D benefit is premised on the notion that individual Medicare beneficiaries should have a choice of private drug plans in order to select a drug benefit that best meets their needs. The statute creates three categories of drug plans: stand-alone plans that offer only prescription drug coverage, Medicare Advantage plans with a drug benefit, and fallback plans. The categories of drug plans are discussed below.

Most significantly, the MMA establishes a low-income subsidy for beneficiaries with incomes up to 150 percent of the federal poverty level and with limited resources. The Act also eliminated, beginning January 1, 2006, all Medicaid drug coverage for the more than 6 million individuals who are dually eligible for both Medicare and Medicaid (dual eligibles). Moreover, it requires states to pay back to the federal government much of the savings they would otherwise realize from their reduced Medicaid obligation to those individuals, and includes other provisions that will affect state budgets.

In the first year of the program, favorable reimbursement rates induced private companies to offer Part D plans throughout the country.[2] It remains to be seen whether they will be as greatly available in the future.

§11.02   ELIGIBILITY FOR PART D COVERAGE

Prescription drug coverage under Part D is voluntary. A beneficiary may purchase Part D coverage if she has Part A or has Part B. Beneficiaries do not have to have both Part A and Part B coverage to choose prescription drug coverage, unless they choose to enroll in a Medicare Advantage plan in which case they must be in both Parts A and B.[3] The beneficiary must enroll in a Part D plan that serves the geographic region in which she resides.[4] Beneficiaries who are incarcerated are not eligible to participate in Part D.[5]

---

[1] Medicare Prescription Drug, Improvement, and Modernization Act of 2003, Pub. L. 108-173 (Dec. 8, 2003), 42 U.S.C.A. §§1395w-101 *et seq.* (2004 Supp.), 42 C.F.R. §423.506.

[2] Information about prescription drug plans will not be available until late September 2006, after the publication of the *2007 Medicare Handbook* for 2007, when CMS enters into final contracts with drug plans. In addition, rules may change as CMS issues additional program guidance to clarify how the Part D program will operate.

[3] 42 C.F.R. §423.30.

[4] 42 U.S.C. §§1395w-101(a)(3)(A), (b)(1)(B)(i).

[5] 42 C.F.R. §§423.4, 423.30(a).

§11.03   CHOICE OF DRUG PLANS

[A]   Prescription Drug Plans

The majority of Medicare beneficiaries who remain in the traditional Medicare program will be able to purchase drug coverage through prescription drug plans (PDPs) that offer only prescription drug coverage. PDPs are offered by sponsoring organizations pursuant to a one-year contract with the Centers for Medicare and Medicaid Services (CMS).[6]

[B]   Medicare Advantage Plans

Individuals who are enrolled in a Medicare Advantage plan established under Medicare Part C must receive their prescription drug coverage through their Medicare Advantage plan, known as an MA-PD. They may not purchase a separate PDP. However, individuals who are enrolled in a Medicare Advantage private fee-for-service (PFFS) plan that does not include a prescription drug option may purchase a PDP for their Part D coverage. Individuals who want to join an MA-PD for the first time must have both Medicare Parts A and B.[7]

[C]   Fallback Plans

Under the MMA, each beneficiary must have a choice of enrollment in at least two plans.[8] One of the plans must be a PDP, and the two plans cannot be sponsored by the same organization. In regions[9] where two drug plans meeting the above requirements are not available, the MMA authorizes creation of a fallback prescription drug plan. Fallback drug plans are more limited in the scope of benefits they can offer; they can only offer the statutory standard benefit.[10] However, in 2006 there were substantially more than two drug plans in each prescription drug plan region, so that CMS did not need to contract with fallback plans. CMS anticipates that sufficient drug plans will be available in 2007 as well.

---

[6] 42 U.S.C. §§1395w-101(a)(1)(A), 1395w-112(b)(1), 1395w-151(a)(14).

[7] 42 U.S.C. §1395w-101(a)(1)(B). Note that individuals enrolled in a Medicare Part C Medical Savings Account (MSAs) may also purchase a PDP to obtain drug coverage.

[8] 42 U.S.C. §1395w-103(a).

[9] CMS has established 34 PDP regions, several of which include more than one state. <http://www.cms.hhs.gov/PrescriptionDrugCovGenIn/Downloads/PDPRegions.pdf>. Each PDP must offer coverage to all beneficiaries in the region that it serves. A PDP may also offer a plan that serves more than one region or that is national in scope. 42 U.S.C. §1395w-111(a).

[10] Id.; §1395w-111(g)(4).

§11.04   THE PART D DRUG BENEFIT

[A]   Covered Part D Drugs

The MMA defines the drugs that are covered under Part D, and therefore the drugs for which payment will be made under Part D, in relationship to their coverage under Medicaid and under other parts of Medicare. A Part D drug is a drug that is approved by the Food and Drug Administration, for which a prescription is required, and for which payment is required under Medicaid.[11] Biological products, including insulin and insulin supplies, and smoking cessation drugs are also covered under Part D.[12]

The MMA excludes from coverage those categories of drugs for which Medicaid payment is optional.[13] Of particular significance to Medicare beneficiaries is the exclusion of drugs for weight gain (ex., used in connection with treating weight loss due to cancer or HIV/AIDS), barbiturates (ex., used to treat seizures in older people), benzodiazepines (ex., used to treat acute anxiety, panic attacks, seizure disorders, and muscle spasms in those with cerebral palsy), and over-the-counter medications. Many of the excluded medications are used by nursing home residents.[14] Note, however, that some of these drugs may be covered if prescribed for a purpose other than those prohibited by MMA.[15] MMA also excludes from Part D coverage those drugs for which payment could be made under Medicare Part A or Part B. CMS has determined that such drugs are excluded from Part D coverage even if the beneficiary does not have coverage under the part of Medicare (either Part A or Part B) which would generally pay for the drug.[16]

Part D plans are not required to pay for all covered Part D drugs. They may establish their own formularies, or list of covered drugs for which they will make payment, as long as the formulary and benefit structure are not found by CMS to discourage enrollment by certain Medicare beneficiaries.[17] Part D plans that follow the formulary classes and categories established by the United States Pharmacopoeia will pass the first discrimination test. However, CMS indicates it will still review formularies to determine whether the placement of specific drugs in each category or class, as well as other benefit design issues, discriminates against

---

[11] 42 U.S.C. §§1395w-102(e)(1), 1396r-8(d), (k).

[12] 42 U.S.C. §§1395w-102(e)(1)(B), (2)(A).

[13] 42 U.S.C. §§1395w-102(e)(2)(A), 1396r-8(d)(2).

[14] The Cost of Being Excluded: Impact of Excluded Medications Under Medicare Part D on Dually Eligible Nursing Home Residents, <www.ascp.com/medicarerx/docs/ASCPPaperExcludedMeds.pdf>.

[15] 70 Fed. Reg. 4193, 4230 (Jan. 28, 2005).

[16] 42 C.F.R. §423.100.

[17] 42 C.F.R. §§423.120(b), 423.272(b).

particular individuals. Plans also have the flexibility to change the drugs on their formulary during the course of the year.[18]

[B] Structure of the Drug Benefit

[1] Introduction

Much of the debate about the MMA centered on the adequacy of the drug benefit itself. However, the discussion did not mention that prescription drug plans are given a great deal of flexibility to design their own benefit structure. Thus, the majority of plans have chosen not to offer the statutory "standard" benefit, and instead offer an alternative benefit structure.[19] Variations in plan benefit structure, along with the substantial number of plans available, have adversely affected the ability of Medicare beneficiaries to compare and choose the plan that best meets their needs.

[2] The Standard Drug Benefit

The MMA establishes a standard drug benefit that Part D plans may offer. The standard benefit is defined in terms of the financial structure of the cost sharing and not in terms of the drugs that must be covered. In 2006, this standard benefit requires payment of a $250 deductible. The beneficiary then pays 25 percent of the cost of a covered Part D prescription drug up to the initial coverage limit of $2,250.[20] The initial coverage limit is calculated based on the total cost of the drugs used by the beneficiary. Once the initial coverage limit is reached, the beneficiary enters a second deductible period known as the "doughnut hole" in which she pays the full cost of her medicine.[21] When her total out-of-pocket expenses for the year, including the deductible and initial coinsurance, reach $3,600, she pays $2 for a generic or preferred drug and $5 for other drugs, or 5 percent coinsurance, whichever is greater.[22] Note that the $3,600 amount is calculated on a calendar year basis; a beneficiary who amasses $3,600 in out-of-pocket costs on December 31 will have to start all over again on January

---

[18] *Medicare Modernization Act 2007 Final Guidelines-Formularies*, <www.cms.hhs.gov/>. <PrescriptionDrugCovContra/Downloads/CY07FormularyGuidance.pdf>.

[19] All prescription drug plans, regardless of their benefit design, are supposed to provide beneficiaries with access to negotiated prices for the covered Part D drugs they include in their formulary, even if the beneficiary is required to pay the full cost of the prescription. 42 C.F.R. §423.104(g)(1).

[20] The beneficiary's share of cost is $500, or 25 percent of the difference between $2,250 and $250. When added to the deductible, the beneficiary's total cost sharing for formulary drugs up to the initial coverage limit is $750.

[21] Once a beneficiary reaches the doughnut hole, she must spend an additional $2,850 on formulary drugs to reach the catastrophic limit. At that point, the beneficiary and the drug plan will have paid a combined total of $5,100 in costs for formulary drugs.

[22] 42 U.S.C.A. §1395w-102(b).

1. The deductible, initial coverage limit, and annual out-of-pocket threshold increase each year by the increase in expenditures for Part D drugs.[23] For 2007, they are, respectively, $265, $2,400, and $3,850.

MMA does not mandate a set premium amount. Premiums are determined by a bidding process and vary from plan to plan and from region to region. Private insurance companies that want to continue participating in the Part D drug benefit must submit new bids each year. Thus, the premiums they charge are likely to change on a yearly basis. Premium amounts will be especially critical for individuals with low incomes, as they will only receive full assistance for plans that offer the standard benefit and that charge the lowest premiums. The national average premium in 2006 is $32.20.

[3] Alternative Coverage and Enhanced Alternative Coverage

Part D drug plans are not required to offer the standard benefit, but can offer alternative prescription drug coverage. Alternative coverage must be "actuarially equivalent" to the standard benefit. In other words, the value of the benefit package must be equal to or greater than the value of the standard benefit package.[24] In an actuarially equivalent plan, the cost sharing varies through the use of such mechanisms as tiered copayments. For example, a beneficiary's share of cost may be less for a generic or preferred brand name drug than for a non-preferred brand name drug. However, a plan that offers an alternative benefit package cannot impose a higher deductible ($265 in 2007) or require a higher out-of-pocket limit ($3,850 in 2007) than required by the standard benefit.

Plans can offer enhanced alternative coverage that might also include changes to the deductible and the initial coverage limit, though the deductible cannot be higher than the $250 set in the statute. Enhanced alternative coverage might also include coverage of drugs that are excluded under Part D or coverage of some drugs in the coverage gap or "doughnut hole." A PDP that wants to offer a drug plan with enhanced alternative coverage in a region must also offer a PDP with the basic benefit package in that region.[25]

[4] Calculating Beneficiary Expenses

As indicated above, only the costs of Part D covered drugs that are included on a plan's formulary count toward the deductible and out-of-pocket limits.[26]

---

[23] 42 C.F.R. §§423.104(d)(1)(ii), (3)(ii). *See* Medicare Part D Benefit Parameters for Standard Benefit: Annual Adjustments for 2007. <http://www.cms.hhs.gov/ MedicareAdvtgSpecRateStats/ downloads/2007_Part_D_Parameter_Update.pdf>.

[24] 42 C.F.R. §§423.4, 423.100, 423.104(e).

[25] 42 C.F.R. §423.104(f).

[26] The regulations discuss beneficiary cost sharing in terms of "covered Part D drugs." 42 C.F.R. §423.104. CMS uses the term to describe Part D drugs that are on a plan's formulary. 70 Fed. Reg. at 4228.

For example, a beneficiary whose only drug expense in January 2007 is $400 for a Part D drug that is not on her plan's formulary will not meet her deductible, and the $4,800 in out-of-pocket expenses she will incur for the year for the non-formulary drug do not qualify her for the reduced cost sharing for high out-of-pocket costs.

Payments that count toward the yearly out-of-pocket limit are referred to as true out-of-pocket expenses, or TrOOP. Only out-of-pocket costs for formulary drugs that are paid for by the beneficiary, a family member, or other person acting on her behalf, or by a state pharmacy assistance program, are considered TrOOP and are counted toward the out-of-pocket limit.[27] Payments made by other insurance, including employer-sponsored plans and AIDS Drug Assistance Programs (ADAPs), do not count toward the limit. Such uncounted payments increase the amount the beneficiary must spend before the reduced cost sharing for high drug expenses begins. In sum, the beneficiary is responsible for paying premiums and the full costs of non-formulary prescriptions, and gets no credit for these payments toward the out-of-pocket limit.

[C]   Access to Pharmacies

A drug plan may establish a network of retail pharmacies with which it enters into contracts in its service area as long as the pharmacies are conveniently located for all enrollees in the drug plan. The network must include access to long-term care pharmacies which serve residents of nursing facilities.[28] A plan that does not offer the standard benefit can offer reduced copayments to enrollees who use its preferred pharmacies. A plan may also offer access to formulary drugs through a mail-order pharmacy.[29]

A Part D plan must provide coverage for formulary drugs purchased at an out-of-network pharmacy if a beneficiary cannot reasonably be expected to obtain the drugs through a network pharmacy. A beneficiary may not use an out-of-network pharmacy on a routine basis. A beneficiary may also have to pay a larger copayment or coinsurance for using an out-of-network pharmacy.[30] Plans may establish policies and procedures, including contracting with pharmacies that are outside of their service areas, to accommodate seasonal residents, often known as "snowbirds" and travelers.[31]

---

[27] 42 U.S.C.A. §1395w-102(b)(4)(C)(ii), 42 C.F.R. §423.100.

[28] CMS developed standards for long-term care pharmacies. *Long-Term Care Guidance*, <http://www.cms.hhs.gov/PrescriptionDrugCovContra/Downloads/LTCGuidance.pdf>.

[29] 42 C.F.R. §423.120(a).

[30] 42 C.F.R. §423.124.

[31] 70 Fed. Reg. 4193, 4249 (Jan. 28, 2005).

§11.05   ENROLLING IN A PART D PLAN

[A]   Introduction

Enrollment in Medicare Part D differs dramatically from enrollment in Medicare Part B, which is also voluntary. A beneficiary who becomes entitled to Part A is automatically enrolled in Part B unless she takes steps to notify the Social Security Administration that she does not want Part B coverage. Enrollment in Part D requires the beneficiary to take affirmative steps to enroll and get Part D coverage. She must first choose a drug plan from the options available in her area. Then, she must enroll through the plan she chooses. If she may be eligible for the low-income subsidy, she must file a separate application for the subsidy either with her state Medicaid agency or with Social Security.

[B]   Enrollment Periods

[1]   Initial Enrollment Period

Individuals who had Medicare Part A and/or Part B when Part D became effective had an initial enrollment period that ran from November 15, 2005, through May 15, 2006. The initial enrollment period for individuals who are first eligible to enroll in Part D on or after March 2006 corresponds to the initial enrollment period for Part B, i.e., the seven-month period running from three months before the month the individual first becomes eligible and ending three months after the first month of eligibility.[32]

[2]   Annual Coordinated Enrollment Period

For 2006, the annual coordinated enrollment period corresponded to the initial enrollment period and ran from November 15, 2005, through May 15, 2006. In 2007 and beyond the annual coordinated enrollment period corresponds to the annual coordinated enrollment period for Part C and will run from November 15 through December 31.[33]

[3]   Special Enrollment Periods

Individuals may be eligible for a special enrollment period[34] if:

• They did not enroll in Part D during their initial enrollment because they had other prescription drug coverage deemed to be "creditable coverage," and they lose the creditable coverage;

---

[32] 42 C.F.R. §§423.38, 407.14.

[33] 42 C.F.R. §423.38(b).

[34] 42 C.F.R. §423.38(c).

- They were given incorrect information concerning the status of their other prescription drug coverage as creditable coverage;

- They were given incorrect information about enrollment by a federal employee;

- They have Medicare and full Medicaid coverage or a Medicare Savings Program (MSP);

- They move out of a plan's service area;

- Their PDP's contract with Medicare is terminated;

- They enrolled in an MA-PD during the first year of eligibility and want to return to traditional Medicare and a PDP;

- They move into, reside in, or move out of a nursing home.

[4] Effective Date of Enrollment

Part D coverage becomes effective:[35]

- January 1, 2006, for individuals who enrolled during November or December 2005;

- The first day of the next calendar month after enrollment for individuals who enrolled between January 1, 2006, and May 15, 2006;

- The same month that Part A and/or Part B coverage becomes effective for individuals who enroll before their month of entitlement to Part A or enrollment in Part B;

- The first day of the next calendar month after enrollment for individuals who enroll after the first month of entitlement for Part A or enrollment in Part B;

- The following January 1, for individuals who enroll during the annual coordinated enrollment period; and

- At the time specified by CMS for individuals who enroll during a special enrollment period.

[5] Involuntary Disenrollment

An individual may be involuntarily disenrolled from a drug plan for reasons similar to the grounds for disenrollment from a Medicare Advantage plan.[36] These include no longer living in the plan's service area, loss of eligibility for Part D, death of the individual, termination of the PDP, failure to pay premiums on a timely

---

[35] 42 C.F.R. §423.40.

[36] *See* discussion on enrollment and disenrollment in the Medicare Advantage chapter of this handbook.

basis, engaging in disruptive behavior that substantially impairs the ability of the plan to arrange for or provide services.[37]

[6] Ability to Change Plan Mid-Year

[i] Changes During the Annual Coordinated Enrollment Period.

All beneficiaries may switch plans once during the annual coordinated enrollment period, which runs from November 15, 2005, through May 15, 2006, and from November 15 to December 31 in subsequent years.[38] For 2006, or for those who enroll during a special enrollment period, enrollment in the new plan becomes effective the following month. After 2006 enrollment becomes effective on January 1 of the next year.

[ii] Changes During Open Enrollment Periods.

Individuals enrolled in a Medicare Advantage (MA) plan also may change plans once during the open enrollment period, which was the first six months of 2006 and is then the first three months of 2007 and beyond. For 2006, beneficiaries who enrolled in an MA-PD could use the open enrollment period (January through June) to change to another MA-PD or to disenroll from the MA-PD and return to traditional Medicare and a PDP. For 2007 and beyond, an enrollee in an MA-PD may use the open enrollment period (January through March) to change to another MA-PD or to disenroll from the MA-PD and return to traditional Medicare and a PDP. Someone who enrolls in an MA plan that does not offer prescription drug coverage may not change to an MA-PD or to original Medicare and a PDP during the open enrollment period. The beneficiary must wait to change plans until the next annual election period.[39]

Beneficiaries with traditional Medicare and a PDP only have an opportunity to change plans after their initial enrollment in 2006. In 2007 and beyond, individuals who enroll in a PDP are "locked in" to their plan for the remainder of the calendar year, even though the plan in which they enroll may change the formulary or cost-sharing arrangements during the year. Enrollees in PDPs must wait until the next annual coordinated enrollment period to switch plans, with enrollment in the new plan becoming effective on January 1 of the following year.

[iii] Special Enrollment Periods.

Beneficiaries may also be eligible to change plans mid-year if they qualify for a special enrollment period described above.

---

[37] 42 C.F.R. §423.44

[38] 42 C.F.R. §423.32(a).

[39] 42 C.F.R. §§422.62(a)(3), (4), (5).

[7] Enrollment Process for Individuals Who Are Eligible for Medicare and Medicaid

The MMA established an enrollment process that provides for automatic assignment into drug plans for individuals who are dually eligible for Medicare and Medicaid (dual eligibles) and who do not choose their own PDP or MA-PD during their initial enrollment period. In addition, dual eligibles are automatically eligible for a continuous special enrollment period and therefore are not ever locked in to a prescription drug plan.[40]

[8] Failure to Enroll on a Timely Basis

[i] Late Penalty.

A beneficiary who does not enroll in a Part D plan within 63 days of her initial enrollment period, and who does not have other "creditable" prescription drug coverage, must pay a late penalty if she subsequently enrolls in a Part D plan. The penalty is assessed at one percent of the national average premium for each month of delayed enrollment, for the remainder of the time in which the beneficiary is enrolled in a Part D plan.[41] Thus, a beneficiary who first becomes eligible for Part D at age 65 but who delays enrolling until age 70 may be assessed a 60 percent penalty on her premium (5 years × 12 months × 1%). Since the penalty is based on a percentage of the average premium each year, the dollar value of the penalty changes as the national average premium changes.

[ii] Creditable Coverage.

Someone who delays enrollment because she has creditable coverage, i.e., coverage through another insurance plan deemed comparable to Part D coverage, will not be assessed a penalty for late enrollment if she later decides to enroll in Part D. A determination of whether coverage is creditable involves an actuarial assessment of whether the other insurance provides coverage of the costs of prescription drugs that equals or exceeds the actuarial value of the prescription drug benefit.[42]

Coverage offered through an employer or union-sponsored health plan, the federal employee health benefits program (FEHBP), Medicaid, a state pharmaceutical assistance program, programs for veterans, and TRICARE may constitute creditable coverage. The entity sponsoring the coverage must inform beneficiaries whether or not the coverage provided meets the definition of creditable coverage.[43]

---

[40] 42 U.S.C. §1395w-101(b)(3)(D); 42 C.F.R. §423.38(c)(4).

[41] 42 C.F.R. §§423.46, 423.286(d)(3).

[42] 42 U.S.C. §1395w-113(b)(5).

[43] 42 U.S.C. §1395w-113(b)(4), 42 C.F.R. §423.56.

Coverage offered through some pre-standardized Medicare Supplemental (Medigap) policies may qualify as creditable, as may coverage through some policies sold in Michigan, Minnesota, and Wisconsin, which are not required to sell the standard policies. The standard Medigap policies H, I, and J do not meet the definition of creditable coverage. Insurers that offer Medigap policies were required to notify their insureds concerning the status of their policies. Beneficiaries are advised to check with their insurers about the status of their policies.

[C] Choosing a Part D Plan

CMS is supposed to provide information to all Medicare beneficiaries to help them choose a Part D prescription drug plan. Information is made available through the *Medicare & You* handbook, through the Medicare toll-free number, and through the Medicare Web site, *www.medicare.gov*. In addition, Part D plan sponsors are required to make available to all individuals eligible to enroll in Part D information about all beneficiary cost sharing, their formulary and cost control mechanisms, their pharmacy network, and their exceptions and appeals process.[44] Beneficiaries who want this information have to check with each drug plan.

Beneficiaries who have retiree health coverage also must contact their former employer or union to determine the effect of enrollment in a Part D plan on their retiree health benefits. Some employers and unions will terminate all retiree health coverage, and not just the drug benefit, for retirees and their dependents if the retiree enrolls in a Part D plan. Dual eligible beneficiaries who are automatically enrolled in a Part D plan and who will lose their retiree health benefits because of their auto-enrollment may need to decline Part D affirmatively if they want the retiree health coverage to continue for themselves and/or their dependents.

§11.06 PREMIUM AND COST-SHARING SUBSIDIES FOR PART D PRESCRIPTION DRUGS FOR LOW-INCOME INDIVIDUALS

[A] Introduction

For the first time in program history, Medicare has a low-income benefit for people with limited incomes and resources. While the Medicaid program has also played a role in paying Medicare's cost sharing for beneficiaries dually eligible for both programs, Medicare has never provided direct low-income subsidies. In its design of the benefit, Congress adopted aspects of the federal Supplemental Security Income program (SSI) and of Medicaid's Medicare Savings Programs (MSPs). Similarly, to administer the benefit, Congress looks to the Social Security Administration and to state Medicaid agencies.

---

[44] 42 C.F.R. §423.128.

[B] The Subsidies

Some form of low-income subsidy (LIS) to help pay costs of Medicare Part D is available to Medicare beneficiaries with incomes up to 150 percent of the federal poverty level (FPL) for a family of the size involved.[45] Subsidies vary according to income, Medicaid status, and institutional status. So-called full subsidy eligible individuals are those with full Medicaid status (full-benefit dual eligibles), those with Supplemental Security Income (SSI) but no Medicaid, those enrolled in one of three Medicare Savings Programs, and individuals with incomes below 135 percent of FPL and countable resources not more than $6,000 for an individual and $9,000 for a couple. Partial subsidy individuals can have incomes up to 150 percent of FPL and resources not more than $10,000 per individual and $20,000 per couple. Resource levels will increase each year based on increases in the consumer price index.

[1] Full Subsidy Eligible Individuals

All full subsidy individuals are entitled to a 100 percent subsidy for the "low-income benchmark premium" (the weighted average of plan premiums for the basic benefit package in the region in which the individual lives), for a plan offering the standard Part D benefit, elimination of the deductible, continuation of coverage through the doughnut hole, and elimination of all cost sharing after they meet the annual out-of-pocket maximum. In addition, their cost sharing is reduced as follows:

- Full-benefit dual eligibles who are institutionalized have no cost sharing at all.

- Full-benefit dual eligibles with incomes up to 100 percent of FPL initially pay no more than $1/generic or preferred brand or $3/non-preferred brand, in 2006; and $1/$3.10 in 2007.

- All other full subsidy individuals initially pay copayments of no more than $2/generic or preferred brand or $5/non-preferred brand, with copayments indexed annually to the cost of Part D drugs in 2006; and $2.15/$5.35 in 2007.[46]

[2] Partial Subsidy Eligible Individuals

Partial subsidy individuals pay a sliding scale premium, a $50 deductible, coinsurance of 15 percent instead of the full 25 percent, including continued coverage through the doughnut hole, and a copayment of no more than $2/generic or

---

[45] 42 U.S.C. §1395w-114.

[46] 42 C.F.R. §423.773(b).

preferred brand or $5/non-preferred brand for all drugs after the out-of-pocket threshold is met.[47]

[3] Deemed Subsidy Eligible Individuals

Certain individuals are treated as full subsidy eligible individuals regardless of their actual income and resources. These are full-benefit dual eligibles, recipients of SSI benefits, and beneficiaries of the three Medicare Savings Programs (MSP): QMB, SLMB and QI.[48]

An initial determination that someone qualifies for the low-income subsidy remains in effect for a full year. As the program becomes more established, however, eligibility determinations may be subject to more frequent review, depending on an assessment of the likelihood of a change in the beneficiary's financial status.[49]

[C] Eligibility Determinations

[1] Where to Apply

Beneficiaries who are not "deemed eligible" have the choice of filing an application for the low-income subsidy (LIS) either at their state Medicaid office or through the Social Security Administration (SSA).[50] Because of strong encouragement by SSA and CMS, the overwhelming majority of beneficiaries apply through SSA.[51] However, though some beneficiaries may prefer SSA offices over state welfare offices, applying at SSA may not always be in a particular individual's best interest, since Medicaid offices screen for other benefits as well,[52] and may have speedier determination time frames and more user-friendly appeals systems.[53] Unlike the Medicaid regulations, the Social Security regulations impose no time restrictions by which SSA must act on applications and appeals.[54]

---

[47] 42 C.F.R. §423.773(d).

[48] 42 C.F.R. §423.773(c).

[49] Final rules were issued on Dec. 30, 2005. 70 Fed. Reg. 77,664 (Dec. 30, 2005) were issued on March 4, 2005. 70 Fed. Reg. 10,558 (Mar. 4, 2005) (stet codified at 20 C.F.R. §§418.3600 *et seq.*).

[50] 42 C.F.R. §423.774(a).

[51] In 2005, to assist with enrollment in the low-income subsidy, SSA sent notices to a large number of Medicare beneficiaries telling them that they may be eligible for the LIS to assist with their drug costs.

[52] 42 U.S.C. §1396a(a)(10); 42 C.F.R. §435.902.

[53] Eligibility regulations proposed by SSA do not include time frames for making eligibility determinations and include a very limited appeals process. 70 Fed. Reg. 10,558 (Mar. 4, 2005) (to be codified at 20 C.F.R. §§418.3600 *et seq.*).

[54] 20 C.F.R. §§418.3110, 418.3220, 418.3230.

In some states, the choice of location for filing the LIS application may determine whether a beneficiary is found eligible for the LIS. State Medicaid offices must screen for eligibility for all Medicaid benefits, including MSP, when an LIS application is filed. In a state with more generous income and/or resource limits for its MSP program, or in a state that does not count support and maintenance provided by others (known as in-kind support and maintenance), someone found ineligible for LIS might still qualify for MSP benefits. By qualifying for MSP benefits, that individual is deemed eligible for the low-income subsidy. If the same individual had applied for LIS through SSA, she would have been found ineligible for LIS without a determination being made about her eligibility for MSP.

[2] Eligibility Criteria

In determining eligibility for the LIS, income is to be determined according to MSP rules, which in turn refer to SSI rules. One improvement over both SSI and MSP rules is the definition of "family size," which requires using a standard that reflects the actual number of dependents in an applicant's household. Dependent is defined as one who relies on the applicant or spouse for at least one-half of her support. Resources are defined as liquid resources, "such as checking and savings accounts, stocks, bonds, and other resources that can be readily converted to cash within 20 days," and real estate that is neither the primary residence of the applicant nor the land on which the residence is located.[55]

[3] Appeals Process

The appeals process for someone who is denied the low-income subsidy depends on where the application is filed. When the Medicaid agency makes the decision, any appeal must follow the procedures used for Medicaid appeals. SSA will use its redeterminations and appeals procedures for the determinations it makes.[56] SSA regulations provide for a telephone hearing or a case review. The preamble indicates that the hearings will not be conducted by Administrative Law Judges who hear other Social Security appeals.[57]

[D] Effect of Eligibility Determination for Low-Income Subsidy[58]

Individuals, other than full-benefit dual eligibles, who are found eligible for the low-income subsidy, must still separately enroll in the Part D plan of their

---

[55] 42 C.F.R. §423.772.

[56] 42 C.F.R. §423.774(c).

[57] 70 Fed. Reg. 77,664 at 77,674 (Dec. 30, 2005).

[58] Note that receipt of the low-income Part D subsidy may affect eligibility and/or benefit amounts in other assistance programs that consider medical expenses in making eligibility and subsidy determinations.

choice.[59] For the initial year of the Part D benefit, CMS facilitated the enrollment of those found eligible for the LIS in a Part D plan and who had not chosen a Part D plan so that their drug coverage became effective May 1, 2006.

§11.07 DUAL ELIGIBLES

[A] Introduction

Among the most dramatic aspects of the Medicare drug benefit legislation is its complete elimination of Medicaid prescription drug coverage for all individuals who are dually eligible for both Medicare and Medicaid. Beginning January 1, 2006, any individual eligible to enroll in a Part D plan who is receiving full Medicaid services cannot receive prescription drug coverage through Medicaid.[60] This is true regardless of whether the individual has actually enrolled in a Part D plan and regardless of whether the plan covers the specific drug needed. Concomitantly, the state cannot receive federal matching payments for such services.

[B] Definition of Dual Eligibles

Dual eligibles are defined as individuals who have coverage under a Part D plan and who are eligible for full Medicaid benefits under any category of a state Medicaid plan. Those with full coverage under a so-called §1115 research and demonstration waiver fall within the definition; individuals receiving prescription drug coverage under a §1115 Pharmacy Plus waiver do not.[61]

[C] Assignment of Dual Eligibles to Drug Plans

Presumably because of dual eligibles' loss of Medicaid drug coverage, Congress required the automatic enrollment in a prescription drug plan of any dual eligible who has not voluntarily enrolled.[62] Dual eligibles are randomly assigned to Part D plans with premiums at or below the average premium for their region. Under revised CMS guidance the effective date of auto-enrollment into a Part D plan for individuals with Medicare who become eligible for Medicaid will be the same as the effective date of Medicaid eligibility. The effective date of auto-enrollment for individuals who become eligible for Medicare and Medicaid in the same month will also be the date of Medicaid eligibility. Under previous

---

[59] Dual eligibles must also apply to a PDP or MA-PD if they do not want to be auto-enrolled in a drug plan or if they want to change the drug plan to which they were assigned.

[60] 42 U.S.C. §1396u-5(d)(1).

[61] 42 C.F.R. §423.772.

[62] 42 U.S.C. §1396u-5(c)(6).

guidance, such individuals could have experienced a gap in prescription drug coverage of several months. New dual eligible individuals who have Medicaid first will be auto-enrolled retroactively to the date of their Medicare eligibility. In all situations, retroactive enrollment raises the possibility that dual eligibles may be required to pay for their drugs out of their own pockets and then be reimbursed.[63]

The Inspector General of the Department of Health and Human Services determined that, in 2006, nearly one-third of dually-eligible beneficiaries were assigned to drug plans that included less than 85 percent of the 178 most commonly used Part D drugs. Some of the drugs excluded from a substantial number of plan formularies (lists of covered drugs) are drugs for high blood pressure, high cholesterol, and pain relief. Only 18 percent of beneficiaries were assigned to plans that covered all 178 drugs, though this did not guarantee that these plans covered all drugs needed by each beneficiary.[64]

Unlike other Medicare beneficiaries, however, duals retain the right to switch plans at any time.[65] Thus, individuals assigned to a plan whose formulary does not include the prescriptions they use may switch to a more appropriate plan. Note, however, in 2006, CMS computer systems could not process changes from one Part D plan to another quickly enough to ensure that coverage under the new plan would become effective on the first day of the month following the change. In addition, CMS records also indicated that some beneficiaries were enrolled in more than one plan, causing some dual eligible individuals to be assessed a premium by the second plan. CMS instituted an enrollment reconciliation process whereby beneficiaries were disenrolled from a Part D plan if CMS records indicated they were enrolled in a different plan unless they affirmatively contacted the plan.[66]

[D] Medicaid Wrap-Around

The elimination of coverage for an otherwise covered Medicaid service represents a substantial departure from the historic Medicare-Medicaid relationship for dual eligibles, under which Medicaid has paid Medicare's cost sharing and provided "wrap-around coverage" for services where, as with home health, Medicare coverage is more limited than Medicaid's or where, as with prescription drugs and long-term care, Medicare coverage is nearly non-existent.[67] The significance of this situation cannot be overstated. Because of the design of the Medicare drug

---

[63] Updated Guidance—Changes to the Effective Date and PDP Notice Requirements for Auto-Enrollment and Facilitated Enrollment—March 17, 2006. <http://www.cms.hhs.gov/States/Downloads/UpdatedGuidance4MAnCostPlanonAEnFE.pdf>.

[64] <http://oig.hhs.gov/oei/reports/oei-05-06-00090.pdf>.

[65] 42 C.F.R. §423.38(c).

[66] <http://www.cms.hhs.gov/PrescriptionDrugCovContra/downloads/EnrollmentReconciliationProcess_03.17.06.pdf>.

[67] For a full discussion of dual eligibility, see **Chapter 10**, Dual Eligibility.

benefit, many dual eligibles have less prescription drug coverage than they had under Medicaid and potentially less protection during appeals processes to challenge denials or other barriers to coverage. Further, they have to make copayments for their prescriptions, with the copayment amounts increasing yearly.

Medicaid can continue to cover for dual eligibles, using both federal and state funding, those drugs that it is permitted but not required by law to cover for any Medicaid beneficiary *and* that are not, by definition, Part D covered drugs. Such drugs include benzodiazepines, barbiturates, prescription vitamins, cough and cold relief drugs, and non-prescription drugs, among others. States also have the option of paying copayments for dual eligibles and/or for drugs that are not on a plan's formulary. However, they will receive no federal matching payments and must use only state funds if they assist dual eligibles with these costs. In 2006 all but one state covered at least some of the excluded Part D drugs.[68]

[E]   Nursing Facility Residents

In addition to the problems that may be experienced by other dually eligible individuals, those who reside in nursing and other long-term care facilities experience problems that arise because of the setting in which they live. For example, there is no assurance that a dually eligible resident who does not choose a plan for herself will be automatically assigned to a plan that includes the pharmacy used by her nursing facility, although all plans are required to include long-term care pharmacies in their networks. Drug plans are not required to provide covered medications in the packaging utilized by nursing facilities or formats utilized by residents; access to medically necessary drugs and drug formats may be provided through the exceptions and appeals processes.[69] Thus, a beneficiary may need to file an appeal in order to get the prescription ordered by the treating physician.

Dually eligible individuals who reside in a nursing facility pay no copayment for their medications. This benefit is not extended to residents of assisted living facilities and others who are receiving home and community-based services pursuant to a Section 1115 waiver. Those individuals must pay the copayments described above for dual eligibles.[70]

[F]   Transitioning into a Part D Plan

When Medicare beneficiaries move from another source of payment for their prescriptions to a Part D plan, they may encounter difficulties caused by changes in formularies and other utilization management tools used by Part D plans to

---

[68] <http://www.cms.hhs.gov/states/EDC/list.asp>.

[69] Long-Term Care Guidance, *supra.*

[70] 42 C.F.R. §§423.772, 423.782(a)(2)(ii). 68 Transitions Process Guidance, <http://www.cms.hhs.gov/pdps/transition_process.pdf> (Mar. 16, 2005).

contain costs. The transition may be particularly difficult for nursing home residents and other dual eligibles, and for beneficiaries with chronic conditions who are stabilized on their current treatments.[71]

All Part D plans are required to establish a transition process for new enrollees who are prescribed Medicare-covered drugs that are not on the plan's formulary.[72] Each plan has the flexibility to design its own process as long as the process is consistent with sub-regulatory guidance issued by CMS. Because CMS only recommended in its initial sub-regulatory guidance that plans consider filling a temporary one-time supply of non-formulary medication for new enrollees, in 2006 many drug plans failed to provide the suggested 30-day transition fill. As a result, many beneficiaries, and in particular dual eligible individuals, were denied coverage for prescriptions. CMS issued additional instructions to drug plans and extended the initial transition period for people who enrolled in the first two months of the program. CMS issued stronger guidance for 2007 that established a minimum set of standards for the transition process. CMS also issued an April 2006 Memorandum that encouraged plans to continue to cover drugs after they are removed from their fomularies for enrollees who are taking the medications.[73]

§11.08   STATE PHARMACEUTICAL ASSISTANCE PROGRAMS

States may choose to provide cost-sharing and wrap-around drug coverage for dual eligibles and other low-income residents through a State Pharmaceutical Assistance Program (SPAP).[74] Any payments made by the SPAP on behalf of a Part D enrollee will count toward the enrollee's true out-of-pocket costs. In other words, SPAP payments for cost sharing and for a plan's covered drugs while the beneficiary is in the "doughnut hole" count toward meeting the $3,600 out-of-pocket limit which, in turn, leads to reduced or eliminated enrollee cost sharing. State Medicaid programs, including Pharmacy Plus waivers under Section 1115 of the Social Security Act, ADAPs, and any other programs where the majority of the funding is from federal sources, cannot be SPAPs.[75]

SPAPs must not discriminate among drug plans with respect to their supplemental coverage;[76] this requirement prevents an SPAP from automatically enrolling subsidy-eligible individuals into one particular drug plan. Plans must coordinate with SPAPs concerning certain basic elements of the drug benefit they offer.

---

[71] Transitions   Process   Guidance,   <http://www.cms.hhs.gov/PrescriptionDrugCovContra/Downloads/CY07TransitionGuidance.pdf>.

[72] 42 C.F.R. §423.120(b)(3).

[73] Transitions Process Guidance, *supra.*

[74] 42 C.F.R. §§423.454, 423.464(e)(1).

[75] 42 C.F.R. §423.464(e)(1)(iv).

[76] 42 C.F.R. §§423.464(e)(1)(ii), 423.464(e)(1)(ii).

§11.09 GRIEVANCE, APPEALS, AND EXCEPTIONS PROCESSES

[A] Grievance Procedures

All drug plans must establish processes for hearing and resolving grievances similar to the process utilized by Medicare Advantage plans under Medicare Part C.[77] Grievances are separate and distinct from appeals and from quality of service complaints filed with a quality improvement organization. Grievances may be filed with the drug plan orally or in writing within 60 days after the incident; plans generally must resolve grievances within 30 days. However, plans must resolve within 24 hours a grievance arising from the plan's decision not to expedite a coverage determination or redetermination under the appeals process.[78]

[B] Coverage Determinations and Appeals

[1] The Coverage and Appeals Process

As directed by Congress, the coverage determination and appeals process for Part D also mirrors closely the process utilized by Medicare Advantage plans.[79] The process begins when the drug plan issues a coverage determination.[80] The beneficiary may request a redetermination, performed by the drug plans, of an unfavorable coverage determination. Individuals who remain dissatisfied after the redetermination can request a further review know as reconsideration; the reconsideration will be performed by the independent review entity (IRE). Following an IRE review, the enrollee may appeal to an administrative law judge (ALJ), then to the Medicare Appeals Council (MAC), and finally to federal court. An expedited review is available if the standards set out in Medicare Part C are met.[81]

Plans must notify enrollees of initial coverage determinations as expeditiously as the enrollee's health condition requires, but no later than 72 hours after receipt of the request. They have seven days in which to notify enrollees of a redetermination decision. Plans must act on requests for expedited coverage determination no later than 24 hours after receiving the request, and on expedited redeterminations within 72 hours.[82] Note that beneficiaries who file an appeal after paying out of pocket for a needed prescription are not eligible for expedited consideration.

---

[77] 42 U.S.C.A. §1395w-104(f). See the Appeals and Grievances of the Medicare Advantage chapter.

[78] 42 C.F.R. §423.564.

[79] 42 U.S.C.A. §1395w-104(g), (h). 42 U.S.C.A. §1395w-104(g), (h).

[80] *See* discussion about notice, *infra*.

[81] 42 C.F.R. §§423.560-423.638.

[82] 42 C.F.R. §§423.568, 423.572, 423.582, 423.590.

Unlike under Medicare Part C, unfavorable redeterminations on Part D claims are not automatically forwarded to the IRE. The beneficiary must file a request for reconsideration with the drug plan within 60 days of the redetermination decision.[83] However, the plan must forward the beneficiary's request to the IRE within 24 hours if it does not act in a timely manner on a redetermination request. The IRE must issue its reconsideration decision within the same time frames noted above for issuing a redetermination.

A beneficiary may file a written request for an ALJ hearing with the entity specified in the IRE reconsideration notice within 60 days of receiving an unfavorable reconsideration determination, provided the amount remaining in controversy meets the threshold requirement.[84] In determining whether the jurisdictional amount is met in a claim involving the refusal to provide a covered drug, CMS projects the costs of the drug based on the number of refills prescribed for the disputed drug during the calendar year. The ALJ hearing is conducted pursuant to the procedures for hearings of Part A and B appeals.[85]

A beneficiary may appeal further to the MAC and then to federal court, following procedures for Medicare Advantage plans.[86]

[2] What Constitutes a Coverage Determination

Coverage determinations that trigger appeal rights include a drug plan's decision not to pay for or provide a medication because the drug is not on the plan's formulary, is not considered medically necessary, is furnished by an out-of-network pharmacy, or is not a drug for which Medicare will pay under Part D. An individual may also appeal when a coverage determination is not provided in a timely manner and delay would adversely affect the health of the beneficiary; a request for an exception is rejected; and the individual is dissatisfied with a decision regarding the copayment required for a drug. A coverage determination may be requested by the beneficiary, her appointed representative, or the prescribing physician.[87]

[C] The Exceptions Process

Part D plans that use formularies to manage drug utilization must also have an exceptions process whereby plan enrollees can seek coverage for a non-formulary drug or request that a formulary drug be provided at a lower tier for cost sharing

---

[83] 42 C.F.R. §423.600.

[84] The amount in controversy, $110 in 2006, may increase yearly based on increases in health costs.

[85] 42 C.F.R. §§423.610, 423.612.

[86] 42 C.F.R. §§423.620, 423.630.

[87] 42 C.F.R. §423.566.

(thereby reducing the copayment or coinsurance).[88] As noted above, denial of an exception request constitutes an unfavorable coverage determination from which appeal rights flow. The importance of the exceptions process cannot be overstated; CMS guidance indicates that the exceptions process will provide all beneficiaries with access to the medically necessary drugs prescribed for them.[89]

In order to get an exception to require the plan to cover a non-formulary drug, the prescribing doctor must show that all of the drugs on any tier of the plan's formulary for treatment of the same condition would not be as effective or would have adverse consequences, or both, for the individual requesting the exception. For this purpose formulary includes the application of cost savings tools, such as dose restrictions, quantity limits, prior authorization, step therapy, and therapeutic substitution requirements, all of which would result in non-coverage for an otherwise coverable Part D drug. If the plan approves the exception request, the drug will be treated as other drugs on the formulary, so that the beneficiary's cost sharing counts toward the deductible and the annual out-of-pocket limit. A beneficiary will not have to file a new exception request each time the prescription is refilled. If the beneficiary renews her membership in the plan after the plan year, the plan has the option of continuing coverage of the medicine.[90] If the plan does not adopt this option, the beneficiary would have to re-apply for an exception the next year.

Plan enrollees may also use the exceptions process to ask that a drug they require be assigned to a lower tier to reduce their cost sharing for the drug when the preferred drug would not be as effective or would have adverse consequences. The exceptions process must address situations where a formulary's tiered copayment structure changes during the year and an enrollee is using a drug affected by the change. However, a plan *does not* have to cover non-preferred drugs at the lower, generic drug co-pay level if the plan maintains a separate tier dedicated to generic drugs. Further, if the plan maintains a formulary co-pay tier in which it places very high cost and unique items, such as genomic and biotech products, it may exclude these very high costs or unique drugs from its exceptions process.[91]

Because exceptions requests are coverage determinations and are governed by the rules for coverage determinations, the plan must act within the time frames for standard coverage determinations (72 hours) or expedited coverage determinations (24 hours), depending on which standards are met. A beneficiary may appeal the denial of an exception request through the appeals process.

Despite its importance, the exceptions process has proven to be both burdensome and lengthy to use. Drug plans may require a doctor's certificate explaining why the plan enrollee needs the non-formulary drug. Each plan has its own criteria for what should be included in the certificate; many plans have different forms a

---

[88] 42 U.S.C.A. §1395w-104(g), (h), 42 C.F.R. §423.578.

[89] Medicare Modernization Act Final Guidelines—Formularies, *supra.*

[90] 42 C.F.R. §423.578(c)(4).

[91] 42 C.F.R. §§423.578(a)(6), (7).

doctor must use depending on the drug in question. CMS has approved a standard exceptions request form developed by the American Medical Association, the Center for Medicare Advocacy, and other groups but has not *required* that plans honor the standard form. Each plan determines how it will evaluate the doctor's determination that the enrollee requires a non-formulary drug, including establishing a process to compare the medical and scientific evidence about the safety and effectiveness of the non-formulary and formulary drugs. Most plans require extensive documentation, sometimes asking for both the beneficiary's own medical records and medical journals. Because the Part D appeals process follows the appeals process for Medicare managed care plans, it involves the exhaustion of multiple layers in order to get a face-to-face hearing.

[D]   Notice and Other Due Process Issues

The prescription drug plan has the responsibility for giving its plan enrollees notice of a change in the formulary or notice that coverage for a requested drug has been denied. The plan must provide written notice of a formulary change, including a change in tiered cost sharing, 60 days in advance of the change to those enrollees who use the prescription, as well as to CMS, prescribing physicians, and pharmacies. The notice must include the change, other available drugs, and a description of the exceptions process. Alternatively, a plan can choose to give an enrollee the 60 days' notice and a 60-day supply of the drug when a refill request is presented to the plan.[92] On April 26, 2006 CMS issued a Memorandum that encourages plans to continue coverage for drugs they take off fomulary for enrollees who have been taking the medications.

It is unclear, however, how enrollees will learn of their rights when coverage of or payment for a prescription is denied at the pharmacy. The regulations place the burden on the plan to provide notice of appeal rights for coverage determinations. CMS states that the pharmacy is not required to provide notice of the reasons for the denial or of the appeals process.[93] Instead, each drug plan must arrange with its network pharmacies to either post at the pharmacy or distribute a generic notice that tells enrollees to contact the plan if they disagree with the information provided by the pharmacist.[94] This approach does not consider the extra burden placed on the enrollee, who must make a special effort to get and then act on the notice, or the practicalities of providing notice when an enrollee uses a non-network pharmacy.

The appeals process also does not provide adequate protection to someone who must appeal to continue receiving coverage of a drug she has been using. Unlike under Medicaid, the MMA does not provide for continued access to the

---

[92] 42 C.F.R. §423.120(b)(5).

[93] 70 Fed. Reg. 4194, 4349-40 (Jan. 28, 2005).

[94] 42 C.F.R. §423.562(a)(3).

medication if an appeal is filed on a timely basis. Thus, dually eligible individuals whose prescription drug coverage will be paid for under Medicare instead of Medicaid will lose an important protection. CMS has indicated in sub-regulatory guidance that Part D plans must provide a continued supply of a medicine to nursing home residents through the exceptions process.

§11.10 CONCLUSION

The Medicare Part D prescription drug program continues to evolve. Advocates should monitor whether plans decide to remain in the program for 2007, and whether those that do change their formularies and/or cost-sharing structures. Low-income subsidy eligible individuals may need to enroll in a different plan if their plan no longer qualifies for a subsidy to pay the entire premium. All enrollees may need to change plans or pursue exceptions if the plan they chose eliminates drugs from its formulary or adds utilization management tools.

BIBLIOGRAPHY

References are to sections.

Books

Henry J. Kaiser Family Foundation: Medicare Chart Book (2001), 7.06[A]
Rozovsky, F., Consent to Treatment: A Practical Guide (1984), 5.04[B]

Journals

AARP Public Policy Institute, *Bridging the Gaps Between Medicare and Medicaid: The Case of QMBs and SLMBs,* Washington, D.C., AARP (Jan. 1999), 10.05[A]

Biles, Brian, *et al., Issue Brief: The Future of Medicare,* The Commonwealth Fund (Nov. 1998), 7.01

Bradford, Glenn E., & Melinda M. Ward, *The Medicare "Super Lien" Revisited,* J. Mo. B. 44 (Jan./Feb. 2000), 9.07[B]

Chiplin, *Breathing Life Into Discharge Planning,* 13 Elder L.J. 1 (2005), 1.05[A][3]

Chiplin, *Medicare Discharge-Planning Regulations: An Advocacy Tool for Beneficiaries,* 29 Clearinghouse Rev. 152 (June 1995), 1.05[A][3]

Chiplin, *The Medicare Limiting Charge: An Issue of Implementation and Enforcement,* 26 Clearinghouse Rev. 167 (1992), 1.05[B]

Chiplin *et al., Choice, Quality, Appeal Rights, and Surrogate Decision Making: A Medicare+Choice Primer,* 32 Clearinghouse Rev. 327 (Nov./Dec. 1998), 3.08[B], 5.04[B]

Families USA, *The Medicare Buy-In: A Promise Unfulfilled,* Washington, D.C., Families USA (Mar. 1993), 10.05[A]

_____, *The Medicare Buy-In: Still a Government Secret,* Washington, D.C., Families USA (Mar. 1992), 10.05[A]

_____, *The Secret Benefit—The Failure to Provide the Medicare Buy-In to Poor Seniors,* Washington, D.C., Families USA (1991), 10.05[A]

_____, *Shortchanged: Billions Withheld from Medicare Beneficiaries,* Washington, D.C., Families USA (1998), 10.05[A]

Gross, David, & Normandy Brangan, Public Policy Institute, Research Group, *Out-of-Pocket Spending on Health Care by Medicare Beneficiaries Age 65 and Older: 1999 Projections,* AARP (Dec. 1999), 10.04[B]

Kane, N., & P. Manoukian, *The Effect of the Medicare Prospective Payment System on the Adoption of New Technology,* 321 New Eng. J. Med. 1378 (1989), 2.09[I]

Moon, Marilyn, *Restructuring Medicare: Impacts on Beneficiaries,* The Urban Institute (Jan. 1999), 7.01

National Health Law Program, *Protecting Residents Against Improper Discharge from Hospitals,* 27 Clearinghouse Rev. 101 (1993), 3.03[B]

National Legal Center for the Medically Dependent and Disabled, *Medical Treatment for the Elderly and Disabled*, 23 Clearinghouse Rev. 1154 (1990), 5.04[B]

Nyzio, Thomas J., *Medicare Recovery in Liability Cases*, S.C. Law. 20-24 (May/June 1996), 9.07[B]

Remler, Dahlia K., & Sherry A. Glied, *What Other Programs Can Teach Us: Increasing Participation in Health Insurance Programs,* Am. J. Pub. Health (Jan. 2003), 10.05[A]

Some States Crack Down on Copays for Dual Eligibles, 6 Eli's Home Care Wk. 196 (Apr. 26, 1999), 10.06[B]

Manuals

Center for Health Dispute Resolution, Medicare Managed Care Reconsideration Process Manual, 2.11[C]

Centers for Medicare & Medicaid Services, HMO/CMP Manual, as revised by Transmittal No. 6 (Mar. 1991), 1.08[B][1]

_____, Medicare Benefit Policy Manual (CMS Pub. 100-02), 3.03[B], 3.03[C], 3.03[D], 3.03[E][1], 3.03[H], 3.05[D], 3.06[A], 3.06[C], 3.06[D], 3.06[E], 5.09[C], 5.09[E], 5.09[F], 5.11[D]

_____, Medicare Carrier's Manual (HCFA Pub. 14-3), 6.03[A], 6.03[D][1], 6.05, 6.07[A], 9.03

_____, Medicare Claims Processing Manual, 1.07[A][2], 3.05[D], 5.05, 6.03

_____, Medicare Coverage Issues Manual (HCFA Pub. 6), 6.03[A], 6.03[D][2]

_____, Medicare General Information, Eligibility, and Entitlement Manual (Pub. 100-01), 3.03[F]]

_____, Medicare Home Health Agency Manual (CMS Pub. 11), 4.03[A], 4.03[B][2], 4.03[B][3][a], 4.03[B][3][b], 4.03[B][4], 4.03[C], 4.04, 4.06[D]

_____, Medicare Hospice Manual (CMS Pub. 21), 5.05, 5.09[C], 5.09[E]

_____, Medicare Hospital Manual (HCFA Pub. 10), 2.08[B], 2.10[C], 3.03[B]

_____, Medicare Intermediary Manual (HCFA Pub. 13), 1.08[A][1], 2.08[B], 3.02, 3.03[C], 3.03[G], 3.07[D], 3.08[B], 3.08[C], 4.03[B][1], 6.05, 7.05[A][2], 9.06, 9.08, 9.09, 9.10[B], 9.10[C]

_____, Medicare Managed Care Manual (CMS Pub. 100-16), 7.01, 7.04[E][5][a]

_____, Medicare Part A Intermediary Manual (CMS Pub. 13-3), 4.06[F], 5.11, 9.07[B]

_____, Medicare Part B Carrier's Manual (HCFA Pub. 14), 2.09[D]

_____, Medicare Quality Improvement Manual (Pub. 100-10), 2.11[A], 2.12[B]

_____, QIO Peer Review Organization Manual (HCFA Pub. 19), 2.10[D], 2.12[B]

_____, Program Integrity Manual (HCFA Pub. 83), 6.03[B], 10.06[E]

_____, Skilled Nursing Facility Manual (HCFA Pub. 12), 3.08[B], 3.08[C]

_____, State Medicaid Manual (HCFA Pub. 45), 10.04[C], 10.05[B], 10.06[B], 10.07[C]

QIO Manual, 2.10[C]

Secretary of Health & Human Services, State Operations Manual (HCFA Pub. 7), Transmittal No. 280 (Mar. 1, 1997), 1.05[A][3]

Reports

Barents Group LLC, *A Profile of QMB-Eligible and SLMB-Eligible Medicare Beneficiaries,* Contract #500-95-0057/Task Order 2, prepared for the Health Care Financing Administration (Apr. 7, 1999), 10.02, 10.05[A]

Briesacher, Becky, *et al., Medicare's Disabled Beneficiaries: The Forgotten Population in the Debate over Drug Benefits,* The Commonwealth Fund (Sept. 2002), 10.03

Dual Eligibles: Medicaid's Role for Low-Income Medicare Beneficiaries, The Kaiser Commission on Medicaid and the Uninsured: Key Facts (Jan. 2005), 10.01

Dual Enrollees: Medicaid's Role for Low Income Medicare Beneficiaries, The Kaiser Commission on Medicaid and the Uninsured: Key Facts (Feb. 2005), 10.01

General Accounting Office, *Employment-Based Health Insurance: Medium and Large Employers Can Purchase Coverage, But Some Workers Are Not Eligible,* GAO/HEHS-98-184 (July 1998), 9.02[B]

_____, *Low-Income Medicare Beneficiaries: Further Outreach and Administrative Simplification Could Increase Enrollment,* GAO/HEHS-99-61 (Apr. 1999), 10.02, 10.04[A], 10.05[A]

_____, *Medicare and Medicaid–Many Eligible People Not Enrolled in Qualified Medicare Beneficiary Program,* GAO/HEHS-94-52 (Jan. 1994), 10.05[A]

Glaun, Kim, *Medicaid Programs to Assist Low-Income Medicare Beneficiaries: Medicare Savings Programs Case Study Findings,* prepared for the Kaiser Commission for Medicaid and the Uninsured (2003), 10.05[A]

Harrington, Charlene, Ph.D., Helen Carrillo, M.S., & Cassandra S. Crawford, M.A., *Nursing Facilities, Staffing, Residents, and Facility Deficiencies, 1997 through 2003* at 16 (Aug. 2004), 10.06[C]

Issue Brief: "Dual Eligibles: Medicaid's Role in Filling Medicare's Gaps, The Kaiser Commission on Medicaid and the Uninsured (Mar. 2004), 10.03

King, Kathleen M., & Mark Schlesigner (eds.), Final Report of the Study Panel on Medicare and Markets, *The Role of Price Health Plans in Medicare: Lessons from the Past, Looking to the Future* (Washington, D.C. National Academy of Social Insurance Sept. ____), 7.01

Medicaid's Role for Low-Income Beneficiaries, The Kaiser Commission on Medicaid and the Uninsured (Jan. 2002), 10.02[C]

Medicaid's Role for Low-Income Beneficiaries, The Kaiser Commission on Medicaid and the Uninsured (Feb. 2001), 10.07[A]

_____, *Variations in State Medicaid Buy-in Practices for Low-Income Medicare Beneficiaries: A 1999 Update,* prepared for the Henry J. Kaiser Family Foundation (Dec. 1999), 10.04[A], 10.05[A], 10.06[B], 10.07[C]

Neumann, Peter J., *et al., Identifying Barriers to Elderly Participation in the Qualified Medicare Beneficiary Program,* Final Report submitted to Health Care Financing Administration (1994), 10.05[A]

TABLE OF CASES

References are to sections.

Legion v. Richardson, 2.04[C]
Levi v. Heckler, 3.03[E]
Linoz v. Heckler, 1.03, 6.03[D][3]
Lormore v. Shalala, 3.03[B]
Lutwin (Healey) v. Thompson, 4.06[E]

Manning v. Utilities Mut. Ins. & Niagara Mohawk Dist. Power Co., 9.07[B]
Mason v. American Tobacco Co., 9.07
Massachusetts Med. Soc'y v. Dukakis, 6.04[B]
Mayburg v. Secretary of HHS, 3.03[E]
McGann v. H & H Music, 9.02[B]
McGill v. Secretary of HHS, 6.08
Meadows v. Cagle's, 9.05[C][3]
Medical Soc'y of N.Y. State v. Cuomo, 6.04[B]
Medicare Beneficiaries Def. Fund v. Memorial Sloan-Kettering Cancer Ctr., 6.04[B]
Morris v. North Haw. Cmty. Hosp., 6.07[F]

New York City Health & Hosp. Corp. v. Perales, 10.06[B]
New York ex rel. Bodnar v. Secretary of HHS, 2.05[A], 3.06[F]
New York ex rel. Holland v. Sullivan, 2.08[B], 3.06[F]
New York ex rel. Stein v. Department of Health & Human Servs., 2.08[B], 3.06[F]

Olson v. Bowen, 3.06[B]
O'Neal v. Shalala, 4.03[A]

Pennsylvania Med. Soc'y v. Marconis, 6.04[B]
Pennsylvania Med. Soc'y v. Snider, 10.06[B]

Perales v. Sullivan, 3.06[B]
Pfalzgraf v. Shalala, 3.06[A], 3.06[B]
Pierce v. Underwood, 6.08
Pilsums v. Harris, 1.07[A][2]
Pope v. Secretary of HHS, 4.03[A]
Powell v. Heckler, 7.04[F][1][f]
Probstein v. Sullivan, 2.08[B]
Public Citizen Inc. v. DHHS, 7.05[A]

Ralabate v. Wing, 10.06[E]
Rehabilitation Ass'n of Va. v. Kozlowski, 10.06[B]
Rosenburg v. Richardson, 3.03[B]
Roth v. Secretary of HHS, 3.06[B]
Rybicki v. Hartley, 9.07

Sarrassat v. Bowen, 1.03, 1.07[A][1], 3.07[D][2]
Sarrassat v. Sullivan, 3.07[A], 3.07[B]
Schisler v. Heckler (Schisler III), 3.06[F]
Schisler v. Heckler (Schisler II), 3.06[F]
Schisler v. Heckler (Schisler I), 3.06[F]
Schweiker v. McClure, 6.07[B]
Scotto v. Bowen, 3.06[B]
Shalala v. Illinois Council on Long Term Care Inc, 6.07[F]
Shepack v. Bowen, 3.03[G]
Situ v. Leavitt, 10.06[A][2]
Smith v. Shalala, 4.04
Sowell v. Richardson, 3.03[F]
Sprague v. General Motors Corp., 9.02[B]
Stearns v. Sullivan, 3.06[B]
Stefanko v. Secretary of HHS, 3.03[G]
Stenger v. Bowen, 3.06[F]
Stephenson v. Shalala, 6.02[D]
Stohler v. Menke, 10.06[B]

TABLE OF AUTHORITIES

References are to sections.

UNITED STATES CONSTITUTION

Amend. V	1.03

UNITED STATES CODE

5 U.S.C.

8905a	9.05[A]

26 U.S.C.

223	7.04[C][4]
4980(b)	9.05

28 U.S.C.

2412	6.08
2412(d)(1)(A)	6.08
2412(d)(2)	6.08

29 U.S.C.

623(g)	9.02[A]
1001 *et seq.*	9.02[B]
1001(c)	9.02[B]
1003	9.02[B]
1021	9.04[B]
1022	9.04[B]
1024(b)	9.04[B]
1051	9.02[B]
1081	9.02[B]
1101	9.02[B]
1132	9.04[B]
1132(a)(2)	9.04[B]
1132(a)(3)	9.04[B]
1144	9.02[B]
1161 *et seq.*	9.02[B], 9.05
1161(a)	9.05[B]
1161(b)	9.05[A]
1162(1)	9.05[B]
1162(2)(A)	9.05[B], 9.05[C][1], 9.05[C][3]
1162(2)(A)(i)	9.05[C][2]
1162(2)(A)(ii)	9.05[B]
1162(2)(A)(iv)	9.05[C][2]

1162(2)(A)(v)	9.05[C][2]
1162(2)(B)	9.05[B]
1162(2)(C)	9.05[B]
1162(2)(D)	9.05[B]
1162(3)	9.05[B]
1162(3)(B)	9.05[C][3]
1162(4)	9.05[B]
1163	9.05[B], 9.05[C][1]
1163(2)	9.05[B]
1166(a)	9.05[B]
1166(a)(2)	9.05[B]
1166(a)(4)	9.05[B]
1167(2)	9.05[B]
1167(3)	9.05[B]
2412	6.08
2412(d)(1)(A)	6.08
2412(d)(2)	6.08

31 U.S.C.

3711	9.10, 9.10[B]

42 U.S.C.

300bb-1 *et seq.*	9.02[B], 9.05
300bb-1(a)	9.05[A]
300bb-1(b)(1)	9.05[A]
300gg	8.10
300gg(c)(1)	8.10
406(b)	6.08
426	2.01
426(a)(2)(C)	1.01
426(b)(2)(C)	1.01
1320c-1 to 1320c-12	2.10[B]
1320c et seq.	2.08[C]
1320c-1	2.10[B]
1320c-3	2.12[B]
1320c-3(e)(2)	2.12[B]
1320c-5(b)(1)	2.10[B]
1320c-12	2.10[B]
1351-3(c)(2)(A)(i) to (vi)	10.06[C]
1382a(b)(2)(A)	10.03
1382a(b)(4)	10.03

CODE OF FEDERAL REGULATIONS

406.32(a)	2.02	408.42	6.02[1]
406.32(b)	2.02	408.43	6.02[1]
406.32(d)	2.02	408.44	6.02[1]
406.32(e)	2.02	408.46(a)	6.02[1]
406.32(f)	2.02	408.46(b)	6.02[1]
406.32(g)	2.02	408.60(b)	6.02[1]
406.33	2.02	409(b)(1)-(9)	3.07[F]
406.34	2.02	409.3	2.05[A]
407.10	6.02[A]	409.10	2.05[B]
407.10(a)(2)(i)	6.02[A]	409.10(b)	2.05[B]
407.10(a)(2)(iii)	6.02[A]	409.11	2.05[B]
407.10(b)	6.02[A]	409.11(a)	2.06[A]
407.12(a)(2)	1.04	409.11(b)	2.06[A]
407.14	11.05[B][1]	409.11(b)(2)	2.06[A]
407.14(a)(1)	6.02[B][1]	409.11(b)(3)	2.06[A]
407.15(a)	6.02[B][2]	409.12	2.05[B]
407.17(b)	6.02[C][1]	409.12(a)	2.06[B]
407.20	9.05[C][5]	409.12(b)	2.06[B]
407.20(b)	9.05[C][5]	409.13	2.05[B]
407.20(c)	9.05[C][5]	409.13(a)	2.06[C]
407.20(d)(2)	6.02[B][1]	409.13(b)	2.06[C]
407.25	6.02[B][2]	409.15	2.05[B]
407.25(a)(1)	6.02[B][1]	409.15(a)	2.06[D]
407.25(a)(2)	6.02[B][1]	409.15(b)	2.06[D]
407.25(a)(3)	6.02[B][1]	409.15(c)	2.06[D]
407.25(a)(4)	6.02[B][1]	409.16	2.05[B], 2.06[E]
407.25(b)	6.02[B][1]	409.18	2.05[B]
407.32	6.02[B][2]	409.18(a)	2.06[F]
407.42	10.04[C]	409.18(b)	2.06[F]
408 Subpart A	2.09[C]	409.19	2.05[B]
408.4(a)	6.02[C][1]	409.20 et seq.	3.02
408.4(b)	6.02[C][1]	409.20	1.05[A][2]
408.8	6.02[C][1]	409.21	3.02
408.20	6.02[C][1], 6.02[C][2][a]	409.24	3.07[A]
		409.27	3.07[A]
408.20(c)(1)	6.02[C][1]	409.30 et seq.	2.11[P], 3.02
408.20(e)	6.02[C][2][a]	409.30-409.34	1.05[A][2]
408.20(e)(1)	6.02[C][2][a]	409.30	3.03[D][2]
408.20(e)(3)(i)	6.02[C][2][a]	409.30(b)(2)	3.03[C]
408.20(e)(3)(ii)	6.02[C][2][a]	409.31	3.03[D][2]
408.20(e)(4)	6.02[C][2][a]	409.31—409.35	3.05[C]
408.21	6.02[C][1]	409.31(a)(1)	3.03[D][1]
408.21(a)	6.02[C][1]	409.31(a)(3)	3.03[D][1]
408.21(b)	6.02[C][1]	409.31(b)	3.02, 3.03[E][1]
408.22	1.04, 6.02[B][2]	409.31(b)(2)	3.03[E][1], 3.03[G]
408.22(a)(1)	6.02[A]	409.31(b)(2)(i)	3.03[D][1], 3.03[F]
408.40	6.02[1]	409.31(b)(2)(ii)	3.03[D][1], 3.03[F]

**SOCIAL SECURITY
AMENDMENTS OF 1972**

**SOCIAL SECURITY DISABILITY
AMENDMENTS OF 1980**

**TICKET TO WORK INCENTIVES
IMPROVEMENT ACT OF 1999**

IRS RULINGS

INDEX

References are to sections.

A

"Accepting assignment," providers
accepting. *See* Medicare
Part B, assignment program
ADMC. *See* Adverse determination
of Medicare coverage
(ADMC)
Administration of Medicare contracts,
2.01[B], 7.01.
See also Medicare
administrative contractor
Administrative law judge hearings,
6.07[C]
generally, 1.07[D]
appealing hospital coverage
denials, 2.11[G]
discovery, permissibility of,
2.11[G], 6.07[K]
evidence at hearing, 2.11[G],
6.07[K]
Medicare Advantage appeal and
grievance process.
See Medicare Advantage
notice of hearing, 2.11[G],
6.07[K]
prehearing/posthearing conference,
2.11[G], 6.07[K]
video teleconference, hearings by,
1.07[D], 2.11[G], 6.07[K]
Adverse determination of Medicare
coverage (ADMC),
10.06[E]
customized items of durable
medical equipment, 10.06[E]
Advocacy for home health services,
4.07

developing a winning appeal.
See Home health care,
winning appeals, developing
skilled nursing facility care.
See Skilled nursing facility
care, problem areas of concern
for the advocate
Ambulance services, 6.03[D][1]
Amyotrophic lateral sclerosis (ALS)
participation of individuals with
ALS, 1.01
Annual Notice to Beneficiaries,
6.06[A]
Appeals. *See also specific parts of
Medicare plan, e.g.,* Home
health care; Hospice care
generally, 1.07
administrative law judge hearings.
See Administrative law judge
hearings
coverage policies, challenges to,
1.07[G]
local coverage determination,
1.07[G]
national coverage
determination, 1.07[G]
Departmental Appeals Board,
review by, 1.07[E], 1.07[G]
discrepancies between Medicare
Act and Health Care Finance
Administration standards,
1.03
expedited access to judicial review,
1.07[F]
judicial review, expedited access
to, 1.07[F]
Medicare Part C plans, 1.07[B]

annual election to participate,
6.04[A]
fees schedules, 6.04[B]
formula for setting physician
fee rates, amendment to,
6.04[B]
participation elections,
6.04[B]
limiting charge amounts,
6.04[B], 6.04[D]
prior determination process,
6.04[C]
private physician contracts,
6.04[D]
attorney's fees, 6.08
"balance bill," 1.05[B][2]
copayments, 1.05[B],
1.05[B][2], 6.02[D]
Qualified Medicare Beneficiary
Program, 1.06[A], 10.03,
10.06[3], 10.07[C]
coverage
generally, 1.05, 1.05[B], 6.01
ambulance services, 6.03[D][1]
durable medical equipment,
6.03[D][2]
exclusions from, 1.05[B],
6.03[B]
listing of covered services,
6.03[A]
local coverage determinations,
6.03[D][3]
local medical review policies
(LMRPs), effect of, 6.03[B]
national coverage
determinations, 6.03[D][3]
preventive services, 1.05[B][1],
6.03[A]
waiver of liability payment for
certain excluded items and
services, 6.03[C]
deductibles, 1.05, 6.02[A], 6.02[D]
Qualified Medicare Beneficiary
Program, 1.06[A], 10.03

eligibility, 1.04, 6.02[A]
enrollment
generally, 1.04, 1.05[B], 6.01
as optional, 1.05[B], 6.02[A]
avoiding gaps in coverage,
6.02[B][1]
declining, 6.02[B][1]
enrollment periods, 6.02[B][1]
organization determinations,
1.07[A][6]
penalty for late enrollment,
6.02[B][2]
special enrollment period (SEP),
6.02[B][1]
Explanation of Medical Benefits.
See Explanation of Medicare
Benefits (EOMB)
filing claims, 6.05
financing of, 1.02, 1.05[B], 6.01
"limiting charge," 1.05[B],
1.05[B][2], 6.04[B], 6.04[C]
Medicare Summary Notices,
6.06[C]
premiums, 1.05[B], 6.02[A],
6.02[C]
Qualified Medicare Beneficiary
Program, 1.06[A], 10.03
Special Low Income Medicare
Beneficiary Program (SLMB),
1.06[B]
representatives, appointment of,
6.08
services, 6.01[A]
Medicare Part C. *See* Medicare
Advantage
Medicare Part D. *See* Prescription
drug coverage
Medicare+Choice. *See* Medicare
Advantage
Medicare Prescription Drug,
Improvement, and
Modernization Act of 2003
(MMA), 1.01[A], 2.01[B],
8.06

States
COBRA continuation coverage,
9.05[A]
guardianship or conservatorship
statutes, 5.04[B]
incapacitated persons, statutes
governing medical decision-
making for, 5.04[B]
Qualified Medicare Beneficiary
Program (QMB) and, 1.06[A],
10.03, 10.07[C]
requirements of employer group
health plans (EGHPs), 9.02[B]
Supplemental Medical Insurance. *See*
Medicare Part B
Surety bonds for home health
agencies, 4.05[E]

T

Telehealth services, 1.05[B][1],
6.03[A]
Travel outside the U.S.
hospital coverage, 2.07[A]
Medigap emergency medical
coverage for, 8.03

U

U.S. Department of Health and
Human Service (HHS), Health
Care Financing

Administration. *See* Health
Care Financing
Administration (HCFA)
Utilization Review Committees,
2.10[A]

V

Video teleconference
hearings held by, 1.07[D], 2.11[G],
6.07[K]

W

Waiver of liability
home health care, 4.06[E]
Medicare Part B excluded items
and services, 6.03[C]
skilled nursing care facility
charges. *See* Skilled nursing
facility care, waiver of
liability of beneficiary
Waiver of Medicare Secondary Payer
Program recovery claims,
grounds for, 9.10[C]
Wheelchairs. *See also* Durable
medical equipment
power wheelchairs, coverage for,
10.06[E]
Workers' compensation programs and
Medicare Secondary Payer
Program (MSP), 9.08